The Theology of John Calvin

The Theology of John Calvin

Charles Partee

Westminster John Knox Press
LOUISVILLE • LONDON

Scripture quotations from the New Revised Standard Version of the Bible are copyright © 1989 by the Division of Christian Education of the National Council of the Churches of Christ in the U.S.A. and are used by permission.

Excerpts from John Calvin's *Institutes of the Christian Religion*, ed. John T. McNeill, trans. Ford Lewis Battles, LCC (Philadelphia: Westminster Press, 1960), is used with the permission of Westminster John Knox Press.

Excerpts from *Calvin's New Testament Commentaries,* David W. Torrance and Thomas F. Torrance, eds. (Grand Rapids: Wm. B. Eerdmans, 1971), is used with the permission of Wm. B. Eerdmans Publishing Company.

Book design by Sharon Adams
Cover design by Eric Walljasper, Minneapolis, MN
Cover art: Stock Montage/Getty Images/Hulton Archive

First edition
Published by Westminster John Knox Press
Louisville, Kentucky

This book is printed on acid-free paper that meets the American National Standards Institute Z39.48 standard. ∞

PRINTED IN THE UNITED STATES OF AMERICA

08 09 10 11 12 13 14 15 16 17—10 9 8 7 6 5 4 3 2 1

Library of Congress Cataloging-in-Publication Data

Partee, Charles.
     The theology of John Calvin / Charles Partee.—1st ed.
        p. cm.
     Includes index.
     ISBN 978-0-664-23119-4 (alk. paper)
     1. Calvin, Jean, 1509–1564.   2. Reformed Church—Doctrines—History—
16th century.   3. Theology, Doctrinal—History—16th century.   I. Title.
BX9418.P375   2008
230'.42092—dc22
                                                                        2008010815

*This book is
dedicated to
Ulrich Mauser
and
Andrew Purves,
Doctors of the Church*

Contents

Preface   xi

Acknowledgments   xix

Considering the Engagement: An Introduction   1
  A. Overview and Scope   1
  B. Three Introductory Conclusions   5
    1. Opponents of Calvin: The Caricatures   5
    2. Proponents of Calvin: The Calvinists   13
    3. Misponents of Calvin: The Assumptions   27
  C. The Structure of the *Institutes*   35
    1. The Four Articles of the Apostles' Creed   35
    2. The Twofold Knowledge of God   36
    3. The Trinitarian God   39
    4. Union with Christ   40
  D. A Word on the Minister of the Word   43

Part One: GOD FOR US

Book I. God the Creator   51
  Introduction to Book I   51
    1. The Scripture   52
      [A Note on Idolatry]   62
    2. The Trinity   64
  A. God's Creation   69
    1. Of Things Invisible   70
      a. The Angels   71
      b. The Devils   73
      A Note on Sin and Evil   75
    2. Of Things Visible   78
      a. The World   79
      b. The Human   80
  B. God's Providence   105
    1. Epicurean Chance and Stoic Fate   109
      a. The Epicureans   109
      b. The Stoics   111

2.	Providence as Universal	113
3.	Providence as Particular	115
4.	Common and Special Grace	116
	Conclusions to Book I	119

Book II. God the Redeemer ... 120
    Introduction to Book II ... 120
        A Personal Note ... 122
    A. Sin: How Total Is Depravity? ... 126
        1. Total and Partial Depravity ... 126
        2. Sin: A Fact without Meaning ... 129
        3. Freedom and Bondage of Will ... 131
        4. Original and Actual Sin ... 133
    B. The Gospel and the Law ... 136
    C. The Person of Christ ... 142
        1. The Eternal and Incarnate Son ... 147
        2. The One Person and Two Natures ... 149
        3. The Body and the Head ... 152
    D. The Work of Christ ... 158
        1. Christ as Prophet ... 163
        2. Christ as King ... 164
        3. Christ as Priest ... 164
    E. Mysticism and Deification: Two Disavowals ... 167
        1. Mysticism ... 170
        2. Deification ... 172
    F. The Narrative of Faith ... 179
    Conclusions to Book II ... 189

Part Two: GOD WITH US

Book III. The Faithful Person(s) ... 193
    Introduction to Book III ... 193
    A. The Work of the Holy Spirit in Faith ... 200
    B. Sanctification through Faith ... 208
    C. The Christian Life of Faith ... 217
        1. Denial of Self ... 217
        2. The Future Life ... 220
        3. The Present Life ... 221
    D. Justification by Faith ... 222
    E. Prayer: The Exercise of Faith ... 233
    F. Predestination: The Certainty of Faith ... 240
        1. Central Dogma ... 244
        2. Reprobation ... 248
        3. Assurance ... 250

G. Resurrection: The Victory of Faith   252
Conclusions to Book III   257

Book IV. The Faithful Community   258
    Introduction to Book IV   258
    A. The Order of the Church   261
        1. The Head and the Body   262
        2. The True and the False   266
        3. The Chosen and the Responsible   269
    B. The Sacraments of the Church   271
        1. Calvin and the Catholics   280
        2. Calvin and the Zwinglians   281
        3. Calvin and the Lutherans   283
    C. The State and the Church   289
    Conclusions to Book IV   295

Breaking Off the Engagement: A Conclusion   297

Calvin's Method in Theology: An Excursus   299
    Introduction   299
    A. Calvin and Reason   304
        1. Natural Reason   306
        2. Sinful Reason   309
        3. Sanctified Reason   310
    B. Calvin and Experience   315
    Conclusion   326

Index of Names   331

Index of Subjects   339

Preface

Because his name continues to be invoked in normative and mythic ways, understanding John Calvin correctly is a recurring challenge. Popular misconceptions of certain kinds appear invincible,[1] but, sometimes and sadly, Calvin is ignorantly dismissed even among the learned. For example, in his survey of world history J. M. Roberts recognizes Calvin's great impact but concludes, "It is not easy to understand the success of this gloomy creed."[2] On the contrary, Calvin's theology is joyful, not gloomy. Moreover, its exceptional quality makes success easy to understand. Altogether the man, his time, his contribution, and his influence represent an immense subject. Formidable but more manageable is an engagement with his theology, which intends to be an accurate description of what the following pages contain. This engagement is centered on the *thought* of John Calvin, which means the concern is not with his *life* (which was rather dull in comparison with Martin Luther) or his *influence* (which was tremendous in comparison with anybody). Moreover, we are not engaged in the fascinating (and endless) game of identifying and evaluating his sources, nor will we often discuss the evolution of his text. That Calvin continued to rethink his expositions (especially in the *Institutes*) and that he stood on the shoulders of many wise people—Christian wise and otherwise—is obvious, but those revisions and those shoulders are not our primary focus. Our purpose is twofold: (1) to survey the full sweep of Calvin's theology and (2) to collect the benefits that accrue. In this regard, it is important to remember that surveyors and miners perform different tasks. Like surveyors, we will cover a lot of ground trying to walk with sure foot along the

1. Friedrich Schiller famously claimed, "Against stupidity the gods themselves war in vain" (Mit der Dummheit kämpfen Götter selbst vergebens), *The Maid of Orleans, Schillers Sämmtliche Werke* (Stuttgart: J. G. Cotta, 1874), III.6.
2. J. M. Roberts, *New History of the World* (New York: Oxford University Press, 2003), 578. For Calvin's impact, see *John Calvin: His Influence in the Western World*, ed. W. Stanford Reid (Grand Rapids: Zondervan Publishing House, 1982).

towpath of Calvin's thought in order to appreciate its special contours, but, unlike miners, we will not dig in any one place expecting to carry away the mother lode.

Several convictions lie behind this effort. First, convinced that Calvin's theology is important for Western intellectual history, I have tried to study him *carefully*. Second, convinced that Calvin has much to teach us, I have tried to read him *sympathetically*. Third, convinced that Calvin has been seriously misrepresented, I have tried to interpret him *correctly*. Fourth, convinced that Calvin deserves to be understood, I have tried to explain him *clearly*. Scholars sometimes think their task is complete when a properly complex interpretation of the subject is presented to the academic guild. I am concerned about proper interpretation—and will be striving for it—but I am also interested in the individual and communal benefits that Calvin's teaching provides. This exposition attempts to present a helpful clarity for all readers rather than an identification of those fascinating complexities that delight scholars and keep them at their desks for long hours writing opaque footnotes to confound each other. Digging a site deeper and deeper can require a laborer to cite wider and wider, making oversight more difficult.

This study may also be useful to those interested in an introduction to Reformed (or Calvinistic) theology in its early and simpler form. When John Calvin appeared in the sixteenth century, Christian theology was already divided between Eastern Orthodoxy and Roman Catholicism. Protestant (or evangelical) theology was emerging with Martin Luther, and in only a few years a "non-Lutheran" alternative Protestant theology began to gain strength. Although Calvin was not the pioneer of Reformed theology, so powerful was his influence that the movement is often called by his name. In the next four centuries Calvinism confronted great challenges and underwent great changes. The question of which changes enhanced the Reformed tradition and which distorted it is a subject of considerable modern interest. Aspects of Calvin and Calvinism are noted here on occasion, and the issue is briefly discussed as the second preliminary conclusion. The debate depends not merely on knowledge and judgment of the later history of the movement but especially turns on the evaluation of original Calvinism. Obviously, an exposition of the theology of John Calvin is essential to an understanding of Calvinism, but it does not finally decide the complicated issue of development or distortion. In addition to the primary concern for a careful exposition of Calvin's theology, these pages include reflection on his thought because following anyone blindly is shortsighted. A study of the past cannot avoid relating historical understanding to modern concerns. Whatever its pretensions, every study of the past involves the present. Put another way, what Calvin says and what he means (or could help us to mean) are not unconnected issues.

Doubtless the study of great thinkers of the past is essential, and striving for pure historical understanding is a worthy goal, but apart from Calvin's personal and historical contribution, he made a tremendous theological contribution. *Solus inter theologos Calvinus.*[3] In 1875 Philip Schaff asserted, "John Calvin [is]

---

3. Cited from Scaliger by Paul Henry, *The Life and Times of John Calvin: The Great Reformer*, trans. Henry Stebbing, 2 vols. (New York: Robert Carter and Brothers, 1851), 185.

the greatest theologian . . . of the giant race of the Reformers, and for commanding intellect, lofty character, and far-reaching influence, one of the foremost leaders in the history of Christianity."[4] A decade later John Tulloch wrote, "Calvin did not know the meaning of dogmatic indecision. His intellectual penetration and directness . . . enabled him at almost every point to maintain a firm footing. And this mere strength of intellectual consistency, traversing the whole ground of Christian truth . . . so as to present a great whole [gave] to his work the influence it secured."[5] A similar evaluation is more recently affirmed by Ward Holder, "Calvin is one of the best theologians the Christian tradition has to offer."[6] Marilynne Robinson makes the point more broadly, adding a comment on Calvin's other work and his humility. "Calvin was a sickly, diligent pastor, scholar, diplomat, and polemicist, who wrote theology of breathtaking beauty and tough-mindedness as well as line-by-line commentary on most books of the Bible. When he died he was buried, as he had asked to be, in an unmarked grave."[7] Doubtless we cherish the best and most beautiful. We admire discipline, intellectual range, and modesty withal, but we study great teachers of the past in large measure for what we can learn from them that is useful to us today. John Calvin provides not only a profound exposition of the various topics of Christian faith but also a splendid outline for theological reflection. The range of questions Calvin raises and the answers he gives is both important and instructive. In short, the theology of John Calvin is not only a permanent, but also a present, resource for Christian understanding and faith.

Since so many agree with so much so far written in this preface, numerous studies of Calvin are readily available. Most of them focus on the fierce certainties of

4. Philip Schaff, "Calvin's Life and Labors," *Presbyterian Quarterly and Princeton Review* 4 (April 1875): 255–56.

5. John Tulloch, *Luther and Other Leaders of the Reformation*, 3rd ed. (Edinburgh: William Blackwood and Sons, 1883), 248.

6. R. Ward Holder, "Calvin's Heritage," in *The Cambridge Companion to John Calvin*, ed. Donald K. McKim (New York: Cambridge University Press, 2004), 266. Benjamin Reist calls the *Institutes* "one of the most comprehensive statements of the understanding of the Christian faith the tradition has given us." In addition, he declares, "[I] have found Calvin's comprehensive study of Christian doctrine a remarkably useful means for introducing students to the task of thinking systematically about the doctrines informing their faith" (Benjamin A. Reist, *A Reading of Calvin's Institutes* (Louisville, KY: Westminster/John Knox Press, 1991), 6, 2.

7. Marilynne Robinson, *The Death of Adam: Essays on Modern Thought* (New York: Houghton Mifflin Company, 1998), 175. Philip Schaff in his *History of the Christian Church*, vol. 8 (Grand Rapids: Wm. B. Eerdmans Publishing Company, 1979 [1910]), 270–95, gathers nearly thirty pages of tributes to Calvin with this introduction, "No name in church history . . . has been so much loved and hated, admired and abhorred, praised and blamed, blessed and cursed, as that of John Calvin." Ernest Renan declared Calvin to be "the most Christian man of his century" (*l'homme le plus chrétien de son siècle*). Henry B. Smith thought, "His errors were those of his own times: his greatness is of all times." Writing at the end of the nineteenth century, Schaff believed of Calvin, "Upon the whole, the verdict of history is growingly in his favor." Karl Barth, considered by many to be the greatest Protestant theologian since Friedrich Schleiermacher, read Calvin carefully and admired him immensely. In a 1922 letter to his friend Eduard Thurneysen, Barth wrote, "Calvin is a cataract, a primeval forest, a demonic power, something directly down from Himalaya, absolutely Chinese, strange, mythological; I lack completely the means [to present his theology] adequately. . . . I could gladly and profitably set myself down and spend all the rest of my life just with Calvin" (*Revolutionary Theology in the Making: Barth-Thurneysen Correspondence 1914–25*, trans. James D. Smart [Richmond, VA: John Knox Press, 1964], 101).

Calvin's Christian faith, virtually ignoring the uncertainties he also illustrates. Calvin is too often seen as authoritarian, even dictatorial—a rigorous theologician. But his theology should be seen as confession in defense of the mystery of God's revelation.[8] When theology is recognized as a humble confessional exposition of the gospel rather than a triumphant explanation of it, the angle of vision is ineluctably shifted. Calvin as a theologian is aware that he can only describe the edges and not the essence of God's mystery. Theology does not present the truth; it seeks to protect the Truth as revealed in Jesus Christ. Of course, with every theologian, Calvin tries to balance head, heart, and hand. Nevertheless, Calvin insists, theological witness comes from the human heart, not merely the head. The gospel "is a doctrine not of the tongue but of life. It is not apprehended by the understanding and memory alone, as other disciplines are, but it is received only when it possesses the whole soul, and finds a seat and resting place in the inmost affection of the heart" (III.6.4).[9] Put another way, the mystical and the dogmatic are two aspects of one theology. "The basic doctrines of the Trinity and Incarnation . . . are mystical doctrines formulated dogmatically."[10] Obviously, John Calvin should also be recognized as a theologian of the heart—a subject reflected very powerfully by Calvin's seal. Surrounding a hand holding a heart is the motto: My heart I offer to thee, O Lord, promptly and sincerely (*Cor Meum Tibi Offero Domine Prompte Et Sincere*).[11] This offering includes a too-seldom-noted confessional modesty, a genuine humility, and expressions of uncertainty, and some places where these virtues seem appropriate to us but do not appear to him. Perhaps on more occasions we might praise his honesty rather than berate his intransigency. Such traits in Calvin are too obvious to miss, but they have been too often dismissed in favor of other theological agendas.

8. Calvin writes to Luther (January 21, 1545) that the true faith cannot "do otherwise than break forth in the confession of faith." See *Letters of John Calvin*, ed. Jules Bonnet, trans. Marcus Robert Gilchrist (Grand Rapids: Baker Book House, 1983 [1850]).

9. References in parentheses are by book, chapter, and paragraph to the *Institutes of the Christian Religion* in the Library of Christian Classics edition (LCC), edited by John T. McNeill and trans. by Ford Lewis Battles, 2 vols. (Philadelphia: Westminster Press, 1960). The Latin and French editions were also consulted. Citations of Calvin's biblical commentaries are by book, chapter, and verse in the latest available English translation. For the Old Testament: *Commentaries of John Calvin*, various translators, 46 vols. (Edinburgh: The Calvin Translation Society, 1843–55). For the New Testament: *Calvin's New Testament Commentaries* ed. David W. Torrance and Thomas F. Torrance, various translators, 12 vols. (Grand Rapids: Wm. B. Eerdmans, 1959–72). When no English translation was available, reference is made to *Ioannais Calvini opera quae supersunt omnia* (CO), ed. by G. Baum, E. Cunitz, and E. Reuss, 59 vols (Brunsvigae: C. A. Schwetschke, 1863–1900). Reist (*Reading of Calvin's Institutes*) speaks of Calvin's "restless creativity" (3) and asserts that the McNeill/Battles edition "makes it possible to watch the seething ferment of Calvin's thought as one reads. In the process the rigid dogmatician of the [popular caricature] disappears" (4).

10. On this subject see Andrew Louth, *The Origins of the Christian Mystical Tradition: From Plato to Denys* (Oxford: Clarendon Press, 1981), xi. Especially to be noted is the influence of Plato on the Christian mystical tradition. For a comprehensive account, see Bernard McGinn, *The Presence of God: A History of Western Christian Mysticism*, 4 vols. (New York: Crossroad, 1997). Volume 1, chap. 3 concerns "Jesus: The Presence of God on Earth."

11. See the note on Calvin's emblem, LCC, I:540. To his friend Farel in August of 1541 Calvin wrote, "But when I remember that I am not my own, I offer up my heart, presented as a sacrifice to the Lord" (*Calvin's Letters*, I:280–81).

Theodore Beza, his friend and successor in Geneva, wrote that of all God's works those persons distinguished for learning and piety deserve to be remembered.[12] Calvin is remembered in prestigious schools that claim to be endowed by him. The large institutions of orthodox Calvinism maintain Calvin's conservative legacy. The small Schleiermacher sodality represents liberal Calvinism, and the edifice of neo-orthodox Calvinism rests its head on Calvin as one of its main pillars.[13] This writer has spent first-class time in all these schools but has earned only degrees of separation. Reformed scholasticism is certainly correct in pointing to Calvin's appeal to reason. Calvin does emphasize piety as the Schleiermachians note, and he takes the Word as seriously as his Barthian interpreters do. However, Calvin's tent is not pegged exclusively in any one of these camps. No-school or Calvin's Calvinism as presented here attempts to read Calvin as directly as possible, recognizing various and mighty fortresses on the horizon, but without assuming Calvin has taken refuge within any of their theological walls or is kept within their castle keep.

No-school Calvinism often writes about Calvin's theology by adopting the Loci method. That is, specific doctrines are examined with no conviction of a common thread running through that holds the individual doctrines together. The best example of this kind of exposition is François Wendel's excellent *Calvin: The Origins and Development of His Religious Thought*.[14] Since Calvin does not clearly identify a "central dogma," this approach avoids the sharp disagreements inevitably arising from any claim for a unitive but tacit organizational principle. The Loci method arranges the beads of Calvin's theology individually on a table where they may be seen but not worn. Separate pearls only become a necklace when they are strung together. Whether on a table or a neck, admiration is properly directed to the jewels exhibited rather than the string hidden.

An attempt to string along a bold synthesis may be added to careful summary. Calvin's Christian faith is founded on the confession that Jesus Christ is Lord, and his Christian theology is based on the conviction that God's elect are united in Christ. This union with Christ is also called "mystical union." As a mystery it

12. "Life of Calvin," in *Calvin's Tracts*, ed. and trans. Henry Beveridge, vol. 1 (Grand Rapids: Baker Book House, 1983 [1844]), xxi.

13. An orthodox Calvinist interpretation is presented by Richard Muller in his *The Unaccommodated Calvin: Studies in the Foundation of a Theological Tradition* (New York: Oxford University Press, 2000). This view is discussed further in the excursus under reason and the introductory section on the Calvinists. The Schleiermacher sodality is represented by Brian Gerrish in essays like "Schleiermacher and the Reformation: A Question of Doctrinal Development," and "Theology within the Limits of Piety Alone: Schleiermacher's and Calvin's Notion of God," in *The Old Protestantism and the New: Essays on the Reformation Heritage* (Chicago: University of Chicago Press, 1982), 179–95, 196–207. Also his *Grace and Gratitude: The Eucharistic Theology of John Calvin* (Minneapolis: Fortress Press, 1993). This interpretation is considered in the excursus under experience. A neo-orthodox view is found in Wilhelm Niesel, *The Theology of Calvin*, 1st ed., trans. Harold Knight (Philadelphia: Westminster Press, 1956). The second German edition of *Die Theologie Calvins* was published by Chr. Kaiser Verlag in 1957 with some significant changes. The term "neo-orthodoxy" may well be questioned for accuracy but is used for convenience.

14. François Wendel, *Calvin: The Origins and Development of His Religious Thought*, trans. Philip Mairet (New York: Harper & Row, 1963).

can be recognized, claimed, and illustrated but—like love or friendship—not ultimately defined, nor can clear and distinct deductions be made from the heart of a mystery. Calvin's confession and his conviction are unified by the work of the Holy Spirit—the bond of union between the Father and Son and the bond of union between God and the believers. In short, union with Christ for the faithful.[15] Put another way, Calvin's thought may be seen as an extended exposition of 2 Corinthians 5:19: "in Christ God was reconciling the world to himself." H. R. Mackintosh suggests that all Christian theology is an interpretation of believing experience from the inside, and oneness with Christ is the *punctum stans*.[16] This conviction cannot be demonstrated scientifically or philosophically, but it can be articulated theologically and its implications confessionally drawn. A number of serious students of Calvin (to be noted later) have made the suggestion that union with Christ is a crucial concept for Calvin,[17] but none has made the effort to demonstrate the foundational role of this doctrine across the total sweep of his theology. Thus, to sound suggestion this effort seeks to add solid exposition. Claiming union with Christ as the only key to unlocking all the mysteries of Calvin's thought would be egregious, but union with Christ is one master key that opens many doors which have been closed for a long time.[18] Since any affirmation without some denial is vacuous, it should be noted that the affirmation of union with Christ automatically denies the absolute and ubiquitous philosophical distinction between subject and object and thus the self separate from God. The concept of union in Christ means that the distinction between divine and human is not finally equivalent to that between objective and subjective. Union with Christ is, of course, a clear biblical witness, but disagreements over the actual existence and possible nature of a unifying thread in Calvin's theology will continue because it cannot be clearly seen. However, such disagreement only indirectly affects the facets we do envision and which shine into the eyes of the soul.

This preface concludes on a more directly personal note. Many writers seek to shroud themselves with the cloak of Olympian objectivity because the admission

---

15. The philosophical basis for this doctrinal exploration appeals to the rejection of the dogmatic method as described by Pepper and the acceptance of the cognitive intuition of a root metaphor. However, for Pepper's philosophical method of hypothesis, Christians must substitute the theological method of confession. In other words, the primary task of theology is to confess the faith aright (Rom. 14:11; 10:9; Phil. 2:11; Matt. 10:32; Luke 12:8; 1 John 4:15) (Stephen C. Pepper, "The Root Metaphor Theory of Metaphysics," *Journal of Philosophy* 32, no. 14 (1935): 365–74.

16. H. R. Mackintosh, "Unio Mystica as a Theological Conception," in *Some Aspects of Christian Belief* (New York: George H. Doran Company, 1923), 118.

17. Typical of this recognition is T. F. Torrance, *Conflict and Agreement in the Church* (London: Lutterworth Press, 1959), 91. "All Calvin's teaching and preaching have to do with salvation through union with Christ in his death and resurrection."

18. To be precise, "union with Christ" is not presented as *the* central dogma based on the older philosophic view of "essence," but as *a* central doctrine around which other doctrines in fact cluster based on the newer (Wittgensteinian) conceptualization of "family resemblances."

of human partisanship on the one hand, or of mortal opposition on the other, raises legitimate suspicions about accuracy and fairness. Although the ideal of pure objectivity is already considerably diminished in our romantic and individualistic age, one of the gnawing holes in this woolly mantle concerns subject selection. Clearly anyone who is willing to devote considerable time and effort to a topic has some kind of interest in it. My conversation with John Calvin goes back a long time. In my early teens, as my curiosity about the great world and the great world of books was taking shape, a pastor extended the immense kindness of taking me with gracious seriousness. When I asked him what I should read in order to get my head and heart properly aligned, he recommended the purchase of Calvin's *Institutes of the Christian Religion*.[19] As a teenager, I had little experience with the intellectual complexity of such topics as prayer and predestination. I was really just beginning to learn the grammar of the discussion and could not grasp the substance of the issues. In addition, and more detrimental to my understanding, was the fact that I had no idea about the structure of the whole. I was trying to study individual trees as I bumped into them with no sense of the shape of the forest. Moreover, I was not sophisticated enough to realize how much my half-formed preconceptions were misshaping what I was reading. Put positively, proper engagement requires understanding the substance of each part, the outline of the whole, and some willingness to be instructed. If John Calvin is regarded as an enemy, his work will be approached with hostility. If he is considered a friend, his work is approached, not uncritically, but with appreciation. I belong to the latter group because I have been engaged with Calvin's theology one way or another for most of my life.

Inevitably, the attempt to discern the real face of John Calvin by looking down into the deep well of history includes some glimpses of my grizzled visage in the ruffled water. From time to time I expect readers to see their own reflections on that same surface.

In any case, this is my report.

---

19. In 1952 I, ambitiously and at considerable financial sacrifice, purchased one hundred pounds of the Great Books of the Western World containing the Great Ideas of the Great Writers. Neither Martin Luther nor John Calvin is included in this set sponsored by a Baptist institution (Chicago) under a Jewish editor (Mortimer Adler) and informed by a Catholic perspective (Thomas Aquinas). This grandiose production was savagely, and (I say with buyer's remorse) accurately critiqued by Dwight MacDonald, "The Book-of-the-Millennium Club," in *Against the American Grain* (New York: Random House, 1962), 243–61. Nevertheless, the first volume correctly recommends the value of a Great Conversation with a Great Mind, which the following pages attempt.

Acknowledgments

First and foremost and always to my wife, Margaret McClure Partee. And our Family.

At various points—President William J. Carl III and Pittsburgh Theological Seminary colleagues: Jack Isherwood, Edith M. Humphrey, John P. Burgess, James E. Davison, John E. Wilson, Byron Jackson, Dale C. Allison, Anita Johnson, Florentina C. Lipuš—and Calvin C. Wilson.

From beginning to end—turning my handwritten, ink-splotched yellow pages into perfect typescript: Kathy Anderson, the coolest cool aide ever.

To my friend and editor Donald K. McKim, whose enthusiasm for Calvin and baseball may surpass my own.

This book is dedicated to two friends: Ulrich Mauser and Andrew H. Purves who ran the theological bases with me.

Considering the Engagement

An Introduction

A. OVERVIEW AND SCOPE

Dragonflies can see in all directions at once, but human vision pays out in a different coign of vantage. The present sight line views Calvin's theology as an exposition of the bold and central Christian conviction, "Jesus Christ is Lord" (Phil. 2:11). Every field of endeavor is defined by ultimate criteria whose ultimacy precludes appealing to more basic and supporting evidence. The Lordship of Christ and the resulting life in him is the fundamental confession of the Christian faith and as such illuminates every corner of Calvin's theology. To ask for reasons for this confession is not to understand what a fundamental confession is. Calvin maintains this essential affirmation not as a basic principle in a philosophy of religion nor as a central dogma in a system of theology, because the final adequacy of principles in theology is replaced by a person, Jesus Christ, and the common view of Calvin interpreted under a single doctrine such as "the majesty, glory or sovereignty of God" is likewise rejected.[1] Too often smooth summaries morph

---

1. Calvin takes principles seriously. He thinks the intellect is rarely deceived in general or essential definitions but often mistaken in the application of the principle to a particular case (II.2.23).

into vicious abstractions that allow the false shepherd to call down thunder on his own flock and lightning on sheep in other folds. Calvin often draws conclusions from principles, but his theology is centered on the person of Jesus Christ, not principles. Minimizing the heart's conviction in favor of a solitary head trip misrepresents Calvin and is the source of most of the caricatures of him. Faith is knowledge of God given in Christ and "both revealed to our minds and sealed upon our hearts through the Holy Spirit" (III.2.7). The hearts of humankind are in God's hand (Com. Gen. 33:4; 35:5). However, in discussing mind and heart Calvin insists that "the Word of God is not received by faith if it flits about in the top of the brain, but when it takes root in the depth of the heart." The mind is illumined by the Spirit of God who also works to confirm the heart. In this confirmation of the heart the Spirit's power is more clearly manifested because it "is harder for the heart to be furnished with assurance than for the mind to be endowed with thought" (III.2.36). In the Commentary on Romans (10:10), Calvin declares, "The seat of faith is not in the head but in the heart." He continues, "I would not contend about the part of the body in which faith is located: but as the word *heart* is often taken for a serious and sincere feeling I would say that faith is a firm and effectual confidence and not a bare notion only."

The famous opening sentence of the *Institutes* declares, "Nearly all the wisdom we possess, that is to say, true and sound wisdom, consists of two parts: the knowledge of God and of ourselves" (I.1.1). This statement denies the sharp modern distinction between objective and subjective. In an important study James Brown correctly points out that the unquestioning modern acceptance of the distinction between subject and object is testimony to the immense influence of Immanuel Kant. This distinction was vaguely adumbrated in Greek philosophy and definitely presented in Descartes's antithesis between thinking and extended substances. "Still it was only in Kant that the modern formulation of the relation clearly emerged and that the terminology in which we still discuss the problems of the relationship was fixed."[2] Whether the Kantian dualism involves a transcendental

---

Nevertheless, it is crucial to recognize that Calvin's theology is based on personal not philosophical categories. Troeltsch claims, "Calvin's basic concept was the majesty of God" (Ernst Troeltsch, *The Social Teaching of the Christian Churches*, trans. Olive Wyon, vol. 2 [New York: Harper and Brothers, 1960], 582). According to H. Bavinck, "The root principle of [Calvinism] is the confession of God's absolute sovereignty" ("The Future of Calvinism," trans. G. Vos, in *The Presbyterian and Reformed Review* 17 [January 1894]: 3). Of greater weight is the observation of John T. McNeill, the doyen of American Calvin scholars; Calvin's theology "has its center in the doctrine of the sovereignty and sublime majesty of God" (John T. McNeill, "The Democratic Element in Calvin's Theology," *Church History* 18, no. 3 [September 1949]: 155). In a helpful article on sovereignty as a principle, David C. Steinmetz ("Calvin and the Absolute Power of God," *The Journal of Medieval and Renaissance Studies* 18 [1988]: 65) first simply declares, "The sovereignty of God is absolute" and then carefully analyzes Calvin's rejection of the medieval distinction between God's absolute and ordained power as too speculative.

2. James Brown, *Subject and Object in Modern Theology* (London: SCM Press, 1955), 19. The same salvo is fired by William M. Thompson, "The Saints, Justification and Sanctification: An Ecumenical Thought Experiment," *Pro Ecclesia* 4, no. 1 (Winter 1995): 17, who writes concerning justification and sanctification, "Calvin's view of this matter is too nuanced, I think, to be adequately explained in these categories of the objective and subjective."

synthesis of objective and subjective need not be decided here. That the subject-object distinction was ontological in Descartes and epistemological in Kant and both in modern thought and neither in Calvin is a sufficient conclusion. In any case, the concept of objective and subjective can be applied to Calvin only with considerable caution. The distinction may be temporarily useful for analyzing some particular parts, but it is too Kantian to be finally adequate for understanding Calvin's theology in general. Calvin's thought is more unitive than dichotomous. Specifically, to the extent that Calvin maintains the doctrine of "union with Christ," he rejects the finality of the modern subject-object dichotomy.

In addition, Calvin's view of true and sound wisdom denies what later becomes the ubiquitous Cartesian dualism separating mankind from Godhead. To the contrary, Calvin affirms in the *Institutes* what God does for us and with us in Jesus Christ. Doubtless, such an appeal to mystery is intolerable in a logical structure, but Calvin knew that Christian faith is not a logical structure. By its nature, union with the Lord Christ does not allow human control of its reality or conceptualization. In the preface to his *Nicomachean Ethics* Aristotle, called the master of those who know, offers a salutary reminder to theologians to expect only the precision a subject-matter admits (I, 1094b). Christians have always known that the most appropriate response to the mystery of incarnation and incorporation is faithful worship,[3] but Paul reminded Timothy that faith and good doctrine go together (Com. I Tim. 4:6). Therefore, theological reflection, like the *Institutes of the Christian Religion*, can serve the beneficial function of aligning the head and the heart.

A word about scope. First, there are legitimate claims for introductory attention devoted to other early non-Lutheran, Protestant thinkers preceding, or contemporary with, Calvin, like William Farel, Huldreich Zwingli, Martin Bucer, and Heinrich Bullinger. The attempt to include them in a single exposition requires the creation of a synthesis external to each individual theologian. While recognizing clearly and accepting happily the contributions of many theologians to the complex development of the Reformed tradition, we can still affirm John Calvin as the greatest systematic thinker among them. A concentrated engagement with his work offers the advantage of dealing with the internal coherence of a single mind in a single text and context. This study does not attempt an extended definition of "Calvinism" before or beyond Calvin since Calvin's own theology is regarded as a complete and sufficient subject.

Second, Calvin wrote more than most of us have the ability or inclination to read, whether in Latin or French or even in English translation. Alone or together, his production of scriptural commentaries, sermons and letters, tracts and treatises is massive and daunting.[4] Considerable attention has been paid to Calvin's

---

3. According to Calvin, "Believers have no greater help than public worship, for by it God raises his own folk upward step by step" (IV.1.5).

4. For a summary and survey, see Wulfert de Greef, *The Writings of John Calvin: An Introductory Guide*, trans. Lyle D. Bierma (Grand Rapids: Baker Books, 1993). See also Jean-François Gilmont, *John Calvin and the Printed Book*, trans. Karin Maag (Kirksville, MO: Truman State University Press, 2005). According to the apposite phrasing of Andrew Pettegree, many of Calvin's letters "are

importance as a biblical commentator, as a polemicist, as a pastor and preacher.[5] It is well to remember Calvin's life's work was ministerial, not academical. The focus here is Calvin's theology as outlined in the *Institutes*. By itself Calvin's *Institutes of the Christian Religion* represents not merely one of the most important core texts of Christian theology, but a complex set of texts in itself. There were major Latin editions in 1536, 1539, and 1559 as well as French translations that reward detailed comparison by those interested in the subtleties of modification. The *Institutes* grew from six chapters in 1536 to seventeen in 1539, and to eighty in 1559. However, and fortunately, through these various editions Calvin devoted a sustained effort to summarizing his developing theology with the result that one can reasonably expect to understand the doctrinal *content* of Calvin's mature theology because of the systematic *context* Calvin himself provided. John Hesselink puts the matter this way: "There is more to Calvin's theology than the *Institutes*. Nevertheless, it is here that we find the reformer's thought expressed in its most comprehensive and ordered manner."[6] The final *Institutes of the Christian Religion* is also massive and daunting in its own way, but it provides a single text to study and by which every exposition can be judged. The following pages are not designed simply as an introduction to nor a summary of Calvin's theology, but rather an engagement with his thought, guided by his own exposition.

Third, the distinction between primary and secondary sources is useful and, therefore, often made. The primary source here is John Calvin and what he wrote. Secondary sources refer to everybody else and what they write—including these pages. The secondary writings on Calvin are voluminous, and one could spend several lifetimes just reading about Calvin without actually reading his own work. Useful surveys of his theology as a whole exist and at varying levels of accuracy and difficulty. Many special studies of particular doctrines are noted herein when they aid insight into the *Institutes*. However, the important task of interpreting Calvin's important interpreters is not a major purpose of this work. An engagement with Calvin himself rather than his scholars means trying to understand and articulate

---

masterpieces of controlled passion, patient advocacy, and clear minded exposition" ("The Spread of Calvin's Thought," in *The Cambridge Companion to John Calvin*, ed. Donald M. McKim [New York: Cambridge University Press, 2004], 213). See also Jean-Daniel Benoit, "Calvin the Letter Writer," trans. G. S. R. Cox, in *John Calvin: Courtenay Studies in Reformation Theology*, ed. G. E. Duffield (Grand Rapids: Wm. B. Eerdmans, 1966), 67–101. Also Douglas Kelly, "The Transmission and Translation of the Collected Letters of John Calvin," *Scottish Journal of Theology* 30 (1977): 429–37.

5. An interesting approach was initiated by Richard Stauffer to compare Calvin the preacher with Calvin the theologian, giving precedence to the sermons over the *Institutes*. See his *Dieu, la creation et la Providence dans le prédication de Calvin* (Bern: P. Lang, 1978).

6. I. John Hesselink, "Calvin's Theology," in McKim, *Cambridge Companion*, 75. In a contrary opinion Michael Walzer, *The Revolution of the Saints: A Study in the Origin of Radical Politics* (Cambridge: Harvard University Press, 1965), 27, declares Calvin was "not primarily a theologian or a philosopher but an ideologist. . . . Detached from the traditional forms of theological and philosophical speculation, Calvin might be described most simply as a practical man of ideas: a French refugee intellectual caught up in Genevan politics." It is true that Calvin made a political impact, but he called his work "Christian philosophy," which meant theology (III.7.1; II.2.26; see chaps. 1 and 2 in my *Calvin and Classical Philosophy* [Louisville, KY: Westminster John Knox Press, 2005]).

what can be learned from a direct and careful reading of his work. Of course, no one is able to think apart from the insights and influences of teachers and studies greatly admired or strongly rejected. Often responsible disagreements among careful students focus the issues of interpretation sharply and helpfully.

B. THREE INTRODUCTORY CONCLUSIONS

Attempting to understand Calvin requires a starting point, behind which is always a stand point. An obvious relation exists between judgment and judge since no one can step completely out of his body or go entirely off her head. Three standing places inform the beginning and shape the ending of this effort. Originally, of course, these conclusions came at the endset of a long process of reflection, but they now orient the mind-set and should be submitted to the reader at the outset before the onset. The first introductory conclusion considers those who have attacked Calvin and the second those who defend him. Calvin's enemies are profoundly wrong in their caricature of him. Additionally and sadly, but not surprisingly, Calvin's friends often believe he says what they want to hear. The relation of Calvin to various Calvinists is a serious and protean subject finally to be narrowed to the question of whether Calvinism is a true development or a real distortion of Calvin's theology. Put another way, a number of Calvin's presumptive family of friends are less faithful to his legacy than his declared enemies. The third introductory conclusion notes three modern assumptive misunderstandings of Calvin's theology.

1. Opponents of Calvin: The Caricatures

The first operating conclusion maintains that Calvin does not deserve the obloquy so often applied to him. Of course no one is above or beyond criticism. When Polonius assures Prince Hamlet that the actors will be treated as they deserve, Hamlet asseverates, "God's bodikens, man, much better. Use every man after his desert and who shall 'scape whipping" (II.2.553–55). Recognition of human weakness, and even its ridicule, may serve a positive function, but the ferocious popular prejudice against Calvin and Calvinism militates against their proper understanding. This fact is nowhere better illustrated than in William Faulkner's *Light in August* (to my mind, the greatest American novel ever written[7]). Faulkner uses Calvinism here (and elsewhere in his writings) as a centrally negative theme.

---

7. In addition to his masterful depictions of Joe Christmas's search for identity, Joanna Burden's outsider status, Percy Grimm's violence, and Rev. Gail Hightower's obsession, Faulkner describes an elemental female in Lena Grove. Equally wonderful is the chap. 1 description of Eula Varner in *The Town*, for whom men chewed their "bitter thumbs": "There was just too much of what she was for any one human female package to contain and hold: too much of white, too much of female, too much of maybe just glory, . . . so that at first sight of her you felt a kind of shock of gratitude just for being alive and being male at the same instant with her in space and time."

The main character, Joe Christmas (with the religiously significant initials), is brutally raised by Simon McEachern and his catechism. A "ruthless man who had never known either pity or doubt."

This negativity usually spills over both Calvin and Calvinism, but sometimes Calvin is set apart and Calvinism alone bears the full brunt of opprobrium. In the careless mind Calvin is considered the dark despot of Geneva whose fearsome shadow blocks all his sympathizers from the light of life. John T. McNeill opines, "Calvin has been so industriously defamed that many on the fringe of the educated world think of him primarily with a certain abhorrence."[8] For example, writing in *Harpers Magazine* (October 1930, 545), R. L. Duffus asserts that Pittsburgh would benefit immeasurably from "one large and comprehensive funeral—it needs to bury John Calvin so deep that he will never get up again." The author is actually attacking Presbyterians in Pittsburgh, whom he believes to be responsible for many things he dislikes. However, there are large numbers of Roman Catholics in New Orleans and large numbers of Lutherans in Minneapolis. The legitimacy and accuracy of criticizing their leadership roles by affirming the value of a large, comprehensive funeral with the deep burial of Thomas Aquinas or Martin Luther pushes hyperbole beyond credible limits.

In some notable instances, angry criticism of Calvinism becomes positively venomous. For example, the acerbic H. L. Mencken writes, "[In America Calvinism] became no more than a luxuriant demonology; even God himself was transformed into a superior sort of devil ever wary and wholly merciless." Mencken excoriates "the throbbing influence of an ever alert and bellicose Puritanism." "The Puritan's utter lack of aesthetic sense, his distrust of all romantic emotion, his unmatchable intolerance of opposition, his unbreakable belief in his own bleak and narrow views, his savage cruelty of attack, his lust for relentless and barbarous persecution—these things have put an almost unbearable burden upon the exchange of ideas in the United States."[9] On a less curmudgeonly day, Mencken might have appreciated the sardonic attack on his unsympathetic evaluation, persuasively mounted by Marilynne Robinson in "Puritans and Prigs." "Puritanism," she writes, "was a highly elaborated moral, religious, intellectual, and political tradition which had its origins in the writing and social experimentation of John Calvin and those he influenced." The popular consensus on the Puritans which Mencken represents "is a great example of our collective eagerness to disparage without knowledge or information about the thing disparaged, when the reward is the pleasure of sharing an attitude one knows is socially approved."[10]

8. John T. McNeill in Richard Stauffer, *L'Humanité de Calvin* (Neuchâtel, Éditions Delachaux et Niestlé, 1964); English trans., *The Humanness of John Calvin*, trans. George H. Shriver (Nashville: Abingdon Press, 1971), 107. Stauffer deals with some of the more learned caricatures of Calvin in his introductory chapter, 19–31. See also Basil Hall, "The Calvin Legend," in *Courtenay Studies*, 1–18.

9. H. L. Mencken, "Puritanism as a Literary Force," in *A Book of Prefaces*, 2nd ed. (New York: Alfred A. Knopf, 1918), 197, 201–2.

10. Marilynne Robinson, *The Death of Adam: Essays on Modern Thought* (New York: Houghton Mifflin Company, 1998), 150, 153.

On a presumably more scholarly level (the title page lists his degrees—B.D., Th.M., Th.D.), Lawrence M. Vance's *The Other Side of Calvinism* (distributed by Vance Publications, 1991) insists that

> Calvinism has established a foothold on theology, and therefore in actuality become the plague and scourge of the Church. . . . The salient determinant [for Vance's writing] is the tremendous damaging nature of the Calvinistic system. Nothing will deaden a church or put a young man out of the ministry any more than an adherence to Calvinism. Nothing will foster pride and indifference as will affection for Calvinism. Nothing will destroy holiness and spirituality as an attachment to Calvinism. There is no greater violation of every hermeneutical, contextual, analytical, and exegetical interpretation of Scripture than Calvinism. (vii, viii)

The same jeremiad against Calvin and Calvinism is passionately continued by Dave Hunt in *What Love Is This? Calvinism's Misrepresentation of God.* Hunt writes, "My heart has been broken by Calvinism's misrepresentation of the God of the Bible whom I love, and for the excuse this has given atheists not to believe in him."[11] Calvinism is defined by the five points of TULIP and with the conviction that the doctrine of limited atonement denies the biblical God of love. Hunt agrees with Vance in regarding with alarm the continuing allegiance to Calvinism of such "evangelical leaders" as John Gerstner, his student R. C. Sproul, D. James Kennedy, Charles Spurgeon, and others. The question, of course, is whether Calvinism misrepresents God or Hunt and Vance misrepresent Calvinism.

Hunt's evaluation can be challenged on sociological, theological, and historical grounds. First, Hunt's debate partners are those he designates as "evangelical leaders." Consequently the views of a large number of highly regarded and appropriately credentialed Calvin scholars are simply ignored, a procedure that does not build confidence in his interpretation. Second, to address only one theological issue, John Calvin believed his teaching on God's eternal election (predestination) was biblical, traditional (Augustinian), and pastoral (comforting). If Hunt had evidenced more understanding of Calvin's intention, his rejection of Calvin's conclusion would be more convincing.

Anyone determined to denounce the worship of Deity and the study of divinity will sooner than later attack John Calvin. In his manifesto *god is not Great,* Christopher (ironically his name means Christ bearer) Hitchens asserts, "According to the really extreme religious totalitarians, such as John Calvin, . . . an infinity of punishment can be awaiting you even before you are born. Calvin's Geneva was a prototypical totalitarian state, and Calvin himself a sadist and torturer and killer. The urge to ban and censor books, silence dissenters, condemn outsiders, invade the private sphere, and invoke an exclusive salvation is the very essence of the totalitarian. [Calvin's followers] are still among us and go by the softer names

---

11. Dave Hunt, *What Love Is This? Calvinism's Misrepresentation of God* (Sisters, OR: Loyal Publishing, 2002), 414. The T.U.L.I.P. is described at book II, section A.

of Presbyterians and Baptists."[12] Judgments like those of Duffus, Mencken, Vance, Hunt, and Hitchens demonstrate that the terms "Calvin" and "Calvinism" are often tarred with the same brush, but a number of scholarly ornithologists see them as birds of quite different feathers. In understandable opposition to Calvin's fierce detractors, his staunch defenders like Émile Doumergue,[13] Emanuel Stickelberger,[14] and Gabriel Mützenberg[15] overemphasize his positive aspects. McNeill offers this stout defense of Calvin:

> To read at large in [Calvin's] letters and treatises was to encounter multiple proofs of a vivid humanness, an outgoing concern for others and enjoyment of association with many of differing social rank, a gentle courtesy with correspondents, and a sturdy loyalty to friends, of whom in youth and age he had a wide circle. This aspect of his personality has been too little regarded, even by many who are familiar with the outlines of his theology. The warmth of his normal relations with his associates; his tenderness toward sufferers from pain or bereavement; his solicitous concern for the members of his correspondents' families; the generous hospitality of his home; his deep and lasting affection for his wife and appreciation of her fine qualities; his resolute commitment to a charitable course in church reform whereby small issues might not become occasions of alienation; his abiding sense of the communion of saints and of the brotherhood of man; these are amply attested elements of his personality which the blots upon his record should not be allowed to eclipse.[16]

Reading Calvin between his detractors and defenders nevertheless generates the impression of overwhelming intensity—an always attractive feature in a great teacher but sometimes an uncomfortable one in a good friend. His seriousness led to the sobriquet, "the Accusative Case," applied in his early years. But, at the end when Calvin died, according to his friend and colleague Theodore Beza:

> There was a general lamentation throughout the city—the whole state regretting its wisest citizen—the church deploring the departure of its faithful pastor—the academy grieving at being deprived of so great a teacher, and all lamenting the loss of one who was, under God, a common parent and

12. Christopher Hitchens, *god is not Great: How Religion Poisons Everything* (Boston: Twelve, 2007), 233–34. Perhaps the nadir of modern obloquy was reached in Aldous Huxley's unsubstantiated claim "that during the great Calvin's theocratic rule of Geneva a child was publicly decapitated for having ventured to strike its parents" (*Proper Studies* [London: Chatto and Windis, 1929], 287).

13. Émile Doumergue, *Jean Calvin, Les Hommes et les choses de son temps*, 7 vols. (Lausanne: G. Bridel et Cie, 1897–1927).

14. Emanuel Stickelberger, *Calvin, A Life*, trans. David Georg Gelzer (Richmond, VA: John Knox Press, 1954).

15. The reprobations of Calvin from the distant past and near present focus Mützenberg's rebuttals. In the chapter dealing with the "true Calvin," Mützenberg appeals to evidences from Calvin's portraits, his friendships (Farel and Viret), his compassion, his sensitivity and vulnerability advancing the theme—"after the darkness light" (*post tenebras lux*)—and concluding that Calvin's theology is alive and well (Gabriel Mützenberg, *L'Obsession Calviniste* [Geneva: Labor et Fides, 1979], 57).

16. Stauffer, *Humanness*, 9–10. Thomas Cahill in his *How the Irish Saved Civilization: The Untold Story of Ireland's Heroic Role from the Fall of Rome to the Rise of Medieval Europe* (New York: Doubleday, 1995), 159, declares McNeill "that most balanced of all church historians."

comforter. . . . Having been a spectator of his conduct for sixteen years . . . I can now declare, that in him all men may see a most beautiful example of the Christian character, an example which it is as easy to slander as it is difficult to imitate.[17]

The Calvin article in the Schaff/Herzog encyclopedia suggests, "Experience shows there is no harder master than a timid man compelled to lead. Again: his ill health must be taken into account. He was a walking hospital. Such men are not apt to be gentle. The wonder rather is that he showed so patient a spirit" (368). Understandably, Calvin inspires more admiration than affection. Beza admits that by nature Calvin was formed for gravity.[18] For that reason Calvin is often pronounced guilty of Carlyle's oft-repeated charge, "The man who cannot laugh is not only fit for treasons, stratagems and spoils; but his whole life is already a treason and a stratagem."[19] Apparently humans are the only creatures God designed with the ability to laugh. The so-called laughter of hyenas and loons does not count since the noises they produce are not occasioned by amusement. Indeed so distinctive is this characteristic of the species that pagan philosophers defined man as a risible animal (*Homo risens*) aware of all sorts of absurdities, interruptions, inconveniences, embarrassments—and weaknesses.[20] Commenting on Philippians 3:1 and recommending "holy joy," Calvin notices the wordplay on concision and circumcision demonstrating to his mind that the Holy Spirit on occasion employs wit and humor.

Interestingly, Mikhail Bakhtin claims, "The sixteenth century represents the summit in the history of laughter."[21] His thesis is chiefly applied to François

---

17. Beza's "Life of Calvin" in *Calvin's Tracts*, ed. and trans. Henry Beveridge, vol. 1 (Grand Rapids: Baker Book House, 1983 [1844]), I, xcvi, c.

18. Ibid., xcviii.

19. Thomas Carlyle, *Sartor Resartus*, Bk. I, 4. This riposte appears to be a rephrase of Lorenzo's comment to Jessica on music (*Merchant of Venice*, V.1.83–85).

20. See Nathan A. Scott Jr., "The Bias of Comedy and the Narrow Escape into Faith," in *Essays on Religion in the Comic Perspective*, ed. M. Conrad Hyers (New York: Seabury Press, 1969), 56. A famous, ponderous, and remarkably unfunny analysis is offered in Freud's *Wit and Its Relation to the Unconscious* in *The Basic Writings of Sigmund Freud*, trans. A. A. Brill (New York: Modern Library, 1938).

21. Mikhail Bakhtin, *Rabelais and His World*, trans. Helene Iswolsky (Bloomington: Indiana University Press, 1984), 101. See Lucien Febvre, *Le Problème de l'incroyance au XVI⁰ siècle: La Religion de Rabelais* (Paris: Éditions Albin Michel, 1968). Calvin and Rabelais are also paired in W. von Wartburg, *Évolution et structure de la langue française* (Tübingen: A. Francke, 1993), 158ff. Writing about Calvin's language Wartburg insists, "La qualité qui domine est sans doute la logique. Calvin énumère les arguments, il les enrégimente et les fait marcher comme une armée rangée en bataille" (164). Calvin is passionate about his subject and he is attempting to persuade, but one may certainly demur from Wartburg's martial imagery. To write reasonably is not to be dominated by logic. Nor is orderly presentation equivalent to an army sweeping into battle. "On retrouve dans ces expressions la passion froide et raisonnée qui dominait cet homme" (166). Among older works on Calvin's contribution to the French language see Abel LeFranc, *Calvin et l'éloquence française* (Paris: Librairie Fischbacker, 1934). More recent studies by Francis Higman include *The Style of John Calvin in His French Polemical Treatises* (London: Oxford University Press, 1967). Also "The Reformation and the French Language," in *L'Esprit Créateur: The French Renaissance Mind: Studies Presented to W. G. Moore* (winter 1976), 20–36. In his introduction to *Three French Treatises*, Higman claims that Calvin's letter to King François I is "one of the most moving pieces of writing in the sixteenth century [and] when Calvin

Rabelais, but includes the declaration that sixteenth-century Protestant leaders used comic forms in writing "to gain popularity, to become accessible to all and to win their confidence."[22] Bakhtin quotes Calvin's colleague, Pierre Viret, to this effect: "I do not deny that the Word of God demands a respectful approach. But it should also be understood that the word of God is not so harsh and austere as to prevent its importance and majesty from being combined with elements of irony, farce, proper playfulness, sharp sallies and jokes."[23] As an example, Doumergue's judgment is cited that Pierre Olivétan's Bible of 1535 reveals a "naive popular humor" that places him "between Rabelais and Calvin; nearer in style to Rabelais, to Calvin in thought."[24] Declaring with Doumergue that "Rabelais and Calvin (and Olivétan) were the creators of French literary prose,"[25] Bakhtin adds, "Even the agelast Calvin wrote a pamphlet about relics with a certain comic overtone."[26] The single, and unusual, word "agelast" summarizes the popular view of John Calvin: a person who does not laugh or smile; someone who cannot enjoy life or the fact that others might be happy.

Certainly one cannot claim Calvin was frivolous or lighthearted, but, as Bakhtin observes, Calvin demonstrates a form of ironic humor in his massively satirical treatise lengthily entitled "Admonition in which it is shown how advantageous it would be for Christendom that the bodies and relics of saints were reduced to a kind of inventory, including those which are said to exist, as well in Italy as in France, Germany, Spain, and other Countries."[27] Of this work there were twenty editions to 1622. In a rare reference to his childhood Calvin expresses the outrage of a small boy observing the poor ignorant women of his parish, unable to distinguish between the figures of saints, murderers, and demons, adorning all alike with garlands.[28] One can only guess at the continuing impact of the child-

---

translated it into French . . . it became perhaps the finest piece of French written until then—not excepting Rabelais" (Jean Calvin, *Three French Treatises*, ed. Francis M. Higman [London: Athlone Press, 1970], 6). Higman writes that no important work of philosophy or theology had been written in French before Calvin's 1541 *Institution de la religion chrestienne*. See also Higman's interesting chapter on music in *The Reformation World*, ed. Andrew Pettegree (New York: Routledge, 2000).

22. Bakhtin, *Rabelais and His World*, 90.

23. Ibid., 100.

24. Doumergue, *Calvin*. 1:121. In the classically ribald *Histories of Gargantua and Pantagruel*, Rabelais refers to "the hypocritical tribes of eavesdropping dissemblers, superstitious pope-mongers, and priest-ridden bigots, the frantic Pistolets, the demonical Calvins, imposters of Geneva . . ." (Depuys elle engendra les Matagotz, Cagotz et Papelars; les maniacles Pistoletz; les demoniacles Calvins imposteurs de Geneve; les enraiges Putherbes, Briffaulx, Caphars, Chattemittes, Canibales et aultres monstres difformes et contrefaicts en despit de Nature) (François Rabelais, *Gargantua and Pantagruel*, trans. Thomas Urquhart and Peter Motteau, Book 4, 32 [Chicago: William Benton, 1952], 274). In a 1533 letter to Francis Daniel, Calvin calls *Pantagruel* "obscene" (*Letters* I, 39).

25. Bakhtin, *Rabelais and His World*, 457.

26. Ibid., 350.

27. *Calvin's Tracts*, I, 189–341.

28. Ibid., 341. Presumably Calvin would object to whatever remained of the lascivious and blasphemous behaviors of the feast of fools. See Ingvild Sælid Gilhus, "Carnival in Religion: The Feast of Fools in France," *Numen* 37 (June 1990): 24–52. Also her *Laughing Gods, Weeping Virgins: Laughter in the History of Religion* (New York: Routledge, 1997).

hood memory of reverently kissing a holy fragment of the Virgin Mary's mother Anna at a monastery near his boyhood home in Noyon.[29] As an adult Calvin notes that among the amazing things an account of relics would reveal is that every apostle had more than four bodies and every saint two or three.[30] Equally amazing anatomically is the display of the foreskin of Jesus at three (!) churches—one in Charrox, one in Rome,[31] and the third in Hildesheim.[32] Again, although only one man carried the cross, if all the pieces were assembled in the same place, one could build a ship.[33] Among the credulous, goat droppings are taken for the beads of the Virgin Mary.[34] Calvin recognizes that since the body of the Virgin Mary is not on earth, no bones can be produced, but the compensation is her breast milk. "Had the breasts of the most Holy Virgin yielded a more copious supply than is given by a cow, or had she continued to nurse during her whole life time, she scarcely could have furnished the quantity which is exhibited." Then Calvin's imagination takes a wild leap as he declares, "I would like to know how that milk . . . was collected, so as to be preserved until our time. We do not read of any person who had the curiosity to undertake the task."[35]

In calling attention to Calvin's humor, Benjamin Warfield admits it is of the "mordant," "pungent," "biting," and "cutting" variety.[36] Warfield quotes Calvin (without indicating the location of the text), "Many—or perhaps we may say, most—men are much more readily helped when they are instructed in a joyous and pleasant manner. . . . Those who have the gift to teach in such a manner as to delight their readers and to induce them to profit by the pleasure they give them, are doubly to be praised."[37]

The polymath Philip Schaff concludes:

> Calvin's character is less attractive, and his life less dramatic than Luther's or Zwingli's. . . . He lacked the genial element of humor and pleasantry . . . stern, severe, unbending, yet with fires of passion and affection glowing beneath the marble surface. His name will never rouse popular enthusiasm. . . . History furnishes no more striking example of a man of so little

29. "Admonition against Relics," *Calvin's Tracts*, I, 328.
30. Ibid., 293.
31. Ibid., 296.
32. Ibid., 340.
33. Ibid., 301.
34. Ibid., 312.
35. Ibid., 317.
36. Benjamin Breckinridge Warfield, *Calvin and Calvinism* (New York: Oxford University Press, 1931), 295–98. See also the remarks on "Calvin and Humor" in chap. 11 of Alain Perrot, *Le Visage Humain de Jean Calvin* (Geneva: Labor et Fides, 1986).
37. Warfield, *Calvin and Calvinism*, 297. Deuteronomy 24:5 mandates that a newly married man is not to be conscripted into the army. "He shall be free at home for one year, to be happy with [his] wife." "That God should permit a bride to enjoy herself with her husband affords no trifling proof of God's indulgence. Assuredly, it cannot be but that the lust of the flesh must affect the connection of husband and wife with some amount of sin; yet God not only pardons the sin, but covers it with the veil of holy matrimony, lest that which is sinful in itself should be imputed to the couple. Nay, God spontaneously allows them to enjoy themselves" (Com. Dt. 24:5). If Calvin's understanding of this passage did not strike him as amusing, even hilarious, it certainly strikes me so.

personal popularity, and yet such great influence upon the people; of such natural timidity and bashfulness combined with such strength of intellect and character.[38]

The profound seriousness of John Calvin is obvious. Human life is beset by calamities whose only antidote is trust in God's abiding providence for the company of the faithful. In addition to this serious disposition Calvin's wretched health undoubtedly precluded a lighter and more joyously playful approach to theological issues.[39] Engaging Calvin does not require the admiration of Doumergue and Stickelberger, but it does not allow the animosity of Vance and Mencken.[40]

Two of the most imprecise words in the intellectual portion of the English language are "Platonism" and "Calvinism."[41] The term "platonic" is quite often used to refer to ideas only very loosely connected to the *Dialogues of Plato*. In the same way, and even worse, the terms "Calvinism" and "Calvinistic" are used so widely, and wildly, as to be almost meaningless. The view that Calvin was the dictator of Geneva wielding the whip of logic and driving a chariot named the *Sovereignty of God* harnessed to mean-spirited steeds called Predestination and Total Depravity is simply wrong.[42] On the contrary, Calvin's *Institutes* represents a reflection on loving "God with all your heart, and with all your soul, and with all your

38. Schaff, *History of the Christian Church*, vol. 8 (Grand Rapids: Wm. B. Eerdmans Publishing Company, 1979 [1910]), 258.

39. Doumergue, *Calvin*, 3:509ff., devotes part of a chapter to Calvin's illnesses. See also Charles L. Cooke, "Calvin's Illnesses and Their Relation to Christian Vocation," in *John Calvin and the Church*, ed. Timothy George (Louisville, KY: Westminster/John Knox Press, 1990), 49–70. In an essay entitled "Calvin's Aging Body in His Maturing Theology" (not yet published), W. Allen Hogge, MD, assesses Calvin's physical condition and concludes it had no impact on his doctrine of providence. Writing to Admiral Coligny's wife on August 5, 1563, Calvin declares that diseases "are to us the messengers of death, we ought to learn to have one foot raised to take our departure when it shall please God" (IV, 331). The second attempt to kill Admiral Coligny in 1572 was successful. Those who cannot forget Calvin's involvement in the burning of the single heretic, Michael Servetus, might also remember the deaths of tens of thousands of faithful Huguenots in the Massacre of St. Bartholomew's Day or read Christopher Marlowe's 1593 drama "Massacre at Paris." On the death of Servetus, see Robinson, *Death of Adam*, 200–206. According to R. H. Murray, *The Political Consequences of the Reformation* (New York: Russell and Russell, 1960), 171, Pope "Gregory XIII proclaimed a solemn jubilee, struck a medal to commemorate the massacre, and ordered Vasari to paint on the walls of the Vatican scenes such as the throwing of the body of Admiral Coligny from the window."

40. A fair presentation of Calvin as husband and father, friend and pastor is found in Stauffer's *Humanness of John Calvin*. Also see the chapters on Calvin's friends and his wife in Perrot, *Le Visage Humain de Jean Calvin*, 11–56.

41. Menna Prestwich correctly observes, "Calvinism is an indispensable term, but it is one which Calvin himself rejected and considered odious" (*International Calvinism*, ed. Menna Prestwich [Oxford: Clarendon Press, 1985], 2). See also *Calvinism in Europe, 1540–1620*, ed. Andrew Pettegree, Alastair Duke, and Gillian Lewis (Cambridge: Cambridge University Press, 1994); *Later Calvinism: International Perspectives*, ed. W. Fred Graham (Kirksville, MO: Sixteenth-Century Journal Publishers, 1994).

42. Basil Hall thinks "Calvinism is essentially a passionate theocentrism: its central dogma is the sovereignty of God." He claims, "What is new with Calvin is the absolute and unqualified assertion of God's sovereignty and man's total corruption as fundamental to right belief" (Basil Hall, *John Calvin: Humanist and Theologian* [London: Historical Association, 1967], 20).

strength, and with all your mind" (Luke 10:27). Moreover, Calvin insists no faith is possible without knowledge of God's kindness toward us (Com. Jon. 3:5), which he and all believers had experienced (III.14.19).

2. Proponents of Calvin: The Calvinists

Generally treated as one phenomenon by its enemies, until recently the received wisdom among most scholars held that the historical movement called Calvinism was discontinuous with the theology of Calvin. Sometimes the term "Calvinian," meaning traceable to Calvin himself, is used in distinction from "Calvinism." Whether continuous or discontinuous, the relation between Calvin and Calvinism is again a basic and hotly debated question. A more intellectually and emotionally charged way of putting the same issue is this: "Is Calvinism a development or a distortion of Calvin's theology?" In his introductory textbook, Justo González declares, "Whereas Calvin started from the concrete revelation of God and always retained an awesome sense of the mystery of God's will, later Reformed Theology tended more to proceed from the divine decrees to particulars in a deductive fashion."[43] Characterizing later Reformed theology is an awesomely complex theological and historical problem, but it can be addressed (1) by comparing the Canons of Dort and the Westminister Confession with the *Institutes*, and (2) by comparing Calvin's practice of theology with those who claim to be his heirs.

On the history of the word "Calvinism," Alister McGrath observes that Protestants thought of themselves as evangelicals, not Calvinists. According to McGrath, the term "Calvinism" was coined by the Lutheran polemicist Joachim Westphal "to stigmatize Reformed theology as a foreign influence in Germany." In dedicating his Jeremiah commentary to Elector Frederick, Lord Palatine of the Rhine, Calvin observes in the preface that his enemies in applying the term "Calvinism" attempt "to affix to your Highness some mark of infamy, [but] they do nothing more than betray their own perversity, and also their folly and disgrace." McGrath concludes that use of the term "Calvinism" to refer to Reformed theology after the death of Calvin is wrong.[44]

McGrath's judgment agrees with the earlier assessment of Protestant scholasticism offered by A. C. McGiffert, who had his own professional troubles with Reformed orthodoxy in America.

> There was little new in the scholasticism of the period. The theology, in spite of many differences in detail, was largely that of the Middle Ages. Reason and revelation were employed in a similar way, and the method of treatment was identical. The reigning philosophy was still that of Aristotle, as understood by the medieval schoolmen, and the supernatural realm was conceived in the same objective and realistic fashion. Compared with that of the Middle Ages,

43. Justo González, *A History of Christian Thought: From the Protestant Reformation to the Twentieth Century*, vol. 3 (Nashville: Abingdon, 1975), 244.
44. Alister McGrath, *The Intellectual Origins of the European Reformation* (New York: B. Blackwell, 1987), 7.

Protestant scholasticism was much more barren, and at the same time narrower and more oppressive.[45]

For some time the main consensus held post-Calvin reformers to be epigonic.[46] When the *con*fessors step down, the *pro*fessors step up. Representing this point of view, H. R. Mackintosh writes:

> Protestant Scholasticism [is] a mood or spirit of theological rigor. [It] appears to be something like a "law" that on any great creative movement, such as the Reformation, there should follow a period of diminished originality but of larger discursive power, in which the gains of the earlier time are, so to speak, catalogued, arranged, and valued. . . . In the process traditional orthodoxy emerged, a distinct historical phenomenon characterized by the fatal tendency to attach an absolute value to dogmatic formulas, to consider faith and assent to creed as virtually one and the same thing . . . without at each point getting back behind the form of sound words to truth as truth is in Jesus. . . . All this brought on a strong inclination . . . to find a solution of hard problems in misplaced rational logic.

In other words, while neither Luther nor Calvin was a philosophical theologian, many of their followers were. The successors of Luther and Calvin are regarded as less prophetic and more academic, more concerned for an intellectual elite gathered in schools than the company of faithful gathered in churches. With a different and inappropriately confident spirit the scholastics represented diminished theological insight but enhanced logical rigor. This trait is indicated by the returning admiration for Aristotle. "A more than ordinarily hurtful feature in traditional orthodoxy, it can now be seen, was the restored predominance of Aristotelianism in Christian theology. . . . On such terms," Mackintosh concludes, "all the romance and glory of the Gospel fade out. The triumphant certainties of the Apostolic faith lapse into rational and necessary axioms, so commonplace and decent that to acquiesce in them is hardly worth a sinner's while."[47]

45. Arthur Cushman McGiffert, *Protestant Thought before Kant* (New York: Charles Scribner's Sons, 1912), 145. McGiffert as a student of Adolf Harnack drank deeply at the well of German liberal theology.

46. Richard Muller objects in the second part of his essay (158), "One of the great ironies of the older scholarship is that it has criticized later Reformed theologians for being epigones, slavish imitators, and then has criticized them still further for failing to imitate" (Richard A. Muller, "Calvin and the Calvinists: Assessing the Continuities and Discontinuities between the Reformation and Orthodoxy," *Calvin Theological Journal* 30, no. 2 (November 1995): 345–75, and 31, no. 1 (April 1996): 125–60. Representing, as I do, the older scholarship, the problem, as it seems to me, is that "later Reformed theologians" imitate each other, not Calvin.

47. See Hugh Ross Mackintosh, "Reformation and Post Reformation Thought," in *Types of Modern Theology: Schleiermacher to Barth* (London: Nisbet & Co., 1956), 6–11. A contemporary objection was leveled by John Milton in his third prolusion "Against Scholastic Philosophy." He requests his auditors "to relax your study of those enormous and near monstrous volumes of the so-called subtle doctors and to be less strenuous in your enjoyment of the warty disputes of the sophists." Milton expects to prove "in my little half hour that the mind is neither entertained nor educated by these studies, nor any good done by them for society" (605). The same theme is repeated in "Of Education." "[I] deem it to be an old error of universities not yet well recovered from the scholastic grossness of

More recently this interpretation is continued by Basil Hall, Brian Armstrong, R. T. Kendall, and Holmes Rolston III. In his essay "Calvin against the Calvinists," Hall argues that Calvin's successors, particularly Theodore Beza, Jerome Zanchius, and William Perkins, distorted the balance of Calvin's theology. Among other changes, they made "Scripture itself into a corpus of revelation in almost propositional form with every part equal to the other parts in inspiration."[48] Brian G. Armstrong writes, "Since the Calvinist thinkers of the late sixteenth and seventeenth centuries rarely even take the trouble to refer to Calvin himself . . . the question then arises whether these orthodox Calvinists can in fact be regarded as proper representatives of Calvin's thought. [I believe] that a careful comparison of [Calvin's] writings with those of representative Calvinists of the seventeenth century reveals a radical change of emphasis . . . so pronounced that at many points the whole structure of Calvin's thought is seriously compromised."[49] Armstrong defines Protestant scholasticism as a "theological approach which asserts religious truth on the basis of deductive ratiocination from given assumptions or principles, thus producing a logically coherent and defensible system of belief." This orientation has an Aristotelian philosophical commitment and employs syllogistic reasoning. Again, reason is exalted to "at least equal standing with faith in theology," involving an interest in metaphysics and a confidence "in abstract, speculative thought." On this view Scripture provides "a unified, rationally comprehensible account."[50] R. T. Kendall's *Calvin and English Calvinism* is primarily focused on the concept of saving faith in William Perkins and its connection to the Westminster Confession, but he disputes "the assumption that Calvin's soteriology was faithfully upheld by the venerable divines who drew up the Westminster Confession and the Shorter and Larger Catechisms."[51] Kendall's sharpest point is that while Calvin believed Christ died for all, Westminster teaches limited atonement—that Christ died only for the elect.

Attempting to rebut Kendall, Paul Helm wrote *Calvin and the Calvinists* to demonstrate "that Calvin and the Puritans were, theologically speaking, at one,

---

barbarous ages, that instead of beginning with the arts most easy . . . they present their young unmatriculated novices at first coming with the most intellective abstractions of logic and metaphysics." Educating "unballasted wits in fathomless and unquiet deeps of controversy" leads some youths to "ignorantly zealous divinity," others to the trade of law—not to contemplate justice and equity but to "pleasing thoughts of litigious terms, fat contentions, and flowing fees." Others "unprincipled in virtue" go into politics. Still others who learned "mere words or such things chiefly as were better unlearned" live a life of unproductive leisure (John Milton, *Complete Poems and Major Prose*, ed. Merritt Y. Hughes [New York: Odyssey Press, 1957], 632).

48. Basil Hall, "Calvin against the Calvinists," in *Courtenay Studies*, 26.

49. Brian G. Armstrong, *Calvinism and the Amyraut Heresy: Protestant Scholasticism and Humanism in Seventeenth-Century France* (Madison: University of Wisconsin Press, 1969), xvii.

50. Ibid., 32.

51. R. T. Kendall, *Calvin and English Calvinism to 1648* (Oxford: Oxford University Press, 1979), 2. James B. Torrance, "Strengths and Weaknesses of the Westminster Theology," in *The Westminster Confession in the Church Today*, ed. Alasdair I. C. Heron (Edinburgh: Saint Andrew Press, 1982), 46 (emphasis in original), sees in Westminster a "decided move to a view where *election precedes grace*, so that the interpretation of the Person and Work of Christ is subordinated to the doctrine of the decrees."

and thus to support the truism that Calvin was a Calvinist." Surely we may assume that Calvin agreed with Calvin. Therefore, the issue is not whether Calvin is a Calvinist, but whether, and in what sense, the Puritans agreed with Calvin. Helm sees the agreement in a "body of teaching" handed down from Calvin to Beza to Knox to Ames and Perkins and achieving classic formulation in the Westminster Confession of 1648. Helm admits there are differences between Calvin and the Puritans but believes the simple explanation is the differences in situation. Thus, the Puritans "developed biblical principles to meet new cases. But it was development from an agreed position, and it was development that was consistent with that position."[52] That Calvin's theology is properly understood as providing the resources for developing "biblical principles" is debatable.

In the introduction to his *Faith with Reason*, Helm insists that religious belief must be able to sustain philosophical scrutiny. Therefore, since philosophy proceeds step by step, argument by argument, religious faith must proceed the same way. We may assume these two "musts" are normative to Helm, but it may be doubted they are descriptive of most people who claim religious beliefs. That is, the majority of believers are sustained by the experience of faith, not by the scrutiny of philosophers. Moreover, faith is more likely experienced by encounter than by argument. As Helm correctly observes, the issue of "reasonable religious belief" is complicated by the fact that "at any one time there are likely to be myriads of ways of defending the rationality of religious belief, depending upon what counts as a defense, what rationality is taken to be, and what a particular religious belief amounts to." Then Helm concludes, "We find in Calvin, I suggest, little or no interest in the rationality of religious belief."[53] This is a puzzling conclusion. How is one to establish the legitimacy of Calvinism's rational principles in the light of Calvin's disinterest in rationality?

Defining Calvinism requires tracing and evaluating the course of theology forward, from Calvin to a later point in history. It also requires tracing and evaluating the course of theology backward, from a later point in history to Calvin. This process requires reevaluating Calvin's successors, especially Theodore Beza.[54]

52. Paul Helm, *Calvin and the Calvinists* (Edinburgh: Banner of Truth Trust, 1982), Preface, 80. In a lecture (at Geneva College, November 21, 2005) entitled "Calvin's Big Idea," Helm referred to the opening lines of the *Institutes* (I.1.1) concerning the knowledge of God and mankind, which he interpreted as "immediately reciprocal." The "big idea" rejects predestination or common grace as Calvin's central dogma. The most serious objections to this interpretation are, first, the unquestioned reliance on a subject-object dichotomy and, second, the ignoring of the centrality of Calvin's doctrine of union with Christ.

53. Paul Helm, *Faith with Reason* (Oxford: Clarendon Press, 2000).

54. Robert Letham, "Theodore Beza: A Reassessment," *Scottish Journal of Theology* 40 (May 1987): 25–40, insists Beza's theology is not so different from Calvin's and therefore Calvinism not so far from Calvin as some suppose. McGrath disagrees. The contrast is clear between the person of Christ in Calvin's theology and the principles of deduction in Beza's theology (Alister E. McGrath, *Reformation Thought: An Introduction*, 2nd ed. (Oxford: Blackwell, 1993), 129–30. Richard A. Muller, "The Problem of Protestant Scholasticism—A Review and Definition," in *Reformation and Scholasticism: An Ecumenical Enterprise*, ed. Willem J. van Asselt and Eef Dekker (Grand Rapids: Baker Academic, 2001), 47, claims McGrath's definition "is a nearly perfect summary of all that was wrong about the older scholarship."

Before turning his career to ecological concerns,[55] Holmes Rolston III wrote *John Calvin versus the Westminster Confession*, arguing that a radical and passionate questioning of the Westminster Confession of Faith was necessary for a defense of Reformed faith. Speaking of the dualisms that made him sick—law and gospel, justice and grace, works and faith—Rolston concludes, "I came to find in my struggle for spiritual health that the disease which afflicted me was a plague that had long infected the Reformed churches. And to my dismay, one of the principal reservoirs of infection was at once the wellspring of faith, The Westminster Confession." Continuing his illness imagery, Rolston declares, "The medicine that broke the fever I was to find in the Reformer himself. It was Calvin who rescued me from the Calvinists."[56] The point could hardly be put more passionately. To be rescued from the Calvinists Rolston insists one must read Calvin.

Among his most powerful points is Rolston's attack on the development of a two-covenant theology "given full confessional status for the first time in the Westminster Confession."[57] According to the Westminster Confession (WC), "The first covenant made with man was a covenant of works, wherein life was promised to Adam, and in him to his posterity, upon condition of perfect and personal obedience" (WC VII, 2). The second covenant is "commonly called the covenant of grace: wherein [the Lord] freely offered unto sinners life and salvation by Jesus Christ, requiring of them faith in him, that they may be saved, and promising to give unto all those that are ordained unto life, his Holy Spirit, to make them willing and able to believe" (WC VII, 3). The first and original covenant was based on obedience and cancelled by sin. God's response to the failure of the covenant of works was its replacement by a covenant of grace based on faith.

The fathers at Westminster began their covenantal thinking not with Abraham and faith and grace but with Adam and creation and nature. They taught that God made a covenant with Adam and Eve conditioned on their obedience. If Adam and Eve had obeyed, or their posterity would obey, God's commandments perfectly, they would be saved by their own obedience through works rather than by God's grace. Because the covenant of works was abrogated by the sin of Father Adam, God *then* made a covenant of grace through faith with Father Abraham. The most grave, pious, learned, and judicious divines gathered at Westminster did not teach that anyone is actually saved by works. In fact, they denied it, but they held out the covenant of works as the original plan of God, which was negated by human sin. This view has produced centuries of disastrous theological consequences. The doctrine of the covenant of works—unrealized and unrealizable—maintains the possibility, an impossible possibility but nevertheless a possibility, that one could—on condition of perfect obedience—be saved

55. See Holmes Rolston III, *Environmental Ethics: Duties to and Values in the Natural World* (Philadelphia: Temple University Press, 1988).

56. Holmes Rolston III, *John Calvin versus the Westminster Confession* (Richmond, VA: John Knox Press, 1972), 6.

57. Ibid., 13.

apart from the grace of God revealed in Jesus Christ and received in faith by the power of the Holy Spirit.

In addition to being unbiblical, the second objection is that Calvin does not employ this distinction. Rolston comments, "Where it was recognized that the concept was not in Calvin, this was considered a positive development of his thought, even with occasional criticism of Calvin for not having adequately formulated the concept." Referring to the covenantal unity between Adam and his posterity, Heinrich Heppe quotes this delightful admission, "Our own Calvin it is true fails to recall such a covenant in his eloquence, only the divine will and ordering by which it was ordained."[58] Such chiding of Calvin seriously misses the point. Rolston claims, "This double Covenant fabric not only modifies, it reverses much of Calvin's thought about Man's primal relationship to God." Third, the covenant of works exalts the primacy of law over grace. Even though negated by sin, the first covenant continues to cast a dark shadow over the divine gift of faith by the human requirement of perfect obedience and the conviction that the covenant of works is still in effect. Charles Hodge, denominated by Rolston as "the nineteenth century's most esteemed American theologian,"[59] suggested that even today anyone who could fulfill the covenant of works would be saved by it without requiring the covenant of grace. In other words, there is a perpetuity of the covenant of works.[60]

In his magisterial study of the New England mind, Perry Miller suggests that coming to America did not result in a development of Calvin's theology but its dissolution. According to the chapter on the covenants of works and grace, when controversy moved from the ecclesiastical to the doctrinal, American Puritans encountered two revolts from those who "had fought originally in their own ranks, or at least were armed with weapons from their arsenals."[61] "Arminianism was a kind of ethical rationalism that had lost the sense of piety, and Antinomianism was an uncontrolled piety without the indispensable ballast of reason; Puritanism looked upon itself as the synthesis of piety and reason and the federal Puritans looked upon the covenant theology as the perfection of that synthesis."[62] The problem focused on divine election and human responsibility—faith and works. Calvin's convictions on the relation between election, the assurance of salvation and the accountability for behavior no longer satisfied the inquiring mind and requiring heart of American Puritans. The solution offered was the theory of the covenant understood as "a mutual agreement between parties upon Article or Propositions on both sides, so that each party is tied and bound to performe his

---

58. Heinrich Heppe, *Reformed Dogmatics*, ed. Ernst Bizer, trans. G. T. Thomson (London: George Allen and Unwin, 1950), 333.

59. Rolston, *Calvin*, 13, 36, 13.

60. Charles Hodge, *Systematic Theology*, vol. 2 (New York: Scribner, Armstrong and Co., 1877), 122.

61. Perry Miller, *The New England Mind: The Seventeenth Century* (Cambridge, MA: Harvard University Press, 1954 [1939]), 367.

62. Ibid., 373.

own conditions,"[63] meaning the omnipotent creator chose to enter a covenant with the human creature. In this way God's sovereignty is affirmed until "[God] alone, of His own unfettered will, proposed that He be chained."[64] God's self-limitation provides room for human action within divine sovereignty. "For God never calleth any unto fellowship with himself in a Covenant of Grace, but ordinarily he first bringeth them into a Covenant of Works."[65]

In sharp criticism Miller asserts that this concept of covenant pictures a God who "is so anxious to win the love of mortals that He will consent to a union upon any terms, upon conditions dictated not by Himself but by mortal reason: 'God will deal with Man in a way agreeable to his nature,' and since man is 'a reasonable creature, and a cause by counsell of his own actions,' the distraught divinity 'treats by making proffers to him, propounding fair and rationall Conditions.'"[66] Mankind, of course, failed to keep the covenant of works, and cannot keep the covenant of grace in deed but only in faith. Therefore, according to the new terms of covenant those who believe in the Redeemer have his righteousness ascribed to them. Miller puts it this way, "Recognizing the now bankrupt condition of the tenant, the landlord guarantees in a new lease to provide him the wherewithal to pay his rent and keep a roof over his head, provided he will believe in the landlord's goodness and show what gratitude he can."[67] God is still the absolute monarch, but God gives humankind a bill of inviolable rights.[68] According to Miller, "The whole intricate argument amounted to: 'though God's grace do all, yet we must give our consent.'"[69] Salvation was understood to be by faith and not by works, but cooperating with grace and performing good faith works were necessary. "The covenanted saint does not supinely believe, but does the best he can, and God will not hold his failures against him; having pledged himself, the saint has taken the responsibility upon himself, and agreed to coöperate with God in the difficult labor."[70] The elect "are covenanted to sainthood, not forced into it, and they are to be saved for trying, not for succeeding, whereas the reprobate are

63. Ibid., 375.
64. Ibid., 379.
65. Ibid., 385. Calvin and the concept of covenant is the subject of Peter A. Lillbeck's *The Binding of God: Calvin's Role in the Development of Covenant Theology* (Grand Rapids: Baker Academic, 2001), who asserts that "the essence of Calvin's conception of the covenant is the notion of the binding of God." This binding is to be understood as self-binding: "God's own act of joining himself with his creatures" (137). Lillbeck thinks that by his treatment of Adam's pre-fall state, "Calvin creates the problem for which a covenant of works is the perfect solution" (288). David A. Weir, *The Origins of the Federal Theology in Sixteenth-Century Reformation Thought* (Oxford: Clarendon Press, 1990), claims a shift away from Calvin's view of the old and new covenants to the covenant of works/covenant of grace distinction. Weir sees a sharp difference between the First Helvetic Confession, which teaches that the Scriptures principally expound God's grace, and the Westminster Larger Catechism a century later, which principally teaches that the Scriptures expound man's duty (154). The Reformed discussions of infra-, supra-, and postlapsarianism are especially interesting. The powerful extension of covenant theory in a legal direction obscured the earlier role of union with Christ.
66. Ibid., 382.
67. Ibid., 377.
68. Ibid., 381.
69. Ibid., 389.
70. Ibid., 383.

eternally damned, not for failing, but for not trying."[71] Grace is not a matter of accomplishment but of intention. The final breathtaking deduction maintains that consent to the covenantal promises entails that "we may go to God and *demand* our salvation of Him."[72]

Miller concludes, "It may seem at first sight that some over-ingenious lawyer, and no man of deep piety constructed this legalized version of Biblical history. . . . But the Puritan divines had not studied dialectic for nothing; give them this broad premise [of covenant theory], backed with copious Scriptural warrants, and they were ready to deduce from it the most gratifying conclusions."[73] In theological terms, "Once more we may marvel at the ingenuity of a contrivance which manages to demand what men cannot give and yet not punish them for failing, which forgives the wrong-doer and yet does not ask the law to go unsatisfied."[74] In historical terms, "The group of Puritans who made up the federal school endeavored to forestall Arminians and Antinomians by their doctrine of the Covenant of Grace, believing it no essential alteration of orthodox theology but a legitimate extension of its implication." "The intellectual history of the century was to prove them sadly mistaken, and their imposition of the covenant doctrine upon the system of Calvin produced at last in the New England theology an altogether different philosophy from any propounded in Geneva."[75] Miller believes that "the horrified ghost of Calvin shuddered to behold his theology twisted into this spiritual commercialism."[76]

In dealing with the same subject Everett Emerson notes, "Covenant theology was chiefly used, to begin with, because it lent itself to an evangelical approach: it made the conversion process as understandable as a business transaction, and it made redemption rest on mutuality. Later Puritans developed its implications into a kind of voluntarism, to the neglect of the Calvinist *doctrines* of irresistible grace."[77] Emerson points out that the covenant of works is an idea that does not appear in Calvin. Nor does salvation as mutuality, although the plural reference to Calvin's doctrines of irresistible grace is puzzling. Both clear and crucial is the conclusion that the greatest danger of covenant theology is the failure to preserve the correct distinction between works and grace. The Puritan conviction that, without observable obedience to the law, the elect could not demonstrate gratitude for their election[78] comes perilously close to confusing sanctification with justification (see these sections in Book III).[79]

---

71. Ibid., 384.

72. Ibid., 389, emphasis in original.

73. Ibid., 378.

74. Ibid., 385.

75. Ibid., 367.

76. Ibid., 389. Calvin is aware of a required righteousness higher than the observance of the law (III.12.1).

77. Everett Emerson, *Puritanism in America, 1620–1750* (Boston: Twayne Publishers, 1977), 57, emphasis added.

78. Ibid., 59.

79. Interestingly, Alister E. McGrath, *Iustitia Dei: A History of the Christian Doctrine of Justification*, 2nd ed. (Cambridge: Cambridge University Press, 1998), 228, claims the development of the

Each of the characteristics, identified with Protestant orthodoxy, is denied in the introduction to *Reformation and Scholasticism*. Among the counterclaims are

1. Scholasticism is a scientific method of research and teaching, and as such does not have a doctrinal content; neither does it have reason as its foundation.
2. There is a continuity between the Medieval, Reformation, and Post-Reformation Era (which is, of course, not to deny that there are many differences).
3. "Aristotelianism" is exceedingly problematic when applied with a broad brush, and should be avoided if used unspecified.
4. Syllogisms are used by any person in a reasoning process (but not always consciously and explicitly), and are therefore, in themselves, not a sign of anything beyond that reasoning process, let alone of Aristotelianism.[80]

In the last several decades the interpretation by the reigning champion has faced mighty and mightily confident challengers like Richard A. Muller and others who work out of his corner.[81] The fight concerns whether Calvin's theology can stand alone or requires completion in "an entire body of true doctrine." According to Muller, "This task was necessary to ensure the survival of Protestantism. The first and second generations of Reformers, the teachers of the first half of the sixteenth century, had been trained in Christian doctrine on the medieval model and had, in their work as Reformers, rendered that model inadequate for the teaching of the next several generations of Protestants." Muller continues, "The Reformers, however, did not provide those generations with a fully developed theological system. Even Calvin's *Institutes* was no more than a basic instruction in the doctrines of Scripture and not a full system of theology written with the precision and detail of the systems of Calvin's own Roman

---

concept of the covenant between God and man came to replace Calvin's Christological view of justification and sanctification. Of course, Calvin deals with the old and new covenants since they are biblical, but the continuity between Calvin and later covenantal theology is questionable.

80. Van Asselt and Dekker, *Reformation and Scholasticism*, 39.

81. For a short summary see Martin I. Klauber, "Continuity and Discontinuity in Post-Reformation Reformed Theology: An Evaluation of the Muller Thesis," *Journal of the Evangelical Theological Society* 33, no. 4 (December 1990): 467–75. In an impressive volume of work Muller offers his approach to an understanding of the reformer in *The Unaccommodated Calvin* (New York: Oxford University Press, 2000). The subtitle *Studies in the Foundation of a Theological Tradition* indicates Muller's primary interest in Calvin as the founder of a theological tradition. In the first paragraph of his preface, Stephen Edmondson, *Calvin's Christology* (Cambridge: Cambridge University Press, 2004), questions the accuracy of anyone's claim "to speak of an unaccommodated understanding of any human being." The essays collected in *After Calvin: Studies in the Development of a Theological Tradition* (Oxford: Oxford University Press, 2003) attack the dichotomizing contrast between Calvin and the Calvinists. The attack continues on a larger scale in *Post-Reformation Reformed Dogmatics: The Rise and Development of Reformed Orthodoxy, ca. 1520 to ca. 1725* (Grand Rapids: Baker Academic, 2003). Volume 1 deals with prolegomena; vol. 2 with Scripture as cognitive foundation; vol. 3 with the divine essence and attributes; and vol. 4 with Trinity. This interpretation clearly stands in the line from Turretin to Hodge to Berkhof, but whether, and in what sense, Calvin heads the line is debatable.

Catholic opponents." And he concludes, "The Protestant theologians of the second half of the sixteenth century—writers like Ursinus, Zanchi, and Polanus—took up the task of writing a complete and detailed system of theology both for the sake of positive teaching and for the sake of polemical defense."[82] Muller accepts the legitimacy of the Reformers' critique of Roman Catholic theology, but he faults them for not providing their descendants with "a fully developed theological system."

Muller asserts, "Scholasticism is rightly defined as a dialectical method of the schools, historically rooted in the late patristic period, particularly in the thought of Augustine, developed throughout the Middle Ages in the light of classical logic and rhetoric, constructed with a view to the authority of text and tradition, and devoted primarily to the exposition of Scripture and the theological topics that derive from it using the best available tools of exegesis, logic, and philosophy."[83] In short, Reformed theology after Calvin employed a scholastic *method* which he opposed, but continued a theological *content* which he approved. This notion that form and content do not interpenetrate strikes me as ludicrous. The way one asks a question may not finally determine the answer, but the former inevitably influences the latter.

Finding Protestant orthodoxy pleasing to his palate, Muller objects to the "distaste of scholasticism" on the part of other diners. Seasoning his complaint with a touch of spice, Muller claims the opposition has been oversalted with "the theological categories of mid-twentieth-century neoorthodoxy." According to Muller, neo-orthodoxy insisted

> the Reformation understood God's revelation as "personal" or as an "event" while scholastic Protestantism understood it as "propositional"; the Reformation was "dynamic," scholasticism, "static"; the Reformers held that Christ alone was "God's Word" and that Scripture was a witness to it, the scholastics assumed ("rigidly," of course) that Scripture was Word and, indeed, verbally dictated by God; the Reformers partook of the gentle spirit of humanism, the scholastics were immersed in the rigors of Aristotelian logic and metaphysics.[84]

In summary, Protestant scholasticism is, or aspires to be, a system based on principles providing arguments derived either from reason or revelation.

Since every theologian aspires to be reasonable, those with whom one disagrees are often labeled rationalistic. Hodge, who studied in Berlin, recognized

82. Richard A. Muller, *Post-Reformation Reformed Dogmatics: The Rise and Development of Reformed Orthodoxy, ca. 1520 to ca. 1725*, vol. 1, 2nd ed. (Grand Rapids: Baker Academic, 2003), 33–34.

83. "Scholasticism in Calvin: A Question of Relation and Disjunction," in *Calvinus Sincerioris Religionis Vindex*, ed. Wilhelm H. Neuser and Brian G. Armstrong (Kirksville, MO: Sixteenth-Century Journal Publishers, 1997), 251. See also Carl R. Trueman, "Calvin and Calvinism," in McKim, *Cambridge Companion*, 225–44.

84. Richard A. Muller, "Problem," in van Asselt and Dekker, *Reformation and Scholasticism*, 45–46, 56, 57–58.

that "Schleiermacher is regarded as the most interesting as well as the most influential theologian of modern times."[85] However, Schleiermacher "succumbed to the attacks which rationalistic criticism had made against faith in the Bible." Since Hodge believed receiving the Bible as a supernatural revelation from God was reasonable, he criticized Schleiermacher for *not* accepting the Bible "as containing doctrines which we are bound to believe on the authority of the sacred writers."[86] Hodge reminds his readers that while "the inward life of a theologian may not be determined by his speculative doctrines, this does not render error less objectionable or less dangerous."[87] Nevertheless, Hodge, the muscular champion of American Reformed orthodoxy, places in a footnote this perfectly charming testimony to the father of modern liberal theology.

> When in Berlin the writer often attended Schleiermacher's church. The hymns to be sung were printed on slips of paper and distributed at the doors. They were always evangelical and spiritual in an eminent degree filled with praise and gratitude to our Redeemer. Tholuck said that Schleiermacher, when sitting in the evening with his family, would often say, "Hush, children; let us sing a hymn of praise to Christ." Can we doubt that he is singing those praises now? To whomsoever Christ is God, St. John assures us Christ is a Saviour.[88]

Hodge charges Schleiermacher with being rationalistic while he himself is only properly rational. Hodge admits, "The ultimate ground of faith and knowledge is confidence in God," but he immediately adds that we must "confide in those laws of belief which God has implanted in our nature." Since it is impossible that God contradict himself, it is likewise impossible that God could reveal something as true which "by the laws of our nature He has rendered it impossible we should believe."[89] Hodge begins with the assurance that theology is a science, and the theologian's task is to collect adequate evidence needed for persuasion of the truth. All the facts of theology are contained in the Scriptures

85. Hodge, *Systematic Theology*, 2:440.

86. Ibid., 441. See the helpful summary of Reformed scholasticism and Hodge's role in it in Jack B. Rogers and Donald K. McKim, *The Authority and Interpretation of the Bible: An Historical Approach* (New York: Harper and Row, 1979), 263ff.

87. Ibid., 442.

88. Ibid., 440. For a comparison of Hodge and Schleiermacher, see B. A. Gerrish, "Charles Hodge and the Europeans," in *Charles Hodge Revisited: A Critical Appraisal of His Life and Work*, ed. John W. Stewart and James H. Moorhead (Grand Rapids: William B. Eerdmans, 2002), 129–158.

89. Hodge, *Systematic Theology*, 1:52. Hodge also suggests a final (not the first!) argument for knowledge of God is the manifestation of God in Christ (346). Hodge seems convinced "the fundamental principle of all true philosophy [is] what we are forced to believe must be true" (341). He continues, "No man can believe in the impossible. And if reason pronounces that it is impossible that the Infinite should be a person, faith in His personality is an impossibility" (348). This latter stricture is addressed to Henry Mansel who, working between Wolff and Kant (and assuming the finality of the subject and object division), concentrates on the conditions of human consciousness recognizing the apparent contradiction between the concept that God is both personal and infinite. Mansel, to my mind, correctly concludes that in important senses thought is not, and cannot be, the measure of belief. Hodge devotes chap. 4 to attack on William Hamilton and Henry Mansel. In his intriguing Bampton Lectures of 1858, Henry Longueville Mansel, *The Limits of Religious Thought Examined* (Boston: Gould and Lincoln, 1859), addresses faith and reason, system and mystery, finite

and the principles properly deduced from these facts such as the axioms: "All truth must be consistent. God cannot contradict himself."[90] Rejecting both rationalism and mysticism, Hodge holds there is a proper office for reason in theology—a "prerogative of Reason."

Christians acknowledge the high prerogatives of reason and a serious responsibility in its proper exercise. "In the first place, reason is necessarily presupposed in every revelation. Revelation is the communication of truth to the mind." Faith is the affirmation of the proposition believed. "Faith involves assent, and assent is conviction produced by evidence." "The first and indispensible office of reason, therefore, in matters of faith, is the cognition or intelligent apprehension of the truths proposed for our reception." "In the second place, it is the prerogative of reason to judge the credibility of a revelation." Hodge defines the credible as that which can be believed rationally, that is, on adequate grounds. He asserts, "A thing may be strange, unaccountable, unintelligible, and yet perfectly credible." What is incomprehensible may not be unreasonable, but what is impossible cannot be true. "[Nevertheless] reason in pronouncing a thing impossible must act rationally and not capriciously."[91]

Returning to Muller, R. S. Clark defines scholasticism as a "technical and logical approach to theological system," subdividing loci into component parts and analyzing them by propositions. Addressing the role of reason in theology after Calvin, Clark objects to the conclusion that fallen human reason is given the same authority as revelation. Likewise reason is not given "an improper instrumental function."

Declaring that the goal of Reformed scholasticism was to provide "an adequate technical theology for schools," Clark suggests, "From this perspective, the discursive method of Calvin's *Institutes* . . . though still propositional, was something of an historical parenthesis in a larger period which was dominated by the scholastic method from the late twelfth century through the late eighteenth century."[92] Applied to Calvin's theology the term "propositional" is simply incorrect, and the term "discursive" is confusing. If by "discursive" Clark means a casual passing from one subject to another in a rambling and digressive manner, the

---

and infinite, absolute and relative to outline the limits of religious thought. Some mysteries, he argues, belong not to reason but to faith. Since a perfect philosophy of the infinite is perfectly unattainable, it must be abandoned. "We can analyze in language what we cannot analyze in thought; and the presence of the language often serves to conceal the absence of the thought" (24). I understand that statement to mean we can separate in reason what we cannot separate in experience: "The truths which guide our practice cannot be reduced to principles which satisfy our reason" (28).

90. Hodge, *Systematic Theology*, 1:15.

91. Ibid., 49–53. Owen Anderson's *Benjamin B. Warfield and Right Reason: The Clarity of General Revelation and Function of Apologetics* (Lanham, MD: University Press of America, 2005), considers Archibald Alexander, Charles Hodge, Warfield, and Cornelius van Til. Given a general family interest in Old Princeton theology, Scottish Common Sense philosophy, reason, natural theology, and apologetics, their internal disagreements are sharp and interesting but convince me that this is not the way to do theology.

92. R. S. Clark, "The Authority of Reason in the Later Reformation Scholasticism in Caspar Olevian and Antoine de La Faye," in *Protestant Scholasticism: Essays in Reassessment*, ed. Carl R. Trueman and R. Scott Clark (Carlisle, Cambria: Paternoster Press, 1999), 111–26, 113, 114, 115–16, 116. In

term does not describe Calvin's careful prose. If "discursive" points to something like Aristotle's distinction between the enthymeme and the syllogism, then Calvin is certainly more rhetorical than dialectical.[93] However, Reformed scholasticism is charged with understanding Calvin as a dialectician rather than a rhetorician.[94] This softer—that is, less rigorously logical—definition of "discursive" does not comport with Clark's emphasis on propositions. Therefore Clark probably intends the stronger definition of discursive reasoning as the process of passing from certain propositions to other truths inferred to follow from them. On this view, inference follows necessarily in deductive reason but only contingently in inductive reason. Given the general direction of Clark's argument concerning Calvin's theology as technical, logical, discursive, and propositional, his admission that the *Institutes* "was something of an historical parenthesis" makes the opposite point. Rather than being "something of an historical parenthesis," the *Institutes* is "exactly an historical exception" to the development of scholastic theology both Protestant and Catholic.

Muller evaluates Calvin's theological efforts not as an attempt to confess the faith but as an attempt to codify the tradition, presumably, believing that the best way to confess the faith is in fact to codify the tradition. Thus Muller views the Gallican Confession (1559), the Scots Confession (1560), the Belgic Confession (1561), and the Second Helvetic Confession (1566) not simply as confessions but as "confessional codifications." On this codifying assumption Muller frames the issue of continuity and discontinuity between Calvin and Calvinism. Within "a broad, confessional definition of the Reformed tradition," John Calvin is regarded not as its greatest theologian, but "as one of its major early codifiers."[95]

---

addressing "The Scholastic Calvin," David C. Steinmetz is kind to the company his essay is keeping in this book. He illustrates Calvin's connection with scholastic theologians of the past, but does not offer an opinion about Reformed scholasticism after Calvin. Moreover, he makes the strong point that while scholastic theology is "theology appropriate to a school," Calvin taught that the church is both a school and a nurturing mother (28). If Calvin thought theology should edify a church family rather than simply a clerical elite, the primary goal declared by Clark of providing an "adequate technical theology for schools" would appear to be discontinuous with Calvin's theology.

93. Robert H. Ayers, "Language, Logic and Reason in Calvin's *Institutes*," *Religious Studies* 16 (1980): 290, recognizes that while "Calvin employs enthymemes, it is always possible from the context to supply the missing premise(s)." The point, however, is not whether a syllogism can be created, but whether Calvin intended one.

94. On rhetoric and dialectic, see my *Calvin and Classical Philosophy*, 4–8. Also Quirinus Breen in "John Calvin and the Rhetorical Tradition," in *Christianity and Humanism* (Grand Rapids: William B. Eerdmans, 1968), 122–23, who claims, "There is a logic in the *Institutes*. In fact, it is full of logic. But the logic is not syllogistic. It is rhetorical logic." Breen notes the enthymeme rather than the syllogism in Calvin's writings. Enthymeme is defined with Quintillian as an incomplete syllogism having one suppressed premise. For Aristotle the enthymeme is a rhetorical syllogism (*Rhetorica*, 1.1356.b.5). According to Willis, "Calvin's thought is not primarily characterized by dialectical diastasis but by rhetorical correlation" (E. David Willis, "Rhetoric and Responsibility in Calvin's Theology," in *The Context of Contemporary Theology: Essays in Honor of Paul Lehmann*, ed. Alexander J. McKelway and E. David Willis [Atlanta: John Knox Press, 1974], 44).

95. Richard A. Muller, "John Calvin and Later Calvinism: The Identity of the Reformed Tradition," in *The Cambridge Companion to Reformation Theology*, ed. David Bagchi and David C. Steinmetz (Cambridge: Cambridge University Press, 2004), 135, 148.

From this conclusion, in its reading of both history and theology one must respectfully but vigorously demur.

In summarizing so complex a topic as Calvin and Calvinism one must recognize that words like "rigid," "narrow," "dogmatic," and "rationalistic" are clearly emotive and opprobious—therefore unclearly precise and descriptive. Were approval being conveyed, "rigid" becomes "strong," "narrow" becomes "focused," "dogmatic" becomes "theological," "rationalistic" becomes "rational." Good and learned people gather and evaluate evidence differently, and collective conviction has individual and societal components. Charles Hodge, Lewis Berkhof, Richard Muller, and their like-minded friends are comfortable appealing to logic and reason, syllogisms, principles and proofs, propositions and adequate evidence, and they believe they have, or would receive, Calvin's approbation. Others of us, living in an uncomfortable world of ambiguities, anomalies, and even antinomies, appreciate Calvin's commitment to mysteries beyond the reach of reason. Not only can this commitment not be set aside, it modifies the other appeals.

The continuity school recognizes significant differences between Calvin and Calvinism, but claims Reformed Orthodoxy as a legitimate development of Calvin's theology rather than a serious distortion of it. Of course, plotting such a trajectory is clearly hazardous, if not downright impossible. No one can say for sure what the "fundamentals" of Calvin's theology would have looked like if they could be "precisely detailed" and applied in another time and place. One group cheers for Calvin *against* the Calvinists and the other cheers for Calvin *with* the Calvinists. Both sides offer reasons for their team preference, but the reasons become persuasive not so much in themselves but in their consonance with one's individual and communal judgments and values.[96]

Protestant scholasticism sees itself as a continuation of the Reformation properly adapted to changing circumstances while preserving the integrity of the Reformation witness. However, each of its constitutive elements is questionably related to Calvin's own text. In addition to a questionable confidence in "system" and the valorizing of a certain kind of "precision" and "detail," the main issue in contention is whether John Calvin offers "a full system of theology." In my language of preference the question is "Does John Calvin offer a faithful systematic reflection on, and confession of, the grace of God revealed in Jesus Christ the Lord?" and my answer is an unqualified "yes." I assume Muller's answer is "no"

---

96. Understanding widely differing interpretations of the same texts by intelligent persons of goodwill may suggest something like "an illative sense." John Hick expounds this idea in connection with John Henry Newman. "The reasoning by which we arrive at many, perhaps most, of the certainties by which we live, does not consist in acquiring Cartesian 'clear and distinct ideas' and perfectly cogent chains of reasoning, but rather in appreciating the drift of a miscellaneous mass of evidence. . . . A great mass of facts fit together in terms of our belief, though no one of them strictly entails it." If illation requires "the capacity to see a large field of evidence as a whole and to divine its significance," obviously different angles of vision will produce differing insights (John Hick, "Faith and the Illative Sense," in *Faith and Knowledge*, 2nd ed. (Ithaca, NY: Cornell University Press, 1966), 69–91. See also Hans Urs von Balthasar, *The Glory of the Lord: A Theological Aesthetics*, trans. Erasmo Leiva-Merikakis (San Francisco: Ignatius Press, 1983), 176.

because he thinks writers like Ursinus, Zanchi, and Polanus were needed to take up "the task of writing a complete and detailed system of theology." In baseball terms Muller regards Calvin as a starter, maybe even a middle reliever, but not a closer. In the adamantine sport of theology, a perfect nine innings on the diamond will probably never be recorded, but sitting squarely behind home plate, and not coming off the wall in left field, I think Calvin pitches a complete, if not perfect, game. Calvin is a systematic thinker but not a system builder. His faith is based on the recognition that Jesus is Lord and we are united with him. Calvin's theology is grounded on Christian convictions, not philosophical (or theological) principles. His exposition is more confessional than argumentative, and while his use of reason is constant, his confidence in reason is not unwavering. The question remains whether a theology that is "technical," "logical," "systematic," and "propositional" is a development of Calvin or a distortion. Calvin's theology is written for the faithful, not the logical. Calvin's theology is not designed to exercise the mental muscles of academically trained professionals but to edify the Christian heart in the community of the faithful. To put the point briefly and sharply, Calvin is not a Calvinist because union with Christ is at the heart of his theology—and not theirs.

3. Misponents of Calvin: The Assumptions

Having considered Calvin's opponents and his proponents, there should be an English word in parallel describing those who misunderstand him. To supply this lamentable lacuna I suggest the neologism "misponent." With the best will toward any text, it is difficult to prevent modern assumptions from creating misunderstandings. This study seeks to demonstrate that the doctrine of union with Christ is close to center stage in Calvin's theology. However, before that curtain goes up, three popular scenes must be removed by this prologue. Intellectual insights sometimes come to us with the freshness of surprise, but much of the time we discover what we are prepared to find. As already observed, when we look down into a well we also see our own reflection, which is to say new insights go into old minds. Studying the work of someone who lived at a different time and place means identifying not only differences in the actual expression of ideas but also differences in the habits of mental association. Most of our life is set within the context of convictions taken for granted. Unexamined assumptions and commitments have powerful effects on student and subject. This situation is unavoidable because each of us thinks within our own time and space and with our own head and heart. Moreover, in reading to learn, we are in large measure selecting a usable past for ourselves. We pass by what has no significance for us and find it difficult to pay much attention to those things that have little applicability to our situation.

John Calvin differs from widely held modern assumptions about his theology concerning three major issues. The first is the relation of system and systematic. The second is the being of God in relation to the knowledge of God, and the third is the knowledge of the self in relation to the knowledge of God. The

understanding and interpretation of Calvin is mightily influenced by unconscious assumptions or conscious decisions on these three topics.

a. System and Systematic

Curiously, both friends and foes of Calvin regard his work as a tightly constructed
system. The benefit for his opponents is that by imploding a section like predestination or total depravity, they can bring down the whole edifice without considering the possible value of other freestanding doctrines. Some proponents
recognize that Calvin himself did not produce a system but believe he gave impe-
tus to the production of one which they regard as essentially the same thing, and
it can be legitimately called by his name. Charles Beard writes, "Christianity has
never before or since been so completely cast into the mold of a system." The popular consensus also accepts Beard's opinion that Calvin thought "Christianity can
be presented in dialectical form [and] can be stated with scholastic accuracy and
tied together by bonds of logic."[97] Calvin is a systematic thinker in striving for
and producing an orderly theological interpretation, but this fact is improperly
designated as a system. Calvin's *Institutes* is more confessional and open-ended,
less rigid, less rational, and less dogmatic than the term "system" usually implies.
In this, Calvin has another important commonality with Plato. Many interpreters
believe both Plato and Calvin produced a cohesive system of thought that can be
comfortably and coherently referred to as Platonism or Calvinism. Of course, a
single mind will produce considerable cohesion. Paul Shorey's fine comment on
Plato applies equally to Calvin. Shorey believes Plato's dialogues demonstrate a
unity of thought. Thus, in the dialogues various sides of one basic theory are
turned to light. He concludes that a careful examination of Plato's writings does
not support the assumption of a series of changes and developments in his
thought.[98] Shorey suggests that Plato's philosophy had taken shape at the age of
thirty or thirty-five.[99] Shorey admits that "the emphasis and center of interest may
shift from dialogue to dialogue—but the doctrine remains the same."[100] Plato may
undergo some minor changes of opinion, but he does not dramatically change his
mind. Plato's works, "though not of course a predetermined systematic exposition,
are the naturally varied reflection of a homogeneous body of opinion, and of a
consistent attitude in the interpretation and criticism of contemporary life."[101]
Shorey regards Plato's *Dialogues* as a unity, but, to be precise, he does not view
Plato's thought as a system because system building is perfectly futile even when
the architect possesses genius.[102] Shorey criticizes the "expositors of Plato [who]
seem strangely oblivious of the limits thus far set to all systems of philosophy. They

---

97. Charles Beard, *The Reformation of the Sixteenth Century in Its Relation to Modern Thought and
Knowledge*, The Hibbert Lectures of 1883, 5th ed. (London: Williams and Norgate, 1907), 295, 296.
98. Paul Shorey, *What Plato Said* (Chicago: University of Chicago Press, 1933), 66.
99. Paul Shorey, *The Unity of Plato's Thought* (Chicago: University of Chicago Press, 1903), 130.
100. Ibid., 178.
101. Ibid., 130–31.
102. Ibid., 134.

treat as peculiar defects of Plato the inconsistencies which they detect in his ultimate metaphysics after they have elaborated it into a rigid system which he with sound instinct evaded by poetry and myth."[103]

Like Plato's *Dialogues*, Calvin's *Institutes* represents a single, searching, and systematic mind at work, but not a system. It is true that many scholars view Calvin's theology as a coherent whole held together by governing principles, but others correctly emphasize Calvin's opposition to systems. William J. Bouwsma takes the terms "system" and "systematic" to be synonymous and rejects both. "I cannot accept the received version of Calvin as a systematic thinker. I do not believe that Calvin ever aspired to the construction of a system, as the term 'system' is commonly understood; as a biblical theologian, he despised what passed for systematic theology in his own time."[104]

Even some who do not think Calvin was obsessed with producing a rational system believe he crafted a central dogma that operates as a philosophical principle or with philosophical principles. Sadly neglecting our union in Christ, Alexandre Ganoczy wrongly claims that "Calvin's fundamental principles in doctrine and practice, his basic intuitions, presuppose opposition between the divine and the human." Although the depth and range of Calvin's confession of our union with Christ should cause him hesitation, Ganoczy concludes, "One may assert without hesitation that for Calvin 'glory to God alone' is the foremost and most basic principle, under whose aegis he undertakes his entire reform program."[105] It is true that in his letter to Sadolet Calvin insists that zeal to illustrate the glory of God is the prime motive of human existence,[106] but this declaration is more doxological than deductive. Likewise, François Wendel insists that "Calvin places all his theology under the sign of what was one of the essential principles of the Reform: the absolute transcendence of God and his total 'otherness' in relation to man." This claim simply ignores Calvin's—to say nothing of the New Testament's—witness to "union with Christ." Wendel continues his overstatement by suggesting, "No theology is Christian and in conformity with the Scriptures but in the degree to which it respects the infinite distance separating God from his creature and gives up all confusion, all 'mixing,' that might tend to efface the radical distinction between the Divine and the human."[107] Of course, Calvin taught God's wholly and holy otherness, but even

103. Ibid., 132.

104. William J. Bouwsma, *John Calvin: A Sixteenth-Century Portrait* (New York: Oxford University Press, 1988), 5. Bouwsma's portrait of "two Calvins" seems unduly fascinated by the metaphors of "labyrinth" and "abyss" to explain Calvin's life and, while dramatic in intention, overstates the role of antithetical impulses, tensions, and contradictions. These metaphors and these contradictions occur to, and in, us all. Calvin's thought demonstrates a central confessional unity and irresolvable logical tensions.

105. Alexandre Ganoczy, *The Young Calvin*, trans. David Foxgrover and Wade Provo (Philadelphia: Westminster Press, 1987), 188, 189.

106. "To Sadolet." The letters from and to Sadolet are cited from vol. 1 of *Selected Works of John Calvin, Tracts*, ed. and trans. Henry Beveridge (Grand Rapids: Baker Book House, 1983 [1844]), 33.

107. François Wendel, 151.

more fundamentally he taught that God is with us in Jesus Christ and in us through the power of the Holy Spirit.

The dilemma of system and systematic is well presented in these remarks of H. R. Mackintosh. "When we speak of the theology of Calvin, it is ten to one we are thinking of his dogmatic system."[108] In contrast, Mackintosh praises Calvin the biblical commentator and insists that "less than any man of his generation, or for many generations after, did [Calvin] attempt to force the rigid formulas of a dogmatic system on the free and living thought of the Bible."[109] Later in his article Mackintosh asserts "mystery there must always be,"[110] but his central conviction remains that of the doctrines of theology "none can, in the last resort, be isolated or incoherent with the rest." According to Mackintosh, "No one belonging to the Reformation epoch had grasped this so powerfully as Calvin; no one had applied it with half his ability or success to doctrinal system-building."[111] The conclusion is, "Thinking out the entire system before he took up the pen, [Calvin] exhibited a complete mastery of logical order and organic reasoning."[112] In this encomium to Calvin's systematic thinking there is an unresolved, and irresolvable, issue between logical order and ineffable mystery to which Mackintosh and many interpreters of Calvin pay insufficient attention. That either Plato or Calvin founded, or thought he had founded, a system in which all or most of the answers were presented or even adumbrated is extremely doubtful. Calvin's theology is not correctly understood as a system of doctrine driven or ultimately guided by reason, but a confession of truth guided by Scripture and driven by faith. Calvin maintains this position consistently, but apparently not with sufficient clarity to convince all his interpreters. Karl Barth sees Calvin's (and perhaps his own) role this way. Calvin was "a conscientious exegete, a strict and tenacious thinker and at the same time a theologian who was indefatigably concerned with the practice of Christian life and life in the church . . . a good teacher . . . who does not hand over to an understanding reader the results of his study, but asks him to take it up and to discover new results in his footsteps."[113] In contrast, J. K. S. Reid wrongly declares "that the very fixity of the systematization achieved by Calvin discouraged development whereas the multitudinous and uncoordinated works of Luther prompted it."[114]

The orderliness of the world and the possibility of understanding God and the world through the right use of reason is a deep-seated conviction for Thomas Aquinas. Calvin does not exhibit the same confidence in the mind's ability to

108. H. R. Mackintosh, "John Calvin: Expositor and Dogmatist," *The Review and the Expositor* (April 1910): 179.
109. Ibid., 182.
110. Ibid., 191.
111. Ibid., 186.
112. Ibid., 185–86.
113. Eberhard Busch, *Karl Barth: His Life from Letters and Autobiographical Texts*, trans. John Bowden (Philadelphia: Fortress Press, 1976), 439.
114. J. K. S. Reid, *The Authority of Scripture: A Study of the Reformation and Post-Reformation Understanding of the Bible* (New York: Harper and Brothers, 1957), 29.

reach God. This is the old and vast question of whether the divine-human relation is a relatively natural correlation or a totally other dissociation caused by sin, or even createdness itself, corrected in either case by grace alone. While Calvin sometimes asserts that God has reasons even if we do not know what they are, a careful reading of Calvin's own text challenges this assumption. Reason itself forces us to see the world in which we live as more disorderly and indecent than Calvin was comfortable admitting. The reality of ambiguity, randomness, logical contradictions, and unanswerable questions also applies to theology. Likewise, Calvin's view of sin and the resulting necessity for humility (II.2.11)[115] forbids complete confidence in the purity of human aspirations toward heavenly things. In his praise of desire for the god Eros, Plato's *Symposium* offered a basic metaphor for the description of religion as the human aspiration for the divine. Calvin accepts human aspiration when he declares, "The chief activity of the soul is to aspire thither" (I.15.6), but aspiration is modified by humility.[116]

Calvin recognized that reason and aspiration have honorable roles in human affairs, but the relation to God is given and maintained in faith. Still, cognitive and conative dissonance troubled Calvin. He worked hard to keep a certain level of confidence in rational order which is instructive, but as Calvin himself often noted, a considerable portion of our world and our theology is not susceptible to reason. This situation should be no great cause for alarm since reformation for Calvin was not only of doctrine but of life, and life is more complex than doctrine.

Calvin's theology is properly concerned for right answers, but his right answers should be understood not as a logically unassailable system of ideas but in terms of their adequacy as a heartfelt confession of faith attempting to protect the mystery of God's revelation. This confessional nature of theology takes precedence over all its rational connections. In its essence, Calvin's theology is not a system explicating rational truth, not even a system rationally explicating revealed truth. Calvin's theology is a systematic offering of faithful witness to the truth revealed by God in Jesus Christ.[117]

---

115. Pierre Marcel, "L'humilité d'après Calvin," *La Revue Réformée*, no. 2 (1960): 33–38.

116. The disconnection between human religion and Christian faith is most powerfully expressed in Barth's "Religion as Unbelief" (Karl Barth, *Church Dogmatics* [*CD*], ed. G. W. Bromiley and T. F. Torrance [Edinburgh: T. & T. Clark, 1957], 297–325).

117. The title of the 1536 *Institute* informs King Francis I that this book is presented as a *confession of faith* (LCC, xxxiii). Garret Wilterdink, in his *Tyrant or Father? A Study of Calvin's Doctrine of God*, 2 vols. (Bristol, IN: Wyndham Hall Press, 1985), is anxious about the logical consistency of Calvin's system. He writes that Calvin's view of God's omnipotence "leads him logically to double predestination and to the immutability and autonomy of grace" (2:89), but in the Bible God is revealed as loving father. Admitting that Calvin nowhere attempts a logical justification of the theological use of paradox, Wilterdink nevertheless concludes, "A paradox to Calvin is an *apparent* contradiction which seems so to us only because the higher truth lies hidden in the mystery of the secret plan of God." Interestingly, in response to the sixth Canon of the Council of Trent, Calvin writes that he abhors paradox (*Ego quum a paradoxis abhorream*). Wilterdink concludes "by his frequent resort to the notion of mystery in dealing with the paradoxical in God's relation to men, Calvin leaves numerous antinomies or contrapuntal themes in his theological teaching" (2:77). A simpler resolution would be to question the adequacy of the concept of system in Calvin, to accept the existence of real contradictions and to understand Calvin's theology as more confessional than logical.

b. The Being of God

Classical philosophy described God (and the gods) by way of eminence from human analogies. If a person is strong, God must be omnipotent. If a person is wise, God must be omniscient. If a person can be good, God must be perfect, as Plato argues in the *Republic* (381b). Famously, Thomas Aquinas follows this pattern in the beginning of the *Summa Theologica*. However, as previously mentioned, Calvin begins the *Institutes* with the sentence, "Nearly all the wisdom we possess, that is to say, true and sound wisdom, consists of two parts: the knowledge of God and of ourselves" (I.1.1). These words summarize two crucial convictions and conclusions that are essential to understanding his theology and where our modern assumptions sharply differ from his. First, Calvin believes that theological reflection properly starts from the *knowledge* of God as revealed in Scripture—a process that he calls the analogy of faith (*analogia fidei*). In contrast, Thomas Aquinas begins his theology in the *Summa Theologica* with the *being* (or existence) of God as reasoned from logic. Giving an account of what can be affirmed about God by the use of human reason is based on the analogy of being (*analogia entis*). According to Thomas, the existence of God and such attributes as simplicity, perfection, infinity, immutability, and unity can be naturally known by reasonable human beings.

This latter method follows the ancient philosophical pattern of discussing what reality is before considering how we know that reality. In philosophy the study of reality or being is called ontology or metaphysics. The study of knowledge is called epistemology. Obviously the analogy of being requires considerable confidence in the abilities of human reason and therefore a natural and general human ability to relate to God. Sometimes this area of study is called natural revelation (what is generally revealed by God in nature) in contrast to divine revelation (what is specifically revealed by God in Scripture). The analogy of being is a sophisticated philosophical idea often taken to divide Roman Catholic from Protestant theology. However, Protestant theology can also begin with a description of the "being" of God. For example, Louis Berkhof's in some circles still influential *Systematic Theology* articulates the principle of being (*Principium essendi*) as the basic prolegomenon to dogmatics.[118] On the basis of this principle the doctrine of God is expounded and is divided into

---

118. Louis Berkhof, *Systematic Theology*, new ed. with the original introductory volume (Grand Rapids: Wm. B. Eerdmans, 1996). Berkhof is a more attractive presentation of the "old Reformed orthodoxy" than displayed in the classic, but incredibly dull, compilation of Heinrich Heppe entitled *Reformed Dogmatics*. Among the characteristic features are (1) the beginning with the doctrine of Scripture, (2) the discussion of the existence and the attributes of God (fifty pages), (3) the decrees of God and predestination prior to the exposition of creation, (4) many chapters on the covenant of works and the covenant of grace, and (5) the understanding of Jesus Christ more as the mediator of the covenant of grace than the revelation of God. Berkhof continues to be influential in one branch of Calvinism. Muller testifies, "With little formal and virtually no substantial dogmatic alteration, orthodox or scholastic Reformed theology appears in the works of Charles Hodge, Archibald Alexander Hodge, and Louis Berkhof," *Post-Reformation Reformed Dogmatics*, 1:29.

1. The Being of God (and)
2. The Works of God.

The former, based on reason, discusses the existence of God and God's attributes both communicable and incommunicable. The final chapter in the section is devoted to the Trinity: God's self-revelation as Father, Son, and Spirit. In contrast, Calvin recognizes no adequate and saving knowledge of God apart from the scriptural revelation of Father, Son, and Holy Spirit. Calvin does not devote many pages to the doctrine of the Trinity (I.13), but the reality of the Triune God is the basic understanding and organizing pattern for reflection about God.

In the century after Calvin, the Westminster Confession began with a description of how God is known on the basis of Scripture. The doctrine of Scripture is articulated in article 1, and the doctrine of God follows in article 2. The teaching of Scripture is understood within the framework of reasoning about being. God is defined in terms of the logical perfection of supreme being as "infinite in being and perfection, a most pure spirit, invisible, without body, parts, or passions, immutable, immense, eternal, incomprehensible, almighty, most wise, most holy, most free, most absolute."

Calvin does not deny but affirms "the being of God" in the common sense that he believes God exists supremely and is the reality who determines all things ("creator of things visible and invisible"). Calvin also, on occasion, affirms the traditional "attributes" of God. However, Calvin thinks speculation about God's being and attributes beyond the witness of the Bible is mistaken. "[It is] not for us to attempt with bold curiosity to penetrate to the investigation of [God's] essence, which we ought more to adore than meticulously to search out" (I.5.9). Calvin means that proper knowledge of ourselves recognizes our ignorance, vanity, poverty, infirmity, and depravity while the knowledge of God reveals that wisdom, virtue, goodness, purity, power, mercy, and righteousness rest in the Lord alone (I.1.1.f.). Among the attributes (or powers or virtues) of God, Calvin often mentions mercy, judgment, and justice. Others include holiness, kindness, goodness, truthfulness, and graciousness. However, for Calvin, these words describe the God revealed in Scripture. They are not the result of rational inferences from the concept of supreme being. We are to understand God's attributes or powers "by which he is shown to us not as he is in himself, but as he is toward us; so that this recognition of him consists more in living experience than in vain and high-flown speculation" (I.10.2).[119]

---

119. Emphasizing God-for-us in the Roman Catholic theological tradition, Catherine LaCugna rejects the ontology of substance in favor of the personalism of revelation. She asserts, "The doctrine of the Trinity . . . summarizes what it means to participate in the life of God through Jesus Christ in the Spirit. [The doctrine] is ultimately therefore a teaching not about the abstract nature of God, nor about God in isolation from everything other than God, but a teaching about God's life with us and our life with each other" (Catherine Mowry LaCugna, *God for Us: The Trinity and Christian Life* [New York: Harper San Francisco, 1991], 1). Although LaCugna cites Calvin only once in a chapter on Thomas Aquinas as an example of reaction to the metaphysical synthesis of scholasticism (144), her

Calvin rejects speculation into the being and attributes of God in favor of what can be known on the basis of scriptural revelation. He begins with the *knowledge* of God rather than the *being* of God; with God's *revelation* (the analogy of faith) rather than with human *reason* (the analogy of being). Calvin continually warns against intellectual speculation about God because what Christians need is not theoretical knowledge concerning the being of God but practical knowledge of the will of God for their lives. According to Calvin there is a human wantonness that tickles many and even drives them to wicked and hurtful speculations (I.14.1). The remedy is to recognize that there is no higher cause than the will of God, which is revealed in Scripture.

c. The Separate Self

The second assumption that modern people do not share with Calvin involves the treatment of divine and human knowledge together rather than separately. Our unexamined view of the "separate self" makes a sharp division between theological and anthropological reflection. In some sense the ancient world ended, and the modern world began, with the new emphasis on individuality that produced panegyrics to human being like Pico della Mirandola's (1463–1494) *On the Dignity of Man*. This great intellectual shift, important enough to require some lines, is often identified with the famous claim of René Descartes (1596–1650) to the effect "I think, therefore I am" (*cogito ergo sum*). This modern "I" problem challenges the most skillful ophthalmologist.

Descartes was concerned with the desire for certainty, and he expected that a process of radical doubt would lead to clear and distinct perceptions resulting in truth. According to Descartes the process of doubting produces the undoubtable conviction that I who doubt exist. This means that I am at least a *thinking substance* (mind). The existence of *extended substance* (body, things, world, etc.) can still be doubted until the existence of *infinite substance* has been demonstrated. This second area of doubt (Does anything exist beyond my mind?) disappears when the existence of God (infinite substance) is demonstrated because the concept of God includes the recognition that a perfect being could not maliciously deceive us about the existence of the world. Thus, the rational process moves from the undoubted existence of (1) self (as mind) to the demonstration of (2) God (as perfect) to the reality of (3) bodies (as objects) because God would not deceive us.

With this rational procedure Descartes expected both to find the truth and to establish the existence of God. It was not his intention to divide God from the self, but to give knowledge of God precedence over knowledge of the self. In Meditation III he wrote, "I see that there is manifestly more reality in infinite substance than in finite, and therefore that in some way I have in me the notion of the infi-

analysis of person (chap. 8), communion, and doxology as the living language of faith have affinities with important themes in Calvin. Of special interest is the section on the concept of self in modern thought from Descartes to the Karls—Barth and Rahner and the Johns—Macmurray and Zizioulas (250ff.). See John D. Zizioulas, *Being as Communion: Studies in Personhood and the Church* (Crestwood, NJ: St. Vladimir's Seminary Press, 1985), and John Macmurray's 1953 and 1954 Gifford Lectures, *The Self as Agent* (London: Faber, 1957), and *Persons in Relation* (London: Faber, 1961).

nite earlier than the finite—to wit, the notion of God before that of myself." In spite of his declared intention, the actual result of Descartes's reflection was to encourage thinkers to begin with the certainty of their own existence and think outward toward all other realities. In practical effect, Descartes teaches in opposition to Calvin, "Nearly all the wisdom we possess, that is to say, true and sound wisdom, begins in one place: the knowledge of ourselves." Calvin did not fall into the Cartesian well. Calvin was, of course, unaware of the developments concerning the idea of a separate self with which we are familiar and that profoundly determine our interests, questions, and investigations. In addition to the Cartesian dualism, the Humean skepticism, the Kantian transcendentalism, and the Freudian critique that mightily influence us were all beyond Calvin's cognizance.

Calvin makes a distinction between divine and human knowledge, but Descartes makes a division. They use similar language but with very different meanings. For Calvin the knowledge of self immediately involves the knowledge of God.[120] Living in the modern world we cannot avoid the megatrend of individuality in our anthropological, psychological, and sociological reflection. However, theological reflection properly begins with the Lordship of Christ, our union with him, and through him our fellowship with the other members of his body who exist to serve the world.

C. THE STRUCTURE OF THE *INSTITUTES*

However readily the specific details of an exposition are comprehended, most of us actually remember its general outline. The overall shape of a work is not only a final aid to the memory but also serves as a useful preliminary guide to understanding. From the first Latin edition of 1536 through the final French edition in 1560 John Calvin continued to revise and expand the *Institutes*, and there has never been complete agreement concerning the organizing structure of his theological presentation. Four suggestions deserve notice.

1. The Four Articles of the Apostles' Creed

The first, and most popular, interpretation is associated with Benjamin Warfield (1851–1921).[121] According to Warfield, "What Thucydides is among Greek, or Gibbon among eighteenth-century English historians, what Plato is among philosophers, or the Iliad among epics, or Shakespeare among dramatists, that Calvin's 'Institutes' is among theological treatises."[122] Warfield asserts that the exposition of Calvin's *Institutes* changed dramatically over the years between 1536

---

120. See Donald J. Wilcox, *In Search of God and Self: Renaissance and Reformation Thought* (Prospect Heights, IL: Waveland Press, 1975). From the title one might expect an analysis of the knowledge of God and the Self. The half-title page cites Calvin on that subject (I.1.1), but the book is a broad intellectual and cultural history of the period.

121. Warfield, "On the Literary History of Calvin's 'Institutes,'" *Calvin and Calvinism*, 373–428.

122. Ibid., 374.

and 1559, but Calvin's "principles never varied." It was before Calvin "had finished his twenty-sixth year that he found himself in full possession of all the productive truths of his theology and never afterwards, during a life of thought and of incessant mental labor, did he find in his work either principles to abjure or elements fundamentally to alter."[123] Warfield continues, "With the edition of 1559 . . . a totally new arrangement was introduced, which reduced the whole to a simple and beautiful order—redacted into four books. . . . These four books treat in turn of the Father, Son, and Holy Ghost, and the Holy Catholic Church. . . . The order was suggested by the consecution of topics in the Apostles' Creed."[124] The view of Calvin as a "theo-logician" concerned with "principles" and Warfield's admiration for "the general adamantine character of his reasoning"[125] is no longer widely accepted. Nevertheless that the four books of the final *Institutes* are ordered under the articles of the Apostles' Creed has much to commend it: I. Holy Father, II. Holy Son, III. Holy Spirit, and IV. Holy Church.

Calvin did indeed write four books, and there are four divisions in the early and ecumenical confession known as the Apostles'. Additionally, Calvin writes, "Thus far I have followed the order of the Apostles' Creed because it sums up in a few words the main points of our redemption, and thus may serve as a tablet for us upon which we see distinctly and point by point the things in Christ that we ought to heed" (II.16.18). However, rather than indicating the expository scheme of the entire *Institutes*, this comment seems to apply only to the immediate discussion. Additionally, the Apostles' Creed outline for the *Institutes* raises several other hesitations. First, a Trinitarian organization must explain why Calvin does not mention the term "Holy Spirit" in the title of Book III. Since Calvin does not clearly indicate that the Holy Spirit is the subject of Book III, the reader must infer this conclusion from an evaluation of the content. Second (and a point to be discussed under the work of the Holy Spirit), this view seems to assume a stronger doctrine of the person of the Holy Spirit than Calvin actually presents. Calvin certainly affirms the *person* of the Spirit, but his emphasis is on the *work* of the spirit. Third, a Trinitarian formulation of a four-book sequence requires that the doctrine of the church have a clear inner dynamic connection with the doctrine of God.

2. The Twofold Knowledge of God

The second view is represented by Edward Dowey,[126] who passes by the formal fourfold division and insists that the real division of Calvin's exposition is the

---

123. Ibid., 390.
124. Ibid., 338.
125. Ibid., 375.
126. See Edward A. Dowey Jr., *The Knowledge of God in Calvin's Theology*, 3rd ed. (Grand Rapids: Eerdmans, 1994 [1951]), especially chap. 2 on "The Duplex Cognitio Domini." See also A. Dakin, *Calvinism* (Philadelphia: Westminster Press, 1946). Seldom cited these days, A. Dakin's purpose is to "send others to the Reformer's monumental work, to be brought in contact with his earnest spirit and feel the mighty sweep of his thought" (6). To accomplish this purpose Dakin offers brief summaries of the doctrines of the *Institutes* organized on the knowledge of God as Creator and Redeemer (224).

twofold knowledge of God as Creator and Redeemer. According to Dowey, "From the point of view of the knowledge of God, which is the foundation of Calvin's theological writing, Calvin's *Institutes* of 1559 contains two, not four, divisions."[127] Dowey is correct in viewing the knowledge of God as twofold (which has ramifications for the doctrine of Holy Spirit), but that this distinction is "the foundation of Calvin's theological writing" may be questioned.

The twofold concept is developed from a statement Calvin added to the final edition of the *Institutes* that Dowey takes to be programmatic. "First, in the fashioning of the universe and in the general teaching of Scripture the Lord shows himself to be the Creator. Then in the face of Christ he shows himself to be the Redeemer" (I.2.1). On this view the first major topic, God the Creator, is discussed in Book I, and the second, the exposition of God the Redeemer, is discussed in Books II, III, and IV.

Within a few months of each other, two books were published on the knowledge of God in Calvin. In an appendix to his revised edition T. H. L. Parker asserts, "Anyone who reads the two works will agree with me that the most striking fact about them lies in their disagreements. Starting from the same evidence, they reach different conclusions." This is especially true of the "principle by which the *Institutes* is to be interpreted."[128] For the *Institutes* as a whole, Parker argues for the fourfold division of the Apostles' Creed. "To impose upon [the *Institutes*] the *duplex cognitio Dei* is to destroy that unity and to make it such a badly arranged book that we should be very surprised that a theologian of Calvin's taste should have professed himself satisfied with it."[129] Parker believes that the *Institutes* reflects a *duplex cognitio* but it is the knowledge of God and the self. "The form that Dowey imposes on [the *Institutes*] does not correspond to the general theme but takes one methodological distinction made in the work and magnifies it into the leading principle to interpret the whole."[130]

The studies of Dowey and Parker, however differently expounded, demonstrate that the twofold distinction between Creator and Redeemer is important for understanding Calvin's view of the knowledge of God. Certainly the work of the Holy Spirit (Book III) and life in the Church (Book IV) are intimately connected with the knowledge of the Redeemer (and also with the Creator), but if Dowey's organizational theory is correct, it is not clear why Calvin devotes two separate books to subsections of his previous topic. Obviously the work of the Holy Spirit is not independent of the person and work of Christ, but Calvin's discussions in Books III and IV indicate a conviction that while these topics are related, they require separate books. Thus, the twofold division of the knowledge of God applied to the entire *Institutes* seems forced.

---

127. Dowey, *Knowledge of God*, 41.

128. T. H. L. Parker, *Calvin's Doctrine of the Knowledge of God*, rev. ed. (Grand Rapids: Eerdmans, 1959), 117.

129. Ibid., 119.

130. Ibid., 121.

In praising and defending his teacher, Brian Armstrong claims, "Dowey's attention to the unquestionably dialectical structure of Calvin's thought lifted much of the research on Calvin to a new level of analysis."[131] Armstrong expands Dowey's "unquestionably dialectical structure" into a dualistic conflict within Calvin's own mind between the two worlds of Renaissance and Reformation. Accordingly, in Calvin's theology "there will always be two poles, two aspects, two dialectical and conflicting elements in each theological topic which he discusses." This conflict is "fundamentally based in a broad, general philosophical dialectic between the ideal and the real."[132] Now using the distinction between real and ideal, Armstrong sees Calvin's concept of sin not as bracketed but as the cataclysmic event that interrupts the relationship with God, creating a constant tension "between the ideal world of God's goodness and the 'real' world where evil triumphs over good."[133] The dualism between ideal and real "which characterizes Calvin's theology is nowhere more clearly seen than in the discussion of the doctrine of justification by faith and its relationship to the doctrine of sanctification." This means, "viewed from the perspective of justification (i.e., viewed in Christ), the individual is pure and holy, accepted and forgiven. On the other hand, viewed from the perspective of sanctification (i.e., viewed in themselves and from the perspective of their actual condition and performance), all believers are still enmeshed in sin, impure and in need of constant forgiveness."[134]

In addition to the dichotomy between ideal and real, Armstrong sees a duality between hypothetical and actual. In another essay, Armstrong repeats the two poles, two aspects, two dialectical and conflicting elements claim,[135] suggesting that "the whole general tenor and structure of Calvin's theology is built around a hypothetical or conditional base."[136] Admittedly, one can find in Calvin a dialectic between ideal and real, universal and hypothetical, necessary and contingent, rhetoric and philosophic, freedom and predestination, divine and human perspectives, justification and sanctification, and so on. However, valorizing the dialectic process in this way overstates the situation. More basic to Calvin's theology is the unity of truth revealed in Jesus Christ. Armstrong moves in the same direction when he writes, "I believe that the nature and force of his use of the hypothetical motif as it relates to his teaching on grace is best perceived and understood when serious attention is given to the role and importance in his the-

131. Brian G. Armstrong, "Duplex Cognitio Dei, Or?: The Problem and Relation of Structure, Form and Purpose in Calvin's Theology," in *Probing the Reformed Tradition: Historical Studies in Honor of Edward A. Dowey, Jr.*, ed. Elsie Anne McKee and Brian G. Armstrong (Louisville, KY: Westminster/John Knox Press, 1989), 135.

132. Ibid., 137.

133. Ibid., 142.

134. Ibid., 149.

135. See also Armstrong, "The Nature and Structure of Calvin's Thought according to the *Institutes*: Another Look" in *John Calvin's Institutes, His Opus Magnum: Proceedings of the Second South African Congress for Calvin Research* (Potchefstroom: Potchefstroom University, 1986), 56.

136. Ibid., 64–65.

ology of the mystical union of the believer with Christ."[137] The unity or duality of Calvin's theology in general and the basis of it in particular remain a warmly debated topic. In the absence of compelling evidence and a comfortable consensus, students of Calvin may be debating a form of the ancient philosophical problem of the One and the Many, of ultimate reality as a unity or plurality.

3. The Trinitarian God

A third view, propounded by Philip Walker Butin maintains the expository outline of the *Institutes* is Trinitarian.[138] This understanding differs from the Warfield theory in two main ways. First, Book IV on the church is understood theologically as a continuation of the exposition of the Holy Spirit (Book III). Second, within the Trinitarian structure, Calvin's anthropology (i.e., his doctrine of man) is articulated "perichoretically." By employing this Greek term (literally, moving around) Butin focuses on the intimate relation between the human and the divine, thereby calling into question the modern view of the self as separate from God. This procedure has the great advantage of taking quite seriously Calvin's treatment of the knowledge of God and ourselves as aspects of one subject rather than two, although it raises important questions about the relation between God's grace, human nature, and the effect of sin. In addition, this dynamic and functional relation allows a stronger emphasis on the work of the persons of the Trinity, which softens the objection that Book III is not structured on the *person* of the Holy Spirit (as Warfield implies) since Book III does in fact focus on the *work* of the Holy Spirit.

According to Butin, Calvin studies can be divided between those that interpret Calvin's view of the divine-human relationship in opposing dialectical terms and those that see a unified Trinitarian exposition.[139] Butin thinks dialectical interpretations "tend to underestimate the significance of Calvin's own explicit and persistent use of *the Trinitarian structure* of the Apostles' Creed *as the organizing paradigm for successive editions of the Institutes.*"[140] Butin's analysis of the human self in connection with the divine Trinity is a major contribution to Calvin studies. However, a Trinitarian outline for the *Institutes* suggests three books rather than four. If Book IV is really a continuation of Book III, the unanswered question is why they are distinguished. Since God is revealed as Father, Son, and Holy Spirit, the human person and the divine persons will obviously be

137. Armstrong, "Duplex Cognitio Dei," 148. The most debatable part of Armstrong's essay is his use of the term "hypothetical," which he seems to have moved into John Calvin from his study of Moïse Amyraut. See Brian Armstrong, *Calvinism and Amyraut Heresy: Protestant Scholasticism and Humanism in Seventeenth-Century France* (Madison, WI: University of Wisconsin, 1969), 143ff.

138. Philip Walker Butin, *Revelation, Redemption, and Response: Calvin's Trinitarian Understanding of the Divine-Human Relationship* (New York: Oxford University Press, 1995).

139. Ibid., 15–16.

140. Ibid., 19, emphasis added.

related in Trinitarian terms. However, a threefold outline for the four books of the *Institutes* is not obvious.

4. Union with Christ

The fourth view, and the one that informs the deeper background of this study, observes a distinction Calvin makes at the beginning of Book III. Calvin writes, "First, we must understand that as long as Christ remains outside of us, and we are separated from him, all that he has suffered and done for the salvation of the human race remains useless and of no value for us. Therefore, to share with us what he has received from the Father, he had to become ours and to dwell within us" (III.1.1). This statement suggests that Calvin's previous exposition was concerned with what Christ does *for* us and the subsequent discussion will treat what Christ does *within* us. In this connection our union with Christ is powerfully affirmed. Since the incarnation, Christians are not allowed to think of themselves apart from Christ in whom, by God's grace, they live. Using this statement as a pivot, the four books of the *Institutes* can be divided into two equal parts:

> Part One: GOD FOR US
> > Book I. God the Creator
> > Book II. God the Redeemer
>
> Part Two: GOD WITH US
> > Book III. The Faithful Person(s)
> > Book IV. The Faithful Community

In Book I Calvin deals with God the Creator and therefore God's creation of and providence for all things, but especially of and for human beings. Calvin is quite eloquent and even passionate in describing the Creator's care for his creature. In Book II, after discussing the creature's sin (chaps. 1–5), Calvin expounds the knowledge of God the Redeemer affirming the central mystery of the incarnation in Chalcedonian terms and avoiding the heresy of Eutychianism more clearly than the heresy of Nestorianism. Having, then, explicated theology proper in Book I and Christology in Book II, he turns not to anthropology but to soteriology. According to Calvin the redeemed sinner receives internally (*Christus in nobis*) God's gift of faith, which is the principal work of the Holy Spirit. Following the exposition of the redeemed sinner in Book III, Calvin treats the redeemed community (and the external means of grace) in Book IV, that is, the church's ministry, sacraments, and relation to the civil government.

The mystery that holds together the confession of God for Us and God with Us is the conviction of God in Us, or, more accurately, We in God. That is to say, the doctrine of the incarnation teaches that in Jesus Christ God became a man, and to him we are united in God's gift of faith. The union of God and a man in Jesus (incarnation) is extended to those who are joined to Christ by God's grace (incorporation). In his commentary on John 16:27 Calvin declares, "The only bond of our union with God is union with Christ."[141] As divine being is known in Christ, so is human being. We are not to think of God or ourselves apart from Christ. "Therefore, that joining together of Head and members, that indwelling of Christ in our hearts—in short, that mystical union—are accorded by us the highest degree of importance. We do not, therefore, contemplate him outside ourselves from afar in order that his righteousness may be imputed to us but because we put on Christ and are engrafted into his body—in short because he deigns to make us one with him" (II.16.19). Union in Christ is both a state and a process. This union with Christ who is one with God is the central and irreducible mystery of Christian faith and life. God is for us in Jesus Christ, and God is with us in Jesus Christ.[142] In a recent article Thomas L. Wenger identifies this view as the new perspective on Calvin and even dignifies it by its own initials (NPC). According to Wenger, the error of the NPC is in realigning the doctrines of justification and sanctification under the rubric of union with Christ. Loyal to the old perspective on Calvin (OPC), Wenger insists the NPC is wrong not only because its proponents (of which I am certainly one) utilize "erratic readings of Calvin," but largely because they (we) do not agree with Richard Muller. Unfortunately Wenger limits his discussion to scholars who interact primarily with Richard B. Gaffin Jr. and Tim J. R. Trumper. Apparently for Wenger the famous baseball progression "from Tinker to Evers to Chance" has its theological parallel "from Oberman to Steinmetz to Muller."[143]

---

141. Even so astute a scholar as Roland H. Bainton, *Hunted Heretic: The Life and Death of Michael Servetus, 1511–1553* (Boston: Beacon Press, 1953), 143, can make the entirely erroneous claim, "For Calvin God was so high and lifted up, so unspeakably holy, and man so utterly unworthy, that no union between God and man could be thinkable." This judgment may summarize Calvin's reputation but not his actual text.

142. See Andrew Purves and Mark Achtemeier, *Union in Christ: A Declaration for the Church* (Louisville, KY: Witherspoon Press, 1999), and the entire discussion of Book III of the *Institutes*.

143. Thomas L. Wenger, "The New Perspective on Calvin: Responding to Recent Calvin Interpretations," *Journal of the Evangelical Theological Society* 50, no. 2 (June 2007): 311–28. One may question the newness of this perspective on Calvin in American theology since John Nevin wrote on union with Christ, both in the Bible and Calvin, at considerable length and with intense passion in the 1840s in his *The Mystical Presence: A Vindication of the Reformed or Calvinistic Doctrine of the Holy Eucharist* (John W. Nevin, *The Mystical Presence and Other Writings on the Eucharist*, ed. Bard Thompson and George H. Bricker [Philadelphia: United Church Press, 1966], 36). Nevin insisted the majesty of the great mystery of union with Christ required the affirmation "that Christ's people are inserted by faith into his very life [involving] to the worthy communicant an actual participation in the substance of his person. . . . The participation is not simply in his spirit, but in his flesh also and blood. It is not figurative merely and moral, but *real, substantial,* and *essential*" (emphasis in original). Swimming against the mainstream of current Calvinism (as represented by Charles Hodge), the systemic import and importance of Nevin's claim may have been neglected because it was attached to sacramental theology. For a wider systematic consideration, see W. Kolfhaus, *Christusgemeinschaft bei Johannes Calvin* (Neukirchen: Kr. Moers; Buchlandlungen des Erziehungsvereins, 1939). A half century ago Paul Van Buren, *Christ in Our Place: The Substitutionary Character of Calvin's Doctrine of Reconciliation* (Grand Rapids: Wm. B. Eerdmans, 1957), divided his work: The Incarnation: Christ's Union with Us; The Atonement: Christ in Our Place; and Incorporation: Union with Christ. More than twenty years ago I suggested a renewed recognition of the importance of union in Christ in Calvin's theology ("Calvin's Central Dogma Again," *Sixteenth-Century Journal* 18 [1987]: 191–99).

David Willis reminds us that the incarnation (or hypostatic union) is the first or prior level of union. The believer's union with Christ is the second or consequent level.[144] Calvin calls this indwelling of Christ in our hearts "mystical union." Nevertheless, Dennis E. Tamburello makes the important point that Calvin "did not see himself as a mystic, nor was mysticism a major focus of concern in his works." Tamburello sees "a relationship between Calvin and the mystical tradition" and "attempts to evaluate the presence of mystical themes in Calvin, particularly in relation to his teaching on union with Christ."[145] However, while the question of historical affinities is always interesting, if Calvin is not a mystic nor much concerned about mysticism, then one must conclude his doctrine of "union with Christ" in the theological foreground is only loosely connected with the central mystical tradition. Also addressing the issue of "Calvin's mysticism," Robinson concludes, "His theology is compelled and enthralled by an overwhelming awareness of the grandeur of God, and this is the source of the distinctive aesthetic coherency of his religious vision, which is neither mysticism nor metaphysics, but mysticism as a method of rigorous inquiry, and metaphysics as an impassioned flight of the soul."[146] Union with Christ for Calvin is not adequately described as mystical because he places so little emphasis on "yearning," nor as completely substantial because essential ontological identity is denied. Union with Christ is real and fundamental, but in a finally ineffable sense.[147]

Christians cannot go beyond or behind or set aside the Lordship of Jesus Christ. Therefore, Calvin teaches the fundamental Christian conviction of the Lordship of Jesus Christ, which by God's grace includes union with Christ. Of course, union with Christ is clearly taught in Scripture. For example, Colossians 3:3–4, which Karl Barth claims as the center of the gospel,[148] reads, "You have died, and your life is hid with Christ in God. When Christ our life appears, then you will appear with him in glory." Certainly John Calvin did not set out to write the *Institutes of the Christian Religion* by deductions from one central theological dogma nor from a basic philosophical principle. The organizing outline suggested here is only claimed to fit comfortably on the *Institutes* and thus to be useful for the purpose of a serious engagement with Calvin's theology. Each of these four views is carefully nuanced and rewards careful study. However, the topic concerns Calvin's interpreters more than Calvin himself. For that reason the outline

144. David Willis-Watkins, "The Unio Mystica and the Assurance of Faith According to Calvin," in *Calvin: Erbe und Auftrag: Festschrift für Wilhelm Heinrich Neuser zum 65. Geburtstag*, ed. Willem Van't Spijker (Kampen: Kok Pharos, 1991), 78.

145. Dennis E. Tamburello, *Union with Christ: John Calvin and the Mysticism of St. Bernard* (Louisville, KY: Westminster John Knox Press, 1994), 22. His chapter "John Calvin on Mystical Union" treats both Bernard and Kolfhaus.

146. Robinson, *Death of Adam*, 188.

147. From the title, one might expect insight into Calvin's view of "union with Christ" from Otto Gründler's "Ingrafting in Christ," in *The Spirituality of Western Christendom* (Kalamazoo, MI: Cistercian Publications, 1976), 169–87, but the essay adds little to the topic of spirituality in general or to the understanding of John Calvin in particular.

148. CD 2.1.149.

of Calvin's theology need not be decided finally nor discussed further than to propose a useful guide for exposition.

D. A WORD ON THE MINISTER OF THE WORD

"Whatever else it was, the Reformation was a great preaching revival, probably the greatest in the history of the Christian church."[149] According to Calvin, God has two ways of teaching. He speaks to us outwardly by the mouth of men and inwardly by his spirit. "These he does simultaneously or at different times, as he thinks fit" (Com. Jn. 14:26). Preaching is the instrument of faith (Com. Eph. 1:13). Indeed, without preaching there can be no faith. "The Church maintains the truth, because in her preaching she proclaims it and preserves it pure and complete and transmits it to posterity" (Com. I Tim. 3:15).

Heiko Oberman argues that the Reformers believed the sermon "forces for itself a way to the heart and mind of the congregation." The sermon is not a preparation for divine encounter; it is itself the encounter with God. "The doors of Heaven and Hell are put in motion by the preached Word." On the contrary for Roman Catholics, in the same way that Dante had to change guides when entering heaven, so the sermon must stop at the portal and point the sinner to the sacraments where true communion between God and human beings is realized. According to Oberman, "The Reformation returned to an understanding of the Holy Spirit as the dynamic presence of God in Jesus Christ." Of course the work of the Holy Spirit in gathering the church cannot be circumscribed, but "the preaching of the Gospel is the specially God-chosen way."[150]

That John Calvin believed himself called of God to the ministry of the Word is a fundamental reality required for understanding him. The gate of life, he claims, is opened only by the Word of God, and the key is put into the hand of ministers of the Word who open the gate for the godly but leave it locked for the ungodly. This latter result is accidental to the gospel, but its reality is designed "to strike terror into the despisers lest they should think they could mock ministers of the Word with impunity" (Com. Mt. 16:19). Leading worship in proclamation, edification, and praise of God is central to Calvin's work, not peripheral.[151] The following catena demonstrates his conviction about the central role of preaching, insisting that the gospel must be proclaimed ceaselessly in the church to the end of the world (Com. II Cor. 5:20). The preaching of the gospel is something in which

149. James Hastings Nichols, *Corporate Worship in the Reformed Tradition* (Philadelphia: Westminster Press, 1968), 29. For a short survey see the chapter on the ministry of the Word by Hughes Oliphant Old, *Worship: That Is Reformed According to Scripture* (Atlanta: John Knox Press, 1984).

150. Heiko A. Oberman, "Preaching and the Word in the Reformation," *Theology Today* 18 (April 1961): 18, 17, 21, 22.

151. The celebration of the sacraments, discussed in Book IV, is not only included in the minister's role, but decisively connected. For the general theme of praise, see Daniel W. Hardy and David F. Ford, *Jubilate: Theology in Praise* (London: Darton, Longman and Todd, 1984). They suggest that Calvin's central focus is the human "living relationship to God in praise" (189).

Christ transfers his own functions to his ministers. "He alone, indeed, has been appointed our teacher by the Father, but he has put pastors and ministers in his place to speak as if out of his mouth" (Com. Acts 13:47). Preachers "are sent, not to strew their words uselessly on the air, or to beat men's ears merely with empty sound, but to bring life-giving light to the blind, to transform men's hearts into the righteousness of God, and to confirm the grace of salvation, which has been procured by the death of Christ" (Com. Acts 26:18). Commenting on 2 Corinthians 13:5 Calvin asserts this verse "shows the relationship between the people's faith and the minister's preaching: for the preaching is the mother who conceives and brings forth, and faith is the daughter who ought to be mindful of her origin." As a means for revealing himself, God appoints the ministry of the Word to serve like a mirror. The angels do not need preaching for they see God's face openly, but we "look upon the likeness of God in the Word, in the sacraments, and, in short, in the whole ministry of the Church" (Com. I Cor. 13:12). This position was already stated in *The Genevan Confession* of 1536. "We receive the true ministers of the Word of God as messengers and ambassadors of God. It is necessary to listen to them as to God."[152] Dealing with the last verse of the Old Testament, Calvin cautions that confidence cannot be simply reposited in preachers. "God sometimes connects himself with his servants, and sometimes separates himself from them: when he connects himself with them, he transfers to them what never ceases to dwell in him; for he never resigns to them his office, but makes them partakers of it only." That is to say, God works through the secret influence of the Holy Spirit (Com. Mal. 4:6). "The external word is of no avail unless animated by the power of the Spirit." Those who fish foolishly for free will carp in vain. "All power of action resides in the Spirit himself, and thus all praise ought to be entirely referred to God alone" (Com. Ez. 2:2).[153]

Interpreting the distinction between letter and spirit Calvin says, "We are ministers of the Spirit not because we hold him bound as captive and not because at our own whim we can confer his grace upon all or upon whom we please, but because through us Christ enlightens men's minds, renews their hearts and wholly regenerates them" (Com. II Cor. 3:6). Christ preached peace not through his own lips but through the apostles as by trumpets. "What they did, not only in his name, and by his command, but as it were in his own person, is justly ascribed to him alone." The gospel's "whole authority comes from recognizing men as God's instruments, and hearing Christ speak to us by their mouth" (Com. Eph. 2:17). Using the four causes as identified by Aristotle, Calvin says the efficient cause of our salvation is the good pleasure of God's will. The material cause is Christ; the final cause is the praise of his grace, and the formal cause is "the

---

152. *Calvin: Theological Treatises*, trans. J. K. S. Reid (Philadelphia: Westminster Press, 1954), 32.

153. Discussing infant baptism, Calvin says that "when the apostle makes hearing the beginning of faith he is describing only the ordinary arrangement and disposition of the Lord which he commonly uses in calling his people." Nevertheless, God uses other ways to call many, "giving them true knowledge of himself by inward means, that is, by the illumination of the Spirit apart from the medium of preaching" (IV.16.19).

preaching of the Gospel, by which the goodness of God flows out to us" (Com. Eph. 1:5, 8).

The reality of Calvin's self-understanding as minister of the Word operates everywhere but is especially evident in the discussion of prayer, sin, and evil, and the excursus on method. Of his attempt to obey the first and special commandment to preachers not to be boring,[154] Breen observes that Calvin's rhetoric differs from the main tradition. "Indeed, he persistently violates a basic rule of rhetoric in that he seldom if ever tries to persuade by pleasing the reader either in what he says or how he says it. Were one to name the most constant excellence of Calvin, it could well be that of vividness; he tries his utmost to keep the reader awake."[155] Higman comments on Calvin's method of "rhetorical logic": "This constant process of orientation of the reader, preparing him for the right reception of each statement, is embedded in the steady line of development, the unfailing continuity of argument provided by the strong connectives."[156] In a May 1555 letter to the pastors of Bern, Calvin wrote, "[Christ] has been pleased to make me a minister." One hundred years ago, surrounded by the stones of St. Peter's Cathedral, Émile Doumergue reminded his auditors that John Calvin was "le Prédicateur de Genève."[157] As a preacher, Calvin's thoughts were never far from his pulpit. Commenting on the importance and worth of the pastoral office in 1 Timothy 3:15, Calvin says that instruction for living in the kingdom of God is preserved in the world only through the church's ministry. "God does not himself come down from heaven to us, nor does he daily send angelic messengers to publish his truth, but he uses the labors of pastors whom he has ordained for this purpose." Faith comes from hearing, and without preaching there can be no faith. The ministry of the Word is an awesome task for godly ministers. The awesomeness of the task should not terrify but stir pastors to greater vigilance because they "by their preaching rescue the truth from darkness and oblivion, falsehoods, errors, impostures, superstitions, and corruption of every kind. . . . This true mark of the church is not found among the papists because they do not think it essential that God's truth be maintained by pure preaching."

Calvin teaches that God wishes to be heard by the voice of his ministers (Com. Is. 50:10). Again, the word that goes out of the mouth of God likewise goes out

---

154. The main characteristic of the humanists was their "pursuit of eloquence," according to Hanna H. Gray, "Renaissance Humanism: The Pursuit of Eloquence," in *Renaissance Essays* from the *Journal of the History of Ideas*, ed. Paul Oskar Kristeller and Philip P. Wiener (New York: Harper Torchbooks, 1968), 199–216. "Calvin's deep convictions bring to his writing a quality of urgency which in some passages takes on an oratorical character. It is much less by formal logic than by enlisting the emotions that he has power to persuade" (LCC, lxx). Later in the same tradition John Witherspoon, "Lectures on Eloquence" (number 13), *The Selected Writings of John Witherspoon*, ed. Thomas Miller (Carbondale: Southern Illinois University Press, 1990), 290, declares, "The intention of all speech or writing, which is but recorded speech, is to persuade, taking the word with latitude."

155. Breen, "John Calvin and the Rhetorical Tradition," 8.

156. Higman, *Style of Calvin*, 104.

157. Émile Doumergue, "Calvin, Le Prédicateur de Genève," Address delivered at the 400th anniversary of Calvin's birth, July 2, 1909.

of the mouth of men "for God does not speak openly from heaven but employs men as his instruments, that by their agency he may make known his will" (Com. Is. 55:11).[158] "A teacher (doctor) is one who forms and instructs the church by the word of truth" (Com. Rom. 12:6). He continues, "The faithful alone really know that God has spoken" (Com. Zech. 6:15). "God's voice fills the whole world [but] his glory is celebrated only in his church because God not only speaks intelligibly and distinctly there, but also there gently allures the faithful to himself" (Com. Ps. 29.9).[159]

The conclusion to be drawn is if God speaks, and if God speaks in the church, then on some subjects sermons are not popularized products of more basic scholarly reflection. Rather scholarly reflection is an academized product of the more basic proclamation of the gospel. In a sweeping generalization, George Hendry claims the Protestant concentration on the authority of Scripture was a "shift of emphasis from the preached word to the written word."[160] Probing the same vein Leith writes, "Calvin thought of preaching as the primary means by which God's presence becomes actual to us and by which God's work is accomplished in individual life and in the community."[161] Thus, for the Christian community sermons are a first-order, not a second-order, activity.

158. In his chapter on the preached word as the Word of God, Roland S. Wallace, *Calvin's Doctrine of the Word and Sacrament* (Edinburgh: Oliver and Boyd, 1953), expounds this orality theme of "two mouths." See Com. Is. 11:4.

159. For Calvin and preaching, see Erwin Mülhaupt, *Die Predigt Calvins, ihre Geschichte, ihre Form und ihre religiösen Grundgedanken* (Berlin: Walter de Gruyter & Co., 1931); T. H. L. Parker, *The Oracles of God: An Introduction to the Preaching of John Calvin* (London: Lutterworth Press, 1947), and *Calvin's Preaching* (Louisville, KY: Westminster/John Knox Press, 1992). John H. Gerstner, "Calvin's Two-Voice Theory of Preaching," *Calvin's Ecclesiology: Sacraments and Deacons*, ed. Richard C. Gamble (New York: Garland Publishing, 1992), 305–16. Jack's unflinchingly severe stance toward those who disagreed with his deductive Calvinism is here contrasted with a winsome compassion for those unable to follow Calvin's advice to preach and pray without notes. Also Victor A. Shepherd, *The Nature and Function of Faith in the Theology of John Calvin* (Macon, GA: Mercer University Press, 1983), 187–206. Karl Barth's massive *Church Dogmatics* may be seen as an exposition of the conviction "God speaks." In *The Word of God and the Word of Man*, trans. Douglas Horton (New York: Harper and Brothers Publishers, 1957), 248–49, Barth declares the Alpha and Omega of Reformed doctrine is: "Speak, Lord, for thy servant heareth." Barth makes a crucial comparison and contrast among the living Word—Jesus Christ, the written Word—Scripture, and the spoken Word—proclamation (*CD* 1.1.4). In the same vein Christoph Schwöbel writes, "Behind the written word is the living word and the written word is meant to become alive again by being spoken." He concludes, "The objective of theological reflection is to provide orientation for the practice of preaching" (Christoph Schwöbel, "Introduction," in Colin E. Gunton, *Theology Through Preaching: Sermons for Brentwood* [Edinburgh: T. & T. Clark, 2001], 4, 5). This book is dedicated to Benjamin William Gunton (1996–98) and includes his father's sermon for his memorial service based on Rev. 14:13: Blessed are the dead who die in the Lord. Of considerable interest is Nicholas Wolterstorff, *Divine Discourse: Philosophical Reflections on the Claim That God Speaks* (New York: Cambridge University Press, 1995).

160. George S. Hendry, "The Place and Function of the Confession of Faith in the Reformed Church," in *The New Man: An Orthodox and Reformed Dialogue*, ed. John Meyendorff and Joseph McLelland (New Brunswick, N.J.: Agora Books, 1973), 28f.

161. John H. Leith, "Calvin's Doctrine of the Proclamation of the Word and Its Significance for Today," in *John Calvin and the Church: A Prism of Reform*, ed. Timothy George (Louisville, KY: Westminster/John Knox Press, 1990), 206. See also John C. Bowman, "Calvin as Preacher," *Reformed Church Review* (1909), 253, who not able to reconcile Calvin's cool logic and fiery ardor, concludes, "Ordinarily the manner of Calvin was calm, refined, dignified, impressive, indicative of the high and

Worship is the heart of Christian life. "For God wishes first of all for inward worship, and afterwards for outward profession. The principal altar for the worship of God ought to be situated in our minds, for God is worshipped spiritually by faith, prayer and other acts of piety. It is also necessary to add outward profession, not only that we may exercise ourselves in God's worship, but offer ourselves wholly to him." (Com. Dan. 3:6). As worship is more fundamental in the church than theology, so kerygmatic proclamation is more basic and often more pertinent than scholarly reflection. Calvin writes, "The first foundation of righteousness is the worship of God. . . . Accordingly, in the First Table [of the Law], God instructs us in piety and the proper duties of religion, by which we are to worship his majesty" (II.8.11). While human beings owe God innumerable things, Calvin summarizes them under four headings: adoration, trust, invocation, and thanksgiving (II.8.16).

In his systematic theology entitled *Doxology: The Praise of God in Worship, Doctrine, and Life*, Geoffrey Wainwright explores the linkages between worship and doctrine. Writing "from faith to faith," he expects to "find echoes in the experience of Christians who seek to praise God in worship, doctrine and life." Wainwright deals briefly with the relation between theology and preaching and with preaching in its liturgical context, but does not consider the possibility that preaching the Word of God might actually be the Word of God as declared in chapter 1 of the Second Helvetic Confession.[162]

In his classic on theology and preaching Heinrich Ott takes the Barthian position that God himself speaks in the spoken word. The task of theology, then, is to evaluate this proclamation. Dogmatics is thus essentially coordinated with preaching. Preaching is an immediate activity, while theology is reflective activity.[163] With this distinction Ott creates a false sequence and a false dichotomy. Homiletics and dogmatics are both reflective, and in oral and written communication both are immediate. With fine insight Brian Gerrish suggests that theology, unlike other academic disciplines, may face its real test in the pulpit, not the lecture room.[164]

---

solemn regard which he cherished for the sacred office whose specific purpose he believed to be the reformation of individual character, and the implanting of a holy, evangelical life in the community." George Johnson, "Calvinism and Preaching," *Evangelical Quarterly* 4 (1932), 245 claims Andreas Gerhard (Hyperius) in 1553 produced the first compend of the Calvinistic view of preaching.

162. Geoffrey Wainwright, *Doxology: The Praise of God in Worship, Doctrine, and Life: A Systematic Theology* (New York: Oxford University Press, 1980), 2, 177–81. Wainwright responds to the denial of the deity of Christ by John Hick and others by treating the worship of Christ as Lord, but his view of Christ as "pattern-setter" is an inadequate conceptualization for Christology (45–70). See also Dietrich Ritschl, *A Theology of Proclamation* (Richmond, VA: John Knox Press, 1960), especially the chapter entitled "The Sermon Is the Word of God." Strangely, the section entitled "Union with Christ" deals with this topic in no theological depth. On the Second Helvetic, see G. W. Locher, "Praedicatio Verbi est Verbum Dei" *Zwingliana* 10 (1958): 47–57, and Edward A. Dowey Jr., "The Word of God as Scripture and Preaching," in Graham, *Later Calvinism*, 5–18.

163. Heinrich Ott, *Theology and Preaching*, trans. Harold Knight (Philadelphia: Westminster Press, 1961). See also Karl Barth, *The Preaching of the Gospel*, trans. B. E. Hooke (Philadelphia: Westminster Press, 1963).

164. B. A. Gerrish, *A Prince of the Church: Schleiermacher and the Beginnings of Modern Theology* (Philadelphia: Fortress Press, 1984), 12.

I take this possibility to be actuality, a commitment apparently shared by Herman Melville's Ishmael, who declares the pulpit is ever this earth's foremost part. "The world's a ship on its passage out, and not a voyage complete; and the pulpit is its prow" (*Moby Dick*, chap. 8). The subject of ministry is treated by Calvin in Book IV of the *Institutes*, but we need to be reminded early and often that Calvin the minister and preacher is with us from beginning to end. The present claim that at least some theological subjects are more properly and helpfully treated in the pulpit than the lecture (or even the seminar) room appears to be more radical than Wainwright, Gerrish, or Ott are willing to accept. But a sermon preached for and within the community of the faithful may be more epistemologically valuable than an essay produced by the barking of a solitary dogmatician. For all the sermon's importance Calvin cautions, "Whatever other people might think, we certainly do not consider our ministry to be so narrowly circumscribed that when the sermon is delivered we may rest as though our task were complete. Those whose blood will be required of us, if lost through our neglect, are to be cared for much more closely and vigilantly (*CO* 5:319). According to Karl Barth, theology's special task is to accompany and evaluate the proclamation of the church (*CD* 1.1.2). To the contrary, theology is itself a form of the proclamation of the church—a worship of God with a special emphasis on the mind (See Com. Mk. 12:30, Mt. 22:37, Lk. 10:27).

PART ONE
GOD FOR US

Book I

God the Creator

INTRODUCTION TO BOOK I

According to Calvin, we cannot know God's essential reality; we can only know God's revelation to us. While the being of God can be intellectually affirmed, it cannot be logically explained. Our knowledge of God is chiefly located in the witness of Scripture that reveals God as Creator and Redeemer. Calvin summarizes, "In the fashioning of the universe and in the general teaching of Scripture the Lord shows himself to be the Creator. Then in the face of Christ he shows himself to be the Redeemer" (I.2.1). Because Calvin has not forgotten the doctrine of Trinity, this "then" is a revelatory not a logical or ontological sequence. The same God is revealed in creation and redemption, in Old and New Testament. Calvin's Christocentric interpretation of the Old Testament is clear in this statement, "God has formed the heavens by his word in such a manner as to prove the eternal Deity of Christ" (Com. Ps. 33:6). Calvin asserts that Christ is held before people in the mirror of the Word (Com. Zech. 9:9). Commenting on John 1:3, "All things were made by him," Calvin writes, "The Father made all things by the Son, and all things are by God through the Son." In Book I Calvin expounds God's work *for us in creation*, and in Book II, God's work *for us in redemption*. As an interpretative device, the twofold knowledge of God as Creator and Redeemer applies most directly and helpfully to this part of the *Institutes*.

In Book I Calvin chiefly considers the knowledge of God as derived from Creation and Providence, but he also treats "the general doctrine of Scripture" and the Trinity. Put another way, before considering what God has done in creating and taking care of the human creature, Calvin discusses briefly *how* we know God (by the general and special revelation in Scripture) and *who* the God is that we know (revealed as Father, Son, and Holy Spirit). Calvin does not address in detail the how question of revelation or the who question of God's personal being. Instead he concentrates on the what questions (God's work in creation and providence). By modern standards Calvin does not provide a complete doctrine of either Scripture or Trinity. He explains to the reader only what is necessary to understand of these subjects concerning the knowledge of God the Creator.

I. The Scripture

Donald McKim rightly observes, "The literature on Calvin and the Scriptures is immense."[1] This situation obtains because for Christians the authority of Scripture is decisive, but the nature of Scripture is divisive. Theoretically, the boundaries of the contemporary debate could range between (1) those who believe the Bible is entirely a divine book, (2) those who regard it as entirely a human book, and (3) those who think the Bible is both divine and human. Practically, the issue is between the Bible as "reliably perfect" (number one) or "perfectly reliable" (number three). The term "reliable" or "perfect" is taken to demonstrate the Bible's nature and provide the answer to its authority. Interestingly, John Calvin is held in such esteem that he is claimed by both sides, and therefore considerable attention has been devoted to his view of Scripture. However, the current issues are not Calvin's, and he should not be forced to answer questions not his own. The nature of the Bible as presently discussed is not Calvin's problem. While his use of the Bible is great, his theoretical remarks on its nature are small and inconclusive, as a brief review of Calvin's interpreters demonstrates. The major interpretative difficulty is that subsequent theologians turned from the living and finally uncontrollable authority of Christ to the written and more controllable authority of Scripture. Calvin maintains a dynamic balance rather than a fixed sequence. "First then, we must hold that Christ cannot be properly known from anywhere but the Scriptures. And if that is so, it follows that the Scriptures should be read with the aim of finding Christ in them" (Com. Jn. 5:39). Even the chosen of the Old Testament "must have a hun-

---

1. Donald K. McKim, "Calvin's View of Scripture," in *Readings in Calvin's Theology*, ed. Donald K. McKim (Grand Rapids: Baker Book House, 1984), 43. McKim suggests Calvin's view of Scripture requires a theological synthesis of the knowledge of God (I.6–9), the work of the Holy Spirit (III.2), and the authority of ministry (IV.8) (50).

dred times succumbed under their evils, had they not Christ before their eyes" (Com. Zech. 9:9). Again, "All divine revelations are correctly designated by the term 'Word of God' so this substantial Word is . . . the wellspring of all oracles. Unchangeable the Word abides everlastingly one and the same with God and is God himself" (I.13.7). Nevertheless, Protestant proclamation was later not considered of sufficient gravity to counterbalance the weight of Roman ecclesiastical tradition.

In terms of his life's work John Calvin is correctly remembered as an outstanding theologian, but he was also a superb scriptural commentator. However, Calvin's actual exegesis of the biblical text is not our present topic, but rather his view of the Scripture as a whole, a subject on which, given its crucial importance, Calvin has remarkably little to say. Calvin believes passionately that the Scripture is God's word. The word of God is the ladder or wings or vehicle by which we fly upward from earth (Com. Hab. 2:1). But this conviction being so fundamental is more asserted and assumed than analyzed and argued.[2]

In interpreting Scripture the Protestant Reformers substituted the authority of the Spirit for the authority of the church and appealed to the heart, not the critical intellect. The Bible "is a book of life through which God speaks directly to the human soul." The church is not the arbiter of the word; rather the word is the arbiter of the church. Protestant interpretation of Scripture began with the historical and grammatical, rejecting needless allegorization and other medieval senses of meaning in favor of the one simple sense that led to Christ. The recent development of the printing press made for a natural, rather than artificial, dissemination of this scholarship. Additionally, the knowledge of Latin alone was recognized as insufficient to understand the Hebrew and Greek Bible. Valuing both the literal-historical and the literal-prophetic sense, the faithful understood "Christ is the point in the circle from which the whole circle is drawn."[3]

Calvin neither devotes a separate chapter nor a sustained discussion to the nature and authority of Scripture, as modern theologians generally do. In Book I.6–10 Calvin deals briefly with the general authority of the Bible in Christian faith and life but concentrates on the special teaching concerning creation. In Book II.6–11 Calvin again focuses on Scripture and at greater length. The primary subject is not a doctrine of Scripture, but the relation of the Old and New Testaments. This situation allows for considerable disagreement among Calvin's interpreters. Here especially we see the handprints of each potter who shapes the interpretative vessel. One might say that the twentieth-century "Bible Battle" occupies the same place that the "Supper Strife" occupied in the sixteenth century.[4] Analyzing the nature and authority of Scripture in Calvin is complicated

2. Not surprising the more basic a conviction the less analysis preferred. See my essay "Calvin's Polemic: Foundational Convictions in the Service of God's Truth," in *Calvinus Sincerioris Religionis Vindex*, ed. Wilhelm H. Neuser and Brian G. Armstrong (Kirksville, MO: Sixteenth-Century Journal Publishers, 1997), 97–122.

3. Robert Grant and David Tracy, *A Short History of the Interpretation of the Bible* (Philadelphia: Fortress Press, 1984), 92, 93, 94.

4. The eucharistic divisions are discussed in the section on the sacraments in Book IV.

by the fact that many people today and the scholars who inform and represent their convictions are deeply committed to a particular doctrine of Scripture believed to be fundamental to all Christian faith and life.

With the other Protestant reformers Calvin rejected allegorical interpretation of Scripture (II.10.10) in favor of the "natural and obvious meaning" (Com. Gal. 4:22–26).[5] Calvin explains the natural and obvious meaning with qualifications such as these: First, clear knowledge of God is to be found in Scripture (I.10.1), which demands study in that school all our lives (I.6.4; I.6.2). Second, in spite of this clarity, encountered difficulty in understanding Christ's words requires fixing on the intention (II.8.26). Third, on the basis of truth revealed in Scripture, philosophical speculation must be avoided (I.11.1). Fourth, nevertheless, ascertaining the true sense of a phrase such as "God's ears" (2 Sam. 22:7) makes a purely literal interpretation impossible. Fifth, scriptural revelation is often accommodated to cultural patterns (IV.15.18). Sixth, "There are many statements in Scripture the meaning of which depends on their context" (IV.16.23). Seventh, while it is difficult to draw an exact line, it is clear that "a sober interpretation of the law goes beyond the words" set down (II.8.8). Calvin believes this "sober interpretation" is realizable, unlike the papists who consider the Scripture "like a nose of wax. . . . It can be turned to anything and no meaning can with certainty be elicited; thus all things will remain perplexed and doubtful, if authority belongs to the Scripture alone" (Com. Jer. 23:17–18).

Hans-Joachim Kraus begins his fine article on "Calvin's Exegetical Principles" by quoting Calvin's conviction concerning the authority of Scripture. "The principal proof of the Scriptures is everywhere derived from the character of the divine speaker" (I.7.4). Enlightened by the illumination of the Holy Spirit, the exegete must exhibit reverence and humility which includes indebtedness to the exegetical tradition of the church." Kraus correctly notes "for all his significant and effective approaches, [the Genevan Reformer] was yet bound by a doctrinal mindset that was oriented to the unity and inner harmony of Scripture." The eight exegetical principles derived from the study of Calvin require: (1) clarity and brevity, (2) the author's intention, (3) his situation, (4) the passage's original meaning, (5) its context, (6) the cautious possibility of meaning beyond the literal, (7) the precise meaning of biblical metaphors, and (8) what Kraus calls "the scope of Christ." Scripture thus must be read with the purpose of finding Christ in it. And it is just here that Kraus does not explicitly acknowledge the implicit, and real, conclusion of his own essay. The goal of Scripture study is personal not principled. That is, we read not to apply exegetical principles accurately but to encounter the living Christ in whom are hid all the treasures of wisdom and knowledge.[6]

---

5. David C. Steinmetz, "John Calvin as an Interpreter of the Bible," in *Calvin and the Bible*, ed. Donald K. McKim (Cambridge: Cambridge University Press, 2006), 285. Calvin "accepted a typological reading of some passages of Scripture, which sounds, on the face of it, very much like what medieval commentators had in mind when they spoke of a double-literal sense." In other words Calvin had a generous view of the plain and natural sense of the text.

6. Hans-Joachim Kraus, "Calvin's Exegetical Principles," trans. Keith Crim, in *Interpretation: A Journal of Bible and Theology* 31 (1977): 18, 17. See also John L. Thompson, "Calvin as a Biblical Interpreter," in the *Cambridge Companion*, 58–73.

A number of his admirers adopted Calvin's nonsequential observations and adapted them to a more philosophical and less historical reading of the Bible. They minimized narrative values in favor of locating logical principles in the text.[7] Crucial as is the narrative, the primary issue is, of course, the subject, Jesus Christ, to whom the narrative witnesses. The scriptural issue in its modern form is illustrated by the Westminster Confession of Faith, which deals with Scripture in Article 1, indicating how essential the doctrine of Scripture is considered to be. Clearly the more profoundly one is involved with a subject, the more difficult separating historical and personal points of view becomes. The serious battle that continues around the doctrine of Scripture inevitably influences our present understanding. Despite being commonly labeled a "thorough-going Fundamentalist,"[8] Calvin's view of Scripture is understood in sharply contrasting ways by scholars.[9] This debate on Scripture, second only to predestination in its warmth, requires some attention.

Jack B. Rogers and Donald K. McKim emphasize Calvin's relation to Christian humanism and the classical rhetorical tradition which "enabled him to accept the accommodated character of biblical language, a concentration on the intent of the author rather than the form of words, and a concern for the cultural context in which the Divine message was encased."[10] Rogers and McKim locate the main problem in the doctrine of Scripture not with Calvin but in the continuing influence of post-Reformation scholasticism which treats Scripture as a compendium of logical propositions and rejects the historical and cultural contexts of biblical statements. Evidence for Calvin's openness to a variety of scriptural interpretations abounds and is typified by his remarks on "It is God that said, Light shall shine" (Com. II Cor. 4:6). "I see," he says, "that it is possible to expound this passage in four different ways." After listing the four possibilities Calvin declares his preference for Chrysostom's understanding "although Ambrose's rendering is also quite suitable." Calvin concludes, "Everyone may use his own judgment."

The conviction that Calvin supports Christian fundamentalism is usually based on the notion that Calvin regards Scripture as inerrant. A. M. Hunter asserts that Calvin replaced the authority of the church by the authority of the Bible. "The Bible therefore is the primary subject of faith seeing that it alone

7. Langdon Gilkey, *Reaping the Whirlwind: A Christian Interpretation of History* (New York: Seabury Press, 1976), 176, correctly observes that "philosophical categories, and especially those of Greek philosophy, play a minor role in Calvin's theology and exert relatively little influence on the development of his main concepts." This means "as in biblical thought generally, God is understood in directly personal categories. As a personal agent in history, he is . . . characterized primarily on the one hand by the *power* of his will to ordain and rule events and, on the other, by the *character* of his will as utterly righteous and supremely loving."

8. Georgia Harkness, *Calvin: The Man and His Ethics* (New York: Henry Holt and Company, 1931), 66. In a 1961 review T. H. L. Parker writes that this book "starts out from the wrong premises, pursues an erring course, and reaches largely mistaken conclusions" (*Scottish Journal of Theology* [1961]: 299).

9. On the inspiration of Scripture, David L. Puckett provides a long footnote on the division of scholars in his *John Calvin's Exegesis of the Old Testament* (Louisville, KY: Westminster John Knox Press, 1995), 45–47.

10. Rogers and McKim, *The Authority and Interpretation of the Bible: An Historical Approach* (San Francisco: Harper and Row, 1979), 99.

presents the positive will of God as He has revealed it to man."[11] According to Hunter, this view requires the logical concomitant of the assertion of the inerrancy of Scripture.[12] In addition Calvin affirms its equal authority and uniform consistency. "Calvin will not allow that there is any evolution of thought or belief exhibited in the Bible. The articles of faith stand as sure in the knowledge of Abraham as in that of Paul."[13] Hunter concludes:

> This view of Scripture was indeed a presupposition necessary to legitimise the construction of a rigid system of Christian doctrine. The Bible was the only source of the materials which went to its making. It must be assumed that, as it constitutes the sole revelation of God, its teaching on all things necessary to be known is complete, sufficient, self-consistent, harmonious, and that from it may be extracted by ordinary processes of reason a system of doctrine capable of logical and luminous statement, any item of which could be substantiated from any pertinent portion of the divine Word.[14]

In Hunter's evaluation, Calvin's view of Scripture is obviously objectionable.

> The Commentaries afford abundant evidence of the embarrassments into which he was driven by his theory [of the inerrancy of Scripture]. Its vindication in detail demanded an amazing amount of strenuous ingenuity, of whose disingenuousness he seems to be as conscious at times as of its unconvincingness. One may say that never did the idea of the verbal inspiration of the Scriptures receive such emphatic refutation as at the hands of this vehement champion, whose frequent transparent evasions, jugglings, and violences are in themselves a confession of its futility.[15]

Since Hunter believes that Calvin teaches the inerrancy of Scripture, he regards evidence to the contrary as transparent evasion of the truth. Disagreeing with

---

11. A. M. Hunter, *The Teaching of Calvin*, 2nd ed. (London: James Clarke and Company, 1950), 75.

12. Ibid., 72. In his groundbreaking study of Charles Dickens, Humphry House, *The Dickens World* (London: Oxford University Press, 1941), 122, refers to "the supposed infallibility of [the Bible] combined with the supposed infallibility of a twice-born judgment." This temper is illustrated in *David Copperfield* by the religion of Mr. and Miss Murdstone which is in fact "a vent for their bad humors and arrogance" (chap. 59). In *Little Dorrit* Mrs. Clennam is represented as a "rigid woman veiled in gloom and darkness, with lightnings of cursing, vengeance, and destruction, flashing through sable clouds" (chap. 5). Arthur, her son, remembers the religion of his parents as "a gloomy sacrifice of tastes and sympathies that were never their own, offered up as part of a bargain for the security of their possessions. [P]enance in this world and terror in the next—nothing graceful or gentle anywhere." (chap. 2). In his essay on "Dickens" in *Soliloquies in England* (New York: Charles Scribner's Sons, 1923), 58–73, philosopher George Santayana suggests the novelist possessed more genius than taste, more fancy than understanding (62). Dickens was essentially insensible to religion; with a most religious disposition he had no religious ideas (59). His portion is "contentment, vision, love, and laughter" (65). "I think Dickens is one of the best friends mankind has ever had" (72). See the article on religion in the superb *Oxford Reader's Companion to Dickens*. Also Dennis Walder, *Dickens and Religion* (London: George Allen & Unwin, 1981), who thinks in *Little Dorrit* Dickens produces his deepest reflection on "Mrs. Clennam's imprisoning Old Testament ethos and Little Dorrit's liberating New Testament spirit."

13. Hunter, *Teaching*, 78.

14. Ibid., 79.

15. Ibid., 76.

Hunter, J. K. S. Reid in his chapter on Calvin in *The Authority of Scripture* devotes careful attention to the state of scholarship. Reid recognizes the widespread view that Calvin's biblicism is based on literal or verbal inerrancy and cites a number of passages supporting that conclusion.[16] However, pointing to ambiguities, Reid also cites a number of passages that do not support inerrancy.

On a more cautious note, Rupert E. Davies affirms that "Calvin nowhere sets out methodically his theory of inspiration [but joins Hunter in concluding] that Calvin committed himself to a completely verbal and mechanical theory of inspiration."[17] Accordingly, Calvin's "doctrine of authority remains essentially one of the absolute, objective supremacy of the Word of God, spoken directly from heaven and in all respects identical with the canonical Scriptures of the Old and New Testaments."[18] Davies concludes, "Only after he has [established the supreme authority of the Scripture] does he feel himself at liberty to proceed to the enunciation of the other doctrines of the Christian faith."[19] The issue turns on the difference between the words "indicate" and "establish." Without question John Calvin believed the Scripture to be the Word of God, and he everywhere indicates its supreme authority for faith and life. However, if Calvin thought he needed to establish the authority of Scripture, a more detailed demonstration of its nature and function would seem to be required.

The passages that Hunter says are evasions are cited by James Barr to demonstrate that Calvin did *not* believe in inerrancy. As an example, Barr points out that Calvin suggests Psalms 74 and 79 were not composed in the time of David. "It is 'probable that many Psalms were composed by different authors after the death of David.'" Moreover, Calvin admits, "It is not easy to determine what calamity is the occasion of Psalm 74. Either the Babylonian attack on Jerusalem, or the desecration of the Temple by Antiochus Epiphanes, could be considered." Likewise, on Psalm 79 Calvin comments, "'This Psalm, like others, contains internal evidence that it was composed long after the death of David.' The probable occasion was either when the Temple was destroyed by the Assyrians (he means the Babylonians) 'or when the Temple was defiled by Antiochus.' 'Its subject agrees very well with either of these periods.'" According to Barr, Calvin seems quite comfortable discussing the historical probabilities of the text without being bound to assert its inerrancy.[20] Certainly Calvin does not assert its historical accuracy. In objecting to an allegorical interpretation of Psalm 19, Calvin also objects to a scientific discourse. David, he insists, is speaking in a homely style accommodated to the rudest and dullest of his hearers (Com. Ps. 19:4).

16. Reid, *The Authority of Scripture: A Study of the Reformation and Post-Reformation Understanding of the Bible* (New York: Harper and Brothers, 1957), 34–35.

17. Rupert E. Davies, *The Problem of Authority in the Continental Reformers: A Study in Luther, Zwingli, and Calvin* (London: Epworth Press, 1946), 114.

18. Ibid., 146.

19. Ibid., 105.

20. James Barr, *Fundamentalism* (Philadelphia: Westminster Press, 1977), 351–52. In Com. Mt. 27:27 Calvin notices that Matthew describes Jesus' robe as scarlet while Mark writes purple (Mark 15:17). He concludes, "We need not sweat over this."

The same point can be illustrated by Calvin's view of the authorship of 2 Peter. Barr continues, "Calvin knows that there has been doubt about the letter in the early church, and he himself thinks that the style is against attribution to Peter. [Calvin says,] 'I do not here recognize the language of Peter. But since it is not quite evident as to the author, I shall allow myself the liberty of using the word Peter or Apostle indiscriminately.'"[21] Barr concludes:

> We have already noted that [Calvin] contemplated with equanimity the date of some Psalms in the Maccabaean era, an opinion now regarded with horror by conservatives, and that his own inclination was to believe that II Peter was not written by the apostle Peter. [Barr continues:] I do not wish to exaggerate the importance of this evidence. It is clear that Calvin was ready to make, in the spirit of the Renaissance, some critical literary judgments on biblical texts. The fact that these limited steps could be made at all suggests that he might have gone farther along this line; in any case it fully demonstrates that *he had no idea that such steps were forbidden or contrary to the faith.* . . . Though these occasional critical decisions were given, they seem to have made no substantial difference to Calvin's total theological method, and they thus remain as isolated particles. But even taken so, and understood minimally and negatively, the fact that Calvin could make them at all sets a huge qualitative difference between him and the modern conservative, for whom it is of the dogmatic essence of the faith that such critical proposals must be rejected, because for him they deny the veracity of God himself. . . . In saying this I readily admit that in other aspects Calvin used much of the language which modern fundamentalists use or imply—the exact words of God, dictation, and so on. But his doctrine of scripture, intense as it was, was not organized as an anti-critical defense.[22]

That Hunter and Barr offer such sharply differing interpretations of Calvin's view of the Bible suggests that Calvin did not develop a doctrine of Scripture at all—at least of the kind that deals with modern questions.

Taking a more balanced and less polemical stance, John T. McNeill[23] notes the distinction between the statement that the Scripture *is* God's word and the conviction that "God's word *is set before* us in Scripture" (I.13.7). The issue can be summarized in the understanding of Calvin's affirmation that Scripture came "by the ministry of men from the very mouth of God" (I.7.5). If the emphasis is placed on Scripture coming from the very mouth of God, some sort of perfection is easier to maintain. If, on the other hand, Scripture comes from a genuine ministry of men, then human imperfections make perfection more difficult to sustain.

McNeill recognizes that Calvin affirms God as the author of Scripture but "on the manner of inspiration of Scripture, [Calvin] is fragmentary and unsystem-

---

21. Ibid., 348–49.
22. Ibid., 173–74 (emphasis added).
23. John T. McNeill, "The Significance of the Word of God for Calvin," *Church History* 28 (1959): 131–46.

atic."[24] Noting that Calvin asserts the church's unity both in the Word and in Christ, McNeill thinks, "In his commentaries, [Calvin] is apt to exploit every passage and does not always bring into harmony his own statements made fragmentarily. Yet for him there is no real inconsistency in saying that the unity of the Church is in Christ alone when he is expounding Ephesians and that it is the Word of God alone when he is lecturing on Micah."[25]

McNeill rightly concludes that Calvin does not offer a "systematic treatment of the relation of the infallible Word to the fallible letter."[26] However, Calvin does insist that as the bearer of God's Word the authority of Scripture does not rest on the judgment of reason nor the validation of the church but on the secret testimony of the Holy Spirit. To Sadolet, Calvin writes, "Learn, then, by your own experience, that it is no less unreasonable to boast of the Spirit without the Word, than it would be absurd to bring forward the Word itself without the Spirit."[27] The relation between Word and Spirit, Calvin summarizes by saying, "For by a kind of mutual bond the Lord has joined together the certainty of his word and of his Spirit so that the perfect religion of the word may abide in our minds when the Spirit, who causes us to contemplate God's face, shines: and that we in turn may embrace the Spirit with no fear of being deceived when we recognize him in his own image, namely, in the word" (I.9.3). The Holy Spirit is thus not considered as creating new doctrines but as making the gospel efficacious in the hearts and minds of the faithful. "The true conviction which believers have of the Word of God, of their own salvation and of all religion, does not spring from the feeling of the flesh, or from human and philosophical arguments, but from the sealing of the Spirit, who makes their consciences more certain and removes all doubt. The foundation of faith would be frail and unsteady if it rested on human wisdom" (Com. Eph. 1:13). According to Calvin, the Word of God cannot be understood apart from the Spirit of God. Word and Spirit are two complementary aspects of God's revelation as "God alone is a fit witness of himself in his word, so also the word will not find acceptance in men's hearts before it is sealed by the inward testimony of the Spirit" (I.7.4).

Warfield shows the deleterious effect of the subject-object dichotomy taken more seriously than it deserves. In his section on the testimony of the Spirit, Warfield suggests Calvin's reader expects a discussion of "the assimilation of special revelation by sinful man," "Calvin, however, is preoccupied with the problem of the accrediting of Scripture." Word and Spirit are conjoined: "The Word supplies the objective factor; the Spirit the subjective factor." Warfield admits that "only in the union of the objective and subjective factors is the result accomplished,"[28] but he does not seem to realize that union in Christ is more basic than this dichotomy.

---

24. Ibid., 139.
25. Ibid.
26. Ibid., 144.
27. "To Sadolet," *Selected Works of Calvin, Tracts*, ed. and trans. Henry Beveridge (Grand Rapids: Baker Book House, 1983 [1844], 1:37.
28. Benjamin Warfield, *Calvin and Calvinism* (New York: Oxford University Press, 1931), 71, 82.

With the theological affirmation of the inner testimony of the Spirit, Calvin mightily modifies the discussion of Scripture.[29] In the introductory volume to his *Systematic Theology*, Berkhof sees the relation between (written) Word and (Holy) Spirit as two essential principles. After developing the principle of being (*principium essendi*) as God, Berkhof treats the Scripture as the principle of external knowing (*principium cognoscendi externum*) and the work of the Holy Spirit as the principle of internal knowing (*principium cognoscendi internum*). Christian theology would seem more focused on divine and human *persons* in relation (*In principio erat verbum . . .*) than on principles of epistemology. Additionally, regarding Word and Spirit as separable principles rather than interlocking confessions and distinguishing between internal and external ways of knowing denies the mystery in which the heart puts down its head to rest in favor of a Procrustean bed that murders sleep. Clearly the reality of Scripture is not under the control of human powers like reason. Whatever the decision about inerrancy and infallibility might be, even the right choice does not advance the sinner's understanding which is entirely ineffectual apart from the Spirit's testimony. God's Word is not apprehended by calculation, even by right doctrine, but only through the mystery of the work of God's Holy Spirit. To support the authority of the Scripture, Calvin points to the grace of style, the grandeur of content, its great antiquity, its accuracy, its marvelous preservation, and so on. But in the final analysis, the authority of Scripture is established by the secret witness of the Holy Spirit by whose work in the exposition of Scripture Christ is conveyed to human beings. For that reason the faithful derive a holy confidence from God's word (Com. Hab. 1:12).

Robert Clyde Johnson recognizes the danger of discussing Word and Spirit separately and then bringing them together.[30] Nevertheless, he believes that Calvin "ascribed the verbal, conceptual substance of the original Biblical documents to God, acting through the Holy Spirit."[31] In exposition Johnson distinguishes two noetic offices of the Holy Spirit. The first is the completed work that God is the author of the Bible, and the second is the continuing work of validating the authority of the Bible.

These disagreements among the scholars should caution readers about easy summaries. Nevertheless, three conclusions seem warranted. First, recent widely divergent interpretations of Calvin on Scripture are often based on modern questions of perfection and reliability that Calvin did not ask and does not answer.[32]

29. Rudolf Otto suggests the "faculty or capacity of divination appears in the language of dogma hidden beneath the fine name 'testimonium Spiritus Sancti internum,' the inner witness of the Holy Spirit." This concept is not analyzed in Calvin but is referred to Schleiermacher and to Kant. Rudolf Otto, *The Idea of the Holy: An Inquiry into the Non-Rational Factor in the Idea of the Divine and Its Relation to the Rational*, trans. John W. Harvey (New York: Oxford University Press, 1958), 145.

30. Robert Clyde Johnson, *Authority in Protestant Theology* (Philadelphia: Westminster Press, 1959), 44.

31. Ibid., 55.

32. Many of today's most contentious biblical issues were not present to Calvin and so he did not address them directly. For that reason Gerhard Ebeling's warning remains especially timely: Theology today must expose itself to the vulnerability, the insecurity, and the risks of dealing seriously with the thought and criticisms of our times, especially the uses of Scripture and reason examining and

Second, the intimate connection between Word and Spirit means Scripture cannot be understood as a purely human activity because the gift of understanding is a work of God's Holy Spirit. McNeill accurately asserts that Calvin "insistently associates Word and Spirit, and views with alarm any tendency to assert the authority of the Spirit . . . away from the Word not less than any reading of the Word of Scripture without the guidance of the Spirit."[33] H. J. Forstman discusses Calvin's exposition of the relation between Word and Spirit in critical detail focused on the concept of authority and commending Rudolf Bultmann's approach.[34] In Book II Calvin deals more clearly with the relation between the written word of Scripture and the living Word revealed in Jesus Christ. The unmistakable affirmation is that Scripture is *personal* witness to Jesus Christ and not *propositional* argumentation for Christian philosophy.

Third, Calvin believed the Bible to be the Word of God, and his task was to expound God's revelation. However, while Calvin's *use* of Scripture is massive, his analysis of its *nature* is slight. In the introduction to the 1560 French edition, Calvin expresses his hope that the *Institutes* "can be a key to open a way for all children of God into a good and right understanding of Holy Scripture" (LCC, 7). The *Institutes* is designed to present "first, a sum of Christian doctrine, and, secondly, a way to benefit greatly from reading the Old as well as the New Testament" (LCC, 8). Calvin's desire to expound the teaching of the Bible is evident and his employment of Scripture for the benefit of readers of the Old and New Testaments is also evident and constant. Since Calvin regarded his work as the exposition of Scripture he made some general remarks about Scripture, but Calvin's so-called doctrine of Scripture must be inferred from his occasional expressions about Scripture as a whole. These occasional comments do not address modern questions, demonstrating how different is Calvin's context of reflection. He asserts and assumes the authority of Scripture but does not offer a sustained analysis and defense of it, avoiding both a literalism that separates the Spirit from the Word and also a fanaticism that concentrates on the Spirit to the exclusion of the Word. It is futile to claim Calvin for one of the sides in the modern "Bible Battle." In addition, Calvin demonstrates the faithful use of the Bible is not required to wait for consensus about its nature. If

---

reexamining our foundations, letting "everything burn that will burn and without reservations await what proves itself unburnable, genuine and true." The willingness to do theology without prior guarantees is "merely the reverse side of the certainty of salvation *sola fide*." Thus, a theology that evades the claims of the critical-historical method does not understand the meaning of the Reformers' doctrine of justification, "even when the formulae of the 16th century are repeated with the utmost correctness. The objection that of course at the time of the Reformation and in early Protestant Orthodoxy the Reformers' doctrine of justification was presented and maintained without knowledge of the critical historical method, merely betrays the basic error of a traditionalism that believes itself relieved by the Reformers' theology from responsible theological labor of its own" (Gerhard Ebeling, "The Significance of the Critical Historical Method for Church and Theology in Protestantism," in *Word and Faith*, trans. James W. Leitch [Philadelphia: Fortress Press, 1963], 51, 57).

33. McNeill, "Significance," 134.

34. See H. J. Forstman, *Word and Spirit* (Stanford, CA: Stanford University Press, 1962).

adopted today, Calvin's understanding would be of considerable contemporary benefit to Christians.[35]

Doubtless, Calvin thought himself a theologian of the Bible, but that designation is not so simple. First, the question of biblical selection is always involved in scriptural answer. Second, reason and experience also play crucial roles in understanding and selection of Scripture. Third, more than four hundred years of interpretative developments in Bible forbid transferring Calvin's insights into our own without considerable modification. Calvin accepted tradition when he thought scriptural intent was clarified, but ecclesiastical tradition, as understood in the Roman Church, was rejected. Interestingly Calvin appreciated and claimed for his theology the best of theological history, which is much the same thing.

As already indicated, Calvin in the main (but not exclusively) appeals his doctrines to Scripture, experience, reason, and tradition (or history), but he does not offer a formula for their relation. Calvin is a biblical, experiential, reasonable, and historical theologian, but all at the same time and in bewildering configurations, which studies of his so-called epistemology seldom admit. Doubtless Calvin thought his theology was scripturally based and he remains one of the great interpreters of the Bible, but his insights cannot simply be repeated as though biblical study had not advanced in crucial ways since the sixteenth century. More to the point, Calvin does not offer an analysis of the use of Scripture in relation to other ways of knowing.

The same conclusion applies to ecclesiastical tradition, or perhaps more accurately phrased, to theological history. Calvin appreciates the history of the church, especially the first five hundred years, but he does not regard tradition as a separate noetic source. Calvin knows a great deal about theological developments in the fathers—East and West. He cites these sources constantly, especially Augustine, when he thinks they agree or disagree with Scripture and the better theological tradition, but apart from serving the cause of Scripture he does not explain the grounds for accepting an appeal to history.

A Note on Idolatry

Having indicated Scripture as the true source of the true knowledge of the true God, Calvin devotes two chapters to idolatry (I.11–12) between his exposition of the general teaching of Scripture (I.6–10) and the doctrine of Trinity (I.13). Idolatry is the human attempt to create a god to honor and worship, and a portion of the *Institutes* often passed over. Neither Niesel, Wendel, Kerr, nor McKim treat this section. Yet Calvin takes the second commandment with great seriousness (cf. II.8.17–21), as Carlos M. N. Eire powerfully demonstrates.[36] Eire makes

---

35. See chap. 13, "The Use of Scripture," in Andrew Purves and Charles Partee, *Encountering God: Christian Faith in Turbulent Times* (Louisville, KY: Westminster John Knox Press, 2000).

36. See especially his chapter entitled "John Calvin's Attack on Idolatry" in Carlos M. N. Eire, *War against the Idols: The Reformation of Worship from Erasmus to Calvin* (Cambridge: Cambridge University Press, 1986), 195–233. As told in his moving autobiography, *Waiting for Snow in Havana: Confessions of a Cuban Boy* (New York: Free Press, 2003), Eire was one of fourteen thousand unaccompanied children airlifted out of Castro's Cuba never to see his father again.

the valuable points that Calvin's attack on idolatry is closely connected with his rejection of Roman Catholic worship as superstitious and idolatrous. For Calvin the reformation of worship was urgent. Again, Calvin is concerned not merely for idolatry on the part of individuals but also for communities. Calvin's crusade against superstition required social support. The most questionable part of Eire's analysis is his confidence in the objective/subjective dichotomy. According to Eire, Calvin's opposition to idolatry is divided into objective and subjective reasons.[37] Likewise "Calvin analyzes the act of worship by separating it into two spheres: the objective and the subjective." Eire concludes, "The two spheres of existence are connected by worship, which is a human act."[38] Two spheres of existence may be a helpful modern distinction for analyzing some parts of Calvin's thought, but must be cautiously invoked.

Calvin insists that human beings left to their own devices without the teaching of Scripture will manufacture idols of wood, stone, gold, or silver and worship them. In strong language Calvin asserts, "This people with fervid swiftness repeatedly rushed forth to seek out idols for themselves as waters from a great wellspring gush out with violent force" (I.11.3). Even more vivid is Calvin's comment that those who live in excrement emit such a stench that they can no longer smell foul odors. These people dwelling in filth (*ordure*) become so accustomed to it that they think themselves among roses.[39] In Calvin's view, "Daily experience teaches that flesh is always uneasy until it has obtained some figment like itself in which it may fondly find solace as in an image of God." In short, human nature "is a perpetual factory of idols" (I.11.8). What the idolatrous mind conceives to be a subject of worship, the hand delivers to the idolatrous eye. Calvin thinks idolatry originates from minds ensnared by a passion for novelty (Com. Dt. 12:29).

For Calvin, worship and honor blend into a single action. Therefore, he does not accept a distinction between *latria* and *dulia*. One cannot worship God and pay homage to saints without taking away some of the honor that belongs solely to God. In addition, the employment of images attacks sound doctrine because images replace true teaching. Idolatry is not only stupid but dangerous. It is silly to render homage to the work of your own hands. Paying tribute to false gods offends the true God, who is not the object of speculation but "the sole and proper witness of himself" (I.11.1). "Surely," Calvin writes, "there is nothing less fitting than to wish to reduce God, who is immeasurable and incomprehensible, to [a human] measure!" (I.11.4). The biblical appearances of God in smoke and flame and cloud are intended as restraining symbols of the incomprehensible divine essence. All graven images dishonor God, replacing pure worship with superstition. According to Calvin, God is revealed in Word and sacrament. God's Word comes to us so fully through Scripture and preaching and the sacraments, that to seek it elsewhere is to enable idols to be the focus of our quest for God.

---

37. Eire, *Idols*, 216.
38. Ibid., 213.
39. "Answer of John Calvin to the Nicodemite Gentlemen concerning their complaint that he is too severe," in *Come Out from Among Them: "Anti-Nicodemite" Writings of John Calvin*, trans. Seth Skolnitsky (Dallas: Protestant Heritage Press, 2001), 101.

Heeding Calvin's urgent and earnest warning against idolatry is continually necessary. The substitution of false idols for the true God is a major intellectual and theological objection to images, but Calvin also objects angrily on the human grounds of modesty. He claims, "Brothels show harlots clad more virtuously and modestly than the churches show those objects which they wish to be thought images of virgins" (I.11.7).[40]

2. The Trinity

Having called attention to the prohibition against *false* gods, Calvin turns to the exposition of the *true* God as triune. The historical development of the doctrine of the Trinity is both crucial and complicated. As Gerald Bray finely writes, "From the beginning, the Christian knowledge of God in Trinity was first experiential and later theoretical, an order of things that has always characterized authentic Christian understanding and confession."[41] The real and central purpose of the doctrine is not to explain the being and work of God but to preserve and protect the monotheistic confession: "Hear, O Israel: The LORD is our God, the LORD alone" (Deut. 6:4) in connection with the conviction "that God is comprehended in Christ alone" (II.6.4),[42] and bound together by the work of the Holy Spirit. The doctrine seeks to understand and expound the biblical revelation of God as Father, Son, and Holy Spirit. In other words, the doctrine of the Trinity is the Christian confession of monotheism. After centuries of discussion the church accepted the formula that God is one substance (*ousia*) and three "persons" (*hypostases*). Each term had a varied and confusing development but were used in the attempt to maintain a proper relation between God's oneness and God's threeness, resulting in the balancing concepts of commonality and distinctiveness. Some events, like the crucifixion, apply to only one person of the Trinity, but others, like creation, refer to all. An overemphasis on the oneness of God leads to the heresy of modalism (one reality manifested in three appearances) and an overemphasis on the three "persons" leads to tritheism (three gods). Every theologian recognizes that the doctrine of the Trinity is an inexplicable mystery.[43]

40. See also David Willis-Watkins, "The Second Commandment and Church Reform: The Colloquy of St. Germain-en-Laye, 1562," in *Studies in Reformed Theology and History* 2, no. 2 (Spring 1994): 44; also John H. Leith, "John Calvin's Polemic against Idolatry" in *Soli Deo Gloria: New Testament Essays in Honor of William Childs Robinson*, ed. J. McDowell Richards (Richmond, VA: John Knox Press, 1968), 111–24. Ulrich Mauser informed me that while Luther was at the Wartburg, Andreas Karlstadt attempted to remove images from churches in response to the prohibition of idolatry. Luther returned to Wittenberg and preached a series of sermons declaring statues and pictures in churches were matters of indifference, not idolatry.

41. Gerald L. Bray, "Out of the Box: The Christian Experience of God in Trinity," in *God the Holy Trinity*, ed. Timothy George (Grand Rapids: Baker Academic, 2006), 39.

42. Warfield thinks Calvin's great contribution to the doctrine of the Trinity "is summed up in his clear, firm and unwavering assertion of the αὐτοθεότης of the Son" (Warfield, "Calvin's Doctrine of the Trinity," in *Calvin and Calvinism;* 284).

43. In his essay on "Calvin's Doctrine of the Trinity" (*Calvin Theological Journal* 25, no. 2 [November 1990]: 168ff.), Thomas F. Torrance addresses the necessity and impropriety of Trinitarian terms.

Calvin accepts the historically orthodox doctrine of the Trinity, but he treats this mystery with such modesty that scholars are obliged to account for the brevity of his discussion. This modesty rather than his putative orthodoxy is the most interesting feature of Calvin's doctrine of Trinity. According to Schaff-Herzog, Calvin did not use the terms "Trinity" and "Person" during his first residency in Geneva because "Calvin was very indifferent to the terminology of theology, so long as the truth was expressed."[44]

In defending Calvin, Karl Barth writes, "[There is] not a vestige of truth in [Peter] Caroli's objection, that Calvin avoided the expressions *trinitas* and *persona*." Then Barth adds in a massive understatement "but it is noteworthy that [Calvin's] interest in this matter is not exactly burning."[45] Emile G. Léonard claims that in Calvin's view the knowledge of God is practical, not philosophical, which means that "Calvin was not greatly interested in the relationship between the Three Divine Persons of the Trinity. In the first edition of the *Institutes* there is no more than an allusion to it."[46] Barth judges that Calvin was more concerned with "the appropriation of salvation" than its "objective presuppositions,"[47] indicating that Calvin accepted the traditional doctrine of Trinity without considering a need for a basic rethinking or restatement of it. Both Niesel and Wendel suggest that the purpose of Calvin's doctrine of the Trinity is to protect his Christology. Wendel writes, "Although devoid of originality, this Trinitarian doctrine constitutes an essential part of the theology of Calvin. It enabled him, notably, to lay the emphasis that he did upon the divinity of Christ."[48] Niesel writes, "The purpose of Calvin's Trinitarianism is to secure the biblical message 'God revealed in the flesh' against false interpretations."[49] In other words, the point Calvin makes is that the God confessed by Trinitarian doctrine is the same as the incarnate Lord attested by Scripture.

Certainly Calvin's doctrine of the Trinity defends his Christology, but a more obvious reason for the brevity of his exposition is the desire to be faithful to Scripture and to resist intellectual speculations about deity. Calvin was not a philosopher in the sense that he thought he had special logical insights to impart to rational persons concerning the general concept of God's tri-unity. Instead Calvin was a teacher within the community of the faithful and believed that God is revealed in Scripture, as Father, Son, and Holy Spirit. To that purpose Calvin cites

44. *A Religious Encyclopedia*, ed. Philip Schaff (New York: Funk and Wagnalls, 1882), 1:367.

45. *CD* 1.1, 477. See Barth's interesting account of Calvin's conflict with Peter Caroli in *The Theology of John Calvin*, trans. Geoffrey W. Bromiley (Grand Rapids: Wm. B. Eerdmans, 1995), 309–45. Caroli charged Calvin and especially Farel with the heresy of Arianism because of their avoidance of the terms "Trinity" and "person." The result of this battle, according to Barth, was Calvin's subjecting himself more directly to the theological continuity of history.

46. Emile G. Léonard, *A History of Protestantism*, ed. H. H. Rowley, trans. Joyce M. H. Reid, vol. 1 (London: Thomas Nelson, 1965), n327.

47. *CD* 1.1, 478–79.

48. François Wendel, *Calvin: The Origins and Development of His Religious Thought*, trans. Philip Mairet (New York: Harper and Row, 1963), 169.

49. Wilhelm Niesel, *The Theology of Calvin*, 1st ed., trans. Harold Knight (Philadelphia: Westminster Press, 1956), 57.

Hilary of Poitiers with approval for using "the natural names" of Father, Son, and Spirit and objecting that to say more is "beyond the meaning of language, above the reach of sense, above the capacity of understanding" (I.13.5). Calvin believes the deity of Father, Son, and Holy Spirit is revealed in Scripture and it is wrong to indulge our curiosity or to speculate about God's essence. Calvin assumes and outlines the traditional doctrine of the Trinity, but while he has a great deal to say about God revealed as Father, Son, and Spirit, Calvin has remarkably little to say about the doctrine of the Trinity as such. This fact suggests that in Calvin's mind the biblical revelation of God as Father, Son, and Spirit and the theological doctrine of Trinity are on different levels. Theological concepts, however important, are to be judged by their capacity to express the truth to which Scripture witnesses.[50]

Since the mystery of the triune relation is above the capacity of human understanding, Calvin warns his reader that the doctrine of Trinity is that place where "if anywhere in the secret mysteries of Scripture, we ought to play the philosopher soberly and with great moderation; let us use great caution that neither our thoughts nor our speech go beyond the limits to which the Word of God itself extends." We must "not take it into our heads either to seek out God anywhere else than in his Sacred Word, or to think anything about him that is not prompted by his Word, or to speak anything that is not taken from that Word" (I.13.21).[51]

Avoiding too-subtle attempts to penetrate into the mystery of the Godhead by evanescent speculations (I.13.19), Calvin bases his teaching on scriptural revelation. The elect are "baptized into the name of the one God who has shown himself with complete clarity in the name of the Father, the Son, and the Spirit. Hence it is evident that in God's essence reside three persons in whom one God is known" (I.13.16). In addition to the biblical baptismal formula, Calvin also

50. Warfield recognizes the Trinity is incomprehensible to the human intellect and therefore not to be measured by human reason. Nevertheless, "the doctrine of the Trinity did not for [Calvin] stand out of relation to his religious consciousness but was a postulate of his profoundest religious emotions; was given, indeed, in his experience of salvation itself." Warfield is aware of a distinction between the reality of God and the doctrine of Trinity but blurs the distinction by regarding doctrine as a statement of the truth rather than a protection of the mystery. Thus, he insists, "[Calvin] never for one moment doubted, we do not say the truth merely, but also the importance for the Christian system, of the doctrine of the Trinity" (Warfield, *Calvin and Calvinism*, 194, 200). McGrath raises the intriguing question whether the doctrine of the Trinity properly plays a foundational role in theology "when it is, in my view, something that we infer from other foundations" (Alister E. McGrath, "The Doctrine of Trinity," in *God the Holy Trinity*, 27).

51. Catherine Maury LaCugna, *God for Us: The Trinity and Christian Life* (New York: Harper San Francisco, 1991), 251, notes some of the complexities in the concept of person: "The Cartesian method isolated the self from the world beyond the self, and presupposed that the self can be a self by itself, apart from relationship with anything or anyone else. Following Descartes, John Locke defined person in terms of self-consciousness, and Leibniz thought of personhood as an enduring self-awareness that is present to itself and knows itself despite external or bodily changes. Kant completed these definitions with the note of morality: A person is a self-conscious moral subject who is responsible for his or her actions. This understanding of person was consistent with the idea of God as unipersonal, the first cause and the ultimate referent of human subjectivity. The tradition (of Latin theology) that has understood God as Supreme Substance gave way to the idea of God as Absolute Subject."

thinks of the scriptural revelation of Word and Spirit as Trinitarian teaching. The Word in this context refers to Jesus Christ, not the Bible. "Therefore, since that there is one God, not more, is regarded as a settled principle, we conclude that Word and Spirit are nothing else than the very essence of God" (I.13.16). In his short discussion of Trinity Calvin is primarily concerned to assert the deity of the Son (13.7–13) and Holy Spirit (13.14–15).

Having affirmed God's essential unity, Calvin insists that we must immediately turn to the threefold scriptural "distinction of the Father from the Word, and of the Word from the Spirit." The Scripture says the Father created all things through the Word which requires that the Father is "somehow distinct from the Word" (I.13.17). Further the distinction is marked by the Son (and not the Father) descending to earth. The Father did not die on the cross, nor was the Father raised from the grave. Scripture distinguishes the Holy Spirit as proceeding from the Father (John 15:26) and Jesus often speaks of the Spirit as another. However, these distinctions among the three persons of the Godhead are not divisions of the divine essence. In other words, unity and distinction are held together in the mystery of God. Calvin says this "passage in Gregory of Nazianzus vastly delights me: 'I cannot think on the one without quickly being encircled by the splendour of the three; nor can I discern the three without being straightway carried back to the one'" (I.13.17). Scripture makes a distinction between Father, Word, and Spirit, but not a division (sed distinctionem non divisionem). This distinction is an unfathomable mystery, but is useful as a matter of order. God is first and the source without beginning. The Son eternally proceeds from the Father, and the Holy Spirit eternally proceeds from both the Father and the Son. This latter understanding is derived from the fact that the "same Spirit is indifferently called sometimes the Spirit of Christ, sometimes the Spirit of him 'who raised up Christ . . . from the dead'" (I.13.18).

Calvin is aware that the doctrine of Trinity is constructed with nonbiblical terms such as essence (οὐσία) and person (ὑπόστασις). In addition, Calvin recognizes that the church's confession of the one divinity of Father, Son, and Spirit causes some people, like Michael Servetus, to raise serious questions about the intellectual and biblical concept of Trinity.[52] Calvin notes that there was also considerable disputation among early theologians. They could not agree among themselves about the Trinity. For example, Jerome claimed that predicating three

52. See Jerome Friedman's fine study, Michael Servetus: A Case Study in Total Heresy (Geneva: Librairie Droz, 1978). R. Willis, Servetus and Calvin: A Study of an Important Epoch in the Early History of the Reformation (London: Henry S. King, 1877), 530, 528–29, sees Calvin as a self-assertive tyrant, pursuing Servetus with relentless rigor because he had addressed Calvin in disrespectful language. Nevertheless, Servetus's "pyre still gleams portentous to the world and even when it burned it was a herald of the dawn of better days to come." The same point of view is expressed by Marian Hillar whose conclusion is announced in his subtitle: The Case of Michael Servetus (1511–1553): The Turning Point in the Struggle for Freedom of Conscience (Lewiston: Edwin Mellen Press, 1997) and Lawrence and Nancy Goldstone, Out of the Flames: The Remarkable Story of a Fearless Scholar, a Fatal Heresy, and One of the Rarest Books in the World (New York: Broadway Books, 2002). Only three copies of Christianismi Restitutio survive.

substances (*substantia*) in God is a sacrilege, while Hilary, to the contrary, insisted it was perfectly orthodox (I.13.5).

Calvin declares that Christians believe in one God understood as "a single, simple essence, in which we comprehend three persons or hypostases. . . . In this way, unity of essence is retained, and a reasoned order is kept, which yet takes nothing away from the deity of the Son and the Spirit" (I.13.20). Calvin thinks the Trinitarian terms finally adopted by the church to express the doctrine were carefully chosen and should not be rashly rejected. Nevertheless, he comes to the amazing conclusion that the doctrine of the Trinity *as a doctrine*, while useful, is not essential if the unity of God and the distinctions among the persons is preserved. Thus he writes, "I could wish [the disputed terms] were buried, if only among all men this faith were agreed on: that Father and Son and Spirit are one God, yet the Son is not the Father, nor the Spirit the Son, but that they are differentiated by a peculiar quality" (I.13.5). Since Calvin believes that Scripture alone is the source of theological truth, our thoughts and words should be *conformed* to Scripture. However, in regard to doctrines like Trinity, we are not *confined* to Scripture because nothing "prevents us from explaining in clearer words those matters in Scripture which perplex and hinder our understanding, yet which conscientiously and faithfully serve the truth of Scripture itself, and are made use of sparingly and modestly and on due occasion" (I.13.3). Calvin returns to this issue in IV.8.16. He rubs the other side of the coin when he objects that some Christian writers needlessly use terms foreign to Scripture (III.15.2).

Calvin does not explain how words (and therefore doctrines made up of them) that conform to Scripture are to be distinguished from those that distort them. Moreover, we are not instructed on how to recognize the "due occasions" when nonscriptural words may be properly used. Additionally, Calvin's reluctance to commit more strongly to the explanation of biblical realities by using nonscriptural words suggests the possibility of considering not the reality but the *doctrine* of the Trinity to be the reverent result of the church's reflection guided by the Holy Spirit. Among the foundational convictions of Calvin's theology is the precedence of the Word over the church—including the church's theological tradition. "All controversies should be decided by [God's] word,"[53] "which demonstrates that our doctrine is sound and must stand because it is the truth of Christ revealed in Scripture and properly interpreted according to the analogy of faith."[54]

In summary, Calvin's exposition of the *doctrine* of the Trinity is concentrated in one small chapter of the *Institutes*. This doctrine is a necessary attempt to confess the Oneness of God who is revealed as Holy Father, Holy Son, and Holy Spirit. Calvin affirms the traditional and orthodox doctrine of one God in three

---

53. "To Sadolet," *Calvin's Tracts*, 1:60. Calvin was not sufficiently aware that the real issue is not Scripture *or* tradition. "What we are confronted with is rather the clash between two concepts of tradition" (Heiko A. Oberman, "Quo Vadis? Tradition from Irenaeus to Humani Generis," *Scottish Journal of Theology* 16 [1963]: 226). The complicated role of tradition in Calvin's thinking is briefly discussed in the excursus.

54. Letter to Francis, LCC, 12.

persons, but his concern is not to explicate the doctrine. Calvin understood that the doctrine of Trinity is not scriptural in the sense that the word "Trinity" is not a biblical term. However, he thought the doctrine served the truth of Scripture and was required by the church to help distinguish between good and bad teachers (I.13.4). Calvin's awareness of the difficulties in conceptualizing the mystery of God (I.13.17) into a doctrine of one substance and three persons makes clear that the *reality of the revelation* of God as Father, Son, and Spirit does not permit a simple and logical formulation.[55] With appropriate modesty Calvin understood the doctrine of Trinity is not designed to explain but rather to protect the mystery of the biblical revelation of God as Father, Son, and Spirit.

A. GOD'S CREATION

At the end of Book I Calvin devotes chapters 14 and 15 to creation and chapters 16 through 18 to providence. Doubtless, Calvin deals with creation before providence because things must exist before they can be governed and nurtured. However, while the exposition of creation occupies the most pages, providence receives the greatest passion. The conviction of God's encompassing providence is very close to the heart of Calvin's theology.

Calvin's discussion of the work of God in creation may be divided into (1) things invisible—the creation of (a) angels and (b) demons—and (2) things visible—the creation of (a) the world and (b) the human. The doctrine of creation is based on faith in God the Creator rather than in scientific or rational confidence in human understanding of the beginning.[56] In Calvin's time, the work of Copernicus was becoming known, but it had little effect on Calvin's theology.[57] Calvin's interest was not in explaining the scientific details of the early history of the world, but rather in confessing God's work of creation.

Calvin thought some general knowledge of God's creation was available to all people, and he based his exposition on the general teaching of Scripture. Assuming the authority of the Bible, Calvin uses its teaching to guide the understanding. Calvin is aware that some Greeks and Romans thought the world was eternal

---

55. It is surely safe to say that the passion expressed in the sonnet lines of John Donne, "Batter my heart, three person'd God" is not directed to the Christian doctrine of Trinity as conceptualized but the reality of God the Father, the Son, and the Holy Spirit as encountered.

56. For a modern discussion of science and religion, see John F. Haught, *Is Nature Enough? Meaning and Truth in the Age of Science* (Cambridge: Cambridge University Press, 2006).

57. See Edward Rosen, "Calvin's Attitude toward Copernicus," *Journal of the History of Ideas* 21 (July–September 1960): 431–41; Robert White, "Calvin and Copernicus: The Problem Reconsidered," *Calvin Theological Journal* 15, no. 2 (November 1980): 233–43; Christopher B. Kaiser, "Calvin, Copernicus and Castellio," *Calvin Theological Journal* 21, no. 1 (April 1986): 5–31; B. A. Gerrish, "The Reformation and the Rise of Science," in *The Impact of the Church upon Its Culture*, ed. Jerald C. Brauer (Chicago: University of Chicago Press, 1968), 231–65; Gary B. Deason, "The Protestant Reformation and the Rise of Modern Science," *Scottish Journal of Theology* 38, no. 2 (1985): 230–33; Alister E. McGrath, *A Life of John Calvin: A Study in the Shaping of Western Culture* (Oxford: Basil Blackwell, 1990), 253–57.

or had emanated from God. In an influential essay Roy Battenhouse mistakenly argues for the compatability of Calvin and Plotinus on creation and providence.[58] Straining for philosophic affinities Battenhouse cites Calvin's praise of God's mighty gifts "by which we are led as by rivulets to the spring itself" (I.1.1). According to Battenhouse, this "metaphor clearly suggests the Neoplatonic concept of emanation."[59] On the contrary, in the Third Ennead where Plotinus considers Fate, Providence, Necessity, Free Will, and Evil, he also refers to common sense. That Calvin's God of history who creates the world has an affinity with Plotinus's philosophic god (or the Good or the One) who "creates" by emanation transgresses my sense of common. In strong opposition to both the eternality of the world and its emanation from God, Calvin insists that God created the world out of nothing. In other words, God did not fashion the world with preexisting material that God did not create. Likewise, the world exists by God's deliberate choice and not as the result of an overflowing of supreme being. The knowledge of God the Creator deals more with *who* we know rather than *how* and *what* we know.

Calvin asserts that the doctrine of creation also requires the doctrine of providence. He declares that to think God would create everything and then abandon the work is foolish. Creation and providence must be understood together. While Calvin's doctrine of creation is expounded in traditional and orthodox sixteenth-century theological terms, his view of providence exhibits more emotional intensity. That we deal with God in everything (I.17.2) is one of Calvin's most central convictions. Creation is the setting for God's dealing with us; providence is the actuality of God's dealing with us.

1. Of Things Invisible

To understand creation Calvin warns that the subject should be approached with a willingness to "remain enclosed within [the] bounds to which God has willed to confine us, and as it were, to pen up our minds that they may not, through their very freedom to wander, go astray" (I.15.1). Monstrous fables, idle questions, and hurtful speculations about the world's beginning must be rejected. Calvin agrees with Augustine[60] that there is no higher cause than God's will, and human beings will get lost unless the Scripture guides them in seeking God.

In this section of the *Institutes*, Calvin explicates, as one would expect, the creation of the world and the human creature, but he begins with the creation of angels and devils—a subject often ignored by modern theologians. Calvin sets out to refute the notions that (1) the angels are nothing more than good impulses in human minds and (2) devils are only evil impulses. The Scripture is clear about the existence of both. At no other place are contemporary thinkers so little inter-

---

58. Roy W. Battenhouse, "The Doctrine of Man in Calvin and in Renaissance Platonism," *Journal of the History of Ideas* 9 (1948): 465.

59. Ibid., 453.

60. Calvin's Augustinianism is demonstrated by Luchesius Smits, *Saint Augustine dans l'oeuvre de Calvin*, 2 vols. (Assen: Van Gorcum, 1957).

ested in Calvin's theological views than his reflections on angels and demons. Special studies devoted to the topic are few, and general surveys of Calvin's thought often ignore the subject completely. The reason for this disinterest undoubtedly reveals more about recent scholarship than about Calvin. In the popular mind, enthusiasm for the angelic and demonic waxes and wanes. From time to time variations on the Faust legend are revived, and angelic visitations are featured with some regularity in cinema. In academic culture the 1992 *Encyclopedia of the Reformed Faith* assumes that Reformed theology in the modern day does not require any definition of angels and demons. The volume contains articles on heaven and hell but not on angels and devils or even Satan. Interestingly, twentieth-century theologian Emil Brunner accepts the existence of demons but not of angels. Brunner thinks angels are a product of the myth-forming imagination, a picturesque way of speaking about God's action. Demons, on the other hand, exist as suprahuman powers of darkness because they help to account for the reality of evil.[61]

Since the Scripture often refers to angels and demons, one would expect all biblical theologians and most systematic theologians to feel some obligation to address the subject. Historically John Milton powerfully fired the imagination of those who read *Paradise Lost*, but presumably theologians should not abandon God's creation of invisible things to poets. Previous to Calvin, Thomas Aquinas produced a famously elaborate discussion of angels and demons (*ST* I.50–64, 106–14).[62] In comparison with Thomas, Calvin's reflection on angels is extremely brief and extremely modest.

a. The Angels

Calvin tells his reader, "I ought to insert something concerning angels" (I.14.3), but the major point of this insertion is not to create scope for cosmological speculations about the nature and purpose of created beings below God and above human beings. Instead Calvin's focus is God's wonderful providence in creating a world so perfectly fitted for human use. The creation and function of angels and devils (chap. 14) is placed between Calvin's discussion of the Trinity (chap. 13) and his explanation of human nature as created (chap. 15). In approaching creation Calvin declares his intention to avoid the fables of the superstitious and the impiety of the scoffers, which means accepting the guidance of Scripture in the obedience of faith and rejecting the wicked speculations of human reason about the beginning of the world. Calvin insists it is wrong to raise questions about the immeasurability of time and space. Nevertheless, in keeping with the

---

61. Emil Brunner, *The Christian Doctrine of Creation and Redemption*, trans. Olive Wyon (Philadelphia: Westminster Press, 1952), chap. 5.

62. In a curious little essay Jacques Maritain, using Aquinas as the standard, argued that "the sin of Descartes is a sin of *angelism*." Descartes "conceived human Thought after the type of angelic Thought" (Jacques Maritain, *Three Reformers: Luther-Descartes-Rousseau* [Westport, CT: Greenwood Press, 1950], 54). See also the chapter "The Angels Who Do His Bidding," in Susan E. Schreiner, *The Theater of His Glory: Nature and the Natural Order in the Thought of John Calvin* (Durham, NC: Labyrinth Press, 1991), 39–53.

assumptions of his time, Calvin believes the world is approximately six thousand years old and that space, however vast, cannot be infinite but has a boundary.

God is declared the Creator of all things visible and invisible, and among the invisible things that God created are the angels. Reflection on the ministry of angels allows the hope in God to be more firmly established. In this reflection a major danger to avoid is the Platonic notion of seeking access to God through angelic intermediaries (I.14.12). Calvin admits that angels do not figure as part of the Genesis creation story, but since they appear later in Scripture as servants of God, it is easy to infer that angels were created by God. God alone is eternal and self-existent; therefore, divinity is falsely attributed to angels. Calvin even warns that to think of the "existence" of the devil is dangerous if one attributes some kind of divinity to the devil apart from God's sovereignty.

According to Calvin, God's word teaches that angels are special creations ordained to carry out God's commands. Investigation beyond that affirmation leads to "empty speculations which idle men have taught apart from God's Word concerning the nature, orders, and number of angels" (I.14.4). Angels are celestial spirits having a real existence without bodily form, and Christ says there are "many legions" of them (Matt. 26:53), but no one can determine the orders or degrees of honor among them. In this warning against speculation Calvin has especially in mind Pseudo-Dionysius the Areopagite who writes of *The Celestial Hierarchy* as if he were an eyewitness to it. In contrast to such empty speculations, Scripture indicates that angels serve "God in exercising God's authority and thus exhibiting his divinity to us." Additionally, angels "keep vigil for our safety, take upon themselves our defense, direct our ways, and take care that some harm may not befall us" (I.14.6).

Calvin suggests that it is not worthwhile to investigate whether individual angels have been assigned to individual believers because caring for us is not the task of one but of all the angels. In fact, those persons who insist on having a single guardian angel place a restriction on God's providence. God uses angels not out of necessity but out of grace, meaning that God often dispenses with their service and works directly through his will alone. Nevertheless, God has bidden innumerable guardians to look after our safety, making us realize the presence of his grace according to our capacity. In an unguarded moment speaking of the image of God, Calvin declares angels, too, were created according to God's image, and concludes our highest perfection is to become like them (I.15.3, also IV.1.4).[63] Calvin's usual teaching is that we are to be conformed to Christ, not angels, because the proper role of angels is not to set us an example but to lead us to Christ.

b. The Devils

According to Calvin, the clearest demonstration of the existence of the devils is found in Matthew 25:41 where Jesus says, "You that are accursed, depart from

---

63. In his commentary Calvin explains more carefully that being like angels means putting aside the weaknesses of the present life (Com. Mt. 22:30).

me into the eternal fire prepared for the devil and his angels." Such expressions of eternal judgment would be meaningless if devils did not exist. The chief reason for considering demonology is to avoid the error of assuming that we do not have more than human enemies and therefore of becoming less vigilant about resisting evil (I.14.19). In an important demonstraton of humility, Calvin admits that God could have created humans unable to sin but refuses to speculate about why this situation did not obtain (II.1.10).[64] Calvin also refuses to entertain the speculative question why an omnipotent God would create an angel (or angels) whom his omniscience knew would rebel.

Beyond the affirmation of the existence of devils, Calvin confesses the Bible is very brief and not very clear. He admits that the "Scripture does not in numerous passages set forth systematically and clearly that fall of the devils, its cause, manner, time, and character" (I.14.16). However, we only need to know what is important to our edification and not superfluous matters that might satisfy our curiosity. Therefore, we should "be content with this brief summary of the nature of devils: they were when first created angels of God, but by degeneration they ruined themselves, and were made instruments of ruin for others" (I.14.16). With this caution in mind, Calvin briefly treats the nature of devils, their work, and their meaning.

Although Satan was created as a good angel, his fall means that Satan's will (*voluntas*) and actions (*conatum*) are entirely and passionately opposed to God. The central problem is the devil was created by God, but Calvin insists Satan's evil nature cannot be attributed to God's creation but to Satan's own perversion of it. In addition to the teaching of Scripture, Calvin appeals to experience for knowledge of the devils. "We experience in all of Satan's deeds what Christ testifies concerning him, that 'from the beginning he was a murderer . . . and a liar' [John 8:44]. The devil opposes the truth of God with falsehoods, he obscures the light with darkness, he entangles men's minds in errors, he stirs up hatred, he enkindles contentions and combat, everything to the end that he may overturn God's Kingdom, and plunge men with himself into eternal death" (I.15.14). By nature Satan is "the author, leader, and architect of all malice and iniquity" (I.14.15), a result not from God's creation but from Satan's choice.

Since the now-fallen nature of devils is fiercely opposed to God's kingdom, their work must also seek the destruction of that kingdom.[65] As presented in

---

64. The conception of a happy fall (*o felix culpa*) has been traced to St. Gregory in the patristic period. The point is that without the terrible fall, the mighty incarnation and glorious redemption would not have occurred. After the fall Milton's Adam is not sure whether to repent or rejoice.

> Much more that much more good thereof shall spring—
> To God more glory, more good will to men
> From God—and over wrath grace shall abound.
>   (*Paradise Lost* 12, 476–78)

See Arthur O. Lovejoy, "Milton and the Paradox of the Fortunate Fall," *Journal of English Literary History* 4, no. 3 (September 1937): 161–79.

65. William Jones, *Finger-Ring Lore* (London: Chatto and Windus, 1877), 520–22, discusses the demons—Mercurial, Jovial, Saturnine, Martial, and Aphrodisiac—which could be shut up and carried about in a finger ring. Perhaps the most famous magical ring belonged to Gyges, mentioned by

Scripture, Satan and the devils are powerful and relentless foes. The Satanic empire wickedly opposes the kingdom of righteousness and sends "great armies" to wage constant war against human beings. However, God has not lost any part of the control of creation to Satan. Calvin recognizes the intractable problem of explaining the existence and power of an evil will antagonistic to an all-powerful and all-provident Creator God. Nevertheless, Calvin asserts that in addition to Satan's perverted nature, his perverted actions require God's will and assent. The history of Job demonstrates that Satan "did not dare undertake any evil act without first having obtained permission" (cf. Job 1:12; 2:6). This and other biblical references demonstrate that "Satan is clearly under God's power" so that even his opposition is dependent upon God's sufferance. On occasions like this Calvin employs the conception of "God's permission," but on other occasions he insists that God does *not* permit Satan's work but actually decrees it. Quoting Augustine with approval, Calvin writes, "God does not permit but governs by his power" (III.23.1). Again, since the will of God is the necessity of all things, God's will of necessity comes to pass (III.23.8). In short, "The figment of bare permission vanishes: because it would be ridiculous for [God] only to permit what he wills to be done, and not also to decree it" (I.18.1). Still, Calvin insists, by making a decree or by giving permission God does not become the author of sin (I.18.4). God is not the author of evil, although sending temptation is "not reckless tyranny, but the execution of his righteous—though obscure—judgement" (Com. Mt. 6:13).

In the Book II section on sin, Calvin devotes chapter 4 to the work of Satan, repeating the distinction between compulsion and necessity and insisting that humans sin necessarily but voluntarily. Again, those whom the Lord does not mercifully guide by his Spirit are justly abandoned to Satan. Nevertheless, the sins that follow abandonment arise from the human will and not outside it (II.4.1). In attempting to explain these contradictory affirmations Calvin claims "no inconsistency in assigning the same deed to God, Satan, and man. [The] distinction in purpose and manner causes God's righteousness to shine forth blameless there, while the wickedness of Satan and of man betrays itself by its own disgrace" (II.4.2). In other words the same event contains the divine will, the satanic will, and the human will. The satanic will moves with malice; the human will is moved by ignorance, if not by sin; the divine and providential will governs both the human and satanic will.

Calvin affirms the omnipotence of God in creation, but denies God is the author of evil. That God did not create Satan to be evil means that Satan's nature and function in opposition to God cannot finally be explained. In partial expla-

---

Plato, which rendered the wearer invisible (*Republic* II.359C, 612B). Sir Walter Scott, *Letters on Demonology and Witchcraft* (New York: Harper and Brothers, 1855), 198, claimed that in opposition to Rome the English Calvinists considered the exorcism of incarnate fiends and evil spirits with scorn and contempt. In his chapter on the age of reformation Paul Carus, *The History of the Devil and the Idea of Evil* (LaSalle, IL: Open Court, 1974), suggests heretic prosecution replaced witch prosecution for a while.

nation Calvin sees the bridle of God's power restraining Satan. Having uncovered "the figment of bare permission," Calvin declares, "[Satan] carries out only those things which have been divinely permitted to him; and so he obeys his Creator, whether he will or not, because he is compelled to yield him service wherever God impels him" (I.14.17). In this sentence Calvin claims that God both permits and compels the actions of Satan. Evil spirits attack all human beings, and while believers are greatly disturbed, they are not destroyed because Christ's victory over death is extended to the members of Christ's body. The wicked, on the other hand, are overpowered and conquered by the devil. The power of Satan's fury is such that humans could not stand apart from Christ's victory and God's providence. "God does not allow Satan to rule over the souls of believers, but gives over only the impious and unbelievers, whom he deigns not to regard as members of his own flock, to be governed by him" (I.14.18). The result is that "conscious of our weakness and ignorance, let us especially call upon God's help, relying upon him alone in whatever we attempt, since it is he alone who can supply us with counsel and strength, courage and armor" (I.14.13).

A Note on Sin and Evil

Calvin treats the existence of evil as part of his teaching on creation, and the existence of sin (discussed in Book II) is treated as part of the doctrine of redemption. As angels contribute to good on earth, so do the devils contribute to a world of evil. Some theologians account for evil as a result of the logical necessity, by which God is also bound, that the good gift of free will must include the possibility of its devastating misuse. Likewise, some theologians regard sin as a necessary result of the happy fall (*felix culpa*), which created the possibility of so great a redemption. In contrast, Calvin deals with both sin and evil as present realities but final mysteries. For many modern thinkers, angels and devils may be safely ignored, but they loom large in popular culture and have an important sermonic function. Since the Bible refers to angels and devils they serve purposes in proclamation that may not require traditional ontological affirmations.

The pressing question is not merely the historical understanding of such references but the personal understanding of their reality. A classic skepticism is expressed by Prince Hal in Shakespeare's *First Part of King Henry IV*. The Welsh mystic, Owen Glendower, declares

> At my nativity
> The front of heaven was full of fiery shapes,
> Of burning cressets; and at my birth
> The frame and huge foundation of the earth
> Shaked like a coward.
> (III.1.12–17)

Glendower then claims,

> I can call spirits from the vasty deeps.

To which Hotspur replies:

> Why, so can I, or so can any man;
> But will they come when you do call them?
> (53–55)

This comment poses the question nicely. We can and do call forth spirits from the vasty deeps, but do they, or can they, come? On this subject Calvin's example is instructive. Unlike some theologians, Calvin does not have a great deal to say about the good and evil angelic orders, leaving the issue more open than closed. After discussing the medieval enthusiasm for angels and demons, Stephen F. Noll points to the "Reformation reserve." He describes John Calvin as a Protestant minimalist and John Milton as a Protestant maximalist.[66] Calvin was aware of the possibility that the experienced facts of good and evil could be reified into accepted fables of angels and devils. That is, the experience of comfort and support in this world could be personalized and projected upon angelic orders in another world. Something like this process has occurred in the symbolic figure of Santa Claus, who without a personal existence nevertheless personifies for some the spirit of the Christmas season. On the other side, the experienced range and reality of pain and evil seem to require a more than natural source. Evil as an ethical abstraction seems inadequate to account for the power of its effects. Thus, a malevolent supernatural being and his demonic minions are thought to exist at counterpurposes to the good and loving God and his angelic hosts. This being is variously known as Satan, Lucifer, and Mephistopheles. And Satan's demonic host in solemn assembly is unforgettably pictured in John Milton's magnificent *Paradise Lost*.

More recently the subject of demons was popularly addressed by M. Scott Peck in his *People of the Lie*.[67] Of special interest is the discussion in chapter 5 of the existence of the devil and of demonic possession requiring exorcism. According to Peck, genuine demonic possession is very rare, but five such cases have been well described by Malachi Martin in *Hostage to the Devil*.[68] Peck writes that he was uncertain about the reality of the devil, but "it was another matter after I had personally met Satan face-to-face. There is no way I can translate my experience into your experience. . . . Conversion to a belief in God generally requires some kind of actual encounter—a personal experience—with the living God. Conversion to a belief in Satan is no different."[69]

---

66. Stephen F. Noll, *Angels of Light, Powers of Darkness* (Downers Grove, IL: InterVarsity Press, 1998), 17.

67. M. Scott Peck, *People of the Lie: The Hope for Healing Human Evil* (New York: Simon and Schuster, 1983).

68. Malachi Martin, *Hostage to the Devil: The Possession and Exorcism of Five Living Americans* (New York: Reader's Digest Press, 1976).

69. Peck, *People of the Lie*, 184.

The subject of angels and devils, of sin and evil, is truly vast and truly complicated. Niesel declares, "The question of God and evil cannot be solved."[70] The most troubling intellectual question is how to understand creation by the all-good, omnipotent, omniscient God of so powerful an adversary to his Holy Will. Calvin addresses this question by insisting that Satan's natural malice cannot be attributed to God's creation but to the perversion of it. Satan chose to rebel against the truth, and the fault is his. This view puts the problem at a different place. If the good and omnipotent God did not directly create the Adversary, at least the good and omniscient God knowingly created an angel with freedom to choose to become the Adversary.[71] This unanswerable question, part of the mystery of sin and evil, has puzzled thinkers for centuries.

A situation, intractable to rational analysis, indicates that the only kind of answers likely to serve will come from another direction than discursive reason. After all, imagination too ranks as a senior faculty member. In "The Tables Turned" William Wordsworth insisted that

> One impulse from a vernal wood
> May teach you more of man,
> Of moral evil and of good,
> Than all the sages can.

He continues

> Our meddling intellect
> Mis-shapes the beauteous forms of things:—
> We murder to dissect.

If our intellect misshapes beauteous forms, presumably it also misshapes hideous forms. Of course, not all analysis is murderous. Moreover, while "vernal woods" may teach us a good deal, Dante was lost in a "dark wood" before he descended into hell, Macbeth died when "Great Birnam Wood [came] to high Dunsinane Hill" (IV.1.93), and the Lady in Milton's *Comus* was left "in the blind mazes of a tangl'd wood" (l. 180).

On many subjects the poets, troubadours, and novelists speak more persuasively to us than the academics.[72] Their language refers to a reality murdered by

70. Niesel, 77. When I learned that my wife's father had been murdered in Africa after fifty years of tremendous missionary service (See *Adventure in Africa: The Story of Don McClure* [Grand Rapids: Ministry Resources Library, 1990]), I went immediately to the phonograph to hear again Mozart's Fortieth Symphony in the tragic key of G minor. We are comforted by the hope that the tragic notes occurring in our lives will likewise be placed in a magnificent harmony.

71. The unconvincing theological distinction between permission, an act of the will, and prescience, an act of knowing, was designed to meet this objection. The same issue reappears in the relation between God's foreknowledge and God's foreordination. This is part of the question whether God can know future, contingent events. If they are known, how contingent can they be?

72. A serious disappointment is Charles Grosvenor Osgood's *Poetry as a Means of Grace* (Princeton, NJ: Princeton University Press, 1941). Rather than an analysis of beauty and divinity, Osgood discusses beautiful lines in Dante, Spenser, Milton, and Sam Johnson.

those who dissect. No doubt fictional characters like Anna Karenina, Ivan Karamazov, the various Little Women, Ralph Nickleby, even Sherlock Holmes and
Irene Adler are, in important senses, more real in our lives than people seated
across the aisle.[73] Surely the most prosaic will admit the statement "True love
ignores the aging process" does not convey the same meaning as:

> Love's not Time's fool, though rosy lips and cheeks
> Within his bending sickle's compass come;
> Love alters not with his brief hours and weeks,
> But bears it out even to the edge of doom.
>   (Shakespeare, Sonnet 116)

The point is, the topic of angels and devils is not so helpfully treated in the class-
room where insoluble questions are endlessly pondered as from the pulpit where
the company of the faithful is challenged and comforted. Angels and devils (and
sin and evil) remain difficult—even impossible—subjects for the scholarly establishment, but poets, painters, cinematographers—and preacher-theologians like
John Calvin—refer to all with powerful effect.[74]

2. Of Things Visible

Entirely too many people with strong opinions about Calvin's view of the human
condition seem quite innocent of this section of the *Institutes* as they hurry by to
denounce his doctrine of "total depravity," which being uncovered is seen as a figment of their own making. Calvin's treatment of God's creation of things visible
includes (a) the world in general and (b) human beings in particular.[75] Since
Calvin lived before the scientific revolution, his ideas of nature and the place of
humankind in nature are very different from modern views. For example, over
the centuries, the necessity of cooperating with nature has become pressing. No
present reader can expect Calvin to be sensitive about contemporary ecological
concerns. The scientific exploitation of nature was just beginning in Calvin's
time, and in common with most theologians, Calvin assumed that nature existed
chiefly for the benefit of mankind. Men and women were an exceptional part of
the natural world, and the emphasis was on the word "exceptional" rather than
on "part."

73. Allan Lazar, Dan Karlen, and Jeremy Salter have written a book entitled *The 101 Most Influential People Who Never Lived* (New York: Harper, 2006).

74. Dorothy Sayers (medievalist, translator of Dante, theologian, mystery writer, creator of Lord
Peter Wimsey) points to the serious virtue of "impenetrable frivolity" in her essay, "Poetry, Language,
and Ambiguity." Her main point is, "A word or phrase is not, and cannot be, an instrument of precision. . . . Poetic language is a web of light, the whole of which is spread through time and space,
and quivers at every touch" (Dorothy L. Sayers, *The Poetry of Search and the Poetry of Statement* [Lon-
don: Victor Gollancz, 1963], 264, 271, 272).

75. For an interesting survey, see Davis A. Young, *John Calvin and the Natural World* (Lanham,
MD: University Press of America, 2007).

a. The World

The caricature of Calvin as one of the brothers grim ignores his description of the world as "this most beautiful theater" in which we should take a pious delight. Calvin believes God created food not only for necessity but for delight. Necessity is part of the purpose of clothing but also comeliness and decency. Our eyes recognize the great beauty of flowers, and our noses take in the sweetness of their smell (III.10.2). Presumably this comment justifies florist shops where on occasion church funds purchase flowers to delight worshipers rather than food to nourish the poor. Moreover, Calvin deduces that God endowed gold and silver, ivory and marble with especial loveliness, from which one assumes the goldsmiths' and the silversmiths' vocation is not devoted to unacceptable luxuriousness. Apart from strict necessity, music, too, provides enjoyment (Com. Gen. 4:20).[76] The works of God are open and manifest in the world. Although the creation "is not the chief evidence for faith, yet it is the first evidence in the order of nature, to be mindful that wherever we cast our eyes, all things they meet are works of God, and at the same time to ponder with pious meditation to what end God created them" (I.14.20). Calvin believes the splendor and magnificence of the heavenly bodies preach "the glory of God like a teacher in a seminary of learning" (Com. Ps. 19:4). The creation of the world, Calvin thinks, has been fully described by Moses in the early chapters of Genesis and amply illustrated by the writings of saintly men such as Basil and Ambrose. For that reason Calvin does not offer a detailed explanation of creation. Indeed, he says, no human explanation is adequate to express the divine wisdom, power, justice, and goodness revealed in the fashioning of the universe.[77] In order to be brief, Calvin only insists that we, first, recognize God's power in the creation of the universe which destines all things for our benefit and, second, recognize with gratitude God's power and grace in ourselves.

What we learn from the history of creation can be summarized this way:

---

76. According to Edith Hamilton, *The Greek Way* (New York: W. W. Norton and Company, 1930), 333, "The Reformation asserted both morality and man's right to think for himself, but denied beauty and the right of enjoyment." Whatever one thinks about the two assertions, the two denials are wrong. On music see H. P. Clive, "The Calvinist Attitude to Music, and Its Literary Aspects and Sources," in three parts of *Bibliothèque d'Humanisme et Renaissance* (1957), 80–102, 294–319 (1958), 79–107. Clive is especially helpful in setting the historical context of Calvin's view of music. Also, Charles Garside Jr., "The Origins of Calvin's Theology of Music: 1536–1543" (Philadelphia: American Philosophical Society, 1979). On the visual arts, see *Seeing Beyond the Word: Visual Arts and the Calvinist Tradition*, ed. Paul Corby Finney (Grand Rapids: Wm. B. Eerdmans Publishing Company, 1999). For a careful discussion of Calvin's view of images in general, see chap. 3 of William A. Dyrness, *Reformed Theology and Visual Culture: The Protestant Imagination from Calvin to Edwards* (Cambridge: Cambridge University Press, 2004). Léon Wencelius, *L'Esthétique de Calvin* (Paris: Société d'édition "Les Belles Lettres," 1937), reads Calvin's theology through the concept of beauty with a major distinction between general and special grace.

77. The same wonder is expressed by Annie Dillard, *Pilgrim at Tinker Creek* (New York: Harper Perennial, 1974), 270. "The universe was not made in jest but in solemn incomprehensible earnest. By a power that is unfathomably secret, and holy, and fleet."

God by the power of His Word and Spirit created heaven and earth out of nothing; that thereupon he brought forth living beings and inanimate things of every kind, that in a wonderful series he distinguished an innumerable variety of things, that he endowed each kind with its own nature, assigned functions, appointed places and stations; and that, although all were subject to corruption, he nevertheless provided for the preservation of each species until the Last Day. We shall likewise learn that he nourishes some in secret ways, and, as it were, from time to time instills new vigor into them; on others he has conferred the power of propagating, lest by their death the entire species perish; that he has so wonderfully adorned heaven and earth with as unlimited abundance, variety, and beauty of all things as could possibly be, quite like a spacious and splendid house, provided and filled with the most exquisite and at the same time most abundant furnishings. Finally, we shall learn that in forming man and in adorning him with such goodly beauty, and with such great and numerous gifts, he put him forth as the most excellent example of his works. (I.14.20)

Calvin's teaching that "God by the power of His Word and Spirit created heaven and earth" (I.14.20) is Trinitarian since he has earlier insisted that the revelation of Word and Spirit demonstrates the reality of the doctrine of Trinity (I.13.16). Calvin is not yet treating redemptive history but only reflecting on the general teaching of Scripture about creation. Calvin's view of the natural world is developed from his understanding of Scripture rather than from cosmological inferences. That the triune God created the world out of nothing means that nothing is coeternal with God and denies emanation theories which hold that the world shares some part of God's substance. This account of creation is based, not on scientific observation, but on theological conviction. The doctrine of creation is part of Calvin's confession of faith in God.

b. The Human

So objectionable and sadly misunderstood is Calvin's view of sin and "total depravity" within it that casual and careless commentators ignore his interpretation of the original glory of creation and its promised restoration. When Calvin makes the transition from the natural to the human world, he cautions that God could well do without all the creatures. Nevertheless, it is a foolish deduction to think that God had no regard to his own glory in creating mankind. "Hence there is nothing absurd in saying that, though he lacked nothing, he yet created the race of men for his own glory."[78] While human being is not necessary to divine being, mankind is important for God's glory. Calvin believes that mankind as originally created was "the noblest and most remarkable example of [God's] justice, wisdom, and goodness" (I.15.1). In the popular mind Calvin's God is pictured as so sovereign as to be arbitrary and cruel. Contemporary culture also demonstrates considerable interest in Calvin's doctrine of mankind understood in terms of the phrase "total depravity." According to this improperly examined

---

78. *Concerning the Eternal Predestination of God*, trans. J. K. S. Reid (Louisville, KY: Westminster John Knox Press, 1997), 96.

assumption, Calvin views every human with dismal suspicion. Over time, Calvin's genuine teaching on total depravity has been so exaggerated as to become a serious caricature. Additionally, the modern interest in sociology and psychology poses a real danger of distorting Calvin's theology. Anthropocentric concern can be focused so narrowly that God and man are isolated from the same interpretive context and the human condition given a prominence that is absent in Calvin. Another way to state this issue is to observe that some contemporary scholars extrapolate Calvin's view of anthropology with the result that the divine connection recedes into the deep background.

For example, Mary Potter Engel claims that Calvin's doctrine of man (or in Engel's language of preference, doctrine of humankind) allows a focus on anthropology apart from theology.[79] Engel recognizes that most students of Calvin (including this one) believe that the self-knowledge of mankind cannot be treated apart from the knowledge of God. In opposition Engel maintains that pervading all Calvin's comments on humankind is a basic distinction between the absolute perspective of God and the relative perspective of humankind. With his ferocious disdain for vain speculation about the being of God in himself, it is impossible to believe that Calvin ever thought we could see anything at all from God's absolute and unaccommodated perspective! The Scripture reveals God's will to us and for us but does not allow us to see from God's perspective. Engel candidly admits there is *no* evidence that Calvin himself was aware of this "fundamental distinction" in his thought[80] and wryly complains that, in expounding these absolute and relative perspectives, Calvin is not always as cooperative[81] nor as careful[82] as one would like. The conclusion adopted here is that Engel has created a distinction in Calvin's theology that Calvin himself not only never considered but would vigorously reject.

To the contrary, the divine-human interconnection is profoundly exemplified not only in the union with Christ but also in creation. Calvin's view of nature and grace is interconnected rather than sequentially distinct as in the Thomistic model. Calvin's expository distinction (I.2.1) between creation and redemption does not mean that human creation can be ultimately separated from salvation. Moreover, his view of the creation of soul and body in Book I is completed by his discussion of the final resurrection of soul and body in Book III. In Book I of the *Institutes* Calvin deals with creation on the basis of "the general teaching of Scripture." This terminology indicates that Calvin is not attempting to produce a neutral cosmology or anthropology based on human "science." Rather—apart from the specific scriptural revelation concerning redemption—there is a general teaching of Scripture about creation which, while it may not satisfy impartial students of the natural and human world, is important for Christians to understand.

79. Mary Potter Engel, *John Calvin's Perspectival Anthropology* (Atlanta: Scholars Press, 1988), 189–91.
80. Ibid., 3.
81. Ibid., 60.
82. Ibid., 160.

Doubtless, in a general way, Calvin discusses our (1) created nature in Book I, (2) our fallen nature in Book II, and (3) our redeemed nature in Book III. However, the main subject in each case is God, not man. For example, the English translation of the *Institutes of the Christian Religion* contains more than fifteen hundred pages, but only fourteen of them are devoted to human nature as created (chap. 15). The point is that Calvin is expounding theology, not anthropology. His teaching about mankind does not stand free of his understanding of God, but depends upon it. Calvin deals with redemption in Books II–IV. In Book I he discusses our knowledge of ourselves in terms of (a) created and fallen nature. The additional major subjects of this short discussion are (b) soul and body, (c) understanding and will, and (d) image and likeness.

Created and Fallen. Turning from the natural creation to the human creation, Calvin asserts the knowledge of ourselves as twofold: (1) of our originally created and upright nature and (2) of the miserable condition to which we are subjected because of sin. Although Calvin often uses the term "nature" unmodified, it is usually clear whether he means created or fallen nature. The first topic, human nature as created, is discussed in I.15. The second, human nature as fallen, is treated in II.1–5. Contrary to almost universal popular opinion, Calvin does not regard sin as a necessary and essential component of the human condition. Sin is treated as a preface to the doctrine of redemption. Calvin does not attempt to indicate or validate the fall as a logical transition between creation and redemption. As we shall see in Book II, Calvin views sin as a practical reality but does not attempt a theoretical justification for it. In other words, Calvin recognizes the fact of sin but does not offer a doctrine of sin.

The declared purpose of the discussion of our created nature is to indicate what God gave to the human race in contrast to what was lost. Additionally, Calvin firmly denies that God is the author of evil. It would seem logical that if God is the creator of everything and evil is something, then God must be the creator of evil. However, Calvin, insisting that God's creation was entirely good, refuses to accept this logic. The good creation included the light of reason to guide human choices. God's creature was endowed with free will, which meant that Adam could have stood if he wished (I.15.8). The same idea is poetically expressed by John Milton in *Paradise Lost* where God declares that Adam was created "sufficient to have stood, though free to fall" (III.96–99).[83] Calvin's conclusion, asserted rather than explained, is that men and women corrupted their own blessings. According to Calvin, Adam and Eve fell so easily because they were not given the constancy to persevere. Ordinarily, the perseverance of the saints is a gift associated with redemption, although there is no logical reason that men and

83. A more complete citation reads,

> . . . and his faithless Progeny: whose fault?
> Whose but his own? Ingrate, he had of mee,
> All he could have; I made him just and right,
> Sufficient to have stood, though free to fall.

women were not created without the ability to sin. Calvin does not attempt to explain the nonbestowal of perseverance (or preservation) in creation. He admits that God might have made "a man who either could not or would not sin at all," and affirms, "Such a nature would, indeed, have been more excellent" (I.15.8). According to Calvin, the answer to nonperseverance lies hidden in God's secret predestination. For now we need only to know the difference between created and corrupted nature.

Soul and Body. Recent theological studies have raised serious questions about the proper understanding of soul and body focused especially on the immense historical influence of the Platonic dualism on Christian thought.[84] Careful attention to Plato's *Dialogues* reveals several differing expositions of soul, but the most famous is found in the *Phaedo*. There Plato taught that the soul and body are two distinct entities. In contrast, modern biblical interpretation emphasizes the unity of soul and body rather than their distinction. Moreover, Plato's view of immortality of the soul and the Bible's view of the resurrection of the body are not obviously compatible convictions. In addition, the reality of sin suggests that death is an enemy, as Paul thought (1 Cor. 15) rather than a friend, as Socrates thought. In the *Apology* (40c), Socrates says there is reason to hope that death is a good thing. In the *Phaedo* Socrates explains to his judges the reason (λόγος) he thinks that after death the true philosopher will attain the greatest blessings in the other land (64a).

In criticizing philosophers, Calvin praises Plato for recognizing the soul as an immortal substance (I.15.6). Nevertheless, whatever philosophical affinities may be adduced, the main point is the soul and body redeemed and restored.[85] Calvin was aware that the philosophers divided the soul into parts but thought their subtleties did not build proper godliness. "I, indeed, agree that the things they teach are true, not only enjoyable, but also profitable to learn, and skilfully assembled by them. And I do not forbid those who are desirous of learning to study them" (I.15.6). Calvin admits that the philosophers' discussion of soul has much to commend it, but they are not aware of the difference between created nature and corrupted nature. Therefore, in order not to become entangled in useless questions, it is sufficient to declare that the human soul consists of two faculties:

---

84. See Edwin Rohde's classic *Psyche*, trans. W. B. Ellis (New York: Harcourt, Brace and Company, 1925). Also Werner Jaeger, "The Greek Ideas of Immortality," *Harvard Theological Review* 52, no. 3 (July 1959): 135–47; and Oscar Cullmann, *Immortality of the Soul or Resurrection of the Dead* (London: Epworth Press, 1958). For a contemporary reflection, see Nancey Murphy, *Bodies and Souls, or Spirited Bodies* (Cambridge: Cambridge University Press, 2006).

85. See my "The Soul in Plato, Platonism, and Calvin," *Scottish Journal of Theology* 22, no. 3 (September 1969), 278–95. Also the fine discussion in Potter, "Immortality and Resurrection" in Potter's *John Calvin's Perspectival Anthropology.* In her article, Margaret R. Miles, "Theology, Anthropology, and the Human Body in Calvin's *Institutes of the Christian Religion,*" *Harvard Theological Review* 74, no. 3 (1981): 303–23, is concerned with "the relationship of Calvin's view of the body to his theology of the Glory of God" (322). One might criticize Miles's conviction that "Calvin had one central interest . . . the 'glory of God'" (303), which allows her to analyze theology and anthropology apart from union with Christ. Nevertheless, going for Miles is the important point that Calvin's belief in the resurrection of the body "is almost an impossible conceptual exercise for us" (323).

understanding and will. Ignorance of sin casts great suspicion on the helpfulness of Plato's view of soul and body. Even more basic for Christian theology than the precise relation of soul and body is the question of whether immortality is to be understood as an innate human possession or a special divine gift. Calvin was, of course, not aware of modern developments in biblical interpretation. Although critical at points, especially regarding their ignorance of sin, Calvin like most theologians East and West was clearly influenced by Plato's view of the immortality of soul. This recognition is overstated by Battenhouse, who thinks Calvinism and Neoplatonism exist in perfect harmony.[86]

Plotinus's view of soul and body expressed in the Fourth Ennead continues this discussion with Plato (especially in Tractate Eight). In each thinker the immortality of soul is an endowment of nature rather than a gift of God. Indeed, Plotinus writes, "Soul must be . . . understood as an emanation from Intellectual-Principle and as holding its value by a Reason-Principle thence infused" (Sixth Ennead, Ninth Tractate). This notion is clearly alien to Calvin. And, of course, neither Plato nor Plotinus teaches resurrection of the body. Plotinus concludes his consideration of soul with a reflection on unity. Only with considerable violence can Plotinus's metaphysical view of the One beyond Being, beyond knowing, beyond Good, and beyond God be connected with Calvin's personal view of union with Christ. According to Calvin, that the human being is composed of body and soul (I.15.2) means that we participate in both the visible and invisible orders. The soul, which comprises reason and will, is our noblest part (I.15.2). Wilhelm Niesel declares that Calvin makes "a clear distinction between the soul and the body," but Niesel also writes, "In spite of this antithesis of the body and the soul, a basic affinity between them arises from the fact that the soul, like the body, is created."[87] Niesel does not explain precisely how we are to understand the relation between "clear distinction" and "basic affinity." Among the continuing issues is that Greek philosophers thought the soul was eternal and immortal in one sense, while Christian theology insisted that the soul was created and immortal in another sense.

Calvin taught that each soul is created by God out of nothing, which means that soul is not an emanation of the divine essence nor is divine being transfused into human being. The result is that immortality is God's direct gift of grace rather than a general bestowal on human nature. The soul has no permanence in itself. If God withdraws his Spirit from the creatures, they perish. "For if God did not conserve the life he has given to man then the death of a man would be exactly the same as that of a horse or dog; for we are not nobler or more worthy, but we owe all to the fact that it has pleased God to give us this special privilege that we will be immortal."[88]

The impact of classical philosophy, especially of Plato and Aristotle, on Christian theology is enormous. Augustine's Christian synthesis of Platonism and

86. Roy W. Battenhouse, "The Doctrine of Man in Calvin and in Renaissance Platonism," *Journal of the History of Ideas*, IX (1948), 447.
87. Niesel, 65.
88. *CO* 53:621.

Aquinas's synthesis of Aristotelianism are immensely influential. One can legitimately claim that Aristotle was Plato's pupil and Aquinas was Augustine's. But if all philosophy is a footnote to Plato and all theology is a footnote to Augustine, then Plato's involvement with thinking in the Western world, direct and indirect, is incalculable. In the sixteenth century Plato was utilized by Protestants as an intellectual counterweight to Catholicism's use of Aristotle. The understanding of the nature of soul and body is one of the chief places where classical philosophy relates to Christian theology.

Understanding and Will. According to Calvin, "The human soul consists of two faculties, understanding and will." In his short exposition for the benefit of believers Calvin simplifies the complex discussion of the classical philosophers on this subject. He teaches that the purpose of understanding was to distinguish good from evil, and the purpose of will was to choose and follow the good and to reject evil (I.15.7). Having made these positive points, Calvin focuses on their loss because the knowledge of original integrity is of little use unless corrupted nature is also recognized (I.15.1). In other words, the created gifts of understanding and will require proper attention to their corruption and restoration. Corruption of the gifts of creation is treated more fully in II.1–5 as a preface to redemption, the subject that occupies the remainder of the *Institutes*. Calvin criticizes the view that man was "commonly thought to be corrupted only in his sensual part and to have a perfectly unblemished reason and a will also largely unimpaired" (II.2.4). So, far from being unblemished, Calvin asserts, "Human reason, therefore, neither approaches, nor strives toward, nor even takes a straight aim at, this truth: to understand, who the true God is or what sort of God he wishes to be toward us" (II.2.18).

In Book I Calvin devotes this very brief discussion to the created gifts of understanding and will, praising them and concluding that the created order was such "that the frame of the universe should be the school in which we were to learn piety, and from it pass over to eternal life and felicity." However, "after the fall of the first man no knowledge of God apart from the mediator has had power unto salvation" (II.6.1). In Book II Calvin insists that these gifts become totally depraved, meaning totally involved. This conviction differs sharply from the Thomistic view that grace does not destroy nature but perfects it. Calvin teaches that understanding and will are entirely subject to sin and no part of them is exempt from sinfulness. Like a crippled limb, humans may and must use their understanding and will, but they cannot be certain when and where they will fail. This fact teaches humility. Indeed, "The foundation of our philosophy is humility" (II.2.11). In this section of the *Institutes* Calvin praises God for the created gifts of understanding and will, but he does not forget their loss due to human sin and their restoration in the new life in Christ.

The relation between human understanding and will as created, fallen, and redeemed also involves God's grace and providence. The most famous sixteenth-century theological exchange was in the 1520s between Martin Luther in his *Bondage of the Will* and Desiderius Erasmus in his *Diatribe concerning Free Choice*.

In 1542 Albert Pighius (*Ten Books on Human Free Choice and Divine Govern-ment*) attacked Calvin's view of free will and providence as presented in chapters 2 and 8, respectively, in the 1539 *Institutes*. Calvin responded in 1543 with *The Bondage and Liberation of the Will: A Defense of the Orthodox Doctrine of Human Choice against Pighius*.[89] Calvin believes the will exists and chooses voluntarily. The will is self-determined, but because the will is corrupt, it is in bondage to sin. However, Calvin's view of will is not expounded merely in the passive voice. For example, Calvin writes, "He alone is truly a believer who . . . relying upon the promises of divine benevolence toward him, lays hold on an undoubted expectation of salvation" (III.2.16). We make God's promises ours by inwardly embracing them (III.2.16). Faith receives and embraces the gospel. Such lan-guage, even in a theological context, suggests an anthropological effort. Putatively it is *we* who do the relying, laying hold on, receiving, embracing, and so on. The philosophical relation between necessity and contingency, fate and fortune, determinism and volition is a question vexed for centuries. Calvin's concern is, first, the deep ravages of sin, and, second, the high danger of pride from putatively meritorious works. In struggling to understand both the freedom and bondage of the human will and the decree and permission of the divine will, Calvin confesses, "In a wonderful and ineffable manner nothing is done without God's will, not even that which is against his will. For it would *not* be done if he did not permit it; yet he does not unwillingly permit it, but willingly; nor would he, being good, allow evil to be done, unless being also almighty he could make good even out of evil" (I.18.3). The freeing response to this human bondage is divine grace—God's grace overcoming sinful nature. The ultimate ground of human confidence is not in the abilities of the mind or the choices of the will, but in the fact that we are not separated from Christ who dwells in us and we in him.

Having praised the original creation of human understanding and will, Calvin concludes that God is comprehended in Christ alone (II.6.4) until such time as we shall see God as he is (II.14.3). God cannot be known apart from Christ because "all thinking about God outside Christ is a vast abyss which immediately swallows up all our thoughts." Those who philosophize about God without Christ are deluded (compare 1 Pet. 1:20; 1 John 2:22). Since Calvin's theology is based on faith, not on reason, the Christian life is not linked by chains of reasoning but guided by faith in Christ, which is the principal work of the Holy Spirit. "We hold ourselves to be united with Christ by the secret power of his Spirit" (III.11.5). "Therefore, that joining together of head and members, that indwelling of Christ in our hearts—in short that mystical union—are accorded by us the highest degree of importance, so that Christ, having been made ours makes us sharers with him in the gifts with which he has been endowed" (III.11.10).

---

89. Edited by A. N. S. Lane, trans. G. I. Davies (Grand Rapids: Baker Books, 1966). See also A. N. S. Lane, "Calvin and the Fathers in His Bondage and Liberation of the Will," in *Calvinus Sin-cerioris Religionis Vindex*.

Image and Likeness. The same dynamic from created to fallen to restored also applies to Calvin's view of the image of God. Mankind was originally created in God's image, which means "that man was blessed, not because of his own good actions, but by participation in God" (II.2.1). The image of God is not to be understood only as a possession but a relationship—and "participation in God" involves "union with Christ." In the fall, while "God's image was not totally annihilated and destroyed in [Adam], yet it was so corrupted that whatever remains is frightful deformity" (I.15.4). Human sin means that the image of God cannot be understood solely in terms of creation or fall but in the true image of God restored in Jesus Christ. In other words, Calvin defines the image more in terms of redemption than creation.[90] Regeneration is nothing else than the reformation of the image of God in the godly, but the second creation of the image in the restoration by Christ is a far more rich and powerful grace (Com. Eph. 4:24). The grace of God exhibited in Christ exceeds all miracles. Indeed the redemption that he has brought surpasses even the creation of the world (Com. Is. 9:6).

Since Christ is the perfect image of God and we are united to him, we are restored to God's image. This summary marks the sharpest possible interpretative difference with Battenhouse, who thinks the fall means "the loss of the divine image originally natural to man. The whole picture is thus strikingly like that of Neoplatonic theory. But further, I think it may be remarked that the loss of this 'image' seems to be for Calvin . . . a more central concern than man's loss of God. That is, fallen man's formlessness rather than his loneliness receives chief attention: the corruption of his nature as man more than the disruption of his fellowship with his creator."[91] In spite of the cautious phrases "may be," and "seems to be," Battenhouse has completely misread Calvin's intention in concluding that Calvin is more interested in the renewal of original nature in ourselves than in the restoration of divine communion in Jesus Christ. In fact, the reverse is true, as conclusively demonstrated by Richard Prins. Prins contrasts "image" to "restoraton," "Adam" to "man," and "Adam" to "Christ," pointing to a limited exposition. "In *The Institutes* there is a whole chapter devoted to the image and soul as created, but there is no section allotted to the image in his discussions of restoration." In other words, Calvin's primary concern is not the lost and found image of God in Adam but the restoration of humankind in Jesus Christ.[92]

---

90. Seeking to bring the visibility of God into the center of Calvin's theology by way of images, Randall C. Zachman, *Image and Word in the Theology of Calvin* (Notre Dame, IN: University of Notre Dame Press, 2007), propounds the centrality of God's self-revelation both *heard* in the revealed Word and *seen* in the created world. This "dually objective" framing of theological centrality displaces the singular and foundational confession of God's revelation in Jesus Christ alone in favor of Jesus Christ as God's living image (chap. 9) and the gospel as his living portrait. Oneness with God consists "of the face-to-face vision of God . . . the restoration of the image and likeness of God" (435). Calvin insists, "A supposed knowledge of God outside Christ will be a deadly abyss" (Com. Jn. 6:46).

91. Battenhouse, "Doctrine of Man," 456–57.

92. Richard Prins, "The Image of God in Adam and the Restoration of Man in Jesus Christ: A Study in Calvin," *Scottish Journal of Theology* 25 (1972): 32.

Based on Genesis 1:27 Calvin teaches that man and woman were created in the image and likeness of God. The two words, "image" and "likeness," do not indicate a difference. Rather, according to Calvin, they simply represent a Hebrew repetition used not for distinction but for emphasis. The primary seat of God's image is "in the mind and heart or in the soul and its powers," although marks of God's glory may also be seen in the body. "The soul is not man, yet it is not absurd for man, in respect to his soul, to be called God's image; even though I retain the principle I just now set forward, that the likeness of God extends to the whole excellence by which man's nature towers over all the kinds of living creatures" (I.15.3). This means "God's image was visible in the light of the mind, in the uprightness of the heart, and in the soundness of all the parts" (I.15.4).

One of the most puzzling features of the study of this section of the *Institutes* is the willingness of scholars to exclude the restoration in favor of analyzing creation and fall. For example, T. F. Torrance, in *Calvin's Doctrine of Man*, correctly observes that Calvin's doctrine of man can only be formulated truly from the standpoint of the grace of God in Jesus Christ. However, Torrance then adds that Calvin also points "out the value of thinking of ourselves *apart from grace*" (italics added) which is explained as a didactic device used by Calvin for effect. On this interpretation Torrance can focus directly on anthropological themes (e.g., the image of God in man [four chapters], the sin of man [three chapters])—in some sense setting aside their theological context. At the same time, Torrance admits that these "moral denunciations of man, apart from the context of grace, . . . do not stand up to [Calvin's] own investigations" and affirms that God's grace is the context of anthropology.[93]

Differently problematic is Mary Potter Engel's virtual omission of the fall from careful analysis in *John Calvin's Perspectival Anthropology*. In attempting to correct, improve, and succeed Torrance's study, she approaches Calvin's view of man along the lines of Marsilio Ficino and Pico della Mirandola as interpreted by Roy Battenhouse. The Renaissance conviction of human perfectability allows the interpreter to pass from creation to redemption, pausing only momentarily to deal with the devastation of sin. Engel treats the fall in eight pages as one of the six controversies surrounding the doctrine of the image of God.[94]

If Calvin's anthropology can be separated from his theology, it would still seem to require following the threefold exposition in the *Institutes*. That is, (1) God's creation of man and woman (treated briefly in I.15), (2) the human reality and effects of sin (treated briefly in II.1–5), and (3) the redemption accomplished by Christ through the power of the Holy Spirit (treated at length in II.6–IV.20). The chief problem with Engel's study, however, is not the balance among these three topics, but the more basic question of whether Calvin's doctrine of man and woman can be abstracted from his doctrine of God without doing interpretive

93. T. F. Torrance, *Calvin's Doctrine of Man* (London: Lutterworth Press, 1949), 18, 19.
94. Engel, *John Calvin's Perspectival Anthropology*, 54–61.

violence to both. Even the most enthusiastic student of Calvin's "anthropology" does not claim Calvin is an anthropologist. John Calvin is a theologian. Therefore, the book jacket claim to challenge "the prevalent bias toward focusing on Calvin's doctrine of God to the neglect of his doctrine of humankind" only adds another bias. Engel's study concentrating on Calvin's doctrine of mankind neglects his doctrine of God. Even more parlous, as previously observed, is Engel's theological (anthropological?) claim that Calvin ever thought he could see things from God's perspective. The charge leveled here is that "Calvin's anthropologists," like Torrance and Engel, in expounding Calvin's doctrine of the created "image of God," have neglected its more important culmination in the redemptive "union with Christ."

Under the general rubric of nature and grace or grace and nature, two aspects of Calvin's "theological anthropology" may be discussed more fully as illustrating first a reflection where going on with Calvin today is not a sound option and second where stopping with Calvin might be a better one. That is, Calvin's point on conscience, however historically representative and interesting, is no longer adequate, while his conclusive ambiguity concerning the so-called point of contact (*Anknüpfungspunkt*) is more adequate than the precision anticipated by those who debated the issue. The discussion with Calvin on conscience stops too soon; the discussion on point of contact goes too far.

The Point of Conscience. Nature and grace or grace and nature is one of those sprawling theological topics that touches everything. Even the order of the two nouns indicates a theological position. Nature and grace follows the order of creation. That is, subsequent to sin's entering God's perfect world and leading to the fall, God's grace was needed to *restore* original nature—roughly the Catholic and Thomistic view. Grace and nature follows the order of redemption. That is, prior to the mystery of sin's entering God's perfect world and leading to the fall, God's grace was already extended in the Eternal Son to *replace* our fallen and sinful nature—roughly the Protestant and Calvinian view. Not only can no subject be isolated from basic conclusions about these two doctrines, but sophisticated nuances appear in unexpected places. To mention only a few, conclusions about the relation of nature and grace reappear in the doctrines of creation and redemption, man and God, sin and fall, election and free will, reason and faith, doubt and certainty, Word and sacraments, law and gospel.[95] In one way or another, every theological page assumes and continues the discussion that this section attempts to bring into clearer (but not less complex) focus.

With his usual elegant balance, Thomas Aquinas declares that grace does not destroy but perfects nature (*gratia non tollit naturam sed perfecit*, *ST* I.8). As a fundamental conviction, both simple and profound, it spreads calmly through his entire theology. The Protestant conviction of "grace alone" sharply rejects this view of "nature and grace." In parallel phrasing Catholic doctrine sees "grace as

---

95. I. John Hesselink, *Calvin's Concept of the Law* (Allison Park, PA: Pickwick Publications, 1992), 236–38, discusses the order of law and gospel or gospel and law.

perfecting nature," while Protestant sees "grace as overcoming nature." However, while the language may be roughly parallel, the theological position is not because the emphasis on nature is different. The Catholic focus is on created nature. The Protestant focus is on fallen nature. The Catholic view of nature as damaged but not destroyed leads first to the possibility and then to the expectation that one may naturally cooperate with grace. Therefore, Thomas draws a distinction between God's operating and initiating grace and human cooperating and responding grace. Both operating and cooperating are God's grace, but cooperating grace is a gift of God infused by God into the soul, which by human effort can become habitual. Following Aristotle, Thomas defines habits as the intrinsic principles of human acts—dispositions of mind or will leading either to good (virtue) or evil (vice). Habits are not innate but learned; they are potential not actual, meaning they can be acquired, developed, lost, or ignored. Habits infused by God constitute the gift of habitual grace (ST I.105.6), which is the principle of meritorious works.

Thomas's view of nature and grace is a way of preserving both the sovereign grace of God and the accountable decisions of humans. Through the sacraments God infuses supernatural habits, but we are responsible for actualizing them. Advancement in goodness requires practice, which in turn requires a disposition (or habit) cultivated to act in certain ways. Calvin thought this view created a dangerously erroneous role for human merit in salvation. Instead of correctly attributing salvation to God's grace alone, one was expected to respond to God's operating grace with cooperating grace. Prior to the sixteenth-century Reformation, two kinds of human merit were discussed: condign merit and congruent merit. Protestants deny both understandings, believing that human beings stand before God not with either condign or congruent merit, but with no merit of their own—rather in the merit bestowed by Jesus Christ in whom they live by the power of the Holy Spirit. Human response to God's grace is not the cause but the consequence of salvation. We cannot stand before God even partially clothed in our faith, piety, or good works. With no merit of our own, we stand before God only in the merit of Jesus Christ to whom we are united.[96]

Calvin expresses his displeasure in the distinction between operating and cooperating grace, passing over the "fanatics" who think grace is distributed to all. Good works, he insists, are enabled "by special grace which only the elect receive through regeneration." Although the Master of the Sentences "attributes the effective desire for good to the grace of God, yet he hints that man by his very own nature somehow seeks after the good—though ineffectively" (II.2.6). Calvin returns to the "worn distinction between operating and cooperating grace" (II.3.11) by commending Augustine's refusal to divide grace between God and us so that the human will has no merit to claim for itself. Calvin thinks the chief problem with the distinction is the meritorious expectation from those who receive the first grace. God's grace is freely and powerfully bestowed and does not

---

96. For a fuller discussion of merit, see Purves and Partee, *Encountering God*, 120–21.

wait to be a coworker with us. God does sometimes withdraw for a short time, but this is not to be understood as God's waiting to see what we will do and does not demonstrate human free will (II.5.13). According to Calvin, "Any mixture of the power of free will that men strive to mingle with God's grace is nothing but a corruption of grace," which means that all actions arising from grace belong to God, who has created a new will to replace the corrupted natural will (II.5.15). In this sense we can say "that we ourselves are fitly doing what God's spirit is doing in us, even if our will contributes nothing of itself distinct from his grace." While Calvin denies that anyone has the power to work in partnership with God's grace, he insists "that after we have by the Lord's power once for all been brought to obey righteousness, *we go forward by our own power and are inclined to follow the action of grace*" (II.3.11, emphasis added). In this way Calvin affirms an appropriate response to God but not a merited grace from God.

According to Carter Lindberg, Luther "learned that the righteousness of God is not a demand to be met by achievement but a gift to be accepted by faith . . . He came to see that salvation is no longer the goal of life but rather its foundation."[97] The Protestant understanding of "grace alone" denies the Catholic view both of infused and cooperating grace and infused and habitual grace. While Catholics believe originally created nature is *damaged* by sin, Protestants insist that originally created nature is *destroyed* by sin. Human depravity is then total in a real but not absolute sense. On the contrary, Thomas teaches that the supernatural virtues (faith, hope, and love) were lost in the fall and can be gracefully restored. The natural virtues (wisdom, moderation, courage, and justice) remain and can be achieved.[98]

Calvin's view of the relation of grace and nature was not satisfactory to some of his putative followers. Otto Gründler points out that later Calvinists, notably Jerome Zanchi, return to the Thomistic category of habitual grace. In dealing with the perseverance of the saints Gründler recognizes that for Calvin the doctrine is ultimately based on union with Christ. However, many Calvinists of the late sixteenth and seventeenth centuries address "the question by reintroducing the Thomistic-Aristotelian *habitus* concept: True faith perseveres in the elect since it is a supernatural substance or virtue infused by God in his elect through the Holy Spirit."[99] Gründler admits "that Calvin nowhere equates *semen fidei* with the Scholastic concept of *habitus infusus* or *virtus infusa*,"[100] but according to Gründler's theological botany, Calvin's view of "the seed of faith" (III.2.21)

---

97. Carter Lindberg, *The European Reformations* (Oxford: Blackwell Publishers, 1996), 66.

98. In his reflection on Christian character (chap. 2) Kirk employs the virtues, expounding the outward signs of Christian life in terms of the cardinal virtues and uses the theological virtues to describe the internal characteristics of the Christian life (Kenneth E. Kirk, *Some Principles of Moral Theology and Their Application* [London: Longmans, Grace and Co., 1920]).

99. Otto Gründler, "From Seed to Fruition: Calvin's Notion of the *semen fidei* and Its Aftermath in Reformed Orthodoxy," in *Probing the Reformed Tradition: Historical Studies in Honor of Edward A. Dowey, Jr.*, ed. Elsie Anne McKee and Brian G. Armstrong (Louisville, KY: Westminster/John Knox Press, 1989), 109.

100. Ibid., 112.

may already contain "the seed of the habitualism which came to fruition a generation later."[101]

Protestantism put together four famous alones, if not logically, at least comfortably: grace alone, Christ alone, Scripture alone, faith alone. There is no comparable emphasis on nature alone because, while not forgetting created nature, the focus of concern was fallen nature. Nevertheless, the concept of *logos* raises the question of whether the knowledge of God comes even partially from nature or entirely by grace. This topic is set within the context of creation, providence, and redemption and specifically involves the extent of sin, and was the subject of the Barth-Brunner debate. Calvin claims that humans are not created in the likeness of beasts because they are endowed "with the light of reason" (Com. Jn. 1.4), meaning that in their present fallen state this light has been turned into darkness and humans are blind. Yet the evangelist "denies that the light of reason is completely put out; for in the darkling gloom of the human mind there still shine some sparks of that brightness" (Com. Jn. 1.5). Calvin is quite aware there are sharply contrasting ideas in this sentence, light and darkness, created and fallen nature, sight and blindness. He concludes that the light shining in the darkness is not meant as praise of fallen nature but to indicate its ineffectuality. Human beings continue to exercise a certain reasonableness, but they cannot reach or even approach God by reason. This situation requires understanding the "two distinct powers of the Son of God." The first appears in the created order of nature. The second appears in the restoration of fallen nature. This understanding is Calvin's conclusion and main point, but on the way to it he mentions two severely damaged, even destroyed, but not absolutely destroyed parts of created nature: the "divine spark" and the conscience. By God's grace these two aspects of created nature remain in fallen nature. Calvin asserts, "There are two main parts in that light which yet remains in corrupt nature. Some seed of religion is sown in all; and also, the distinction between good and evil is engraven in their consciences" (Com. Jn. 1.5). Calvin insists, "There is within the human mind, and indeed by natural instinct, an awareness of divinity" (I.3.1). Because this sense of deity is inscribed in every heart, no one has an excuse for denying the existence of God. Those who do deny God are struck in their consciences with the vengeance of divine majesty. That is, "the worm of conscience, sharper than any cauterizing iron, gnaws away within" (I.3.3).[102]

How brightly these two lights shine in the darkness of corrupt nature involves a basic judgment on Calvin's doctrines of creation and redemption, nature and

---

101. Ibid., 109. Calvin employs the concept of habit in debate with Pighius, *Bondage and Liberation of the Will*, book 6, 378.

102. Robert A. Greene, "Synderesis, The Spark of Conscience in the English Renaissance," *Journal of the History of Ideas* 52, no. 1 (January–March 1991): 195–219, traces the "*worm* of conscience" from Augustine's interpretation (*City of God* 21:9) of Isaiah's undying worm (66:24). On conscience itself Greene asserts that "for every echo of the medieval tradition [in Calvin] there is a devastating rejection of it." He concludes, "The spark of conscience is apparently snuffed under this onslaught" (204). The worm of conscience wriggles into Chaucer's "Physician's Tale" and Shakespeare's *Richard III* (I.3.222).

grace, but before one tries too hard to understand Calvin's view of natural knowledge of God, Serene Jones with considerable tranquillity points out that Calvin often refutes his own arguments.[103] The complexity of deciding whether Calvin actually believed in a naturally innate knowledge of the existence of God suggests that "a rhetorical reading of Calvin's position can shed new light on this debate";[104] specifically the "logical inconsistency" of a created sense of divinity which is obliterated by sin "serves as a warning signal that Calvin may have purposes other than strictly logical ones in thus framing his topic."[105] Jones believes too few interpreters consider "the possibility that Calvin intended these chapters on 'natural knowledge' to serve rhetorical functions that are not necessarily wedded to concerns for logical precision, conceptual clarity, or systematic rigor."[106] Jones concludes the attempt to give a systematically important role to the sense of divinity "will not succeed precisely because Calvin does not elaborate a systematized epistemology with respect to this notion of 'innate knowledge.'"[107]

In an earlier reflection on the seed of religion and conscience, Edward A. Dowey Jr. admits the sense of divinity "is not very closely defined in Calvin's thought,"[108] and conscience receives a "baffling variety of expressions."[109] Nevertheless, Dowey confidently concludes that Calvin employs the subjective-objective split. "Calvin's conception of the revelation in creation corresponds to the doubleness, the subjectivity and objectivity, which is one of the elemental characteristics of mental life."[110] Applying this debatable subject-object dichotomy to Calvin, Dowey thinks both the sense of divinity and the conscience are elements in the subjective revelation in creation. According to Dowey, the sense of divinity (or seed of religion) is the direct revelation of God to the soul of man as creature.[111] Its empirical effects "are (1) the universality of religion, which because of sin means the universality of idolatry, accompanied by (2) the servile fear of God and (3) the troubled conscience."[112]

Alvin Plantinga, an American philosopher, takes the *sensus divinitatis* to mean that "one who follows Calvin here will . . . hold that a capacity to apprehend God's existence is as much part of our natural noetic or intellectual equipment as is the capacity to apprehend truths of logic, perceptual truths, truths about the past, and truths about other minds."[113] Doubtless it is natural that a modern

103. Serene Jones, *Calvin and the Rhetoric of Piety* (Louisville, KY: Westminster John Knox Press, 1995), 159.

104. Ibid., 155.

105. Ibid., 158.

106. Ibid., 159.

107. Ibid., 162.

108. Edward A. Dowey Jr., *The Knowledge of God in Calvin's Theory*, 3rd ed. (Grand Rapids: Eerdmans, 1994 [1951], 50.

109. Ibid., 57.

110. Ibid., 50.

111. Ibid., 56.

112. Ibid., 53.

113. Alvin Plantinga, "Advice to Christian Philosophers," in Michael D. Beaty, *Christian Theism and the Problems of Philosophy* (Notre Dame, IN: University of Notre Dame Press, 1990), 26–27.

Christian philosopher would posit a natural knowledge of God's existence apprehended by reason, but a British philosopher, also interested in Calvin, comes to
the opposite conclusion. In a section dealing with Calvin and Plantinga on the
sensus divinitatis, Paul Helm writes, "'Reformed' epistemology takes encouragement from the fact that in Calvin one finds very little attention given to the proofs
of God's existence." Plantinga understands Calvin to teach belief in God as part
of the human noetic structure. Helm counters, "There is no evidence from the
passage cited (or from any similar passages) that Calvin has in mind the rationality of religious belief, or the nature of religious knowledge."[114] While Calvin
does declare that all humans are endowed with the light of reason, he also claims
that the light of reason is darkened by sin. In either case, the seed of religion does
not blossom into saving faith.

Concerning conscience, the second light remaining in corrupt nature, Calvin
asserts that even "in the densest darkness of ignorance this tiny little light
remained, that men recognized man's conscience to be higher than all human
judgements" (IV.10.5).[115] Even the heathens testified, "Conscience is like a thousand witnesses" (Com. Gen. 4:7). Conscience is defined as an inner forum—a
certain mean between God and man, which represents God's judgment
(III.19.15). According to John Milton, God declares,

> And I will place within them as a guide
> My Umpire *Conscience* Whom if they will hear,
> Light after light well us'd they shall attain,
> And to the persisting, safe arrive.
> (*Paradise Lost* 3:194–97)

Calvin thinks, "Conscience refers to God. A good conscience, then, is nothing
but inward integrity of heart" (III.19.16). Conscience is invoked not merely for
the knowledge of God's will, but also for the certainty of faith. Faith turns on the
chief hinge that God's promises of mercy are true in us. "We make them ours by
inwardly embracing them." This statement sounds like "cooperating grace,"
which Calvin rejects, but Calvin draws the conclusion that this assurance "renders the conscience calm and peaceful before God's judgment" (III.2.16).

---

114. Helm, *Faith with Reason* (Oxford: Clarendon Press, 2000), 84, 85. See also Paul Helm, "John
Calvin, the *Sensus Divinitatis* and the Noetic Effects of Sin," *International Journal for the Philosophy
of Religion* 43 (1998): 87–107.

115. According to Thomas Aquinas, conscience is a dictate of reason (*ST* I.II, q.19a.5) meaning
practical reason, not the will or speculative reason. Informed by the intellectual virtue of prudence
an individual applies the judgment of conscience to conduct (*ST* I.II, q.19a.3). Thomas makes a distinction between synderesis (the principle behind the act) and conscience (which refers to the act
itself). The word "conscience" is often used to refer to both, but synderesis is a habit. According to
Reginald Garrigou-Lagrange, *Beatitude*, trans. Patrick Cummins (St. Louis: B. Herder, 1956), conscience is a spark enkindled by the Creator in the human being and cannot be lost unless reason itself
is lost. He concludes that conscience even when it is invincibly erroneous is the voice of God (306).
As Thomas says (III Quodlibet, 27), "Every judgment of conscience, be it right or wrong, be it about
things evil in themselves or morally indifferent, is obligatory, in such wise that he who acts against
his conscience always sins."

Dowey asserts that the conscience "given in the created order [is] a universal endowment, part of man as man, an element of the *imago Dei*" specifically concerned with the distinction between good and evil.[116] Dowey sees conscience as "deeply imbedded both in Calvin's utterly non-redemptive 'natural' theology and in the very heart of his conception of justification by faith and of sanctification, as a category which brings into proper focus the 'natural' and the soteriological, the knowledge of the will of God the Creator in its relation to the will of God as Redeemer."[117] Conscience is both a knowledge of the law of God and at the same time a knowledge of the law of nature. If, and to the extent that, Calvin develops an "utterly non-redemptive 'natural' theology" and an utterly soteriological supernatural theology, it seems strange that their relation is brought into proper focus by the faculty of conscience with its "baffling variety." Against Dowey, the ultimate relation between creation and redemption is not a principle nor a faculty but a person, Jesus Christ the Lord.

In agreement that Calvin appeals to conscience without careful analysis, David Bosco asserts, "Issues tend to be analyzed with concentrated precision when they are deemed crucial to his conception of Christian life." "Yet nowhere in the *Institutes* does conscience receive an extended treatment." Bosco concludes, "Thus our examination, organized around the metaphors of conscience as court and the assaulted conscience [as worm?] and probed with the analytical tool of the three elements of conscience [derived from contemporary ethical philosophers], strongly supports the assertion that Calvin had a coherent view of conscience." The precise meaning of "coherent" is debatable in the light of Bosco's insistence that Calvin ignored the conative element of conscience and his immediately following and apparently reluctant admission that Calvin's account "may at times be lacking in systematic development." In fact Bosco's conclusion is easily reversed on his own grounds. Because Calvin does not develop his view of conscience in a systematic way, his comments may be taken in a number of directions, but such developments are interpretation, not exposition.[118]

Surely theological assertions about conscience need reconsideration. In an early and typically apodictic deliverance Karl Barth denigrates the calculating reason (*rechnende Vernunft*) in favor of conscience thusly: "The reason sees the small and the larger but not the large. It sees the preliminary but not the final, the derived but not the original, the complex but not the simple. It sees what is human but not what is divine." In contrast, "Conscience is the perfect interpreter of life, what it tells us is no question, no riddle, no problem, but a fact—the deepest, innermost, surest fact of life: God is righteous." Barth concludes, "Conscience, as everybody knows, may be reduced almost to silence or crushed into oblivion; it may be led astray to the point of folly and wrongdoing; but it remains

---

116. Dowey, *Knowledge of God*, 56.
117. Ibid., 64–65.
118. David Bosco, "Conscience as Court and Worm: Calvin and the Three Elements of Conscience," *Journal of Religious Ethics* 14 (1986): 353.

forever the place, the only place between heaven and earth, in which God's righteousness is manifest."[119]

In a more recent study, Randall C. Zachman offers a detailed study of Calvin's view of conscience. Zachman is interested in the relation of Luther and Calvin on the concept of conscience and most especially on the role of the testimony of a good conscience in the doctrine of the assurance (or certainty) of faith. Defining conscience, Zachman cites Calvin's commentary on Genesis 4:9: "As often, then, as the secret compunctions of conscience invite us to reflect upon our sins, let us remember that God himself is speaking with us. For that interior sense by which we are convicted of sin is the peculiar judgment seat of God, where he exercises his jurisdiction." Zachman continues his emphasis on conscience as the very voice of God by paraphrasing Calvin's definition this way, "Since the conscience arises from the awareness of divine judgment, the testimony of the conscience should be regarded as the judgment we receive from God before God's tribunal" (III.19.15). Conscience is more usually understood not as the direct voice of God but the accusing witness to sin arising from an innate sense of divine judgment. The passage concludes that conscience "is a certain mean between God and man, because it does not allow man to suppress within himself what he knows but pursues him to the point of convicting him." Zachman's exposition of Calvin's view of conscience is functional in the sense that he works within the intellectual framework Calvin provides. This procedure is perfectly legitimate as historical theology, but not as systematic theology. In other words, some systematic reflection on the continuing usefulness of the concept of conscience in theology in the light of Freud's critique would seem essential.[120]

In a 1960s reflection on conscience, Gerhard Ebeling begins by asserting that we are clumsy beginners in this language school. "That is why we are theologians and think humbly enough of ourselves but very highly of our task." Ebeling then declares, "The call of conscience as such is not by any means the voice of God," suggesting "that *the root of the phenomenon of conscience* lies in the basic ontological determination of man as the being whose relation to himself is that of joint cognizance." . . . "Strictly man does not 'have' a conscience, but he is conscience. . . . Conscience indeed both accuses and is also the very experience of being accused."[121]

Even before Freud there were recognized difficulties in the notion that conscience is the voice of God or the privileged voice of human wisdom. One of the

119. Karl Barth, *The Word of God and the Word of Man*, trans. Douglas Horton (New York: Harper and Brothers Publishers, 1957), 9, 10.

120. Randall C. Zachman, *The Assurance of Faith: Conscience in the Theology of Martin Luther and John Calvin* (Louisville, KY: Westminster John Knox Press, 2005), 100, 101. Breasted defines conscience as a social force for morality. When early people "became conscious of a function of human intelligence, which discriminated between right and wrong conduct, they involuntarily applied to it the old word 'heart,' meaning the moral discernment exercised by the heart." Under that name, "conscience" began its history as a social force (James Henry Breasted, *The Dawn of Conscience* [New York: Charles Scribner's Sons, 1935] 395).

121. Ebeling, "Theological Reflexions on Conscience" in *Word and Faith*, 421, 418, 417 (emphasis in original).

clearest examples that a foolish, pompous, stupid man will have a pompous, foolish, stupid conscience is seen in the exchange between the marvelously winsome Elizabeth Bennet and the perfectly sycophantic Rev. William Collins. Urgently urged not to attack Fitzwilliam Darcy, Mr. Collins says to Elizabeth, "You must therefore allow me to follow the dictates of my conscience on this occasion, which leads me to perform what I look upon as a point of duty. Pardon me for neglecting to profit by your advice, which on every other subject shall be my constant guide, though in the case before us I consider myself more fitted by education and habitual study to decide on what is right than a young lady like yourself" (Jane Austen, *Pride and Prejudice*, chap. 18).[122]

Questions about the reality and role of the seed of religion are asked in the theological context of original creation and original sin. The question of conscience, however, also has a clinical context. Paul L. Lehmann concludes his *Ethics in a Christian Context* with a summary of Calvin's view of the role of conscience in Christian freedom, which involves "the operational consequences of the knowledge of God which had been under discussion in the first two books [of the *Institutes*]." In his chapter entitled "The Decline and Fall of Conscience," Lehmann writes, "The semantic, philosophical and theological pilgrimage of conscience begins with the Greek tragedians of the fifth century before Christ and ends with Sigmund Freud." Lehmann analyzes the views of Aquinas, Kant, and Calvin, which hold in a general way that conscience is the voice of God in a human life. Calvin thinks the conscience properly refers to God alone (III.19.16). "Therefore, just as works concern men, so the conscience is nothing but an inward uprightness of heart" (IV.10.4). "Scripture shows that God's promises are not established unless they are grasped with the full assurance of conscience" (III.13.4).[123] Freud, on the contrary, insists that conscience is trained and determined by human society, not divine directive. In the light of Freud's clinical studies, Lehmann concludes, "Ethical theory must either dispose of the conscience altogether or completely transform the interpretation of its significance."[124]

122. In an interesting essay entitled "The Conscience of Huck Finn," Jonathan Bennett discusses the conflict in Huck's mind between obeying the established slavery laws and his friendship for Jim, the real hero of the adventures of Huckleberry Finn. Sadly, this magnificent classic is being rejected because Mark Twain employs the now-taboo N-word. Harold Bloom, whose colossal erudition impresses his judgments with great weight, opines that the opening of chap. 19 in *The Adventures of Huckleberry Finn* is the finest paragraph ever written by an American. Bennett's discussion contrasts the conscientiousness of Nazi Heinrich Himmler with the conscience of Jonathan Edwards, Calvinist theologian and philosopher, whose view of sinners in the hands of an angry God Bennett judges worse than Himmler's morality (*Philosophy* 49 [1974]: 131). In "The Facts Concerning the Recent Carnival of Crime in Connecticut" Mark Twain tells of a man who encounters his conscience appearing as a small fiend "covered all over with a fuzzy, greenish mold" who "only sat there leering at me with joy and contempt, and placidly chuckling" declaring, "It is my business—and my joy—to make you repent of everything you do." This story was called to my attention by my son, Charles. Samuel L. Clemens, as erstwhile I, had a bad conscience about his pipe smoking, to which the top floor of his Hartford house was devoted.

123. See J. Peter Pelkonen, "The Teaching of John Calvin on the Nature and Function of the Conscience," *Lutheran Quarterly* 21 (1969): 74–88.

124. Paul L. Lehmann, *Ethics in a Christian Context* (New York: Harper and Row, 1963), 365, 327. See also the magisterial study of C. A. Pierce, *Conscience in the New Testament* (London: SCM Press, 1958), especially his brief discussion of choice (προαίρεσις) and conscience (συνείδησις), 126ff.

It is easy to see that with the sense of divinity Calvin desired to protect the conviction that impressed on the original creation is an awareness of the Creator. The notion of conscience is designed to protect a continuing relation between Creator and creature, and a responsibility of the latter to the former. Nevertheless, I think the answer to the options posed by Lehmann is to dispose of the concept of conscience altogether. At the very least the teaching of the eminent ethicist, Jiminy Cricket, recommending that we let our conscience be our guide must be rejected.

The Point of Contact. Nearly every interpretation of Calvin discusses the famous Barth-Brunner debate.[125] The general issue concerns the relation of nature and grace and closely related subjects like operating and cooperating grace. Put briefly, Brunner believes in a "natural grace" that Barth denies. Specifically, insofar as Calvin is concerned, the topic is the relation between the natural knowledge of God and the revealed knowledge of God. Karl Barth, emphasizing the centrality of God's special revelation, almost (or entirely) denies the validity of natural knowledge. On the other hand, Emil Brunner, while asserting the primacy of the scriptural revelation, nevertheless affirms the reality of some natural knowledge. In discussing Calvin's view of "the image of God," Brunner writes, "Calvin considers this remnant of the *imago Dei* to be of great importance. One might almost say that it is one of the pillars supporting his theology. For he identifies it with nothing less than the entire human, rational nature, the immortal soul, the capacity for culture, the conscience, responsibility, the relation with God, which—though not redemptive—exists even in sin, language, the whole of cultural life." Barth responds, "The possibility of a real knowledge by natural man of the true God, derived from creation, is, according to Calvin, a possibility in principle, but not in fact, not a possibility to be realized by us. One might call it an objective possibility, created by God, but not a subjective possibility, open to man. Between what is possible in principle and what is possible in fact there inexorably lies the fall. Hence this possibility can only be discussed hypothetically: *si integer stetisset Adam*" (*Inst.* I.2.1).[126]

When this debate focuses directly on Calvin, various conclusions are possible because Calvin does not unambiguously support either Brunner's or Barth's conclusions. Wisely, Calvin leaves unresolved, because unresolvable, the central issue of this debate. Barth is correct that Calvin has little to say on natural theology; Brunner is correct that Calvin has something to say on natural theology.

Recently Trevor Hart has addressed the topic in a chapter entitled "The Capacity for Ambiguity: Revisiting the Barth-Brunner Debate." According to

125. The debate seems to have achieved iconic status when Joan E. O'Donovan (without mentioning Calvin at all) can turn to it "with a view to clarifying their implications for theological ethics," especially for the definition of the human concluding in favor of Barth "that the transcendental-relational, Christological-Trinitarian conceptualization is the most theologically adequate and efficacious defense of human being" (Joan E. O'Donovan, "Man in the Image of God: The Disagreement between Barth and Brunner Reconsidered," *Scottish Journal of Theology* 39, no. 4 [November 1986]: 449, 435).

126. See *Natural Theology: Comprising "Nature and Grace" by Prof. Dr. Emil Brunner and the Reply "No" by Dr. Karl Barth*, trans. Peter Fraenkel (London: Centenary Press, 1946), 41, 106.

Hart, "The focus of this fierce disagreement was a fundamental question concerning the relationship between nature and grace, creation and redemption, state and church."[127] To Hart's list, divine and human, philosophy and theology, revelation and reason, freedom of will and bondage to sin, and even evangelism and social action might be added. Hart calls helpful attention to the differences between the two theologians in defining "capacity," but he does not sufficiently address the role of "ambiguity" in theology, which is crucial for comprehending Calvin.

Hart points out that the first requirement for understanding the debate between Barth and Brunner is to recognize its historical context in the 1930s. The German nation was still recovering from the First World War, and Karl Barth was reacting against his professors and the theology of Friedrich Schleiermacher. Most especially Barth's witness to the otherness of God encountered the election of Adolf Hitler and the rise of National Socialism. As the dark clouds of the Second World War gathered, the social, political, and theological situation led to the Confessing Church movement and the Barmen Declaration of 1934.[128] Barth vigorously opposed what he saw as accommodation of God to the nation-state, meaning Christians could derive their message from both divine revelation and natural reason. Concerning the quarrel with Brunner, Hart concludes, "It is important, when reading Barth's harsh and unrelenting response, to keep [this historical context] firmly in mind. Otherwise the passion and invective may seem unprovoked and inappropriate."[129] The theological issues can now be separated from the political context in which they were originally debated. Whatever needed to be said in that time, a somewhat cooler response is now appropriate. Barth, and some others but not all, recognized early the depraved nature of National Socialism and resisted

127. Trevor Hart, *Regarding Karl Barth: Essays toward a Reading of His Theology* (Cumbria, UK: Paternoster Press, 1999), 139.

128. A fine and moving survey is presented by Arthur C. Cochrane, *The Church's Confession under Hitler* (Pittsburgh, PA: Pickwick Press, 1976). Among the most harrowing accounts of the Nazi time are Jean-François Steiner, *Treblinka* (New York: New American Library, 1979), and Robert Jay Lifton, *The Nazi Doctors: Medical Killing and the Psychology of Genocide* (New York: Basic Books, 1986). See also Alan D. Beyerchen, *Scientists under Hitler: Politics and the Physics Community in the Third Reich* (New Haven, CT: Yale University Press, 1977), and Robert P. Ericksen, *Theologians under Hitler: Gerhard Kittel, Paul Althaus and Emanuel Hirsch* (New Haven, CT, and London: Yale University Press, 1985). Hirsch, the most impenitent Nazi, was "arguably the most gifted mind in German theology in the twentieth century." Jack Forstman, *Christian Faith in Dark Times: Theological Conflicts in the Shadow of Hitler* (Louisville: Westminster/John Knox, 1992), 216. Forstman's study indicates the theological social, political, and personal complexities of this time in Germany. See also Jean-Loup Seban, "The Theology of Nationalism of Emanuel Hirsch," *The Princeton Seminary Bulletin* 7, no. 2 (1986), 157–76, and Klaus Scholder, *The Churches and the Third Reich*, trans. John Bowden, 2 vols. (Philadelphia: Fortress, 1988).

129. Hart, *Regarding Karl Barth*, 148–49, 150. One hapless victim of this academic debate between the professors was Brunner's doctoral student Günter Gloede, whose *Theologia Naturalis bei Calvin* was published in 1935 (Stuttgart: Kohlhammer). Karl Barth's doctoral student, Wilhelm Niesel, called Gloede's book "a most comprehensive work" but nastily concluded, "This fullness, however, cannot conceal a disastrous lack of scholarly depth, so evident as to make his arguments invalid" (Niesel, 16–17). A more positive view of Gloede's work is given by Edward A. Dowey Jr., *The Knowledge of God*, 265–66, another doctoral student of Brunner.

wherever they were able. This included rejecting the conviction that Hitler's rise to power was to be understood as a revelation of God.

In his *Church Dogmatics* Barth claims that Brunner accepts "'a point of connection (*Anknüpfungspunkt*) for the divine message in man' undestroyed by sin, a questioning after God, 'natural to man.'"[130] Barth rejects Brunner's point of contact and Brunner's conception of the other task of theology, namely, a consideration of the person being addressed. Since Brunner insists that God the creator has established a point of contact with human beings,[131] Hart analyzes their difference of emphases under the category of "capacity." The difference could also be discussed under the uses and limitations of philosophy.

Barth concedes that human beings are not sticks or stones.[132] All people have a capacity for God in that very minimal sense. Nevertheless, Barth insists on the discontinuity between the Creator and creature requiring "a clear distinction being drawn between what is true of a person *as a creature*, by virtue of nature on the one hand, and, on the other, as the object and recipient of God's self-giving in grace." It is instructive that here Hart raises a pointed question and offers an ambiguous answer in the same sentence. He asks whether Barth's view of discontinuity allows "any genuine continuity to be acknowledged between God and humanity." His answer assumes there is a kind of genuine continuity, but "it is from moment to moment a matter of God's gracious action in the life of the particular creature, and never something which the creature possesses as such."[133] This answer contains the question of continuity-capacity in another form and assumes an answer that Brunner thought should be discussed. Since God's revelation allows and requires a human response, presumably this response can be analyzed, at least to some extent, even if God both establishes and maintains the human capacity to respond. When Barth rejects the language of "a human capacity for God," it is difficult to understand the phrase "God's gracious action *in* the life of a particular creature."

Brunner responded to Barth's attack in an irenic spirit, believing "there is between me and Barth no difference of opinion, except the one on the side of Barth that there is a difference of opinion."[134] Brunner agrees that the original image of God in humanity has been destroyed, but he is not willing to understand "destroyed" in an absolute sense. That is, the human capacity to be related to God has not become an incapacity. "No one who agrees that only human sub-

---

130. *CD* I.1.29.

131. Dealing with accommodation Brian Armstrong simply ignores Barth and repeats Brunner's point without argumentation. "[S]ince the end of theology is that we are led to the worship and adoration of God, it is essential that we apprehend what we can about the marvelous goodness of God in accommodating himself to our finitude by investing his mark on creation and so providing a *point of contact* with his creatures" (Armstrong, "Duplex Cognitio Dei," in *Probing the Reformed Tradition*, 144 [emphasis added]).

132. That human beings are not sticks or stones seems to come from Homer by way of Plato. "Friend, I am a man, and like other men, a creature of flesh and blood, and not 'of wood or stone' as Homer says" (Plato, *Apology*, 34e).

133. Hart, *Regarding Karl Barth*, 143.

134. Ibid., 151.

jects but not sticks and stones can receive the Word of God and the Holy Spirit can deny that there is such a thing as a point of contact for the divine grace of redemption."[135]

In addition to the argument over this "point of contact" Brunner championed a reflective prolegomena as another task of theology. On the contrary, Barth saw any discipline preliminary to dogmatics as an illegitimate task. According to Barth, dogmatics is not properly concerned to discuss the possibility of divine revelation but only its actuality.[136] In volume 1 of his *Dogmatics*, Brunner devotes more than one hundred pages to "Prolegomena." Declaring "Faith is the encounter with [Jesus Christ] not submission to a doctrine about Him," Brunner eschews traditional "Apologetics" as an unfortunate discipline. In its place he suggests Eristic theology, which he defines as "the intellectual discussion of the Christian Faith in the light of the ideologies of the present day which are opposed to the Christian message." In other words, Eristic theology attacks the reigning ideologies of each era, specifically "the self-understanding of the unbelieving 'natural' man."[137] Brunner's program requires the theologian to understand how the natural man thinks. The theologian must study and be willing to discuss philosophy, even though from a special angle. Thus, one of Brunner's early books was entitled *The Philosophy of Religion from the Standpoint of Protestant Theology*.[138]

135. *Natural Theology*, 31. Randall C. Zachman, "The Awareness of Divinity and the Knowledge of God in the Theology of Calvin and Schleiermacher," in *Revisioning the Past: Prospects in Historical Theology*, ed. Mary Potter Engel and Walter E. Wyman Jr. (Minneapolis: Fortress Press, 1992), 131–46, expounds together, and sees considerable continuity at a formal level among, Calvin's concept of the awareness of divinity, Schleiermacher's feeling of absolute dependence, and Brunner's point of contact (145). Zachman claims "the awareness of divinity is best understood as being a function of the conscience itself" (136–37), but the theological adequacy of the historical definition of conscience after Freud is just as "mysterious and elusive" as the sense of divinity.

136. Richard A. Muller, *Post-Reformation Reformed Dogmatics: The Rise and Development of Reformed Orthodoxy, ca. 1520 to ca. 1725*, vol. 1 (Grand Rapids: Baker Academic, 2003), 29, suggests that Protestant orthodoxy is relevant for Karl Barth because of his "sensitivity" to the importance of prolegomena. Given Barth's vigorous rejection of prolegomenon to theology, this is a strange use of the word "sensitivity."

137. Emil Brunner, *The Christian Doctrine of God*, trans. Olive Wyon (Philadelphia: Westminster Press, 1950), 510, 98, 101. In his *General Revelation* (Grand Rapids: Wm. B. Eerdmans, 1955), G. C. Berkouwer deals with Barth and his early opponents on natural theology. Barth, he says, thought the claim to know God apart from Christ was based on the analogy of being, which is the cardinal doctrine of the Roman Catholic Church and the invention of the antichrist (28).

138. On their differences see Daniel D. Williams, "Brunner and Barth on Philosophy," *Journal of Religion* 27 (1947): 241–54. Williams devotes most of his analysis to Brunner but concludes both are wrong because what is required is a theology that is both Christian and philosophical at the same time. See Emil Brunner, *The Philosophy of Religion from the Standpoint of Protestant Theology*, trans. A. J. D. Farrer and Bertram Lee Woolf (London: James Clarke, 1958). Karl Barth's view of the relation of Protestant theology and philosophy is helpfully gathered and translated in *The Way of Theology in Karl Barth: Essays and Comments*, ed. H. Martin Rumscheidt (Allison Park, PA: Pickwick Publications, 1986). Barth's brother, Heinrich, was an accomplished philosopher, and while Karl possessed a sophisticated knowledge of philosophy, his use and appreciation of the discipline was very different from his brother's and from Brunner's. Writing about the mystery of God's "worldliness," Barth indicates that God's speaking is never clearly marked off from other worldly events. Then he advises, "And let us not forget that theology in fact, so surely as it avails itself of human speech, is also a philosophy or a conglomerate of all sorts of philosophy" (*CD* 1.1.188). Brunner wanted to discuss in specific detail the use and abuse of philosophy in theology which Barth was willing to do only occasionally rather than systematically.

Brunner's Kierkegaardian attack on the essential sufficiency of reason apart from revelation[139] was based on his confidence that true understanding of the human condition led to the longing for God. Barth saw this question of "self-understanding" as unacceptable anthropology and not proper theology. He charged not only Brunner but more justly Friedrich Gogarten and Rudolf Bultmann with capitulating to "existential philosophy," and "trying to understand faith as a human possibility, or, if you will, as grounded in a human possibility, and therefore you are once again surrendering theology to philosophy."[140] Barth believed most passionately that prolegomena is not a question of what must be said before engaging in theology. Rather, prolegomena is properly "the things that must be said *first.*"[141]

Brunner agrees that the "old creation is not capable of the new creation—that is, there is nothing in the old Adam, the flesh which could simply be developed or extrapolated to posit the new Adam." Brunner also agrees "that the original image of God in man has been destroyed, that the *justitia originalis* has been lost." Nevertheless, he argues there is a kind of grace in nature, a "natural grace," if you will. Otherwise, revelation and redemption float in the air above us. That Barth's God is too much *over* us and too little *in* us was an early and persistent criticism. Brunner insists that we must be able to speak meaningfully about a "point of contact" for the saving action of God in humanity. Brunner explains the point of contact is not to be understood as a natural human possession. So far he agrees with Barth, but then Brunner employs the ancient philosophical distinction between form and matter. This abstraction allows Brunner to declare that while the "material" image of God is entirely lost, the "formal" image of God remains. There is then a human capacity to hear the Word of God which the Word creates. This assertion is having the point at issue both ways. Brunner wants to talk about the divinely created human capacity to hear. However, Brunner's "formal" image refers to this divinely created capacity to be addressed by God as natural. According to Brunner, "Only because humans can hear and understand the divine address is God able to speak to them."[142] Barth insists that the capacity to hear is a matter of God's grace, not of human nature—even a formal image as distinguished from a material image.

Brunner asserts that theology is not divine revelation but a product of the human capacity for rational thought in the service of the gospel. "The question is not whether there be such a positive relation between human reason and divine revelation, but in what it consists." Brunner charges that his opponents' view of human incapacity "has reached such a pitch of intensity that it becomes sheer nonsense." He concludes with the paradoxical and confessional doctrine of

139. Emil Brunner, *Revelation and Reason: The Christian Doctrine of Faith and Knowledge*, trans. Olive Wyon (Philadelphia: Westminster Press, 1946).

140. Letter to Bultmann, cited in Bruce L. McCormack, *Karl Barth's Critically Realistic Dialectical Theology: Its Genesis and Development, 1909–1936* (Oxford: Clarendon Press, 1995), 410.

141. *CD* 1.45.

142. Hart, *Regarding Karl Barth*, 152, 153, 158.

"personal communion"—God's gift requires a God-given human capacity to respond.[143] God's speaking to humans assumes their created capacity to hear. Brunner objects that Barth "quotes some twenty times from my pamphlet the words *Offenbarungsmächtigkeit des Menschen* (the human capacity for revelation) which I not only have never employed at all, but which I, as much as he, detest as heretical. The phrase I did use was that of *Wortmächtigkeit* (capacity for speech and understanding)."[144]

The debate between Brunner and Barth is, as Hart suggests, about "capacity." However, this question has almost nothing to do with the interpretation of Calvin's theology because their disagreement concerns a subtle and shifting question that Calvin neither posed nor answered. Both Barth and Brunner thought they saw the issue clearly and their debate is instructive as a modern disagreement between Reformed theologians on nature and grace and more especially the meaning of "Grace Alone." However, insofar as their debate concerned Calvin, Brunner and Barth read their own sharp conclusions about prolegomena and point of contact into Calvin's more open formulations.

The common background of this debate is the Thomistic view of "habitual grace" which all three Reformed theologians reject. According to Thomas Aquinas, grace *perfects* nature (*ST* I.8) which means nature is understood in fundamental continuity with grace. The Protestant version of this axiom, based on the conviction that the fall has not merely damaged but destroyed original nature, is that God's grace *overcomes* sinful human nature. Since Thomas believes nature is perfected by grace, he teaches a distinction between operating and cooperating grace. Cooperating grace is a gift of God infused by God into the soul (the doctrine of justification) and becomes habitual grace (the doctrine of sanctification), which is the principle of meritorious works.

Calvin explicitly rejected Thomas's optimistic view of a comfortable cooperation between God's gracious gift and the necessary human response to it. As Calvin phrases the question that Barth and Brunner debated, "It has not yet been demonstrated whether man has been wholly deprived of all power to do good (Barth's view), or still has some power, though meager and weak; a power, indeed, that can do nothing of itself (Brunner's view), but with the help of grace also does its part" (Thomas's view) (II.2.6). Calvin, Brunner, and Barth all reject the conclusion that "doing our part" means that "we cooperate with the assisting grace of God, because it is our right either to render it ineffectual by spurning the first grace, or to confirm it by obediently following it" (II.2.6). Thomas understands God's grace infused in humans becomes "habitual grace." Thomas writes, "The

143. Emil Brunner, *Man in Revolt: A Christian Anthropology*, trans. Olive Wyon (Philadelphia: Westminster Press, 1957), 536, 534, 541, 527.

144. Paul Lehmann, "Barth and Brunner: The Dilemma of the Protestant Mind," *Journal of Religion* 20 (1940): 124–40, supporting Brunner asserts that the great theological achievement of the Reformers was to maintain the dialectical relation between original and sinful humanity. Post-Reformation this distinction was compromised by fundamentalists and modernists. According to Lehmann the dilemma of the Protestant mind is that Barth is right in his attack on "natural theology" and wrong in his defense of "revealed theology."

term *habitus* [habit] is derived from *habere* [to have]. Now habit is taken from this word in two ways: in one way, inasmuch as man or any other being, is said to *have* something; in another way, inasmuch as something is disposed in a particular way either in regard to itself or in regard to something else" (*ST* I.II q.49.1).[145]

The three Reformed theologians reject the concepts of both infused grace and habitual grace. Calvin, Brunner, and Barth likewise reject the category of merit, congruent and condign, as opposed to a proper understanding of grace alone. Human beings come before God in the grace revealed in Jesus Christ and with no merit of their own. Grace is entirely God's gift and does not depend on human cooperation. This conviction is based on "taking sin seriously." Sin destroys rather than merely damages the natural relation to God. "Humans," Barth insists, "can no more contribute anything to that knowledge of God which alone saves them than they can bring anything to the throne of grace in order to secure divine favor."[146] So strongly does Barth emphasize actuality against any discussion of potentiality that he declares, "Grace is an event of personal approach, not a transferred tangible state of soul." Barth continues, "We do not regard [faith] as in any sense a possibility belonging to man."[147]

Turning to Brunner, Barth insists that "Man's capacity for God . . . has really been lost."

> The reconciliation of man with God in Christ includes in itself or else begins with the fresh establishment of the lost "point of contact." This point of contact is, therefore, not real outside faith but only in faith. In faith a man is created by the Word of God for the Word of God, existing in the Word of God, not in himself, not in virtue of his humanity and personality, nor from the standpoint of creation, for what is possible from the standpoint of creation from men to God has actually been lost through the Fall. Thus this point of contact also, like everything became real in faith, i.e. through the grace of reconciliation, can only be spoken of theologically, and not theologically and philosophically.[148]

Since Protestants believe grace overcomes nature instead of perfecting it, they generally understand God's grace to *replace* rather than merely *restore* fallen nature. However, the distinction between sin damaging or destroying our original nature is not absolute. Calvin insists that something of reason and will remains undestroyed in the human race (II.2.12). From this affirmation one can infer a natural human capacity to think and to choose, which God's grace having created and preserved employs without infusing, or—more precisely—reinfusing.

---

145. In his *Treatise on Christian Doctrine*, the Puritan poet-theologian John Milton moves in a Thomistic direction. Chapter 21 is devoted to engrafting in Christ. Engrafting is defined as a *habit* (!) produced by God, meaning that the understanding is restored in great part to its original clearness and the will restored to its original liberty.
146. Hart, *Regarding Karl Barth*, 150.
147. *CD* 1.44, 272–73.
148. Ibid., 273–74.

Granted "replacement" as the preferred term, one would still assume a capacity for replacement to be necessary even if maintenance is defined as continual replacement. Protestants believe that God's grace alone so creates the conditions for human response that it is not appropriate to speak of cooperating grace. This doxological language intended to give all glory to God is finally unable to define precisely the role of giver and receiver. Barth rightly wants to defend the sovereign grace of God revealed in Jesus Christ to us. Brunner rightly wants to defend the sovereign grace of God revealed in Jesus Christ not only over us, not only to us, but also in us. Barth understands Brunner to give into human possession (or capacity) a gift that has been stripped from the divine hands. Brunner understands Barth to deny that God's gift truly encounters human being. Calvin seems to have recognized that theological language appropriate to praise and glorify God the giver is not able and not necessary to define the capacity (or noncapacity) of the one being gifted as precisely as Barth and Brunner desire. The fine fury of Barth's "Nein" according to Brunner, and to me, ameliorated considerably over the years. In reviewing the *Doctrine of Man* in *Church Dogmatics* (3.2), Brunner claims the "new Barth" agrees with the "old Brunner." That is, Barth now admits a real human value in non-Christian wisdom the "wiser among the wise of this world." This "common ground" of Barth's is equivalent to Brunner's "point of contact."[149]

B. GOD'S PROVIDENCE

As the doctrine of creation exhibits God's power, the doctrine of providence exhibits God's grace. Calvin insists these doctrines belong together because the same God who creates the world also cares for it. Additionally, God's providential grace for all the world includes the human world. For that reason providence involves predestination, understood as special grace applied to the faithful. Calvin's view of predestination will be treated with more detail in the place where he locates it (Book III), but the recognition that providence and predestination (or eternal election) are interlocking doctrines is crucial to proper understanding.[150] The immensely learned Josef Bohatec asserts that predestination is Calvin's central teaching (*Zentrallehre*) but not in the sense of his dogmatic point of departure. On the contrary, the doctrine of providence is Calvin's root metaphor (*Stammlehre*).[151] The main theological concern in this portion of the *Institutes* is the relation between universal providence (sec. 2) and particular providence (sec. 3), but there are two other important issues—one philosophical

149. Emil Brunner, "The New Barth: Observations on Karl Barth's *Doctrine of Man*," trans. John C. Campbell, *Scottish Journal of Theology* 4 (1951): 123–35.
150. David F. Wright indicates this connection with the phrase "predestinating providence" ("Calvin's Role in Church History," in McKim, ed., *Cambridge Companion*, 287).
151. Josef Bohatec, "Calvins Vorsehungslehre," in *Calvinstudien: Festschrift zum 400. Geburstage Johann Calvins*, ed. J. Bohatec (Leipzig: Rudolf Haupt, 1909), 414.

(sec. 1) and one theological (sec. 4).[152] The philosophical issue is discussed in terms of the Epicureans and Stoics. The theological distinction between common and special grace is discussed last because the issue chiefly belongs to Calvin's interpreters rather than to Calvin himself.

For Calvin, to call God the Creator means that God governs all things, that we are God's children, and can expect all good things from God. The creation of the world demonstrates God's providential love for human beings. "[God] willed to commend his providence and fatherly solicitude toward us in that, before he fashioned man, he prepared everything he foresaw would be useful and salutary for him. How great ingratitude would it be now to doubt whether this most gracious father has us in his care, who we see was concerned for us even before we were born" (I.14.22). In her study of nature and natural order in Calvin entitled *The Theater of His Glory*, Susan E. Schreiner begins with the centrality of the doctrine of providence to Calvin's great concern for order, also treating the historical context of Calvin's attacks on Stoic and Epicurean errors. Among other helpful discussions are those on secondary causality, angels, the image of God, natural law, and redemption. The sharpest difference between Schreiner's interpretation and the present one is her conclusion: "All of his arguments show the same overriding concern: the attempt to find an indisputable foundation upon which to affirm that a reliable God controls a rational universe. The argument to which Calvin returned most frequently was based on the unchangeable nature of God's attributes."[153] Calvin is confessing the Christian faith more than advancing arguments to support it. Moreover, the God he finds is more sovereign and mysterious than reliable and comprehensible. The universe, while orderly, is beyond human concepts of rationality, and Calvin has relatively little to say about God's attributes. The foundation of his doctrine of providence is God's love. The divine attributes do not serve as a logical starting point from which one must rationally conclude that God continues "to care for and govern his creation."

Calvin devotes three chapters to the doctrine of providence following his exposition of creation (I.16–18). In declaring that "ignorance of providence is the ultimate of all miseries; the highest blessedness lies in the knowledge of it" (I.17.11), Calvin reveals one of his most profoundly held convictions. Forstman correctly observes that the exposition of providence approaches more nearly the tone of ecstasy than any other section of the *Institutes*.[154] In his fine survey of the doctrine Benjamin Farley asserts, "The providence of God is a doctrine of faith.

---

152. In surveying providence from Plato to Schleiermacher, Richard Baepler suggests Plato's affinity with all Christian thinkers in that Plato "set down life in a rational and providentially ordered universe" (Richard Baepler, "Providence in Christian Thought" in *The Caring God: Perspectives on Providence*, ed. Carl S. Meyer and Herbert T. Mayer (St. Louis: Concordia Publishing House, 1973), 45–66.
153. Schreiner, *Theater of His Glory*, 33.
154. Forstman, *Word and Spirit*, 98. The cool, rational, scholastic exposition in Heppe's chapter (12) on "Providence" detailing the threefold activity of preservation, concurrence, and government, of primary and secondary causes, contingency and necessity strikes a very different tone from Calvin's passionate celebration of God's care for all things.

It is neither a postulate of reason or science nor a philosophical position. It is a conviction of faith, based on revelation."[155] Dealing with Augustine and Calvin under the rubric of traditional views of providence, Langdon Gilkey addresses Calvin's understanding of prosperity and adversity, concluding, "God's providence uses the events of history to bring his elect inwardly and so freely to their promised eschatological destiny." Calvin is aware that the tragedies of life are real calamities. Only an eschatological solution is possible. Within God's ordaining providence human life is directed to a transcendent goal.[156]

In the three major revisions of the *Institutes* (1536, 1539, 1559) Calvin attempted to explain this conviction more clearly, adding, rearranging, synthesizing.[157] In 1536 providence is treated as part of the belief in God the Father, Creator. What God has "once established, so now he sustains, nourishes, activates, [and] preserves . . . Therefore whatever may finally happen, we are never to doubt or lose faith that we have in him a propitious and benevolent Father, and no less are to await salvation from him."[158] In this edition, election or predestination is mentioned in connection with the church. Those who are called to be the people of God are also called into the one holy catholic church. Calvin demonstrates the closeness of providence and predestination (and sanctification!) in this comment, "As many as have been chosen [*electus*] by God's eternal providence to be adopted as members of the church—all these are made holy by the Lord."[159]

In the edition of 1539 Calvin devotes an entire chapter to predestination and providence, in that order. He begins with the observation that the covenant of life is not equally preached to all, and where it is preached is not equally received. The fact that some reject and others accept the gospel is referred to the mystery

---

155. Benjamin Wirt Farley, *The Providence of God* (Grand Rapids: Baker Book House, 1988), 18.

156. Gilkey, *Reaping the Whirlwind*, 183. Gilkey believes the modern consciousness of history was "formed largely by Augustine and later developed by Calvin" (159). Gilkey's interpretation, tinted or tainted by the theology of Paul Tillich, regards providence as "that symbol which describes the activity or 'role' of God in the world as a whole over the entire course of time" (160). He claims Calvin is interested in doctrines only as they provide "a symbolic framework for faithful obedience" (177). Calvin did not think his doctrine of providence was the exposition of a symbol system but the proclamation of the gospel truth. Among Gilkey's other writing is the splendid *Shantung Compound* (San Francisco: Harper Collins, 1966). As a young college graduate Gilkey went to China to teach, following in the steps of the once-famous Horace Tracy Pitkin, who was murdered in the Boxer Rebellion. Gilkey, interned by the Japanese, wrote a fascinating account of his experiences and observations, including the death of the great Eric Liddle, subject of the movie *Chariots of Fire* and a fine biography (Russell W. Ramsey, *God's Joyful Runner* [South Plainfield, NJ: Bridge Publishers, 1987]). *Shantung Compound* stands with other imprisonment classics, including Dostoevsky's *Notes from the Underground*, and Helmut Gollwitzer, *Unwilling Journey, A Diary from Russia*, trans. E. M. Delacour (London: SCM Press, 1953). Ernest Gordon's *Through the Valley of the Kwai* (New York: Harper and Brothers, 1962) is a harrowing account of the railroad of death made familiar by the movie *The Bridge on the River Kwai*. See also Karl and Debbie Dortzbach, *Kidnapped* (New York: Harper and Row, 1975). Debbie's mother was the first-grade teacher of our two oldest children.

157. The development of a doctrine in the mind of a theologian through years of reflection is always interesting to trace. Calvin's development of his doctrine of providence is an improvement. The same cannot be said of his eucharistic doctrine.

158. John Calvin, *Institution of the Christian Religion (1536)*, trans. and annotated by Ford Lewis Battles (Atlanta: John Knox, 1975), 66–67.

159. Ibid., 78–79.

of divine wisdom. Everyone is not created equally; "rather eternal life is foreordained for some and eternal damnation for others" (III.21.5). Calvin insists that
this view brings great comfort because predestination "builds up faith soundly,
trains us to humility, elevates us to admiration of the immense goodness of God
towards us, and excites us to praise this goodness."[160] Providence is defined as
God's governance of the world determining what he will do by his power and
executing it by his will.

The final edition of the *Institutes* in Latin (1559) and French (1560) represents a third stage. Here the main exposition of providence precedes predestination. Calvin does not explain his reasons for this new location, although he
declares in the preface to the 1559 edition of the *Institutes* that he "was never satisfied until the work had been arranged in the order now set forth" (LCC, 3).
Providence is treated as the completion of the doctrine of creation and predestination is part of the perception of the grace of Christ. One may, with Bohatec,
regard providence as Calvin's foundational doctrine, but Calvin's strong doctrine
of providence is here understood to be based on his even stronger conviction of
union with Christ.

Although Calvin's expositions of providence and predestination are widely
separated in 1559, the most important theological point is their continuing commonality. In broad terms providence is concerned with God's work in creation;
predestination is concerned with God's work in redemption. Since the Creator
and Redeemer is one God and the created and redeemed being is one person, it
is essential to recognize that the God who elects by his providence also provides
for his elect. In other words, God's special or particular providence for the elect
is indistinguishable from predestination. Among the basic doctrines that may be
distinguished but not divided are creation and redemption, providence and predestination, justification and sanctification.

In his final exposition of the doctrine of providence Calvin attacks the Epicurean and Stoic view of providence, clarifies the meaning of universal providence, and asserts the crucial theological role of particular providence. In one
form or another, God's relation to what happens in the world is a very old problem. In the ancient world the Epicureans (whose name is now associated with the
search for pleasure) championed the idea that the world was governed by chance
or fortune. They believed that things happen in unpredictable ways without reasons or causes. Therefore, a happy result might occur if one got "lucky." To the
contrary, the Stoics (now associated with lives of somber resignation) believed
everything that happened was determined and therefore occurred by necessity or
fate. In an important sense, providence for Christians may be understood as a
golden mean between the extremes of Epicurean chance and Stoic necessity. Epicureans believed that the world is the product of sheer chance (fortune). Therefore the world is neither designed nor governed. Everything that happens is a
matter of pure luck. Stoics argued that the world is the result of inexorable deter-

160. *Concerning the Eternal Predestination of God,* 56.

minism. Free will is an illusion since every effect has a fixed cause (fate). Christians deny Stoicism and Epicureanism and see the doctrine of providence as another way of affirming God's love.

While some thinkers attempt to affirm God the Creator without affirming God as Governor and Preserver, Calvin teaches that God as Creator is not properly understood unless we pass on to providence. If God were not Creator it would be difficult to believe that God cares for human affairs, but since God is the Creator one should also be persuaded that God takes care of his works. According to Calvin:

> To make God a momentary Creator, who once for all finished his work, would be cold and barren, and we must differ from profane men especially in that we see the presence of divine power shining as much in the continuing state of the universe as in its inception. . . . Faith ought to penetrate more deeply, namely, having found him Creator of all, forthwith to conclude he is also everlasting Governor and Preserver—not only in that he drives the celestial frame as well as its several parts by a universal motion, but also in that he sustains, nourishes, and cares for, everything he has made, even to the least sparrow [cf. Matt. 10:29]. . . . All parts of the universe are quickened by God's secret inspiration. (I.16.1)

Providence is simply defined as God's governance of all events (I.16.2). This governance requires for its proper understanding the rejection of the Epicurean view of fortune and the Stoic view of fate. While Calvin's doctrine of providence is often connected to Stoicism, he vehemently denies the association. Calvin insists that God's providence excludes chance and necessity.

1. Epicurean Chance and Stoic Fate

a. The Epicureans

Epicureanism, like Stoicism, is a philosophy of salvation that seeks human happiness in a proper relation to the world. The Epicureans were (and are) popularly thought to teach that the world is randomly governed by fortune, thereby denying divine purpose and order. The Stoics were (and are) popularly understood to believe that the world is rigidly ruled by necessity, in effect denying human freedom and responsibility. Calvin opposes both views. Interestingly, Calvin was aware that the Stoics make some room for freedom by their refusal to apply providence to small things. Likewise, Calvin recognized the Epicureans had a view of both chance and necessity, insisting they cannot excuse their actions by objecting they are constrained by the necessity of divine predestination (III.23.8). Against the Epicureans he insists that everything is governed by God. Against the Stoics, who insist that everything is governed by God, Calvin attacks their ignorance of God's particular providence. According to Calvin, those who do not understand the providence of God are fools. Among these fools he places Aristotle and the Epicureans, as the following quote demonstrates.

We find that some of the greatest of philosophers were so mischievous as to devote their talents to obscure and conceal the providence of God, and, entirely overlooking his agency, ascribed all to secondary causes. At the head of these was Aristotle, a man of genius and learning; but being a heathen, whose heart was perverse and depraved, it was his constant aim to entangle and perplex God's overruling providence by a variety of wild speculations; so much so, that it may with too much truth be said, that he employed his naturally acute powers of mind to extinguish all light. Besides, the prophet not only condemns the insensate Epicureans, whose sensibility was of the basest character, but he also informs us that a blindness, still greater and more detestable, was to be found among these great philosophers themselves. (Com. Ps. 107.43)

Epicurus believed that the gods exist, but being perfect they did not create the world and being perfectly happy they can have no concern or care for it. The universe is without divine cause and without divine design. To the atomic theory of Democritus, Epicurus added radical contingency with the notion that the atoms have a random capacity to swerve away from the straight line of fall. To the contrary, Calvin objects: "What good is it to profess some sort of God who has cast aside the care of the world only to amuse himself in idleness? What help is it, in short, to know a God with whom we have nothing to do?" (I.2.2). Calvin insists, "Nobody seriously believes that the universe was made by God without being persuaded that he takes care of his works" (I.16.1). "We must know that God's providence, as it is taught in Scripture, is opposed to fortune and fortuitous happenings. Now it has been commonly accepted in all ages, and almost all mortals hold the same opinion today, that all things come about through chance. What we ought to believe concerning providence is by this depraved opinion most certainly not only beclouded, but almost buried" (I.16.2). Calvin then offers the following situations that are commonly supposed to illustrate good or bad luck. "Suppose a man falls among thieves, or wild beasts; is shipwrecked at sea by a sudden gale; is killed by a falling house or tree. Suppose another man wandering through the desert finds help in his straits; having been tossed by the waves, reaches harbor, miraculously escapes death by a finger's breadth. Carnal reason ascribes all such happenings, whether prosperous or adverse, to fortune."

In opposition Calvin concludes, "Anyone who has been taught by Christ's lips that all the hairs of his head are numbered [Matt. 10:30] will look farther afield for a cause, and will consider that all events are governed by God's secret plan" (I.16.2).

Calvin summarizes his objections to the Epicureans in the following comment:

[The Epicurean] philosophy was to think that the sun is two feet wide, that the world was constructed out of atoms, and by trifling like that, to destroy the wonderful craftsmanship which is seen in the fabric of the world. If they were refuted a hundred times, they had no more sense than dogs. Although, briefly, they admitted that there were gods, yet they imagined them to be idle in heaven and to be applying to magnificence of living, and that their blessing consisted in idleness alone. As they used to deny that the world was divinely created, as I have just said, so they supposed human affairs are turned by chance, and are not governed by the providence of heaven. To them the greatest good was pleasure, not obscene and unbridled pleasure indeed, but yet such as by its attractions more and more ruined men already naturally inclined to the indulgence of the flesh. The immortality of souls was like a fairy tale to them, so that the result was that they freely allowed the indulgence of their bodies. (Com. Acts 17.28)

Contrary to the Epicurean view, the world is governed by God and in God's governance is our hope and consolation. Calvin concludes, with Basil the Great, that "fortune" and "chance" are pagan terms with whose significance the minds of the pious ought not to be occupied (I.16.8). The believer "permits every part of his life to be governed by God's will" and does not complain of his lot. There are "many chance happenings to which we are subject," such as disease, plague, war, storm, poverty, but whatever happens is ordained by God. Although these calamities are declared "chance happenings," Calvin concludes, "Especially let that foolish and most miserable consolation of the pagans be far away from the breast of the Christian man; to strengthen their minds against adversities, they charged these to fortune. . . . On the contrary, the rule of piety is that God's hand alone is the judge and governor of fortune, good or bad, [and] with most orderly justice deals out good as well as ill to us" (III.7.10).

b. The Stoics

Calvin's first book (published April 4, 1532) was a commentary on Seneca's *De Clementia*. The young humanist praises the Stoics "who attribute the superintendance of human affairs to the gods, assert providence, and leave nothing to mere chance." He criticizes, "The Epicureans, although they do not deny the existence of the gods, do the closest thing to it; they imagine the gods to be pleasure-loving, idle, not caring for mortals. They think everything happens by mere chance."[161] The Stoics did not entirely deny chance, but sought to rise above its power by reason. Seneca reasons thusly, "Of what avail is philosophy, if God rules the universe? Of what avail is it, if Chance governs everything? For not only is it impossible to change things that are determined, but it is also impossible to plan beforehand against what is undetermined; either God has forestalled my plans, and decided what I am to do, or else Fortune gives no free play to my plans." Whatever the truth might be, whether fate binds us inexorably, whether God arranges everything, or whether chance tosses us about, philosophy "will teach us to follow God and endure Chance."[162]

Since the Stoics believed that the world was ruled by Providence, they considered the Epicureans to be atheists. Cicero complains, "There are and have been philosophers who hold that the gods exercise no control of human affairs what-

---

161. *Calvin's Commentary on* Seneca's *De Clementia*, ed. and trans. Ford Lewis Battles and André Malan Hugo (Leiden: E. J. Brill, 1969), 28–31.
162. Seneca, *Epistulae Morales*, 90.1.5.

ever. But if their opinion is the true one, how can piety, reverence or religion exist?"[163] Cicero has Quintus define fate as follows, "By Fate I mean the same that the Greeks call εἱμαρμένη, that is, an orderly succession of causes, wherein cause is linked to cause and each cause of itself produces an effect."[164] Both Greek and Roman Stoics thought salvation could be found in the austere philosophical quest to "follow nature." This Nature or ultimate reality is variously named God, Fate, Necessity, or Providence to which human beings are related by reason (*logos*). Of all the classical thinkers the Stoics had the most developed concept of providence since the word only appears twice in the New Testament (Acts 24:2; Rom. 13:14). In an important sense the Stoics created the doctrine of providence (Greek πρόνοια, Latin *providentia*).

Calvin's doctrine of providence or predestination is often charged with being a Christian version of the Stoic view of necessity that all things happen in an inexorable nexus of causes and effects. Calvin complains that those who say his view of providence is the same as the Stoic dogma of fate attack him falsely and maliciously. Fate, he insists, is a concept that oppresses God's truth. Calvin distinguishes his doctrine of providence from the Stoic doctrine of fate by insisting as follows:

> We do not, with the Stoics, contrive a necessity out of the perpetual connection and intimately related series of causes, which is contained in nature; but we make God the ruler and governor of all things, who in accordance with his wisdom has from the farthest limit of eternity decreed what he was going to do, and now by his might carries out what he has decreed. From this we declare that not only heaven and earth and the inanimate creatures, but also the plans and intentions of men, are so governed by his providence that they are borne by it straight to their appointed end. (I.16.8)

In his fine article P. H. Reardon demonstrates that the young Calvin was at home in the world of Stoic thought on providence but not preoccupied with it.[165] Reardon correctly notes that the "Christocentricity of God's Providence in Calvin's thinking is not to be overlooked"[166] and concludes "that Calvin, in spite of certain similarities with the Stoic view of Providence, was moved by a different spirit and directed by another insight. [Calvin's view] was inspired by the biblical belief in God's action in history."[167]

As one would expect, in commenting on Acts 17:16–17. Calvin deals at some length on Paul's encounter with the "customary impudence" of the Epicureans and the "subtle and fallacious arguments" of the Stoics. Nevertheless, after sharply rejecting the Epicurean view of fortune and the Stoic view of fate, Calvin returns

163. *De Natura Deorum*, 1.2.3.
164. *De Divinatione*, 1.55.125.
165. P. H. Reardon, "Calvin on Providence: The Development of an Insight," *Scottish Journal of Theology* 28, no. 6 (December 1975): 519, 523.
166. Ibid., 531.
167. Ibid., 533.

to a puzzling proximity with both. While Calvin rejects the Stoic concept of necessity, he teaches that all things are determined by God.[168] We shall return to this topic in the discussion of predestination. Concerning Epicurean fortune, Calvin writes,

> Yet since the sluggishness of our mind lies far beneath the height of God's providence, we must employ a distinction to lift it up. Therefore I shall put it this way: however all things may be ordained by God's plan, according to a sure dispensation, for us they are fortuitous. Not that we think that fortune rules the world and men, tumbling all things at random up and down, for it is fitting that this folly be absent from the Christian's breast! But since the order, reason, end and necessity of those things which happen for the most part lie hidden in God's purpose, and are not apprehended by human opinion, those things, which it is certain take place by God's will, are in a sense fortuitous. (I.16.9)

This comment suggests that some events appear to be contingent and one may act as if they are, but one may not believe in fortune because necessity is hidden in God.[169]

2. Providence as Universal

In developing his doctrine of providence, Calvin accepts the traditional distinction between universal (or general) and particular (or special) providence. The former emphasizes that God created and keeps all things in their continuing reality. Special providence focuses on direct care for individual things. In making this distinction one might expect universal providence as the wider and more inclusive category to be developed as the context for the narrower category, particular providence. This conclusion is so logical that many students erroneously believe that Calvin thought the same way. The distinction between common and special grace is motivated by the underlying conviction that Calvin is a rationalist building a theological system. Wilhelm Niesel correctly observes that "Calvin's theology does not proceed by successive thoughts."[170] The insight that Calvin's

---

168. Concerning foreordination, Robert Ayers charges that Calvin falls into the pit of inconsistency and obscurity. "There are passages which clearly support the view that everything that happens, happens by necessity (cf. I.16.1, 2, 3, 4, 5, 6, 7, 8, 9; II.2.1; II.4.7; III.4.34) and yet there are also passages in which Calvin exhorts his readers to apply their minds and efforts to sincere repentance, to strive towards the goal of perfection, to have a zeal for daily progress, to exercise patience as they await a blessed hope, to render an account of their lives, and to lead sinners to repentance (III.3.25; III.6.2, 3, 4; III.7.1; III.25.1, 7; IV.12.8)" (Robert H. Ayers, "Language, Logic and Reason in Calvin's *Institutes*," *Religious Studies* 16 [1980]: 283–84). Ayers is quite right about Calvin's language judged from a logical and reasonable point of view. However, Calvin's thoughts need not be judged by philosophical canons of logical coherence but by theological accuracy in confession.

169. For a more extended discussion see my *Calvin and Classical Philosophy* (Louisville, KY: Westminster John Knox Press, 2005), chaps. 7–9.

170. Niesel applies this comment to the relation of Creator and Redeemer. He writes, "Calvin's theology does not proceed by successive thoughts, as though the recognition of a Savior God were inferred from the recognition of a Creator God" (71).

theology does not proceed by "successive thoughts" applies to universal and particular providence in the sense that Calvin does not infer the latter from the former, although a number of "Calvinists" think he does or should.

Calvin certainly asserts God's universal providence. However, while Calvin firmly believes in God's universal providence, he focuses on special providence because he thinks more in experiential and personal terms than in logically impersonal categories. Logical deduction is often defined as moving from the general to the particular while induction moves from the particular to the general. The advantage of deduction is that if the general category is established, then the special category can be developed within it. The process of induction on the other hand requires that each step beyond the particular be correct in order to arrive at a general conclusion. Deduction is the way of rationalism and the intellect; induction is the way of empiricism and experience. By his interpreters Calvin's theology as a whole is often explicated as a rational system of thought, and this approach is especially evident in his doctrine of providence. Nevertheless, however logical and necessary it may appear, to explain and expand Calvin's view of universal providence (or common grace) as the context for his doctrine of special providence distorts his theology. Calvin writes, "I do not wholly repudiate what is said concerning universal providence provided they in turn grant me that the universe is ruled by God, not only because he watches over the order of nature set by himself, but because he exercises especial care over each of his works" (I.16.4). Clearly Calvin affirms universal providence, but even more clearly he insists on God's special providence for each of his works.[171] The following citation makes this point perfectly clear. "The providence of God [is extended] in a general sense to all creatures, that by arguing from greater to less he may prove that we are kept under his special care." Philosophers "conceive of a diffuse kind of providence, as if God had no concern for individual creatures. But Christ asserts, that each single creature is distinctly under God's hand and protection, that nothing may be left open to chance" (Com. Mt. 10:29). General or "greater" providence is affirmed but the purpose of doing so is to express God's "special care." Philosophers are aware of a universal or "diffuse kind of providence" but "Christ asserts, that each single creature is distinctly under God's hand."

According to Calvin, the Scripture praises God's *general* providence, but particular events are testimonies to God's *singular* providence, especially for mankind. Three things are to be noted, says Calvin (I.17.1): First, God's providence applies to the future as well as the past. Future events indeed appear fortuitous to us, but in our hearts we know that God turns every event whatever way he wills. "God's will is the highest and first cause of all things because nothing happens except from his command or permission" (I.16.8). Here God's command, decree, and permission seem to be equivalent for Calvin (cf. I.18.1). Second, God's providence "is the determinative principle of all things in such a way

---

171. See chap. 9, "Calvin on Universal and Particular Providence," in my *Calvin and Classical Philosophy*.

that sometimes it works through an intermediary, sometimes without an intermediary, sometimes contrary to every intermediary." Finally, God's providence reveals God's "concern for the whole human race, but especially his vigilance in ruling the church, which he deigns to watch more closely."

3. Providence as Particular

Every Christian theology has some kind of doctrine of God's general or universal providence. Disagreements begin with the specificity of the application of providence. Often a comfortable gap is allowed between general and special providence, which is thought to encourage the exercise of human responsibility and accountability. Calvin's conviction about the particularity of God's providence closes this gap. Providence generally refers to God's universal care of all the world but in Calvin's theology God's particular care of everything in the world receives strong emphasis. Since Calvin does not deny universal providence, the concept may be expanded by the will and conviction of the interpreter.

Nevertheless, careful attention to the text demonstrates Calvin's passion to insist that each thing and each person is in God's hand. God is known in creation and providence. Calvin insists, "We see the presence of divine power as much in the continuing state of the universe as in its inception" (I.16.1). The sun and seasons are so governed by the special providence of God that no drop of rain falls without his command (I.16.5). No wind arises or increases without God's will (I.16.7). The splendor of divine providence is also revealed by infants. "David exclaims that infants still nursing at their mothers' breasts are eloquent enough to celebrate God's glory for immediately in coming forth from the womb, they find food prepared for them by his heavenly care." According to Calvin the availability of mothers' milk is determined by God's providence. Experience, he says, plainly demonstrates "that some mothers have full and abundant breasts, but others' are almost dry, as God wills to feed one [baby] more liberally, but another more meagerly" (I.16.3). On this trip down mammary lane Calvin's doxological intention is praiseworthy, but his biological understanding is faulty.

Such enthusiastic statements about special providence could be understood as absolute divine determinism but Calvin insists that God

> who has set the limits to our life has at the same time entrusted to us its care; he has provided means and helps to preserve it; he has also made us able to foresee dangers; that they may not overwhelm us unaware, he has offered precautions and remedies. Now it is very clear what our duty is: thus, if the Lord has committed to us the protection of our life, our duty is to protect it; if he offers helps, to use them; if he forewarns us of dangers, not to plunge headlong; if he makes remedies available, not to neglect them. . . . The Lord has inspired in men the arts of taking counsel and caution, by which to comply with his providence in the preservation of life itself: Just as, on the contrary, by neglect and slothfulness they bring upon themselves the ills that he has laid upon them. (I.17.4)

God's particular care for every human being makes impossible a conceptual separation of providence from predestination. So perspicacious a scholar as Wendel suggests, "Predestination can in fact be regarded as in some respects a particular application of the more general notion of Providence."[172] The phrase "in some respects" provides a slight latitude for interpretation, but the conclusion here is to the contrary. At the pulsating heart of Calvin's theology is the conviction that Jesus Christ is Lord and by God's grace his elect are indissoluably united with him. Providence should therefore be regarded as a universal application of the more crucial notion of predestination. In other words, providence is the doctrine of predestination applied universally to the world, and predestination is the doctrine of particular providence applied directly to individuals.

Calvin certainly affirms a doctrine of universal providence, but he declares that only believers can trace the workings of divine providence. Commenting on the mouths of babes and sucklings (Ps. 8:2), Calvin declares the tongues of infants hanging on the breast and not yet able to speak are nevertheless eloquent in celebration of God's providence. "The providence of God, I confess, shines forth principally for the sake of the faithful, because they only have eyes to behold it." Calvin warns of the dangers of "vain subtleties" for those who do not use the doctrine rightly (I.17.1). Still he affirms God's care of all things with the assumption that most people agree. While universal providence undoubtedly forms the background for Calvin's understanding, it is not the primary focus of his exposition. In summary, Calvin does not first explain universal providence and then turn to special providence. Rather he assumes that God's universal providence is generally understood and accepted, placing a profound emphasis on particular providence, which reappears later in the *Institutes* as eternal election or predestination. Calvin declares that no one understands God's providence properly except those who recognize that in everything we deal with God (I.17.2).

4. Common and Special Grace

That the categories Calvin uses to explain God's providence are not uniform should cause no surprise. The question is whether going farther down that road leads to a pleasant vista or a tangled wood. Calvin maintains the fundamental conviction that in everything we deal with God (I.17.2), but his discussion of common and special grace is multiform. For example, P. H. Reardon appreciates the categories Calvin employed in his 1545 *Treatise Against the Libertines*. In this work Calvin considers God's governance under three aspects. The first is the order of nature as established by God. The second is God's direction of all things, helping his servants and punishing the wicked. Believers understand this aspect of providence to be both universal and special. The third aspect is God's governance of the faithful by the Holy Spirit. Reardon observes, "Nowhere are his

172. Wendel, 178.

distinctions on the subject [of providence] so clear as in the *Treatise Against the Libertines.*"[173]

Another set of categories is advanced by Étienne de Peyer who thinks, "General Providence gives to human nature its plenitude and completion. Particular Providence directs the effects of this nature. Saving Providence brings to man the elements of a new nature or of nature restored." De Peyer believes that particular providence is identical with common grace. Thus he outlines Calvin's doctrine of providence as (1) general providence, (2) particular providence or common grace, and (3) special providence or saving grace.[174] Calvin does discuss general or universal providence and special or particular providence, also general or common grace and special grace, but Calvin does not develop his doctrine of providence as sharply in the categories de Peyer suggests. Calvin's basic distinction is twofold rather than tripartite. Common grace ought to be associated with universal providence and special grace with particular providence.

Of more historical and theological importance are the views of those who seek to improve Calvin's exposition of providence by developing a comprehensive doctrine of common grace. Hermann Bavinck thinks that Calvin finds the will of God revealed in the Bible and in the world. "Though this gracious and omnipotent will of God is made known in the Gospel alone and experienced in faith only, nevertheless it does not stand isolated, but is encompassed, supported, and reinforced by the operation of the same will in the world at large. Special grace is encircled by common grace."[175] It is not clear how Bavinck understands the modifiers "alone" and "only" in the context of "encompassed, supported, and reinforced," but it is clear he is expanding the concept of common grace.

A great deal of attention has been devoted to common grace by some Calvin scholars. They enlarge and schematize Calvin's profoundly held but not deeply analyzed remarks on the closely related topics of natural or general revelation, universal providence, and common grace. Herman Kuiper claims that Calvin is the discoverer of the doctrine of common grace whose purpose is to deny the dichotomy between nature and grace represented to some extent by Luther but mainly associated with Thomas Aquinas. Calvin accounted for the good found in the unregenerate with the concept of common grace. "He was the first theologian who made a clear-cut distinction between common and saving grace, between the operations of the Spirit of God which are common to mankind at large and the sanctifying work of the same Spirit which is limited to God's elect." Kuiper admits the term "common grace" is used by Calvin only four times.[176] In

---

173. Reardon, "Calvin on Providence," 529–30; see also my *Calvin and Classical Philosophy*, 126–27.

174. Étienne de Peyer, "Calvin's Doctrine of Providence," *Evangelical Quarterly* 10 (1938): 37.

175. Hermann Bavinck, "Calvin and Common Grace," *Calvin and the Reformation* (New York: Fleming H. Revell Co., 1909), 126.

176. Herman Kuiper, *Calvin on Common Grace* (Grand Rapids: Smitter Book Co., 1928), 2. Kuiper did not find a single instance in which Calvin actually used the term "common grace" (*gratia communis*) and only four where *gratia* and *communis* are connected (Com. Am. 9:7; Com. Col. 1:20; Com. Heb. 1:5; and Com. Rom. 5:18) (177–78).

Romans Calvin declares, "Paul makes grace common to all men, not because it in fact extends to all, but because it is offered to all" (Com. Rom. 3:18). On John 3:27 Calvin comments, "No one can receive anything except what is given him from above." This "gift" is a special illumination, not a common endowment of nature (II.2.20). As God's gifts are special not common, so are the virtues of pagans not common gifts of nature, but special graces of God, which God bestows variously (II.3.4). The point is that Calvin does not deny but affirms a kind of common grace, but in a general way.[177] Nevertheless he is chiefly concerned to confess God's special or particular grace and not chiefly concerned to create a system of compatible concepts.

Since the order of logic posits that the larger category includes the smaller category, Calvin's doctrine of providence might be enlarged in the direction of a comprehensive doctrine of common grace. However, it is important to the correct understanding of Calvin's theology to recognize that Calvin himself did not do so. Calvin asserts God's universal providence but his main emphasis is on God's particular providence or special grace. According to Calvin God watches over the order of nature but exercises special care over each of his works (I.16.4). Calvin's chief insistence is that all things are directly governed by God's will. This discussion involves the terms "universal" and "particular providence" and "common" and "special grace," but common grace is not the presupposition and context of special grace.

One could admit that Calvin's own exposition of the doctrine of providence in the *Institutes* focuses chiefly on particular providence, and still insist that further theological reflection requires an extended exposition of universal providence. Obviously this conclusion cannot be resolved by appeal to the text since there is textual agreement. The issue remains whether the development of a more comprehensive doctrine of universal providence improves Calvin's theology. This is a theological judgment based in part on the conviction that Calvin's theology represents a logical system in which expanding his statements clarifies rather than distorts them. Certainly Calvin affirms God's universal providence, but he does not develop this concept as a presupposition to particular providence. Instead Calvin's doctrine of providence directly addresses Christian believers and only incidentally general mankind. The proper interpretation of the text demonstrates that Calvin, being a theologian and not a philosopher, is faithful in confessing God's direct care of all things and wise in not trying to determine precisely the

177. See also Abraham Kuyper, *De Gemeene Gratie*, 3 vols. (Pretoria: Hoveker and Wormser, 1902–4): Hermann Bavinck, *De Algemeene Genade* (Kampen: G. Ph. Zalsman, 1894); Cornelius van Til, *Common Grace* (Philadelphia: Presbyterian and Reformed, 1947); H. Henry Meeter, *Calvinism: An Interpretation of Its Basic Ideas* (Grand Rapids: Zondervan, 1939), 69–77. See also William Masselink, *General Revelation and Common Grace* (Grand Rapids: Eerdmans, 1953): chap. 5 on common grace, chap. 7 on Calvinistic philosophy. Also the essay by A. Lecerf, "Le protestantisme et la philosophie," in *Études Calvinistes* (Paris: Delachaux et Niestlé, 1949), 107–13; J. M. Spier, *What Is Calvinistic Philosophy?* trans. Fred H. Klooster (Grand Rapids: Eerdmans, 1953); and William Young, *Toward a Reformed Philosophy* (Grand Rapids: Piet Hein, 1952).

level of direct or indirect care various degrees of nonbelievers receive because they are logically included in the phrase "of all things."

CONCLUSIONS TO BOOK I

Among the benefits to be derived from Book I of Calvin's *Institutes* is, first, the irenic recognition that the continuing *use* of Scripture does not require an exhaustive formulation of its *nature*. Second, sharp warnings about false gods are always necessary and urgent. Third, the church and its theologians would be more respectable if they were more responsible in affirming ineffable mystery in exposition of their doctrine of the Trinity. However, the two main themes of Book I are our knowledge of God the Creator and our knowledge of the Creator's providence.

Calvin does not explicate a theology of nature even relatively independent of specifically human interests and concerns, saying, for example, "God himself has shown by the order of creation that he created all things for man's sake" (I.14.22). From our present perspective in the midst of ecological crisis brought on in large measure by imperious and impervious human self-centeredness, this is to be regretted. Nevertheless Calvin's doctrine of creation, although a confession of faith, has its own integrity not being subsumed under the doctrine of providence. That is, unlike Schleiermacher, Calvin's view of creation is not asserted entirely on the basis of the human experience of providence. For Calvin the knowledge of God's work is known from the testimony of Scripture as well as human experience.

Within the context of God's creation, Calvin develops his doctrine of God's providence with considerable passion. Perhaps the most unexpected result of this section is Calvin's reversal of universal and particular providence. Calvin does not deny—rather, he affirms—universal providence, but his strongest emphasis is on particular providence. In fact so emphatic is his insistence on particular providence that it is difficult, if not impossible, to separate from his doctrine of predestination since both are examples of God's loving care for the faithful.

Book II

God the Redeemer

INTRODUCTION TO BOOK II

Book II involves two of the most important and interlocking and ineffable Christian doctrines: Trinity and Christology. Trinitarian doctrine combines the concept of one substance (or essence) and three persons, claiming a unity that is tri-unity. This relation addresses the mystery of God in terms of the proper *unity of essence* (ὁμοουσία, περιχώρησις) (*consubstantialitas*, or *coessentialitas*) and also the proper *distinction of persons* (οἰκονομία, ἰδιοποίησις) (*persona*, or *discrimen*). Christological doctrine combines the concept of one person and two complete natures—a real unity in real duality. The debate led through the heresies of the Ebionites, the Gnostics, Origen, the Monarchians, the Adoptionists, Arius, Apollinaris, Nestorius, and Eutyches until the orthodox formula adopted at the Council of Nicaea (325), which was supplemented at the Council of Chalcedon (451). This formulation is not an explanation but a confession. Its lasting purpose is not to satisfy the mind, but to protect the heart of the central mystery that in Jesus Christ God was reconciling the world to himself (2 Cor. 5:19).[1]

---

1. Three post-Calvin revolutions continue to influence modern culture in powerful ways. The historical revolution raises fundamental questions about the nature and proper authority of the Bible.

The knowledge of God the Redeemer is the main subject of the *Institutes* Book II. Calvin's exposition begins with a reflection on the fact of sin from which much of the caricature of Calvin and Calvinism derive. Major topics thereafter include the gospel and the law, the one person and two natures of Christ, and the work of Christ discussed in three offices: prophet, king, and priest. Following Calvin's exposition of the person and work of Christ is the best place to consider the issues of mysticism and deification in Calvin, followed by the narrative of faith using the Apostles' Creed as an outline.

That the fact of sin forms no part of the actual knowledge of the Redeemer is obvious. Sin is the reality from which human beings require redemption, but the reality of the Mediator is not exhausted in the work of the Redeemer. In a historical sense, sin is preliminary to redemption, but in a theological sense, sin is a foreign body. The fact that Calvin begins his exposition of God the Redeemer by discussing human sin in five chapters is noteworthy. Among theologians, the fall is most often treated as the human distortion of divine creation rather than as a prologue to divine redemption. Traditionally the fall is assigned meaning, even if negative meaning, as the occasion that brings redemption. Calvin does not make these common connections.

Among the sections contributing directly to the knowledge of God the Redeemer, Calvin teaches that the gospel precedes the law, asserting that God's grace is extended to human beings *before* they are instructed how to behave. This conviction reverses the central Lutheran view that law precedes grace. Second, while Calvin explains the orthodox view of Jesus Christ as one person in two complete natures, he places a distinctive emphasis on the humanity of Christ. Third, with the three offices, Calvin offers a dynamic and functional account of the work of Christ in connection with the previous section, which was focused on the person of Christ. As prophet, Christ brings an end to all prophesies by his perfect teaching; as king, Christ rules over death, the devil, and the world; and as priest, Christ reconciles us to God by his holy obedience. In the fourth section Calvin explains atonement within the narrative of the Apostles' Creed.

Calvin insists that the created order was such "that the frame of the universe should be the school in which we were to learn piety, and from it pass over to eternal life and felicity." However, "after the fall of the first man no knowledge of God apart from the mediator has had power unto salvation" (II.6.1). Therefore, God is comprehended in Christ alone (II.6.4) until such time as we shall see God as he is (II.14.3).

Early in Book I Calvin asserted that the knowledge of God is twofold: the Lord who shows himself as Creator is also seen as Redeemer in the face of Christ

---

The social revolution raises fundamental questions about sexual nature and proper roles and proper language for men and women. The christological revolution raises fundamental questions about the nature(s) and role(s) of Jesus Christ. Essentially this revolution is an attack on the adequacy of the Chalcedonian formulation. Barth recognizes this formulation is confessional. "The statement that Jesus Christ is the One who is of divine and human essence dares to unite that which by definition cannot be united" (*CD* 4.2.61). For a discussion of the hypostatic union, see *CD* 4.2.60–69.

(I.2.1). In Book II, following the description of sin, Calvin turns to the second fold dealing with what God has done for us in Jesus Christ. This exposition of the knowledge of God the Redeemer also begins the exposition of ourselves as redeemed, to which the remainder of the *Institutes* is devoted. Calvin's "anthropology" thus includes a threefold knowledge of ourselves: as created, as corrupted, and as redeemed. Importantly, the knowledge of our corruption is treated existentially but is denied ontological reality.

A Personal Note

For many years I thought Calvin's exposition of Christ was one among many doctrines rather than the basic conviction on which his entire theology rests. With nodding acceptance I had read past statements like we know God clearly in the person of Christ.[2] That Jesus was more than the mightiest of the prophets (Mark 1:7) had been affirmed from childhood, as was some kind of vague notion of two natures later located more technically in the fundamental mystery of hypostatic union (*unio hypostatica*). The text that finally exploded in my mind was Calvin's declaration that "Christ was the true Jehovah" (I.13.9). He continues:

> Moreover, if apart from God there is no salvation, no righteousness, no life, yet Christ contains all these in himself, God is certainly revealed. And let no one object to me that life and salvation have been infused with Christ by God for Christ is not said to have received salvation, but to be salvation itself. . . . The name of Christ is invoked for salvation; therefore it follows that he is Jehovah. . . . And to have it more plainly understood that "the whole fullness of divinity dwells bodily" in Christ [Col. 2:9], the apostle confesses that he introduced no other doctrine among the Corinthians than knowledge of him, and that he has preached nothing but this [I Cor. 2:2]. (I.13.13)

I had read these statements a number of times, but I remember vividly the first time I felt the full force of their stupendous claim. In spite of what I understood and accepted as the orthodox view of Trinity and incarnation, I realized that I still maintained some kind of vestigial subordination of the Son to the Father. As a response to these passages in Calvin, I spent considerable time reflecting on whether my own theology allowed me to make so brief and bold a declaration as "Christ is Jehovah." I decided that the confession "Jesus Christ is Lord" (Phil. 2:11; 1 Cor 12:3) (which I did accept) was in fact equivalent to "Jesus Christ is Jehovah" (which I now accept). I concluded that I agreed with Calvin in believing "God is comprehended in Christ alone" (II.6.4), meaning God is like

2. The complete citation reads, "For how can any mortal man ascend to the height of God unless he is raised on high by his hand? God in Christ descended to the lowliness of men to stretch out his hand to them. . . . Whoever aspires to know God without beginning at Christ must wander in a labyrinth . . . because everyone is deprived of all right knowledge of God who leaves Christ [but] whoever directs his mind and all his senses to Christ will be led straight to the Father. We clearly behold God in the person of Christ" (Com. Jn. 8.19).

Christ, not that Christ is like God. Perhaps the simplest and clearest evidence of identification is prayer addressed to Christ which is only appropriately directed to God (I.13.13). Calvin is not being hyperbolic when he interprets the phrase, "They shall look to me whom they have pierced" to demonstrate that the essence of the Father and the Son is the same. This denies the blasphemy that the Father is the only true God and Christ is some kind of God, too. The Father and the Son are one and the same God (Com. Zech. 12:10).

This conclusion is neither obvious nor easy. Even so careful a scholar as J. K. S. Reid, while recognizing Calvin's Christocentrism, still maintains that his theology contains a "comprehensive principle." He writes, "It is wrong to represent Calvin as exalting the sovereignty of God at the expense of a real interest in Jesus Christ. The comprehensive principle of his theology is, of course, God's sovereignty; but when one asks concerning the content of which this is the framework, he is led by Calvin straight to Christ. Calvin's theology is theocentric in no sense that precludes Christocentricity."[3] Reid is certainly correct that no intellectual principle can replace Christ in Calvin's theology, but interpreting Calvin through a comprehensively abstract intellectual principle like the sovereignty of God runs the great risk of substituting the abstract principle for the concrete person of Jesus Christ the Lord.

The Christian faith begins in God's presence with us (Matt. 1:23). God is revealed in and as Jesus Christ (2 Cor. 5:19). That is, God is fully revealed in Christ (Col. 1:19). Thus, Calvin writes, "Christ is the one and only foundation of the Church" (Com. 1 Cor. 3:11, cf. IV.2.1), "hence all thinking about God without Christ is a vast abyss which immediately swallows up all our thoughts" (Com. 1 Pet. 1:20). Emil Brunner makes this confession:

> The Christian Faith is not other than (*nichts anderes als*) faith in Jesus Christ. Therefore the whole of Christian theology is not other than (*nichts anderes als*) the explication of faith in Christ. Hence faith in Jesus Christ is not simply part of this faith, and Jesus Christ is not one "subject" among other subjects in the Christian Creed. The doctrine of God, of His Nature and of His Will, of the Creation and the Divine government of the world, of man as created in the Image of God and as sinner, of the Old Covenant as promise and the preparation for the New—all these doctrines are various moments in the one faith in Jesus Christ.[4]

3. Reid, *Authority of Scripture*, 52.
4. Emil Brunner, *The Christian Doctrine of Creation and Redemption*, trans. Olive Wyon (Philadelphia: Westminster Press, 1952), 2:239. The same point is made by Thomas F. Torrance. "In Jesus Christ we meet the very embodiment of the majestic Sovereignty of God breaking into the world to claim it for himself, the coming of *Immanuel* (עמנואל), God himself to be with us and one of us, and specifically *Yeshua* (ישוע), meaning *Yahweh-Savior*, for, 'he shall save his people from their sins.' He is the *Lord Jesus*, the divine Savior of mankind, [who is not] a kind of 'double' for God in his absence, but the incarnate presence of *Yahweh*, the Lord God himself. . . . We come to know Christ today as the Lord and Savior in the same way as the disciples and their converts came to know him at the very beginning, when they called upon Jesus to save them from their sins, worshiped him, and prayed to him, and glorified him, as *Jesous Kyrios* (Ἰησοῦς κύριος), thereby accepting the designation of him as *Yahweh*, the very name God had given himself in his unique revelation to Israel when he delivered them redemptively out of their bondage in Egypt" (Thomas F. Torrance, *The Christian Doctrine of God, One Being Three Persons* [Edinburgh: T. & T. Clark, 1996], 51).

Such statements on the centrality of Jesus Christ are not to be understood as expressions of an essential tenet, not even as the most essential tenet. Confessing Jesus Christ as Lord is not the first item on a list of essential beliefs. Rather, God's revelation in Jesus Christ is the foundational reality of essential faith. He is the basis for, the ground of, and the truth from which all essential tenets derive. In the human realm, fact and interpretation cannot be entirely separated, though they are not the same. Similarly, in theology Christ and Christology are not the same. Reality properly precedes all interpretations of it. While there is no knowledge of Jesus Christ that is not christological, Jesus Christ is never exactly identical with our doctrines concerning him. Even christological doctrine is required to bow the knee before the person of Jesus Christ.

The confession "Jesus Christ is Lord" is at once the most fundamental, most far-reaching, and most remarkable of Christian claims.[5] Ultimately the coalescence of its historical, ontological, epistemological, and behavioral components seems to be a miracle—at least the conviction of its truth remains mysterious. In short, the church's one foundation is Jesus Christ her Lord. Christians worship God revealed in, through, and as Jesus Christ. This is the basic truth from which all doctrines, including the so-called essential tenets, derive. Essential tenets protect the church's confession of her one Lord, but they cannot replace the foundational encounter with him which occurs in experience and issues in service.

With the exposition of Christology, the general, and generally unthreatening, discussion of God's being and works moves to the specific, and specifically demanding, question of God's relation to Jesus of Nazareth.[6] Attempting to understand the experience that "in Christ God was reconciling the world to him-

5. The scorn the great historian Edward Gibbon pours on the conviction of Christ's Lordship in his impressively rolling prose is nonetheless savage for being lofty. According to Gibbon, "The theologian may indulge the pleasing task of describing Religion as she descended from Heaven, arrayed in her native purity. A more melancholy duty is imposed on the historian. He must discover the inevitable mixture of error and corruption which she contracted in a long residence upon earth, among a weak and degenerate race of beings." Included in the results a historian must recognize that Christian divines in rejecting the observance of the Mosaic law pronounced "with the utmost caution and tenderness a sentence of condemnation so repugnant to the inclination and prejudices of the believing Jews." In reviewing the history of christological reflection, Gibbon deals chiefly with the Gnostics and the Ebionites, expressing some sympathy for the latter. "The unfortunate Ebionites, rejected from one religion as apostates and from the other as heretics . . . insensibly melted away either into the church or the synagogue" (Edward Gibbon, *Decline and Fall of the Roman Empire*, vol. 1 (Chicago: William Benton, 1952), chap. 15: 179, 182, 183).

6. In the relative context of the world's religions, the absolute claim, "I am the way, and the truth, and the life" (John 14:6) must be faced. If Christ is Lord, he is more than Kant's example or Hegel's symbol. In his address of July 15, 1838, delivered before the senior class at Harvard Divinity School (from which he had earlier graduated), Ralph Waldo Emerson, *The Spiritual Emerson: Essential Writings*, ed. David M. Robinson (Boston: Beacon Press, 2003), complained that "the first defect of historical Christianity" is its exaggeration of the personal. "It has dwelt, it dwells, with noxious exaggeration about the *person* of Jesus" (71, emphasis in original). On a different subject, "Threnody," Emerson's attempt to console himself on the death of his son, "the deep-eyed boy," demonstrates the thinness of hope in transcendental philosophy and is one of the saddest poems I know.

self" (2 Cor. 5:19) led to the development of the doctrine of incarnation, which has both natural and supernatural components. As John E. Smith writes, "No one, I believe, will deny that this doctrine is a legitimate and absolutely essential part of Christian theology." Moreover, apart from traditional biblical or devotional language, a restatement of the doctrine looks something like this: "There is an event or series of events within recorded human history which we describe as the appearance of the Christ, and this event is both a legitimate part of the historical process and a unique revelation of the meaning (in the sense of divine purpose) of that process as a whole." Smith observes that the definition contains words like "event," "unique," and "history," which have both ordinary, commonsense meanings as well as more carefully reflective ones. In other words, "We do not and cannot learn, for example, the meaning of a concept like 'unique' from the Bible alone without recourse to an analysis of our general human experience."[7] Granting the importance of ordinary, commonsense meanings, there are also confessions of faith that go beyond ordinary common sense. According to Calvin, Paul calls Christ, "'the image of the invisible God,' meaning by this, that it is through him alone that God, who is otherwise invisible is manifested to us . . . The word 'image' is not used of his essence, but . . . Christ is the image of God because he makes God in a manner visible to us." This is a powerful weapon against the Arians. "The sum is, that God in himself, that is in his naked majesty, is invisible; and that not only to the physical eyes, but also to human understanding; and that he is revealed to us in Christ alone, where we may behold him as in a mirror. For in Christ he shows us his righteousness, goodness, wisdom, power, in short, his entire self. We must, therefore, take care not to seek him elsewhere; for outside Christ everything that claims to represent God will be an idol" (Com. Col. 1:15). Any "supposed knowledge of God outside Christ will be a deadly abyss" (Com. Jn. 6:46).[8]

7. John E. Smith, *Reason and God: Encounters of Philosophy with Religion* (New Haven, CT: Yale University Press, 1961), 153, 154.

8. Paul van Buren's Basel dissertation written under Karl Barth, *Christ in Our Place: The Substitutionary Character of Calvin's Doctrine of Reconciliation* (Grand Rapids: Eerdmans, 1957), was a helpful contribution to Calvin studies. The main focus is the atonement interpreted by the substitutionary theme of Christ in our place. His emphasis on Christ as substitute is one-sided and the remarks on the "penal substitutionary" doctrine (142) inadequate. Additionally, the Christian narrative is set in motion more by the bad news of human sin than the good news of God's grace. Moreover, in eschewing careful engagement with other scholars, van Buren needlessly deprives himself of challenges from other minds. Nevertheless, the exposition in part 1 of the incarnation as Christ's union with us and part 3 of incorporation as our union with Christ is sound. As is the following testimony of the foreword: "This study in Calvin has strengthened my conviction that as Christ is the center of our faith, so Christology is the *determining* center of all theology." The most far-reaching and disturbing question reads, "Is the work of Christ to be understood as having gained the *reality* of salvation, or only as having opened up its *possibility*?" (32, emphasis in original). In response, van Buren sets aside Calvin's doctrine of predestination and concludes, "Christ's work, in itself, remains for Calvin an unfilled possibility" (143). The former is impossible; the latter is implausible. Not long after his Calvin book, van Buren wrote *The Secular Meaning of the Gospel* (New York: Macmillan, 1963), which associated him with the death-of-God theology of the 1960s. See Charles N. Bent, *The Death-of-God Movement* (New York: Paulist Press, 1967).

A. SIN: HOW TOTAL IS DEPRAVITY?

In the popular mind Calvin and Calvinism are associated with predestination and total depravity. For that reason, any proper understanding must address the question in some detail: "Just how total is depravity and what does it mean?" The correct and short answer is that Calvin's "doctrine of total depravity" is neither total nor a doctrine. The crucial distinction is that by "total" Calvin means totally susceptible to sinfulness but not totally situated in sin. In addition and equally surprising, sin is declared to be accidental. Calvin believes in free will, although he prefers not to use the term. Moreover, while original sin is affirmed, actual sin is also emphasized. Calvin's teaching about sin is here examined under four headings. First, by following our noses we take a quick sniff at the T.U.L.I.P. and the question of total depravity. Second, Calvin offers the remarkable insistence that sin is adventitious. Third, Calvin's view of the freedom and bondage of the will is briefly examined. Fourth, the role of original and actual sin is considered.

1. Total and Partial Depravity

John Calvin's doctrine of sin is often regarded as so severe that "Calvinism" can be used as a synonym for the gloomiest possible evaluation of the human condition and its most dreary prospects. Robinson writes both correctly and ironically, "We speak as though John Calvin invented the Fall of Man, when that was an article of faith universal in Christian culture."[9] Based on the conviction that Calvin taught the total depravity of all human beings, this view of sin is represented by the framework of the famous (or infamous) acrostic T.U.L.I.P., a device used by both friend and foe as a faithful summary of Calvin's theology. For example, Gary Scott Smith writes, "For the purposes of this study, we will define a Calvinist as one who adheres to the theology of John Calvin primarily as set forth in his *Institutes of the Christian Religion*." At this point Smith and I are on the same page, but then he turns over a new leaf: "This theology is popularly summarized in five points often referred to by the acronym TULIP—Total depravity, Unconditional election, Limited (or definite) atonement, Irresistible grace, and Perseverance of the saints." Smith recognizes, "These points were not formulated by Calvin but by the Synod of Dort in 1619 about fifty years after his death, in response to the challenges of Jacob Arminius to his teachings." Nevertheless, Smith accepts this popular summary as an accurate and adequate summary.[10] Even those who argue that TULIP is useful are not likely to insist that so short a summary is an adequate reflection of the range and nuance of Calvin's theology. Moreover, those who think the acronym is accurate must admit that

9. Marilynne Robinson, *The Death of Adam: Essays on Modern Thought* (New York: Houghton Mifflin Cmpany, 1998), 151.
10. Gary Scott Smith, *The Seeds of Secularism: Calvinism, Culture, and Pluralism in America, 1870–1915* (Grand Rapids: Christian University Press, 1985), 4. Obviously the TULIP mnemonic was created by an English-speaking person.

the interpretive importance of order and context does not and cannot come to full bloom in this TULIP.[11]

On the other hand, the TULIP summary commends itself for several reasons. First, many people already know and accept it. Second, as a mnemonic device it is clever and easy to remember. Third, an important synod in the Netherlands produced the five Canons of Dort which, by a slight rearrangement of sequence, can be made to assert each of the points of TULIP. Fourth, tulips today remind us of Holland although they were introduced into Europe by the Turks.[12] Fifth, Dutch Calvinists accept the Canons of Dort, indicating the existence of a living

---

11. Among the more interesting expositions of TULIP Calvinism is Richard J. Mouw's *Calvinism in the Las Vegas Airport* (Grand Rapids: Zondervan, 2004). The opening chapter entitled *"Hardcore TULIP"* describes a scene in the movie *Hardcore*, set in the Las Vegas airport, where George C. Scott, playing an agonized Calvinist named Jake Van Dorn, explains the theology of TULIP to a teenage prostitute named Niki, played by Season Hubley. While Mouw defends each of the doctrines represented by TULIP, he admits "that, when stated bluntly, they have a harsh feel about them. To articulate them 'with gentleness and respect' takes some effort" (14). He is especially hesitant about limited atonement. Not so Paul Helm, "The Logic of Limited Atonement," in *Scottish Bulletin of Evangelical Theology* 3, no. 2 (Autumn 1985): 47–54, who, defending logic and reason, sees doctrine as argument, not confession. See also Jonathan H. Rainbow, *The Will of God and the Cross: An Historical and Theological Study of John Calvin's Doctrine of Limited Redemption* (Allison Park, PA: Pickwick Publications, 1990). Gentle respect leads Mouw to keep his powder dry with the Heidelberg Catechism rather than firing away with the Canons of Dort. The movie *Hardcore* was written and directed by Paul Schrader, a graduate of Calvin College, where Richard Mouw taught for seventeen years. Schrader also wrote *Taxi Driver* and both wrote and directed *American Gigolo*. Another well-known Calvin College alumnus who satirized his Calvinistic background was the great humorist Peter De Vries. See his "TULIP" in *No, But I Saw the Movie* (Boston: Little, Brown & Company, 1946), 1–16. His Rev. Andrew Mackerel claims, "[The Dutch Calvinists] were hairsplitters the like of which an ordinary human being in our time is totally unlikely to hear. 'One Dutchman, a Christian; two Dutchmen, a congregation; three Dutchmen, heresy'" (*The Mackerel Plaza* [Boston: Little, Brown & Company, 1958], 31). Growing up among Dutch Calvinists Reverend Mackerel moves away from that background to become pastor of the "People's Liberal" church, and his story begins with an angry telephone call to the zoning board objecting to a newly installed sign which he can see from his study window. The sign read, "Jesus Saves." In contrast, in the profoundly moving *The Blood of the Lamb* (New York: Penguin Books, 1961 [1985]), written as his only daughter, Emily, died of leukemia, De Vries wrote, "I came to understand a few things about what people believe. What people believe is a measure of what they suffer" (25). See also Roderick Jellema, *Peter De Vries: A Critical Essay* (Grand Rapids: Wm. B. Eerdmans, 1966). Cruelly jesting at the reality of pain, Lord Byron writes, "As I suffer from the shocks / Of illness, I grow much more orthodox" (*Don Juan*, Canto 11, 5).

12. As an exotic footnote, this information on the tulip is provided by Lord Kinross. Sultan Ahmed's

> Seraglio during the winter was regaled with *helva fêtes*, social gatherings in which philosophical symposia, together with poetry recitals, dancing, Chinese shadow plays, and prayers were accompanied by the distribution of sweets, otherwise helva. But when the winter was over there was now introduced for the Sultan's delectation a spring fête which developed largely into a festival of tulips. Ahmed had a great love for flowers—for the rose, the carnation (which his moustache was said to resemble), the lilac, the jasmine. But it was eventually the tulip that captured his fancy above all the rest. Its name in Turkish was *lale*, held to have a sacred significance from its resemblance to "Allah," and the reign of Ahmed III became known to posterity as *Lale Devri*, or the Reign of the Tulip. The tulip was a wild flower of the Asiatic steppes which had strewn the path of the Turks throughout their centuries of westward migration. It was Busbecq, the Austrian imperial ambassador of the sixteenth century, who as a keen botanist first introduced the tulip to the West, taking tulip bulbs back to

community more disposed to affirm than to deny—or even to question—the validity of the TULIP acrostic.[13]

That TULIP represents the Calvinistic theology of the Synod of Dort can scarcely be doubted. Additionally, if one assumes that the historical development of Calvinism was in the main an enhancement of Calvin's theology, rather than a distortion of it, there is no need to review the adequacy of the Canons of Dort or the later Westminster Confession as faithful expressions of Calvinistic theology. Furthermore, since a goodly number of the godly people interested in Calvin's theology (and thus in this book) are also loyal to either Dort or Westminster or both, some tiptoeing around the TULIP might be appropriate.

While crucial to the history of Calvinism, a detailed analysis of the Synod of Dort (1618) or the Assembly at Westminster (1644) is clearly outside the scope of a study of the *Institutes* of Calvin (1560). The extremely important question whether, and in what ways, later Calvinism improved or distorted Calvin's theology is addressed in the introduction and need not be treated here. The present purpose only requires the observation with which both sides would agree. Calvin's theology does not start with total depravity. Since Calvin locates his discussion of sin at the beginning of Book II, clearly he does not begin the *Institutes* with it.

Calvin can, and certainly does, paint his portrait of human beings in the darkest colors, giving some credence to the emphasis on the power of the vice grip. For example, he writes, "I have said that *all parts* of the soul were possessed by sin after Adam deserted the fountain of righteousness." Again the soul's "*entire nature* is opposed to supernatural grace." Yet again, no part of mankind "is immune from sin and *all that proceeds* from him is to be imputed to sin" (II.1.9, emphases added). On the other hand, Calvin also says, "We grant that God's image was *not totally annihilated and destroyed* in [Adam], yet it was so corrupted that whatever remains is frightful deformity" (I.15.4).

As usual Thomas Aquinas has an elegant solution to the issue of total and partial depravity. The fall destroyed the supernatural virtues: faith, hope, and love,

---

Flanders on his journey home. Its European name was derived from the nickname the Turks gave it: *tulbend*, or "turban" in the Persian language. Not long afterward the tulip was imported by European merchants and propagated in large quantities in Holland, where in time some twelve hundred varieties of it were known. This gave rise in the seventeenth century to a craze of tulipomania among the Ottoman elite, in the course of which fortunes were made and lost from rare tulip bulbs, and the tulip became known as "the gold of Europe."

From Lord Kinross, *The Ottoman Centuries: The Rise and Fall of the Turkish Empire* (London: Jonathan Cape, 1977), 378–79. Jack Goody, *The Culture of Flowers* (Cambridge: Cambridge University Press, 1993), 188–89, under the title "tulipomania," deals with commercial and theological aspects of flowers.

13. R. B. Kuiper, *As to Being Reformed* (Grand Rapids: Wm. B. Eerdmans, 1926). In his chapter on "Christianity and Calvinism" Kuiper claims the five points of Calvinism were sponsored by the Genevan Reformer. He concludes, "Calvinism is the most nearly perfect interpretation of Christianity. In the final analysis, Calvinism and Christianity are practically synonymous. It follows that he who departs from Calvinism is taking a step away from Christianity. . . . For in the last instance the fundamentals of Calvinism are also the fundamentals of the Christian religion" (88, 91).

which are restored by God's grace alone. The natural virtues: wisdom, courage, moderation, and justice were seriously damaged, but not totally destroyed. They remain as essential natural components of human being. By the exercise of free will, the natural virtues can, and should, be improved. Carlos Eire reads Calvin in a Thomistic direction. Sinful humanity's "natural gifts have been corrupted and his spiritual gifts have been completely taken away."[14] Calvin's remarks lend some plausibility to this understanding. For example, Calvin says sin destroyed the supernatural gifts of faith and love and damaged the natural gifts, which means "something of understanding and judgment remains as a residue along with the will." The fall did not totally wipe out reason, nor did the will perish (II.2.12). The remaining residue includes vestiges of truth, equity, and order. However, when Calvin is describing the fall directly rather than defending God's mercy to the fallen creature, he carefully avoids placing even relatively sound capacities in the natural human apart from God's special grace. In other words, for Calvin, unlike Thomas, grace does not perfect created nature but restores fallen nature. The proper resolution of this dilemma is not a doctrine of operating and cooperating grace as in Thomas (ST, I.2.111ff.). Rather, by total depravity Calvin means totally susceptible to sin but he says, "I grant that not all these wicked traits appear in every man"; therefore he continues, "Yet one cannot deny that [all these wicked traits lurk] in the breast of each" (II.3.2).

2. Sin: A Fact without Meaning

Remarkably, for Calvin sin is defined as an accident. Sin "is an adventitious quality which comes upon man rather than a substantial property which has been implanted from the beginning" (II.1.11). This definition owes something to Aristotle's distinction between reality and actuality (substance) on the one hand and contingency and possibility (accident) on the other.[15] Sin is a fact for Calvin, but an inexplicable fact. Since sin is defined as an accident, it cannot become a substantial doctrine. Human depravity cannot be regarded as a central dogma in John Calvin's Calvinism. Sin has devastating consequences, but no positive meaning.

The threefold outline of much popular theology assigns an important meaning to sin. That is, (1) God created everything good, but (2) man and woman abused the good gift of free will, thereby falling into sin.[16] (3) In response to sin God sent Jesus Christ to redeem the world. According to this scheme, sin is the pivotal event between creation and redemption that both requires and explains the incarnation. Calvin takes the fact of sin with absolute seriousness, but sin as accident does not have meaning. The popular three-step theology which moves

14. Carlos M. N. Eire, *War against the Idols: The Reformation of Worship from Erasmus to Calvin* (Cambridge: Cambridge University Press, 1986), 203.

15. This distinction is employed often against Pighius in *The Bondage and Liberation of the Will.* Human corruption is accidental, not substantial (Book II, 263).

16. Usually not addressed is the difficulty of a physical transmission of a moral failure or the legitimacy of guilt transferred to a person for actions occurring centuries before.

from God's creation to sin's destruction to Christ's restoration understands human sin as a logically necessary part of salvation history. In contrast, Calvin's five small chapters on sin are not essential to the relation between Creator and Mediator. Rather the discussion of sin is inserted between the knowledge of the Creator (Book I) and Redeemer (Book II). For Calvin sin is a terrible reality, but it is not a major division of his theology. Calvin should be understood as a theologian of God's grace, not of human sin.

The setting of Calvin's main account of sin is not as a pivotal discussion between creation and redemption, but rather a bracketed discussion between the knowledge of God the Creator and the knowledge of God the Redeemer. The fact of sin affects both kinds of knowledge, but sin is not part of either. Sin is treated as a strange or foreign object in the body of Calvin's theology, having no necessary connection to Creator or Mediator although the Mediator is the Redeemer.

If sin were meaning-full it would not be sin. The presence of sin and evil in a world created by an omnipotent, omniscient, and loving God is incomprehensible.[17] Calvin refuses to give sin an ontological grounding or justification. "[The orthodox faith] does not admit that any evil nature exists in the whole universe. For the depravity and malice both of man and of the devil, or the sins that arise therefrom, do not spring from nature, but rather from the corruption of nature" (I.14.3). Calvin passionately refuses to make the logical inference from God's omnipotence to God's responsibility for sin. Without being able to challenge the premises, he denies the conclusion insisting that it is impious to think of the sovereign God as the author of evil, but he cannot claim it is illogical. In some sense, then, Calvin's view of sin is both accidental and unreasonable. Calvin insists that "all things take place by God's determination" (III.23.6), meaning that "God foreknew what end man was to have before he created him, and consequently foreknew because he so ordained by his decree" (III.23.7). "Accordingly, man falls as God's providence ordains, but he falls by his own fault" (III.23.8). Calvin can criticize the unbridled use of reason in theology (II.2.18) and asserts the will of

17. In a chapter entitled "The Riddle of Sin," G. C. Berkouwer agrees. He writes, "Sin, for the Christian, is unreasonable, idiotic, and incomprehensible in the light of God's love as *now revealed*." "Sin itself, in its source and cause, can never be explained." "One can only affirm that there is no *reason* and no sensible *motive* for man's sin. . . . One cannot find sense in the senseless and meaning in the meaningless" (G. C. Berkouwer, *Sin* [Grand Rapids: Wm. B. Eerdmans, 1971], 144, 131, 134). Utilizing Gabriel Marcel's distinction between "problem" and "mystery," George Dennis O'Brien suggests the *problem* of the justification of suffering cannot properly be raised because of the primacy of the *mystery* of "the existential relation of God and man" which "cannot be avoided or transcended" and blocks "any literal meaning to the qualitative characteristics of power and goodness which are used to generate the dilemma [of justification]." O'Brien declares, "The final answer is what God *is* in Christ" (emphasis in original) (George Dennis O'Brien, "Prolegomena to a Dissolution to the Problem of Suffering," *Harvard Theological Review* 57, no. 4 [October 1964]: 322, 316, 323). I take the term "existential relation" to be equivalent to "union with Christ." For a more recent theological/philosophical reflection on Christology, sin, and horrendous evils as a *distinct* category, see Marilyn McCord Adams, *Horrendous Evils and the Goodness of God* (Ithaca, NY: Cornell University Press, 1999), and *Christ and Horrors: The Coherence of Christology* (Cambridge: Cambridge University Press, 2006).

God as the final standard (III.22.11). However, most of the time he assumes that God has "reasons" even if we do not know what they are. "It would be claiming too much for ourselves not to concede to God that he may have reasons for his plan that are hidden from us" (II.11.14). In connection with the reality of sin, Calvin simply refuses to carry his reflection to its logical conclusion. Sin is a fact, but it is an accidental fact, which means it has no ultimate meaning.[18] Additionally, while Calvin takes sin with utmost seriousness, the victory over sin is absolute. In that context, his teaching of "total depravity" properly understood can be considered a cheerful doctrine.

3. Freedom and Bondage of Will

In the sixteenth century among early Protestants, bondage of the will to sin was considered a liberating doctrine. Any kind of confidence in human free will led to questions about its proper exercise and immediately to uncertainty and therefore anxiety about one's salvation. Assurance of faith meant understanding redemption can only be found in God's grace and not at all in human merit. Sin did not totally deprive human beings of will but of soundness of will (II.3.5). Since the fall of Adam all are alienated from God by sin. "I readily allow that a certain remnant of life remains in man's soul. For understanding and judgment and will and all the senses are so many parts of life. But since there is no part which aspires to the heavenly life, it is not surprising if the whole man is accounted dead so far as the Kingdom of God is concerned" (Com. Jn. 5.25). God's grace is not extended on the basis of our merit. On the contrary, "The first part of a good work is will; the other, a strong effort to accomplish it; the author of both is God" (II.3.9). Freedom can be an intolerable burden, as famously argued by the Grand Inquisitor in Fyodor Dostoevsky's *The Brothers Karamazov*. When the notion of freely choosing and faithfully following God's way becomes a frightening responsibility, the proclamation that God's grace rescues men and women from an impossible situation is comforting good news. The issue, of course, is the relation between divine sovereignty and human freedom. Two perils must be avoided. If divine sovereignty is overemphasized, the result is complete resignation. If human freedom is overemphasized, the result is brazen confidence or abject fear. Calvin's astounding conclusion is that we should accept our freedom but not boast of it. He observes that some theologians teach there

---

18. Among the famous cries of the heart is Dorigen's agonized question concerning evil and God's providence in "The Franklin's Tale" of Chaucer's *Canterbury Tales*. As she waits anxiously for the return of her seagoing husband, Arveragus, whom she loved more than her own life, Dorigen cannot understand why a loving, perfect, and omniscient God would allow "grisly, fiendish, black rocks" in his world on which have perished "a hundred thousand bodies of mankind." To her mind those rocks do not benefit man, nor bird, nor beast. Among other similar outcries that immediately come to mind are Ivan's challenge to Alyosha in the chapter "Rebellion" of *The Brothers Karamazov*. See also Nicholas Wolterstorff, *Lament for a Son* (Grand Rapids: Eerdmans, 1987); and chap. 10, "The Accident of Sin," in Andrew Purves and Charles Partee, *Encountering God: Christian Faith in Turbulent Times* (Louisville, KY: Westminster John Knox Press, 2000).

is no freedom to choose between good and evil, but we are free to act wickedly. Others "teach that man, despoiled of the powers of free will, takes refuge in grace alone. At another time they provide, or seem to provide, him with his own armor" (II.2.9). Calvin thinks the danger of all discussion of free will leads to celebrating human achievement and robbing divine honor.

According to Calvin, pride was the beginning of all evils and disobedience was the beginning of the fall. In this section of the *Institutes*, Calvin contrasts pride with humility. The great danger of a discussion of free will is that it fosters pride. In contrast, "The foundation of our philosophy is humility . . . so if you ask me concerning the precepts of the Christian religion, first, second, third, and always I would answer, 'Humility'" (II.2.11).[19] Bondage of will in Calvin does not obviate responsibility and accountability: "Obviously, man's ruin is to be ascribed to man alone; for he, having acquired righteousness by God's kindness, has by his own folly sunk into vanity" (II.1.10).[20]

The topic of free will was famously and historically addressed by Augustine and Pelagius in the fifth century. During the Reformation Martin Luther responded to Erasmus with a powerful attack entitled *Bondage of the Will* (1524). Until then many thought Erasmus was supportive of Luther's challenges to Rome. By some Erasmus was thought to lay the egg that Luther hatched. Erasmus came out of his shell and cracked the egg by writing *The Freedom of the Will* in order to distance himself from the Lutheran movement. In his teaching on total depravity and bondage of the will Calvin is essentially following Augustine and Luther and not creating a so-called Calvinistic doctrine. At the end of the Reformation period the issue returned in the Arminian controversy, which led in the next century to the charge that John Wesley was "Arminian."[21] John Calvin's absolutely pessimistic view of total depravity was taken to deny the possibility of human perfection in this life, while John Wesley's resolutely optimistic view was taken to encourage Christian perfection in this life. It is not really clear whether Wesley thought of Christian perfection as a possession or a process. But, whatever the degree of expectation, it was a hope.[22]

19. The Greek idea of *hubris* includes the intoxication of mind found in those most certain it does not apply to them.

20. In a powerful contemporary vindication of Calvin's position, Robinson writes, "the belief that we are all sinners gives us excellent grounds for forgiveness and self-forgiveness, and is kindlier than any expectation that we might be saints, even while it affirms the standards all of us fail to attain." Modernity has replaced this vision "with an unsystematic, uncritical and in fact unconscious perfectionism, which may have taken root among us while Stalinism still seemed full of promise, and to have been refreshed by the palmy days of National Socialism in Germany, by Castro and by Mao. . . . Gross error survives every attempt at perfection and flourishes. No Calvinist could be surprised. No reader of history could be surprised" (Robinson, *Death of Adam*, 156).

21. On Arminianism, see Herbert Darling Foster, "Liberal Calvinism: The Remonstrants at the Synod of Dort in 1618," *Harvard Theological Review* 16, no. 1 (January 1923): 1–37.

22. Benjamin B. Warfield wrote a thousand pages attacking perfectionism and defending the Reformers' "miserable-sinner Christianity." According to Warfield, the Roman Catholics, Arminians, Wesleyans, Quakers, and others join in this assault on the Reformers' doctrine of sin and grace (Benjamin Breckinridge Warfield, *Perfectionism*, 2 vols. [New York: Oxford University Press, 1931–32]). In 1958 Samuel G. Craig edited and shortened Warfield's work (Grand Rapids: Baker Book House),

Calvin's most important practical, as opposed to theoretical, discussion of the behaviors expected of Christian life is found in his exposition of sanctification and justification in Book III. The general conclusion is that sanctification is a life-long process and cannot be completed on this earth. However, in this "Wesleyan moment" of Calvin's theology he suggests the possibility of a perfection before death. Citing Augustine, Calvin writes, "The grace of persisting in good . . . is given to us in order that we may will, and by will may overcome concupiscence. . . . The original freedom was to be able not to sin; but ours is much greater, not to be able to sin." This is *not* "a perfection to come after immortality," but connected with human will and God's grace. "Surely the will of the saints is so much aroused by the Holy Spirit that they are able because they so will, and that they will because God brings it about that they so will" (II.3.13). In this discussion Calvin seems to suggest (against the I [Irresistible grace] of T.U.L.I.P.) that grace is resistible! Grace is "offered by the Lord, which by anyone's free choice may be accepted or rejected." However, Calvin continues, "It is [God's] grace which forms both choice and will in the heart, so that whatever good works then follow are the fruit and effect of grace." In Calvin's theology, good works come not by our choice or by our nature, but by God's grace (II.5.8).

In summary, because the idea of even restricted freedom produces a foolish assurance, Calvin says that to designate our wicked acts as "freedom of the will" is to label a slight thing with a proud name (*superbus titulus*) (II.2.7). The notion of freedom of the will is always in danger of robbing God of his honor. Calvin admits it is possible to speak of freedom of will without misunderstanding, but he prefers not to use the idea (II.2.8).

4. Original and Actual Sin

The primary purpose of Calvin's doctrine of original sin is to reaffirm the bondage of the will. The purpose of the doctrine of the unfree will is, as we have seen, to demonstrate that human beings can recover what they have lost by sin only through God's grace revealed in Jesus Christ. Calvin refers to his earlier affirmation that nearly all wisdom consists of the knowledge of God and ourselves (I.1.1) in order to point out the knowledge of ourselves has a two-part dialectic. First, we must consider our original nature and the natural excellence which comes from God's creation and involves the purpose of our creation and the good gifts bestowed on us. This reflection leads to meditation on divine worship and the future life. Second, we must also recognize our fallen nature and the misery of our condition, which should bring us humility and shame. In this connection

---

adding a summary talk to students entitled "Entire Sanctification." Warfield believed in entire sanctification but not that it could occur in this life. Although despising Wesleyanism, Albrecht Ritschl championed Christian perfection (*Die christliche Vollkommenheit*). English translation in *Bibliotheca Sacra* 35:140 (October 1878), 656–80. As a boy I always wondered whether I was totally depraved as my father suspected or on the way to perfection as my mother hoped.

Calvin cites the classical recommendation to "know thyself," which too often leads to pride since the philosophers contemplate only our best qualities. Philosophers are aware of human evil, but they "hold as certain that virtues and vices are in our power [thus] we seem to do what we do, and to shun what we shun, by free choice." Some of these philosophers even accept life as a gift of the gods, but regard the way humans live as their responsibility. "This is the sum of the opinion of all philosophers: reason which abides in human understanding is a sufficient guide for right conduct; the will, being subject to it, is indeed incited by the senses to evil things; but since the will has free choice, it cannot be hindered from following reason as its leader in all things" (II.2.3).

According to Calvin, the philosophers "locate the will midway between reason and sense" (II.2.2). Reason is defined as the guide for a good life, while sense is a lower impulse that leads to error and baseness. The will is free to follow either the reason or the appetites. The philosophers are aware that living according to reason is not easy, but they insist it is possible. Right reason leads to right conduct if the will follows, but the will is too often tempted toward evil by the senses. Nevertheless the will can freely choose to follow reason. Free will entails that both virtue and vice are within our power. In contrast to the philosophers, theologians recognize that the original state no longer obtains because sin has damaged both reason and will, but theologians have been misled not only by their desire to receive the approval of philosophers but also by their fear that asserting an unfree will would lead to slothfulness. Calvin objects that too many theologians agree with or waffle in the house of the philosophers. In fact, "all the ancients, except Augustine, so differ, waver or speak confusedly on [free will], that almost nothing certain can be derived from their writings" (II.2.4).

Calvin thinks "blind self-love is innate in all mortals" (II.1.2), and for that reason, "There is, indeed, nothing that man's nature seeks more eagerly than to be flattered" (II.1.2). Nevertheless, "Since in the person of the first man we have fallen from our original condition, [we must remember] that primal worthiness cannot come to mind without the sorry spectacle of our foulness and dishonor presenting itself by way of contrast" (II.1.1). Calvin recognizes that the ancient doctors taught obscurely about original sin (II.1.5), and there was much debate surrounding the doctrine. "For all to be made guilty by the guilt of one" is not easy to accept. Nevertheless Adam's sin caused his own death, consigned all people to ruin, and even "perverted the whole order of nature" (II.1.5). Some modern theologians disagree with Calvin about the extension of sinfulness to nonhuman nature. Calvin thinks the disobedience of Adam led not simply to the ruin of the human race but means that all creatures are subject to corruption (Rom. 8) because "they are bearing part of the punishment deserved by man, for whose use they were created" (II.1.5).

Calvin offers this definition: "Original sin, therefore, seems to be a hereditary depravity and corruption of our nature, diffused into all parts of the soul, which first makes us liable to God's wrath, then also brings forth in us those works which Scripture calls 'works of the flesh' [Gal. 5:19]" (II.1.8). Due to original sin,

human nature cannot be extolled in such a way as to make us satisfied with ourselves and forgetful that in God we "may recover those things which we have
utterly and completely lost" (I.1.1). "Here, then, is the course that we must follow if we are to avoid crashing upon these rocks: when man has been taught that
no good thing remains in his power, and that he is hedged about on all sides by
most miserable necessity, in spite of this he should nevertheless be instructed to
aspire to a good of which he is empty, to a freedom of which he has been deprived"
(II.2.1). At this point Calvin once again pushes beyond the limits of logic by
declaring both that no good thing remains in our power and that we should aspire
to a good which is not present with a freedom which we do not possess.[23] Such
assertions without obvious rational coherence may be called paradoxical or contradictory. In either case, as affirmations they are integral parts of Calvin's theology. This situation applies most dramatically in the relation between completed
justification and continuing sanctification, defined as twin graces, as we shall discuss in Book III.

Dealing with Adam's fall in the exposition of predestination and addressing
the relation of God's decree and God's permission, Calvin confesses with Augustine that "the will of God is the necessity of things." This means "the first man
fell because the Lord had judged it to be expedient; why he so judged is hidden
from us. Yet it is certain that he so judged because he saw that thereby the glory
of his name is duly revealed." The human race falls as God's providence ordains
but falls by their own fault. According to Calvin we are wasting our time and
God's patience in seeking the cause of God's decree when we should contemplate
our corruption. On this question, "The craving to know [is] a kind of madness"
(III.23.8). Calvin is aware that this answer does not satisfy the impious who still
"growl and mutter." Nevertheless, Calvin continues to insist that the calamities
decreed for some are the results of their faults (III.23.9).

Without doubt Calvin teaches a strong doctrine of original sin. However, he
also sounds a cautionary note—perhaps especially useful for preachers and pastors. We are not to understand that human beings are guiltless and do not deserve
the curse that falls upon them. It is true that Adam's sin infected all of us, but we
are all sick in ourselves. There is considerable danger that a too-forceful presentation of original sin will allow Adam and Eve to be blamed for the original sin
in a way that excuses all others from their actual sin. The delicate balance between
justification and sanctification, bondage and freedom of the will, also applies to

---

23. In his classic *The New England Mind: The Seventeenth Century* (Cambridge: Harvard University Press, 1954 [1939]), 367, Perry Miller sees both American "Arminianism" and "Antinomianism" as a reaction against Calvin's perceived ethical absolutism, which "seemed to these critics devoid
of any grounds for moral obligation: what duties could be exacted from ordinary men when everything depended upon a mysterious decree of election." By 1600, American divines felt obligated to
answer the question, "If I am not elected, I can do nothing and why should I try?" Miller observes
that "Calvin himself had simply brushed aside such frivolous cavils, magisterially declaring, "'Man,
being taught that he has nothing good left in his possession, and being surrounded on every side with
the most miserable necessity, should nevertheless, be instructed to aspire to the good of which he is
destitute.'"

original and actual sin. Calvin suggests that contemplating the doctrine of original sin so overwhelms us that we are forced to throw ourselves entirely upon the mercy of God. However, Calvin also insists that we "are guilty *not* of another's fault but of our own" (II.1.8). This comment indicates that humans cannot blame only Adam and Eve for *original sin*. Everyone must accept personal responsibility for *actual sin*.

The main issue for Calvin is how Christ's righteousness and life are restored to us. Those who deny original sin think our actual sin has not been transmitted from Adam but occurs only in imitation of Adam. If that were true, Christ's righteousness would be ours by imitation, not communication. Calvin exclaims, "who can bear such sacrilege!" The proper relationship is this: "Adam, implicating us in his ruin, destroyed us with himself; but Christ restores us to salvation by his grace" (II.1.6). Calvin recognizes the depth of sin, but he does not rejoice in it, as some of his critics suggest. His major point is not human depravity but divine grace.

B. THE GOSPEL AND THE LAW

After five chapters on sin, Calvin turns in the next six to gospel and law. Educated as a lawyer, Calvin has an insider's appreciation of the crucial role of law in human society, especially with regard to equity and order, both extremely high values for him. However, Niesel rightly claims, "If with the usual prejudices about the legalism of Calvin we come to his writings and really read them, it is just here [in Book II] that we shall find what a lot we have to unlearn."[24] The main and specific point Calvin makes in this section of the *Institutes* is that grace takes precedence over law. The first caution to readers is to resist the temptation to focus on the topic of gospel and law to the neglect of their basis, unity, and purpose, which is the knowledge of God the Redeemer. Christ alone is the end of the law and prophets (Com. Mt. 17:3). Every doctrine of the law, every command, every promise points to Christ (Com. Rom. 10:4). The gospel does not supplant the law but ratifies it (II.9.4). The law guides our life like a candle, but Christ is the sun of righteousness dispelling the darkness (Com. Dan. 9:25; Com. Mal. 4:2). This discussion of gospel and law is most emphatically part of Calvin's Christology. The focus is not on Scripture itself but the role of the gracious gospel and the gracious law in the revelation of the Mediator and Redeemer. The second caution requires the recognition that the subject of gospel and law is not equivalent to New and Old Testaments. Calvin finds gospel in the Old Testament and law in the New Testament.[25] The third caution points out that the central dynamic between gospel and law in Calvin's theology does not allow an analysis

---

24. Wilhelm Niesel, *The Theology of Calvin*, 1st ed., trans. Harold Knight (Philadelphia: Westminster Press, 1956), 92.

25. On the unity of the Old and New Testaments, see Hans Heinrich Wolf, *Die Einheit des Bundes: des Verhältnis von Alten und Neuen Testament bei Calvin* (Neukirchen: Kr. Moers, 1958). Whenever the word "covenant" appears, Calvin affirms that we should think "grace" (Com. Is. 55:3).

of law even relatively separate from grace using categories like eternal, divine, natural, and positive law in the way Thomas Aquinas does.[26] Niesel and Wendel each treat this subject in two chapters. The first deals with the law of God, the second with the Old and New Testaments, but dual analysis obscures the christological unity of Calvin's exposition. Moses and the prophets are, he thinks, true teachers because "the law is nothing but a preparation for the Gospel" (Com. Jn. 10:8).

The central theological point of these chapters is that God's grace is the result of God's love and is extended to humanity before instruction in behavior is given.[27] Even more important is Calvin's focus on Jesus Christ as the promise of the law and the fulfillment of the gospel. Martin Luther wrote, "Nearly the entire Scripture and the knowledge of all theology depends upon the correct understanding of law and gospel."[28] However, Luther emphasizes more strongly than Calvin both the sequence of law to gospel and the role of law as demand rather than promise. In early editions Calvin began this part of the *Institutes* with the Old Testament, observing the historical pattern of treating the Old and then the New Testament. In the final edition, he changed the order from historical to theological to emphasize more strongly the common witness of law and gospel to Christ. Historically the law precedes and prepares for the gospel, but the gracious law is God's promise of salvation and the gracious gospel is God's fulfillment of that promise. In his earlier writings Calvin followed Luther's emphasis on and order of "law before gospel," but later, Calvin teaches that grace precedes law. This sequence contains another flashpoint for Calvin interpretation. By careful scholars Calvin's so-called legalism was never considered graceless. The law and the gospel are both grace-full but in different ways. The issue remains priority and emphasis, which is distorted in the Westminster Confession's distinction between the covenant of works and the covenant of grace as discussed in the section on Calvin and the Calvinists. The role of law in the covenant of works is a post-Calvin topic.

In Book I Calvin discussed the knowledge of God the Creator, but because of sin this knowledge is useless without the gift of faith "setting forth for us God our Father in Christ" (II.6.1). In Book II Calvin declares his purpose is not yet to discuss faith in Christ in detail (II.6.1.4). God calls us to faith in Christ because "we cannot by contemplating the universe infer that [God] is Father." After "the fall of the first man no knowledge of God apart from the Mediator has had power

26. See Karl Barth, "Gospel and Law," in *God, Grace and Gospel*, trans. James Strathearn McNab (London: Oliver and Boyd, 1959), 1–27. Also, John T. McNeill, "Natural Law in the Teaching of the Reformers," *Journal of Religion* 26 (1946): 168–82. Gessert asserts that Calvin's real mentors are the Hebrew prophets, not the statesmen of Greece and Rome. While Calvin occasionally implies one of Thomas's four kinds of law, his primary concern is the divine law (Robert A. Gessert, "The Integrity of Faith: An Inquiry into the Meaning of Law in the Thought of John Calvin," in *Scottish Journal of Theology* 13 [1960], 247–61).

27. See I. John Hesselink, "Law and Gospel or Gospel and Law? Calvin's Understanding of the Relationship," *Calviniana: Ideas and Influence of Jean Calvin*, ed. Robert V. Schnucker (Ann Arbor, MI: Sixteenth-Century Essays and Studies, 1988), 13–32.

28. Weimarer Ausgabe of *Luther's Works*, 7:505.

unto salvation." According to Calvin, the electing grace of God revealed in the Old Covenant "taught believers to seek salvation nowhere else than in the atonement that Christ alone carries out" (II.6.2). The new covenant is a confirmation of the old covenant (Com. Mt. 5:17). Since Christ is the central content of both the Old and New Covenants, Calvin devotes an entire chapter (II.10) to explaining, "The covenant made with all the patriarchs is so much like ours in substance and reality that the two are actually one and the same. Yet they differ in the mode of dispensation" (II.10.2). The difference between the two covenants is discussed in II.11, but the conclusion is, "The Old Testament fathers (1) had Christ as pledge of their covenant, and (2) put in him all trust of future blessedness" (II.10.23).

On this Christocentric focus David Puckett writes, "[Calvin] believed Christian exegetes, in their eagerness to relate the Old Testament to Christian doctrine, were often guilty of twisting the text to an unnatural interpretation." Nevertheless while Calvin was concerned to respect the literary and historical context of the Old Testament, "He insists that Christ is the true substance of the Old Testament."[29] Calvin admits the christological center was not clearly taught in Moses. Still in the messianic lineage of David it was clearly evident that God willed to be propitious to the human race through the Mediator. Citing Habakkuk 3:13; 2 Kings 8:19; Isaiah 7:14; 55:3–4; Ezekiel 34:23–25; 37:24, 26; Hosea 1:11; 3:5; Micah 2:13; Amos 9:11; Zechariah 9:9; and Psalm 28:8–9 Calvin states, "Here I am gathering a few passages of many because I merely want to remind my readers that the hope of all the godly has ever reposed in Christ alone" (II.6.3). Scripture teaches that faith in God is faith in Christ. "Believe in God, believe also in me" (John 14:1). Calvin comments that faith properly mounts up from Christ to the Father, but "although faith rests in God, it will gradually disappear unless he who retains it in perfect firmness intercedes as Mediator." God is the object of faith but "unless God confronts us in Christ we cannot come to know that we are saved." In comparison with the immensity of God's glory, human beings are like grubs crawling on earth, which means that "apart from Christ the saving knowledge of God does not stand" (II.6.4).

Having emphasized the primacy and priority of God's grace revealed in Jesus Christ, Calvin turns to the role of law. As Calvin reads the Old Testament, the law was added some four hundred years later to the covenant made by God with Abraham. The purpose of this addition was not "to lead the chosen people away from Christ; but rather to hold their minds in readiness until his coming" (II.7.1). According to the apostle, Christ is the end of the law unto salvation to every believer (Rom. 10:4) which means that even the ceremonial laws, vain exercises in themselves, and now "abrogated not in effect but only in use" (II.7.16), were designed to lift the minds of the Jewish people to Christ.

Turning from the law's purpose to its effects, Calvin suggests that the moral law would produce eternal salvation if it could be completely observed (II.7.3).

29. David L. Puckett, *John Calvin's Exegesis of the Old Testament* (Louisville, KY: Westminster John Knox Press, 1995), 6, 140–41.

In this line Calvin veers closest to the Westminster Confession's concept of a once-valid-but-now-rejected covenant of works. However, Calvin's comment is directed to the gracious purpose of the law in the context of his insistence that the teaching of the moral law, which includes the Decalogue and Jesus' summary, by being so far above human capacity makes its fulfillment impossible. Calvin defines "impossible" as "what has never been and what God's ordination and decree prevents from ever being" (II.7.4). Calvin returns to the praise of the gracious law in describing the Christian life in Book III. "The law of God contains in itself that newness by which his image can be restored in us [but] our slowness needs many goads and helps" (III.6.1). Again, "The law of the Lord provides the finest and best disposed method of ordering a man's life" (III.7.1).

Calvin insists that while the law cannot be perfectly obeyed, it serves three functions: punitive, protective, and pedagogical. The first function of the law is to punish sinners. The second function is to protect society. The third and principal function of law is to teach believers how to live.[30] This subject is continued in the discussion of sanctification—the doctrine of the holy life in Book III (3–10).

The first use of the law is to warn, inform, convict, condemn, and finally to destroy sinners. For believers this punitive function of the law produces a misery that teaches humility. Through this use of the law, believers come to recognize "they are not fit to receive Christ's grace unless they first be emptied" (II.7.11). Second, the law restrains evil people from enacting with their hands what their minds have conceived. The dread of the law's punishment does not change the hearts of these evildoers, but restraining them is necessary for public tranquillity. Because of the folly of the flesh, believers too need the restraining function of the law. "For all who have at any time groped about in ignorance of God will admit that it happened to them in such a way that the bridle of the law restrained them in some fear and reverence toward God until, regenerated by the Spirit, they began wholeheartedly to love him" (II.7.11). The third use of the law is pedagogical. That is, the law teaches believers what the will of God is and encourages them to follow it. Among sinners the law threatens and condemns, but among saints the law guides by its precepts and comforts by its promise of grace. The law guides the faithful toward salvation (Com. Ps. 19:7). Strangely, Wendel looks askance at this exposition of God's gracious law guiding believers. Unaccountably he writes, "It is here that the author of the *Institutes* has laid himself the most widely open to the reproach of legalism so often laid against him."[31] On the contrary, John Hesselink in his thorough study insists, "For Calvin, as we have seen, the law is a dynamic entity primarily expressive of the gracious will of God for the benefit of his people." Hesselink focuses primarily on the third use of the law

30. Luther clearly explicated two uses of the law, but Calvin and Melanchthon employed three. Gerhard Ebeling's "On the Doctrine of the *Triplex Usus Legis* in the Theology of the Reformation," in *Word and Faith*, trans. James W. Leitch (Philadelphia: Fortress Press, 1963), 62–78, deals only with Luther and Melanchthon.

31. François Wendel, *Calvin: The Origins and Development of His Religious Thought*, trans. Philip Mairet (New York: Harper and Row, 1963), 200.

but provides a fine discussion of natural law and conscience.[32] In addition, he affirms the centrality of Christ in the covenant of grace and denies the so-called covenant of works. "There is, moreover, ultimately only one covenant and that covenant is the covenant of grace. In this regard, there is an important difference between Calvin and later Reformed theology which also taught a covenant of works."[33]

One of the most warmly debated topics in theology generally and in Calvin studies particularly is the doctrine of natural law.[34] The subject is framed in large measure by the Stoic confidence in nature as guide. Another part of the problem in Calvin is discerning the precise meaning and distinction between created and fallen nature. Calvin equates the natural law and the moral law when he asserts, "The Lord has provided us with a written law to give us a clearer witness of what was too obscure in the natural law" (II.8.2). Since the inward or natural law is the same as the moral law, Calvin devotes one of his longest expositions to the Ten Commandments. The goal of the law is to mold human life to outward honesty and to inward righteousness (II.8.6). "Whatever he requires of us . . . we must obey out of natural obligation. But what we cannot do is our own fault. If

32. In her chap. 4 Susan Schreiner also treats natural law and conscience in connection with the vestiges of the image of God remaining after the fall and their role in society. Especially valuable is the historical review of natural law and the conclusion, "Calvin was not interested in natural law in and of itself. He did not develop a 'theology of natural law' but rather, used the principle of natural law as an extension of his doctrine of providence" (*The Theater of His Glory: Nature and the Natural Order in the Thought of John Calvin* [Durham, NC: Labyrinth Press, 1991], 94).

33. I. John Hesselink, *Calvin's Concept of the Law* (Allison Park, PA: Pickwick Publications, 1992), 277, 88. Hesselink concludes his study by quoting Calvin to the effect that we must set reason aside and submit to the Holy Spirit in order to hear Christ living and reigning in us (III.7.1). This summary includes the correct observation, "The law is not the gospel, but it serves the gospel; it is an indispensable part of the gospel." And this puzzling one: "In a sense, [the law] is prior to and more comprehensive than the gospel, for it was the mode of God's relationship to humanity prior to and apart from sin" (285). In two overlapping essays, "Calvin's Doctrine of the Covenant of Grace," *Reformed Review* 15, no. 4 (May 1962): 1–12, and "The Covenant of Grace in Calvin's Teaching," in *Calvin Theological Journal* 2, no. 2 (November 1967): 133–61, Anthony A. Hoekema agrees with Hesselink that Calvin does not teach the covenant of works directly but thinks "the spiritual truths underlying this doctrine are found in Calvin." Disagreeing with Perry Miller's conclusions about the covenant of grace in Calvin and Calvinism, Hoekema insists "Calvin was as much concerned about the responsibility of man as about the sovereignty of God" (134). Hoekema judges that the covenant is unilateral in origin but bilateral in fulfillment. "The covenant of grace has its origin wholly in the undeserved grace of God, but, when once established, that covenant imposes mutual obligations on both God and man" (140). This affirmation of "mutual obligations" and the view of God's promises as conditional undervalues the reality of union with Christ, the unconditional gift of grace, and the work of the Holy Spirit in the Christian life.

34. In his classic survey of political theory George H. Sabine devotes three chapters to natural law but does not discuss the subject in connection with the early Protestant Reformers. Hugo Grotius gave this definition of natural law: "The law of nature is a dictate of right reason, which points out that an act, according as it is or is not in conformity with rational nature, has in it a quality of moral baseness or moral necessity; and that in consequence, such an act is either forbidden or enjoined by the author of nature, God" (George H. Sabine, *A History of Political Theory*, 3rd ed. [New York: Holt, Rinehart and Winston, 1961], 424). Even though Grotius himself appeals to God, in the seventeenth century naturalism and rationalism begin to detach from theology. See the excursus for remarks on "right reason." See also Kai Nielsen, "The Myth of Natural Law," *Law and Philosophy*, ed. Sidney Hook (New York: New York University Press, 1964), 122–43.

our lust in which sin reigns so holds us bound that we are not free to obey our Father, there is no reason why we should claim necessity as a defense, for the evil of that necessity is both within us and to be imputed to us" (II.8.2).

Josef Bohatec's magisterial study *Calvin und das Recht* was published in 1934 as Adolf Hitler was coming to power in Germany.[35] Additionally, Karl Barth and Emil Brunner were debating the broad topic of natural theology and the narrower topic of natural law within it, as previously discussed. Among the conclusions now to be drawn is that the political situation in the Third Reich and the theological responses to it overrode the clear evidence of Calvin's text. For example, Arthur Cochrane expresses his allegiance to Barth's view of natural law[36] but admits the force of McNeill's criticism to this effect: "The assumption of some contemporary theologians that natural law has no place in the company of Reformation theology cannot be allowed to govern historical inquiry or to lead us to ignore, minimize, or evacuate of reality, the positive utterances on natural law scattered through the works of the Reformers."[37]

Returning to the topic a couple of years after Cochrane, David Little offers both an unsatisfactory compliment and analysis. Calvin is praised for not overdoing his natural law theory but also for not rejecting or neglecting the idea altogether. Little's interest appears to be not so much in Calvin as on prospects for natural law theory among Christians, which he thinks will require (1) empirical generalizations about human nature applied cross-culturally and historically, (2) movement from these generalizations to behavioral prescriptions, (3) an understanding of the moral reliability of human nature corrupted by sin, and (4) a relation between natural moral obligation and Christian moral obligation.[38]

Following his exposition of the three uses of the law, Calvin discusses its two results. He declares, "In our discussion of the knowledge of ourselves we have set forth this chief point: that empty of all opinion of our own virtue, and shorn of all assurance of our own righteousness . . . we may learn [(1)] genuine humility and [(2)] self-abasement. Both of these the Lord accomplishes in his law" (II.8.1). Calvin's strong conviction about the need for humility before God and his abhorrence of pride is clear, but this summary of the law in two results appears to be only one. That is, humility and self-abasement seem to be two names for the same virtue.

In the final edition of the *Institutes*, Calvin added a chapter affirming again that while Christ was known to the Jews under the Law, he was clearly revealed only in the gospel (II.9). This chapter emphasizes further the role of both law and gospel in pointing to Christ. Calvin also expresses a wide hope for God's ancient chosen people. John's statement, "'No one has ever seen God; the only begotten

35. Josef Bohatec, *Calvin und das Recht* (Feudigen: Buchdruckereri u. Verlagsanstalt, 1934).

36. Arthur C. Cochrane, "Natural Law in the Teachings of John Calvin," *Church-State Relations in Ecumenical Perspective*, ed. Elwyn A. Smith (Louvain: Duquesne University Press, 1966), 180.

37. McNeill, "Natural Law," 168.

38. David Little, "Calvin and the Prospects for a Christian Theory of Natural Law," in *Norm and Context in Christian Ethics*, ed. Gene H. Outka and Paul Ramsey (New York: Charles Scribner's Sons, 1968), 175–97.

Son, who is in the bosom of the Father, has made him known' [John 1:18] does not exclude the pious who died before Christ from the fellowship of the understanding and light that shine in the person of Christ" (II.9.1). Calvin declares that "the word 'gospel,' taken in the broad sense, includes those testimonies of his mercy and fatherly favor which God gave to the patriarchs of old" (II.9.2).

The chief and often-neglected subject of Calvin's discussion of law and gospel in Book II is Jesus Christ. The point Calvin makes is that Christ is the content of both law and gospel but in different ways. Christ is revealed as promise in the law and as fulfillment in the gospel. However, even in Christ's fulfillment there remains a promise. While Christ has entirely accomplished our salvation, "the enjoyment thereof ever lies hidden under the guardianship of hope, until, having put off corruptible flesh, we be transfigured in the glory of him who goes before us" (II.9.3). On this "already" and "not yet," Calvin comments, "These two things agree rather well with each other: we possess in Christ all that pertains to the perfection of heavenly life, and yet faith is the vision of good things not seen" (II.9.3).

C. THE PERSON OF CHRIST

The full title of Book II is "The Knowledge of God the Redeemer in Christ, First Disclosed to the Fathers under the Law and Then to us in the Gospel." After the bracketed five chapters on sin, Calvin begins his Christology proper with an explication of the revelation of Christ in the gospel and the law, as we have just seen. In the present section Calvin expounds the doctrine of Christ with the more traditional topics of the person (II.12–13) and work (II.14) of Christ. In the former Calvin affirms the orthodox Chalcedonian doctrine that Christ is one person in two natures. In the second Calvin explains the three offices of Christ: the prophetic, the kingly, and the priestly. These two sections represent the usual distinction between the person and work of Christ. The former is a more static reflection on Christ's being—who Christ is. The latter is a more dynamic reflection on Christ's ministry—what Christ accomplishes. This distinction is only for convenience in teaching. As Jansen observes, "Christian theology must ever insist that Jesus' person and work interpret each other in indissoluble unity."[39] The interpretative problem is that the orthodox formula of "one person and two natures" is an intractable mystery, and as it is impossible to imagine that Christ's personal being can be explained with precision, so it is impossible to think his personal action can be explained adequately within human categories. This mystery leads to reflection on Calvin's doctrine of accommodation usually considered in connection with Scripture, but even more pertinent to Christology.

In the introduction to his recent book on Calvin's Christology, Stephen Edmondson necessarily notes and predictably claims that all previous studies of

---

39. John Jansen, *Calvin's Doctrine of the Work of Christ* (London: J. Clark, 1956), 13.

this topic are incomplete.[40] He then declares, "For Calvin, Christ's person and office are two sides of the same coin, so that, just as we must understand Christ's person functionally, so, too, must we understand his office personally. That is what it means to say that Christ is the Mediator: it is to tie person and office inextricably together."[41] Nevertheless, Edmondson in making a distinction between the substantial self and the functional self tilts toward emphasizing work over person, asserting, "The central pattern of Calvin's Christology [is] that Christ mediates the covenant in history through the threefold office of priest, king and prophet."[42] His interpretation insists the office of mediator is the center of Calvin's Christology because Calvin privileges Christ's work over his person.[43] Being mediator seems a function of the person rather than a function attached to a person. The key to understanding is that things "which apply to the office of the mediator are not spoken simply either of the divine nature or of the human." Nevertheless, Christ's mediatorial functions requiring his human nature were exerted *before* the incarnation (II.14.3). Commenting on Hosea 12:4, Calvin writes, "Christ, the eternal wisdom of God, did put on the character of a mediator, before he put on our flesh. He was therefore then a mediator and in that capacity he was also an angel. He was at the same time Jehovah, who is now God manifested in the flesh" (see also Com. Zech. 1:18). Calvin believes Christ's divinity was silent "whenever it was the business of the human nature to act alone in its own terms in fulfillment of the office of mediator" (Com. Mt. 24:36). Moreover, Jesus' growth in wisdom and God's favor refers to his human nature (Com. Lk. 2:40) as does his manifestation in the form of a servant (Com. Phil. 2:7). In this emphasis Calvin follows Augustine and Thomas (*ST* III.26.2), who assert that Christ is mediator as he is a human being. Augustine declares that God having become a partaker of our humanity affords us access to participation in his divinity (*City of God* 9:15).

Edmondson's emphasis on the work of the Mediator raises two immediate questions. First, does the strong focus on the role of Mediator, which is presumably prior to sin, lead inevitably to some diminution of the role of Redeemer, which is responsive to sin? After all, Redeemer is the term employed in the title of Book II. Second, and of potentially surpassing seriousness, to privilege Christ's

40. Stephen Edmondson, *Calvin's Christology* (Cambridge: Cambridge University Press, 2004), 3.
41. Ibid.
42. Ibid., 41. Jill Raitt, "Calvin's Use of Persona," in *Calvinus Ecclesiae Genevensis Custos*, ed. Wilhelm H. Neuser (New York: Verlag Peter Lang, 1984), employs three broad categories: person as office, person as "somebody," and person in reference to Trinity. Nevertheless, she asserts their inaccuracy because Calvin never used the word "person" to refer to a static mode of being. "Rather than begin with ontology and proceed to derived activity, Calvin preferred to begin with activity and proceed to the relations such activity indicated" (286).
43. Edmondson writes, "I take as the center of Calvin's Christology his repeated titular definition in the 1559 *Institutes* of Christ as the Mediator and articulate the form and content of Calvin's teaching around this central focus. . . . A variety of implications are entailed by Calvin's choice of this central moniker for Christ [including that for] Calvin, a focus on Christ as Mediator makes the doctrine of Christ's office in its relation to Christ's work the fundamental organizing principle in his Christology" (*Calvin's Christology*, 5).

work over his person can lead to an instrumental Christology in which Christ's work of salvation replaces his person as mediator and savior. This dangerous view was held by Friedrich Schleiermacher in the nineteenth century and John Hick in the twentieth. Surely union in Christ is not to be understood as union with Christ's work. In any case, Calvin exposits person before work. Edmondson affirms person this way: "Though our primary interest may be in what Christ has done for us, we cannot properly conceive of this activity if we do not also understand who Christ is."[44] At the same time he insists, "[Calvin's] Christology turns not on questions of who Jesus was, but rather around the axes of what Christ has done to save."[45] A more felicitous expression of the relation between person and work and the roles of Mediator and Redeemer is offered by David Willis, who asserts Calvin uses the word "Mediator" in a twofold sense, identifying "the Redeeming Mediator in the flesh with the Mediator who is the Eternal Son of God."[46] In other words, God the Mediator is apprehended in God the Redeemer (I.2.1). The person-and-work sequence need not be crucial for interpretation, but it can be. For example, in his 1927 book, *The Mediator*,[47] Emil Brunner employed the more traditional pattern of treating person, then work. In volume 2 of his 1949 Dogmatics, Brunner treats first the work of Christ and then his person.[48] Beginning with the work of Christ can improperly focus on the benefits of Christ to the neglect of his person, indicating interest selfishly concentrated on what Christ does for us without properly reverent attention to Christ in himself.[49]

The Protestant Reformers did not set out to reform the doctrine of Christ *as such*; they reaffirmed the christological decisions of the patristic period. Wendel is correct that "[Calvin] adopts in full the dogma of the two natures of Christ and the current explanations of the relation between the two natures."[50] The doctrine of "Scripture alone" did not imply the rejection of the historical development of doctrine (the Trinity, the two natures of Christ, etc.) because the Reformers believed that these developments faithfully served the truth of Scripture. In this essential way the Reformers accepted "tradition." The topics cannot be finally separated, but the primary focus of the Protestant Reformation was soteriological rather than christological. The question was not "Who is Jesus Christ?" because this question was regarded as correctly answered in the patristic period. The question was, "How does he save us?"

44. Ibid., 88.

45. Ibid., 42.

46. Willis, *Calvin's Catholic Christology: The Function of the So-called Extra Calvinisticum in Calvin's Theology* (Leiden: E. J. Brill, 1966), 99.

47. Emil Brunner, *The Mediator: A Study of the Central Doctrine of the Christian Faith*, trans. Olive Wyon (New York: Macmillan Co., 1934).

48. Emil Brunner, *The Christian Doctrine of Creation and Redemption*, trans. Olive Wyon (Philadelphia: Westminster Press, 1952).

49. See Barth's note criticizing Melanchthon on the benefits of Christ (*CD* 1.1.28, 259).

50. Wendel, *Calvin: The Origins and Development*, 215.

Calvin affirms Jesus Christ is both fully God, fully a man, and entirely one person. Each of these assertions is an ineffable mystery but altogether a necessary confession of the Lordship of Christ. In explanation of this confession Calvin rejects the overemphasis of Christ's divinity expounded by Andreas Osiander (discussed in the section on justification) as well as the overemphasis on Christ's humanity of Francesco Stancaro. "Stancarism," as Joseph Tylenda points out, "was neither a system of theology nor a new confession of faith, but a single idea." Accepting the Father, Son, and Holy Spirit as "the only one and true God, of one essence, of one will and of one operation," Stancaro concluded that our Lord Jesus Christ, true God and true man, is mediator according to his humanity alone. To the contrary Calvin insisted Christ is the Son of God in respect to both natures and therefore mediator in both natures.[51]

Although he affirms traditional Chalcedonian orthodoxy, Calvin's exposition of the person and natures of Christ is probably the most difficult part of the *Institutes* to understand and evaluate in terms of the text itself because so much depends on Calvin's emphases, which, in turn, involve what he does not say and in relation to views he does not discuss. In other words, understanding what Calvin is affirming requires knowing what he is tacitly denying. The three most notable features of Calvin's Christology are first the brevity of his discussion of the Trinity, including the doctrine of incarnation. The second is Calvin's emphasis on the continuing integrity of Christ's human nature. The third is the problem of accommodation. While Calvin affirms the orthodox one-person-in-two-natures formulation of Chalcedon, his emphasis on the humanity of Christ is remarkable. A crucial part of this doctrine of the humanity of Christ is expounded in Book IV in the chapter on the Eucharist. The result is that although both Luther and Calvin affirmed the orthodox doctrine, their different emphases led to fierce controversies over Christology.

These disagreements became obvious when Joachim Westphal attacked the Zurich Consensus, which Calvin and Bullinger had worked out. Calvin replied to Westphal in three treatises and then gave up continuation of the debate as unprofitable. According to Wendel, "Calvin and Westphal helped to envenom the controversy by the way they conducted it [but it was their] enthusiastic and often blundering allies who gave the lamentable quarrel its vast extension and its irresoluble character."[52] The lasting result of the debate appears in Article VIII of the Lutheran Formula of Concord (1577), which mentions the Eucharistic controversy between "the sincere theologians of the Augsburg Confession and the Calvinists, who had, moreover, perturbed other theologians." This controversy extends to the person of Christ and differing positions on the subtleties of the communication of attributes, which involves the proper understanding of the relation

---

51. See the two articles by Joseph Tylenda, "Christ the Mediator: Calvin versus Stancaro," *Calvin Theological Journal* 8, no. 1 (April 1973): 5; and "The Controversy on Christ the Mediator: Calvin's Second Reply to Stancaro," *Calvin Theological Journal* 8, no. 2 (November 1973): 137.

52. Wendel, *Calvin: The Origins and Development*, 104.

between Christ's human and divine natures. The *Concordia* charges Calvinists with a defective view of the hypostatic union, teaching "the combination that takes place when two boards are glued together, where neither confers any thing on the other nor receives any thing from the other." According to the Lutherans, the proper union and communion of the two natures can be illustrated by the similitude of a blade glowing in a fire. Such a knife will both cut and burn. According to Calvin there is an irreducible duality between Christ's divinity and humanity. Thus, "We hold that Christ, as he is God and man, consists of two natures united but not mingled" (II.14.4). Again, Calvin writes, "For we affirm his divinity so joined and united with his humanity that each retains its distinctive nature unimpaired, and yet these two natures constitute one Christ" (II.14.1). Rejecting both the metaphors of the two boards and the fiery blade, Calvin substitutes our two eyes. Our left and right eyes are each real and each visionary, but they are not the same. Nevertheless, almost always they bring to us a single sight (Sermon on I Tim. 3:16; *CO* 53:326).[53]

In sum, Lutheran theology sees an unacceptable duality in Calvinistic Christology; Calvinistic theology sees an unacceptable unity in Lutheran Christology.[54] Since acceptable Christology maintains the unity of person and the duality of natures, the fine tuning of the distinctions is more confessional than analytic. Edmondson asserts, "The *communicatio idiomatum*, in other words, is a means to express Christ's unity, not to explain it."[55] In his fine study of this doctrine, Willis writes that Calvin's discussion of the communication of attributes indicates "Calvin's awe before the mystery and his distaste for speculation set limits to his inquiry into what, in retrospect, may be called the ontological foundation of the Incarnation." Willis concludes, "For Calvin, the *communicatio idiomatum* is primarily a hermeneutical tool to keep in balance the varied Scriptural witness to the One Person, but it rests upon and presupposes the hypostatic union."[56]

The present reflection on Calvin's view of the person of Christ is treated under three headings: (a) the Eternal and Incarnate Son, (b) the One Person and Two Natures, and (c) the Body and the Head. However, before proceeding, a note on language is necessary.

Prior to the widespread adoption of inclusive language, the phrase "fully God and fully man" was the traditional expression of christological doctrine. It was then

---

53. The christological debate between Lutherans and Calvinists continues today. The subjects of "ubiquity" and "local presence" are more fully considered in Book IV as part of the Supper Strife.

54. In discussing this mystery Joseph N. Tylenda, "Calvin's Understanding of the Communication of Properties," *Westminster Theological Journal* (Fall 1975), concludes, "For Calvin, an attribute of one nature is *assigned* to the person of Christ, though designated by his other nature; for Luther the attribute of one nature is *granted* to the other nature" (64–65, emphasis added).

55. Edmondson, *Calvin's Christology*, 216. Edmondson offers a helpful short summary of this doctrine (214) which is the subject of Willis's important study.

56. Willis, *Calvin's Catholic Christology*, 67.

assumed that the term "man" did not exclude women. This view has recently changed.[57] However, the older language had a theological advantage in that the word "man" is usefully ambiguous referring both (1) to mankind in general (or humankind as some now prefer) and (2) to a specific human being. The newer language affirming Jesus Christ as fully divine and fully human (or God-human) can be theologically confusing, if not heretical. Concerning the manhood, Jesus Christ is, of course, to be understood in full identity with general humanity, but he was also a single and real person. Replacing "man" with the term "human," whatever its contemporary linguistic comfort value to some and awkwardness to others, is theologically inferior because it does not prevent a purely symbolic or idealistic understanding of Christ's humanity. In other words, in the new linguistic situation the humanity of Christ can be understood as pointing to an ideal example rather than a real individual.

Concerning the Godhead, the orthodox view insists Jesus Christ is not divine in the adjectival sense that he is *like* God, rather in the substantial sense he is the *same* as God or equal to God. Even the noun phrase "the divinity of Christ" can be understood to refer to Christ's likeness to God rather than his equality with God (Phil. 2:6). A more accurate term is the Deity of Christ, but to declare either Jesus Christ is fully deity and fully human in one person or fully deity and fully a human in one person is still stilted for some and can be misleading. For some English speakers the noun "deity" is not yet clearly parallel to the adjective "human," although "human" is now used often as a noun replacing "man," and will doubtless in time, if not already, connote both humanity in general and a single human being. The point is the orthodox formula confesses the full Deity of Jesus Christ and the full humanity of Jesus Christ, the latter meaning that he was a single real human being and that he represented all human beings when he took the sins of the world upon himself.

1. The Eternal and Incarnate Son

Many Christians wrongly believe the statement "Jesus Christ is the Son of the Eternal God" to be perfectly correct. To the contrary, the early church insisted that "Jesus Christ is the *Eternal* Son of the Eternal God." In addition to defending the doctrine of Trinity, this crucial adjective calls attention to the distinction between Christ the Mediator and Christ the Redeemer. The Christian conviction that God

---

57. See Brian Wren, *What Language Shall I Borrow? God-Talk in Worship: A Male Response to Feminist Theology* (New York: Crossroad, 1989). I learned a great deal about my own unexamined assumptions from Ursula K. LeGuin, *The Left Hand of Darkness* (New York: Ace Books, 1969). Her Gethenians do not see each other as male or female. They may choose to be either and during their lifetime both. When the mother of several children may be the father of several more, my comfortable categories collapse.

is revealed in Christ (2 Cor. 5:19) led to reflection on the eternality of the Son. According to John's Gospel, Jesus Christ the Word was with God in the beginning and was God. The eternal son was concealed in God infinitely before the foundation of the world and, after being obscurely outlined to the patriarchs under the Law, was at length more fully manifested in the flesh (Com. Jn. 1:1).[58] This confession of eternal sonship in turn led to a distinction between Christ as Mediator and Christ as Redeemer. Calvin believes the distance between the Creator and the creature is so great, a Mediator was *always necessary* to draw humankind near to God. In the creation of the universe the Word is set forth as intermediary (I.13.7). Since we are not able to ascend to God, Calvin says that "it was necessary [though not of simple or absolute necessity] for the Son of God to become for us 'Immanuel, that is, God with us'" (II.12.1). Still, he was the Son of God before the creation of the world.

Since Christ is the Mediator, looking to him alone is the principal mark of faith. However, because of sin and fall, what was once the unbridgeable distance between God and mankind has now become an impassable gulf. Nevertheless, the revelation of Christ is not simply the result of God's response to human sin. "Even if man had remained free from all stain, his condition would have been too lowly for him to reach God without a Mediator" (II.12.1). Calvin asserts "that in the original order of creation and the unfallen state of nature Christ was set over men and angels as their Head" (II.12.4), but Calvin refuses to carry this affirmation into a speculation. The conviction Christ would have become a man if mankind had not needed redemption, Calvin regards as idle speculation since it is contrary to fact. The notion Christ might have taken on human flesh for the purpose of showing love toward those who are *not* lost, Calvin rejects as a useless inquiry since in fact all are lost. In actuality the fall is set "between man's first origin and the restoration we obtain through Christ" (II.12.7). Calvin spends little time trying to describe the contrary-to-fact situation of a sinless world in no need of a redeemer. The correct understanding is the incarnation was *not* forced on God by human sin. God's grace would have been extended to humanity in Jesus Christ the Mediator even if the role of Redeemer had not been required. The confession of the Eternal Son of the Eternal God *before* the historical incarnation is a powerful declaration of the mystery of God, fostering humility and forbidding speculation. At the same time it is a salutary reminder that the person and work of Christ cannot be restricted to the history of Israel and the church.[59]

---

58. For the eternal Son in the Synoptic Gospels, see Simon J. Gathercole, *The Preexistent Son: Recovering the Christologies of Matthew, Mark, and Luke* (Grand Rapids: Wm. B. Eerdmans, 2006).

59. Karl Barth's section on "The Eternal Son" in his *Church Dogmatics* (1.1.11) is based on the deity of Christ. Barth admits the dogma of Christ's divinity is not found in the biblical texts. Nevertheless "the divinity of Christ is to be regarded not as a derivative, but as a *fundamental* statement." "No reflection can claim to be the basis of this assumption, no reflection can call this assumption in question. Any reflection can but start from it and return to it" (*CD* 1.1, 475). Calvin, on the other hand, assumes the Scripture teaches the divinity of Christ in many places, just not at Isa. 4:3 where that interpretation is, he thinks, an ingenious gloss.

2. The One Person and Two Natures

In his Commentary on I Timothy (3:16) Calvin addresses the immensity of the mystery of the Godhead, affirming, "The most fitting description of Christ's person is contained in the words, 'God manifested in the flesh.'" Paul asserts the reality of the two natures, their distinction and their unity in one person. "In this single phrase the true and orthodox faith is powerfully armed against Arius, Marcion, Nestorius and Eutyches." The biblical declaration that Jesus Christ is Lord came to include the patristic confession of the eternality of the Son, the incarnation, and the doctrine of two natures in one person. This development did not follow a logical but a historical order. That is, the issues were differently considered at different times and places. The orthodox conclusion that Jesus Christ is fully God and fully a man was asserted in the Nicene Creed and reaffirmed in the Chalcedonian formula. Calvin repeats the formulation this way: "For we affirm [Christ's] divinity so joined and united with his humanity that each retains its distinct nature unimpaired, and yet these two natures constitute one person" (II.14.1). Once agreed, this understanding was not seriously challenged until recent times. Nevertheless, the general consensus of orthodoxy always left room for special emphases.

In the context of his exposition of the knowledge of God the Creator and within the discussion of the Trinity, Calvin affirms the classical doctrine that Jesus of Nazareth is true God (I.13). He reasserts this affirmation in his Book II christological discussion but now in the context of the incarnation of true God in true man. Agreeing with the patristic doctrine that Jesus Christ is one person in two natures, Calvin expounds the deity of Christ, the humanity of Christ, and those biblical passages that comprehend both natures at the same time (II.14.3). In the introduction to his commentary on John's Gospel, Calvin says the Synoptics emphasize the humanity of Jesus (his body) while John emphasizes the divinity of Christ (his soul). According to Calvin, John's Gospel is the key to open the door to understanding the others.

In dealing with his divinity Calvin declares, "Since all the fullness of the Deity dwells in Christ, there is no God apart from him" (Com. I Jn. 2:22). Again, "We must hold this principle that Christ was true Jehovah from the beginning. The Son of God is the same in essence with the Father, and is with him the only true God (Com. Zech. 11:14)." "Let us account it sufficient that God has formed the heavens by his word in such a manner as to prove the eternal deity of Christ" (Com. Ps. 33:6). Christ gives clear witness to his deity first because Christ does not judge in a human way and second because he makes himself the author of election. Christ testifies that those who were chosen before the creation of the world were chosen by himself. "Such a remarkable demonstration of His divine power should affect us more deeply than if the Scripture had called him God a hundred times" (Com. Jn. 13:18).

Calvin also confesses the humanity of Christ who so identified with us he was not embarrassed to admit a stain in his own genealogy resulting from incestuous intercourse among his ancestors (Com. Mt. 1:3). This condescension means that in touching his side and hands Thomas confesses Christ as Lord and also calls him God. Through his humanity we arrive at the divinity of Christ starting from the nearer knowledge. By the Christ-man we are led to the Christ-God, our faith "apprehending Christ on each, born in a stable, and hanging on a cross, it goes on to the glory of his resurrection and then at length to his eternal life and power, in which shines his divine majesty. Yet . . . we cannot know Christ aright as our Lord without the knowledge of his divinity immediately following" (Com. Jn. 20:28). According to Calvin, in his secret divinity Christ "is no better known to us than is the Father. But he is said to be the express image of God because in him God has entirely revealed himself, inasmuch as his infinite goodness, wisdom, and power appear in him substantially" (Com. Jn. 14:10). This means there is no reason to try to probe the secrets of heaven when God provides for our weakness by coming near in the person of his son. We should look to him alone when concerned for the heavenly protection of our salvation. For in Christ the face of God the Father otherwise hidden far away appears to us so that the naked majesty of God shall not engulf us with its infinite brightness (Com. Jn. 5:22).

In confessing Jesus Christ as a singular person, Calvin comments that Christ shows his divinity by commanding the angels, since he could not issue orders to angels without being God himself. Also in presenting himself in human form to Daniel we see a foreshadowing of incarnation (Com. Dan. 8:16). Although God and man are united in one person, Calvin insists it does not follow that human nature received what is peculiar to divine nature (Com. Lk. 2:40). The relation of one nature to the other nature in one person led to the doctrine of the communication of the properties.

The Christologies of Luther and Calvin are similar in believing God is known in Christ who is both God and man in one person. However, the two natures are differently emphasized. These differences are complicated but fundamental and important. Interestingly, while the sharpest difference between Calvin and Lutheran theology is in Christology, the historical battle was over the Eucharist. According to Wendel, "Whenever Calvin comes to speak of the person of the Christ, he takes care to place emphasis simultaneously upon the unity of the God-man and upon the distinction between the two natures." Both Calvin and Luther insist that Christ is not separated from God but "in Luther's case the tendency to underline the unity of the Christ is far more pronounced than in Calvin's, so much so that Luther has sometimes been accused of monophysitism." In distinction from Luther, "Calvin affirms equally and more clearly still that the distinction between the two natures is indispensable."[60] Wendel correctly calls attention to the genuine distinction between the two natures in Calvin's theol-

---

60. Wendel, *Calvin: The Origins and Development*, 219. An entirely opposite conclusion on Christ's real humanity is drawn by Battenhouse, "Doctrine of Man," 460, who sees in Calvin a tendency toward monophysitism or the denial of Christ's true humanity. Calvin's Christology "suggests, as I read it, accommodation rather than orthodox incarnation. Christ seems essentially a deity playing a stage part, putting on a mask of humanity as a temporary expedient, educational in purpose."

ogy, but he does not adequately explain Calvin's view of the full reality of both natures in one person which leads to the integral and risen humanity of Jesus.[61]

Calvin places a special emphasis on the genuineness of Christ's human nature and therefore his efficacy for us. Having treated Christ's true divinity in I.13.7–12, Calvin deals with his true humanity in Book II. The so-called *extra Calvinisticum* contains a defense of Christ's real humanity, as Willis puts it: "That the Eternal Son of God was not restricted to the flesh does not mean he was not united to it. To confess the unity of the two natures in One Person is to confess that mysterious way in which he who was boundless in majesty and power joined himself to that which was weak and limited."[62] Christ was made *from* woman rather than *by* woman (II.13.3). He became "a lowly and despised man" (II.13.2), yet remained "without fault and corruption" (II.13.4). Human generation is of itself not unclean, but Christ was sanctified by the Spirit for the purpose of joining himself to base and ignoble men. "For we know that the children of God are not born of flesh and blood but of the Spirit through faith" (II.13.2). Christ who was the true and natural son of God before the creation of the world (II.14.5–6) was made man that we might be made children of God by adoption and grace. Christ, then, possesses by nature the Sonship that we receive as a gift (II.14.6).

Both Luther and Calvin vigorously denied they were either Nestorian or Eutychian. Nevertheless, Reformed theology thought the Lutheran view tended toward Eutychianism, and led to a denial of the real humanity of Jesus. Lutheran theology thought Reformed theology tended toward Nestorianism and led to the denial of real personal unity. Of course, Christ is one person, but Calvin emphasized that the one person consists of two distinct natures, so Christ's humanity never disappears into his divinity. This conviction is powerfully evident in the eucharistic emphasis on Christ's ascended humanity and his life-giving flesh and blood. Although affirming Jesus Christ is one person, Calvin also affirms both his full divinity and full humanity. This duality even extends to his humanity! In

---

61. Wendel, *Calvin: The Origins and Development*, 224. In his *Divine Comedy* the great Italian and Roman Catholic poet Dante Alighieri addresses Christology at the end of the *Purgatorio* (Canto 29f.) and again in the final vision of the *Paradiso* (Canto 33). In the former the presence of Christ is symbolized by the appearance of a Griffon which is one creature but seen as half eagle and half lion. In purgatory the vision of Dante the pilgrim is not yet entirely clear. He sees the Griffon reflected in the eyes of the Blessed Beatrice. Most Protestants have difficulty with the general theological role of Beatrice in the *Divine Comedy*, but Dante describes a fascinating effect. The pilgrim cannot maintain the proper visual image of the two natures of the Griffon because one continually slides into the other, indicating that Jesus Christ is seen now as God and now again as a man. The brilliant image of the Griffon is central to the heavenly procession in Purgatory but does not appear at all in Paradise. In the final and beatific vision the pilgrim looks into the Godhead and sees not only three lights that are one light, but also a human form in God, suggesting a risen humanity in God. A serious question may be asked concerning the metaphor of beatific vision as adequate for the afterlife. An everlasting and therefore continuing kingdom of God might be a stronger image for poets and theologians to contemplate. In any case, Dante can go no further in imagining Trinity and incarnation and their relation to humanity. Calvin speaks of an "immediate vision of the Godhead" in dealing with the unity of the person of the mediator "seated at the right hand of the Father" (II.14.3), but the context is a christological testimony, not a celestial theory.

62. Willis, *Calvin's Catholic Christology*, 63. The point is sometimes made that Christ is wholly God (*totus Deus*) but not the whole of God (*totum Dei*).

his commentary on Galatians (3.13) Calvin says, "There are two things to be considered, not only in the person of Christ, but even in his human nature. The one is that he was the unspotted Lamb of God, full of blessing and grace. The other is that he took our place *and thus became a sinner* and subject to the curse, not in himself indeed, but in us; yet in such a way that it was necessary for him to act in our name" (emphasis added). Calvin affirms Christ was sinless, but he asserts that, in an important sense, we must also say he became a sinner. "There is nothing strange in the fact that Christ, who was to be made a curse upon the cross for us, should take upon himself our uncleanness, even to the extent of being accused for our sakes, although he was free of fault or sin (Com. Lk. 2:22)." Reformed theology has maintained this point not merely to avoid docetism, but as necessary to salvation. Christ *as sinner* stood in our place.[63] As Edmondson observes, "Our union with God is dependent on the unity and humanity in Christ."[64]

3. The Body and the Head

To this point the christological confession deals with time. How can one person be understood to live in two complete and different natures at the same time? An answer was advanced in the conception of a communication of properties between the human and divine (*communicatio idiomatum*).[65] Calvin approves the doctrine because he understands the Scripture to speak of Christ (1) sometimes attributing to him what belongs only to his humanity, (2) sometimes attributing to him what belongs only to his divinity, and (3) sometimes what embraces both natures but fits neither alone (II.14.1).[66] The same issue is also raised in terms of space. That is, how can the same person, the head of the body, be understood to live simultaneously in two different places, heaven and earth? The phrase "This is my body" occurs in the celebration of the Lord's Supper but is also a topic in the doctrine of Christ. While "the Body of Christ" is most familiarly associated in the New Testament with the church, the body is also an issue in the doctrine of Christ. Modern christological discussions sometimes make a distinction between "the Jesus of history" and "the Christ of faith": Jesus being the human name and Christ being the divine title. This distinction can be placed on the two natures—human and divine—of the one person Jesus Christ.

63. This daring thought is explored by Paul van Buren, *Christ in Our Place: The Substitutionary Character of Calvin's Doctrine of Reconciliation* (Grand Rapids: Wm. B. Eerdmans, 1957), 40–47.

64. Edmondson, *Calvin's Christology*, 218. Edmondson thinks, "No one sensitive to the Nestorian heresy would wish to speak of an independent human nature in Christ, so, of course, Calvin's understanding of Christ's human nature is bound up with its relation to his divinity." Presumably Edmondson in denying an *independent* human nature also affirms an *integral* human nature.

65. See Wendel, *Calvin: The Origins and Development*, 221–24. According to Raitt, "Calvin taught that the communication of idioms occurs only through the person of the mediator and never between the natures themselves" (Jill Raitt, "The Person of the Mediator: Calvin's Christology and Beza's Fidelity" in *Occasional Papers of the American Society for Reformation Research*, vol. 1 (December 1977), 53.

66. For a reflection on the two natures one person, *filoque, communicatio idiomatum*, and *extra Calvinisticum*, see Willis, *Calvin's Catholic Christology*, 81–82.

The question is how can one person—one human person—be truly and fully God? Calvin's assertion of this mystery came to be called the *extra Calvinisticum.* Calvin declares the incarnation does not mean that the deity left heaven to hide in a human body. Rather, "Here is something marvelous: The Son of God *descended from heaven* in such a way that, *without leaving* heaven, he willed to be borne in the virgin's womb . . ." (II.13.4, emphasis added). The purpose of the incarnation is that God's grace alone has ordained that "the office of Redeemer was laid upon [Christ] that he might be our Savior" (II.16.1). Christ stands in our midst to lead us little by little to a firm union with God (I.15.5). The Christ who died obediently in the place of the sinner acquired righteousness for us and entered heaven in our flesh. Thus in him we already possess heaven. This effect does not extend to all mankind since faith intervenes to engraft us spiritually into the body of Christ (II.13.2), a notion that is developed in Book III. The whole Christ is present everywhere, says Calvin, but not in his wholeness. For in his flesh he is contained in heaven until he appears in judgment (*Institutes* II.13.4; IV.17.30). Calvin rightly calls this subject a mystery, which we confess both in encounter with Christ who is present to us and also seated at the right hand of God. This dual affirmation is fundamental to Calvin's doctrine of the Lord's Supper.

The so-called *extra Calvinisticum* reappears in Calvin's exposition of "local presence" in the Lord's Supper and is discussed there. For now it is clear that Calvin denied the divine ubiquity of Christ, as the Lutherans taught it, in favor of the humanity of Christ who descended from heaven yet never left heaven. In the light of these logically contradictory christological affirmations concerning the communication of human and divine attributes, Karl Barth suggests that no resolution is possible between the opposing Lutheran and Reformed views. We cannot say one is right and the other wrong. The truth about the reality of Jesus Christ, according to Barth, does not allow a single conceptualization (either Lutheran or Calvinist), so if there is to be an evangelical theology at all, these two understandings must remain.[67] However, the problem is not to confess the adequacy of any conceptualization, but whether any conceptualization is adequate to the confession. Christians confess the Lordship of Christ. Their theologians try to protect this confession by conceptualizing the hypostatic union, the *communicatio idiomatum,* to protect the oneness of person and the *extra Calvinisticum* to protect the twoness of natures, but each affirmation remains a mystery. As Raphael cautions Adam in Milton's *Paradise Lost,* perfect knowledge is beyond the capacity of angels to declare or humans to grasp:

> to recount Almighty works
> What words or tongue of Seraph can suffice
> Or heart of man suffice to comprehend?
> Yet what thou canst attain . . .
> shall not be withheld

67. *CD* 1.2, 171.

Thy hearing, such Commission from above
I have receiv'd, to answer Thy desire
Of knowledge within bounds; beyond abstain
To ask.
(*PL* 7.112–21; see also 5.563–76)

On this theme Calvin asks with some heat, "Who even of slight intelligence does not understand that, as nurses commonly do with infants, God is wont in a measure to 'lisp' in speaking to us? Thus such forms of speaking do not so much express clearly what God is like as accommodate the knowledge of him to our slight capacity" (I.13.1). When he says the sabbath was profaned by the priests, he is speaking imprecisely. "Christ was adapting himself to his hearers" (Com. Mt. 12:5).

This concept addresses the problem of a biblical statement that seems to contradict a dogmatic conviction. For example, in a classic passage in *The City of God*, Augustine deals with traits like anger and repentance ascribed to God in the Scripture but embarrassing for the theological mind to contemplate. Rather than questioning the grounds for his rejection of these characteristics, Augustine explains their use and value. The anger of God does not, he claims, inflame God's mind nor disturb God's unchangeable tranquillity. "His thought and reconsideration also are the unchangeable reason which changes things; for He does not, like man, repent of anything He has done, because in all matters His decision is as inflexible as His prescience is certain." Augustine assumes without question that God's perfection requires unchangeableness. "But," he continues, "if Scripture were not to use such expressions [as the anger of God], it would not familiarly insinuate itself into the minds of all classes of men, whom it seeks access to for their good, that it may alarm the proud, arouse the careless, exercise the inquisitive, and satisfy the intelligent; and this it could not do, did it not first stoop, and in a manner descend, to them where they lie."[68] Augustine does not explain why the intelligent should be satisfied with descriptions which they must transpose from accommodation to the weakness of the human mind (God's anger) to the truth of which the human mind is capable (God's unchangeableness). On the same subject Calvin insists that statements about God's love and hostility are not said falsely (II.16.3), but they are beyond "our feeble comprehension" to understand.

The concept of accommodation in Calvin has been addressed by Edward Dowey, Ford Lewis Battles, and David F. Wright. According to Dowey, "Accommodation is of two varieties: (a) the universal and necessary accommodation of the infinite mysteries of God *to finite comprehension*, which embraces all revelation, and (b) the special, gracious accommodation *to human sinfulness* which is connected with the work of redemption." Dowey's primary interest in accommodation is its noetic quality. Of God's truth we can know only what is accommodated to our small capacity as (1) creature and (2) sinful creature. In both situations we are taught humility before God's mystery. Dowey concludes, "This

---

68. Augustine, *The City of God*, trans. Marcus Dods (Chicago: Encyclopedia Britannica, 1952), 15:25.

concept of accommodation with respect to all knowledge of God, whether meant in principle for man as creature or as sinner, is the horizon of Calvin's theology."[69] However important the concept of accommodation is to the knowledge of God and ourselves, this is an overstatement. Calvin's theological horizon is not limited to epistemological considerations. Knowing takes its place within the soteriological context of atonement, requiring confession of what God has done for us (faith) and requiring obedience to God's will for our lives (love).

In contrast to Dowey, Battles treats accommodation not in epistemological but in rhetorical terms. Battles believes after Calvin's conversion he exchanged human rhetoric for divine rhetoric. "Thus, the starkest inconsistencies in Scripture are harmonized through rhetorical analysis, within the frame of divine accommodation, to human capacity; but, more than merely serving as an apologetical device, this method unlocks for Calvin God's beneficent tutelage and pedagogy of his wayward children." Battles points out that (1) the apparent teaching of Scripture asserts God has a mouth, ears, eyes, hands, and feet, while (2) the true teaching is God's infinite and spiritual essence. The role of (3) accommodation between appearance and reality is that God descends far beneath his loftiness and speaks to us in terms of our slight capacity to understand. Still Battles thinks accommodation is Calvin's fundamental way of explaining God's revelation, which is calculated to our capacity[70] for the purpose of leading us to Christ. In other words, accommodation is treated less epistemologically and more soteriologically. Calvin makes this point firmly. "Irenaeus writes that the Father himself infinite becomes finite in the Son, for he has accommodated himself to our little measure lest our minds be overwhelmed by the immensity of his glory." This statement does not subordinate the Son to the Father. "It means nothing else than that God is comprehended in Christ alone" (II.6.4).

In his exposition Battles makes two important points. First, in the *Institutes* Calvin never uses the noun *accommodatio* but always the verbs *accommodare* or *attemperare*. This usage indicates that accommodation is not a state of knowledge as with Dowey but a divine action, "God was Accommodating. . . ." Second, Battles in a refreshing admission declares, "It may be that we have succumbed to the temptation of putting the concept of accommodation too much at the center of Calvin's thought and of trying to organize everything around this notion. Yet, if this be a faithful interpretation, accommodation would seem (even when Calvin does not explicitly advert to it) his fundamental way of explaining how the secret,

---

69. See Edward A. Dowey Jr., *The Knowledge of God in Calvin's Theololgy*, 3rd ed. (Grand Rapids: Eerdmans, 1994 [1951]), 4–17.

70. Ford Lewis Battles, "God Was Accommodating Himself to Human Capacity," *Interpretation: A Journal of Bible and Theology* 31 (1977): 19–38, reprinted in *Interpreting John Calvin*, ed. Robert Benedetto (Grand Rapids: Baker Books, 1996). According to Battles, capacity (*captus*) is the key word for Calvin. He suggests "that be the theme of a separate investigation" (130), which so far as I know Battles did not undertake. Obviously, a study of Calvin's view of human capacity would benefit the Barth-Brunner debate, which focused on that issue.

hidden God reveals himself to us."[71] In support Zachman claims, "There is nearly universal agreement that this description of the role of accommodation in Calvin's theology is accurate."[72] If his judgment is accurate, I must be classified among the "nearly" because I regard the concept as rhetorically useful but logically incoherent.

David Wright thinks condescension is the hallmark of all God's dealing with humanity. "That is why the motif, or cluster of motifs, of divine accommodation takes us to the heart of Calvin's theology."[73] Wright's essay aims to place the concept of accommodation "within the body of [Calvin's] theology, to ascertain its functional importance, particularly in relation to his understanding of God," pointing out that when Origen and Augustine "found something in Scripture that was patently unworthy of God if taken literally" they resorted to allegory, while Calvin invoked divine accommodation.[74]

In his helpful listing of Calvin's various appeals to accommodation, one is especially troubling: the accommodation to barbarity. "This is accommodation not merely to humanity *qua* humanity, or to sinful humanity, but to barbarity, the crudity and cruelty of a primitive stage of human history." As examples Wright cites God's permission for Hebrew slavery (Lev. 25:39–40), for the monstrous dissolution of the bond of slavery only by the violation of marriage (Exod. 21:1–6), and for a father to sell his daughter into slavery (Exod. 21:7–11).[75] Wright concludes that God controls revelation completely "but at the cost of self-limitation, sometimes to such an extent that the true knowledge of God and his will is largely veiled . . . Too often in the Pentateuch Calvin claims that what Moses in the name of God instructed or allowed the Israelites was a travesty of God's perfect law. *The real truth was as much masked as exposed by the text.*"[76]

Theologians work between bold confidence and abject humility. Karl Barth put the issue memorably. "*As ministers we ought to speak of God. We are human, however, and so cannot speak of God. We ought therefore to recognize both our obligation and our inability and by that very recognition give God the glory.*"[77] Wright rightly claims the ability to recognize biblical passages that are unworthy of God if taken literally and appeals to accommodation for their interpretation. Difficult as is the theory of accommodation actually applied to Scripture in the context of human understanding, more difficult still is its application to Christology in the

71. Battles, *Interpreting John Calvin*, 118.

72. Randall C. Zachman, "Calvin as Analogical Theologian," *Scottish Journal of Theology* 51, no. 2 (1998): 162. Zachman thinks Battles left two major questions unaddressed. The first: *how* does accommodation take place? The second: *why* does accommodation take the form it does? The suggested answer is found in terms of the analogy and anagoge between the sign and the reality signified.

73. David F. Wright, "Calvin's Accommodating God," in *Calvinus Sincerioris Religionis Vindex*, ed. Wilhelm H. Neuser and Brian G. Armstrong (Kirksville, MO: Sixteenth-Century Journal Publishers, 1997), 18.

74. Ibid., 5, 7.

75. Ibid., 10, 11.

76. Ibid., 18–19 (emphasis added).

77. Karl Barth, *The Word of God and the Word of Man*, trans. Douglas Horton (New York: Harper and Brothers, 1957), 186 (emphasis in original).

context of divine incarnation. The problem is usually ignored by using the term "accommodation" for the former and "condescension" for the latter.

Calvin confesses "that God is comprehended in Christ alone" requires understanding "the Father, himself infinite, becomes finite in the Son, for he has accommodated himself to our little measure lest our minds be overwhelmed by the immensity of his glory" (II.6.4). Calvin recognizes that Scripture sometimes attributes to Christ what belongs only to his human nature, sometimes attributes to him what belongs only to his divine nature, and sometimes what embraces both natures but fits neither alone (II.14.1). Presumably these confusing attributions are designed to accommodate the knowledge of Christ to our slight capacity. After the close of the New Testament, several centuries elapsed before the christological formula (two natures one person) was devised and accepted at Nicaea. However, if the biblical premises were accommodations, it would seem the dogmatic conclusions must be likewise. The solution, I think, requires the evaluation of theological language not for its strict logical coherence but for its adequacy in protecting confessional mysteries.

The problem accommodation theorists overlook is the difficulty of recognizing and then establishing the difference between real truth and accommodated truth. The concept of accommodation assumes that the precise truth is beyond human capacity and must be masked—additionally that God, not content with this situation, offers an explanation which humans can recognize is not perfect but only useful given our small capacity. This raises the question whether all revelation is accommodated, and if so leading to the problem of our recognizing the point where limited knowledge becomes false. Certainly the accommodation of the glorious truth of God to the small capacity of the finite and sinful mind is not supposed to inculcate falsehood by reduction (although see Com. Mt. 12:5). Nevertheless, ordinary human minds have such various capacities that various levels of accommodation are required. Somewhere down the line of accommodation to human understanding, positive error will be impossible to avoid—if not in divine intention, then at least in human reception.

Reflection on acceptable christological conceptualization is a crucial task, but such reflection demonstrates with exceptional clarity both the necessity and the inadequacy of theological constructions. To the best of its ability the Christian church must protect the central miracle of its confession of faith from distortion, but the requirements for protection and confession do not produce analytical clarity. The usual explanation for this problem is that God's reality is beyond human reason but not contrary to it. Since this pious confidence in reason is grounded in itself, a superior stance accepts as impenetrable mysteries the relation of "persons" in the doctrine of the Trinity and the precise relation between the two natures in the incarnation. The hypostatic union can be passionately confessed but not rationally explained. Theological reflection aims at protective and confessional adequacy, but this entails intellectual formulations that will remain provisional.

The unfathomable complexities of the larger, and somewhat more distant, mysteries of Trinity and incarnation become even more evident in the smaller, and closer, mysteries of dealing with the mind and will of Jesus Christ. To the question of whether Jesus had two minds—one human, one divine—Calvin teaches that the union of the two natures in Christ means Christ who knew all things was yet ignorant of some things as a man. Otherwise he could not experience grief and anxiety as we do (Com. Mt. 24:36). To the question of whether Jesus had two wills—one divine, one human—Calvin rejects the monothelite heresy by answering, "In Christ there exists a remarkable example of balance between the wills of God and of man; they differ from each other without conflict or contradiction" (Com. Mt. 26:39). In these struggles to understand the one person and two natures Calvin claims in a charming comment that Christ slept naturally as a tired human being but his divinity stayed awake to watch over him (Com. Mt. 8:23). Reflecting on "the child grew" (Luke 2:40) Calvin insists Christ was subject to human ignorance. Although "he was one person of God and man, it does not follow that he was given anything that was properly divine."

The conviction that God was in Christ reconciling the world to himself (2 Cor. 5:19) led to the protective doctrines of Trinity and incarnation. The two-natures-one-person doctrine led in turn to the question of whether Jesus with two natures had two minds or being one person had one theanthropic mind. Later, the same question arose concerning one will (monothelitism) or two wills (dyothelitism). One will was the orthodox position for some years until it was declared unorthodox at the Sixth Ecumenical Council meeting at Constantinople in AD 680. Obviously these decisions were determined by appeal to conviction and not by appeal to evidence, since mysteries of this magnitude are not susceptible to evidentiary hearing. On an even smaller scale of preference one may begin exposition with the person of Christ, as Calvin did, or with the work of Christ, as Edmondson thinks Calvin meant.

D. THE WORK OF CHRIST

The primary work of Christ as Redeemer is to create atonement between the Holy God and sinful humanity. Granted its importance, Christians have strangely never been able to produce a single and common understanding of this central theological affirmation. Strictly speaking, various more or less acceptable theories of atonement are available, but no consensus doctrine of atonement has ever been produced. Historical theories of atonement can be summarized in various ways. For example, Irenaeus's view is characterized as dramatic and dualistic; Anselm's view is called objective and rational; Abelard's, subjective and moral. In turn these interpretations are interpreted by numerous studies—one of the best known being Gustaf Aulén's classic *Christus Victor*.[78] Another way of divid-

---

78. Gustaf Aulén, *Christus Victor: An Historical Study of the Three Main Types of the Idea of Atonement*, trans. A. G. Hebert (New York: Macmillan, 1951).

ing theories of atonement is between those that posit a change in God and those
that posit a change in mankind. In the early church Origen and Irenaeus thought
atonement brought about a change in God's relation to the creature. Origen
spoke of a ransom paid to cancel Satan's claim on sinners. Irenaeus thought Christ
recapitulated all the steps of human life and by his obedience reversed the fall
into sin. In the Middle Ages, Anselm taught that sin had dishonored God and
that Christ had restored God's honor by rendering satisfaction to God. Also in
the Middle Ages, and to the contrary, Peter Abelard insisted that God is not angry
with his sinful human creatures. Therefore, the purpose of Christ's suffering is
not to change God's attitude but to manifest God's love for mankind and set an
example to follow. In more recent times McLeod Campbell offered a theory of
vicarious repentance. Perfect repentance for sin, he thought, would produce sufficient atonement for it. On this interpretation, the work of Christ is not actually suffering for sinners but vicariously repenting for them, thus producing
forgiveness.[79]

The narrative of theology often moves from an epistemological basis in Scripture to the being and work of God followed by a discussion of sin and then
redemption from sin followed by the person and work of Christ. In contrast
Calvin expounds the knowledge of God the Creator and then the knowledge of
God the Redeemer, but he does not devote a separate exposition to a doctrine of
atonement. This approach convinces many scholars that Calvin does not have a
single, unified doctrine or theory of atonement, and neither Niesel nor Wendel
lists "atonement" in their subject index. Robert A. Peterson addresses "Calvin's
doctrine of the atonement" under the rubric of God's love, claiming, "It is therefore not surprising that [Calvin's] theology tugs at the heart, as well as challenges
the mind." In addition to expectable chapters on incarnation and Christ's threefold office, Peterson explicates six biblical atonement themes: Jesus was the obedient second Adam, the victor, the legal sacrifice, the historical sacrifice, the
meritor of grace, and an example in his death on the cross. He concludes that
Calvin did not formulate a theory of the work of Christ but expounded the threefold office and these six biblical themes without synthesizing them.[80] If Calvin
did not formulate a theory of the work of Christ, it seems puzzling to speak of
his doctrine of atonement. However, Peterson may be recognizing that Calvin's
theology is more generally confessional than precisely theoretical. Each section
of the *Institutes'* Book II contributes to the confession that God is for us as
Redeemer. This sentiment is profoundly expressed in the doxology that concludes
the penultimate chapter. "We see that our whole salvation and all its parts are
comprehended in Christ. . . . If we seek salvation, we are taught by the very name

---

79. John McIntyre lists twelve different theories (he calls them models) of atonement in
The Shape of Soteriology: Studies in the Doctrine of the Death of Christ (Edinburgh: T. & T. Clark,
1992), 26ff.

80. Robert A. Peterson, *Calvin's Doctrine of the Atonement* (Phillipsburg, NJ: Presbyterian and
Reformed Publishing Co., 1983), 85. Edmondson, *Calvin's Christology*, 112, agrees that Calvin did
not produce a single theory of atonement.

of Jesus that it is 'of him'" (II.16.19).[81] In this chapter Calvin asserts that atonement is based on "the whole life of Christ" (II.16.5).

The subject of Book II of the *Institutes* is the knowledge of God the Redeemer. In the entire course of promise (chaps. 6–11), person (12–14), work (15), and life (16–17) the Redeemer effects atonement, but Calvin does not articulate a distinctive doctrine of the atonement. The following quotation is characteristic of Calvin's exposition:

> The mark of adoption rightly excels all other testimonies of God's love. The infinite love of God toward the world was the reason for the incarnation, but if cause precedes effect an apparent contradiction arises. That is, God loved the world before its redeemer was appointed. It is a wonderful goodness of God and incomprehensible to the human mind, that God was benevolent towards men whom he could not but hate and removed the cause of the hatred that there might be no obstruction to his love. And indeed, Paul tells us that we are loved in a double sense in Christ. First, because the Father chose us in him before the creation of the world (Eph. 1:4). Secondly, because in him also God has reconciled us to himself and shown that he is gracious to us (Rom. 5:10). See how we are both enemies and friends until atonement has been made for our sins and we are restored to favor with God. . . . No one will ever feel that God is favorable to him unless he understands that God is appeased in Christ. But as all taste for God's love vanishes when Christ is taken away, we may safely conclude that, since by faith we are engrafted into his body, there is no danger that we shall be cut off from the love of God (Com. Jn. 17:23).

Calvin begins with God's love, which results in the incarnation. He pauses to notice the logical problem of caring for, rather than hating, sinners before their redeemer was provided. Scripture teaches that the elect are chosen both prior to creation and after reconciliation, meaning they are both friends and enemies of God until sin is removed by atonement and the faithful are united to Christ.

In disagreement, a number of scholars believe Calvin has a strong forensic doctrine of atonement resembling Anselm's and emphasizing not divine love but human sin and law. Emil Brunner recognizes that God through his love creates the atonement, but Brunner asserts that Calvin followed Anselm in elaboration of the idea of penal expiation.[82] In a more recent example, F. W. Dillistone claims

---

81. After Calvin the topic of the order of salvation (*ordo salutis*) takes on a more prominent role— for example, in the Westminster Confession. Based on Calvin's great dictum, "Our whole salvation and all its parts are comprehended in Christ" (II.16.19), Richard B. Gaffin Jr. *Resurrection and Redemption: A Study in Paul's Soteriology* (Grand Rapids: Baker Book House, 1987), 135, 139, concludes, "The first and, in the final analysis, the only question for the Pauline *ordo* concerns the point at which and the conditions under which incorporation with [Christ] the life-giving Spirit takes place." Nevertheless, Gaffin's interest in the "dogmatical consequences" of the resurrection of Christ in Paul's soteriology involves considerable discussion of the *ordo salutis*.

82. Brunner, *Mediator*, 471, 458. On rational grounds Anselm insists, "I do not seek to understand that I may believe, but I believe in order to understand" in *Proslogium* I in *St. Anselm Basic Writings*, trans. S. W. Deane, 2nd ed. (LaSalle, IL: Open Court, 1962). (See also Karl Barth, *Anselm fides quaerens intellectum: Anselm's proof of the existence of God in the context of his theological scheme* [Pittsburgh, PA: Pickwick Press, 1975].) This "faith seeking understanding" requires a

Calvin, after Anselm, is "the next most famous figure in the history of the legal interpretation of atonement." According to Dillistone, the key terms in Anselm belong to *civil* law—debt, liability, compensation, honor, price, payment, merit. In Calvin the key terms belong to *criminal* law—punishment, death, the curse, wrath, substitution, surety, merit, imputation. The general, shorthand summary of the two so-called legal interpreters of atonement associates the term "satisfaction" with Anselm and "substitution" with Calvin. Dillistone asserts that Calvin's view of atonement, "with minor variations, remained dominant in Reformed theology until well into the nineteenth century."[83]

Paul Fiddes follows this commonly received interpretation, concluding that Calvin gives an absolute place to law, and, therefore, builds a theory of atonement on the principle of divine justice, which Fiddes designates as the "penal substitutionary" theory and, employing the subjective-objective distinction, dismisses as too "objective." If Calvin takes "union with Christ" as seriously as I insist, this dichotomy is called into serious question. Fiddes himself acknowledges Calvin teaches union with Christ, but—in total opposition to the present view—insists "this experience is completely separated from atonement. It is a life of increasing sanctification which *follows* justification as a second stage" (emphasis in original).[84]

---

confidence in logic which is important for Anselm's theological method and apologetics. Anselm thinks it is evident that "the rational mind alone, among all created beings, is capable of rising to the investigation of [Supreme Being]" (*Monologium*, 66). According to Anselm, all Christians should accept the truth of the Christian faith but should also seek reasons for it. For that reason Anselm produced his metaphysical and soteriological arguments. The former, the ontological argument for the existence of God, asserts that the mind can think of a something than which nothing greater can be conceived. This greatest thing (God) must exist in reality rather than merely in the mind, or it would not be the greatest. Anselm's second famous argument concerns the birth, life, and death of Jesus under the title *Cur Deus Homo?* (Why God Man?). His argument can be summarized under five points: (1) Human obedience is owed to God the Creator. Therefore, to commit sin is to dishonor God. (2) Justice demands that God must be recompensed for this dishonor or the offenders must be punished. (3) However, everlasting punishment defeats the purpose of creation. Therefore, God must save some humans. (4) Since God only is great enough to render proper satisfaction for the offense committed and only mankind owes it, a God-man is necessary. (5) Jesus Christ as a human being owed obedience to God, but not his death. Therefore, Anselm concludes the death of Jesus was not a punishment but a rendering of satisfaction. With the notable exception of Norman Malcolm in his much-discussed essay, "Anselm's Ontological Arguments," *Philosophical Review* 69 (January 1960): 41–62, most scholars think Anselm's ontological argument founders not on logic but on the fact that existence is not a logical predicate. The soteriological argument depends on an *intellectual* confidence in the calculations of reason and also an unexamined *social* assumption of the application of chivalry's canons to God's honor—neither of which is shared by Calvin. In these arguments Anselm appeals to logical necessities rather than a narrative of historical events—to what the head can fathom rather than to what the heart can believe.

83. F. W. Dillistone, *The Christian Understanding of Atonement* (Philadelphia: Westminster Press, 1968), 195, 196.

84. Paul S. Fiddes, *Past Event and Present Salvation: The Christian Idea of Atonement* (Louisville, KY: Westminster/John Knox Press, 1989), 103, 97, 99, 100. In his essay entitled "Atonement and 'Saving Faith'" in *Theology Today* (April 1960–January 1961): 181, 183, Brian A. Gerrish emphasizes the "happy exchange" in Luther and Calvin. That is, "First and foremost, the Christian is one who has been united with Christ so intimately that an exchange of qualities has somehow taken place." Gerrish admits that the two major reformers use language implying penal substitution and forensic imputation, but rightly insists their concept of faith includes and transcends these and all other legalistic terms.

On the interpretation of Dillistone and Fiddes, Anselm teaches satisfaction (Christ pays the debt of honor) while Calvin teaches substitution. That is, in penal substitution Christ pays the penalty of sin by satisfying God's justice. Edmondson, on the other hand, while explicating Calvin in terms of Anselm's satisfaction theory, also employs Paul van Buren's view of Christ in our place. Appealing to the ubiquitous subjective-objective categories, Edmondson suggests that Christ's appeasing God's wrath by satisfying God's righteousness "is typically called an 'objective' understanding of Christ's Atonement, and it is prevalent throughout Calvin's work. At the same time Calvin consistently balances this emphasis with a more 'subjective' approach, recognizing that, through sin, we . . . cut ourselves off from God." He concludes, "thus, throughout my argument, the subjective and objective dimensions of Christ's work as Mediator have been reiterated—that God effects that covenant in his history and he draws God's chosen into that covenant in faith through his history."[85] In addition to denigrating the importance of union with Christ, all these theories present a significant problem in assuming that forgiveness is a dilemma for God.

One major difficulty in formulating a doctrine of atonement is avoiding the assumption of a separation between God-the-angry-Father-Creator and God-the-atoning-Son-Redeemer. George H. Kehm sees a tension between Calvin's understanding of God as loving Father and God as avenging judge. The popular consensus views Calvin's sinners, like those of Jonathan Edwards, in the hands of an angry God dangling like a spider over the fires of hell. Puzzling over the role of the blood of Christ and the symbolism of defilement, Kehm observes, "The idea of a legal process in which there can be a substitution of an innocent person to suffer the penalty for another has the *appearance* of something that is rationally ordered (even if the underlying concept of justice is not only odd but incoherent)." Kehm insists, "As an 'explanation' of how the death of Christ reconciles sinners to God, the [penal substitutionary] theory is untenable," concluding with Paul Ricoeur "that the theory of satisfaction is 'only a second-degree rationalization of a mystery whose center is not punishment but the gift.'"[86] Kehm complains that Calvin has not solved the problem, but Calvin recognizes "some sort of contradiction" in speaking of the wrathful God's gracious sending of the *person* of the Redeemer with the intention of providing forgiveness before the *work* of redemption has been accomplished. Calvin is quite aware of God as both friend and enemy, as cited previously in his comment on John 17:23. The expression that God is our enemy until he is reconciled to us by Christ is to be understood as "accommodated to our capacity that we may better understand how miserable and ruinous our condition is apart from Christ" (II.16.2). Calvin is content to apply his theory of accommodation to the appearance of contradiction without further analysis.

85. Edmondson, *Calvin's Christology*, 93, 227.
86. George H. Kehm, "Calvin on Defilement and Sacrifice," *Interpretation* 31, no. 1 (January 1977): 42, 48.

Calvin is very much aware of the depth of the sin to which we descend and the height of the law to which we aspire, but the saving work of Christ is primarily explained in terms of his three offices (or more precisely the threefold office) of prophet, king, and priest. Undoubtedly the purpose of Calvin's exposition is to expand the traditional and more static doctrine of one person in two natures in order to include the more dynamic work of Christ as summarized in the three offices. He declares, "Faith ought not to be fixed on the essence of Christ alone (so to speak), but ought to attend to his power and office, for it would be of little advantage to know who Christ is, if this second point were not added, what he wishes to be toward us, and for what purpose the Father sent Him" (Com. Jn. 1:49). Clearly, an understanding of Christ's person is not sufficient without a discussion of Christ's work. This topic is organized in the final edition of the *Institutes* around the three offices. Commenting on 1 Corinthians 1:30, Calvin declares, "There is scarcely another passage in Scripture which gives a clearer description of all the offices of Christ." First, in Christ we obtain perfect *wisdom*. Second, in his name we are made *righteous* before God because his obedience is imputed to us. Third, Christ is our *sanctification* because we who are by nature unholy are born again by his Spirit that we may be holy. Fourth, Christ was given to us for redemption.

According to John F. Jansen, when Calvin devotes a separate chapter (II.15) to the work of Christ, he appears to be the first theologian to employ the trifold office in a systematic way.[87] In this practice he was followed by some Lutheran and most Reformed theologians. Naturally, as the doctrine of the three offices became commonplace in systematic theology, objections to it and defenses of it arose. However, we need not pursue the earlier or later history of the doctrine. For Calvin Christ as prophet presents God to us; as king he rules over us; and as priest he represents us to God. The single reality of these three offices consists in the integrity of the person and work of the Messiah.

1. Christ as Prophet

The prophetic office of Christ involves the fulfillment and termination of this role among God's people. The teaching of God's will is completed and brought to an end in the perfect revelation in Christ. "Christ is the only teacher of the Church" (Com. Jn. 15:20). In the Commentary on Micah 4:3, Calvin says the true teaching office belongs to God. God is the chief and the only teacher. Again, "The Father willed the supreme teaching office to be in Christ alone" (Com. Jn. 20:21). While God's chosen people were provided with an unbroken line of prophets, their hope for full understanding depended on the coming of the Messiah. The Messiah was anointed as were the prophets of the Old Testament;

---

87. Jansen, *Calvin's Doctrine*, 16. Robert Mackintosh, *Historic Theories of Atonement* (London: Hodder and Stoughton, 1920), 269, thinks the three offices became of real doctrinal significance when remodeled by Albrecht Ritschl and McLeod Campbell.

however, "the perfect doctrine he has brought has made an end to all prophesies." "That is, outside Christ there is nothing worth knowing, and all who by faith perceive what he is like have grasped the whole immensity of heavenly benefits" (II.15.2).

2. Christ as King

To the Psalmist's question, "Who is this king of glory?" Calvin answers, "The Son of God, clothed with our flesh, has now shown himself to be king of glory" (Com. Ps. 24:8). Calvin believed David as a king was a type of Christ (Com. Hos. 8:4). Therefore, in discussing kingship in Judah, Calvin says, "[This] is the right view of the subject: for Christ at length appeared, on whose head rests the true diadem or crown, and who has been elected by God, and is the legitimate king, and who, having risen from the dead, reigns, and now sits at the Father's right hand, and his throne shall not fail to the end of the world; nay, the world shall be renovated, and Christ's kingdom shall continue, though in another form, after the resurrection, as Paul shows to us; and yet Christ shall be really a king forever" (Com. Am. 9:11). Calvin recognizes that in speaking of God Micah does not mention Christ by name, but we should nevertheless "conclude that Christ is true God [and] he is the supreme King of his Church" (Com. Mic. 4:3). Christ's eternal kingdom is not of this world. It is spiritual, which means that Christ is "the eternal protector and defender of his church" and of each individual. The same eternal protection that applies to the church inspires hope after this life for "a joyous and peaceful life, having rich possessions, being safe from all harm, and abounding with delights such as the flesh commonly longs after" (II.15.4). Because Christ is king, "We shall always be victorious over the devil, the world, and every kind of harmful thing" (II.15.4). "Thus it is that we may patiently pass through this life with its misery, hunger, cold, contempt, reproaches, and other troubles—content with this one thing: that our King will never leave us destitute" (II.15.4).

Calvin adds in the "perfect glory the administration of the Kingdom will not be as it now is" (II.15.5). With this reflection Calvin interprets the scriptural references to the completion of the messianic work. First Corinthians 15 reads, "When he hands over the kingdom to God the Father" (v. 24) and "The Son himself will . . . be subjected . . . that God may be all in all" (v. 28). Calvin concludes that sitting at the right hand of the Father means on Christ is bestowed the name above every name (Phil. 2:9–11). The application of the term "Lord" and the execution of judgment both indicate the kingly duties of Christ. In fact, "the full proof will appear at the Last Judgment, which may also be properly considered the last act of his reign" (II.15.5).

3. Christ as Priest

Calvin declares, "The priesthood belongs to Christ alone" (Com. I Jn. 2:1). Calvin interprets Christ's priestly work primarily in terms of Hebrews 7–10, employing the bold assertion that Christ is the officiating priest and the sacrifice offered. The terrors experienced by Pilate's wife testified to the innocence of Jesus and that his punishment was not deserved (Com. Mt. 27:19). "The priestly office belongs to Christ alone because by the sacrifice of his death he blotted out our own guilt and made satisfaction for our sins" (II.15.6). "God's righteous curse bars our access to him, and God in his capacity as judge is angry toward us. Hence, an expiation must intervene in order that Christ as priest may obtain God's favor for us and appease his wrath" (II.15.6). In the Old Testament the priest was not allowed to enter the sanctuary without a blood sacrifice (Heb. 9:7). In an amazing development Christ becomes both priest and sacrifice because only Christ was worthy to *make* the offering and to *be* the offering that brings reconciliation.

Calvin concludes his one-page exposition of the priestly office with a two-sentence attack on the papists who, not content with Christ's priesthood and once-for-all sacrifice on the cross, assume they must sacrifice Christ anew each day in the Mass. Observing that Calvin employs only two offices in the 1536 *Institutes* (*CO* 1:68), Jansen writes, "In spite of the fact that Calvin suggests the formula of the three offices in the later editions of his *Institutes* and *Catechism*, he does not himself make any real use of the formula." Jansen bases this conclusion on the fact that the triple formula never occurs in Calvin's biblical commentaries.[88] Jansen points out that references to Christ as king and priest are abundant. For example, "It was indeed an inestimable honor, that the Son of God, when about to commence his reign and priesthood, had chosen Capernaum for the seat of his palace and sanctuary" (Com. Mt. 11:23). The division Jansen makes between Calvin, the systematic theologian, and Calvin, the scriptural exegete, is persuasive up to a point, but some of the force is removed if one considers that the threefold office is useful for Calvin's exposition rather than necessary to it.

Since "priest," "king," and "prophet" are important biblical words, it is not surprising that theologians should apply them to Christ—sometimes as a twofold office, priest and king, like David, and sometimes as a triple office: "king of kings, priest of priests, prophet of prophets . . ."[89] Calvin recognizes that the three offices were not unknown to earlier theologians. "The papists use these names, too, but coldly and rather ineffectually, since they do not know what each of these titles contains" (II.15.1).

Calvin bases the three offices not on a typological synthesis of three separate Old Testament orders but by interpretation of the title "Christ" or anointed. He writes, "John did not seize upon an empty and unmeaning title to adorn the Son of God, but included under the name 'Christ,' all the offices which the prophets ascribed to Him" (Com. Jn. 20.31). Again, "For we know that under the law prophets as well as priests and kings were anointed with holy oil." He admits "that Christ was called Messiah especially with respect to, and by virtue

---

88. Jansen, *Calvin's Doctrine*, 59, 73.
89. Petrus Chrysologus (d. 450) quoted by Jansen, *Calvin's Doctrine*, 31.

of, his kingship. Yet his anointings as prophet and as priest have their place and must not be overlooked by us" (II.15.2). These citations demonstrate that Calvin's interpretation of the work of Christ begins with the reality of Christ and then looks back to the Old Testament to aid understanding. Calvin does not start with the Old Testament and then treat Christ as a typological fulfillment of its ideals.

Of course, the revelation of atonement involves the prophetic office, but the accomplishment of atonement is primarily a priestly sacrifice and kingly conquest (Com. Acts 17:22).[90] Modern theologians usually attach their discussion of atonement to the priestly office, a procedure that appeals to the scriptural description of Christ as both high priest and lamb in the book of Hebrews. Christ is the sacrificing officer as well as the sacrificial offering. "For it is the office of Christ to take away sins and for this end He was sent by the Father; and it is by faith that we partake of Christ's virtue" (Com. I Jn. 3:5).

As the incarnation demonstrates God's love, the crucifixion illustrates God's love for mankind and wrath against human sin. These conclusions (including accommodated truths) point to the confessional rather than logical nature of theological reflection. Since various theories of the atonement are available, a variety of affirmations and denials exist alongside them. Not surprisingly, some of the severest opponents of one theory are the proponents of another. The absence of a theoretical consensus indicates that Christians confess, rather than understand, atonement with God revealed and wrought by Jesus Christ and confirmed by the power of the Holy Spirit.

The central point is that Calvin does not produce a doctrine of atonement but articulates themes in the work of Christ that contribute to an understanding of reconciliation. Even more importantly, Calvin does not understand reconciliation in subjective-objective categories but in terms of union with Christ.[91] In 1923 H. R. Mackintosh asserted, "I should like to put forward the plea that Union to Christ is the fundamental idea in the theory of redemption. It is from this center alone, as it seems to me, that we can interpret luminously all the problems which gather round justification and sanctification."[92] The accuracy of this observation becomes even clearer in the discussion of sanctification and justification in Book III and makes the point again that union in Christ is not a new perspective in Reformed theology. The conclusion is that Calvin does not present a logically coherent doctrine of the atonement. Rather, in attempting to confess the faith aright, Calvin offers this programmatic summary: "Christ was given to us by God's generosity, to be grasped and possessed by us in faith. By partaking of him, we principally receive a double grace: namely, that being reconciled

90. Cf. Jansen, *Calvin's Doctrine*, 40.

91. Paul Tillich declares, "Atonement therefore necessarily has an objective and a subjective element" which means a correlation between divine offer and human acceptance (Paul Tillich, *Systematic Theology*, vol. 2 [Chicago: University of Chicago Press, 1957], 170).

92. H. R. Mackintosh, "Unio Mystica as a Theological Conception," in *Some Aspects of Christian Belief* (New York: George H. Doran Company, 1923), 108.

to God through Christ's blamelessness, we may have in heaven instead of a Judge a gracious Father; and secondly, that sanctified by Christ's spirit we may cultivate blamelessness and purity of life" (III.11.1). By God's grace the elect are united to Christ in faith and by partaking of him receive the double grace of justification and sanctification. In other words, what God does *for* us in the person and work of Christ (Book II), God does *in* us with justification and sanctification by the work of the Holy Spirit (Book III).

E. MYSTICISM AND DEIFICATION: TWO DISAVOWALS

The concept of deification applied to Calvin might have some plausibility if the reality of Father, Son, and Holy Spirit is understood in a Sabellian direction. However, since Calvin's hope is located in Christ, the goal is participation in him, not divinization. In other words, a sharply focused Christology precludes a blurry deification. Having professed Calvin's dogmatical theology to rest on his mystical theology and having with no uncertain trumpet sounded the note of union with Christ as a central theme, it becomes necessary to deny Calvin's connection with both mysticism and deification. This exclusion is not immediately obvious since A. Schlemmer is correct in thinking faith itself is a form of mysticism.[93] Another Francophone, Carl A. Keller, calls in his ringing agreement with the work to hand by insisting on the importance of Calvin's doctrine of union with Christ. However, Keller also thinks the reformed tradition has neglected "la splendeur de la divinisation, de la participation vivifiante à la vie et à l'œuvre du Christ, de l'union mystique."[94] Certainly "mystical union" with Christ is near "au cœur de la pensée du Réformateur," but Calvin is improperly connected to Pseudo-Dionysius and the mystical tradition. Additionally, the sadly one-sided view that Calvin teaches only that we are "born in sin and inclined to evil" is not corrected by asserting the splendor of divinization. In my view Keller is correct in choosing the subjects for his analysis of Calvin's theology but wrong in the conclusions he draws from them. Union with God is established not instrumentally but "substantially" by union with Christ through the work of the Holy Spirit.

Similarly, while supporting the present thesis that "emphasis upon union with Christ can be called the hallmark of both Reformed doctrine and Reformed spirituality,"[95] Julie Canlis bases this conclusion on the observation of "a slow but steady reversal of theological trends, an openness to see Calvin in terms of

93. A. Schlemmer, "Y a-t-il un mysticisme Réformé?" *Foi et Vie* (1935): 755.

94. Carl A. Keller, *Calvin Mystique: Au Cœur de la pensée du Réformateur* (Geneva: Labor et Fides, 2001), 175.

95. Julie Canlis, "Calvin, Osiander and Participation in God," *International Journal of Systematic Theology* 6, no. 2 (April 2004): 172. In his *Reformed Symbolics: A Comparison of Catholicism, Orthodoxy, and Protestantism*, trans. David Lewis (Edinburgh: Oliver & Boyd, 1962), Wilhelm Niesel devotes a chapter to "Union with Christ" and calls this doctrine both the basic confession of the Reformed churches (181) and a basic doctrine of Calvin (184). I claim "union with Christ" is the basic *confession* of Calvin and a basic *doctrine* of the Reformed churches.

[1] mystical union or [2] deification." As evidence of the former, Canlis cites my essay on union with Christ,[96] and of the latter, Carl Mosser on deification,[97] who takes his orientation from the declaration of 2 Peter 1:4 that believers may become partakers of divine nature. According to Mosser, in commenting on this text Calvin appeals to Anselm. "Calvin's implicit reasoning is that God is that than which nothing greater can be conceived, i.e. the greatest possible being. Therefore, partaking of his divine nature is that blessing than which nothing more excellent can be conceived; i.e. the greatest possible blessing." Thus he entitles his essay, "The Greatest Possible Blessing: Calvin and Deification." Questionable is the accuracy of the logical move ("Calvin's implicit reasoning") from greatest possible being to greatest possible blessing. Mosser claims, "In concert with the patristic writers Calvin views the believer's partaking of the divine nature as a kind of deification." On the contrary, Calvin's emphasis is not on participation in the divine essence but only in the union with Christ effected by the work of the Holy Spirit. Mackintosh defines Christian mysticism as "the action of the Holy Spirit, whereby the *substance* of believers is joined most closely, though without intermixture to the *substance* of the Holy Trinity and the flesh of Christ." The work is assigned to the Holy Spirit joining divine and human substances (without mixture) including a strong reference to the flesh of Christ. Mackintosh recognizes that the term "substance" often means only the highest degree of reality, but asserts the category of substance should be put aside and the subject thought out in terms of personality.[98] This means we must "learn to be satisfied with Christ because in him we find God the Father also, as he communicates himself to us by his Son." The reason Calvin offers here is that "when we think of God apart from a mediator, we can only conceive of him as being angry with us" (Com. II Cor. 5:19).

In debate with Osiander, Calvin agrees that Father, Son, and Holy Spirit dwell in us, yet this truth is "perversely twisted by Osiander; for he ought to have considered the manner of the indwelling—namely, that the Father and Spirit are in Christ, and even as the fullness of deity dwells in him, so in him we possess the whole of deity." The truth is we are "united with Christ by the secret power of his Spirit" (III.11.5). I take this comment to affirm a "trinitarian indwelling" understood and confessed christologically. In my judgment, mystical union and deification in Calvin are not two doctrines but one. Union with Christ alone permits and defines the discussion of theosis. Obviously I am open to seeing Calvin in terms of mystical union, but this is not mysticism as ordinarily understood. Moreover, I think deification applied to Calvin's theology is a misnomer for exactly the reason Canlis advances as a caution. Unless deification "is clearly

96. Charles Partee, "Calvin's Central Dogma Again," *Sixteenth-Century Journal* 18 (1987): 191–99.
97. Carl Mosser, "The Greatest Possible Blessing: Calvin and Deification," *Scottish Journal of Theology* 55, no. 1 (2002): 40, 41.
98. Mackintosh, "Unio Mystica," 100, 102. In the discussion of Trinity, deification, justification, and especially Eucharist, the precise meaning of substance is as important to recognize as it is difficult to determine.

anchored in sonship—our participating in a form of the Son's relationship to the Father by grace—then it does not do justice to Calvin."[99] In other words, Calvin's view of union with Christ is mystical union but not mystical experience. Union with Christ does not, of course, make us the same as God (that would be pantheism), but also not even like God if the humanity of Christ and the work of the Holy Spirit are not properly confessed. In short, to deny mysticism and deification, as commonly and essentially understood, in application to Calvin, actually advances and enhances his view of union in Christ.

Every theological doctrine, having spiritual content, may be taken in a mystical direction. Calvin praises the concept of union with God and confesses mystical union. Union with Christ is the "marvelous exchange" by which Christ becoming the Son of man with us makes us sons of God with him (IV.17.2). Again, "With a wonderful communion, day by day, he grows more and more into one body with us, until he becomes completely one with us" (III.2.24). Nevertheless, Calvin is too little interested in the analysis of his own experience for a mystic and too much interested in the reality of Christ's humanity for a divinizer. Evaluating the same evidence, scholars come to different conclusions. Some employ the term "divinization," convinced it does not transgress the proper boundaries of Calvin's theology; others, including me, believe deification does not respect the proper boundaries of Calvin's theology. If because of sliding definitions the exclusion of Calvin from the mystics and divinizers cannot be conclusively demonstrated, it may be persuasively illustrated that in their ordinary range of meaning mysticism and deification are inaccurately applied to Calvin's theology. This evaluation is evident in his polemic against Osiander, as we discuss in the section on justification. Although, once again, and especially here, there is no consensus among the learned.

Mysticism and divinization are related and extremely complicated subjects. In a clever phrase, W. T. Stace reminds us that dealing with concepts so nebulous, "It is better to be vaguely right than to be precisely wrong."[100] To their general relation one could argue that mysticism is a possibility leading to deification or that deification is an actuality leading to mysticism. In a more specific analysis within the Christian context, equally vast questions must be addressed to the proper and improper relation of God the Father to God the Son as well as God the Creator and Redeemer to the freedom of the creature in general and the choice of the elect in particular.

99. Canlis, "Calvin, Osiander and Participation," 184. The mystical union between the believer and the Lord and between the Father and Son cannot be known by idle speculation but only when Christ pours his life into us by the secret efficacy of his Spirit (Com. Jn. 14:20).

100. W. T. Stace, *Mysticism and Philosophy* (London: Macmillan, 1960), 6. Pioneers in the academic study of mysticism include William James, Evelyn Underhill, and Rudolf Otto. They were followed by Stace, R. C. Zaehner, and Ninian Smart. Rudolf Otto's *Mysticism East and West*, trans. Bertha L. Bracey and Richenda C. Payne (New York: Meridian Books, 1957), contains an interesting chapter on deification as justification (*unio substantialis*), as well as essays on Fichte and Schleiermacher. For noting the dialectic between doctrine and experience, see Ninian Smart, *The Religious Experience of Mankind* (New York: Charles Scribner's Sons, 1969).

1. Mysticism

In the chapter on mysticism and theology in her classic study, Evelyn Underhill asserts the centrality of the dogmas of Trinity and incarnation for institutional Christianity, which attempts to exhibit their meaning in time and space. Mystical philosophy, on the other hand, seeks to demonstrate their meaning in eternity. Underhill concludes that in ecstasy the mystic experiences as one the Holy Spirit within and the Transcendent Spirit without.[101] Whatever might be the role of doctrine, the fascination of the mystical experience is most characteristic of the central tradition as demonstrated by Underhill's subtitle, "Man's Spiritual Consciousness," and its development in chapters dealing with self-awakening, self-purification, self-illumination, voices, visions, recollection, contemplation, ecstasy, rapture, and so on. John E. Smith writes, "It is generally admitted that mysticism is an essentially individual and personal form of spirituality which must be studied in and through the expression of individual experience."[102]

At the foundation of his theology Calvin affirms the believer's union with Christ as a gift of the Holy Spirit (II.2.17; III.2.35 and *passim*).[103] In this simple sense Calvin's exposition of doctrine rests on his mystical theology because rational reflection is vacuous without apprehension of spiritual reality. However, this broad definition of mysticism includes not only Calvin, but also every Christian theologian making mysticism (or spirituality) a term of such sweeping generalization and such sprawling application that any exclusion would be difficult to maintain. Stace claims that exalting the mind's perception of itself as unitary consciousness or universal self is "the source of all doctrines of 'union with God' or 'identity with Brahman' . . . whether they are expressed in pantheistic, nihilistic, or theistic language. Emptiness, the Void, Nothingness, the desert, the dark night, the barren wilderness, the wild sea, the One—these are all equivalent expressions of the same experience of an absolute unity in which there are no empirical distinctions, and which is indifferently to be regarded as the pure essence of the indi-

101. Max Dominicé, *L'Humanité de Jésus d'après Calvin* (Paris: Je Sers, 1933), 47, describes the incarnation as full Christian mysticism. Evelyn Underhill, *Mysticism: A Study in the Nature and Development of Man's Spiritual Consciousness* (New York: Meridian Books, 1955), 107–8. In responding to Stace's statement that "there are *no* Protestant mystics," Anne Fremantle and W. H. Auden found that many Protestants agreed with Stace. "Calvinists, *en masse*, thought that even if there were mystics, there shouldn't be any" (*The Protestant Mystics* [Boston: Little, Brown & Co., 1964], vii). Fremantle includes Luther as a Protestant mystic, but not Calvin.

102. John E. Smith, "William James's Account of Mysticism; A Critical Appraisal," in *Mysticism and Religious Traditions*, ed. Steven T. Katz (Oxford: Oxford University Press, 1983), 247. This focus is demonstrated by Martin Buber: "Now from my own unforgettable experience I know well that there is a state in which the bonds of the personal nature of life seem to have fallen away from us and we experience an undivided unity" (*Between Man and Man*, trans. Ronald Gregor Smith [New York: Macmillan, 1965], 24).

103. Canlis suggests, "Calvin's genius was to perceive that without a genuine role for the Holy Spirit, you cannot help but have a fusion or divine overwhelming of some sort" ("Calvin, Osiander and Participation," 172).

vidual soul or the pure essence of the universe."[104] Calvin is not interested in the mind's perception of itself, nor identity with Brahman. Additionally, he is no worshiper of nature and therefore not a nature mystic. Unlike William Blake (*Auguries of Innocence*), Calvin does not see the world in a grain of sand nor heaven in a wildflower, although he recognizes God's wisdom and power is displayed in the smallest plant (Com. Ps. 19:1). It is impossible to imagine Calvin writing these lines:

> Are not the mountains, waves, and skies, a part
> Of me and of my soul, as I of them?
> (Byron, *Childe Harold's Pilgrimage* III.75)

Additionally, Calvin, unlike Plotinus and Augustine, is little influenced by Plato outside the grandiose aphorism that everyone is either a Platonist or an Aristotelian.[105] Moreover, Calvin's putative mysticism is not consonant with Plotinus's view of the One. Calvin knows the personal name of his God.[106] Calvin's view of knowledge and the testimony of the Holy Spirit is different from Augustine's illuminationism. Musing on the mystery of evil in connection with certain books of the Platonists, Augustine confesses that he "entered into my inward self" and beheld with love and awe "above my mind, the Light Unchangeable" (*Confessions* 7.10).[107]

Intriguingly, W. R. Inge sees the revival of interest in mysticism as a rediscovery of the testimony of the Holy Spirit as the primary ground of faith. Obviously, the work and testimony of the Holy Spirit is important to Calvin. However, Inge also claims that "the essence of mysticism is the experience of coming into immediate relation with the higher Powers, whether these are called the One, as by the Neoplatonists, or by the names of Asiatic divinities, or, as in Christianity, are identified with the divine Christ or the Holy Spirit." That in its purest form mysticism is just prayer might not be entirely objectionable to Calvin, but not in this pluralistic context.[108] Significantly, Calvin affirms the term "mystical union" in polemic against Osiander's view of it (III.11.10), but Calvin's view of "mystical

---

104. Stace, *Mysticism*, 109–10. Conceiving himself to be charting a lone course, Stace focuses his analysis on "mystical experience" and its relation to traditional philosophic problems. He emphasizes that the mystic possesses an "inner subjective certainty" which produces neither demonstrations nor disproofs as these terms are ordinarily understood. According to Stace, many writers assume that mysticism is a religious phenomenon and thus "simply define the mystical consciousness as 'union with God'" (341).

105. On Plato and Aristotle in Calvin, see my *Calvin and Classical Philosophy* (Louisville, KY: Westminster John Knox Press, 2005), esp. chaps. 7 and 8.

106. The same stricture applies to Wordsworth's vague "presence that disturbs me with the joy / Of elevated thoughts, a sense sublime," a something "Whose dwelling is the light of setting suns" ("Lines Composed above Tintern Abbey," 94–97).

107. See Phillip Cary, *Augustine's Invention of the Inner Self: The Legacy of Christian Platonism* (Oxford: Oxford University Press, 2000). Cary draws a distinction between Augustine's exaltation of the inner private self and the objective meaning and power of Christ's flesh, which he defines as the fundamental issue of Christian thought (x).

108. William Ralph Inge, *Christian Mysticism* (New York: Meridian Books, 1899 [1956]), vi, viii. See also his *The Philosophy of Plotinus* (London: Longmans, Green and Co., 1923).

union" is union with Christ through faith, which is a gift of the Holy Spirit, not an achievement of luminous presence resulting from entering the inward private self as with Augustine, and not restricted to Christ's divine nature as with Osiander. While Calvin is most usually evaluated as a dogmatical theologian, he can with some effort also be interpreted as a mystical or spiritual theologian. Certainly his faith can be described as spiritual, even mystical in a certain sense, but his theology is dominantly confessional and exegetical, focused not on his experience but on the Lordship of Christ.[109]

2. Deification

The elevation of the deification doctrine arises from, or is accompanied by, "a strong emphasis on the theme of 'Union with Christ' and a depreciation of legal or juridicial images in soteriology."[110] In this study the latter two are present but the former is marked absent. Carl Mosser points out, "'Mystical union' is very often a technical phrase for deification from at least the time of Pseudo-Dionysius."[111] This connection between mysticism and deification is also declared by R. C. Zaehner. "In Christian terminology mysticism means union with God." He defines mysticism as "praeternatural experiences in which sense perception and discursive thought are transcended in an immediate apperception of a unity or union which is apprehended as lying beyond and transcending the multiplicity of the world as we know it."[112] Deification, often judged to be a major difference between Christian theology East and West, may be shortly described as the believer's reception by grace of what the Christ is by nature. For example, Athanasius taught, "The Son of God became man, that we might become God."[113] Gregory of Nazianzus claimed that the Risen Christ "still pleads even now as man for my salvation, for he continues to wear the body which he assumed, until he makes me God by the power of his Incarnation."[114] In a con-

---

109. In his study of *The Spirituality of John Calvin* (Atlanta: John Knox Press, 1974), 99, Lucien Joseph Richard seeks to provide a conceptual analysis of Calvin's "personal assimilation of the salvific mission of Christ." Richard maintains that "the major themes of Calvin's spirituality [are] knowledge of God and of man; the necessity of honoring the glory of God, demanding, on the part of man, faith, service and obedience; total dependence upon God's word incarnated in Christ, and the practical attitude of man expressed in piety and worship." Doubtless, this summary has a strong component in "personal assimilation," but the themes are more clearly expounded in terms of theological reflection than personal experience.

110. Bruce McCormack, "Participation in God, Yes, Deification, No: Two Modern Protestant Responses to an Ancient Question," in *Denkwürdiges Geheimnis: Beiträge zur Gotteslehre: Festschrift für Eberhard Jüngel zum 70. Geburtstag*, ed. Ingolf Ulrich Dalferth, Johannes Fischer, and Hans-Peter Grosshans (Tübingen: Mohr Siebeck, 2004), 347. Indicating his conclusion in the title, McCormack analyzes the topic in Karl Barth and Eberhard Jüngel.

111. Mosser, "Greatest Possible Blessing," 50.

112. R. C. Zaehner, *Mysticism—Sacred and Profane: An Inquiry into Some Varieties of Praeternatural Experience* (London: Oxford University Press, 1961), 32, 198–99.

113. *On the Incarnation* I.108.

114. *Oration* 30.14 in *Select Library of Nicene and Post-Nicene Fathers of the Christian Church*, 1st series (Grand Rapids: Eerdmans, 1989), 7:315.

temporary definition Robert G. Stephanopoulos writes, "Theosis . . . is the aim and purpose of the Christian life: union and free communion with God. . . . In no sense must theosis be understood in pantheistic terms, as the mystical return of the divine to the Divine or the ontological commingling of the divine with the human nature." He continues, "Deified man is man renewed, re-created and transfigured into the son of God by grace, whereas God remains inviolate, sovereign and inaccessible in His unknowable and unapproachable essence."[115]

The term "deification" is derived from Plato's *Theaetetus* (176A). Plato thought since evil hovers around the earth, we ought to fly away to heaven, which is to become like God *as far as this is possible*.[116] Likeness to God for Plato meant becoming holy, just, and wise. Looking askance at the pagan connections with deification, Adolf Harnack writes, "The highest blessing bestowed in Christianity is adoption into the divine sonship, which is assured to the believer, and is completed in participation in the divine nature, or more accurately, in the deification of man through the gift of immortality."[117] According to Dionysius the Areopagite, "Deification (θέωσις) is a certain assimilation and unification with God in so far as possible" (ἡ δὲ θέωσις ἐστιν ἡ πρὸς θεὸν ὡς ἐφικτὸν 'ἀφομοίωσις τε καὶ ἕνωσις).[118] The issue for caution and analysis identified overtly by Plato and Pseudo-Dionysius and covertly by all others is presented in the phrase "in so far as possible." For Christian theologians, union with God must be understood in a Trinitarian dynamic.

Scudding before the wind in his essay "Sailing to Byzantium," Joseph McLelland breezily asserts that on the decisive point of mystical union, "Calvin is one with our Orthodox brethren in their idea of *theosis*."[119] Scholars advocating deification in Calvin tend to concentrate on his view of participation in God (cf. II.2.1).

---

115. Robert G. Stephanopoulos, "The Orthodox Doctrine of Theosis," in *The New Man: An Orthodox and Reformed Dialogue*, ed. John Meyendorff and Joseph McLelland (New Brunswick, NJ: Agora Books, 1973), 149–50, 152. In her study of Aquinas and Palamas, A. N. Williams claims the union of God and humanity is an infallible marker of theosis "when this union is conceived as humanity's incorporation into God, rather than God's into humanity" (*The Ground of Union: Deification in Aquinas and Palamas* [New York: Oxford University Press, 1999], 32).

116. Curiously, when Calvin cites this idea he omits the "as far as possible" phrase (I.3.3).

117. Adolf Harnack, *History of Dogma*, trans. Neil Buchanan (New York: Dover Publications, 1961 [c. 1900], 3.164. On the background, see Jules Gross, *The Divinization of the Christian According to the Greek Fathers*, trans. Paul A. Onica (Anaheim, CA: A & C Press, 2002 [1938]). The chapter on Pseudo-Dionysius is entitled "The Mysticism of Divinization." The history of deification from metaphor to dogma is carefully expounded by Norman Russell. Especially helpful is his chapter on the earliest Christian model: participatory union with Christ (Norman Russell, *The Doctrine of Deification in the Greek Patristic Tradition* [Oxford: Oxford University Press, 2004], 1).

118. Dionysius the Pseudo-Areopagite, *The Ecclesiastical Hierarchy*, trans. Thomas L. Campbell (Washington, DC: Catholic University Press, 1955), 1.3.

119. Joseph C. McLelland, "Sailing to Byzantium: Orthodox-Reformed Dialogue: A Personal Perspective" in *New Man*, 16, 17, observes correctly, Calvin's "mystical conviction was soon forced underground in Reformed theology" by the sad fact "that Calvin's disciples did not reckon such living union so important as subscription to creeds (intellectual assent to certain propositions) or conformity to standards of behavior (external assent to a certain ethos)." "[The] new scholasticism aimed at precision and systematization: the church of those living-in-Christ had become a school of students progressing in doctrine."

Foundational to Calvin's theology are the doctrines of Trinity, incarnation, the original image of God in creation, and the restored image of God in sanctification. Moreover, terms such as "communion," "fellowship," "indwelling," "ingrafting," "adoption," "imputation," even "infusion" are equally central to his thinking. Nevertheless, deification overstates the situation. Calvin does on occasion employ the phrase "union with God."[120] For example, in III.25.2 Calvin praises Plato's recognition that the highest human good is "union with God," but he criticizes Plato for not knowing that happiness depends on Christ's resurrection. A more complex notion is encountered in the description of Christ's kingly office in terms of the consummation at the Last Judgment ("the last act of his reign") when the Son will deliver the kingdom to his God and Father (1 Cor. 15:24). Calvin says if we wander from God for a short time "Christ stands in our midst, to lead us little by little to a firm union with God" (II.15.5). Based on the unity of the Son with the Father Calvin asserts, "We infer that we are one with Christ: not because He transfuses his substance into us, but because by the power of His Spirit He communicates to us His life and all the blessings He has received from the Father" (Com. Jn. 17:21).

Wendel thinks Calvin's radical distinction between the two natures of Christ leads him to reject "anything that might have led to any deification of man, even by way of Jesus Christ and even in his person."[121] On a similar note and in a fugue of musical terms, F. W. Norris plays on the themes that "deification should be viewed . . . as an ecumenical consensus, a catholic teaching of the church, best preserved and developed by the Orthodox." He judges Harnack's strictures against deification as the off-key rendition of a "poorly-read Protestant." According to Norris, "Koinonia, fellowship with God, is actually deification, participation in God." He continues, "We Christians have the promise of participating in the divine nature. [This] does not mean that we become God as the Father, Son, and Holy Spirit are God. *Our participation in the divine nature is in God's energies, not the essence.*"[122] Presumably aware of Calvin's teaching of our participa-

120. Barth rightly observes, "the Christian does not claim the fulness of the union of God with man for his own experience and self-consciousness, but professes that other, the Mediator, in whom it has taken place for him" (*CD* 4.2.57). See the references to "union with Christ" listed by Dennis E. Tamburello, *Union with Christ: John Calvin and the Mysticism of St. Bernard* (Louisville, KY: Westminster John Knox Press, 1994), 111–13.

121. Wendel, *Calvin: The Origins and Development*, 259.

122. F. W. Norris, "Deification: Consensual and Cogent," *Scottish Journal of Theology* 49, no. 4 (1996): 422, 418, 413, 417, 428 (emphasis added). The distinction of divine essence and energies is to read Calvin through the eyes of Gregory Palamas, among others. If union with God is not hypostatic, not substantial, but "union through the uncreated energies," the result seems impersonal. Both distinction and result are difficult—if not impossible—for Reformed theologians to understand or accept. Its design appears to be the avoidance of pantheism, which Reformed theologians suspect anyway. R. C. Walls, "St. Gregory Palamas," *Scottish Journal of Theology* 21 (1968): 446–47, 441, suggests the possibility that Gregory has "dragged the theology of salvation through the crack in the door left ajar by II Peter's phrase 'partakers of the divine nature.'" Still, Walls thinks that the "bold distinction between essence and the energies of God" defends the scriptural revelation of the knowability of the unknowable God (441), which is a return to the gospel of grace—the gift of God himself in Christ.

tory union with Christ, Norris nevertheless excludes Calvin from those who accept divinization. "John Calvin seems to have avoided teaching deification or not known of it."[123]

To the contrary, Carl Mosser, while admitting that deification is not a prominent theme in Calvin, insists the doctrine is truly present. "Christ unites believers to God because in his person God and humanity are already united." Citing II.15.5, Mosser concludes, "This intimate union is not merely union with Christ as human mediator, but with God." Mosser bases his argument for deification in Calvin on conclusions he draws from Calvin's development of the image of God, union with the Mediator, baptism, Eucharist, glorification, Trinity, and 2 Peter 1:4. The point to notice, however, is Calvin's cautionary phrases that are emphasized in the following citation. "God makes himself ours so that all his possessions become *in a sense* ours. . . . We should notice that it is the purpose of the Gospel to make us sooner or later like God; indeed it is *so to speak* a kind of deification." This does not mean we "cross over into God's nature so that his nature absorbs ours." On the contrary, the holy apostles said, "We shall be partakers of divine immortality and the glory of blessedness, and thus we shall be *in a way* one with God *so far as our capacity allows*" (Com. II Pet. 1:4). In the divine-human relation Calvin describes a union maintaining both intimacy and distance, and avoiding the assertion of identity more carefully than the enthusiastic divinizers.

At the end Mosser offers a guarded conclusion. Deification is not a major element in Calvin's theology. Thus, to his question, "Can we then speak of 'Calvin's doctrine of deification'?" he answers, "no and yes." He admits that on this subject Calvin "did not employ the boldest language of the Church fathers" and "does not explicitly draw this conclusion [but] his reasoning inescapably leads to it . . . Glorified believers can appropriately be designated gods."[124] From commonly recognized premises a doctrine of deification in Calvin is a deduction that Mosser considers good and I consider unnecessary.

Addressing the same topic, J. Todd Billings makes the useful distinction between a doctrine and a theme—recognizing that a doctrine of deification in Calvin must go beyond the exposition of biblical themes like union, participation, and adoption. Billings correctly affirms the importance of union with Christ. "Calvin describes participation in the transformative, vivifying union with Christ. Particularly in his theology of the Lord's Supper and baptism, believers participate in Christ as they are ingrafted into Christ's body, becoming one with Christ." Billings understands this oneness as the "fundamental union of divinity and humanity." He thinks, "Calvin's development of the biblical themes of union, adoption, ingrafting, and participation give a strongly 'catholic' character to his theology of deification." At the same time Billings, in my judgment, stumbles off the straight line of sober judgment when he insists that Calvin's doctrine of deification is distinctive because "participation in Christ is impossible

---

123. Norris, "Deification," 420.
124. Mosser, "Greatest Possible Blessing," 46, 43, 53, 52.

without imputation; participation in the life-giving *substantia* of Christ in the sacraments is inseparably linked with ecclesial unity and love; full humanity as humanity united with God means that partitive, synergistic understandings of grace and the Spirit must be rejected." Even more debatable is the claim that "union with God through Christ leads to deification as the fullest manifestation and final end of humanity." Calvin does write in debate with Osiander that union with God is "the true and highest perfection of dignity" (II.12.6), but this union with God is not understood with Christ as merely instrumental. Union with God is not *through* Christ but *in* Christ. Billings thinks, "The core objection [to his view] is that Calvin systematically opposes humanity and divinity such that a transformative union between the two becomes unthinkable." For anyone who reads Calvin and notices his doctrine of union with Christ, whatever the difficulties of its understanding, the issue cannot be the systematic opposition of humanity and divinity. The question is rather whether deification is the proper description of the transformative union. Billings recognizes that union "does not make us 'consubstantial with God' like a fourth member of the Godhead," nor by an inflowing of God's substance, "but by the grace and power of the Spirit" (I.15.5).[125] The equivalency of the concept of theosis and the conviction of union with Christ continues to be asserted. Myk Habets writes, "For Calvin, the concept of theosis comes closest to what is more commonly in the West termed 'union with Christ.' It has been argued that the *unio mystica* is central to Calvin's theology. If this is true, then logically the doctrine of theosis is also of importance to Calvin's theology."[126]

In addition to crucial but delicate differences of christological affirmation, Calvin most clearly rejects the anthropological concept of cooperative will associated with theosis. Stephanopoulos writes, "Theosis is not only an eschatological potentiality, but the fulfillment of a long and intense ascent by the Christian person who strives to live in Christ and acquire the gifts of the Holy Spirit in this present life. It is the completion of an arduous moral and spiritual *askesis* of the regenerated Christian as he strives, by faith and grace, to achieve union with God." He continues, "Individual human hypostases must each personally, responsibly and by faith, appropriate the work of Christ in cooperation with the sanctifying grace and gifts of the Holy Spirit." And concludes, "Through constant repentance and faithful obedience to God's will the believer operates with divine grace for sanctification and theosis."[127] Calvin flatly rejects this idea of cooperation represented in the Sixth Session of the Council of Trent (Sixth Decree). The notion that we cooperate in justification is one of "the inanities which the sophists are wont to babble in the schools." On the contrary, faith is the gift of God "as well in its beginnings as its increase, even to its final perfec-

125. J. Todd Billings, "United to God through Christ: Assessing Calvin on the Question of Deification," *Harvard Theological Review* 98, no. 3 (2005): 325, 317, 321, 324, 334, 317, 324.

126. Myk Habets, "Reforming Theosis," in *Theosis: Deification in Christian Theology*, ed. Stephen Finlan and Vladimir Kharlamov (Eugene, OR: Pickwick Publications, 2006), 146–67, 148.

127. Stephanopoulos, "Orthodox Doctrine," 149–50, 156–57, 158.

tion."[128] However union is described, Calvin insists it is a divine bestowal, not a human achievement. As such, union with Christ is an actuality of grace, not merely a possibility of providence.

These conflicts among the scholars concerning Calvin's relation to the doctrines of mysticism and deification demonstrate that opposite conclusions can be drawn from common evidence. Certainly union with Christ and union with God are not different concepts in Calvin. "We can be fully and firmly joined with God only when Christ joins us with him" (II.16.3). The only bond of our union with God is union with Christ (Com. Jn. 16:27). For Calvin, understanding union with God means understanding union with Christ. Therefore, some such balancing of denial and affirmation as presented by John Murray seems appropriate. "Union with Christ does not mean we are incorporated into the life of the Godhead." At the same time, "It is union . . . with the Father and with the Son and with the Holy Spirit that union with Christ draws along with it."[129] Likewise, Emil Brunner regards the theology of Friedrich Schleiermacher as mystical (see his *Das Wort und die Mystik*), but the "unity of God's self-communication and human self-understanding"—the mystical union with Christ can rightly be described as "Christ-mysticism." "The *pro nobis* ('on our behalf') of faith in the Cross is identical with the *in nobis* ('in us') which is one with the speaking of the Holy Spirit." This Christ-mysticism means primarily faith in Christ.[130] In an earlier work Brunner declares that faith in Christ is genuinely contrary to mysticism, meaning that Christ-mysticism is not ordinary mysticism. According to the apostle Paul, the point of unity, "the center of the entire New Testament is personal communion (*Persongemeinschaft*) with Jesus Christ, the living Lord through the Holy Spirit. That is also the center of Reformation theology, namely in its Calvinistic form, the doctrine of the *insertio* or *insitio* in Christ." Again, Brunner declares, "In bringing this communion with Christ to prominence, Calvin has gone so far that he places it above faith."[131] Brunner supports the peripheral role of traditional mysticism in Calvin as well as the central importance of union in Christ. The concept of union with Christ is also central in Brunner's own theology, but it is not so evidently conceptualized and explicated as is the attack on the subject-object antithesis, in favor of the I-Thou relationship associated with Martin Buber, through the development of "Truth as Encounter."[132]

Admittedly Calvin's doctrine of union with Christ has a "mystical" rather than "logical" source. In a broad sense, union with Christ is experienced rather than deduced by the faithful. One can therefore correctly speak of "Christ-mysticism"

128. "Acts of the Council of Trent with the Antidote," in *Calvin's Tracts*, III.110, 120.

129. John Murray, *Redemption—Accomplished and Applied* (Grand Rapids: Wm. B. Eerdmans, 1955), 208, 212. See the chapter on union with Christ.

130. Emil Brunner, *The Christian Doctrine of the Church, Faith, and the Consummation*, trans. David Cairns (Philadelphia: Westminster Press, 1962), 205, 408.

131. Emil Brunner, *Vom Werk des Heiligen Geistes* (Zurich: Zwingli-Verlag, 1935), 34, 33.

132. Emil Brunner, *Truth as Encounter*, trans. Amandus W. Loos and David Cairns (Philadelphia: Westminster Press, 1964).

but only insofar as the focus remains the Lordship of Christ rather than the experience of the mystic. Likewise, Calvin teaches a thoroughly Trinitarian union with God through union with Christ by the power of the Holy Spirit. This doctrine can be called deification if deification is defined *not* as becoming God but becoming like God *as far as possible*. In debate with Osiander, Calvin asserts that we are not consubstantial with God (I.15.5). The question presented for Calvin interpretation becomes, "How far is it possible to become like God?" In my judgment, an accurate reading of Calvin precludes divinization as the conclusion of his doctrine of sanctification. Interestingly, some scholars from the other church of the Reformation interpret Luther in terms of "union with Christ," which is denominated the "Finnish breakthrough." This understanding rejects neo-Kantian presuppositions which allowed faith to be defined only as volitional obedience rather than as ontological participation. This new emphasis in Luther studies rejects a purely forensic understanding of justification (*Christus pro nobis*) in favor of participation (*Christus in nobis*). One result is a new regard for Orthodox theology and its analogous view of deification (theosis), which the Lutherans treat in connection with the doctrine of justification rather than sanctification where Reformed theologians deal with the topic. Tuomo Mannermaa defines theosis thusly: "Divine life has manifested itself in Christ. In the church, understood as the body of Christ, human beings participate in this life and thereby partake of 'the divine nature' (II Pet. 1:4)." This Lutheran affirmation seems to me more acceptably focused on union with Christ than the language of the Orthodox theologians.[133]

Without careful Trinitarian development the concept of union with God ordinarily leads from a powerful mystical aspiration to a vague hope for deification—insofar as that achievement is deemed possible. Unmodified by considerable caveats, the concept of deification does not protect the reality and result of the Christian confession of incarnation, resurrection, ascension, and session in flesh and Calvin's Trinitarian exposition of union in Christ involving not only the natures and person of the Son but also the will of the Father and the work of the Spirit. As he begins his exposition of communion with Christ in Book III of the *Institutes*, François Wendel correctly places both mysticism and divinization outside the contours of Calvin's theology. "There is no question, when Calvin is speaking about union or communion with Christ, of any absorption into Christ, or any mystical identification that would diminish human personality in the slightest degree, or draw Christ down to us. The author of the *Institutes* had already shown himself too hostile to any glorification or deification of man, and of earthly and sinful man above all, to be suspected of trying to revert to this by

___

133. Tuomo Mannermaa, "Justification and Theosis in Lutheran-Orthodox Perspective," in *Union with Christ: The New Finnish Interpretation of Luther*, ed. Carl E. Braaten and Robert W. Jenson (Grand Rapids: Wm. B. Eerdmans Publishing Company, 1998), 26. Rainer Hauke, *Gott-Haben—um Gottes Willen: Andreas Osianders Theosisgedanke . . .* (Frankfurt am Main: Peter Lang, 1999), is interested in justification as deification. He concludes the Osiandrian model of possessing essential righteousness failed in favor of righteousness as imputed.

a roundabout way."[134] The same point is made by Niesel: "This *unio mystica* must be clearly distinguished from the mystical union with the Divine, described by the mystics. According to them, man is released from the material world, stripped of all opposition to God, and so finally reaches and loses himself in the Supreme Being. . . . The mystical union spoken of by Reformed theologians . . . is something quite different." The relationship is not Creator and creature but Savior and sinner. "It is not a doctrine of being (ontology) but a doctrine of salvation (soteriology)." The possibility of the human merging into the divine simply does not arise. When this is forgotten, as in pietism and romanticism (à la Schleiermacher), the role of Jesus Christ is assailed and imperiled. "Theology is changed into mysticism."[135]

F. THE NARRATIVE OF FAITH

In a general way Calvin discusses Christ the Mediator in chapters 12 through 15. In chapters 16 and 17 the emphasis is on Christ the Redeemer and the salvation he acquires for us. In both instances, the christocentric focus of Calvin's theology is very clear. He reminds the reader, "The moment we turn away even slightly from [Christ], our salvation, which rests firmly in him gradually vanishes away" (II.16.1). "Hence we can be fully and firmly joined with God only when Christ joins us with him. If, then, we would be assured that God is pleased with and kindly disposed toward us, we must fix our eyes and minds on Christ alone. For actually, through him alone we escape the imputation of our sins to us—an imputation bringing with it the wrath of God" (II.16.4). In his oft-quoted doxological summary Calvin declares:

> We see that our whole salvation and all its parts are comprehended in Christ. We should therefore take care not to derive the least portion of it from anywhere else. If we seek salvation, we are taught by the very name of Jesus that it is "of him." If we seek any other gifts of the Spirit, they will be found in his anointing. If we seek strength, it lies in his dominion; if purity, in his conception; if gentleness, it appears in his birth. For by his birth he was made like us in all respects that he might learn to feel our pain. If we seek redemption, it lies in his passion; if acquittal, in his condemnation; if remission of the curse, in his cross; if satisfaction, in his sacrifice; if purification, in his blood; if reconciliation, in his descent into hell; if mortification of the flesh, in his tomb; if newness of life, in his resurrection; if immortality, in the same; if inheritance of the Heavenly Kingdom, in his entrance into heaven; if protection, if security, if abundant supply of all blessings, in his Kingdom; if untroubled expectation of judgment, in the power given to him to judge. In short, since rich store of every kind of good abounds in him, let us drink our fill from this fountain, and from no other. Some men, not content with him alone, are borne hither and thither from one hope to another;

---

134. Wendel, *Calvin: The Origins and Development*, 235.
135. Niesel, *Theology*, 184–5.

even if they concern themselves chiefly with him, they nevertheless stray from the right way in turning some part of their thinking in another direction. Yet such distrust cannot creep in where men have once for all truly known the abundance of his blessings. (II.16.19)

This quotation concludes Calvin's chief exposition of Christology, the subject of Book II. In chapter 14 (section C above) Calvin expounded the one person and two natures of Christ. In chapter 15 (section D above) he treated the work of Christ in three offices. Obviously the person and work of Christ belong together, and Book III of the *Institutes*, which describes the work of the Holy Spirit, is not ultimately separated from the work of Christ. In chapter 16 Calvin emphasizes that Christ abolished sin and wrought atonement by his whole life (II.16.5). The knowledge of God the Redeemer is concluded *historically* using article 2 (the christological affirmations) of the Apostles' Creed.

Calvin is not especially interested in the origin of the Apostles' Creed, believing "the only point that ought to concern us [is] that the *whole history of our faith* is summed up in it succinctly and in definite order" (II.16.18, emphasis added). Before beginning his historical exposition, Calvin deals with the relation between God's love and wrath, making the confusing point that "in a marvelous and divine way [God] loved us even when he hated us" (II.16.4). Calvin insists, "There is a perpetual and irreconcilable disagreement between righteousness and unrighteousness" which means that God cannot receive sinners completely. On the other hand, he says, "Because the Lord wills not to lose what is his in us, out of his own kindness he still finds something to love" (II.16.3). Human wickedness had not entirely destroyed God's work, therefore, "He knew how, at the same time, to note in each one of us what *we* had made, and to love what *he* had made" (II.16.4).

Since human beings are sinful, they are lost, condemned, and dead. Therefore, they must seek salvation outside themselves. God is a righteous judge with the power and will to demand satisfaction (*satisfactio*) for the human abrogation of his divine law (II.16.1). However, God is not only a righteous judge but a loving father, which means his judgment on sin is anticipated by his mercy revealed in Jesus Christ. Calvin recognizes that the sending of the Son by the Father is already a pledge of forgiveness even before the work of reconciliation was undertaken, much less accomplished. According to Calvin, God's love for us is established, grounded, and declared in Christ. This means, quoting Augustine, that "it was not after we were reconciled to him through the blood of his Son that he began to love us. Rather, he has loved us before the world was created, that we might be his sons along with his only-begotten Son—before we became anything else" (II.16.4). In other words, God loved us even though we sinned against him. Christ abolished our sin because of God's love; Christ did not abolish our sin in order to allow God to love us.

Calvin admits that to place forgiveness before reconciliation appears to be a contradiction. Indeed, the Scripture teaches that God was our enemy until we were reconciled by the death of Christ, but Calvin understands this teaching to be accommodated to our small capacity (II.16.2). Since for Calvin God dwells in impenetrable mystery (III.2.1; III.6.16), it is arrogant to speculate about his essence. We cannot know God in himself, but only God in relation to us. In Jesus Christ God reveals to us what we need to know and believe—God accommodating to our capacity. Calvin declares succinctly, "God cannot be comprehended by us except as he accommodates himself to our standard" (Com. Ez. 9:3–4). The scriptural verses about the relation of God's mercy and wrath are designed to meet our need to feel the fear of God's wrath upon us before we experience the mercy revealed to us in Jesus Christ. Once we learn "that apart from Christ, God is, so to speak, hostile to us and his hand is armed for our destruction; [then we can] embrace his benevolence and fatherly love in Christ alone" (II.16.2). In Hunter's striking phrase, "It is the part of faith to believe that behind the veil mercy and judgment kiss one another."[136]

Calvin recognizes that logically God's wrath and our condemnation should be in effect until our reconciliation was accomplished by Christ. However, Calvin also realizes that the incarnation is an indication of God's intention to forgive sin even before the life of Jesus on earth or the crucifixion and resurrection take place. While the love of God the Father anticipates the reconciliation of God the Son, nevertheless, until Christ dies for us, we remain unrighteous and cannot be fully joined to God. Through Christ alone (his one person in two natures, his anointed work as priest, king, prophet, and his accomplished work: "crucified under Pontius Pilate," etc.), we escape the imputation of our sins and the wrath of God. Therefore, to receive assurance of our forgiveness "we must fix our eyes and minds on Christ alone" (II.16.3). Traditionally, Protestants teach that humans become righteous by *imputation*, not by *impartation*. There are serious difficulties with each of these views. In imputation God declares a believer forgiven, but this is a judicial fiction since the person does not become essentially or substantially holy. Critics of impartation argue that the fact of continuing sinfulness demonstrates true holiness is not a human possibility. Calvin continues to use the language of imputation, but the categories of both subjective impartation and objective imputation should be rejected in favor of Calvin's own emphasis on Christ for us (Book II) and Christ in us (Book III). By insisting that assurance of forgiveness is found in Christ alone, Calvin comes near to moving this discussion beyond the categories of imputation and impartation to union with Christ. Righteousness before God is God's gift of faith based on union with Christ. Sinful natures and sinful actions are forgiven in the new life made possible by his resurrection victory.

From this point onward the chapter follows the Apostles' Creed, which, as Calvin observes, passes at once from the birth of Christ to his death and resurrection. The death of Christ is to us a cause for joy, not sorrow (Com. Zech. 12:12). Scripture, he says, defines the way of salvation more exactly as peculiar and proper to Christ's death (II.16.5). That is, Christ died for our sins (Rom. 4:25), so we are justified by his blood and reconciled through his death (see Rom. 5:9–10). The

---

136. A. M. Hunter, *The Teaching of Calvin*, 2nd ed. (London: James Clarke and Company, 1950), 53.

conclusion is that "for us the substance of life is set in the death of Christ" (II.16.5). Nevertheless, it is curious that Calvin combines the suffering under Pontius Pilate with the crucifixion and omits the first three phrases of the Apostles' Creed. Doubtless, Calvin thought he had already dealt sufficiently with "[I believe] in Jesus Christ His only Son our Lord," but it is not obvious why he also ignores the second line concerning the conception by the Holy Spirit and the third, "born of the Virgin Mary." Calvin affirms these three phrases, of course, but in other places.

Calvin begins his exposition with the phrase "suffered under Pontius Pilate," insisting that for salvation it was essential that Christ die *in the place* of sinners, meaning that although he was innocent, he accepted the burden of sin and suffering. "To make satisfaction for our redemption a form of death had to be chosen in which he might free us both by transferring our condemnation to himself and by taking our guilt upon himself" (II.16.5). According to Calvin, it is a mystery how our stain and punishment are somehow cast on Christ and cease to be imputed to us. The form of his death by crucifixion is likewise a mystery. We are taught that he who knew no sin was made sin for our sake (2 Cor. 5:21). That is to say, "The Son of God, utterly clean of all fault, nevertheless took upon himself the shame and reproach of our iniquities, and in return clothed us with his purity" (II.16.6). Because of God's grace his sacrificial death brought satisfaction so that "we might cease to be afraid of God's wrath." Calvin reminds his reader that while Christ bore human sins he did not break under them. The shameful cross, he declares, is also a triumphal chariot.

Calvin emphasizes not merely what Christ needed to do but what we need to believe. We need to keep in mind and heart both Christ's sacrifice and our cleansing. According to Calvin we could not believe confidently "that Christ is our redemption, ransom, and propitiation unless he had been a sacrificial victim. Blood is accordingly mentioned wherever Scripture discusses the mode of redemption" (II.16.6) because Christ's shed blood is both a satisfaction for us and cleansing of us.[137]

The second phrase, "dead and buried," teaches again that Christ took our place and by dying redeemed us to life. Christ's "whole life was nothing but a sort of perpetual cross" because he learned obedience through what he suffered (III.8.1). Due to our union with Christ, his death and burial confer a twofold blessing on us: liberation from death and mortification of the old man. However, "No language can fully represent the consequences and efficacy of Christ's death" (Com. Eph. 5:2).

To the third phrase, "the descent into hell," Calvin devotes more attention than to any other part of the Apostles' Creed. He accepts that the phrase was not original but a later insertion. Its use only gradually became customary. Still, Calvin believes that the descent into hell points to "the useful and not-to-be

137. See Richard Mouw's interesting chapter "Preaching the Blood" in *The Smell of Sawdust: What Evangelicals Can Learn from Their Fundamentalist Heritage* (Grand Rapids: Zondervan, 2000).

despised mystery of a most important matter" (II.16.8). Some had argued that "hell" should be understood as the "grave," and therefore Christ's descent into the grave simply repeats the statement that he was buried. Calvin rejects the idea that the phrase is either careless or useless, but he also rejects the interpretation that Christ descended to the souls of the patriarchs who had died under the law in order to free them from prison. This story, says Calvin, is often repeated and defended, but it is still only a story. The verse about Christ's preaching to the spirits in prison (1 Peter 3:19) Calvin understands to teach that both the godly and the ungodly are aware of Christ's death.

The correct explanation is that Christ "stood accused before God's judgment seat for our sake" (II.16.12), which means Christ did not die a common death. Calvin sees David as a type of Christ and thinks the phrase "my strength is dried up" adumbrates Christ's descent into hell because excessive grief dries up the vital moisture of the body (Com. Ps. 32:15). Christ died more than a bodily death. That is, he took the place of *all* evildoers and suffered *all* the punishments, including death, that God in his wrath inflicted upon the wicked. Christ's body was given as the price of our redemption, but he paid an even greater price in the sufferings of his soul. Christ truly dreaded the pangs of death and experienced profound anguish over the possibility of being forsaken by God. This is not to say that God was ever actually angry at his Son, but for our sake, Christ, like us, experienced fear, sorrow, and dread before the wrathful and avenging God (II.16.11). His human fearfulness does not detract from his heavenly glory because since Christ is obedient, his weakness is not a vice. In summary, the descent into hell points to the uncommon and dread-full death which Christ died and instructs us on how much our salvation cost the Son of God.

The fourth topic is "resurrection from the dead." Of course, Christ's death and resurrection belong together. The terms are linked by synecdoche meaning that either word standing alone involves the other. With that caution in mind, Calvin's discussion of Christ's resurrection focuses on Christ's victory and our faith. Christ's resurrection is a mirror of our life (Com. Hos. 6:2). Our salvation is completely accomplished in Christ's death, by which (1) "we are reconciled to God, (2) his righteous judgment is satisfied, (3) the curse is removed, and (4) the penalty paid in full" (II.16.13). However, while his death destroys our sin and death, his resurrection displays his heavenly power and supports our faith. "The power of God, which guards us under faith, is especially revealed in the resurrection" (II.16.13). As Christ died and was raised from the dead, so we, being united to him, die with him and are raised with him. Thus our resurrection is guaranteed by his because he died the same death as other human beings "and received immortality *in the same flesh* that, in the mortal state, he had taken upon himself" (II.16.13, emphasis added).[138]

---

138. The affirmation of resurrection in the selfsame flesh is found in these Reformed confessions: The Scots Confession, articles 11 and 25; the Heidelberg Catechism, answer 49; the Second Helvetic Confession, article 11; the Westminster Confession, article 32.

The resurrection victory is followed by the glorious ascension, the fifth phrase, whereby Christ's kingdom is truly inaugurated. "Christ's ascension into heaven ought to establish our faith in eternal life" (Com. Rom. 10:6). He continues, "When we hear of the ascension of Christ, it instantly comes to our minds that he is far removed from us; and so indeed he is, with respect to his body and human presence [but] he nevertheless fills all things, and that by the power of his Spirit." According to Calvin, the Scripture clearly testifies concerning the ascension "that he was *in his humanity* received up into heaven, where he dwells until he descends to judge the world."[139]

Although his body is contained in heaven, his spiritual presence is shed abroad because the right hand of God encompasses heaven and earth (Com. Eph. 4:10). Until the ascension Christ's presence had been confined to the flesh, but with his bodily absence he poured out his Spirit to help his people and to scatter his enemies. "As his body was raised up above all the heavens, so his power and energy were diffused and spread beyond all the bounds of heaven and earth" (II.16.14). Christ remains with us according to the presence of his majesty but after the ascension his physical presence is described as "seated at the right hand of the Father." The resurrection was not complete until Christ entered the heavenly life by ascending to the right hand of the Father in order to draw believers to himself (Com. Jn. 20:17). Since Christ is in heaven in our minds we should dwell with him outside this world. Nevertheless, "as it would be rash and foolish to mount up beyond the heavens, and assign to Christ a station, or seat, or place of walking in this or that region, so also it is a foolish and destructive madness to drag him down from heaven by any carnal consideration so as to seek him on earth" (Com. Phil. 3:20). This view of both a heavenly localized body and a universally ubiquitous presence is vehemently developed in Calvin's eucharistic theology. McLelland opines, "Here is the crux of the Reformed position, in all its splendid ambiguity. It turns on the doctrine of Ascension." Attempting to define heaven and earth and describe the spiritual power emanating from the glorified humanity of Christ, he claims, "The Reformers were in deep waters here—as are we all."[140] We may be in deep waters, but a better image might be "spaced out."

The sixth topic, the session at the right hand of the Father, does not simply mean that Christ was blessed. Nor does it matter that Stephen saw him standing rather than sitting (Acts 7:55). Christ's session is not about the posture of his body, but about the majesty of his authority. Christ was raised by his Father to the sovereignty of heaven to sit at the Father's right hand (Com. Ps. 31:4). This phrase indicates that the Father delegates to the Son the tasks of ruling and governing. Being seated at the right hand thus means being invested with lordship

139. *Short Treatise on the Holy Supper*, 165.

140. J. C. McLelland, "Meta-Zwingli or Anti-Zwingli? Bullinger and Calvin in Eucharistic Concord," *Articles on Calvin and Calvinism*, ed. Richard C. Gamble, vol. 13 (New York: Garland Publishing, 1992), 154.

over heaven and earth. "The purpose of that 'sitting' [is] that both heavenly and earthly creatures may look with admiration upon his majesty, be ruled by his hand, obey his nod and submit to his power" (II.16.15).

According to Calvin, that Christ was raised in the flesh and "entered heaven in our flesh" (II.16.16) means that heaven is not only a future hope but a present possession because of our union with Christ. Second, having returned to the Father, Christ is our constant advocate and intercessor standing in his righteousness between the Father's eyes and our sins. Third, the ascension indicates the victory over God's enemies, which gives us the confidence to wait patiently until he returns to judge the living and the dead.

Christ's final act, Calvin's seventh topic, is to come down from heaven "in the same visible form in which he was seen to ascend" (II.16.17) for the purpose of calling the living and the dead to the final judgment. Calvin understands this judgment to be a wonderful consolation because Christ, our advocate, is not coming to condemn us. In fact our judge is our redeemer. Thus, his promise of eternal blessedness is fulfilled in his judgment.

Calvin's exposition of redemption, and therefore atonement, is focused on the Redeemer's person, work, and life, the latter outlined by the Apostles' Creed, which results in union with Christ. The basis of this confession for Calvin is the orthodox faith in the reality of the divine and human nature in the one person of the Mediator/Redeemer. For some time this conviction, and therefore the traditional conception of atonement, has been under such sharp attack that the situation warrants a few paragraphs.

In his influential reorientation of theology, Friedrich Schleiermacher offered a very different view of atonement focused on the believer and the believing community's experience of sin and grace, into which his conception of the person and work of Christ is fitted. With this post-Kantian emphasis on experience, the first part of *The Christian Faith* develops the concept of religious self-consciousness, and the second part explicates the religious self-consciousness as determined by the antithesis of sin and grace. Sequencing so strongly from sin to grace rather than from grace to sin almost inevitably places the primary emphasis on human misery rather than divine love. In any case, with his view of God-consciousness Schleiermacher expected to avoid the difficulties arising from the attempt "to define the mutual relations of the divine and the human in the Redeemer."[141] Additionally, he claims his "mystical" view is the true mean between a "magical" and "empirical" view.[142]

I take Schleiermacher to hold a fairly traditional confidence in the supernatural (Kant's noumenal realm), but his expository focus is on the natural (Kant's phenomenal realm). So I understand his comment, "The maxim everywhere

141. Friedrich Schleiermacher, *The Christian Faith*, ed. H. R. Mackintosh and J. S. Stewart (New York: Harper & Row, 1963), 397.
142. Ibid., 429.

underlying our presentation [is] that the beginning of the Kingdom of God is a supernatural thing, which, however, becomes natural as soon as it emerges into manifestation."[143] Whatever Schleiermacher's personal faith may be, his exposition of that faith is almost entirely restricted to its phenomenal dimensions, as the following summary indicates:

> We cannot say, either, that Christ fulfilled the divine will *in our place* or *for our advantage.* That is to say, He cannot have done so *in our place* in the sense that we are thereby relieved from the necessity of fulfilling it. No Christian mind could possibly desire this, nor has sound doctrine ever asserted it. Indeed, Christ's highest achievement consists in this, that He so animates us that we ourselves are led to an ever more perfect fulfillment of the divine will. Not only so; but He cannot have done it in the sense that the failure to please God which is present in us in and for ourselves, should or could, as it were, be covered by Christ's doing more than was necessary to please Him. For only that which is perfect can stand before God; hence even Christ Himself had (to put it so) nothing to spare, which could be distributed among us, whether we regard the completeness of His fulfillment in outward acts (which, moreover, for reasons which will emerge more clearly later, would be quite un-Protestant) or whether we regard only the purity of the inward sentiment.[144]

Redemption, then, addresses the condition of God-forgetfulness or the constraint of the feeling of absolute dependence or the lack of God consciousness. The term, "redemption," signifies passively the release of this constraint and actively "the help given in the process by some other person."[145] In this latter process redemption is effected by Christ through the communication of his sinless perfection (sec. 88). According to Schleiermacher, "to ascribe to Christ an absolutely powerful God-consciousness, and to attribute to Him an existence of God in Him are exactly the same thing. . . . We posit the God-consciousness in His self-consciousness as continually and exclusively determining every moment, and consequently also this perfect indwelling of the Supreme Being as His peculiar being and His inmost self."[146] In other words, Schleiermacher treats the person and work of Christ as explanation of the Christian awareness of divine grace which results in fellowship with the Redeemer. In a famous definition he declares, "Christianity is a monotheistic faith, belonging to the teleological type of religion, and is essentially distinguished from other such faiths by the fact that in it everything is related to the redemption accomplished by Jesus of Nazareth."[147] In spite of this "everything" claim, Schleiermacher's view of the Redeemer differs sharply from Calvin's not only in his redefinition of the mutual relations of the divine and human nature in Christ but also in the saving efficacy of his God-consciousness.

---

143. Ibid., 430.
144. Ibid., 456 (emphasis in original).
145. Ibid., 54.
146. Ibid., 387, 388.
147. Ibid., 52.

A more recent, and more radical, solution to the difficulties of logical conceptualization is to deny atonement altogether. Motivated in large measure by a commendable concern to respect the beliefs of adherents of other world religions, John Hick thinks the solution precipitates a new interpretation of Christology concentrated primarily on the work of Christ. Rejecting the Chalcedonian formula, Hick, echoing Kant, believes Jesus Christ is a godly man but not the God-man.[148] The belief that God became incarnate is not only a myth but specific to certain cultures. In *God Has Many Names* Hick asserts it would be unjust for the Creator of all to choose one people and their history in preference to another.[149] The work of Christ, then, is not to save sinners but to set before them an example of God's love to follow. According to Hick, the atonement must be reinterpreted, but he means abandoned. Hick admits that the doctrine has considerable emotional power but insists it is finally unintelligible. In an essay entitled "Evil and Incarnation," he affirms that the doctrine of the atonement is the traditional answer to the evil of sin, but finds serious problems involved with this "time-honored notion." First, the idea that the death of Jesus transformed God's relation to humans so as to enable God to love us contradicts Jesus' own revelation of God's love. Second, the Christ event as the single act of God leading to salvation, whether conceived of as objective or subjective (moral influence), is Christian triumphalism. Third, if God is not impassible, then presumably God is fully involved in the human condition already and there is no need of an incarnation for God to be among us.

Hick recognizes that the Christian story of redemption by the blood of Christ has had a rich emotional history and has inspired splendid poetic expressions. He thinks no Christian who has ever lived within the evangelical thought-world can read or sing without emotion William Cowper's lines set to music in the hymn "There Is a Fountain Filled with Blood":

> There is a fountain filled with blood
> Drawn from Emmanuel's veins;
> And sinners, plunged beneath that flood,
> Lose all their guilty stains.

Nevertheless, Hick concludes, while this strand of the Western religious heritage may be well loved, the notion of the salvation of the world by the blood of Christ is highly culture-specific. The church's later attempts to rationalize ancient Hebrew conceptions of blood sacrifice reflect various stages of

---

148. Two seminal christological essays appeared in *God and the Universe of Faiths: Essays in the Philosophy of Religion* (London: Macmillan, 1973). This neo-Arian interpretation continues in *The Myth of God Incarnate*, ed. John Hick (London: SCM Press, 1977), and *The Metaphor of God Incarnate: Christology in a Pluralistic Age* (Louisville, KY: Westminster/John Knox Press, 1993). See also Hick's 1986–87 Gifford Lectures, *An Interpretation of Religion: Human Responses to the Transcendent* (London: Yale University Press, 1989).

149. John Hick, *God Has Many Names* (Philadelphia: Westminster Press, 1982), 31. Obviously, this view must contend with the Old Testament teaching of Israel as the chosen nation (Gen. 15; Exod. 6:7) and with the New Testament teaching that Christians are a "chosen race," a "holy nation," "God's own people" (1 Pet. 2:9).

European intellectual and social history. Except as a metaphor for God's love, incarnation and atonement are both unintelligible. Hick argues the statement that God became flesh and dwelt among us full of grace and truth (John 1:14) is not actually or literally true.[150] In a short summary, Hick believes God's love is revealed *by* Christ but not *in* Christ. The primary reality is God's love exemplified in but not indigenous to Christ's person. Christ's work is not atonement but example. The statement "God was in Christ reconciling the world to himself" (2 Cor. 5:19) means that in Christ we see God's love displayed, but not God's face revealed.

According to Emil Brunner, no selection among the different interpretations of the meaning of Christ's crucifixion leads to a single correct view because the crucial elements cannot be combined into a logical theory. The necessary components of atonement do not produce a coherent "theory" but a series of "pictures." The first picture is colored red by the Old Testament sacrificial system. The sacrificial cultus was a living fact for the early church, meaning that the flow of blood was considered necessary to restore mankind to God. The second picture involves punishment and suffering. The obedient Son of God stood in the place of the sinner and by his stripes we are healed. Third, by bearing their iniquities Christ's obedient death cancels the sinners' debt. Fourth, the cross achieves the deliverance of humankind from the powers of darkness. Fifth, in the blood of Jesus a new covenant is established. "The 'Blood of the New Covenant,' the blood shed on the cross is not only the sign but also the means by which the new relation with God, the new communion with God is created."

Brunner insists these five elements are not *theories* but *pictures* that blend and intermingle, concluding, "None of these conceptions, by itself is adequate; and even when they are all combined they do not constitute a clear intellectual unity." Nevertheless, the death of Jesus on the cross is the *necessary* revealing, atoning, and redeeming act of God, although we cannot say precisely why that must be so. "All these ideas of sacrifice and atonement, of vicarious punishment, of the payment of a debt, the rescue of man from slavery to the power of darkness, of the establishment of the new covenant by the true Passover Lamb, are pointing to 'something' beyond. . . . The mystery of the 'must,' of that necessity, is the mystery of the cross as God's saving act."[151] If Brunner is correct, Calvin is wise to view atonement as the saving work of the Redeemer without trying to produce a logically compelling doctrine of atonement. Calvin is clear that salvation is found in Christ, emphasized in the blood of atonement and the flesh of Eucharist. But this is finally a confession, not an explanation.[152]

---

150. *Incarnation and Myth: The Debate Continued* (Grand Rapids: Eerdmans, 1979), 77–84.

151. Brunner, *Creation and Redemption*, 283–87.

152. Relating incarnation, union, and atonement, Robert Letham writes, "Union with Christ is, in fact, the foundation of all the blessings of salvation. Justification, sanctification, adoption and glorification are all received through our being united to Christ." Earlier Letham has puzzlingly criticized Karl Barth for "an exaggerated focus on Christ" when Barth makes what appears to me the same point (Letham, *The Work of Christ* [Downers Grove, IL: InterVarsity Press, 1993]), 80, 29).

CONCLUSIONS TO BOOK II

In Book I of the *Institutes* Calvin deals with the knowledge of God the Creator. Book III concerns the reception of the Lord's benefits. Since Calvin accepts the central Christian conviction that Jesus Christ is Lord, his heartfelt gratitude for the love of God revealed in Christ is most powerfully expressed in Book I in the doctrine of particular providence. In Book III this same gratitude is expressed in the doctrine of particular predestination, as we shall see.

In Book II Calvin focuses on the knowledge of the Lord Jesus Christ explicated in terms of the gospel and the law, the one person and two natures of Christ, his work under three offices, and finally the witness to him of the Apostles' Creed. Each of these topics concerns the knowledge of God the Redeemer and must be approached through faith, which means erasing the brushstrokes that paint Calvin as an exceptionally rigorous advocate for the use of law and reason in theology. The center of Calvin's faith is the Lord Jesus Christ, who, by God's grace, was for our sake incarnate, suffered, crucified, dead, buried, risen, ascended, seated at the right hand of majesty, and will return in glory and mercy.

PART TWO
GOD WITH US

Book III

The Faithful Person(s)

INTRODUCTION TO BOOK III

The rationale for marking a division in the *Institutes* between Books I and II on the one hand, and Books III and IV on the other was discussed in the introduction. Book I deals with God for us as Creator and Book II with God for us as Redeemer. The latter contains Calvin's Christology, the "objective" basis of redemption. Book III explains the "subjective" reception of the grace of Christ in terms of *persons*, and Book IV continues the exposition of faith in Christ developed now in terms of "outward helps" to the *community*. These outward helps not only beget and increase faith but gather and hold the faithful community together. In earlier formulations the words "God for us" summarized Books I and II while "God in us" was applied to Books III and IV. This terminology for part 2 is theologically accurate, and Calvin uses it constantly (cf. II.1.1), but the idea of God-in-us may suggest some sort of divinity resident (and bound) within human being—a divine spark (λόγος σπερματικός), as Stoicism taught. This conception is not entirely misleading because something of the image of God remains even after the fall, but Calvin also insists that what remains is "horribly deformed" by sin. Protecting the *objectivity* and *freedom* of God's presence to persons and the community might be better expressed with the phrase "God *with* us" because God's presence depends on the divine initiative, not human will. Calvin emphasizes divine gift and not the human possession of it.

In summary, part 1 of this study deals with God for us as Creator (Book I) and Redeemer (Book II). Part 2 considers God with us as faithful persons (Book III) and as a faithful community (Book IV). Of course, these distinctions are employed to serve the convenience of exposition, because the reality is beyond formulaic conception. For example, the doctrine of the Trinity distinguishes between Father and Son but also identifies the one God as Creator and Redeemer. God and man are distinguishable, but human beings are united to God in Christ—a reality more to be adored than to be understood.[1] Commenting on Ephesians (5:32) concerning the union between Christ and the church, Calvin admits, "I am overwhelmed by the depth of this mystery, and with Paul am not ashamed to acknowledge in wonder my ignorance. . . . Reason itself teaches us whatever is supernatural is clearly beyond the grasp of our minds. Let us therefore labor more to feel Christ living in us, than to discover the nature of that communion."

Likewise, an individual believer can be distinguished from the community of believers, but through the work of the Holy Spirit individuals live and flourish in profound connection with the community.[2] Modern readers must be careful not to impart contemporary concepts of individuality and the self into centuries where they are dissimilar. Most emphatically the term "faithful person" is not to be taken as a "separate self" in the modern sense. The ideas that self and society are twin-born and the problem of recovering a sense of community are different issues now than in Calvin's time. In Book III Calvin insistently uses the first-person plural. The suggested distinction between Books III and IV is that the latter deals with the church (a way of looking at outward helps for faithful persons) and the former with faithful persons—a category that includes individuals. It is also important to recognize that the distinction between parts 1 and 2 find their unity in Jesus Christ who is confessed to be both God *for* us and God *with* us and *in* whom we live and move and are. Book IV expounds the work of the Holy Spirit in the faithful community (ecclesiology), and Book III is concerned simultaneously (not sequentially) with faith, the work of the Holy Spirit in faithful individuals (soteriology).

Calvin indicates the transition from Book II to Book III by addressing the question, "How do we receive those benefits which the Father bestowed on his

1. In a helpful review of "Calvin's Doctrine of Our Union with Christ" Seng-Kong Tan (*Quodlibet Online Journal of Christian Theology and Philosophy* 5, no. 4 (October 2003), http://www.Quodlibet.net, overemphasizes the role of principles in Calvin's thinking, such as *distinctio sed non separatio*. Axioms may be applied to Calvin's theology, but he was attempting to confess the faith, not to defend the principles.

2. Langdon Gilkey, *Reaping the Whirlwind: A Christian Interpretation of History* (New York: Seabury Press, 1976), 185, writes, "The unique power of Calvinism as a religious force transformative of the Western society lay in its dual emphasis on the individual and on the community. . . . The individual in Calvinism is given an unprecedented strength, autonomy and creative role," but individuals are not isolated from community.

only-begotten Son—not for Christ's own private use, but that he might enrich [us]?" "Faith ought not to be fixed on the essence of Christ alone (so to speak), but ought to attend to his power and office, for it would be of little advantage to know who Christ is, if this second point were not added, what he wishes to be toward us, and for what purpose the Father sent him" (Com. Jn. 1:49). To understand faith we must first "understand that as long as Christ remains outside of us, and we are separated from him, all that he has suffered and done for the salvation of the human race remains useless and of no value for us." In other words, what Christ has done *for* us must also be done *in* us because "all that he possesses is nothing to us until we grow into one body with him" (III.1.1). In short, the faithful are united to Christ.

The centrality of this doctrine is emphasized by Karl Barth. Union with Christ "has a comprehensive and basic significance for Calvin. Indeed, we might almost call it his conception of the essence of Christianity." According to Barth this idea may surprise those informed by the still current legend that Calvin was the great champion of the great distance between divine and human being. Calvin's doctrine of union has two aspects. It is first and comprehensively the sanctification of man, and second, within this it is also man's justification. Barth thinks the significance of this doctrine grew on Calvin:

> The real advance has obviously been made when we come to the INSTITUTIO of 1559, in which *unio cum Christo* has become the common denominator under which Calvin tried to range his whole doctrine of the appropriation of the salvation achieved and revealed in Christ. For now in the Third Book, before he can speak of faith, of conversion and renewal, of the *vita hominis christiani*, of *abnegatio nostri* as its sum, of the necessary bearing of the cross, of the relation between this and the future life, then—and only then—of justification, of Christian freedom and prayer, of eternal election as the ultimate presupposition of the whole, and finally of the future resurrection, according to the view attained in 1559 he has first to make it plain how it can come about at all that what God has done for us in Christ, as declared in the Second Book, can apply to us and be effective for us. The answer given in the noteworthy opening chapter of the Third Book is to the effect that it comes about through the *arcana operatio Spiritus*, which consists in the fact that Christ Himself, instead of being *extra nos*, outside the man separated from Him and therefore irrelevant to us, becomes ours and takes up His abode in us, we for our part being implanted into Him (Rom. 11:17) and putting Him on (Gal. 3:27).[3]

We come to enjoy Christ and all his benefits because of "the secret work of the Spirit" who is the bond by which Christ effectually unites us to himself" (III.1.1).[4] The purpose of human life is to be united to God (Com. Hab. 2:4). The end of the gospel is union with God. There can be no communion without love, and progress in faith requires cleaving to God (Com. I Jn. 2:5).

---

3. *CD* 4.3.2, 550–51.
4. On Calvin as the theologian of the Holy Spirit, see I. John Hesselink's Appendix in *Calvin's First Catechism* (Louisville, KY: Westminster John Knox Press, 1997), 177–87.

Book III treats the reception, benefits, and effects of the grace of Christ, but the discussion contains a number of surprises. Wendel expresses the situation this way:

> The order of the subjects expounded in the Third Book of the *Institutes* is rather surprising at first sight. Having indicated that "the things which have been said concerning Jesus Christ are of profit to us through the hidden operation of the Holy Spirit," the author speaks of faith and of regeneration by faith: to this he adds chapters on penitence and on "the life of the Christian man." It is only then that he comes to deal with justification by faith and the emptiness of works, and then with Christian freedom, prayer, predestination, and finally with the resurrection. The majority of commentators have been struck by this somewhat unaccustomed order and have tried to give reasons for it, especially to explain why Calvin placed his developments upon justification after the exposition of regeneration.[5]

Wendel is quite right in what he says about the order of Calvin's exposition, but the more crucial question is what Calvin means by the "secret work of the Holy Spirit." "The order of subjects expounded in the third book of the *Institutes*" is indeed surprising, but the context of subjects within the work of the Holy Spirit is even more so.

In approaching this section, two immediate warnings are necessary. First, many theologians devote separate attention to a "Doctrine of Man." For example, Louis Berkhof in his *Systematic Theology* deals with the doctrine of God (being and works) in part 1 (180 pages). Part 2 (124 pages) is titled "The Doctrine of Man in Relation to God" and discusses the original state, the sinful state, and the covenant of grace (which replaces the covenant of works). Berkhof treats human beings as more distant from divine being than Calvin does. In addition, his Christology *follows* his anthropology. For Berkhof the person and work of Christ (110 pages) is part 3. In contrast, Calvin's Christology (Book II) *precedes* what could be very loosely called his "theological anthropology" (Book III). One might expect to find "Calvin's anthropology" located in his exposition of faithful persons, but, in opposition to the relatively freestanding anthropological discussions developed by theologians like Berkhof, Calvin's discussion of faithful individuals is seen within the work of the Holy Spirit!

The second caution requires recognition of Calvin's emphasis on the *work* of the Holy Spirit. As noted in the discussion of Trinity, Calvin affirms the eternal

---

5. François Wendel, *Calvin: The Origins and Development of His Religious Thought*, trans. Philip Mairet (New York: Harper and Row, 1963), 233. This quotation notices faith, regeneration by faith, and justification by faith. Likewise, Victor A. Shepherd, *The Nature and Function of Faith in the Theology of John Calvin* (Macon, GA: Mercer University Press, 1983) in an unbalanced discussion, deals with justification (six pages), sanctification (four pages), and predestination (fifty-seven pages) in connection with faith briefly and correctly defined as the gratuitous gift of God, meaning that Jesus Christ is both the author and object of faith. In fact, Calvin's understanding of faith as gift is the hinge for *all* the doctrines of Book III.

deity and essence of the Spirit rather briefly and even cursorily (I.13.14–15). In Book III he focuses on dynamic relations rather than static distinctions, passing by ontological discussions of substance in favor of functional and personal categories of action. Calvin writes, "God the Father gives us the Holy Spirit for his Son's sake, and yet has bestowed the whole fullness of the Spirit upon the Son to be minister and steward of his liberality. For this reason, the Spirit is sometimes designated "Spirit of the Father," sometimes "Spirit of the Son" (III.1.2). Christ is called the "inner school master" and the Holy Spirit the "inner teacher" in the same paragraph (III.1.4). According to Calvin's basic conviction, "The Holy Spirit is the bond by which Christ effectually unites us to himself" (III.1.1). Without the Spirit, "Christ, so to speak, lies idle because we coldly contemplate him as outside ourselves. . . . But he unites himself to us by the Spirit alone" (III.1.3). And in being united to Christ, Calvin affirms that the Spirit "so breathes divine life into us that we are no longer actuated by ourselves but are ruled by his action and prompting" (III.1.3). The Commentary on Romans teaches that "we must either deny Christ, or confess that we become Christians by his Spirit" (8:9). The Spirit sets us apart to God by ingrafting into the body of Christ (Com. I Cor. 1:2). In the Commentary on Zechariah (4:6), Calvin declares the word "Spirit" means power. Butin notes the problem of reconciling the concepts of power and person, concluding, "Let it suffice to point out that a developed understanding of the Spirit as 'person' (in the most common Western understanding of that term) is foreign, not only to the New Testament, but even to the authoritative trinitarian views of the ecumenical councils."[6] Calvin says, "No one is fit to offer sacrifices to God, or to do any other service except one who has been molded by the hidden operation of the Spirit. Willingly indeed we offer ourselves and our all to God, and build his temple; but whence is this voluntary action, except that the Lord subdues us and thus renders us teachable and obedient?" (Com. Hag. 1:14). Apparently, Calvin believes the hidden operation of the Holy Spirit does not interfere but enhances voluntary action.

In such statements, individual and separate identities of the divine and human are difficult to locate and maintain. Moreover, it is impossible to decide the distinction between the doctrine of the work of the Holy Spirit or the benefits the believer derives from it because Calvin does not differentiate sharply between the

---

6. Philip Walker Butin, *Revelation, Redemption, and Response—Calvin's Trinitarian Understanding of the Divine-Human Relationship* (New York: Oxford University Press, 1995), 181n1. In the *Congrégation sur Divinité de Iésus-Christ* (*CO* 47: 473), Calvin notes that in the doctrine of the Trinity the word "person" is not used in an ordinary way. Karl Barth avoids the concept of person, preferring "mode of being" (*CD* 1.1, 406–7). In a radically untraditional approach G. W. H. Lampe, *God as Spirit* (Oxford: Clarendon Press, 1977), 225, suggests replacing the Trinitarian model with the unifying concept of God as Spirit. The conceptualization of divine unity meant that "the Trinitarian distinctions, which had originally been developed in order to affirm that Jesus is God, and yet to deny that God is Jesus, as it were without remainder, and at the same time to preserve what the Bible was believed to say about another, distinct, area where God encounters men, no longer had any content."

Spirit and the Father, nor between the Spirit and the Son, nor indeed between the Spirit and the Self.[7] This concept of the Holy Spirit as the bond between Father and Son and between God and the faithful is of ancient lineage, especially represented in Augustine.[8]

Following the biblical revelation of Father, Son, and Holy Spirit, the doctrine of Trinity was several centuries in developing, and the deity of the Holy Spirit was only declared at the Council of Constantinople in AD 381. Augustine devoted his great work *De Trinitate* to reflection on this subject. The mystery of the Trinity, of course, lies beyond human comprehension, and its formulation bristles with intellectual difficulties. Comprehending the divine essence (οὐσία, *essentia*) being impossible, the relation of the divine persons to either the divine essence or to each other cannot be precisely understood. More directly, the employment of the term "person" (ὑπόστασις, *persona*) is complicated and even confounding in its application to the Holy Father, the Holy Son, and especially to the Holy Spirit. Calvin only repeats the confusion when he writes, "'Person,' therefore, I call a 'subsistence' in God's essence, which, while related to the others, is distinguished by an incommunicable quality" (I.13.6). The meaning of "person" when applied to the Holy Spirit is a special issue. Obviously the Son is a person in the ordinary human sense of the word, and Father is a personal term in a way that Spirit is not. It is useful to remember that Calvin much prefers to refer to God as "Father" rather than as "Being." Nevertheless, that the triune God relates to human beings in a personal way does not legitimate the descriptive accuracy of the ordinary-language term "person" on every level.[9]

---

7. Quite helpful on each of these subjects is George S. Hendry's *The Holy Spirit in Christian Theology* (Philadelphia: Westminster Press, 1956), but especially the chapter on the Holy Spirit and human spirit. H. Wheeler Robinson concludes his reflection on the Holy Spirit with an analysis of personality, addressing the strong objection of Professor Pringle-Pattison that popular theology "has succeeded in transforming the profound doctrine of the Spirit, as the ultimate expression of the unity and communion of God and man, into the notion of another distinct Being, a third center of consciousness mysteriously united with the other two." Robinson needlessly impoverishes his study by setting aside Scripture and tradition and adopting the line of Kant and Schleiermacher in desiring "to lay stress upon the value and validity of religious experience and to develop their theology on the basis of the religious consciousness." Nevertheless, the criticism of understanding the Holy Spirit as "another distinct Being, a third center of consciousness" is apt (H. Wheeler Robinson, *The Christian Experience of the Holy Spirit* [New York: Harper and Brothers, 1928], 268, vi). This problem is discussed without clarifying the issues by B. J. Engelbrecht, "The Problem of the Concept of the 'Personality' of the Holy Spirit According to Calvin," in *Calvinus Reformator: His Contribution to Theology, Church and Society* (Potchefstroom, SA: Potchefstroom University, 1982), 201–16. Even John Milton worried about this issue, concluding that since the Holy Spirit was sent by the Father and the Son he was inferior in rank to both the Father and Son. In addition, the Holy Spirit cannot act of himself or in his own name, and can never be made the object of an invocation (Maurice Kelley, *The Great Argument: A Study of Milton's De Doctrina Christiana as a Gloss upon Paradise Lost* [Princeton, NJ: Princeton University Press, 1941], 107–8, 110).

8. Bernard de Margerie, *The Christian Trinity in History*, trans. Edmund J. Fortman (Still River, MA: St. Bede's Publications, 1975), 110–21.

9. Clement C. J. Webb deals linguistically, historically, philosophically, and theologically with this crucial concept in the 1918–19 Gifford Lectures entitled *God and Personality* (London: George Allen and Unwin, 1919), but with very slight attention to the Holy Spirit. Among his important discussions is the emphasis on individuality and rationality resulting from the view of Boethius, who

This problem is clearly exhibited in the *Summa Theologica*. Aquinas produces first a treatise on God as unity followed by a treatise on Trinity. The latter exposition begins with the *procession* of the divine persons and ends with the *mission* of the divine persons. Working with the ancient philosophical puzzle of the One and the Many and utilizing the Aristotelian categories of substance and attributes, Thomas asks, "Whether the word 'Person' should be said of God?" (*ST* 1, q.29. a.3). Thomas admits that the word "person" is *not* used of God in Scripture, but since he defines God as the supremely perfect, self-subsisting being of a rational nature, he concludes the term "person" is properly applied to God. This conclusion raises a difficulty because the word "person" applied to God is predicated plurally of the Three in contrast to the nature of the names belonging to the essence (a.4). John Zizioulas dissents from this tradition, pointing out that theologians like Thomas wrongly assume the formulation of the doctrine of Trinity as "one substance, three persons" (μία οὐσία, τρία πρόσωπα) to mean the ontological reality of God is primarily located in the one substance rather than in the divine persons. To the contrary, Zizioulas insists that patristic theology identifies the being of God with the "person" of the Father.[10] Even better than appealing the issue to the Western or the Eastern fathers would be a careful exegesis of the biblical witness to Father, Son, and Spirit and the relatively successful attempts of various theologians to articulate and protect that mystery.

Consonant with the doctrinal consensus of the church and the intellectual categories established to expound it, Calvin certainly affirms the Holy Spirit as the third "person" of the Trinity. He writes, "If the Spirit were not a subsistence in God, choice and will would not be ascribed to him. Paul, therefore, very clearly attributes to the Spirit divine power, and shows that He resides hypostatically in God" (I.13.14). Calvin concludes, "It is quite clear that in God's essence reside three persons in whom one God is known" (I.13.16). Nevertheless, in much the same way as Book II accepts the deity of Christ and emphasizes his humanity, so Book III accepts the person of the Spirit and emphasizes his work, expressing the dynamic activity described in the Scripture rather than the ontological, impersonal, and static conceptuality derived from theology influenced by philosophy.[11]

---

defined person as the individual subsistence of a rational nature (*persona est naturae rationabilis individua substantia*). Additionally, Webb claims only so far as personal relations exist between the worshiper and God can God be properly described as "personal" (lecture 3). In his 1924–25 Gifford Lectures, Lewis Richard Farrell asserts, "In fact no one has ever been able to imagine a divine personal power that in its nature, attributes, and activity was wholly non-human; also we find that the farther the ideal recedes from the human sphere the less is its value for real and practical religion" (*The Attributes of God* [New York: Oxford University Press, 1925], 61). In his final chapter Farrell argues that abstract metaphysical attributes like eternity, immutability, and infinity present special difficulties.

10. John D. Zizioulas, *Being as Communion: Studies in Personhood and the Church* (Crestwood, NJ: St. Vladimir's Seminary Press, 1985), 40–41.

11. The standard study of Calvin's doctrine of the Holy Spirit remains Werner Krusche, *Das Wirken des Heiligen Geistes nach Calvin* (Göttingen: Vandenhoeck & Ruprecht, 1957). The work of the Holy Spirit in faith, union, and communion with Christ is noted on pp. 265–72, including the judgment that his concept of mystical union does not make Calvin a mystic. Given the essentially dynamic conceptualization of the doctrine of the Holy Spirit, all Christian theology, including

Book III is lengthily entitled "The Way in Which We Receive the Grace of Christ: What Benefits Come to Us from It, and What Effects Follow." The evident and crucial point is that the work of the Holy Spirit continues the exposition of the Lordship of Christ. As T. F. Torrance finely puts it, "The Holy Spirit does not speak to us of himself but only of what he has received from the Son, and only in order to make known the Father in the Son and the Son in the Father (John 16:13. cf. 14:26, 15:26; Inst. I.9.1; III.2.34; IV.8.8, 11, 13; IV.10.18)."[12] The subject of Book III is the grace of Christ focused on *our* reception of, benefits from, and effects resulting which come to us by the work of the Holy Spirit. The small chapter that introduces Book III is massively misunderstood when faith is defined apart from union with Christ. Calvin declares the Holy Spirit is "the inner teacher by whose effort the promise of salvation penetrates into our minds [meaning] that faith itself has no other source than the Spirit" (III.1.4). Without the Holy Spirit, "Christ, so to speak, lies idle because we coldly contemplate him as outside ourselves [until Christ] unites himself to us by the Spirit alone" (III.1.3). This union with Christ is obtained through the supernatural gift of faith, which is "the principal work of the Holy Spirit" (III.1.4). The chief subject of the *Institutes* Book III is faith, but not human faith as it might be anthropologically analyzed. In the following comment Wendel seems to give permission to study faith apart from Christ. "Faith may indeed be an absolutely free gift of God; it is no less surely ours, once we have received it."[13] Calvin, on the other hand, asserts that faith has no value in itself but only as the instrument by which we obtain the righteousness of Christ (III.18.8). The focus on faith is not primarily as a human possession, but as a gift of God's grace revealed in Jesus Christ with benefits effected through the work of the Holy Spirit. Calvin discusses this gift under the major headings of faith, sanctification, justification, prayer, predestination, and resurrection.

A. THE WORK OF THE HOLY SPIRIT IN FAITH

Because faith is the work of the Holy Spirit, no human person is assigned a simple and individual responsibility for its possession. The gift of faith is God's to bestow as God chooses because faith is not our possession by nature (III.2.35). This Godly presumption of Calvin's results in an exposition of the doctrine of faith by far the most extensive in the *Institutes*. Faith covers Book III generally,

---

Calvin's, can be expounded in terms of the work of the Holy Spirit. Several themes, identified in these pages with Calvin, receive considerable systematic development by Alan Torrance, chiefly in conversation with Barth. They include the crucial divine-human concept of "person," the importance of moving beyond *analogia entis* and *analogia fidei* to *analogia communionis*, and the doxological role of worship in constructive dogmatics (especially chap. 5) (Alan J. Torrance, *Persons in Communion: An Essay on Trinitarian Description and Human Participation* [Edinburgh: T. & T. Clark, 1996]).

12. T. F. Torrance, "Calvin's Doctrine of the Trinity," 186.

13. Wendel, *Calvin: The Origins and Development*, 263.

but is explicitly designated in chapter 2 and the chapters entitled regeneration by faith (III.3–5), justification by faith (III.11–19) and prayer as the chief exercise of faith (III.20). Calvin admits the word has many meanings (III.2.13), but his chief insistence is that faith is a singular gift of God (III.2.33) in the revelation of Christ, and the principal work of the Holy Spirit. Faith is the result of heavenly grace, lest anyone should glory in any birth other than that of the Spirit (Com. Mk. 3:20). "[Faith] is the proper and entire work of the Holy Spirit," with the result that we are (1) instructed by the Word, (2) the Word is confirmed by the sacraments, and (3) our hearts are opened for the reception of Word and sacrament (IV.14.8). "Faith is called the only work of God because by it we possess Christ and become sons of God, so that he governs us by his Spirit" (Com. Jn. 6:29). The content of the gift of faith is Christ himself because faith does not reconcile us to God unless faith joins us to Christ (III.2.30). "The whole substance of our salvation is not to be sought anywhere else than in Christ. . . . The true looking of faith is placing Christ before one's eyes and beholding in him the heart of God poured out in love" (Com. Jn. 3:16). Again, "Our salvation comes from faith, which ties us to God, and the only pathway is our insertion into the body of Christ, to live by his Spirit, and also to be ruled by him" (Com. Jas. 2:14). "We know we are God's children by the sure pledge of faith in Christ and the seal of adoption by the Holy Spirit" (Com. I Jn. 3:19). This Trinitarian confession—God's children pledged in Christ and sealed by the Holy Spirit—defines faith and explains its theological role. "By the word *faith* he means the first principles of religion and any doctrine that has been found not to correspond with these is condemned as false" (Com. Rom. 12:6).

Calvin insists that apart from Christ no one is loved by God (III.2.32) because God loves us with the same love he bestows on his son. "Apart from Christ [we are] hated by God and he only begins to love us when we are united to the body of his beloved son" (Com. Jn. 17:26). Faith is a work in divine but not in human terms. It is not an individual accomplishment. Faith depends on God alone (Com. Hab. 2:4), and the sole pledge of God's love is Christ (III.2.7). The whole human race is deprived of God's blessings, which can only be obtained by faith in the gospel; all are blind until enlightened by faith; all are slaves of Satan's tyranny until freed by faith; all are hostile to God and liable to death until their sins are remitted by faith. "Accordingly there is nothing more wretched for us than to be without Christ and faith" (Com. Acts 26:18).

God's special gift is that we possess Christ and he possesses us. "That Christ should be formed in us is the same as our being formed in Christ" (Com. Gal. 4:19). In this way Calvin strongly and essentially identifies faith and union with Christ. According to Calvin's summary, "Christ, when he illumines us into faith by the power of his Spirit, *at the same time* so engrafts us into his body that we become partakers of every good" (III.2.35, emphasis added). It is remarkable, Calvin asserts, "that believers live outside themselves, that is, in Christ. This can only be if they hold true and substantial communication with him. Christ lives in us in two ways. The one consists in his governing us by his Spirit and directing all our actions. The other is what he grants us by participation in his righteousness, that, since we can do nothing of ourselves, we are accepted in him by God" (Com. Gal. 2:20). Such statements and the following are difficult to overemphasize. Calvin insists, "That joining together of Head and members, that indwelling of Christ in our hearts—in short, that mystical union—are accorded by us the highest degree of importance, so that Christ, having been made ours, makes us sharers with him in the gifts with which he has been endowed" (III.11.10). He continues elsewhere, "We cannot know by idle speculation what is the sacred and mystic union between us and him and again between him and the Father, but that the only way to know it is when he pours his life into us by the secret efficacy of the Spirit" (Com. John 14:20). Calvin appeals both the mystical union and the work of the Holy Spirit to the experience of faith. "Nothing relating to the Holy Spirit can be learned by human reason, but that he is known only by the experience of faith" (Com. John 14:17). In Calvin's theology, union with Christ is a central reality, not a mere metaphor or a pious hope.[14]

His doctrine of faith is crucial to proper interpretation of Calvin, whose most famous and succinct definition is introduced with the claim that "understanding mixed with doubt is to be excluded." Faith is "a firm and certain knowledge of *God's* benevolence toward us, founded upon the truth of the freely given promise in *Christ* both revealed to our minds and sealed upon our hearts through the *Holy Spirit* (III.2.7, emphasis added). This Trinitarian affirmation of faith teaches that the knowledge of God's benevolence and Christ's truth is completed by the work of the Holy Spirit revealing to our minds and sealing upon our hearts. Thus, faith is the gift by which the Holy Spirit leads the elect into the light of the gospel (III.1.4). However, important as the Trinitarian relation is, even more notable is the fact that faith and union with Christ being virtually synonymous means faith is not under human control in initiation or achievement.

According to modern dispositions and assumptions, faith is correlative and interactive. Against Calvin, faith is today understood, at least in part, as *my* faith. Since theology requires listening and questioning so faith is assumed to include both gift and response. Calvin affirms a human response to the divine gift, but he credits the response to the work of the Holy Spirit in order to avoid all self-gratulation or -glorification. Faith is not a human choice made habitual but a divine blessing made continual by union with Christ. Correctly regarding faith as a divine miracle of incorporation and denying Osiander's view of union with Christ as a mixing of divine and human substance, Wilhelm Niesel defines faith as "the turning of persons (Hinwendung des Menschen) to Christ which is the work of the Holy Spirit."[15]

14. For Calvin, Doumergue declares simply, "Faith is a mystical union" (Émile Doumergue, *Le Caractère de Calvin*, 2nd ed. [Neuilly: La Cause, 1931], 54). Doumergue's *Calvin,* 320, contrasts Luther's lyrical mysticism with Calvin's more sober temperament. Calvin thought God's prophets (like himself) were of a sedate and composed mind (Com. Ez. 3:14). Nevertheless, on the secret witness of the Holy Spirit, Doumergue thinks Calvin sings "un véritable cantique mystique" (*Le Caractère,* 57).

15. Niesel, *The Theology of Calvin*, 1st ed., trans. Harold Knight (Philadelphia: Westminster Press, 1956), 123.

Early in his exposition Calvin describes firm faith as our embracing and resting in God's mercy with steadfast hope. This remark about embracing and resting seems to involve human cooperation with God's grace, but Calvin immediately declares many people today are dangerously deluded about the true character of faith. God is not properly understood as the object of faith because Christ who is both God and man is our intermediary. "As God he is the destination to which we move; as man, the path by which we go. Both are found in Christ alone" (III.2.1). Statements that seem to require human choice are rather focused on divine adoption. Calvin asserts that to suppose persons attain faith by their own efforts is an absurd fiction. Faith is "the unique gift of the Spirit" (III.2.8).[16]

The Trinitarian concept of faith in Calvin's theology is clearly demonstrated by his refusal to locate its discussion among the human virtues. We are to understand that all the virtues are gifts of God (III.14.2–3). "Even though the life of man be replete with all the virtues, if it is not directed to the worship of God, it can indeed be praised by the world; but in heaven it will be sheer abomination" (III.3.7). Today the word "virtue" is often restricted to chastity or currently acceptable sexual behaviors. However, the concept of virtue once ranged over the good life both in actual conduct and ideal aspiration. For Plato, Aristotle, and Aquinas virtue is a basic moral principle whose exposition originates in the *Dialogues* of Plato, continues in the *Ethics* of Aristotle, is mentioned in Augustine,[17] and forms a major section in Thomas Aquinas's *Summa Theologica*.

In classical ethical reflection, virtue (ἀρετή) led to human excellence. The list of virtues required varied—and in Plato sometimes included holiness—but in general the four classical (or natural) virtues were moderation (σωφροσύνη), courage (ἀνδρεία), justice (δικαιοσύνη), and prudence (φρόνησις), sometimes translated as practical wisdom.[18] In traditional Christian thought, as represented by Aquinas and his poetic disciple, Dante, ethical reflection expounded the seven, adding to the four natural or classical virtues the three supernatural or Christian virtues: faith, hope, and love. According to Aquinas, sin removed these supernatural virtues, which grace must restore—grace perfecting nature. The natural

---

16. In an extremely helpful and wide-ranging analysis of being "in Christ," J. K. S. Reid suggests Karl Barth "stands as representative of a view opposed to that of all who think of faith as a human possession or contribution to be offered as a condition prior to the enjoyment of salvation" (*Our Life in Christ* [Philadelphia: Westminster Press, 1963], 82). In taking this stance Barth merely adopts Calvin's standpoint.

17. In praising the "spark of reason," the image of God in mankind that survived the fall, Augustine claims our rational nature provides the capacity to foster the four classical virtues (*City of God* 22.24). In book 1 of his *Christian Doctrine*, Augustine deals with faith, hope, and love.

18. A brief discussion of ἀρετή as human excellence from Socrates to Plato to Aristotle to Aquinas and Roman Catholic moral philosophy is found in Thomas E. Hill, *Ethics in Theology and Practice* (New York: Thomas Y. Crowell Company, 1956), chap. 8. On the interesting relation of σοφία and φρόνησις, see Richard C. Trench, *Synonyms of the New Testament* (London: Macmillan & Co., 1880), 281–82. See also *The Cardinal Virtues: Aquinas, Albert, and Philip the Chancellor*, trans. R. E. Houser (Toronto: Pontifical Institute of Medieval Studies, 2004). In addition to the translated texts, the introductory historical survey of the pagan philosophers, Christian fathers, and masters of the schools is especially helpful.

virtues were central to ethical discussion in classical times and with the addition of the supernatural virtues, central in Christian times, but—so far as I know—Calvin never refers to the virtues in this formation.[19] In the *Institutes* Calvin twice lists three virtues that are actually two. At III.14.2 Calvin cites moderation and then justice and equity, which appear to be the same. At II.8.11, after mentioning equity, Calvin includes continence and temperance, which are the same classical virtue, also adding fortitude and prudence (III.14.3). Instead of using the seven virtues as a framework for ethical discussion, Calvin dismisses them all as worthless if they do not lead to worship of the true God (III.3.7). Calvin's view of the relation of faith and virtue contrasts strongly with Aquinas's. Among the sharpest differences is Thomas's treatment of virtue, including faith, in his Treatise on Habits. Calvin does not make the Thomistic distinction between infused and acquired virtue, nor between formed and unformed faith (III.2.8–10). Additionally, Calvin insists that "love is an accessory or inferior aid, a prop to our faith, not the foundation on which it rests" (Com. I Jn. 3:19).[20]

One might too hastily conclude that Calvin exalted the Protestant virtue of faith over the Catholic virtue of love, but in Calvin's mind, faith is not reducible to a virtue. Additionally he insists all virtues are gifts of God. Virtues do not come from the excellences of human nature but by the gift of divine grace (II.3.3–4). In declaring no true virtues exist apart from true faith (III.14.3), Calvin affirms the preeminence of faith. More important still is Calvin's definition of faith as the work of the Holy Spirit uniting the believer to Christ.

Calvin's view of faith's unique preeminence is one of his foundational convictions.[21] Salvation is a result of faith alone, which is entirely a gift of God. In a contrary opinion Cardinal Sadolet, seeking to return the Genevans to the Roman Church, argued that salvation was achieved within the church by faith issuing in works, which means that the human desire and intention to perform works pleasing to God is also essential. Sadolet wrote, "We hold that in this very faith love

19. Calvin scholar Benjamin W. Farley has very little to say about Calvin in his study of virtue. See *In Praise of Virtue: An Exploration of the Biblical Virtues in a Christian Context* (Grand Rapids: Wm. B. Eerdmans, 1995). In a personal letter of September 2006 Farley suggests that in various and numerous places Calvin recommends all the virtues but never uses the seven-virtue scheme. In a wide ranging and sympathetic study of Aquinas and Calvin, Dutch Calvinist Arvin Vos points out concerning faith and virtue that in Thomas formed and unformed faith are one habit, but formed faith is a virtue while unformed faith is not. Vos's discussion of the seven virtues focuses on the extent of damage resulting from the fall and concludes with a quotation from *ST* 1–2, q.85, a.2: "Because he is rational, it belongs to man *to act in accord with reason, which is to act virtuously.* For sin to cause man to cease to be rational is impossible, since he would then no longer be capable of sinning. It is not possible, then, that this good be totally taken away" (emphasis added). Vos's subtitle indicates the centrality of Thomas's agenda to which Calvin and other Protestants offer critique. The previous quotation demonstrates how different is Calvin's view of faith, virtue, reason, and sin (Arvin Vos, *Aquinas, Calvin, and Contemporary Protestant Thought: A Critique of Protestant Views on the Thought of Thomas Aquinas* [Grand Rapids: Wm. B. Eerdmans, 1985], 31, 142–46).

20. On faith and love see my "Calvin's Polemic Foundational Convictions in the Service of God's Truth," in *Calvinus Sincerioris Religionis Vindex*, ed. Wilhelm H. Neuser and Brian G. Armstrong (Kirksville, MO: Sixteenth-Century Journal Publishers, 1997), 111–13.

21. On the subject of essential tenets, see ibid., 97–122.

is essentially comprehended as the chief and primary cause of our salvation."[22] On the contrary, Calvin insists faith precedes love (III.2.41). Love is an accessory or inferior aid to faith (Com. I Jn. 3:19). He continues, "Scripture teaches salvation depends on God's free adoption. We do not first love God but are chosen by God through the atonement effected in Jesus Christ."[23] "God's mercy is not restricted to those who attempt to prove themselves worthy of it by good works."[24] "The Law and the Prophets give first place to faith and whatever pertains to the lawful worship of God, relegating love to a subordinate position" (II.8.53). Calvin makes the same point in his commentary on 1 Corinthians 13:13. "Love is said to be greater here, not in every respect, but because it will last forever, and now has a primary role in keeping the church in being." Nevertheless, according to Calvin, the Papists are wrong to infer that love is of more value in justification than faith. Faith properly understood in its fullness is not only the mother of hope, but love itself is produced by faith.

Calvin recognizes that some people do not seem to receive the gift of faith, a subject treated more directly under the doctrine of predestination. Prior to that discussion Calvin observes, "We see that not all indiscriminately embrace that communion with Christ which is offered through the Gospel" (III.1.1). Among the rejectors are some who think they are elect. Calvin declares, "The reprobate are sometimes affected by almost the same feeling as the elect," what Calvin puzzlingly calls "the lower working of the Spirit" (III.2.11), an assertion that makes distinguishing between certain and uncertain faith a crucial matter.

The conviction that salvation is not conditional but certain is an almost forgotten mark of the Protestant Reformation. According to Calvin, doubting the certainty of one's salvation is sinful. We do not understand the goodness of God apart from full assurance (III.2.16). "[F]aith is not content with a doubtful and changeable opinion . . . but requires full and fixed certainty" (III.2.15). If salvation were not certainly known to believers, election "would have been a doctrine not only lacking in warmth, but completely lifeless." In summary, Calvin insists, "Our faith is nothing, unless we are persuaded for certain that Christ is ours, and that the Father is propitious to us in Him. There is, therefore, no more pernicious or destructive conception than the scholastic dogma of the uncertainty of salvation" (Com. Rom. 8:33, 34).[25]

Susan E. Schreiner asserts that some of the most pitched battles in the Reformation concerned "certitude." "Indeed, it can be argued that certainty was the fundamental theological locus of the sixteenth century." Additionally she observes,

22. "From Sadolet," *Calvin's Tracts*, ed. and trans. Henry Beveridge (Grand Rapids: Baker Book House, 1983 [1844]), 1:10.

23. "To Sadolet," *Calvin's Tracts*, 44.

24. Ibid., 33.

25. The Council of Trent, which formulated the Catholic response to the Protestant Reformation, held, "No one [can] state with absolute certainty that he is among the number of the predestined" (Council of Trent, chap. 11). See "The Certainty of Salvation" in Andrew Purves and Charles Partee, *Encountering God: Christian Faith in Turbulent Times* (Louisville, KY: Westminster John Knox Press, 2000).

"All sixteenth-century polemics appealed to the Spirit as the agent of certainty."[26] Heppe agrees. "The certainty of salvation and assurance of the state of grace is the most essential sign of faith and the most direct effect produced by it in the consciousness of the elect person." However, Heppe locates certainty against the background not only of the object of faith but also the covenant of works focused in human consciousness, not union with Christ. He asserts, "The believer is certain not only of the truth of the object of faith, but also of the fact that his subjective faith is real faith and that by it he really possesses salvation and enjoyment of the covenant of grace."[27] Addressing this issue Jack Forstman begins his essay with Doumergue's claim that Calvin was "tormented by an incomparable need for certitude."[28] He then returns to his longtime concern for Word and Spirit in Calvin, declaring, "Calvin's obsession with certainty inevitably causes one to focus on his conviction that the Bible as a whole is true."[29] Forstman sees in Calvin two sources for knowledge of God: the objective Bible and the subjective relational self. In this coupling of the knowledge of God and the self, "It appears that theology is at the same time anthropology and vice versa."[30] Calvin's conviction about God and self should, Forstman thinks, lead directly to a "discussion of faith where the distance between God or Christ and human beings collapses by action of the Holy Spirit."[31] In suggesting that salvation becomes effectual in the collapse of distance between subject and object Forstman seems near to a foundational affirmation of union with Christ. However, veering off he claims Calvin does not move in that direction because of his concern for the principle of biblical authority. This is a serious error in judgment on Forstman's part.

Union with Christ is exactly the direction Calvin's theology moves. For Calvin certainty is not to be found in a principle or a book but a person. That is, in union with Jesus Christ. Our task is "to establish with certainty in our hearts that all those who, by the kindness of God the Father, through the working of the Holy Spirit, have entered into fellowship with Christ, are set apart as God's property and personal possession" (IV.1.3). Furthermore, Calvin is more interested in fidelity than coherence. Forstman's agenda is more rational and historical than christological

26. Susan E. Schreiner, "'The Spiritual Man Judges All Things': Calvin and the Exegetical Debate about Certainty in the Reformation," in *Biblical Interpretation in the Era of the Reformation*, ed. Richard A. Muller and John L. Thompson (Grand Rapids: Wm. B. Eerdmans Publishing Company, 1996), 215, 190.

27. Heinrich Heppe, *Reformed Dogmatics*, ed. Ernst Bizer, trans. G. T. Thomson (London: George Allen and Unwin, 1950), 536.

28. Doumergue, *Calvin*, 4:60. Doumergue's comment is more complex than the simple torment of certainty. "Il est là tout entier, logique, allant jusqu'au fond des questions; pratique, uniquement préoccupé de piété; tourmenté par un besoin incomparable de certitude; unissant dans un mélange rare les raisons et les sentiments; précédant Pascal, pour invoquer ces raisons que la raison ne connaît pas, et précédant aussi les théologiens modernes de l'expérience chrétienne: 'Je ne ditz autre chose que ce qu'on chacun fidèle expérimente de soy.'"

29. See H. J. Forstman, *Word and Spirit* (Stanford, CA: Stanford University Press, 1962), and "Coherence and Incoherence in Calvin's Theology," in *Revisioning the Past: Prospects in Historical Theology*, ed. Mary Potter Engel and Walter E. Wyman Jr. (Minneapolis: Fortress Press, 1992), 113.

30. Forstman, "Coherence and Incoherence," 115.

31. Ibid., 116.

and confessional. He asserts that for those properly affected by developments since the Enlightenment, "Calvin's assault on human reason is horrible indeed."[32] Additionally Forstman thinks Calvin's unsophisticated view of biblical authority is deeply troublesome and incoherent. He concludes, "However acceptable that view may have been in the sixteenth century, it is difficult to see how it can be other than deeply troublesome in the twentieth, at least with twentieth-century persons who have something of a global perspective and a critical consciousness."[33] Forstman himself does not avoid incoherence in the following two "only's." According to Forstman, Calvin sees two sources of the knowledge of God: the objective Bible and the subjective relational self. On the one hand Forstman suggests that action of the Holy Spirit in faith should collapse the distance between the divine and the human. Nevertheless, he asserts, "Certainty is found *only* in being related to Christ, through whom the good things of God are extended toward us."[34] Then, Forstman also claims, "God's acting, speaking, and thinking are reliably found in one place *only*: Holy Scripture."[35]

Calvin's use of reason, whether a vicious assault or an accurate employment, depends on one's definition and confidence in reason itself and is a constant issue for interpretation. If logical coherence is the single standard of the proper use of reason, then Calvin's view of certainty is an excellent example of his assault on reason. However, if faithful witness to the experience of believers be admitted, the definition of reasonableness must be broadened. On the one hand, Calvin declares faith is "sure and firm," neither doubtful nor confused. Faith "requires full and fixed certainty, such as men are wont to have from things experienced and proved" (III.2.15). On the other hand, Calvin asserts, "Unbelief is, in all men, always mixed with faith" (II.2.4).

In recognizing the fact of unbelief among believers, Calvin acknowledges two sides to the statement, "I believe and yet have unbelief." He recognizes these halves appear to contradict each other, but insists all of us experience both (Com. Mk. 9:24). Calvin continues, "Therefore the godly heart feels in itself a division because it is partly imbued with sweetness from its recognition of the divine goodness, partly grieves in bitterness from an awareness of its calamity; partly rests upon the promise of the gospel, partly trembles at the evidence of its own iniquity, partly rejoices at the expectation of life, partly shudders at death" (III.2.18). The conflict between certainty and doubt "is what every one of the faithful experiences in himself daily, for according to the carnal sense he thinks himself cast off and forsaken by God while yet he apprehends by faith the grace of God" (Com. Ps. 22:2). Human beings will always find matters for doubt if they look to their own merits (Com. Ps. 31:3). Our carnal sense tells us we are forsaken by God, but faith apprehends the grace of God. Living by faith we "stand before God in the sure confidence of divine benevolence and salvation" (III.2.15).

32. Ibid., 127.
33. Ibid., 119.
34. Ibid., 128.
35. Ibid., 125.

Believers "are more strengthened by the persuasion of divine truth than instructed by rational proof [meaning] the knowledge of faith consists in assurance rather than in comprehension" (III.2.14).

Calvin does not appeal his view of certainty to the logic of human reason but to the work of the Holy Spirit. Since believers are "sealed with the Holy Spirit," the assurance which believers have of their own salvation comes from the Holy Spirit "who makes their consciences more certain and removes all doubt." "Let us remember," Calvin writes, "that the certainty of faith is knowledge, but it is acquired by the teaching of the Holy Spirit, not by the acuteness of our own intellect" (Com. Ps. 3:19). Certainty is based not on the self but on Christ. When Christians look at themselves, the result is trembling and despair, but they are called to communion with Christ and assured of salvation as members of his body (Com. I Cor. 1:9). Calvin thinks this reality is *not* to be understood as oscillation! The Papists say, "If you contemplate Christ, there is sure salvation: if you turn back to yourself, there is sure damnation." The fact of doubt and unbelief is not an alternation between confidence and despair since "Christ is not outside us but dwells within us." Salvation comes to us "because he makes us, ingrafted into his body, participants not only in all his benefits but also in himself" (III.2.24). Assurance of salvation is possible because faith is christologically rather than anthropologically based. Observing that union with Christ is the foundation of the assurance of faith, David Willis asserts, "That is clear: the assurance of faith comes from focussing on Christ and not on ourselves apart from him."[36]

In summary, faith is sure, firm, and confident knowledge based on God's mercy and faithfulness revealed in Jesus Christ to whom the faithful are sealed by the Holy Spirit. "It will not be enough for the mind to be illumined by the Spirit of God unless the heart is also strengthened and supported by his power." Both in the mind and in the heart, "Faith is a singular gift of God" (III.2.33).

B. SANCTIFICATION THROUGH FAITH

Calvin's doctrine of sanctification is a facet of his theology that glitters with purest ray serene. Misunderstood by many of his followers, Calvin teaches that sanctification is the result of God's grace irresistibly effected by the work of the Holy Spirit. Having explained "how faith possesses Christ, and how through it we enjoy his benefits" (III.3.1), Calvin turns to the "double grace" of regeneration through faith and justification by faith (III.11.1). Commenting on 1 Corinthians 1:30 he says, "We cannot be justified freely by faith alone, if we do not at the same time live in holiness. For those gifts of grace go together as if tied by an inseparable bond, so that if anyone tries to separate them, he is, in a sense, tearing Christ to

---

36. David Willis-Watkins, "The Unio Mystica and the Assurance of Faith According to Calvin," in *Calvin: Erbe und Auftrag: Festschrift für Wilhelm Heinrich Neuser zum 65. Geburstag*, ed. Willem Von't Spijker (Kampen: Kok Pharos, 1991), 77.

pieces." In fact there is an inseparable bond among Jesus Christ, grace, faith, justification, and sanctification. Calvin declares justification to be "the main hinge on which religion turns" (III.11.1), but the relation between justification and sanctification is "the basic principle of the whole doctrine of salvation, the foundation of all religion" (Sermon on Luke 1:5–10; *CO* 46:23). Refusing to separate these fraternal, but not identical, twins is crucial for understanding Calvin.[37] If justification is too strongly emphasized Calvin is moved in a Lutheran direction; if sanctification is too strongly emphasized Calvin is moved in a Wesleyan direction. Proper understanding also requires attention to expository order, the precise relation to justification, and especially the recognition that sanctification is the irresistible work of the Holy Spirit. Calvin concludes this section with a lengthy polemic against the Roman view of the sacrament of penance.[38]

Justification is defined as "the remission of sins and the imputation of Christ's righteousness" (III.11.2), meaning we are not righteous in ourselves nor can we become righteous through works. Rather, we are reckoned as righteous by virtue of union with Christ (III.11.3). "There is no sanctification apart from communion with Christ" (III.14.4). This union with Christ in Calvin's mind is not exclusively defined as a state, it is also a process. We will never reach full union "until this flesh, which is involved in many remnants of ignorance and unbelief, shall have been laid aside" (Com. Eph. 4:13). In the Genevan Confession the child is taught to answer: "It is little to have begun unless you continue. For it behooves us to be disciples of Christ up to the end, or rather without end."[39] Spiritual birth is not the work of a moment (Com. Jas. 1:19). "Christ stands in our midst, to lead us little by little to a firm union with God" (II.15.5). The old nature is gradually put to death when we are ingrafted into Christ (Com. Rom.

---

37. Alfred Göhler, *Calvin's Lehre von der Heiligung* (Munich: Chr. Kaiser Verlag, 1934), devotes part 2 to the relation between sanctification and justification, emphasizing the unity of the double grace grounded in the saving work of Christ. In considering the two doctrines, Boisset does not follow nor interpret Calvin's sequence. More seriously, in asserting sanctification to be sequential from predestination, he ignores union with Christ as the basis of both (Jean Boisset, "Justification et Sanctification chez Calvin," in *Calvinus Theologus,* ed. W. H. Neuser [Neukirchen: Neukirchen Verlag, 1974], 137). In considerable detail Dennis E. Tamburello in his *Union with Christ* connects justification and sanctification with union in Christ. The point is nicely put by Case-Winters. "Calvin is as much a theologian of sanctification as of justification. He in fact held . . . these two together. Calvin assumed that our justification will have real effects in our lives, that we will be *regenerated*; and that faith will necessarily issue in good works. Yet neither our faith nor our works are our own . . . rather they are, equally, gifts of God. For Calvin . . . sanctification is not primarily about good works, but about 'union with Christ'" (Anna Case-Winters, "Joint Declaration on Justification: Reformed Comments," in *Concord Makes Strength: Essays in Reformed Ecumenism,* ed. John W. Coakley [Grand Rapids: Wm. B. Eerdmans, 2002], 91 [emphasis in original]. See also our chapters entitled "The Finality of Forgiveness" (Justification) and "The Struggle for Saintliness" (Sanctification) in Purves and Partee, *Encountering God.*

38. In a general way Calvin uses the term "repentance" to indicate the turn from the old life and regeneration for the turn to the new life. Still, he writes, "Repentance is nothing else but a reformation of the whole life according to the law of God" (Com. Hos. 12:6). Some of the insights contained in this section were learned in discussion with Ariane Arpels-Josiah.

39. "The Genevan Confession," in *Calvin: Theological Treatises,* trans. J. K. S. Reid (Philadelphia: Westminster Press, 1954), 130.

6:6). Again, sanctification "does not take place in one moment or one day or one year; but through continual and sometimes even slow advances God wipes out in his elect the corruptions of the flesh, cleanses them of guilt, consecrates them to himself as temples renewing all their minds to true purity that they may practice repentance throughout their lives and know that this warfare will end only at death" (III.3.9). "It is not enough to have embraced only once the grace of God, unless during the whole course of your life you follow his call" (Com. Rom. 11:22). Moreover, "We also see, that it is not enough that God should speak once, and that we should once receive his word, but there is need that he should rouse us again and again; for the greatest ardor grows cold when no goads are applied" (Com. Hag. 1:13).

Given the definition of justification as "main hinge," scholars have expended considerable ingenuity explaining why the exposition of sanctification precedes rather than follows justification. The normal, logical, and historical progression is from justification to sanctification, which Calvin uses when he writes that in the presence of God the pious mind "feels itself quickened, illumined, preserved, justified, and sanctified" (I.13.13). Logically, God first forgives our sins and only then mandates the holy life. One plausible theory for the reversal in the *Institutes* suggests that Calvin anticipates and wishes to obviate Roman Catholic objections that the Protestant view of justification by faith alone leads to a denial of the fruits of the Spirit and the holy life. Calvin complains that too many people "fancy their faith to be buried in their hearts, and bring forth no fruit of their profession" (Com. Dan. 3:28). A better possibility, often actualized, is the concern that Protestants might accept the activity of God in justification with such eagerness as to become inattentive to their own responsibility in sanctification. According to Calvin, believers are justified by faith alone, but the imputation of righteousness is not to be separated from the actual holiness of life (III.3.1).

Calvin asserts, "The whole life of Christians ought to be a sort of practice of godliness, for we have been called to sanctification" (III.19.2). Regeneration he defines as "a singular gift of God" (III.3.21), the true turning of our life to God consisting of mortification of the flesh and vivification of the Spirit (III.3.9), finding their unity in Christ. That is, in baptism the faithful participate in Christ's death and in his resurrection they receive eternal life. Calvin insists that repentance is the gate to the school of Christ (Com. Jn. 4:16) which does not precede but flows from faith (III.3.1). The gift of faith includes the forgiveness of sins, salvation, life, and everything that we obtain in Christ (III.3.19). We are not united to God because of our holiness but because we are united to him we become more and more holy. Calvin objects that certain Anabaptists think they have been restored to perfect holiness and in following the Spirit no longer need to bridle the lust of the flesh. In response Calvin declares we recognize one Christ and one Spirit of Christ who is "the author of love, modesty, sobriety, moderation, peace, temperance, truth" (III.3.14). Nevertheless, even in a saint there remains a "smoldering cinder of evil" that can burst forth in flame at any time (III.3.10). Sin does not reign in the saints, but sin continues to dwell. Thus, "far removed from perfection, we must move steadily forward, and though entangled in vices, daily fight against them" (III.3.14).

Since Calvin is developing a confession of faith rather than a system of philosophical theology, he emphasizes what needs to be learned first rather than what must be posited first as the basis for deductions. By dealing with regeneration before justification Calvin helps the reader, while glorifying the divine role, to pay attention also to the human role. Having dealt with the relation between faith in Christ and union with Christ, he treats the *continuing process* of sanctification which is accomplished *with* us before he discusses the *completed fact* of justification, which is accomplished *for* us. This distinction between state and process is helpful but not absolute. These are confessional rather than logical categories. For example, Pierre Marcel writes, "Justification is based on what Christ has done *for* us; sanctification, upon what He does *in* us—it is a work in which, in a certain sense, the believer co-operates."[40] Calvin teaches that our justification occurs *outside* us in Christ's work *for* us. Our sanctification is the work of the Holy Spirit *within* us. However, Calvin rejects the concept of cooperation (II.2.6) insisting that the human will is responsive (which is the work of the Holy Spirit) but not in itself cooperative (as a work of the human being). The work of the Holy Spirit empowers the human will but does not cancel it. Any discussion of human freedom must avoid two errors. First, to be avoided is the denial of human responsibility leading to complacent acceptance of sin. Second, the affirmation of human responsibility leading to confident acceptance of merit for salvation is likewise wrong. Calvin's amazing answer to this dilemma is that no good thing remains in human power, yet "in spite of this [a person] should nevertheless be instructed to aspire to a good of which he is empty, to a freedom of which he has been deprived" (II.2.1). This conundrum is addressed again in conversation with Augustine, whom Calvin understands to teach that "the human will does not obtain grace by freedom, but obtains freedom by grace." By grace the human will is converted, by grace it is directed, and by grace it continues in good (II.4.14). The point again is Calvin's denial of the modern concept of subject and object in his affirmation of union in Christ.

While sanctification and justification are discussed in separate chapters, they constitute one subject. As Karl Barth, following Calvin, observes, "We are not dealing with a second divine action which either takes place simultaneously with [justification], or precedes or follows it in time."[41] Justification and sanctification are one in divine origin and one in human experience, but two for the purpose of analysis. Since justification is accomplished once-for-all by the work of Jesus Christ and sanctification is being accomplished day-by-day through the work of the Holy Spirit, the doctrines are single in confession but dual in explanation. As indicated, this distinction is a matter of strong emphasis but not of exclusive

40. Pierre Marcel, "The Relation between Justification and Sanctification in Calvin's Thought," *Evangelical Quarterly* 27 (1953): 134 (emphasis in original).
41. *CD* 4.2, 502.

definition. Justification also has a progressive dimension, extending from calling to death (Com. Rom. 8:30). The title of II.14, "The Beginning of Justification and Its Continual Progress," makes clear that justification is not simply a static condition. Again, as John Murray points out, "To think of sanctification exclusively in terms of a progressive work" is a mistake.[42]

Subject and object, human being and divine being according to modern dispositions of understanding tend toward either/or. Calvin's view of union with Christ is a divine-human relation that is both/and. This conclusion is powerfully expounded by Philip Butin, who declares the crucial issue in Calvin's doctrine of sanctification is the role of the Holy Spirit. Put another way, how does the work of the Holy Spirit impact the human will? "How can what God does in us also and simultaneously be authentically *human* response?" According to Butin this question is in important respects the central problem of his book. He proposes a more interactional and relational model for theology—a "new appreciation for Calvin's perichoretic understanding of the trinitarian character of the divine-human relationship."[43]

An essential feature of Butin's reflection on Calvin's "Trinitarian paradigm" is the dynamic extension indicated in his subtitle: "Calvin's Trinitarian Understanding of the Divine-Human Relationship." In this fine study Butin argues that the Trinity is the basis (chap. 4, focused on the Father), pattern (chap. 5, focused on the Son), and dynamic (chap. 5 focused on the Spirit) of God's relationship with humanity. By expounding the positive Butin has convincingly illustrated the negative. That is, to assume Calvin teaches a modern individualistic view of the separate-from-God self is a serious error. According to our sinful nature there is a real difference between God and humanity, but the radical separation is overcome by God's grace. Moreover, given the final impenetrability of the divine Trinity by the human mind, the relationship of divine-human is a reverent confession rather than a confident conclusion. Additionally, the exposition of the dynamic work of the Holy Spirit rewards careful study. Butin's main title indicates the Trinitarian work of the Father in revelation, the work of the Son in redemption, and "the *divine dynamic* of the divine-human relationship, through explication of the role of the Holy Spirit in [Calvin's] theology of human response." In another place Butin states that Calvin "consistently refuses to countenance . . . any way of framing the problem of human response to God that assumes that genuinely human action must be autonomous from or independent of God's enablement." At the same time the previous quotation points to the role of the Holy Spirit in human response.

Butin calls attention to "a discernable shift of emphasis" from Book II to Book III. While denying the reality, Butin admits the appearance that Book III "appears to shift attention to the human side of the divine-human relationship." Proper

---

42. John Murray, "Definitive Sanctification," *Calvin Theological Journal* 2 (April–November 1967): 5–21. What is most characteristic of "definitive sanctification" is death to sin and resurrection to life brought about by union with Christ (12).

43. The term περιχώρησις (perichoresis), employed in the understanding of "persons" in the Trinity, means "flowing around" and is helpfully used by Butin to assert mutuality.

understanding requires recognition of the Holy Spirit as bond between the Father and Son and between God and the believer. He writes:

> The point to be noticed throughout Calvin's development of the theme of the Spirit as bond is the explicit qualitative continuity that is implied between Christ's relationship with the Father (in the Spirit), and the church's relationship with Christ (in the same Spirit). In both cases, the Spirit constitutes the relationship, as its bond. . . . In short, the bond of Christ's relationship with God the Father is identical to the bond of the believer's relationship with God the Son, because in both cases that bond is God the Holy Spirit.

In some sense humans receive the revelation of the Father and redemption in the Son, but they render response through the work of the Holy Spirit. Calvin insists, "We ourselves are fitly doing what God's Spirit is doing in us, even if our will contributes nothing of itself distinct from his grace" (II.5.15). Butin concludes, "Where Christian believers are concerned, there is no intrinsic incompatibility between attributing the same human actions primarily and fundamentally to God's grace, and yet concurrently (in a second and wholly derivative sense) to human beings." In both act and being Calvin insists on the "bold inclusion of believers in the 'perichoresis' of the divine life through their participation in Christ by the Holy Spirit."[44]

Appealing to the work of the Holy Spirit, God's action within human action is simultaneously that person's action. The work of the Holy Spirit provides both divine indwelling and human empowering. Apart from Christ we have no ability to do good. According to Calvin, "The first part of a good work is will; the other, a strong effort to accomplish it; *the author of both is God*" (II.2.9, emphasis added). God bends, shapes, and forms the will, but Calvin insists we both act and are acted upon (II.5.14).

Karl Barth asserts, "There can be no doubt that in practice [Calvin's] decisive interest is primarily in the problem of sanctification." Indeed, we might regard it is established beyond any doubt that, as distinct from Luther, Calvin must be called the theologian of sanctification.[45] Sometimes it is said that Lutherans shout "Justification!" and whisper "Sanctification." If so, Calvin is distinct from Luther in his strong doctrinal emphasis on living the holy life to the glory of God. In Protestantism the mandate to lead the holy life does not carry the expectation that it can be accomplished apart from the direct grace of God, and even then not in this earthly life. No work of ours contributes to sanctification. In the context of an exposition of assurance of faith, Calvin states, "There can be no genuine assurance before God unless his Spirit produces in us the fruit of love. All the same . . . no one should conclude from this that we must look to our works for our assurance to be firm" (Com. I Jn. 3:19). Nevertheless, Calvin speaks of

---

44. Butin, *Revelation, Redemption, and Response*, 93, 127, 15–16, 53, 93, 76, 83, 78, 43.
45. *CD* 4.2, 509.

"the grace of good works." When Protestants affirm justification by faith alone, they do not deny the efficacy of good works nor the evidence of the fruits of the Spirit. Intensity of belief cannot be considered an adequate substitute for integrity of behavior. Thus, Calvin believes the saints are able to draw some comfort and confidence by remembering and even proclaiming their innocence and uprighteousness (III.14.18).

Wilhelm Niesel deals with this issue at some length in rejecting the *syllogismus practicus*.[46] The practical syllogism is a Protestant version of condign merit. Catholic conviction holds that with grace bestowed a person is able to merit glory. The Protestant question is whether the existence of gifted faith produces tangible signs of election. According to Calvin, "Purity of life is rightly regarded as the illustration and evidence of election" (Com. II Pet. 1:10). Since Protestants believe justification is not complete without sanctification, salvation by faith alone cannot occur without the works of faith. Some think this conclusion allows believers to look to their works for some kind of assurance of faith. Berkouwer's chapter on election and the certainty of salvation is almost entirely devoted to the practical syllogism which "originates from the Biblical connection between justification and sanctification by the Holy Spirit."[47] It is not, he says, a syllogism of reason but a syllogism of faith. Barth declares that Calvin's cautious approach to good works in relation to faith in the assurance of salvation was abandoned by Beza, Gomarus, the men of Dort, and Wolleb, leading to the dangerous consequences inherent in the practical syllogism. "Calvin, for his part, did not find himself in the dilemma merely because it escaped him. A happy inconsistency led him to believe that he could unify the christological beginning and the anthropological conclusion of his thinking." One might also think a strong doctrine of union with Christ would obviate the dichotomy. Barth says as much himself in substituting faith in Christ for self-examination and self-evaluation.[48]

Niesel thinks Calvin's remarks on this issue do not develop a doctrine but only make a concession to Roman theologians. Calvin "concedes that our works can be for us signs that we are in a state of grace, provided that we have first assuredly and sufficiently recognized our salvation to lie in the Word of God and in Christ."[49] In his presence I would not disagree with my esteemed teacher (for one semester) but the grace of good works is a legitimate aspect of sanctification, not a concession to Rome. Saving faith, as a gift of the Holy Spirit, leads to works, but works do not lead to saving faith. Good works are in no sense the *cause* of salvation but in every sense its *consequence*. For many this situation is easy to comprehend. When adult children visit the parental home, they find useful work to do *not* in order to *become* a child of that household but as an expression of grat-

---

46. Niesel, *Theology of Calvin*, 170–81. See also his "Syllogismus Practicus," in *Aus Theologie und Geschichte der Reformierten Kirche: Festgabe für E. F. Karl Müller* (Neukirchen: Kr. Mörs, 1933), 158–79.

47. G. C. Berkouwer, *Divine Election* (Grand Rapids: William B. Eerdmans, 1960), 295, 293.

48. *CD* 2.2.338, 340.

49. Niesel, *Theology of Calvin*, 174.

itude for *being* beloved members of the family. This work is neither intended nor understood as a *cause* of the relationship but rather a *because* of the relationship, and may be contemplated with some satisfaction on the drive back home. Calvin insists the kingdom of heaven is not the reward of our works. It is not the servants' wages but the sons' inheritance (III.18.2). Based on our union with Christ, Calvin's development of the process of sanctification affirms that we are not justified by works but also not without works. Good works are "the fruit and effect of grace" (II.3.13). Calvin returns to the proper understanding of good works in his exposition of justification (III.11.13–20; III.14; III.15).

The exposition of sanctification concludes with a lengthy rejection of the Roman theologians' views of confession and satisfaction (III.4) and indulgences and purgatory (III.5). According to Roman theology as expressed by the Council of Trent under the decree of justification (chap. 14), the sacrament of penance, is absolutely necessary for salvation. Penance requires the acts of contrition, confession, and satisfaction. Contrition is defined as "a sorrow of mind and a detestation for sin committed" with a further distinction between perfect contrition motivated by love of God and imperfect contrition motivated by fear of hell. Oral confession to a priest is also deemed necessary for salvation. By the sacrament of penance eternal punishment is canceled, but temporal punishments may still be required. Fastings, prayers, almsgiving, and other pious exercises of the spiritual life produce satisfaction.

Concerning contrition, Calvin thinks the bitterness of our sorrow for sin will never correspond with the magnitude of the offense and therefore can never provide the necessary assurance of pardon. Second, confession of sin should not be restricted to confession to priests. Rather, "We should lay our infirmities on one another's breasts, to receive among ourselves mutual counsel, mutual compassion, and mutual consolation" (III.4.6). Additionally, since "in every sacred assembly we stand before the sight of God and the angels," Christian people should "practice humbling themselves through some public rite of confession" (III.4.11). Both private and public confession of sin is useful, but "confession of this sort ought to be free so as not to be required of all, but to be commended only to those who know that they have need of it. Then, that those who use it according to their need neither be forced by any rule nor be induced by any trick to recount all their sins" (III.4.12).

Satisfaction, the third aspect of penance, means that in order to merit God's pardon a person must make compensation for his or her transgressions. Calvin insists this view of cooperating grace and the production of works deprives Christ of his proper honor and the burdened conscience of every possibility of assurance. "Over against such lies [Calvin places] freely given remission of sins" (III.4.24). Christ alone provides the forgiveness of sin, demonstrating that "there is no other satisfaction whereby offended God can be propitiated or appeased" (III.4.26).

According to Calvin indulgences made the "soul's salvation the object of lucrative trafficking, the price of salvation reckoned at a few coins, nothing offered free of charge." This fact "can truly serve as a proof of how deeply men were immersed for centuries in a deep night of errors" (III.5.1). The doctrine of indulgences maintains that the treasury of merits accrued by Christ, the apostles, and martyrs is under the custody, dispensation, and delegation of the Bishop in Rome. On the contrary, Calvin insists forgiveness of sins and holiness of life are found in Christ alone. Likewise, purgatory is a place where expiation of sins is sought apart from the blood of Christ with the consequence that "purgatory is a deadly fiction of Satan, which nullifies the cross of Christ, inflicts unbearable contempt upon God's mercy, and overturns and destroys our faith" (III.5.6).[50]

In summary, Calvin defines sanctification as a gift of God's grace revealed in Jesus Christ through faith. The glory of God requires affirmation of God's irresistible love, irresistible faith, irresistible justification, *and* irresistible sanctification. However, the term "irresistible" is here used primarily to praise God's sovereign grace not to calibrate human response or responsibility. The concept of irresistibility denies condign merit and Lombard's understanding of operating and cooperating grace. Calvin writes that Peter Lombard, "the Master of the Sentences . . . taught: 'We need two kinds of grace to render us capable of good works.' He calls the first kind 'operating,' which ensures that we will effectively will to do good. The second he calls 'co-operating,' which follows the good will as a help." Calvin objects strongly to this distinction. "The ambiguity in the second part offends me, for it has given rise to a perverted interpretation. They thought we co-operate with the assisting grace of God, because it is our right either to render it ineffectual by spurning the first grace, or to confirm it by obediently following it" (II.2.6). The essays from an Orthodox and Reformed dialogue, published in 1973, paired Robert Stephanopoulos for the Orthodox on deification (theosis) with John Beardslee for the Reformed on sanctification. If, and to the extent that, these doctrines can be usefully compared, the striking difference—for Calvin at least—is that while we receive we do not cooperate with God's assisting grace.[51]

Some Reformed theologians, in learning that justification is entirely a divine work, assumed sanctification was mostly a human work. While rejecting the Roman view of operating and cooperating grace, they understood justification as humanly passive and sanctification as active. According to Heppe, sanctification is "man's effort, lasting his whole life to live in thought, word and action solely according to God's good pleasure and for His glory." Holiness is defined as a disposition suited to God infused into the heart, and sanctification is regarded as the continuation of justification to gradual completion. The chapter on sanctification in Heppe's

50. On the question of purgatory see Heinrich Quistorp, *Calvin's Doctrine of the Last Things*, trans. Harold Knight (Richmond, VA: John Knox Press, 1955), 102–7.

51. Although Beardslee takes his bearings from Reformed orthodoxy, his vision is not limited to that perspective. He insists that the human being who is sanctified is, and remains, a human being—like Christ but never becomes Christ. "Reformed theology has always been suspicious of any form of pantheism, and has feared some aspects of Greek theology for this reason" (146–47). The Greek theologians deny pantheism, but the Reformed theologians suspect them of pantheism anyway. See John W. Beardslee III, "Sanctification in Reformed Theology," in *The New Man*, 132–48. For some discussion of Stephanopoulos, see the section on deification.

Reformed Dogmatics strikes me as more Roman than Reformed.[52] In a praiseworthy attempt to safeguard human responsibility and accountability, this reading of the doctrine sadly but not surprisingly slights the confessional glorification of the work of the Holy Spirit. Although the believer is both involved and responsible, sanctification is not the task of the believer but the work of the Holy Spirit.

C. THE CHRISTIAN LIFE OF FAITH

Between Calvin's exposition of sanctification and justification in Book III stand four little chapters sometimes published separately under the title, *The Golden Booklet of the True Christian Life*. Calvin says the desired agreement between God's righteousness and human obedience requires considerable discussion, but he excuses himself from this task with his famous claim, "By nature I love brevity."[53] Nevertheless, Calvin outlines "a pattern for the conduct of life in order that those who heartily repent may not err in their zeal" (III.6.1). The point is that the exposition of the Christian doctrine of sanctification is followed by a practical exposition of the Christian life. In the same way the Christian doctrine of justification leads to a practical discussion of Christian freedom (III.19).

The foundation of the Christian life, Calvin insists, is the command to be holy as God is holy because holiness is the bond of our union with God. Calvin immediately adds communion is not the result of our holiness rather our holiness is the result of being endued with God's holiness (III.6.2). Calvin also declares Christ is the bond of our adoption as children of God. Therefore, a wicked life is rejection of both Creator and Savior (III.6.3). Christian perfection is not possible in this life, but we should strive to make progress toward that goal remembering "when today outstrips yesterday the effort is not lost" (III.6.5).

According to Calvin's outline, the Christian life requires denial of the self, meditation on the future life, and a proper use of the present life.[54]

1. Denial of Self

On contemporary scales self-denial does not weigh nearly so heavily as self-expression or self-esteem. Calvin, however, considers self-denial a great gain, not a serious loss. Since we belong to God, the denial of ourselves is the sum of Christian life. Because of sin, neither the human reason nor human will is a

52. Heppe, 570, 565. See my essay "The Reformed Doctrine of Irresistible Sanctification," in *Essentialia et Hodierna: Acta Theologica* 2002, Supplementum 3: In Honor of P. C. Potgieter, 107–24.
53. A few years after Calvin, Polonius declaimed that he would be brief "since brevity is the soul of wit / And tediousness the limbs and outward flourishes" (*Hamlet* II.2.90–91). Thomas Jefferson once told a correspondent, "I could have written a shorter letter if I had more time."
54. See Alfred Göhler, "Das christliche Leben nach Calvin," *Evangelische Theologie* 4 (1937): 299–325. To many of the subjects of Book III, but especially to this section, Ronald S. Wallace devotes considerable discussion in his *Calvin's Doctrine of the Christian Life* (Grand Rapids: Wm. B. Eerdmans, 1961).

sufficient guide for the Christian life. Rather, reason should "give way to, submit, and subject itself to, the Holy Spirit so that the man himself may no longer live but have Christ living and reigning within him" (III.7.1). Seeking to promote God's glory removes such evils as pride, arrogance, ostentation, avarice, desire, and lasciviousness. This self-denial is a way to one of Calvin's core affirmations that we deal with God in everything. "Accordingly, the Christian must surely be so disposed and minded that he feels within himself it is with God he has to deal throughout his life" (III.7.2; cf. I.17.2).

The denial of self has two references. First, and partly, to mankind, and second, and chiefly, to God. As an acute observer Calvin recognizes that in trying to hide our vices from other people we also convince ourselves that our personal vices are slight. Additionally, "There is no one who does not cherish within himself some opinion of his own pre-eminence" (III.7.4). Self-denial, then, requires us to understand "that whatever benefits we obtain from the Lord have been entrusted to us on this condition: that they be applied to the common good of the church" (III.7.5). The result of this first part of self-denial is the mandate "to look upon the image of God [in everyone] which cancels and effaces their transgressions, and with its beauty and dignity allures us to love and embrace them" (III.7.6). To serve God means to serve God's creatures (Com. Ps. 16:3). "Faith by itself cannot please God since it cannot even exist without love for the neighbor" (Com. Hos. 6:6). Calvin asserts that our resources ought especially to be employed for the benefit of the poor, criticizing those who "waste their resources on every kind of luxury, others upon the palate, others upon ornaments, others upon fine houses" (Com. Phil. 4:18). Calvin is obliged to affirm the punishment of sinners, which he does in the section on resurrection, but this conclusion of concern for and behavior toward other people must modify the canard that Calvin smugly and even glee-fully consigns the reprobate to their predestined hell. Calvin insists that Christians pray not just for other believers but for all persons. "For what God has determined concerning them is beyond our knowing except that it is no less godly than humane to wish and hope the best for them" (III.20.38).[55]

Self-denial before God, the second and chief aspect of belonging to God, means accepting both good and evil from God's hands with calm assurance and expectation of eternal victory. Since desirable outcomes in this life rest entirely on God's blessing, "We shall not dash out to seize upon riches and usurp honors through wickedness and by stratagems and evil acts, or greed, to the injury of our neighbors" (III.7.9). In dealing with God in everything Calvin speaks of "the many chance [!] happenings to which we are subject" (III.7.10). These include diseases, plague, war, ice and hail, poverty, the death of wife, parents, children, and neighbors. The ungodly are frightened at the noise of a falling leaf, but even the godly man knows "that his life hangs only by a thread, and is encompassed

---

55. For a discussion of the contribution of Edwardsean Calvinism to American Universalism, see Ann Lee Bressler's chapter, "Calvinism Improved," in *The Universalist Movement in America 1770–1880* (Oxford: Oxford University Press, 2001), 9–30.

by a thousand deaths, and who, ready to endure any kind of affliction which shall be sent upon him, and living in the world as if he were sailing upon a tempestuous and dangerous sea, nevertheless bears patiently all his troubles and sorrows, and comforts himself in his afflictions, because he leans wholly upon the grace of God, and entirely confides in it" (Com. Ps. 10:6). Because of such inevitable troubles Calvin devotes an entire chapter (III.8) to bearing the cross believing "whomever the Lord has adopted and deemed worthy of his fellowship ought to prepare themselves for a hard, toilsome, and unquiet life" (III.8.1). In the Commentary on Matthew (16:24) Calvin declares that the disciples had a horror of the cross, but Christ taught them the necessity of denying themselves and the voluntary bearing of the cross. Human life in general is subject to common troubles, but the elect choose to bear the cross as imitators of Christ. As Christ was led through earthly tribulations to heavenly glory, so will his disciples be. Our Lord bore his cross to demonstrate obedience to the Father, but there are many other reasons for us to bear the cross, which include the humbling of our pride and complacency, the learning of patience in the present life, and hope for the future. Calvin asserts that in "the very harshness of tribulations we must recognize the kindness and generosity of our Father toward us, since he does not even then cease to promote our salvation" (III.8.6). We must commit our lives to God's care not only for this life but for the life to come (Com. Ps. 31:5).

Suffering under the cross demands patience and hope, but it does not require indifference or cheerfulness nor lead to the iron philosophy of the Stoics. Pain, poverty, illness, disgrace, and death cause in us natural feelings of sadness, bitterness, groaning, and weeping, but they will be dispelled by the spiritual joy of knowing that "none of these things happens except by the will and providence of God" (III.8.11). Calvin defines patience by making a distinction between the philosophic view of necessity and the Christian view of God's employment of afflictions to benefit salvation. In these comments Calvin struggles with the sole causality witnessed in some parts of Scripture which attributes both good and evil to God. Calvin recognizes the pain of disgrace, contempt, and injustice, thus allowing natural tears to be shed at the deaths of our dear ones. "But the conclusion will always be: the Lord so willed, therefore let us follow his will" (III.8.10).

Having declared the tragedies of life to be "chance happenings" and insisting that God is not the author of evil, Calvin feels compelled to offer God's compassionate chastisement as a reason for human suffering. Again, struggling with this issue in the commentary on 1 Peter 3:18, Calvin says we should not have to suffer for our evil deeds because Christ suffered for us. Nevertheless, we should bear persecutions with equanimity, understanding that we are not suffering for our faults but for righteousness' sake. "It is a great thing for us to be made conformable to the Son of God when we suffer without cause, but there is an additional cause for consolation in that the death of Christ had a happy issue, because though he suffered through the weakness of the flesh he yet rose again through the power of the Spirit." On Calvin's own showing this inquiry could simply throw up its hands at the declaration of "chance happenings" in this life and move to a consideration of the future life.[56] However, Calvin's view of God's governance does not permit him to stop at this place of unknowing. Calvin teaches the believer to have confidence that whatever happens is ordained and governed by God's will. Therefore the pagan notion of "fortune" (which seems to be just another word for "chance happenings") must be rejected. In any case, "the rule of piety is that God's hand alone is the judge and governor of fortune, good or bad, and . . . with most orderly justice deals out good as well as ill to us" (III.7.10).

2. The Future Life

Calvin discusses the future life before the present life, presumably because he does not want to emphasize the historical progression from present to future, but rather the theological reality that hope in the future life provides for the present life. The property of faith is "to take encouragement for the future, from the experience of past favor" (Com. Gen. 19:20). At the same time, "it is profitable to the pious to be thus unsettled on earth; lest, by setting their minds on a commodious and quiet habitation, they should lose the inheritance of heaven" (Com. Gen. 20:1). Calvin writes, "The chief assurance of faith rests in the expectation of the life to come, which has been placed beyond doubt through the Word of God" (III.2.28). Again, our salvation rests upon the resurrection and reign of Christ in glory. Having attacked the Papists' view of faith as imaginative speculation, Calvin insists that approach to God would be dread-full apart from Christ the Mediator who delivers us from sin and fear. "Therefore since our salvation depends on the resurrection of Christ and his supreme power, faith and hope find here what can support them" (Com. I Pet. 1:21).

This section on the future life anticipates the concluding chapter of Book III on the final resurrection. However, meditating on the future life in the context of the Christian life indicates not merely a future hope but a present reality. In a kind of eschatological verification of God's grace Calvin declares death to be the great distinction "between the reprobate and the sons of God, whose condition in the present life is commonly one and the same, *except that the sons of God have by far the worst of it.*" Moses (whom Calvin thought wrote Genesis) wanted Abram to have "not only a long, but a placid old age, with a corresponding joyful and peaceful death" through knowing a better life awaited him (Com. Gen. 25:15, emphasis added).

---

56. Some suffering, like toothache, is recognizably beneficial when it leads to preventive dental care. However, as harrowingly presented in the chapter entitled "Rebellion" in Fyodor Dostoevsky's *Brothers Karamazov*, the death of children is especially difficult (and I think impossible) to reconcile into any acceptable theodicy. In my view, evil is not a problem to be solved but a mystery to be endured. For example, I cannot explain why our adopted son has cerebral palsy and mental retardation. To my mind the very best attempt to understand evil is John Hick's *Evil and the God of Love* (New York: Harper and Row, 1966). But when a scholar with so much learning and sensitivity concludes with an "Irenaean view" of God's providence, I am willing to accept that no satisfactory conclusion can be attained in this life.

The connected themes of meditation on life and death are of considerable antiquity.[57] Herodotus wrote, "Call no man happy till you know the nature of his death" (*Clio* 1.32). The closing lines of Sophocles' *Oedipus Tyrranus* read

> Of no mortal say
> "That man is happy," till
> Vexed by no grievous ill
> He pass Life's goal.

Plato's immensely influential dialogue, *Phaedo*, concerned with life after death, considers the life of philosophy as one long rehearsal (μελέτη) of dying (64a). In *The City of God* (12.10) Augustine declares that the whole of life is nothing but a race toward death. In his meditation upon death nearer Calvin's time, Thomas à Kempis declares, "Blessed is he that always has the hour of his death before his eyes, and daily prepares himself to die" (*Imitation of Christ* 1.23).

Calvin addresses the theme of life's vanity by suggesting that the human situation would not be superior to the animal kingdom except for the hope of life after death. Because the human mind and heart are dazzled by earthly allurements, God offers continual proof of earth's miseries (III.9.1). "The Lord has ordained that those who are one day to be crowned in heaven should first undergo struggles on earth" (III.9.3). We should remember that even our miseries will be blessed (III.2.28). Therefore, God permits his followers "often to be troubled, and plagued either with wars or tumults, or robberies, or other injuries . . . sometimes by exile, sometimes by barrenness of the earth, sometimes by fire, sometimes by other means, [God] reduces [his faithful] to poverty" (III.9.1). However, death will not terrify believers because faith seeks what nature dreads. Indeed "no one has made progress in the school of Christ who does not joyfully await the day of death and final resurrection" (III.9.5).

Like most Christian theologians, Calvin believes the complete and perfect restoration of this present life will take place in the future life. Living by faith the believer seeks God alone, and leaving the world, fixes his mind on heaven (Com. Hab. 2:4). Indeed, Martin Schulze in an overstatement claimed meditation on the future life to be the principal idea in Calvin's system.[58] More accurately Quistorp writes, "The hope of Christians is rooted in their fellowship with Christ," which means "through faith they are incorporated in His body."[59]

3. The Present Life

Calvin thinks discussions of the present life slip into error on opposite slopes: one is mistaken rigor and the other is mistaken indulgence. Since life is a pilgrimage

---

57. See Josef Bohatec, *Budé und Calvin: Studien zur Gedankenwelt des französischen Frühhumanismus* (Graz: Hermann Bohlaus, 1950), 415–30.

58. Martin Schulze, *Meditatio futurae vitae* (Leipzig: Dieterichische, 1901).

59. Quistorp, *Calvin's Doctrine,* 20. Quistorp offers a helpful critique of Schulze's attempt "to classify Calvin as a stoic-humanist pessimist (with a Christian outlook)" strongly influenced by Plato and Erasmus, 51ff.

to the heavenly kingdom, the traveler must avoid sliding down either side. The overly strict allow only the use of the most necessary goods in this life. "According to them," Calvin says, "it would scarcely be permitted to add any food at all to plain bread and water" (III.10.1). The overly lax under the pretext of freedom move to licentious indulgence. The correct use of earthly benefits in the present life is directed to the end for which God created them. As expected, Calvin thinks God provides present happinesses for the purpose of rising above them to the contemplation of eternal bliss (Com. Is. 1:20). It is not the will of God to feed his faithful people in this world like swine but to give them by means of earthly things a taste of the spiritual life (Com. Zech. 10:3). Additionally and surprisingly to those who glimpse only a gaunt and grim-visaged Calvin is his insistence that God's gifts serve both necessity and delight. Since God is the giver of all good things, (1) some people must learn to bear their abundance moderately (III.10.3–4), (2) others with slender means must learn patience, and (3) all must account for their stewardship of the gifts bestowed upon them (III.10.5). Finally, on the basis of God's calling to each person Calvin warns against the restless and discontented desire to change stations.

In a delightful concatenation Calvin insists that God created food "not only to provide for necessity but also for delight and good cheer." Clothing is necessary but also produces comeliness and decency. Grasses, trees, and fruits are both useful and beautiful. The paragraph concludes with this rhetorical flourish:

> Has the Lord clothed the flowers with the great beauty that greets our eyes, the sweetness of smell that is wafted upon our nostrils, and yet will it be unlawful for our eyes to be affected by that beauty, or our sense of smell by the sweetness of that odor? What? Did he not so distinguish colors as to make some more lovely than others? What? Did he not endow gold and silver, ivory and marble, with a loveliness that renders them more precious than other metals or stones? Did he not, in short, render many things attractive to us, apart from their necessary use? (III.10.2)

D. JUSTIFICATION BY FAITH

Faith is the work of the Holy Spirit (III.1–2) resulting in the double grace of regeneration and justification. Treating first sanctification by faith and the holy life, the *second* of the double graces (III.3–10), Calvin then turns in the second place to the *first* grace, justification by faith, which includes a long exposition of good works, and concludes with a short discussion of Christian freedom. The transition from sanctification to justification is marked by emphasizing the centrality of Christ for both. "Christ was given to us by God's generosity, to be grasped and possessed by us in faith. *By partaking of him*, we principally receive a double grace: namely, that being reconciled to God through Christ's blamelessness, we have in heaven instead of a judge a gracious Father; and second, that sanctified by Christ's spirit we may cultivate blamelessness and purity of life"

(III.11.1, emphasis added). After defining justification and its basis in Christ, the most salient feature of Calvin's exposition is the understanding of the relationship of the double grace. The next commanding topic is Calvin's view of participation as seen in the tension between imputation and impartation. Many interpreters make the enormous error of explaining Calvin's doctrine of justification by forensic imputation alone and apart from union with Christ.

As already noted, justification, with Calvin as with Luther, is "the main hinge on which religion turns" (III.11.1).[60] According to the general understanding, Luther recognized the centrality of justification and Calvin worked out its forensic dimensions. This traditional view is presented with a kindly spirit by Thomas Coates in "Calvin's Doctrine of Justification." Coates begins with the venerable conclusion that Luther's doctrine has more warmth and intensity of feeling. "Calvin's treatment of the doctrine of justification seems cold, abstract, logical, and judicial; Luther's was warm, concrete, and spontaneous." Still, when "John Calvin directed all the powers of his great intellect to the logical and systematic exposition of this fundamental Christian doctrine, [he left] nothing to be desired in lucidity of presentation, in effectiveness of argumentation, and in the thoroughness of its application." Calvin drives home his conclusion "with the hammer blows of irresistible logic." Determined to read Calvin as cold and abstract in defense of the glory and sovereignty of God, it is impossible to take Coates off the hook when he makes the stupendously spurious statement that Calvin has "little room" for the doctrine of union with Christ. This means, according to Coates, that Calvin's claims for the role of mystical union, for ingrafting into the body of Christ and participating in his righteousness (III.11.10), while very significant, are also unique. This view is flat-out wrong, and Coates's "little room" for union with Christ must be unlocked and thrown wide open. Nevertheless, with generous condescension Coates suggests, "Nowhere, perhaps, does Calvin's dependence on Luther appear more clearly, and perhaps by the same token, nowhere does Calvin's theology come so close to genuine warmth."

His lens coated with the common logical and legalistic smudges, Coates sees "the dominant emphasis in Calvin's exposition of the doctrine of justification [as] its *forensic* character." The sinner is declared righteous outside himself, but while Coates acknowledges its basis in the work of Christ he asserts "Calvin's stress on the legal aspect of justification—a judicial act by which God as Judge, absolves the accused."[61] This forensic emphasis is continued by Bruce McCormack. McCormack thinks the current theological pressure of doctrines like union with Christ, regeneration, and sanctification threaten to push justification out of sight. Nevertheless, "Calvin's doctrine of justification is easily stated and unproblematic in itself. . . . For Calvin, justification is a *forensic* or legal concept. That is to

60. Luther says that justification is the master and prince, the Lord, the ruler and judge over all kinds of doctrines (WA 39.l.205).
61. Thomas Coates, "Calvin's Doctrine of Justification," *Concordia Theological Monthly* 34, no. 6 (June 1963): 325–34, 333–34, 325, 331, 327, 327–28 (emphasis in original).

say, it is a term that finds its home in the setting of a court trial" with the resulting remission of sins and imputation of Christ's righteousness. This formulation "quickly became the standard Protestant view."[62] Obviously the notion of imputation is alive and well, but standing alone it does not adequately characterize Calvin's doctrine of justification. Calvin certainly employs the term, but he has not exchanged the living room of God for the courtroom of law. That is to say, union with Christ is more basic than forensic declaration.

While Calvin in general agrees with Luther on justification, there are significant differences, helpfully pointed out by Alister E. McGrath. Calvin, like Luther, believed in the personal union of Christ and the believer. Incorporation is fundamental for justification. Distinct but inseparable, sanctification and justification are two consequences of incorporation into Christ. McGrath asserts, "Like Luther, Calvin stresses that faith is only implicated in justification to the extent that it grasps and appropriates Christ. [It will] be clear that Calvin is actually concerned not so much with justification, as with incorporation into Christ (which has, as one of its necessary consequences, justification)."[63] Nevertheless as we have seen, Calvin places a stronger, systematic emphasis on the holy life. Regarding justification, Calvin declares, "Faith is something merely passive, bringing nothing of ours to the recovering of God's favor but receiving from Christ that which we lack" (III.13.5). Justification is an *act*; sanctification is a *process*. Faith is the instrument by which we receive the righteousness of Christ (III.18.8).

Calvin defines justification this way: "The sinner, received into communion with Christ, is reconciled to God by his grace, while, cleansed by Christ's blood, he obtains forgiveness of sins, and clothed with Christ's righteousness as if it were his own, he stands confident before the heavenly judgment seat" (III.17.8). However, before we can stand before God's throne, Christ has stood in the person of the sinner, reckoned among the criminals, but declared righteous by the judge. This substitution is our acquittal, meaning that God's righteous anger no longer hangs over us (III.2.5). Justification is God's acceptance on the basis of remission of sins and the imputation of Christ's righteousness (III.11.2). Beginning with

62. Bruce L. McCormack, "Justitia aliena: Karl Barth in Conversation with the Evangelical Doctrine of Imputed Righteousness," in *Justification in Perspective: Historical Developments and Contemporary Challenges*, ed. Bruce L. McCormack (Grand Rapids: Baker Book House, 2006), 171.

63. Alister E. McGrath, *Iustitia Dei: A History of the Christian Doctrine of Justification*, 2nd ed. (Cambridge: Cambridge University Press, 1998), 224, 225. For Luther and Calvin see Karla Wübbenhorst, "Calvin's Doctrine of Justification: Variations on a Lutheran Theme," in McCormack, *Justification*, 99–118. According to McGrath, after Calvin's death the theological interest shifts further away from justification to predestination as the central doctrine of the Reformed Church (226). Additionally, as earlier noted, the concept of a legal covenant between God and man came to replace Calvin's christological view of justification and sanctification (228). In his comprehensive study Tjarko Stadtlund, *Rechtfertigung und Heiligung bei Calvin* (Neukirchen-Vluyn: Neukirchener Verlag, 1972), provides a helpful survey of the previous literature dealing with these topics together, including the important observation by Schneckenburger that for Lutheran theology, union with Christ is the result of the process of justification while for Reformed theology union with Christ is the condition for the process of justification (118). While reversing Calvin's order of exposition, Stadtlund recognizes the centrality of union with Christ for both sanctification and justification (118–24).

human sin, Calvin moves to union with Christ resulting from the divine grace of forgiveness, which cleanses and clothes the sinner with Christ's righteousness. As sinners the human race is God's enemy until their sins are forgiven and they are restored to grace through the one and only mediator, Jesus Christ (III.12.3). Those whom God receives into union with Christ the Lord justifies (III.19.21). No one is righteous in himself, but the righteousness of Christ is communicated by imputation (III.11.23).

The order of justification is that God deigns to embrace the sinner, which leads to the acknowledgment that we have been reconciled to God by Christ's righteousness and not by our works (III.11.16). Since God loves only those whom he justifies, the faithful—justified by the righteousness of Christ—are accounted righteous *outside* themselves (III.11.11), although Calvin has already insisted that the benefits of Christ must be received "within us." Calvin thinks there is no doubt that he who is taught to seek righteousness outside himself recognizes he is destitute of righteousness in himself, leading to the conviction that "our righteousness is not in us but in Christ" and "we possess it only because we are partakers in Christ" (III.11.23).

Calvin's introductory chapter on justification offers a brief definition, then sharp rejections of "essential righteousness" (III.11.5–12) (which Calvin calls Osiander's "strange monster" [III.11.5])[64] and the Scholastics on good works (III.11.13–20). In the *Institutes* Calvin responds to Osiander at I.15.3–5 on creation, II.12.4–7 on incarnation, and III.11.5–12. The last section focuses on justification and our "essential righteousness" with the role of Christ's divine nature in the immediate background. Calvin found himself uncomfortably between Andreas Osiander, who taught Christ is Savior according to his divine but not his human nature (III.11.8), and Francesco Stancaro, Osiander's opponent and erstwhile colleague at Königsberg, who taught Christ is Mediator according to his human but not his divine nature.[65] Osiander believed that human beings created in God's image means that God dwelt essentially in Adam. The fall, then, was the loss of the essential indwelling of the Son of God in his divine nature. This view Calvin regards as a foolish and perverse curiosity, a wild dream, a contrary-to-fact speculation. Speculations about creation, he thinks, should not replace the facts of redemption. An apparent subtext is Calvin's defense of the role of Christ's priestly work (III.11.8). Our mediator is our redeemer clothed with flesh and reconciling God and man with the sacrificial shedding of blood (II.12.4). The image of God should be understood as gracious gift rather than a natural possession.

---

64. David C. Steinmetz devotes a short surveying chapter to Osiander in *Reformers in the Wings*, 2nd ed. (Oxford: Oxford University Press, 2001), 64–69. Emanuel Hirsch, *Die Theologie des Andreas Osiander: und ihre Geschichtlichen Voraussetzungen* (Göttingen: Vandenhoeck and Ruprecht, 1919), 258n24 complains that Osiander's doctrine of *inhabitatio*, which depends on faith and has absolutely nothing physical about it, is overlooked by Calvin in his remarks at III.11.10.

65. James Weis, "Calvin Versus Osiander on Justification," in *Articles on Calvin and Calvinism*, ed. by Richard C. Gamble, vol. 5 (New York: Garland Publishing, 1992), 354.

Calvin's central objection is Osiander's christological truncation. Calvin concludes that if our righteousness derives solely from Christ's divine nature, then it is a work shared equally with the Father and Spirit. Certainly Calvin's doctrine of the Trinity affirms Trinitarian intimacy, but justification is properly the distinctive work of the Mediator, not the Father or Spirit. Additionally, the doctrine of incarnation forbids an improper distinction between the divine and human nature. Our justification, as Calvin says, "is surely peculiar to the person of the Mediator, which, even though it contains in it the divine nature, still has its own proper designation by which the Mediator is distinguished from the Father and the Spirit" (III.11.8). In Christ's human nature, specifically in his flesh, our justification is accomplished. "Paul has established the source of righteousness in the flesh of Christ alone" (III.11.9). This view of flesh points to the doctrine of the church as the Body of Christ and to the Lord's Supper. "The flesh of Christ is like a rich and inexhaustible fountain that pours into us the life springing forth from the Godhead into itself" (IV.17.9).

In my judgment, if Calvin had any predilection toward a doctrine of deification (theosis), it would appear in discussion with Osiander. This debate involves explosively loaded terms like "imputation," "impartation," "ingrafting," "infusion," "insertion," "communion," "justification," "sanctification," "righteousness," "participation," "fellowship," and most especially "essence" and "substance." Calvin agrees with Osiander that we are one with Christ, but this affirmation does not mean "Christ's *essence* is mixed with our own." Osiander thought union with Christ meant participating in Christ's divine nature. According to Calvin, Osiander "pretends that we are *substantially* righteous in God by the *infusion* both of his essence and of his quality." Calvin charges that growing into union with Christ through the power of the Holy Spirit is replaced in Osiander's theology by a transfusion of Christ's substance into us, making us "essentially righteous."

Calvin is at considerable pains to reject Osiander's emphasis on the distinction of Christ's divine nature in favor of the personal (hypostatic) unity of the two natures, but "substantial" often only means "real."[66] The distinction between real and substantial union is not entirely clear in comments like the following: "To comprehend aright what it meant that Christ and the Father are one, take care not to deprive Christ of his person as mediator." He is the head of the body and joined to the members. "The unity of the Son with the Father is . . . diffused through the whole body of believers. From this, too, we infer that we are one with Christ; not because he transfuses his substance into us, but because by the power of his Spirit he communicates to us his life and all the blessings he has received from the Father" (Com. Jn. 17:21). According to Wendel, until Osiander's writ-

---

66. H. R. Mackintosh, "Unio Mystica as a Theological Conception," in *Some Aspects of Christian Belief* (New York: George H. Doran Company, 1923), 100, 101, points out that in Calvin's time the category of substance indicated "the highest degree of reality." A substantial union between God and a person "was the deepest and most real that the human mind could imagine." The debate over the proper definition of substance continues. See Michael J. Loux, *Substance and Attribute: A Study in Ontology* (Boston: D. Reidel, 1978).

ings began to appear, Calvin had not been aware that his own view of justification in union with Christ by God's gift of faith could be understood in Osiander's framework.[67]

In a key passage, as expressed in the French edition of 1560, Calvin writes that Christ lives in us and not outside us. We are joined by an indissoluble bond becoming daily united more and more with him into one and the same substance (*une mesme substance*) (III.2.24).[68] Calvin also speaks of the secret union (*arcanam coniunctionem*) by which God revives us by his Spirit and transfers his power to us. We are ingrafted into the likeness of his death and resurrection. In this way, "We pass from our own nature into his" (Com. Rom. 6:5). However, this ingrafting and the resulting substantial union does not include the possession of "essential righteousness" as Osiander thought. That righteousness belongs to Christ by nature and to us only by imputation protects Christ's divinity from confusion with our humanity. The central assertion of justification in Christ by participation is "that our righteousness is not in us but in Christ, that we possess it only because we are partakers in Christ." And this righteousness is communicated to us "by imputation" (III.11.23).

Of this debate Julie Canlis sprightly writes, "In the late 1540s [Osiander] did more than stir the theological waters: he threatened to sink the Reformation boat."[69] Clearly Calvin decided to sail away before Osiander's craft capsized and (to overload the nautical image) fired a passing salvo at Osiander, charging him with being "perversely ingenious in futile inventions," mingling heaven and earth by extending God's created image to both body and soul (I.15.3). Moreover, the true image of God is not to be found in the old Adam but in the restoration of sinners obtained through Christ, the second Adam (I.15.4). Additionally, righteousness is not derived "by an inflowing of [Christ's] substance, but by the grace and power of the Spirit" (I.15.5). Union with Christ is the work of the Holy Spirit, not the mixture of substances (III.11.5). The image of God is more accurately understood in terms of redemption than creation; justification by the work of the Holy Spirit than by the substance of Christ. Calvin regards as a vain speculation Osiander's view that the incarnation would have been necessary even without Adam's sin. Calvin says Christ the Mediator cannot be separated from

67. Wendel, *Calvin: The Origins and Development*, 236. J. Todd Billings, "United to God through Christ: Assessing Calvin on the Question of Deification," *Harvard Theological Review* 98, no. 3 (2005): 332, makes the point that "while Calvin is usually cautious in his use of extrabiblical theological language, at times he was quite daring in the way he would speak about union with Christ through participation in his substance."

68. The note on this passage in Jean-Daniel Benoit's French edition of the 1560 *Institutes* indicates Calvin used the word "substance" to express the reality of a thing and not in the philosophic and technical sense of scholastic theology. It describes our union with Christ. Our oneness with Christ is not a transfusion of substance but the work of the Spirit. "The beginning of a blessed life is when we are all governed and live by the one Spirit of Christ" (Com. Jn. 17:21).

69. Julie Canlis, "Calvin, Osiander, and Participation in God," *International Journal of Systematic Theology* 6, no. 2 (April 2004): 169. She also affirms that Calvin's followers traded the primacy of union with Christ "for a chronological *ordo salutis*, making union dependent upon prior 'steps' in the soteriological process" (172–73).

Christ the Redeemer because "the Mediator never was promised without blood" (II.12.4); "these two were joined together by God's eternal decree" (II.12.5).[70]

In addition to the obviously differing christological understandings, Calvin's concept of imputation is both subtle and crucial. Osiander—upholding, as he thought, the Protestant doctrine of justification—rejected a purely arbitrary, forensic, and imputed righteousness in favor of an "essential righteousness." Calvin rejected Osiander's "essential righteousness," but he taught an "entire righteousness" (III.11.11). Entire righteousness means, "When we come to Christ, we find in him the exact righteousness of the law, and this also becomes ours by imputation" (Com. Rom. 3:31). Again, "We are not righteous in ourselves but in Christ. The gift of righteousness is not an endowment but an imputation" (Com. Rom. 5:17). Calvin understood union with Christ to mean an imputed righteousness that was righteousness without exception. Calvin insisted our righteousness was outside us in Christ, but he also writes, "Christ is *not* outside us but dwells within us" (III.2.24, emphasis added). In a central confession Calvin declares that we are to think of Christ dwelling in us. "For we await salvation from him not because he appears to us afar off, but because he makes us, ingrafted into his body, participants not only in all his benefits but also in himself." Christ is so communicated to us that we are made one with him (III.2.24). While Calvin uses the concepts of ingrafting and infusion, imputation and impartation, he nevertheless insists Osiander wrongly concludes our righteousness is essentially *in* us rather than outside us in Christ from whom it is both imputed and imparted to us.

The difficulty with understanding Calvin's view of imputation is well illustrated by two comments of Wendel's, the first emphasizing duality; the second, unity. On the one hand, he writes, "The logical consequences of the doctrine of the imputation of the righteousness of Christ is that never, not even after the remission of our sins, are we really righteous." Wendel thinks this point addresses Calvin's fear of deification. On the other hand, "Imputation and union with Christ are, rather, two inseparable aspects of one and the same divine grace: the one is not possible without the other."[71] This same tension also appears in Canlis's discussion. Osiander rejected a doctrine of justification that was only forensic in declaration without change in existence, while "Calvin accepted a purely forensic notion of justification." At the same time, "Instead of Osiander's justification by the divine essence within, Calvin insisted that we participate in Christ's own *human* righteousness (*iustitia Christi*) through being united with him." The sharp point to note is that Calvin's purely forensic imputation (if such it be) is profoundly modified by the reality of participation in Christ. Addressing the tension between imputation and impartation Canlis concludes, "Unfortunately, Calvin's focus on salvation *extra nos* has primarily come to mark the Protestant tradition,

---

70. According to Gunter Zimmerman, Calvin misunderstood Osiander, and they have much in common. "Calvins Auseinandersetzung mit Osianders Rechtfertigungslehre," in *Kerygma und Dogma* 35 (July–September, 1989): 236–56.

71. Wendel, *Calvin: The Origins and Development*, 259, 258.

rather than his equally warm and vibrant theology of participation."[72] Addressing this topic from a Roman Catholic perspective, Bill Thompson, in an interesting phrase, finds Calvin "less unclear than Luther" in his distinction between justification and sanctification, signaling their unity by participation in Christ through the Spirit. What is very clear is Thompson's recognition that justification is not a reality captured by terms like "imputation" or "forensic." The reality of union with Christ "underlies not only sanctification but also justification" and is the key to avoiding extreme forensicism. There are both imputational and transformative dimensions to justification. Of special merit (in a Protestant sense) is Thompson's reflection on the assurance of salvation.[73] In any case, however one assesses a later bifurcation, it is essential to recognize Calvin's omnipresent affirmation of union with Christ both within and without us.

In developing the concept of "participation" Canlis suggests, "The union of which Calvin speaks is the union spoken of by the Fathers and dubbed *theosis*— our being brought to God, by God."[74] Concerned with the question of deification in Calvin, J. Todd Billings also addresses union with Christ, Osiander, justification, and Calvin's "wide-ranging theology of participation." Since Billings believes "a forensic notion of pardon is the necessary prerequisite for . . . a life of sanctification," he charges Canlis with underestimating "the decisive importance of imputation for Calvin in the Osiander controversy, downplaying Calvin's 'forensic' dimensions in an effort to retrieve his theology of participation." According to Billings, this underestimation of Calvin's forensic dimension also applies to Joseph McLelland and on the same point. Emphasizing participation in Christ's righteousness, McLelland laments the diminution of the mystical in favor of the legal dimension in later Calvinism. On the contrary, according to Billings, Calvin's view of participation in Christ is both deeply legal and deeply mystical. Apparently, the "correct estimation" maintains, "In Calvin, the 'forensic' imputation of Christ's righteousness and the mystical union with Christ are held in the closest possible relationship—one is unthinkable without the other."[75] This declaration bypasses the strains in the relationship of impartation and imputation, leaving the issue bridged by assertion rather than explanation. These foregoing and overlapping evaluations suggest that Calvin taught both imputation and impartation. So I understand the statement: "See how being reconciled to God by the sacrifice of Christ, we both are accounted and are righteous in him."[76] In debate with Osiander, Calvin emphasizes that our righteousness is outside ourselves in Christ and therefore must be imputed to us by God. At the same time, being united to Christ we possess the benefits he imparts.

72. Canlis, "Calvin, Osiander, and Participation," 171, 175, 174, 176.
73. William M. Thompson, "Viewing Justification through Calvin's Eyes: An Ecumenical Experiment," *Theological Studies* 57 (1996): 447, 451, 453, 464.
74. Canlis, "Calvin, Osiander, and Participation," 181.
75. Billings, "United to God," 326, 327, 329.
76. Calvin on Trent, *Calvin's Tracts* 3.152–53.

While Calvin actively declares justification to be passive (III.13.5), sanctifica-tion is not so, but both regeneration and justification "are conferred on us by Christ." In this their christocentric nature is clear. Calvin immediately adds, "and both are attained by us through *faith*" (III.3.1), which he has already defined as a gift of God and the principal work of the Holy Spirit. This "attainment of ours" including "to us," "on us," "in us," and "by us" would seem to include our cooperation with God, at least to the extent that we choose to receive what God wills to confer. However, Calvin does not view the human role in this way. According to Calvin, faith, meaning our human faith, is passive in that we bring nothing of our own to the recovering of God's favor but receive from Christ what we lack (III.13.5). This, it seems to me, is the language of doxology, not analy-sis. "Faith of itself does not possess the power of justifying, but only in so far as it receives Christ" (III.11.7). Faith in this sense is an earthen vessel, but the trea-sure is the gold hidden in it. Similarly, the pot that does not make us rich should not be confused with the gold that does. Such statements contrasting vessel and treasure, reality and imputation sound dual, but the imputation of Christ's righ-teousness is a real gift and not a forensic fiction. We are not our own but belong to Christ and are united to him. "We hold ourselves to be united with Christ by the secret power of his Spirit" (III.11.5). To cite again, "Therefore, that joining together of head and members, that indwelling of Christ in our hearts—in short that mystical union—are accorded by us the highest degree of importance, so that Christ, having been made ours makes us sharers with him in the gifts with which he has been endowed" (III.11.10).

Turning from Osiander to the Romanists, Calvin affirms justification out-side us in Christ, but we are not outside Christ since by God's gift of faith we participate in Christ.[77] Calvin rejects Osiander's idea of infusion as essential righteousness and also the Council of Trent's view of infusion as inherent righ-teousness.[78] However, his chief concern is to establish justification by God's grace through faith alone and not by works. Calvin thinks human beings can only with the greatest difficulty be induced to leave the glory of righteousness to God alone.

---

77. Canlis, "Calvin, Osiander, and Participation," 169, 170, says the concept of "participation" has been typecast as mystical, platonic, and un-Reformed. Her point is Calvin uses "participation" in a nonontological, nonsubstantial way.

78. See anathema 11 of the canons attached to the sixth session. According to the Canons and Decrees of the Council of Trent, both "ingrafted" and "infused" are necessary for the definition of "justification." "In justification itself, along with the remission of sins, man receives, through Jesus Christ, in whom he is ingrafted, all these things infused at the same time, viz., faith, hope, and char-ity" (see *Calvin's Tracts* 3.96). Thomas W. Casteel, "Calvin and Trent: Calvin's Reaction to the Coun-cil of Trent in the Context of His Conciliar Thought," *Harvard Theological Review* 63 (1970), writes, "The sharpest and most extensive refutation of the Council of Trent . . . was left to John Calvin" (100) and the refutation of the decree on justification and the thirty-three related canons occupy a third of the entire work (105). Craig B. Carpenter is correct in observing that "to seemingly every objection-able point related to justification raised by Roman Catholics from total depravity to the necessity of assurance, Calvin responds by developing his doctrine of union with Christ" (Craig B. Carpenter, "A Question of Union with Christ? Calvin and Trent on Justification," *Westminster Theological Journal* 64 [2002], 384).

While the Scholastics praise Christ in the beginning, at the end they teach "men are justified partly by the grace of God and partly by their own works; thus only showing themselves somewhat more modest than Pelagius was."[79] Calvin charges the Papists with impossibly mixing the grace of Christ and the merit of works. "Whoever wants to have a half-Christ loses the whole" (Com. Gal. 5:2).[80]

Against the Scholastics Calvin draws a strong distinction between works righteousness and faith righteousness. Many people believe justification is the result of faith *and* works, but Calvin insists that as long as any particle of works righteousness remains, so does some occasion for sinful boasting (III.11.13). Righteousness is not the meritorious result of good works but solely the result of Christ's righteousness gracefully and faithfully bestowed upon us (III.11.16). Nevertheless, Calvin declares that one whose life is pure and holy satisfies God's judgment and may be justified by works! Sinners are excluded from the righteousness of works and are saved only by grasping the righteousness of Christ through faith and, clothed in it, appear in God's sight as righteous. "The righteousness of good works depends on the fact that God by pardon approves them" (III.18.5).

"[Justification is] the acceptance with which God receives us into his favor as righteous men. And we say that it consists in the remission of sins and the imputation of Christ's righteousness" (III.11.2), which Calvin summarizes as "We are reckoned righteous before God in Christ and apart from ourselves" (III.11.4). In addressing Cardinal Sadolet, Calvin identifies justification by faith as "the first and keenest subject of controversy between us." Justification is the result of God's mercy in forgiving sinners through faith alone in Christ alone in whom salvation is completed. Then Calvin expresses the central paradox of his doctrine of good works in relation to justification: "We deny that good works have any share in justification, but we claim full authority for them in the lives of the righteous. . . . If you would duly understand how inseparable faith and works are, look to Christ."[81] We are not devoid of good works but are made righteous apart from them (III.11.1). "Since we see that every part of our salvation stands outside of us, why is it that we still trust or glory in works? . . . Christ is for us both righteousness and life, and that this benefit of righteousness is possessed by faith alone" (III.14.17). According to Calvin, the Council at Trent ascribes to human free will some "natural" movement apart from direct, divine grace. In contrast, Calvin declares, "We certainly obey God with our will, but it is with a will which he has formed in us."[82]

79. Calvin on Trent, *Calvin's Tracts*, 3.108.

80. In his chapter "The Process of Justification," *The Harvest of Medieval Theology: Gabriel Biel and Late Medieval Nominalism* (Cambridge, MA: Harvard University Press, 1963), 156, Heiko Augustinus Oberman writes of Gabriel Biel, "First and most important, Biel is convinced that man can, without the aid of grace, *ex puris naturalibus*, love God above all else, for his own sake." Dealing with the riddle of election, Oberman observes, the doctrine of predestination is the "most revealing indicator of the understanding of the doctrine of justification" (185). Since Calvin treats justification before predestination, one might argue that the doctrine of justification is the most revealing indicator of what the doctrine of predestination will be.

81. To Sadolet, *Calvin's Tracts*, I.41, 43.

82. Calvin on Trent, *Calvin's Tracts*, III.147–48.

Concerning works, Calvin asserts, to the extent anyone is satisfied with his own righteousness, he impedes God's mercy. This mistake is occasioned by comparing ourselves with other people. With lofty scorn he charges and attacks the Roman view of partial righteousness. "If then an adulterer refrains from theft, and lays out in alms some of his wealth, they will have this to be charity, and declare it to be acceptable" (Com. Hag. 2:12). We should consider God's own righteousness, with the result we direct our one hope to Jesus Christ whose compassion is our merit. Calvin insists when faith is gloriously extolled, works are not thereby grievously denigrated. Faith and good works are inseparable, but justification is the result of faith, not works. Christ contains both justification and sanctification in himself, but they should be distinguished. We are not justified by works but not without works, "since in our sharing in Christ, which justifies us, sanctification is just as much included as righteousness" (III.16.1). "Justification is withdrawn from works, not that no good works may be done, or that what is done may be denied to be good but that we may not . . . ascribe salvation to them. For our assurance, our glory, and the sole anchor of our salvation are that Christ the Son of God is ours" (III.17.1). Since we are sinners, even our good works are sinful. However, our sins being forgiven, "the good works that now follow are appraised otherwise than on their own merit. For everything imperfect in them is covered by Christ's perfection" (III.17.8). Our pardon occurs since "God contemplates us and our all in Christ. . . . Therefore, as we ourselves when we have been engrafted in Christ are righteous in God's sight because our iniquities are covered by Christ's sinlessness, so our works are righteous and are thus regarded because whatever faith is otherwise in them is buried in Christ's purity, and is not charged to our account. Accordingly, we can deservedly say that by faith alone not only we ourselves but our works as well are justified" (III.17.10).

Divine justification leads to human freedom, but when freedom is mentioned, Calvin thinks passions boil and wild tumults arise. Nevertheless Christian freedom is a necessary part of doctrine and is "*especially an appendage of justification*" without which "neither Christ nor gospel truth, nor inner peace of soul, can be rightly known" (III.19.1, emphasis added). The crucial point is that freedom is subordinated to love, which is in turn subordinated to faith, the gift of God (III.19.13). Christian freedom is thus a product of Christian justification, but justification is not the result of freedom. Christian freedom consists of three parts. The first is to advance beyond any hope of being justified by works that fulfill the righteousness of the law. "We should, where justification is being discussed, embrace God's mercy alone, turn our attention from ourselves, and look only to Christ" (III.19.2). The law functions in calling us to sanctification, but justification depends on the righteousness of Christ and makes us free.

The second freedom is the recognition that to be free from the dread of the law is to be free to the guidance of the law. Calvin explains with this image: Those bound by the yoke of the law are like servants required to fulfill their assigned tasks every day. Children are more gently treated, not hesitating in their love to offer parents "incomplete and half-done and even defective works" with the expectation that those who are justified by faith will have their works justified as well (III.19.4–5).

The third part of Christian freedom is to understand adiaphora. The world contains some "indifferent things" (ἀδιάφοροι), which may be chosen or rejected at will. To be avoided is the conscience becoming overconscientious and over-scrupulous. For example, "If any man should consider daintier food unlawful, in the end he will not be at peace before God, when he eats either black bread or common victuals, while it occurs to him that he could sustain his body on even coarser foods." Likewise, if one scruples to use linen sheets, she will be anxious about hemp and finally about tow (III.19.7). Tranquillity of conscience is the acceptance of unmerited righteousness conferred as a gift of God (III.13.3).

To be precise, some foods, some drinks, some garments being more expensive than others could theoretically undermine the righteous use of personal resources.[83] Calvin's society was not so mobile as today, and he assumed everyone, whether slenderly, moderately, or plentifully, should be content to live in station. Still, Calvin appreciated the good things of life and a modest aspiration for their acquisition. "Surely ivory and gold and riches are good creations of God, permit-ted, indeed appointed, for men's use by God's providence." We have never been forbidden to laugh, to add new possessions to old, to eat heartily, to delight in music, or to drink wine (III.19.9). In these observations Calvin is recommending a commonsense, orderly moderation in the freedom produced by justification, avoiding offending weaker consciences as much as possible. "We must at all times seek after love and look toward the edification of our neighbor" (III.19.12).

E. PRAYER: THE EXERCISE OF FAITH

Calvin's exposition of prayer is the single longest chapter in the *Institutes* and a fact strange indeed if "everything is predestined" as Calvin's doctrine of predesti-nation is usually misunderstood. That John Calvin's personal faith and public witness is practical and experiential rather than speculative and logical is nowhere better demonstrated than in his exposition of the miracle of prayer. Profoundly aware that God already knows what we need, is not hindered from coming to our aid, and yet desires to hold conversation with us, Calvin offers instruction on prayer, which is the exercise of faith and the practice of predestination.[84]

83. The category of "indifferent things" is important to affirm but difficult to illustrate. I suggest that the decision arranging bathroom tissue to roll over the top or from the bottom of the dispenser is truly a matter of perfect indifference, however much some persons might insist on the one rather than the other.

84. This chapter of the *Institutes* is reprinted with a helpful introduction by I. John Hesselink in *John Calvin, On Prayer: Conversation with God* (Louisville, KY: Westminster John Knox Press, 2006). At a minimum, according to Calvin, prayer should be offered when we awake in the morning, when we begin our daily work, when we sit down to a meal, when we finish eating, and when we retire at night (III.20.50).

Perhaps the most surprising feature of this long chapter is its focus on the practice rather than the theory of prayer.[85] More obviously than usual Calvin is expressing the logic of the heart, not the mind. Prayer is something Christians do more than discuss. For them prayer is a given, not a problematic. Calvin thus offers practical instruction about performance rather than explanations of theoretical difficulties. In other sections of the *Institutes* Calvin discusses doctrines with the assumption that the truth is presented on which practice can be based. Here, to the contrary, the behavior is in the foreground and the basis in the background.[86] Nevertheless, the basis is clear, as Graham Redding observes, "Prayer is not so much a technique that can be imparted and mastered as the outworking of a relationship as Christ lives in his disciples and they in him." This relationship is "a reconciling, sanctifying union" with the mediator which makes prayer *through* Christ, *in* Christ and *with* Christ.[87]

Modern theological discussions of prayer attend especially to its intellectual difficulties. According to P. R. Baelz, "It is notorious that every book on prayer has a chapter on its difficulties."[88] These difficulties are sympathetically discussed by David Basinger, whose title poses the question, "Why Petition an Omnipotent, Omniscient, Wholly Good God?"[89] So severe are these problems that Immanuel Kant thought petitionary prayer as a means of grace was a superstitious illusion in which a reasonable person would be embarrassed if caught.[90] This skeptical point of view received episcopal approval in Bishop John A. T. Robinson's *Honest to God* chapter on "Worldly Holiness," which presents a nonreligious understanding of prayer. Prayer is defined not as address to God but "openness to the ground of our being."[91] Friedrich Heiler declares, "The element in prayer which is objectionable

85. Niesel, *Theology of Calvin*, 156, correctly observes, "In the *Institutes* Calvin gives instruction about prayer rather than a doctrine of prayer." Ronald S. Wallace agrees by entitling his chapter, "Prayer as the Principal Exercise of Faith," in *Calvin's Doctrine of the Christian Life* (Grand Rapids: Wm. B. Eerdmans Publishing Company, 1959). Commenting on Eph. 6:18 Calvin declares prayer is a unique privilege and the chief exercise of faith.

86. Curiously Berkhof's *Systematic Theology* has almost nothing to say on prayer. In sharp contrast, Warfield thinks "[Calvinism] is capable of being put into a single sentence; and that one level to every religious man's comprehension. For Calvinism is just religion in its purity." Warfield concludes that true religion is most fully expressed in the attitude of prayer and continues, "Other men are Calvinists on their knees; the [true] Calvinist is the man who is determined that his intellect, and heart, and will shall remain on their knees continually, and only from this attitude think, and feel, and act" (Benjamin B. Warfield, "What Is Calvinism," in *Selected Shorter Writings*, ed. John E. Meeter [Nutley, NJ: Presbyterian and Reformed Publishing Company, 1970], 389, 390).

87. Graham Redding, *Prayer and the Priesthood of Christ in the Reformed Tradition* (London: T. & T. Clark, 2003), 287. Redding criticizes federal Calvinism and the Westminster Confession in chap. 3.

88. P. R. Baelz, *Prayer and Providence* (London: SCM Press, 1968), 12. In his essay on "Philosophy and Christology," D. M. Mackinnon considers the possibility that in the knowledge of God one "may have to turn his back on more than the silly respectabilities of so-called religious philosophy," suggesting "the fundamental language of religion is prayer," in *Essays in Christology for Karl Barth*, ed. T. H. L. Parker (London: Lutterworth Press, 1956), 288–89.

89. David Basinger, "Why Petition an Omnipotent, Omniscient, Wholly Good God?" *Religious Studies* 19 (1983): 25–41.

90. Immanuel Kant, *Religion within the Limits of Reason Alone*, trans. Theodore M. Greene and Hoyt H. Hudson (New York: Harper and Brothers, 1960), 183.

91. John A. T. Robinson, *Honest to God* (Philadelphia: Westminster Press, 1963), 102.

to the philosopher [is] the thought of an influence brought to bear on God."[92] Critics have especially in the mind the prayer of petition which is generally accompanied by the assumption that "prayer changes things."[93] The issue is whether an immutable, omnipotent, and omniscient God needs (or can accept) information and advice from the creature. John Milton answered,

> But prayer against his absolute Decree
> No more avails than breath against the wind,
> Blown stifling back on him that breathes it forth.
> Therefore to his great bidding I submit.
> (*PL* 11.311–14)

William Brown, citing Kirsopp Lake, opines, "Prayer, to our fathers, was primarily petition, the process by which God 'was induced to do otherwise than he would have done if prayer had not been used.' But modern science, with its clearer revelation of the laws of life, has made this view no longer possible to modern men." Brown is sure that prayer results in appreciation, fellowship, creativity, discipline; he is not certain about "the vexed question of petition in prayer."[94] In his chapter entitled "Changing Things and God," David Willis affirms, "The mystery of prayer is thus the mystery of God's love for us" [with the result that] "not to pray confidently in Christ is not to take God at his Word." Willis also flatly declares, "Prayer does not change things. Prayer changes people who change things."[95]

92. Friedrich Heiler, *Prayer: A Study in the History and Psychology of Religion*, trans. Samuel McComb (London: Oxford University Press, 1932), 99. Voltaire is quoted that the only fitting prayer is one of submission (92). Mark Twain, the greatest American humorist, was deadly serious in his opposition to much of Christianity, yet see his *Joan of Arc*, which he considered his best book. In one of his gentler forays against Christian theology, Twain describes Huck Finn's encounter with prayer (*The Adventures of Huckleberry Finn*, chap. 3). According to Huck,

> Miss Watson she took me in the closet and prayed, but nothing come of it. She told me to pray every day, and whatever I asked for I would get it. But it warn't so. I tried it. Once I got a fish-line, but no hooks. It warn't any good to me without hooks. I tried for the hooks three or four times, but somehow I couldn't make it work. By and by, one day, I asked Miss Watson to try for me, but she said I was a fool. She never told me why, and I couldn't make it out no way. I set down one time back in the woods, and had a long think about it. I says to myself, if a body can get anything they pray for, why . . . can't the widow get back her silver snuff-box that was stole? Why can't Miss Watson fat up? No says I to myself, there ain't nothing in it.

93. H. H. Farmer, *The World and God: A Study of Prayer, Providence, and Miracle in Christian Experience* (New York: Harper, 1939), 129, 134, notes that petition is the most often questioned element, but insists petition is "the heart and center of prayer." H. D. Lewis, *Our Experience of God* (New York: Macmillan Company, 1959), 246, contains two interesting chapters on this subject. The first is entitled "Miracle and Prayer"; the second, "Petitionary Prayer." Both insist, "The hardest philosophical problems present themselves when we consider the petitionary aspect of prayer." Lewis seems to believe that prayer is always a miracle and petitions are sometimes granted.

94. William Adams Brown, *The Life of Prayer in a World of Science* (New York: Association Press, 1927), 7, 131. On the vexed question of whether God can change, see J. K. Mozley, *The Impassibility of God: A Survey of Christian Thought* (Cambridge: Cambridge University Press, 1926).

95. David Willis, *Daring Prayer* (Atlanta: John Knox Press, 1977), 18, 14, 120. On this issue I disagree with my old tennis buddy, also on the question, more difficult of resolution each passing year, regarding who won the most games.

John Calvin might be assumed to be among the foremost theologians in rejecting the prayer of petition with its suggestion that the mind of God or the history
of things could be changed (cf. Com. Gen. 6:6). However, Calvin regards petition as necessary, not futile, while defining prayer as "the practice of predestination."[96] To exempt "changing things" is an overly truncated interpretation of this
statement. Calvin defines prayer as the exercise of predestination, but the latter
doctrine, usually regarded as inexorably static, has an active and petitionary component as is evident in this citation: "The reason why Paul enjoins us both to
pray and to give thanks without ceasing is, of course, that he wishes all men to
lift up their desires to God, with all possible constancy, at all times, in all places,
and in all affairs and transactions, to expect all things from him and give him
praise for all things" (III.20.28).

In his first *Institutes* (1536), Calvin wrote that all things *must* come to pass by
God's will whether we ask for them or not (108). Nevertheless, we ought not only
to desire these things but to request them. For an individual to ask God to do
what God knows we need and will do anyway would seem to be an exercise in
acceptance rather than a request for special action. In addressing the issue of
divine sovereignty and human responsibility, Calvin thinks no genuine problem
exists because prayer is based on union with Christ effected through the work of
the Holy Spirit. All prayer to God is offered in Christ's name. "For in calling God
'Father' we put forward the name 'Christ'" (III.20.36). Contrary to Calvin's
christological conception of prayer is the more anthropological understanding
represented by Bouyer, who writes, "Prayer . . . by definition cannot be a divine
act since it is, above all, the act of man in the presence of God."[97] Calvin writes,
"We cannot call on God rightly and sincerely except by the guidance and teaching of the Holy Spirit; for he it is who not only dictates our words, but also creates groanings in our hearts. . . . It then follows, that we do not pray through the
impulse of our own flesh, but when the Holy Spirit directs our hearts, and in a
manner prays in us" (Com. Jer. 29:12).

Calvin begins his chapter by affirming that in Christ God offers happiness to
replace our misery. In Christ, God "opens to us the heavenly treasures that our
whole faith may contemplate his beloved Son, our whole expectation depend
upon him, and our whole hope cleave to and rest in him." It remains, then, "for
us to seek in him, and in prayers to ask of him, what we have learned to be in
him" (III.20.1). Prayer is the means by which "we reach those riches which are
laid up for us with the Heavenly Father" (III.20.2). Of course God knows what
we need and is able to help us unasked, but, Calvin insists, "those very things
which flow to us from his voluntary liberality he would have us recognize as

---

96. "The practice of this doctrine [predestination] ought also to flourish in our prayers" (*Huius
doctrinae praxis in precibus quoque vigere debet*). See my "Prayer as the Practice of Predestination," in
Calvinus Servus Christi, ed. Wilhelm H. Neuser (Budapest: Presseabteilung des Ráday-Kollegiums,
1988), 245–56.

97. Louis Bouyer, *Introduction to Spirituality*, trans. Mary Perkins Ryan (New York: Desclee,
1961), 59.

granted to our prayers." Both things are true: God watches over us unceasingly and he awaits our prayers (III.20.3).

Calvin teaches that "prayer rightly begun springs from faith, and faith [springs] from hearing God's Word" (III.20.27). Prayer should be framed according to four rules: reverence, sincerity, humility, and confidence. Aware that true humility and confident hope are "apparently contrary," Calvin insists that "repentance and faith are companions joined together by an indissoluble bond, although one of these terrifies us while the other gladdens us." Prayer arises from and contains both the contradictory emotions of fear and faith. "That is, [believers] groan under present ills and anxiously fear those to come, yet at the same time take refuge in God, not at all doubting he is ready to extend his helping hand." Confidence is so essential that Calvin exclaims, "It is amazing how much our lack of trust provokes God if we request of him a boon that we do not expect" (III.20.11). Having taught earlier as an illustration of the necessity of humility that "to pray rightly is a rare gift" (III.20.5), Calvin concludes with forceful confidence, "Only that prayer is acceptable to God which is . . . grounded in unshaken assurance of hope" (III.20.12). A positive description of the intercessory role of Jesus Christ is followed by a negative view of the role of the saints. After a short reflection on private and public prayer, the remaining pages are devoted to an exposition of the Lord's Prayer as an example for believers to follow.

In each of the major editions of the *Institutes*—1536, 1539, 1559—Calvin devotes a separate chapter to prayer that involves an introduction, exposition, and conclusion. The introduction includes such affirmations as the will of God is revealed in Christ alone to faith; that no glory belongs to human beings (and thus saints are not to be invoked as though Christ has failed); that we are commended to offer prayers of both petition and thanksgiving; and that God has promised to hear us. The major portion of the chapter is an exposition of the Lord's Prayer, and the conclusion asserts that the will of God will be done according to the laws of divine providence. Faith in Christ as the principal work of the Holy Spirit (III.1.4) includes the fruit of faith, namely prayer: "the unique privilege with which God honors his children." According to Calvin, "The true test of faith lies in prayer," and "While the Spirit testifies to us that we are children of God, He at the same time pours this confidence into our hearts, so that we dare invoke God as our Father" (Com. Rom. 8:16). Thus the whole of prayer is attributed to the grace of the Holy Spirit who is our teacher in prayer (III.20.5). Faith precedes prayer since we must believe before we can pray (Com. Jas. 1:6). That is to say, it is confidence in the promise of God that opens our mouth to pray (Com. Rom. 8:16), and the gift of true faith therefore leads to prayer (Com. Acts 1:14).

These quotations indicate that Calvin's understanding of prayer has a Trinitarian form: it issues from faith—the gift of the Holy Spirit; founded in union with Christ; through whom the faithful approach and invoke a loving Father (Com. Rom. 8:16). The whole of prayer is attributed to the grace of the Holy Spirit (Com. Rom. 8:26; see III.20.5). Apart from Christ no one can approach God in prayer (Com. Jn. 14:14) because only through Christ can God be called Father (Com.

Is. 63:16). "We do not pray to God properly unless we are persuaded for certain in our hearts that he is our Father" (Com. Rom. 8:16). Since Calvin believes that God does not hear the prayers of sinners (Com. Jn. 9:31), the faithful must pray with the confidence that their prayers are always heard and answered (Com. I Jn. 5:14). "Confidence is necessary in true invocation and thus becomes the key that opens to us the gate of the kingdom of heaven" (Com. Eph. 3:12).

Calvin thinks it would be a fatal presumption to rush into the presence of God until we have learned that our prayers are sanctified by Christ (Com. Heb. 8:3). Our prayers are heard because they are united with the prayer of Christ, whose atoning work includes continual intercession for us (III.20.28–29). God's providence includes "both the will and power to take the best care of us" (III.20.2); but "we see that to us nothing is promised to be expected from the Lord, which we are not also bidden to ask of him in prayers." Calvin is aware that the omniscient God who governs heaven and earth in love and power does not need to be reminded of what we need, nor the all-provident God to be stirred to action on our behalf. This is not a problem, he thinks, because the performance of our duty to lay our desires before God is not for God's sake but for ours.

Remarkably Calvin thinks there is an "easy answer." What God "has determined to give, of his own free will and even before he is asked, he promises to give all the same, in response to our prayers." This posing of the question and its answer is worth quoting at greater length.

> Here is the sufficient remedy to remove and to cleanse the superstition now condemned. Is not the source of the folly, which makes many think they shall succeed if they weary God with many words, that they imagine Him to be like a mortal man, who needs to be told and advised? Anyone who is persuaded that God not only cares for us, but also knows our necessities, and anticipates our prayers and our worries before He is told of them, this man will forget his long-windedness and will be content if he makes his prayers as long as it helps the practice of his faith. To approach God in a rhetorical fashion, in order to move Him by power of address, he will recognize to be absurd and laughable. But if God knows what we need before we seek it, there might appear to be no benefit in prayer. If of His own accord He is ready to help us, what need have we to interject our prayers that might get in the way of the spontaneous course of His providence? There is an easy answer, in the very purpose of prayer, for the faithful do not pray to tell God what He does not know, or urge Him to His duties, or hurry Him on when He delays, but rather to alert themselves to seek Him, to exercise their faith by meditating upon His promises, unburdening their cares by lifting good for themselves into His bosom, and finally to testify that from Him alone, all good for themselves and for others is hoped and asked. As for Himself, what He has determined to give, of His own free will and even before He is asked, He promises to give all the same, in response to our prayers. Keep hold of both points, then: our prayers are anticipated by Him in His freedom, yet what we ask we gain by prayer. (Com. Mt. 6:8)

For many of us this is *not* an "easy answer," but it is instructive to see how Calvin works on it. Commenting on "Work out your own salvation with fear and trembling: for it is God who works in you both to will and work," Calvin attacks the assurance that comes from blind confidence in our own strength instead of depending completely on the grace of God. "It is God who works" means that we can do nothing except through the grace of God alone. Calvin then distinguishes two principal parts in any action: the will and the effective power, and *both are wholly ascribed to God.* That is to say, God is not merely the author of the beginning and the end, but also of the middle. Calvin rejects what he calls the sophistical attempt to harmonize God's grace and human free will by conceiving free will as a human movement with peculiar and separate capacity. Since "work is ascribed to God and man in common [Pelagians and Papists] assign half to each. In short, from the word 'work' they derive free-will; and from the term 'salvation,' the merit of eternal life." The proper understanding is that God brings to perfection those godly affections that he has inspired in us. Both goodwill and good action should be ascribed to God's free mercy. Calvin admits that such a denial of human free will causes many to "indulge themselves the more freely in their vices, but this is not the fault of the doctrine which should produce carefulness in our hearts" (Com. Phil. 2:13). It is our duty to ask of God even for those things that seem to come from our own hands (III.20.44). When Calvin remembers, he accepts the view that God is immutable (I.17.12) and rejects the possibility that prayer changes God (III.20.43). Additionally, the course of events being under God's all-wise, all-knowing, all-loving control does not need to be changed.[98] However, God attends to prayer because not to do so would deny his nature (Com. Ps. 65.1). God not merely hears and responds to our prayers but promises to provide what we require on the basis of prayer. Thus "those very things which flow to us from [God's] voluntary liberality he would have us recognize as granted to our prayers" (III.20.3). Calvin insists that we, like David, are to pray for pardon although we are already pardoned. This exercise is necessary because "it is plain that there is no inconsistency in having a persuasion of the grace of God, and yet proceeding to supplicate his forgiveness" (Com. Ps. 51:9).

The clearest illustration that Calvin's exposition of prayer follows the logic of his heart rather than his head is the confession that our confidence is grounded in God (III.20.11) because salvation is based on communion with Christ who has *changed* (!) the immutable God's throne from dreadful glory to wonderful grace (III.20.17). "We have the heart of God as soon as we place before him the name of his Son" (Com. Jn. 16:26). "The sole end and legitimate use of prayer . . . is that we may reap the fruits of God's promises" (Com. Ps. 119:38), and while we dare not ask more than God would freely bestow (Com. Ps. 91:15), it is not in vain to require God to behave toward us as he has promised (Serm. Dt. 26:16–19) and to refer to God all our needs (Com. Ps. 17:1), and even our wants as children familiarly address their father. Not that we tell God what He does not know or argue with God about our needs, but that our cares may be lightened

---

98. Nevertheless, a Sermon on Deut. 9:13–14 (*CO* 26:682) suggests that in the birth of John the Baptist the course of nature is changed by prayer.

and we have confidence that we will obtain whatever we request in faith (Com. Ps. 10:13).

F. PREDESTINATION: THE CERTAINTY OF FAITH

Because eternal election is so often regarded as Calvinism's "central dogma," cannonade against predestination is a primary objective for Calvin's opponents (human depravity being a secondary target). This point is well made by Lyman H. Atwater: "The distinguishing mark of Calvinism which usually ensures the appellation from friend and foe, is the doctrine of the divine foreordination, or predestination of all events in a manner and within limits exclusive of fatalism, but inclusive of the contingency of second causes, and the freedom of rational and accountable creatures." Certainly, Calvin's foes will not allow the exclusion of fatalism and the inclusion of contingency and freedom, which his friends, like Atwater, defend in terms of system, principle, and reason.[99] According to his enemies Calvin's view of eternal election produces a cowardly retreat from human freedom and responsibility, but among Calvin's Corps constituency predestination is a favorite redoubt from which one bravely advances along the lines of divine sovereignty, justice, and mercy. Both interpretations often mistakenly assume eternal election is a logical deduction from the concept of omnipotence.

The volumes devoted to predestination are indeed voluminous, but too seldom noticed is the christocentric basis of Calvin's confession of predestination, the mystery it exhibits, and the comfort it provides as the following citation summarizes:

> Let us learn that we cannot be assured of our salvation except by faith. For if someone asks, "How do I know whether I am saved or damned?" this question demonstrates he does not know it is faith we must have (and not assurance) in God through Jesus Christ. Do you really want to know you are elect? Regard yourself in Jesus Christ. For those who by faith are truly in communion with Jesus Christ can be perfectly assured that the eternal election of God applies to them and they are his children. Whoever finds himself in Jesus Christ and is a member of his body by faith is assured of his salvation. When we wish to know this fact, we are not to mount higher to inquire about things hidden from us to this hour. But behold God descends to us in the revelation of his Son as if to say, "Here I am. Contemplate me and know that I have adopted you as my children." When we receive this witness of salvation brought to us by the Gospel we know and are assured that God has elected us.[100]

In this repetitive statement Calvin asserts eternal election is received in the gift of faith defined as communion in Christ which produces assurance.

99. Lyman H. Atwater, "Calvinism in Doctrine and Life," *The Presbyterian Quarterly and Princeton Review* 4 (January 1875): 75, 83, 85.

100. *Congrégation sur l'élection éternelle, CO* 8:114.

Calvin believes, "If our faith is not founded on the eternal election of God, it is certain that our faith would be ravaged by Satan at every moment" (Serm. on Eph. 1:3–4)—but those who examine predestination as taught in the Word "reap the inestimable fruit of comfort" (III.24.4). Calvin insists he teaches "nothing not borne out by experience: that God has always been free to bestow his grace on whom he wills" (III.22.1). God alone opens the eyes of blind minds (Com. Lk. 19:42). In commenting on Ephesians 1, Calvin says, "The full certainty of salvation consists in the fact that through the gospel God reveals his love to us in Christ." This fact is confirmed in the eternal election of God by which our adoption takes place before our birth. Thus, believers "know that they were saved, not by any accidental or unforeseen occurrence, but by the eternal and unchangeable decree of God." The divine freedom is further confirmed by the fact that we are chosen outside ourselves—in Christ. "It is not from the sight of our deserving, but because our heavenly Father has engrafted us, through the blessing of adoption, into the body of Christ." The mercy of God is nowhere declared more sublimely than in predestination, which Calvin illustrates according to Aristotle's four causes: the final cause is God's grace and glory; the efficient cause is the good pleasure of God's will; the material cause is Christ by whom the love of God is poured out to us; and the formal cause is preaching by which Christ through whom we come to God is communicated.

The chief and head of the modern problem with Calvin's doctrine of predestination is his confession that "Man falls according as God's providence ordains, but he falls by his own fault" (III.23.8). Thinkers today are not only puzzled but offended by this profession. Calvin nevertheless affirms that the cause behind the elect is God. The real and remote cause behind the reprobate is also God, but the real and proximate cause of reprobation is the self. Calvin credits God with ordaining the fall and the resulting reprobation for which mankind, not God, is to blame. Although this juxtaposition of ideas mightily discomfits some, they reside side by side in Calvin's mind because he finds them in Scripture.[101]

Calvin knows that in the Old Testament God chooses Isaac over Ishmael (Com. Gen. 21:12) and Ephraim over Manasseh (Com. Gen. 48:20). And, most directly, "Jacob have I loved but Esau have I hated" (Com. Mal. 1:2–3, cf. Rom. 9:13). Calvin concludes, "If, then, we cannot determine a reason why [God] vouchsafes mercy to his own except that it so pleases him, neither shall we have any reason for rejecting others, other than his will. For when it is said that God hardens or shows mercy to whom he wills, men are warned by this to seek no

---

101. The paradoxical tension between God's choice of the elect and the elects' choice of God is expressed this way in the Westminster Confession: "This effectual call is of God's free and special grace alone, not from anything at all foreseen in man, who is altogether passive therein, until being quickened and renewed by the Holy Spirit, he is thereby enabled to answer this call, and to embrace the grace offered and conveyed in it" (10.2). Apparently, the elect are passive in receiving grace but, once quickened and renewed by the Holy Spirit, become active in answering the call and embracing the grace. Effectual calling is irresistible "yet so as they come most freely, being made willing by his grace" (10.1).

cause outside his will" (III.22.11). This so-terrific statement must act as a soporific for those who perpetuate the canard about Calvin's logic. Thomas J. Davis cites Leroy S. Rounder: "Calvin, obsessed with the need for clarity and logical consistency, carefully crafted an increasingly monstrous doctrine [predestination] which even he found hard to believe."[102]

Calvin maintained that his exposition of election was scriptural, true to God's mystery and therefore necessary and profitable to be taught to the comfort of the company of faithful relying entirely on God's grace revealed in Jesus Christ. In his most-often-cited short definition, Calvin writes, "We call predestination God's eternal decree, by which he compacted with himself what he willed to become of each man. For all are not created in equal condition; rather, eternal life is foreordained for some, eternal damnation for others. Therefore, as any man has been created to one or the other of these ends, we speak of him as predestined to life or to death" (III.21.5). These words read in isolation and without attention to modifying contexts are quite objectionable to modern sensibilities. Among mental dispositions today, eternal decrees, unequal creations, foreordination to life or death are not readily acceptable. However, not sufficiently noticed is that modern sensibilities in their turn are also not without difficulties.

That choosing for or against Calvin's teaching offers neither a clear nor an easy alternative is demonstrated by the famous preacher Charles Haddon Spurgeon (1834–92). In his sermon entitled "A Defense of Calvinism," Spurgeon divides the theological world into Arminians and Calvinists. All of us, he thinks, are born Arminian in that we assume we are seeking God when in fact God is seeking us. "I suppose there are some persons whose minds naturally incline toward the doctrine of free-will. I can only say that mine inclines as naturally towards the doctrines of sovereign grace." That salvation is of the Lord is an epitome of Calvinism. Spurgeon testifies, "I believe the doctrine of election because I am quite certain that, if God had not chosen me, I should never have chosen Him; and I am sure that He chose me before I was born, or else He never would have chosen me afterwards; and He must have elected me for reasons unknown to me, for I never could find any reason in myself why He should have looked upon me with special love."

To this point Spurgeon is following Calvin's confession, but he admits he admires both the Calvinist George Whitefield and the Arminian John Wesley, reasoning that the "system of truth revealed in the Scriptures is not simply one straight line, but two," including both divine providence presiding over all things and human free will to choose. "That God predestines and yet that man is responsible are two facts that few can see clearly." Granting this paradox, one could emphasize election with Calvin or choice with Wesley as doxological confession, but Spurgeon concludes, "They are two lines that are so nearly parallel that the

---

102. Thomas J. Davis, "Preaching and Presence: Constructing Calvin's Homiletical Legacy," in *The Legacy of John Calvin*, ed. David Foxgrover (Grand Rapids: Calvin Studies Society, 2000), 84, 86. In opposition to Rounder, Davis points to the real presence of Christ (which seems equivalent to the Lordship of Christ being a function of that reality) and union with him as "the crux of Christian existence."

human mind which pursues them farthest will never discover that they converge, but they do converge, and they will meet somewhere in eternity, close to the throne of God, whence all truth doth spring." Having the issue both ways is to beg the question. Asserting convergence beyond the limits of the human mind means Spurgeon's conclusion is rhetorical, not rational, and establishes no logical basis for his assertion that preaching Christ and him crucified is simply Calvinism. "It is a nickname to call it Calvinism; Calvinism is the gospel, and nothing else."[103]

Predestination, shortly defined as God's unfailing and unflagging care for his chosen, is a mystery of divine love confessed, not to drive toward despair or fruitless speculation, but to exalt the grace of God by denying the saving efficacy of human merit. Calvin thinks predestination "builds up faith soundly, trains us to humility, devotes us to admiration of the immense goodness of God towards us, and excites us to praise this goodness."[104] Predestination is part of the confession of the range and intensity of God's care for his faithful people. All Calvin's doctrines are connected but some, like creation and redemption, justification and sanctification, providence and predestination, are especially interlocking. In exposition of the work of the Holy Spirit in Book III, Calvin links union with Christ and faith, sanctification and justification, prayer and predestination. At the deepest levels of his theology the subject-object dichotomy is replaced by union with Christ. Nevertheless, the distinction is helpful in understanding emphases. Calvin wants his reader to understand that faith and election, sanctification and justification, prayer and predestination are all to be credited to God. Union with Christ, justification, and election are more the "objective" facts, while faith, sanctification, and prayer involve some "subjective" action. Especially to be noted is Calvin's insistence that election precedes faith. "Election, as Paul testifies, is the mother of faith" (III.22.10). However, his exposition of faith (chap. 2) precedes election (chaps. 21–24)! Predestination is not developed in Book I in terms of the doctrine of creation nor in Book II as part of the doctrine of redemption, but at the end of Book III within the saving work of the Holy Spirit.

A number of Calvin's followers did not respect his location of predestination. They took the intense conviction of God's salvific care, cut it loose from its mooring in the believer's humble attempt to understand the implications of the gift of faith, and let it float upriver to drop anchor in the doctrine of God. For example, the Westminster Confession, a hundred years later, deals with the Scripture in article 1, with God in article 2, and election in article 3. (Jesus Christ is article 8!) At Westminster predestination is developed *before* the doctrines of creation, redemption, faith, and so on. In Calvin, eternal election is properly an attempt from the believer's perspective to understand God's love for those whom God chooses. According to Westminster the doctrine is an attempt, from God's perspective, to explain the eternal choice of those whom God will love. Put

---

103. Charles Spurgeon, "A Defense of Calvinism," http://www.spurgeon.org/calvinis.htm, 1, 2, 8, 9, 5.
104. *Concerning Eternal Predestination*, 56.

another way, predestination in Calvin deals with *our experience* of God's grace; in Westminster it deals with *God's bestowal* of grace. We can understand something of the former, but we can only guess about the latter. Doubtless, eternal love for the elect *and* eternal election of the loved are united in God, but Calvin is often wrongly regarded as one who knew and taught a great deal about God's eternal election and nothing of God's eternal love. In fact, the doctrine of predestination is about God's love.

In the popular mind Calvin and predestination are inextricably linked. With this doctrine, according to Hunter's striking phrase, Calvin brought upon himself and his system "cataracts of horrified abuse."[105] More carefully considered, predestination is neither a logical deduction nor the central doctrine. Niesel correctly observes, "All mere thinking about eternal predestination as an idea in itself leads us into uncertainty and despair." Calvin agrees: "They are mad who seek their own or others' salvation in the labyrinth of predestination" (Com. Jn. 6:40). Niesel continues, Calvin's theology is not "a system of thoughts about God and man proceeding from the one thought of the utter dependence of man on God. Metaphysical speculation about the ground of the world and its relation to the creature, however powerful and impressive, and revelational theology of which the only aim is to lead us to the Lord, are nevertheless mutually exclusive."[106] Calvin declares, "Human curiosity renders the discussion of predestination, already difficult in itself, very confusing and even dangerous. No restraints can hold it back from wandering in forbidden bypaths and thrusting upward to the heights. If allowed, it will leave no secret to God that it will not search out and unravel" (III.21.1). "The predestination of God is truly a labyrinth from which the mind of man is wholly incapable of extracting itself" (Com. Rom. 9:14). Without attempting a blanket statement, the following pages attempt to cover the subject examining the threads of central doctrine, the issue of reprobation, and the question of assurance.

1. Central Dogma

Famously and incorrectly Alexander Schweizer claimed predestination as the central dogma of Reformed Christianity.[107] On the contrary, partisans of this posi-

---

105. A. M. Hunter, *The Teaching of Calvin*, 2nd ed. (London: James Clarke and Company, 1950), 84. One of the oddities of historical theology is that Calvin, who wrote a *Treatise on Free Will* (*Against Pighius*), should have his name so closely associated with predestination, while Luther, who wrote on *The Bondage of the Will*, is not.

106. Niesel, *Theology of Calvin*, 161, 159–60. Wendel's discussion of predestination is especially helpful in tracing the doctrine's historical development and its pastoral emphasis. Wendel, *Calvin: The Origins and Development*, 289, asserts that in Calvin's view, predestination "was never to be discussed as an indulgence in metaphysical speculations, but to throw a fuller light upon the doctrine of justification by grace alone and give a theological basis for ecclesiology." The earlier part of the statement is more accurate than the latter. Eternal election throws a fuller light on Calvin's view of faith connected to union with Christ, which includes justification and sanctification.

107. Alexander Schweizer, *Die Protestantischen Centraldogmen in ihrer Entwicklung innerhalb der Reformierten Kirche*, vol. 1 (Zurich: Orelli Fuessli, 1854), 57.

tion hold a leash on the wrong dogma. Eternal election is a crucial component of the more basic confession of God's grace made sure in union with Christ. As previously noted, Calvin's convictions about predestination are clearly adumbrated in his discussion of providence.[108] The result in both cases is that Calvin is describing the believer's experience of the loving care of God the Creator and God the Redeemer in the world in general and in human life in particular.[109] Already cited is Bohatec's formula that providence is root metaphor (*Stammlehre*) and predestination is central doctrine (*Zentraldogma*). Wendel makes the point this way:

> After Alexander Schweizer in 1844 and Ferdinand Christian Baur in 1847 had claimed that predestination was the central doctrine of Calvin's theology and that all the originality of his teaching proceeded from it, historians and dogmaticians went on for three-quarters of a century repeating that affirmation like an article of faith which did not even need to be verified. It is true enough that Calvin attributed great importance to predestination in both its forms—election and reprobation—and that he never shared the point of view of Melanchthon, who thought it a subject hardly suitable for discussion. In the different editions of the *Institutes* Calvin gave it more and more space and, in consequence of attacks that were made upon the doctrine, he was moved to defend it in several special writings, notably in the *Congrégation sur l'élection éternelle* of 1551 (published in 1562) against Jérôme Bolsec, and in the second work against Pighius which appeared in 1552 as the treatise *Upon the Eternal Predestination of God*. But to recognize that Calvin taught double predestination, and underline its dogmatic and practical interest, is not to say that this must be taken to be the very center of his teaching.[110]

Additionally, eternal election is not a logical deduction from the sovereignty of God nor the cornerstone of his theological edifice, but it is the continuation of his doctrine of faith. As Heinz Otten observes, "Calvin in his treatment of predestination never starts from the doctrine of God so that he would perhaps construct the gracious election from the idea of sovereignty and sole efficacy of God,

---

108. For a more detailed discussion of this point, see the chapter "Calvin on Universal and Particular Providence" in my *Calvin and Classical Philosophy* (Louisville, KY: Westminster John Knox Press, 2005). Interestingly, Doumergue, in his volume 4 of his great *Jean Calvin*, devotes only seven pages (111–18) to providence in his discussion of the doctrine of God and sixty-five pages to predestination in a separate section (351–416).

109. According to Karl Barth, "The really vital core, the secret both of history and of our existence, is our response to the fact of election" (Barth, *The Word of God and the Word of Man*, trans. Douglas Horton [Boston: Pilgrim Press, 1928], 58).

110. Wendel, *Calvin: The Origins and Development*, 263–64. In his 1535 *Loci Communes* (Corpus Reformatorum 21.452) Melanchthon says the topic of predestination is useless and confusing. In opposition Calvin thinks Scripture teaches eternal election, and it would be blasphemous to be content with brutish ignorance under pretense of modesty (III.2.3). Further, Christians should not be deterred by scoffers since avoiding their scorn would require keeping secret "the chief doctrines of the faith," such as the deity of Son and Spirit and the creation of the universe (III.21.4). Luther strongly defended double predestination against Erasmus and never revoked his view.

but rather predestination is for him a part of soteriology."[111] I confess it is inexplicable to me that anyone who has followed Calvin's exposition to this point should only now be surprised and find here Calvin's conclusions insufferable. Objections to Calvin's conception of predestination should be raised with his understanding of the doctrines which it enhances, most especially the Lordship of Christ, union with Christ, particular providence, and faith.

In his own lifetime there were objections to Calvin's view of eternal election, and as a result he devotes four chapters (III.21–24) to its explanation. In spite of this effort, a common interpretation maintains that his "central dogma" is the glory (or sovereignty) of God, and eternal election (or predestination) is its rationally necessary implicate. The terms "glory" and "sovereignty" are not exactly equivalent, although they are often used interchangeably. Glory as a biblical word applied to God fosters awe and worship but does not encourage calculations and deductions. Sovereignty, on the other hand, with its political overtones and its philosophical undertones of the Absolute, seems almost to require logical inferences to be drawn.

Among the more sympathetic attempts to expound Calvin's doctrine of predestination is A. M. Hunter's. Thinking the "sovereignty of God" is Calvin's master-thought, Hunter takes aim at a halfhearted and half-minded defense by denying that the "primary postulate of sovereignty" is presented in terms of inflexible logic. Hunter writes, "Calvin had a vivid and profound sense of the Divine majesty, but, while seeking to communicate it to others, he would not set it before them as the supreme object of their contemplation; that would be to plunge them into an awe that was mingled with terror. The principal thing was to be sure of His paternal goodness. . . . Ever [Calvin] seeks to root faith in the grateful recognition of God's goodness to us in Providence and grace."[112]

Hunter concludes there are two ways of thinking about God in Calvin. The first, and most dominant, descends "upon the world from a conception of God which might find support in Christ but which did not start from Him; in the other he ascended from Christ to God or rather with Christ to God." The latter means the "God whom he posited was not the fruit of the speculation which was his peculiar abhorrence, but a Being not merely depicted in Scripture but reflected in life and religious experience." Still, Calvin "*entered the sphere of theological thought with the doctrine of predestination deeply imbedded in his heart.* It would be difficult to say whether his idea of God imposed upon him his doctrine of predestination or, rather, his acceptance of predestination as explaining life

---

111. Heinz Otten, *Calvins Theologische Anschauung von der Prädestination* (Munich: Chr. Kaiser, 1938), 87. That predestination is a deduction from omnipotence is argued by H. Bois, "La Prédestination d'après Calvin," in *Études sur la Réforme* (Paris: Librairie Armand Colin, 1919), 674–76. Against the view of Calvin as a speculative thinker G. Oorthuys, "La Prédestination dans la Dogmatique Calviniste," in *De l'élection Eternelle de Dieu* (Geneva: Éditions Labor, 1936), 213, writes, "Calvin refused to be a philosopher. He wanted to be a theologian, a teacher of Holy Scripture, purveyor of the Good News, preacher of Christ, witness of the faith, nothing more."

112. Hunter, *Teaching*, 50.

forced upon him his idea of God." In any case, "The sovereignty of God domi-nates Calvin's thought and forms the citadel into which he retreats whenever hard pressed by antagonists, yet he conceives of it as acting through various attributes, or, as it were, from different centres of His Being." The range of sovereignty defined apart from Jesus Christ and conceived by Hunter to operate sometimes as justice and wrath, sometimes as mercy and love, produces both an erroneous and blurred focus. Hunter thinks Calvin "shows signs of being uneasily conscious of this himself, protesting, as he frequently does, that there must be some point of view, could we only reach it, from which the appointments of each of these various attributes might be reconciled with the demands of the rest, or rather that, did we know all of God, we should see that there was no inner contradic-tion at all, and that when God is just, He does not cease to be merciful, or when He is wrathful, He does not cease to be loving."[113] In this way Hunter tries to combine confidence and humility, to blunt the hard-edged conception of the sov-ereignty of God in Calvin from a rationalistic speculation in favor of the scrip-tural depiction reflected in the experience of the faithful. Nevertheless, whether clear or blurred, the conception of the sovereignty of God, while it might be intended as doxology, lends itself to abstract deduction and leads to an abstract predestination apart from God's love revealed in Jesus Christ.

Every thinker struggles with the intellectual difficulties of predestination, but the resolution is not Hunter's "double-minded Calvin." Proper interpretation begins with the recognition that Calvin believes and thinks more in biblical/personal than philosophical/abstract categories. United by the work of the Holy Spirit, Calvin's central confession is "Jesus Christ is Lord," and his central conviction is "union with Christ." God is revealed and known as Creator and Redeemer. The Redeemer bestows the gift of faith (the principal work of the Holy Spirit) upon those who are chosen for redemption. This gift of faith involves the "double graces" of justifica-tion, a once-for-all event, and sanctification, a continuing-for-life process. In the context of God's loving care for all creation, eternal election is Calvin's reflection on the mystery of "those who are chosen for redemption."

Not only is predestination misunderstood as Calvin's central dogma based on the inexorable decree of God whose sovereignty and power it demonstrates to right reason, but also misunderstood when not recognized as the love of God revealed in his Christ. "If we seek God's fatherly mercy and kindly heart, we should turn our eyes to Christ, on whom alone God's Spirit rests." It is insane to seek apart from Christ what we obtain in him alone. Since we have been chosen in him,

> We shall not find assurance of our election in ourselves; *and not even in God the Father, if we conceive him as severed from his Son.* Christ then is the mir-ror wherein we must, and without self-deception may, contemplate our own election. For since it is into his body the Father has destined those to be

113. Ibid., 51.

engrafted whom he has willed from eternity to be his own, that he may hold
as sons all whom he acknowledges to be among his members, we have a sufficiently clear and firm testimony that we have been inscribed in the book
of life if we are in communion with Christ. (III.24.5, emphasis added)

2. Reprobation

Eternal election is much easier to affirm and accept than eternal reprobation, but
"those whom God passes over, he reprobates (*Quos Deus preterit, reprobat*)"
(III.23.1). According to Calvin, "God declares that he wills the conversion of all,
and he directs exhortations to all in common" (III.3.21). Commenting on
1 Corinthians 1:8, Calvin says even in our doubting we ought to be certain that
God will never give us up. We must make the judgment in love "that as many are
called, are called to salvation." In summary, "Sincere Christians should entertain
good hopes about all who have come onto the right way of salvation, and are stay-
ing the course, even though they are still beset by many maladies."

Based on this conviction Calvin begins his discussion of predestination in the
Institutes from the preacher's puzzled experience. "In actual fact, the covenant of
life is not preached equally among all men, and among those to whom it is
preached, it does not gain the same acceptance, either constantly or in equal
degree" (III.21.1). More dramatically, he writes, "If the same sermon is preached,
say, to a hundred people, twenty receive it with the ready obedience of faith, while
the rest hold it valueless, or laugh, or hiss, or loathe it" (III.24.12). The preaching of the word is effectual only upon the illumination of the Spirit (III.24.2).
Since God's mercy is offered both to the godly and the wicked through the gospel,
it is faith, defined as the illumination of God, that distinguishes between the
pious and the impious (III.24.17).

Struggling with this issue in the commentary on 1 John (2:19), Calvin says
that there are three degrees of gospel profession: those who pretend godliness
without integrity; those whose hypocrisy deceives themselves, and the truly faithful who "carry a testimony of their adoption firmly fixed in their hearts." In grap-
pling with the division between elect and reprobate, between some and all, Calvin
says the gospel addresses all in general, but the gift of faith is rare (III.22.10). It
is certainly true that Calvin considered reprobation more than a possibility or an
empty classification. On the basis of Scripture he asserted that Ishmael, Esau,
Pharaoh, Saul, and Judas (Com. Jn. 2.62) were reprobate, concluding this destination serves the glorification of God's name (III.23.6). Nevertheless, he insists
that "we are reconciled to God is proper to the Gospel [but] that unbelievers are
adjudged to eternal death is accidental (*accidentale*)" (Com. Jn. 20:23). "Experience teaches that God wills the repentance of those whom he invites to himself"
(III.24.15). His mercy is extended to all provided they seek it, but only those
whom he has illuminated seek his mercy (III.24.17).

Calvin thinks it plain that salvation comes to pass by God's bidding. "Salvation is freely offered to some while others are barred from access to it, [the result

is] at once great and difficult questions spring up, explicable only when reverent minds regard as settled what they may suitably hold concerning election and pre-destination. A baffling question this seems to many. For they think nothing more inconsistent than that out of the common multitude of men some should be pre-destined to salvation, others to destruction" (III.21.1).

> God once established by his eternal and unchangeable plan those whom he long before determined once for all to receive into salvation, and those whom, on the other hand, he would devote to destruction. We assert that, with respect to the elect, this plan was founded upon his freely given mercy, without regard to human worth; but by his just and irreprehensible but incomprehensible judgment he has barred the door of life to those whom he has given over to damnation. Now among the elect we regard the call as a testimony of election. Then we hold justification another sign of its man-ifestation, until they come into the glory in which the fulfillment of that election lies. But as the Lord seals his elect by call and justification, so, by shutting off the reprobate from knowledge of his name or from the sancti-fication of his Spirit, he, as it were, reveals by these marks what sort of judg-ment awaits them. (III.21.7)

Calvin clearly believes that damnation is the predestination of some persons. This fact is important to know, because otherwise, "We shall never be clearly per-suaded, as we ought to be, that our salvation flows from the wellspring of God's free mercy until we come to know his eternal election, which illumines God's grace by this contrast: that he does not indiscriminately adopt all into the hope of salvation but gives to some what he denies to others" (III.21.1). This conclu-sion does not lead to arrogance, "For as we know not who belongs to the num-ber of the predestined or who does not belong, we ought to be so minded as to wish that all men be saved" (III.23.14). Too often neglected is Calvin's insistence that God's "secret judgments surpass our comprehension. For those who seemed utterly lost and quite beyond hope are by his goodness called back to the way; while those who more than others seemed to stand firm often fell." Given the limitations of our judgment, we should exercise "a certain charitable judgment whereby we recognize as members of the church those who by confession of faith, by example of life, and by partaking of the sacraments, profess the same God and Christ with us" (IV.1.8).

Accepting the biblical category of reprobation, Calvin denies its application to believers:

> Satan has no more grievous or dangerous temptation to dishearten believ-ers than when he unsettles them with doubt about their election, while at the same time he arouses them with a wicked desire to seek it outside the way. I call it "seeking outside the way" when mere man attempts to break into the inner recesses of divine wisdom, and tries to penetrate even to high-est eternity, in order to find out what decision has been made concerning himself at God's judgement seat. For then he casts himself into the depths of a bottomless whirlpool to be swallowed up; then he tangles himself in innumerable and inextricable snares; then he buries himself in an abyss of

sightless darkness.[114] For it is right for the stupidity of human understanding to be thus punished with dreadful ruin when man tries by his own
strength to rise to the height of divine wisdom. And this temptation is all
the deadlier, since almost all of us are more inclined to it than any other.
(III.24.4)

3. Assurance

Calvin is aware, "Many persons dispute all these positions which we have set forth,
especially the free election of believers; nevertheless, [he insists] this cannot be
shaken." Some think God distinguishes among persons by foreknowledge of their
merits, meaning God adopts those foreseen to be worthy of grace and damns those
foreseen to be inclined to evil. Calvin objects to this point of view (III.22.1–6),
placing both election and reprobation in God's will. God's foreknowledge and
foreordination are not different. "When we attribute foreknowledge to God, we
mean that all things always were, and perpetually remain, under his eyes, so that
to his knowledge there is nothing future or past, but all things are present. And
they are present in such a way that he not only conceives them through ideas, as
we have before us those things which our minds remember, but he truly looks
upon them and discerns them as things placed before him. And this foreknowledge is extended throughout the universe to every creature" (III.21.5).

To magnify God's grace, Calvin insisted on eschewing entirely a human role
in salvation. Salvation in the beginning is God's initiative and in the end is God's
accomplishment.

> Now it behooves us to pay attention to what Scripture proclaims of every
> person. When Paul teaches that we were chosen in Christ "before the cre-
> ation of the world" [Eph. 1:4a], he takes away all consideration of real worth
> on our part, for it is just as if he said: since among all the offspring of Adam,
> the Heavenly Father found nothing worthy of his election, he turned his
> eyes upon his Anointed, to choose from that body as members those whom
> he was to take into the fellowship of life. (III.22.1)

Predestination must be confessed not as a mere matter of God's prescience or general governance but as an expression that neither God's arm nor God's love is fore-
shortened. Calvin could not believe that God flew about like a bird, anxious and
uncertain, waiting to alight on human decisions.[115] In denying election as God's
foreknowledge of human merits to be accrued, Calvin declares God to be the
active author and not the idle observer of salvation (III.22.6). Election is not a
matter of permission but decree, and we must understand that "God's will is so
much the highest rule of righteousness that whatever he wills, by the very fact

114. Our poets are much impressed by the tradition that the flames of hell are dark. Robert Her-
rick writes, "The fire of Hell this strange condition hath / To burn, not shine (as learned Basil saith)"
("Noble Numbers," *The Poems of Robert Herrick* [London: Oxford University Press, 1951], 410).
According to Milton, the dark fires of hell produce "no light, but rather darkness visible" (*PL* 1.64).

115. *Concerning Eternal Predestination*, 67.

that he wills it, must be considered righteous" (III.23.2). God has mercy upon whomever he wills, and he hardens whomever he wills (Com. Rom. 9.18).

Predestination is not a theoretical exposition of God's power but a practical understanding of God's providence applied to the chosen ones. Predestination is an affirmation of the ultimate victory of God's irresistible love. The confession that God's love for God's elect is unfailing and unflagging raises many problems for the understanding, among them the correct relation between God's sovereign holy will and our sinful human wills, but also between the chosen and not chosen. The result produces not steps of logic but moments of confession, which include both the assurance of pardon and the certainty of one's salvation.[116]

Calvin understands there are those who wish to avoid all mention of predestination, but he believes that in the Word of the Lord "we have a sure rule for the understanding. For Scripture is the school of the Holy Spirit, in which, as nothing is omitted that is both necessary and useful to know, so nothing is taught but what is expedient to know. Therefore we must guard against depriving believers of anything disclosed about predestination in Scripture, lest we seem either wickedly to defraud them of the blessing of their God or to accuse and scoff at the Holy Spirit for having published what it is in any way profitable to suppress" (III.21.3). This means, "We should not investigate what the Lord has left hidden in secret, [but also] we should not neglect what he has brought into the open, so that we may not be convicted of excessive curiosity on the one hand, or of excessive ingratitude on the other" (III.21.4). Calvin concludes, "Let this, therefore, first of all be before our eyes: to seek any other knowledge of predestination than what the Word of God discloses is not less insane than if one should purpose to walk in a pathless waste [cf. Job 12.24], or to see in darkness. And let us not be ashamed to be ignorant of something in this matter, wherein there is a certain learned ignorance" (III.21.2). In short, Calvin believed his doctrine of predestination was biblical in origin and mysterious in conceptualization.

All Christians believe in some form of "election," because 2 Thessalonians teaches that "God chose you as the first fruits for salvation" (2:13), and the Gospel of John declares, "You did not choose me but I chose you" (15:16). Most surely agree that salvation is initiated by God's choice. The apostle Paul wrote, "[God] chose us in Christ before the foundation of the world to be holy and blameless before him" (Eph. 1:4). On the other hand, the Scripture also appeals to human choice in verses like "If you are unwilling to serve the LORD, choose this day whom you will serve" (Josh. 24:15), or "The kingdom of God has come near; repent, and believe in the good news" (Mark 1:14).

One option is to understand election as a divine possibility requiring human decision. Using a modern example, God broadcasts good news twenty-four hours a day on a special frequency. In addition, God created human beings with the

---

116. A. N. S. Lane, "Calvin's Doctrine of Assurance," in *Vox Evangelica* 11 (1979): 32–54. In this helpful essay one might judge too much time is spent with W. H. Chaulker's 1961 Duke University thesis and too little time focused on Christ who is discussed as the *fifth* ground of assurance.

ability to hear and installed a permanent receiver in each heart. However, the divine radio station has not been preset but must be individually dialed up. On this view salvation is a universal offering, but not a personal gift of God. God can be praised for salvation in general, but each person is responsible for his or her salvation in particular. To change and challenge the image, many people think the God of Hosts has prepared a very specific guest list for the great banquet and is not waiting anxiously to see who comes through the door.

The Scripture teaches, and the theological tradition reflects, a dual destiny for the human race: heaven or hell. Obviously John Calvin did not invent the problem of understanding the pre- or postdestiny of the elect and the reprobate. Perhaps the most elegant resolution to the problem is offered by Thomas Aquinas (and maintained by millions of people). This view holds that God predestines the elect to grace, and the elect respond to God's operating grace with cooperating grace (which in its own complicated way is a result of God's gift). Thus, the elect are *predestined* to grace but, in some sense, *earn* glory.[117] This solution grants the primary initiative in salvation to divine operating grace but in a secondary way involves human cooperating grace, which, while not apart from divine grace, suggests a role for human responsibility.

Calvin denied predestination to grace as below divine honor and cooperating grace as above human capacity (III.22.9). Calvin sees predestination to grace as synonymous with predestination to glory. Salvation belongs to God's grace-full foreordination alone and not to divine foreknowledge of human choices made in relative independence. Calvin writes, "No one who wishes to be thought religious dares simply deny predestination, by which God adopts some to hope of life, and sentences others to eternal death. But our opponents, especially those who make foreknowledge its cause, envelop it in numerous petty objections" (III.21.5).

The attempt to understand God's eternal election will undoubtedly remain a subject of debate in years to come as it has been in years past. However, human explanation follows after the divine mystery of predestination seen as part of the confession of the gift of faith, which is the principal work of the Holy Spirit uniting the believer to Christ.

G. RESURRECTION: THE VICTORY OF FAITH

After four chapters on election, Book III concludes with a discussion of the promise and hope of resurrection of the body based on union with God. Our union with Christ is not merely a matter of following his example, but of being ingrafted into his death, which is inseparable from his resurrection. This means our death will be followed by our resurrection (Com. Rom. 6:5). With this treatment of the redemp-

---

117. See my "Predestination in Aquinas and Calvin," in *Reformed Review* 32, no. 1 (Fall 1978): 14–22.

tion of soul and body, Calvin completes his exposition of their creation in Book I. Accordingly, the brief discussion of resurrection was deferred to this place in order that readers could learn that Christ is both the author of our salvation and the example of our resurrection. "By his resurrection, he completed the whole work of our salvation. . . . For this reason Christ's resurrection alone is often set before us to confirm our assurance of salvation" (Com. Rom. 10:9). This is especially true of the Gospel according to John, which "emphasizes more the doctrine in which Christ's office and the power of his death and resurrection are explained" (Intro. to John). Thus "with our eyes fixed on Christ we wait upon heaven, and nothing on earth hinders [the faith, love, and hope of the godly] from bearing us to the promised blessedness" (III.25.1). Calvin teaches, "They alone receive the fruit of Christ's benefits who raise their minds to the resurrection" (III.25.2). The point is well summarized in T. F. Torrance's foreword to the English edition of Heinrich Quistorp's *Calvin's Doctrine of the Last Things.* "Calvin's main teaching about eschatology can be formulated by saying that eschatology is the application of Christology to the work of the church in history. . . . Calvin's teaching here pivots upon the doctrine of union with Christ. Because we are united to Christ and participate in his risen humanity, eschatology is essential to our faith."[118]

Recognizing that the hope of resurrection from the dead is powerfully scorned by some and painfully doubted by others, Calvin responds to three objections. First, the chiliasts attempt to limit the reign of Christ to one thousand years based on their understanding of Revelation 20:4. This view is wrong because "all Scripture proclaims that there will be no end to the blessedness of the elect or punishment of the wicked" (III.25.5). Second, some have thought that death requires the resurrection of both soul and body. To the contrary, the soul, formed after the image of God, is immortal. Third, some teach that while souls are immortal they will be clothed with "new bodies." Calvin thinks the notion of new bodies denies the resurrection of the flesh. He admits, "It is difficult to believe that bodies, when consumed with rottenness, will at length be raised up in their season. Therefore, although many of the philosophers declared souls immortal, few approved the resurrection of the flesh" (III.25.3). However, Calvin says, faith overcomes these doubts with two helps: one is Christ's resurrection and the other is God's omnipotence.[119]

---

118. Quistorp, *Calvin's Doctrine*, 8.

119. One of the most famous doubters was David Hume. On Sunday, July 7, 1776, James Boswell, being too late for church, visited Hume who was "just a dying." Although lean and ghastly, Hume was calm and even cheerful. Boswell suggested there might be a life after this one, to which Hume replied "that it was a most unreasonable fancy." Taken aback, Boswell asked if "the thought of annihilation never gave him any uneasiness." He said, "Not in the least." Unnerved, Boswell confesses he was "assailed by momentary doubts while I had actually before me a man of such strong abilities and extensive inquiry dying in the persuasion of being annihilated." However, Boswell recollected his "excellent mother's pious instructions" and kept the faith (James Boswell, "An Account of My Last Interview with David Hume, Esq.," in Norman Kemp Smith, ed., *David Hume: Dialogues Concerning Natural Religion* [New York: Bobbs-Merrill, 1987], 76–79).

Calvin has taught that the principal work of the Holy Spirit is faith, which leads to the election of the faithful in Christ and through him to their victory over death. In support Calvin cites Colossians 3:3–4: "You have died, and your life is hidden with Christ in God. When Christ who is your life is revealed, then you will also be revealed with him in glory."[120] This promise is violently besieged by temptations to renounce future for present benefits. Among the philosophers only Plato recognized the highest good as union with God but he did not understand its true nature (III.25.2).[121]

Reflection on resurrection begins with the recognition that the resurrection of Christ is the basis of our hope for resurrection. Our union with Christ involves his assumption and redemption of our nature and his victory over death for our sake. On this subject Calvin admits, "I am only touching upon what could be treated more fully and deserves to be set out more brilliantly," but the point is "to separate [Christ] from ourselves is not permissible and not even possible, without tearing him apart" (III.25.3). Because we are united in Christ, we participate in his victory over death, meaning that he "received again the mortal body which he had previously borne" (III.25.7). Because Christ is raised in a perfect body, he "will come on the Last Day as judge to conform our lowly inglorious body to his glorious body" (III.25.3). The resurrection of Christ demonstrates the power of the Holy Spirit, who gives life to all believers. In short, Christ's resurrection is the basis for the resurrection of the elect.

The second aid to faith in the resurrection is the conviction of God's almighty power. Citing Paul, Calvin points out that all things are subject to God, who promises a future life and is able to preserve us until it is bestowed. This power enables God to change our lowly body to be like Christ's glorious body (cf. Phil. 3:21). Since this event is an "incalculable miracle" that overwhelms our senses, Calvin cites a number of biblical passages alluding to the resurrection. "But let us remember that no one is truly persuaded of the coming resurrection unless he is seized with wonder, and ascribes to the power of God its due glory" (III.25.4). In this exposition Calvin again declares that the fall of mankind resulting in death is accidental (*accidentalis*) (III.25.7). Moreover, in affirming the immortality of the soul and the mortality of the body, Calvin concludes that the resurrection restores to vigor at God's command the *selfsame body* that died. The Scripture does not "define anything more clearly than the resurrection of the flesh that we now bear" (III.25.7), which may again be noted is crucial to understanding the Lord's Supper.

Having developed the fact of the final resurrection, Calvin turns to a description reminding his readers that the nature of our union with God means "the souls of the pious, having ended the toil of their warfare, enter into blessed

---

120. Karl Barth, *CD*, II.1, 149, calls this passage the essence of the gospel.
121. As the *Phaedo* brilliantly demonstrates, Plato hoped for the immortality of the soul but not for the resurrection of the body.

rest, where in glad expectation they await the enjoyment of promised glory, and so all things are held in suspense until Christ the Redeemer appear" (III.25.6). It is a great mystery, but "the Lord will share his glory, power and righteousness with the elect [and] will somehow make them to become one with himself" (III.25.10).

In resisting vain speculation about the situation of the soul in its "intermediate state" Calvin asserts, "It is foolish and rash to inquire concerning unknown matters more deeply than God permits us to know" (III.25.6). Nevertheless, in addition to the resurrection of the selfsame body, Calvin affirms the suffering of the reprobate and the consolation to the elect of Christ's presence. Although held in some suspense the souls of the pious enter into a blessed rest to await the enjoyment of the promised glory. Curiously, Calvin's very first theological work was devoted to the intermediate state.[122] In his *Psychopannychia* Calvin attempted to refute the Anabaptist view that souls separated from the body by death slept until the final judgment. According to Calvin, on dying the faithful enter immediately into the kingdom of God (cf. III.25.6). Wendel summarizes, "This rest is not a sleep; it is conscious, and the faithful are sharing in the Kingdom of God; but they will not be able to enter into the final glory until after the Judgment."[123]

The manner of resurrection is a mystery, and prickly speculations about thorny questions must be carefully avoided. Still, Calvin insists that the resurrection body is both the *same* and *different*. We are raised *in the same flesh* in which we died, but its quality is *different*. Obviously a fuller explanation of the relation of same and different would be helpful, but apparently this intellectual puzzle does not interest Calvin. He makes a distinction between body and soul and asserts that death is the severing of body and soul (III.25.8). Nevertheless, since both body and soul are of God, it is a monstrous error to "imagine that the souls will not receive the same bodies with which they are now clothed but will be furnished with new and different ones" (III.25.7). Christ "does not call forth new matter from the four elements to fashion men, but dead men from their graves" (III.25.7). With the assertion of the resurrection of the same flesh, Calvin is not attempting to explain the precise nature of same and different but to protect the necessary confessional identity of the sinner and his judgment. The one who is forgiven must be the same one who sinned. Thus, the atonement body and the resurrected body are not different. Of course, Calvin recognized the natural decay of the physical body after death, but in reference to three elements insisted, "Since God has all the elements ready at his bidding, no difficulty will

122. George H. Tavard, *The Starting Point of Calvin's Theology* (Grand Rapids: Wm. B. Eerdmans Publishing Company, 2000). This work is often translated "Sleep of the Soul" but παννυχίς indicates wakefulness. See Willem Balke, *Calvin and the Anabaptist Radicals*, trans. Willem Heynen (Grand Rapids: Eerdmans, 1981).

123. Wendel, *Calvin: The Origins and Development*, 287.

hinder his commanding earth, water, and fire to restore what they seem to have consumed" (III.25.8).

In addition to the insistence on same and different, Calvin also thought that the heavenly life would contain gradations. That is, everyone would *not* receive an equal measure of glory (III.25.10);[124] each person is specially treated. "In short, as Christ begins the glory of his body in this world with manifold diversity of gifts, and increases it by degrees, so also he will perfect it in heaven" (III.25.10).

Calvin's summary of the final resurrection indicates that Christ is present, the elect are consoled, and the reprobate are tormented. These tortures are figuratively expressed in Scripture by physical things such as darkness, weeping, gnashing of teeth, unquenchable fire and brimstone, the undying worm gnawing at the heart. However expressed, the essential condition of the reprobate is alienation from God, as Calvin paraphrases 2 Thessalonians 1:9: "The faithless 'shall suffer the punishment of eternal destruction, excluded from the presence of the Lord and from the glory of his might'" (III.25.12). Overwhelmed by God's marvelous grace, Calvin also maintains a strong conviction of God's stern judgment. Calvin recognizes that the Apostles' Creed mentions only the resurrection to life, but he asserts the resurrection to judgment as well—a subject uncongenial to modern taste. According to Calvin, "To be consumed by death would be a light punishment if they were not brought before the Judge . . . whose vengeance without end and measure they have provoked against themselves" (III.25.9).

The most thorough study of Calvin's doctrine of last things remains Heinrich Quistorp's. He observes that neither Luther nor Calvin produce "any coherent system of eschatology, but rather they treat the last things from time to time at relevant points in their scriptural exegesis and preaching and in their exposition of the creed (apart from the special polemical work of Calvin, the *Psychopannychia*)." The result of this neglect was disastrous since Protestant theology "became more and more de-eschatologized, or rather subjected to a perverse spiritualization and individualization of eschatology." Devoting major attention to the immortality of the soul and the general resurrection, Quistorp begins with an exposition of hope declaring that as Luther is the theologian of faith, Calvin is the theologian of hope.[125] Certainly Calvin points in this direction with his insistence that the goal of resurrection is the ineffable splendor of eternal happiness which is fulfilled when death is swallowed up in victory (III.25.10).

---

124. One of Dante's most spectacular effects in the *Paradiso* is the hierarchy of bliss contained in nine levels of heaven. Each person is supremely happy at the level attained, neither envying those above nor scorning those below. Piccarda Donati lives in the lowest order of Paradise, but her joy is complete and her contentment perfect. Dante asks, "Do you not desire to be in a more exalted place?" She answers, "Brother, our love quiets our wills and makes us desire only what we have and thirst for nothing else" (*The Divine Comedy of Dante Alighieri*, trans. Charles Eliot Norton [Chicago: William Benton, 1952], Canto III, 65, 70–72 paraphrased).

125. Quistorp, *Calvin's Doctrine*, 12, 11.

CONCLUSIONS TO BOOK III

The *Institutes* Book I expounds the knowledge of God the Creator and mainly discusses the doctrines of creation and providence. Book II concerns the knowledge of God the Redeemer chiefly in gospel and law, the two natures, and the three offices. Book III applies the benefits of Christ to faithful persons. This section is not anthropology but soteriology. In the context of the secret work of the Spirit, Calvin explains the crucial doctrine of faith as the principal work of the Holy Spirit, which includes sanctification and the Christian life, justification and Christian freedom, prayer and predestination. Book IV turns from these internal to the external means of grace: the church, the sacraments, and the civil government.

Book IV

The Faithful Community

INTRODUCTION TO BOOK IV

The final book of the *Institutes* concerns the community of the faithful, expounding the "outward helps [that] beget and increase faith within us, and advance it to its goal" (IV.1.11). These outward helps are discussed under the rubrics:

A. The order of the church, which emphasizes a doctrine of the variety of gifts which leads ultimately to the parity of believers and the parity of ministry (IV.1–13).

B. The sacraments of the church, in which Calvin's rejection of the Roman conception of seven sacraments points to a pathway diverging from the Catholics, Lutherans, and extreme Zwinglians, but he, like they, stumble over the cobblestones of the concept of substance (IV.14–19).

C. The church in relation to the state (IV.20). To my mind, and sadly, Calvin's conclusions on this subject are theologically comforting and practically dissatisfying.

Benjamin Milner claims that the special significance of Calvin's doctrine of the church is that we must think of the church "as the history of the restoration of order in the world." This order is to be understood "dialectically, as referring simultaneously to the Word and the Spirit." The created order, which was disordered by the fall, is restored by the creation of the church.[1] For Calvin the church is God's answer to the world's disorder. The modern assumption to the contrary looks at the world with an unblinking "I." Among the megatrends developed over the centuries since the sixteenth, "individualism" and its boon companion "diversity" stand out. From this observation platform the importance of community unity and loyalty is blurred and makes the context of belonging to and in the church, as expounded by Calvin, more difficult to appreciate and easier to amalgamate to modern concerns. For example, Ernst Troeltsch sees Calvinism as daughter to mother Lutheranism. In his central doctrine of predestination Calvin is regarded as Luther's pupil and offers "only the logical and systematic presentation of the fundamental element of Lutheran doctrine." This development leads to the second-leading Calvinistic idea, that of religious individualism. Lutheranism, according to Troeltsch, does not think out predestination to its ultimate consequence of the impossibility of losing God's grace and with the result that anxiety about salvation disappears. "The Calvinist knows that God's election cannot be lost, and will therefore have to direct his efforts, not to himself, but to the task of fashioning the world and the community after God's will. His obligation is not to hold to God, but, on the contrary, to be himself upheld by God." Troeltsch misapprehends Calvin's doctrine of eternal election in suggesting an individual may be isolated "in the time preceding the working out of his election." However, he is correct that the doctrine of predestination places the believer "into a fellowship which is mutually supporting, enduring, criticising, and improving, and such fellowship is, in every case, as in Israel's, defined to be a fellowship of the people."[2] Calvin's doctrine of the church and his conviction that union with Christ includes fellowship and service with other members of Christ's body refutes any strong notion of "reformed individualism."

For some recent thinkers Calvin's concern for the church is pushed aside in favor of his influence on social developments, especially democracy, and on economic developments, especially capitalism. In such studies the real interest is not Calvin's theology, but the impact (true or imagined) that his doctrine and its adherents had on the topic under consideration. According to Calvin, "The whole order of nature would be subverted, unless God preserved the church. For the creation of the world would serve no purpose if there were no people to call upon God" (Com. Ps. 115:17).

1. Benjamin Charles Milner Jr., *Calvin's Doctrine of the Church* (Leiden: E. J. Brill, 1970), 194–96, 4.
2. Ernst Troeltsch, "Calvin and Calvinism," *The Hibbert Journal* 8, no. 1 (October 1909): 104, 108–9, 119.

It is well to remember that Calvin was a pastor, as Benoit powerfully demonstrates. Writing under the ferocities, brutalities, and deprivations of World War II, Benoit shows Calvin concerned for the care of souls in similarly terrible times. Calvin's concern is evident in his letters to prisoners and martyrs brought low and to those born high like Edward VI, king of England; the formidable Jeanne d'Albret, queen of Navarre; and Admiral de Coligny, murdered during the Massacre of St. Bartholomew's Day. Additionally, Benoit treats doctrines such as prayer, divine providence, human depravity, and the Lord's Supper for their pastoral impact, emphasizing Calvin's authority and humility in the role of pastor— *la délicatesse de son âme.*[3]

"Pastoral care," as John Leith reminds us, "is not only comfort for the bereaved, forgiveness for the guilty, and help for the sick and needy; it is preeminently the renewal of life in the image of Christ."[4]

Calvin's doctrine of the church is irrefragable evidence that beliefs issue in behaviors. The life of faith requires a community of faith, and communal life requires structure. Indeed, according to some scholars, Calvin's greatest contribution was not narrowly theological but broadly organizational.[5] Calvin's organizational influence is undoubtedly real and important for interpreting him, but that focus produces a different book. The social implications and implementations of Calvin's theology is a massive subject, requiring a perspective of its own, but in the *Institutes* the church is Calvin's final, not first, subject.

Book IV can receive a briefer discussion here for three reasons. First, there is a dynamic and overlapping relationship between Book III concerned with faithful persons and Book IV concerned with faithful community. For example, the doctrine of eternal election applies to the chosen persons of Book III as well as the chosen people of Book IV. Likewise, church discipline is an application of the doctrine of sanctification, and so on. Doctrines such as prayer, worship, predestination, and Christian life expounded in Book III in more individual terms need not be pursued again in their more communal aspects.[6] Second, a great deal of Book IV is devoted to polemics against the Catholics, Lutherans, or Anabaptists. The details of Calvin's counterarguments need not be traced except where the controversy about truth is part of the presentation of truth. Third, while of a certain interest, the long historical disquisitions of Book IV need not be traced.

---

3. Jean-Daniel Benoit, *Calvin, Directeur d'ames: Contribution A l'Histoire De La Piété Réformée* (Strassbourg: Éditions Oberlin, 1947), 245.

4. John H. Leith, *An Introduction to the Reformed Tradition* (Atlanta: John Knox Press, 1977), 82. Leith discusses the differences among Presbyterian, Episcopal, and Congregational forms of church government in chap. 5.

5. See Williston Walker, *John Calvin, the Organizer of Reformed Protestantism 1509–1564* (New York: Schocken Books, 1969 [1906]).

6. In the royal quartos of his masterwork, *Jean Calvin*, Doumergue devotes vol. 4 to the topics of the *Institutes* Books I, II, III. Volume 5 deals at great length with the topics of Book IV.

A. THE ORDER OF THE CHURCH

Calvin's passionate commitment to the church is well expressed in this prayer:

> Grant, Almighty God that since thou hast at this time deigned in thy mercy
> to gather us to thy Church, and to enclose us within the boundaries of thy
> word, by which thou preservest us in the true and right worship of thy
> majesty,—O grant, that we may continue contented in this obedience to
> thee: and though Satan may, in many ways, attempt to draw us here and
> there, and we be also ourselves, by nature, inclined to evil, O grant, that
> being confirmed in faith, and united to thee by that sacred bond, we may
> yet constantly abide under the guidance of thy word, and thus cleave to
> Christ thy only-begotten Son, who has joined us for ever to himself, that we
> may never by any means turn aside from thee, but be, on the contrary, con-
> firmed in the faith of the gospel, until at length he will receive us all into his
> kingdom. Amen.[7]

Institutes Book III is a discussion of the faith by which we are united to Christ
and obtain salvation and eternal blessedness. Book IV treats the "outward helps"
needed to beget and increase faith. This new topic is a new occasion to emphasize anew that Christ is the foundation of the church (Com. I Cor. 3:11) and we
are united to him. Indeed, "unless he is united to us, the Son of God reckons
himself in some measure imperfect" (Com. Eph. 1:23). Once again Calvin
insists, "Our true completeness and perfection consists in our being united into
the body of Christ" (Com. Eph. 4:12). Moreover, "Apart from the body of Christ
and the fellowship of the godly, there can be no hope of reconciliation with
God. . . . It follows that strangers who separate themselves from the church have
nothing left for them but to rot amidst their curse" (Com. Is. 34:24). We are "the
spiritual and mystical body of Christ," which means there are different members
with different functions but all together are connected to form a unity (Com. I
Cor. 12:12). This union is to be understood so that "if we are to be true members of Christ, we grow into one body by the communication of his substance"
(Com. Eph. 5:30).

In full Trinitarian definition the church is the communion of saints composed
of all those "who, by the kindness of God the Father, through the working of the
Holy Spirit, have entered into fellowship with Christ" (IV.1.3). The church is
the divinely ordained fellowship in which Christ encounters the elect through
the ordinary means of Word and sacrament. According to Calvin, "The blessed
and happy state of the church always had its foundation in the person (*persona*)
of Christ" (II.6.2). "True completeness and perfection consists of our being
united into the body of Christ" (Com. Eph. 4:12). In this section, union with
Christ is emphasized not merely as individual but as a communal reality. "No
hope of future inheritance remains to us unless we have been united with all other

7. Preceding Com. Hos. 4:19.

members under Christ, our Head" (IV.1.2). The source of our communion (κοινωνία) with each other is based on "the fact that we are united to Christ so that 'we are flesh of his flesh and bone of his bones.'" Together we have communion with the blood of Christ when he ingrafts us into his body so he may live in us and we in him (Com. I Cor. 10:16). So intense is the union of head and body that Calvin illustrates it with a very violent image. The body dies when severed from the head "just as a man's life is ended when his throat is pierced or his heart mortally wounded" (IV.2.1).

In a similitude more gentle, Calvin describes life in the faithful community with a maternal illustration. "There is no other way to enter into life unless this mother conceive us in her womb, give us birth, nourish us at her breast, and lastly unless she keep us under her care and guidance until, putting off mortal flesh, we become like the angels. Our weakness does not allow us to be dismissed from her school until we have been pupils all our lives" (IV.1.4). Calvin agreed with Cyprian that one cannot have God for Father without the church as Mother (IV.1.2).

By reputation and in caricature John Calvin is a firm believer in decency and in order (1 Cor. 14:40). The proper ordering of the church—its government, its leaders, and its powers—is of paramount importance (IV.1.1). For our purposes three themes are raised: (1) the head and the body, including the role and divisions of ministry; (2) the true and the false, including the distinguishing marks of the church and their application. Finally, (3) the chosen and the responsible, including the maintenance of discipline among the elect.

1. The Head and the Body

The scriptural figure of head and body is central to Calvin's doctrine of the church. This twofold discrimination points to the mystery of union with Christ, but it also points to the distinction between divine and human being. Since Christ is head of the body, no mortal can arrogate any part of that role to himself. The headship of Christ is not transferable (IV.6.9). Geddes MacGregor rightly observes that Calvin invests the body of Christ with "immense significance."[8] The very life of the members of the body requires the head, but the church as the body of Christ is not the extension of the incarnation. In other words, ministry is a gifted service, best understood as the laity of all believers, rather than as an ordained status that could be understood as the priesthood of all or some believers. Put another way, Calvin distinguishes the gifts for office bearing in the church but he does not separate those who receive them from the

---

8. Geddes MacGregor, *Corpus Christi: The Nature of the Church according to the Reformed Tradition* (Philadelphia: Westminster Press, 1958), 53ff. According to J. A. T. Robinson, *The Body: A Study in Pauline Theology* (Chicago: Henry Regnery Co., 1952), 9, 50, the theological conception of body is distinctive to the apostle Paul. "One could say without exaggeration that the concept of the body forms the keystone of Paul's theology." He adds, "To say that individuals are members of a person is indeed a very violent use of language—and the context shows that Paul obviously meant it to be violent."

body where they are to be used. Allan Farris makes the interesting suggestion that, while taking Book IV into account, discovering Calvin's basic teaching on the laity requires study of Book III.[9]

Calvin emphasizes Christ's headship with both architectural and anatomical tropes. As part of an edifice complex, Calvin says Christ is a stone of stumbling, a rock of offense, and most especially the head of the corner or chief cornerstone. There is no building without this foundation (Com. I Pet. 2:7–8). Again, Christ is also head of the body. This metaphor denotes the highest authority and cannot be crassly applied to the pope (Com. Eph. 1:22). The pope cannot be head of the church because "the name of head is too noble to be transferred to any mortal man under any pretext, especially without the command of Christ" (Com. Col. 1:18). With the papacy one man sets himself against the head, placing himself apart and above the other members (Com. Eph. 4:15). Since the headship of Jesus Christ is not vested nor invested in any mortal, the Roman priestly hierarchy is denied in favor of equality of ministry determined not by a handheld sacrament of ordination, but by the divinely bestowed variety of God's gifts. "We are not just a civil society, but, having been ingrafted into the body of Christ, we really are members one of another. Therefore every one of us should realize that whatever his gift, it has been given to him for the upbuilding of all the brethren; and with that in mind he should devote it to the common good and not suppress it, burying it within himself so to speak, or use it as if it were his private possession" (Com. I Cor. 12:27).

Calvin believes orderly government is necessary in all ages (IV.3.8), but because of our weakness God equips the saints for the work of ministry through pastors who preach the heavenly doctrine (a subject already noted in the introduction). William Robinson claims that in asserting implicit faith to be deficient when it had been deemed sufficient for laypersons, Calvin made real faith the same for both clergy and laity. Faith in God requires explicit recognition of God's goodness, not implicit reliance on the faith of others. It is absurd to label real ignorance tempered by genuine humility as true faith. "For faith consists in the knowledge of God and Christ, not in reverence for the church" (III.2.2–3). He continues, "The two words *kleros* (clergy) and *laos* (laity) appear in the New Testament, but, strange to say, they denote the same people, not different peoples."[10] In other words, all Christians are God's laity and all Christians are God's clergy, but there is only one great high priest who has passed through the heavens; Jesus the Son of God and Christ "was made a High Priest forever" (Com. Heb. 5:4).

---

9. Allan L. Farris, "Calvin and the Laity," *Canadian Journal of Theology* 11, no. 1 (1965): 54–67, 62.

10. William Robinson, *Completing the Reformation: The Doctrine of the Priesthood of All Believers* (Lexington, KY: College of the Bible, 1955), 12, 17. See Hendrik Kraemer, *A Theology of the Laity* (Philadelphia: Westminster Press, 1958). Especially helpful is the chapter on the laity in history. Less successful, because less radically analyzed, is the situation of "clericalized laity" or "ordained lay persons."

Calvin rejected the sacramental ordination of priests as understood and practiced in the Roman tradition. Ordination is a sign of the dignity of the ministerial office in the church (IV.3.16), not a separate status. Ministry is a gifted function. The keys of the kingdom are not locked into the church and its clergy class but refer simply to the preaching of the gospel, and "with regard to men it is not so much power as service. For Christ has not given this power actually to men, but to his Word, of which he has made men ministers" (IV.11.1). I understand these statements to mean that humans do not *share* Christ's offices but *serve* them by proclaiming him.

According to Calvin the church's common ministry is best served by dividing some tasks into offices according to gifts. The *Draft Ecclesiastical Orders* of 1541 declare "four orders of office instituted by our Lord for the government of the church."[11] They consist of pastors, doctors, elders, and deacons. In the *Institutes* from 1543 onward, Calvin recommends three ministerial orders. The order of presbyters comprises pastors and doctors; the elders are charged with the censure of morals and the exercise of discipline; the deacons are committed to the care of the poor divided into those who distribute alms and those who care directly for the sick and poor (IV.4.1; IV.3.8–9).

The office of pastor "is to proclaim the Word of God, to instruct, admonish, exhort and censure, both in public and private; to administer the sacraments and to enjoin brotherly corrections along with the elders and colleagues." Among other things, calling to the office of pastor requires an examination in both doctrine and life. Pastors should maintain good doctrines and good habits. Leadership in the church requires skill in teaching based on profound learning. To be excluded is volubility without depth, defective utterance, insufficient mental ability, and those out of touch with ordinary people. Calvin advises persons without these gifts to go off and sing to themselves. Additionally, everyone is burdened with ordinary faults, but leaders should not "have a name that is held in infamy and besmirched by some scandalous disgrace" (Com. I Tim. 3:2).

The duty of doctors, the second order, is instruction of the faithful in true doctrine that the purity of the gospel not be perverted by ignorance or evil opinions. The office of doctor of the church developed in connection with the rise of universities. Calvin sees the doctoral ministry in connection with Christ's office of prophet. "For as our teachers correspond to the ancient prophets, so do our pastors to the apostles" (IV.3.5). Calvin acknowledges some interpreters think pastors and doctors are the same office and agrees to some extent but still maintains that the two offices should not be confounded. Doctors needed a superior knowledge of Scripture; a knowledge of languages, the humanities, and sound doctrine; but they had no liturgical, homiletical, pastoral, sacramental, or disciplinary responsibilities. Calvin taught, "Teaching is the duty of all pastors; but there is a particular gift of interpreting Scripture so that sound doc-

11. *Calvin: Theological Treatises*, trans. J. K. S. Reid (Philadelphia: Westminster Press, 1954), 58.

trine may be kept and a man may be a doctor who is not fitted to preach" (Com. Eph. 4:11).[12]

Calvin notes that all who govern in the church are called presbyters, which includes pastors and elders (Com. Jas. 5:14). Nevertheless, the third order, that of ruling elder, consists of those who are not charged with preaching but are elected to join with pastors in the spiritual government of the church (IV.11.1). "Their office is to have oversight in the life of everyone, to admonish amicably those whom they see to be erring or to be living a disordered life, and where it is required, to enjoin fraternal corrections themselves and along with others." They should be "of good and honest life, without reproach and beyond suspicion, and above all fearing God and possessing spiritual prudence."[13] In session with the pastors, elders have the duty to exclude from fellowship "manifest adulterers, fornicators, thieves, robbers, seditious persons, perjurers, false witnesses," and so on (IV.12.4).

The diaconate is the fourth order of ministry and sometimes the nursery from which presbyters are chosen (Com. I Tim. 3:13). The deacons were to care for the poor and sick. According to Calvin, there were two kinds of deacons in the ancient church. The first received, disbursed, or held goods for the sake of the poor. The second cared directly for the poor. The former are characterized by simplicity, that is, faithful administration; the latter by cheerfulness, "that they may not, as very often happens, spoil the services which they render by their morose attitude" (Com. Rom. 12:8).

Calvin grants that the saints could be made perfect in one moment, but God wills that they should grow in the church and by way of these offices to be taught through human means (IV.1.5). Troeltsch correctly observes that "all offices are duties, but none are privileges."[14] Salvation is the work of God, but since God chooses to employ ministers and preaching "as his instruments for that purpose, he ascribes to them what is his, so joining the power of his Spirit with the activity of man" (Com. Gal. 4:19). The pastor, as a humble servant of the Word, is God's ambassador and mouth, to be received as an angel and as Christ himself (Com. Gal. 4:14). The offices in the church are connected to gifts for the church, and the church is ruled by the preaching of the Word. "That we have ministers of the Gospel is [Christ's] gift; that they excel in necessary gifts is his gift; that they execute the trust committed to them, is likewise his gift" (Com. Eph. 4:11). The ministry of reconciliation is not an exclusive assignment, but it is a most remarkable description of the role of ministers sent as messengers to declare God's goodwill toward us. Other persons can certainly bear witness to God's grace, but it is a special duty of ministers (Com. II Cor. 5:18). Calvin claims earthly teachers are doubly useful since they test our obedience and calm our anxiety. Otherwise, we might be driven away if God thundered at us directly (IV.1.5). In the meantime those who in a teachable spirit attend to ministers ordained by God are properly edified.

12. Robert W. Henderson, *The Teaching Office in the Reformed Tradition: A History of the Doctoral Ministry* (Philadelphia: Westminster Press, 1962), 16–31.

13. Ibid., 63.

14. Troeltsch, "Calvin and Calvinism," 120.

Rejecting the Roman view of hierarchy and priesthood, Calvin does not employ the phrase "priesthood of all believers."[15] According to Wilhelm Pauck, with his doctrine of the priesthood of all believers Luther subducted the distinction between clergy and laity, but the conception of ministry made the parity of believers difficult to maintain.[16] Niesel suggests that "the notion of the priesthood of all believers too easily misunderstood as the common possession of all the necessary gifts, is not Calvin's view."[17] Calvin's emphasis is rather on the diversity of gifts which are so distributed that each person has a limited portion (Com. Rom. 12:6). Not everyone is equally endowed (IV.8.11), but all gifts are to be used for the common good (Com. I Cor. 12:4). The ability to lead others is itself a good gift of God. "The political distinction of ranks is not to be rejected, for natural reason itself dictates this for the purpose of eliminating confusion; but whatever shall have this object in view will be so arranged that it may neither obscure the glory of Christ, nor serve tyranny or ambition, nor prevent the cultivation among the ministers of brotherhood with equal liberties and rights" (Com. Num. 3:5).

The parity of ministers suggests the parity of believers: "For we who are defiled in ourselves, yet are priests in him, offer ourselves and our all to God, and freely enter the heavenly sanctuary that the sacrifices of prayers and praise that we bring may be acceptable and sweet-smelling before God" (II.15.6). The note accompanying this text in LCC declares that Calvin's comments on the priesthood of all believers, while rare and unsystematic, are substantially the same as Luther's view. On the contrary, I think Calvin's comments lead in the direction of the laity of all believers in service of the one great high priest, Jesus Christ. Interestingly there are questions about Calvin's own ordination. Calvin functioned as a pastor, but "neither Beza nor Colladon ever uses any form of the words *ordination* or *consecration* to describe Calvin's admittance to the office of pastor."[18] Additionally, the Reformed modesty about priestly claims for its clergy is reflected in its unwillingness to accept the deification of its members as earlier discussed.

2. The True and the False

According to McNeill, "No writer has ever extolled the Holy Catholic Church with greater zeal than Calvin."[19] Calvin thought, "Schism is the worst and most

15. G. D. Henderson, "Priesthood of Believers," *Scottish Journal of Theology* 7 (1954): 6. T. F. Torrance, *Royal Priesthood: A Theology of Ordained Ministry*, 2nd ed. (Edinburgh: T. & T. Clark, 1993), xv, 35.

16. Wilhelm Pauck, "The Ministry in the Time of the Continental Reformation," in *The Ministry in Historical Prespectives*, ed. H. Richard Niebuhr and Daniel D. Williams (New York: Harper and Brothers, 1956), 112.

17. Wilhelm Niesel, *The Theology of Calvin*, 1st ed., trans. Harold Knight (Philadelphia: Westminster Press, 1956), 203. John R. Crawford, "Calvin and the Priesthood of All Believers," *Scottish Journal of Theology* 21 (1968): 145–56, thinks Niesel oversimplifies.

18. Farris, "Calvin and the Laity," 55, 56.

19. John T. McNeill, "Calvin as an Ecumenical Churchman," *Church History* 32, no. 4 (December 1963): 379–91, 380.

harmful evil in the church of God" (Com. Jn. 9:16). It "is always disastrous to leave the church" (IV.1.4). In fact, "separation from the church is the denial of God and Christ" (IV.1.10). Therefore, Calvin insisted that the Protestants were reformers of the church, not its deformers. Calvin asserts against Cardinal Sadolet "that all we have attempted has been to renew the ancient form of the church, which, at first distorted and stained by illiterate men of indifferent character, was afterwards criminally mangled and almost destroyed by the Roman pontiff and his faction."[20] Union with Christ requires the hearts of all believers to be united in his praise and their tongues joined in harmony. God "will not allow his glory to be sounded amid discord and controversy" (Com. Rom. 15:5). For this reason no church should be turned in on itself. "On the contrary, all of them should be extending the right hand to each other, to promote their fellowship with each other . . . as the concern for unity demands" (Com. I Cor. 14:36).

Given the necessity for real unity, it becomes imperative to distinguish between the true and the false church. The true church is found "wherever we see the Word of God purely preached and heard, and the sacraments properly administered [and, presumably, received] according to Christ's institution, there it is not to be doubted, a church of God exists" (IV.1.9).[21] Calvin explains his doctrines of Word and sacrament at great length, but applying them to a church is difficult. According to Calvin the Scripture uses the term "church" in two ways, sometimes referring to the invisible church seen only by God and sometimes to the visible church seen by us. In this latter "are mingled many hypocrites who have nothing of Christ but the name and outward appearance" (IV.1.7). However, since our judgment is limited in scope it must be charitable in application. We should "recognize as members of the church those who, by confession of faith, by example of life, and by partaking of the sacraments, profess the same God and Christ with us" (IV.1.8). In this world we cannot expect a church without blemish which satisfies our standards. "The point is that anyone who is obsessed by that idea, must cut himself off from everybody else, and appear to himself to be the only saint in the world, or he must set up a sect of his own with other hypocrites" (Com. I Cor. 1:2). So long as the marks of the true church are recognizable, while not perfectly, the church cannot be rejected "even if it otherwise swarms with many faults" (IV.1.12). In a letter of January 13, 1555, Calvin writes to the English exiles in Frankfurt, "In the Anglican liturgy, such as you describe it to me, I see there were many silly things. [However] if there lurked under them no manifest impiety [they are] to be endured for a time."

At this point Calvin again appeals to the useful but difficult distinction between fundamental and nonfundamental beliefs already noted as the third part of Christian freedom. Calvin clearly applies the notion of adiaphora to ethical and ceremonial matters. Of the former he mentions as indifferent the eating of

20. To Sadolet, in *Selected Works of John Calvin, Tracts*, ed. and trans. Henry Beveridge (Grand Rapids: Baker Book House, 1983 [1844]), 231.

21. For a helpful summary, especially on the marks, see G. S. M. Walker, "Calvin and the Church," *Scottish Journal of Theology* 16 (1963): 371–89.

meat, the use of holidays and vestments, dinner napkins and pocket handker-chiefs, white and black bread, sweet and flat wine, fresh and impure water. The latter refers to Roman ceremonies that are human inventions become supersti-tions and condemned by Scripture and Christ himself (IV.10, esp. IV.10.22). Additionally, it is indifferent whether the Lord's Table is set with leavened or unleavened bread, red or white wine (IV.17.43).[22]

Calvin is not so clear about indifferent doctrines which being only partially true are not exactly false. Calvin might have regarded some ideas as indifferent not merely in use but in reality (metaphysical adiaphora). Additionally, there might be ideas that humans must regard as indifferent because no one is able to deter-mine their truth or falsity (epistemological adiaphora). However, Calvin does not consider these options. Predictably he objects to including the doctrines of Trin-ity, predestination, and free grace as *choses indifférentes*.[23] The category of doctri-nal adiaphora is not exactly the same issue as fundamental versus nonessential doctrines. Nevertheless, Calvin charges Melanchthon with extending "the dis-tinction of nonessentials (*res medias et indifferentes*) too far. Several of those things which you consider indifferent are obviously repugnant to the word of God."[24] Although on such issues as predestination and free will Calvin seems to have exer-cised a certain charity and forbearance, and in spite of the fact that Calvin has the highest regard for Melanchthon's scholarship[25] and cherishes his friendship, Calvin's perception of truth here denies Melanchthon the right to decide on things indifferent. In his heart Calvin seems to believe that no doctrine that he consid-ers certain and important could ever be regarded as anything less than true.

This confidence makes Calvin's refusal to identify one essential doctrine or one set of essential doctrines a crucial factor in understanding the application of the marks of the true church. Calvin says that any society that has a pure min-istry of the Word and a pure celebration of the sacraments may be safely embraced as church. However, he immediately qualifies this comment by insisting that faults which damage the purity of Word and sacrament ought not to estrange us from communion with those in a defective church. The reason for continuing fellowship is that "not all the articles of true doctrine are of the same sort." Some doctrines are more necessary to know than others. In contrast to these necessary doctrines, some disputed doctrines, such as the place of the soul after death, are nonessential matters and do not break the unity of faith. In addition to recog-nizing the category of "nonessential doctrines," Calvin also apparently means that not all true doctrine is essential doctrine. In other words, some true doctrines are more fundamental than other true doctrines!

22. See T. W. Street, "John Calvin on Adiaphora: An Exposition," doctoral dissertation, Union Theological Seminary, 1954. Also, E. F. Meylan, "The Stoic Doctrine of Indifferent Things . . . ," *Romantic Review* 8 (1937): 135–45.

23. Letter of February 20, 1555. *Letters of John Calvin*, ed. Jules Bonnet, trans. Marcus Robert Gilchrist (Grand Rapids: Baker Book House, 1983 [1858]).

24. Letter of June 18, 1550.

25. The three treatieses against Westphal are cited from volume 2 of *Selected Works of John Calvin*, ed. and trans. Henry Beveridge (Grand Rapids: Baker Book House, 1983 [1849]), 3.354.

Then Calvin offers examples of what he means by "the proper principles of religion." They are: "[1] God is one; [2] Christ is God and the Son of God; [3] our salvation rests in God's mercy; [4] and the like" (IV.1.12–13). This summary ends with the remarkably vague imprecision of "and the like." In the Commentary on 1 Corinthians he seems to expand this comment. The Corinthians "held on to the fundamental doctrine (*doctrina fundamentalis*)—[1] the One God was worshiped by them and [2] was invoked in the name of Christ—[3] they rested their confidence of salvation in Christ, and [4] they had a ministry that was not wholly corrupt" (Com. I Cor. 3:12). The fourth phrase is new and might replace "and the like" in the previous formulation. If so, the *Institutes* is an extended exposition of these heads of doctrine. Book I teaches that "God is one." That Christ is God and the Son of God is explained in Book II. Book III develops the theme that our salvation rests in God's mercy, and true ministry is the subject of Book IV.

Calvin's main concern in this discussion of true and false is to avoid the scandal of schism, warning that those who are "imbued with a false conviction of their own perfect sanctity" should not lightly spurn the society of those they judge less holy (IV.1.13). At the same time those "who lead a filthy and infamous life may not be called Christians, to the dishonor of God, as if his holy church were a conspiracy of wicked and abandoned men" (IV.12.5).

3. The Chosen and the Responsible

Calvin's doctrine of the Christian church, like that of the Christian person, is an extension of his communal and individual confession of union with Christ. By metonymy, confession stands for faith (Com. Heb. 4:14) and faith and election stand together as God's gifts uniting the head and the body. Calvin begins by explaining that the communion of saints means the church "stands by God's election, and cannot waver or fail any more than his eternal providence can" (IV.1.3). "We must leave to God alone the knowledge of his church, whose foundation is his eternal election" (IV.1.2), but we are to understand "that from the creation of the world there was no time when the Lord did not have his church" (IV.1.17). With these statements in place, unless he intends to deny Calvin's theology entirely, it is difficult to follow Geddes MacGregor's judgment, "There is no doubt that Calvin was methodologically in error when he so closely tied his doctrine of the church to his predestinarian doctrines."[26] More correctly and to the contrary, Ray Petry asserts, "Calvin felt that the vitality of this '*communio sanctorum*' was heightened not impaired by the doctrine of predestination. . . . The doctrine of election, as Calvin saw it, did not paralyze action but inspired it."[27] The grace of God issuing in the gift of faith and resulting in union with Christ would be impossible to understand without the provision of a fellowship of support.

---

26. MacGregor, *Corpus Christi*, 48.

27. Ray C. Petry, "Calvin's Conception of the 'Communio Sanctorum,'" *Church History* 5 (1936): 227–38, 229, 231.

Having praised God's grace in choosing members of the body of Christ and identified the marks by which the company of the faithful can distinguish the true church from the false, Calvin turns to the responsibilities of the chosen. Benoit calls divine sovereignty and human responsibility, "la grande antinomie calvinienne."[28] This grand antinomy is illustrated by the application of discipline. Being chosen does not mean sitting on a throne; it means going to work. While God protects his church, the faithful are expected to do their part. The same dynamic found between justification and sanctification appears between the chosen people and their obedience. Calvin writes to Sadolet that there are three things necessary for the safety of the church: doctrine, discipline, and sacraments, to which a fourth should be added—ceremonies that exercise the people in proper piety.[29] Proper piety, the fourth necessity, requires proper hearing of the Word of God. It does not involve the practice of wandering from station to station contemplating idols. Calvin thinks so many crosses of wood, stone, silver, and gold erected here and there in churches only blind the eye to the light of the world (I.11.7). Doctrine is primarily a matter of belief; discipline and ceremony are primarily matters of behavior; and the sacraments are both. All are important for the upbuilding of the church.

According to Calvin, "As the saving doctrine of Christ is the soul of the church, so does discipline serve as its sinews" (IV.12.1). Sound discipline is an appendix to true teaching (Com. Mt. 18:18). Nevertheless, Calvin does not include discipline as a third mark of the church, although discipline is so marked by the Scots Confession (art. 18) and the Belgic Confession (art. 29). Church discipline serves three purposes. First, it excludes from the holy church those who lead a filthy and infamous life in order that God not be dishonored. Second, good people should not be corrupted by constant commerce with the wicked. Third, those who come under discipline should be led to repent and amend their lives (IV.12.5).

Calvin once described the work of pastors in a threefold formulation. First, they must instruct the people in pure doctrine. Second, they must administer the sacred mysteries, and third, they must keep and administer upright discipline (IV.3.6). For the exposition of discipline he divides the church into two orders: clergy and people, defining clergy as those who perform public ministry in the church (IV.12.1). All should submit to the common discipline, but it is appropriate that gentler discipline apply to laity and stronger discipline to clergy as leaders in the church. However, many of the rules in effect among the Papists—such as priestly celibacy—are harmful innovations repugnant to Scripture (IV.12.22–23). Church discipline should be properly exercised to obviate scandal, but the church, while not perfect, is holy if it is daily advancing toward that goal (IV.1.17). "Neither the vices of the few nor the vices of the many in any way prevent us from duly professing our faith there in ceremonies ordained by God.

28. Benoit, *Calvin, Directeur d'ames*, 83–84.
29. To Sadolet, *Calvin's Tracts*, 38.

For a godly conscience is not wounded by the unworthiness of another, whether pastor or layman, nor are the sacraments less pure and salutary for a holy and upright man because they are handled by unclean persons" (IV.1.19).[30] In short, our own imperfections indicate the need for forgiveness.

Thomas Hall seems hot under the spleen about Calvin's view of the church. According to Hall, Calvin's church is no democracy of believers but a divine organization for ruling thoughts and conduct. The glory of Protestant ethics is founded by Luther and developed by Kant. For "Calvin the soul finds out which church has the sacrament and the word and submits wholly to it."[31] To my mind Calvin's presentation of the ministry of Christ and his people, his remarks on the marks of the church, and his gentle application of church discipline are sensible, kindly, loving, and grace-full.

B. THE SACRAMENTS OF THE CHURCH

The threads that held together the church's sacramental theology were already unraveling before Calvin entered the fray. Nevertheless, with his doctrine Calvin hoped to bring concord from discord, requiring first an exposition of sacramental reality and then an explanation of the relation of that view to the Romans, the Zwinglians, and the Lutherans. As one would expect, Calvin's discussion of the sacraments brings fresh encounters with old themes such as the mystery of God's revelation, faith, the work of the Holy Spirit, spiritual flesh (or glorious body), Holy Spirit, and most emphatically union with Christ. According to Calvin, that we are members of his flesh, and of his bones, is not exaggeration but simple truth. "If we are to be the true members of Christ, we grow into one body by the communication of his substance. In short, Paul describes our union to Christ, a symbol and pledge of which is given to us in the holy supper. . . . Paul declares that we are of the members and bones of Christ" (Com. Eph. 5:30). Again, Christ is the fountain from which our life flows. "The Father is the origin of life, but the fountain from which we must draw it is Christ." As Christ "is the unique image of the invisible God, as he is the only interpreter of the Father, as he is the only guide of life, indeed, as he is the life, the light of the world and the truth, we necessarily vanish away into our own inventions so soon as we depart from him." By our engrafting into Christ we are made one with God (Com. I Jn. 5:20). Even in such passionate and foundational confessions of faith concerning union with Christ, Calvin understandably employs, and then fatally attempts to explain sacramental reality in the common transactional currency of "the communication of

30. The concept that the pure ordinances of the church are not damaged by the impure character of the officiating minister is difficult to explain convincingly to a new bride, eyes choked with tears, who has just learned that the pastor who performed her wedding ceremony was a long-term adulterer.

31. Thomas C. Hall, "Was John Calvin a Reformer or a Reactionary?" *The Hibbert Journal* 6, no. 1 (October 1907): 173, 180.

his substance." As confession, Calvin's eucharistic doctrine is extremely helpful, but as explanation is very difficult if not totally useless, a condition shared by all the sectaries of the century.

Concepts like substance, presence, and participation—crucial here—were also central to other discussions such as deification and justification. New themes include the relation of the "sacraments" of the Old with the New Covenants, the relation of the invisible Word: living (in Jesus Christ), and spoken (in preaching)—with the visible Word: written (in Scripture), and exhibited (in the sacraments). Among the many complexities are the questions of the absolute or relative necessity of the sacraments for Christian life, the definition of true and real; of sacrament and sacramental; of Eucharist (the sacrament) and eucharistic (thanksgiving); of sacrifice, sign, seal, symbol, figure, instrument, pledge; of commemoration and communion; the relation of proclamation to sacrament; and the meaning and value of Calvin's doctrinal development. In these fathomless depths the twists and turns of themes can be glimpsed but cannot be fully pursued.

Calvin defines a sacrament as "an outward sign by which the Lord seals on our consciences the promises of his good will toward us in order to sustain the weakness of our faith; and we in turn attest our piety toward him in the presence of the Lord and his angels and before men" (IV.14.1). The same point is made by Augustine, who teaches that a sacrament is "a visible sign of an invisible grace."[32] This aspect is sometimes called "objective." These signs of God are also exercises of our piety, and thus denominated "subjective."[33] Together they represent sublime and spiritual realities which the Latins call "sacraments," the Greeks call "mysteries" (IV.14.2), and the Hebrews call "covenants" (IV.14.6). Since God's promises precede the sacraments, the latter are appendices of the gospel, serving the purpose of confirming and sealing the promises.

According to Calvin, God gave various signs to assure believers, such as the tree of life for Adam and Eve (Gen. 2), the rainbow for Noah (Gen. 9), the smoking fire pot for Abraham (Gen. 15), the wet and dry fleece for Gideon (Judg. 6),

---

32. On signs, see Christopher Elwood, *The Body Broken: The Calvinist Doctrine of the Eucharist and the Symbolization of Power in Sixteenth-Century France* (New York: Oxford University Press, 1999). As the subtitle indicates, Elwood is interested in the eucharist as "one focal religious symbol [contributing] to the birth, nurture, and full flowering of social and political revolution" (3). The eucharist is important, he says, because it "was the central symbol defining power in the late medieval and early modern periods" (4). Calvin's contribution was "a radically new interpretation of the way in which the signs of the eucharist operated" (5). The single chapter devoted exclusively to Calvin on the Lord's Supper deals also with its propaganda purpose and effect.

33. B. A. Gerrish, "Calvin's Eucharistic Piety," in *Calvin and Spirituality*, ed. David Foxgrover (Grand Rapids: Calvin Studies Society, 1995), 57, makes the important and convincing point that Calvin's piety is not predestinarian but eucharistic. Gerrish's "Sign and Reality: The Lord's Supper in the Reformed Confessions," *The Old Protestantism and the New: Essays on the Reformation Heritage* (Chicago: University of Chicago Press, 1982), 122–23, states that both Zwingli and Calvin made a distinction between sign and reality (to avoid their merging as in Roman Catholicism and Lutheranism), but Zwingli sees a difference between sign and reality. Calvin's position is "the exact opposite of Zwingli's: "*because* a sacrament is a sign, *therefore* it bestows what it signifies." The main point of this intriguing essay is to suggest three types of eucharistic theology in the Reformed Confessions: Zwingli's, Calvin's, and Bullinger's.

circumcision (Gen. 17), the cloud and sea, the spiritual rock (1 Cor. 10:1–5), and so on. These signs may be called sacramental, but the ordinary means of grace are the two sacraments established by the Lord (IV.14.19). The Lord's Supper is the sign and seal of our *sanctification* in Christ through the work of the Holy Spirit, and Baptism is the sign and seal of our *justification* before God in Christ.

Christ's baptism was a visible symbol of his kingly anointing for the purpose of standing among us "to lead us little by little to a firm union with God" (II.15.5). "Baptism is the sacrament of faith." Therefore, in his doctrine of Trinity, he connects God, faith, and baptism. The faithful are baptized into the name of the Father, Son, and Spirit (I.13.16). Baptism, he continues, is a mystery (IV.16.1), but in baptism "we are buried together with Christ, so that we may become dead to the world and to the flesh, and may live to God" (Com. I Pet. 3:21). Baptism is our engrafting into the body of Christ so that we are joined together to live in him (1 Cor. 12:13). We become one with him and also grow up into the body of Christ (Com. Rom. 6:3). Again, "Baptism is the once-for-all sign of the initiation by which we are received into the society of the church, in order that engrafted in Christ, we may be reckoned among God's children" (IV.15.1). This initiation both declares our faith in the engrafting and makes our confession of it before others. In the sacrament "God affirms his grace to us with this sealing, so those who offer themselves for baptism in turn ratify their faith, as if by appending their signature" (Com. Mt. 28:19). Baptism is not a "christening," if that means simply a human service of baby naming. Baptism is a recognition of the divine *incorporation* into the holy triune name—the new covenant with Christ, our high priest, in his own blood made visible (Com. Heb. 9:11, 12, 15). Baptism brings three things: (1) a sign and symbol of our cleansing (IV.14.3); (2) a sign and symbol of our engrafting into the death and life in Christ (IV.14.5); and (3) a testimony to our union with Christ. In short, "all the gifts of God proffered in baptism are found in Christ alone" (IV.15.6). As Niesel correctly observes, "The first two of these gifts depend wholly upon the third."[34]

Over time sacramental action becomes customary and its meaning traditional. If Calvin had been less anxious about admitting the role of tradition and the power of practice, his weak reasons for infant baptism might be more consonant with his strong convictions.[35] As it is, the long chapter (IV.16) defending the practice against the Anabaptists cites an anagogy with circumcision in the covenant of promise (IV.16.1). Additionally, Christ's blessing of little children indicates the duty of the church to provide a parent with the opportunity "to

---

34. Niesel, *Theology of Calvin*, 220.

35. Calvin thinks devotion demands decorum. Behaviors toward sacred things should exhibit modesty, piety, and reverence—not "trifling pomps which have nothing but fleeting splendor" (IV.10.29). The best guide is the nourishment of mutual love. Religion does not consist in a woman's shawl. If a woman rushes off in such haste to help a neighbor "she does not offend if she runs to her with head uncovered" (IV.10.31). Additionally, if a cool head gets cold, there is nothing wrong if the preacher first uncovers his head to obey Paul's injunction and then puts his skullcap back on so as not to catch cold (Com. I Cor. 11:4). The rule of modesty and the established custom of the region dictate what is to be done in such matters.

mark his child with the symbol of the covenant" (IV.16.9).[36] Dealing with the Ethiopian eunuch, Calvin grants that adults are ingrafted by faith, but the children of the godly are born children of the church because Our Father is also their Father (Com. Acts 8:37). To become heirs of life we must have communion with Christ (IV.16.17), and while young children may not have obvious understanding of, or faith in, the mystery of spiritual regeneration, they may, if it please God, receive "a tiny spark at the present time [which God] will illuminate in the future with the full splendor of his light" (IV.16.19).[37] In this way the cleansing of baptism asserts forgiveness of sins not only past but present and future, meaning that while we cannot presume on God's indulgence toward sin, we can have confidence in God's mercy.

Calvin locates the mystery of baptism and Eucharist in the work of the Holy Spirit. "If the Spirit be lacking, the sacraments can accomplish nothing more in our minds than the splendor of the sun shining upon blind eyes, or a voice sounding in deaf ears" (IV.14.9). The power is in the Spirit not the sacrament. While the reality and truth are joined to the sign in that God chooses to work by outward means, nonetheless "we obtain only as much as we receive in faith" (IV.15.15). Faith, of course, has been defined as the principal work of the Holy Spirit (III.1.4). As Egil Grislis points out, the sacraments are instruments in God's hand. They are not to be identified with substance in the Catholic sense nor with symbol in the Zwinglian sense.[38]

Calvin emphasizes that the proclamation of the Word and the celebration of the sacraments belong together as the ordinary means of grace, but their exact relation is a question Calvin never answers satisfactorily. Calvin declares the two sacraments are *another* aid to our faith. The primary aid is the Word (preached and heard) and the secondary aid is the sacraments (administered and received). In the Genesis Commentary he writes, "The preaching of the gospel is called the kingdom of heaven, and the sacraments may be called the gate of heaven, because they admit us into the presence of God" (28:17). In themselves the sacraments do not contain and cannot confer grace since nothing is offered "through the sacraments [other] than what is offered by God's word and received by [the

---

36. François Wendel, *Calvin: The Origins and Development of His Religious Thought*, trans. Philip Mairet (New York: Harper and Row, 1963), 328, dismissively declares, "Since it was not possible for [Calvin] to adduce a single New Testament passage containing a clear allusion to infant baptism, he had to be content with indirect references and analogies drawn from circumcision and Christ's blessing of the children."

37. For a major essay on a minor topic, see Barbara Pitkin, "'The Heritage of the Lord': Children in the Theology of John Calvin," in *The Child in Christian Thought*, ed. Marcia J. Bunge (Grand Rapids: Wm. B. Eerdmans, 2001), who concludes, "Calvin, like many intellectuals and reformers of his day, was intensely interested in children and child rearing" (162). Unlike "his own spiritual descendant, Friedrich Schleiermacher," Calvin does not idealize the faith of children but "he did consider the youngest infants capable of not merely manifesting but indeed *proclaiming* God's glory" (164, emphasis in original).

38. Egil Grislis, "Calvin's Doctrine of Baptism," *Church History* 31 (1962): 54. Grislis thinks the consistency of Calvin's doctrine of baptism requires reinterpretation of the doctrine of election, which "is a very central theme of Calvin's thought" (57).

believer] in true faith" (IV.14.14). "For we know that justification is lodged in Christ alone, and that it is communicated to us no less by the preaching of the Gospel than by the seal of the sacrament, and without the latter can stand unimpaired" (IV.14.14). Nevertheless, since we are of the flesh, our faith is feeble and would fall except that our merciful Lord "condescends to lead us to himself even by these earthly elements, and to set before us in the flesh a mirror of spiritual blessings" (IV.14.3). Again, "The sacraments have the same office as the Word of God" (IV.14.17). The sacraments are appendages to the preaching of the gospel (Com. II Cor. 5:18). They have no hidden power in themselves to confer the grace of God upon us. Of themselves sacraments do not bestow grace, but they testify to it.

The sacrament of baptism is defined as the initiatory sign and seal of the ingrafting of the faithful into the triune name of God. More difficult is the question of the eucharistic contribution to the reality of union in Christ. Should the eating of Christ's flesh be understood as a metaphor for the "spiritual reception" of believing?

When Calvin declares the Lord's Supper to be "an appendage of the Gospel" (see IV.14.3), Gerrish gently chides him for a description applied "a little misleadingly."[39] The sacraments as "inferior aids" sound Zwinglian and lead Wendel to conclude that they possess a "secondary and supplementary character," thus excluding "any essential union between the sacramental elements and grace."[40] However, Calvin rejects Zwingli's view of bare commemoration in favor of real communion, which seems to require an additional gift. Calvin says, "If it is true that a visible sign is shown to us to seal the gift of something invisible, we should accept the symbol of the body and assuredly trust that the body itself is also no less given to us" (Com. I Cor. 10:16). Gerrish summarizes, "Whatever changes there may have been over the years in Calvin's sacramental theology, he does not seem to have wavered on this cardinal point: the holy banquet is a sign and pledge of union with Christ."[41] Still, "Calvin insists that we do not merely recall Christ's benefits in the supper: we actually receive them. The supper is a gift, it does not merely remind us of a gift. The crucified Lord is the risen Lord who invites us to his table and bids us receive: 'Take, eat, this is my body.'"[42]

The main and continuing disagreements with Calvin's teaching, Gerrish suggests, swim around his concept of the efficacy of sacramental signs and the sacramental presence of Christ's body and blood. There is well-nigh acclamatory agreement on the main point that union with Christ is at the heart of Calvin's eucharistic piety, but the most formidable difficulty may be phrased as

39. Gerrish, *Grace and Gratitude: The Eucharistic Theology of John Calvin* (Minneapolis: Fortress Press, 1993, 158.
40. Wendel, *Calvin: The Origins and Development*, 312, 316.
41. Ibid., 133. Kilian McDonnell, *John Calvin, the Church, and the Eucharist* (Princeton, NJ: Princeton University Press, 1967), devotes chap. 5 to union with Christ as a sacramental and ecclesiastical concern.
42. B. A. Gerrish, "John Calvin and the Reformed Doctrine of the Lord's Supper," *McCormick Quarterly* 22, no. 2 (January 1969): 93.

understanding "the life-giving flesh of Christ,"[43] which is clearly illustrated in this confusing explanation made more difficult with its appeal to substance: "Though I confess that our souls are truly fed by the substance of Christ's flesh, I . . . repudiate the substantial presence which Westphal imagines. . . . The flesh of Christ gives us life, [but] it does not follow that his substance must be transferred into us. This fiction of transfusion being taken out of the way, it never came into my mind to raise a debate about the term substance. . . . By the secret virtue of the Holy Spirit life is infused into us from the substance of his flesh."[44]

In his fine study tracing Calvin's sacramental theology from the *Institutes* of 1536 to 1559, Thomas J. Davis opposes the view that sees no important modifications of doctrine between 1536 and 1559 despite the obvious development in both size and content. According to Davis, Calvin's eucharistic teaching was ambiguous in 1536, but by 1559, as the result of years of exegetical work and controversies, he had "developed concepts of the life-giving flesh of Christ and the work of the Holy Spirit in joining Christ and the Christian." In support Davis analyzes the complicated concept of substance, which he thinks Calvin denies in 1536 and affirms in 1559, concluding that the changes between 1536 and 1559 are important improvements. If the concept of substance is misleading, as I think, its development should be understood as an unnecessary obfuscation.

According to Davis, "What Calvin holds at the beginning of his career as a doctrine of the Eucharist is but a starting point for much determined and dedicated intellectual and spiritual endeavor." Chiefly, Calvin "goes from denying substantial partaking [of Christ] to strongly affirming it, linking that participation in the body of Christ to the very means of salvation." This substantial partaking signifies that "the Christian is joined to Christ himself, as mediator, which means in the flesh in which he won salvation for his church." Davis concludes, "By the time of the 1559 *Institutes*, it is clear that Calvin believes that in the Supper one truly partakes of the flesh and blood of Christ through the power of the Holy Spirit." "It is clear that he does mean Christ's literal body. . . . Calvin emphasizes that the flesh of the ascended Christ is true human flesh." "Thus, the reality of the Supper of which the believer partakes is the human flesh of Jesus Christ." Davis's summary of "Calvin's Mature Eucharistic Theology" rightly concentrates on union with Christ (see IV.17.1) insisting that "Calvin has set up his theology so that the definition of being a Christian is to be in union with Christ."

43. In discussing Christ's two natures Calvin observes that God does not have blood and cannot suffer while Christ does both (II.14.2). Calvin speaks of the life-giving *blood* of Christ in explaining the scriptural employment of synecdoche (Com. I Cor. 12:13) (Gerrish, *Grace and Gratitude*, 160). On the flesh Gerrish comments, "It is not at all surprising that stalwart Reformed divines have sometimes been not merely puzzled but offended by Calvin's talk about the communication of Christ's life-giving flesh" (190). G. S. M. Walker, "The Lord's Supper in the Theology and Practice of Calvin," in *John Calvin: Courtenay Studies in Reformation Theology*, ed. G. E. Duffield (Grand Rapids: Wm. B. Eerdmans, 1966), 133–34, speaks of two paradoxes: "Although communion is a spiritual act, it involves an actual sharing in Christ's flesh and blood, and although his body has now ascended physically into heaven, we are none the less able to make contact with it through the Spirit."
44. *Westphal*, 2:277.

However, to the question, "How does Calvin explain this great mystery of union with Christ?" Davis answers, "By explaining the sacrament of the Eucharist." Understandably partial to his own subject, the emphasis still seems misplaced. The proper emphasis should be that union with Christ explains the Eucharist rather than the reverse.[45]

Contrary to Davis, H. R. Mackintosh claims:

> The exposition of the sacraments contained in the edition of 1536 is much superior to those of 1539 and 1559. It is clearer, closer to the New Testament and almost totally free from unintelligibly mysterious elements. The reader is swept on by the overwhelming fervor and momentum of the whole, and left finally with the conviction that these few pages offer an incomparably wise and warm delineation of what baptism and the Lord's Supper mean, or at all events ought to mean, for all who have laid heart and mind open to the love of God in Jesus Christ our Lord.

Mackintosh concludes, "Calvin's merit lay rather in his magnificent refutation of the mass, coupled with his convincing assertion of the objective reality of Christ's presence." The problem is Calvin's "praiseworthy effort to keep step with Luther . . . leads him, it must be confessed, to lay a false emphasis, in the higher reaches of his theory, on the reception by the communicant of the real flesh and blood of Christ, as distinguished somehow from the spiritual reception of Christ himself."[46] Calvin describes our participation in Christ as a wonderful exchange (*mirifica commutatio*) in "becoming Son of Man with us, he has made us sons of God with him" (IV.17.2). The reality of this common union is, of course, exactly the issue, to which a (merely) "spiritual reception" was considered Zwinglian and inadequate.

Granting the later likelihood of inexplicable explanations offered in defense, the three elements of Calvin's later eucharistic doctrine cited by Davis are essentially in place in the 1536 *Institutes*. In the very first section Calvin declares that

45. Thomas J. Davis, *The Clearest Promises of God: The Development of Calvin's Eucharistic Teaching* (New York: AMS Press, 1995), 79, 84, 86, 212, 110, 204, 206, 214, 202.

46. H. R. Mackintosh, "John Calvin: Expositor and Dogmatist," *The Review and Expositor* 7, no. 2 (April 1910), 185, 194, 193. Caroline Walker Bynum, *The Resurrection of the Body in Western Christianity, 200–1336* (New York: Columbia University Press, 1995), 56, 111, suggests a deep link "between early eucharistic theology and the doctrine of the resurrection. Eucharist, like resurrection, was a victory over the grave." Among some patristic theologians, "Eucharist is central to salvation because by digesting it we became indigestible to natural process." She continues, "To rise with all our organs and pieces intact is a victory over digestion—not only the digestion threatened by torturers and cannibals but most of all that proffered by natural process itself. [The eucharist] came to be seen as a palpable assurance that our flesh unites with the undigested and indigestible flesh of Christ in heaven." A similar connection between resurrection and eucharist is made by Michael Welker. From a provocative section entitled "The Offensive Reality of the Risen Jesus Christ as the Key to Understanding the Supper" he moves in part 2 to consider the meaning of Christ's presence. "In the Supper, Jesus identifies his externally perceivable, earthly vitality with the bread and the wine: I am giving you that in which I live here on earth." Attempts to understand this gift focusing on the elements of bread and wine are "long and full of conflict." Welker discusses real presence as Lutheran, spiritual presence as Zwinglian, and personal presence as a way forward to praise of God and reconciliation with God and with each other (Michael Welker, *What Happens in Holy Communion?* trans. John F. Hoffmeyer [Grand Rapids: Wm. B. Eerdmans, 2000], 89).

our merciful Lord leads us to himself with earthly elements, "and *in the flesh itself* causes us to contemplate the things that are of his Spirit." The term "substance" is both affirmed and denied.[47] Additionally, Christ assumed our true flesh, suffered in our true flesh, rose in our true flesh and ascended to heaven in our very flesh. Moreover, the heavenly locality of that body is stated. "It is the unchanging true nature of a body to be contained in a place, to possess its own dimensions and to have its own shape." At the same time, Christ's reign is not "bounded by any location in space." The second section is concerned with the continuing problematic of the relation between Word and sacrament, and the fourth explains the disputed role of the Holy Spirit.[48] Aptly citing Aristotle's *De Caelo* (294B) to the effect that we are all inclined to direct our inquiry not simply by the matter itself, but by the views of our opponents, Gerrish thinks Calvin's disagreements with Roman Catholics, Zwinglians, and Lutherans became more and more burdensome and influential, perhaps leading him away from his own proper insights.[49] Most especially the general use of the term "substance" led all the theologians of the sixteenth century to confuse rather than to confess the eucharistic mystery of common union or communion.

Since the mystery of union with Christ is at the heart of the Lord's Supper, mystery and "unintelligibly mysterious elements" will remain. This is not surprising since Calvin says, "If anyone should ask me how [the flesh of Christ in the Supper] takes place, I shall not be ashamed to confess that it is a secret too lofty for either my mind to comprehend or my words to declare. And, to speak more plainly, I rather experience than understand it" (IV.17.32). In a letter to Peter Martyr Vermigli, Calvin insists that we draw life from the flesh and blood of Christ, but an explanation of this mystery is not possible.[50] Again, commenting on "This mystery is great" (Eph. 5:32), Paul "implies that no language can do it justice. . . . Those who refuse to admit anything on this subject beyond what their own capacity can reach, are very foolish. When they deny that the flesh and blood of Christ are offered (*exhiberi*) to us in the Lord's Supper, they say: 'Define the manner or you will not convince us.' But I am overwhelmed by the depth of this mystery, and with Paul am not ashamed to acknowledge in wonder my ignorance." Calvin refers to the mystery of the Lord's Supper many times in chapter 17 (including IV.17. 1, 7, 9, 31, 33, 36), insisting, "I do not measure the mystery of the Supper by human reason, but look up to it with devout admiration."[51]

Calvin begins his discussion with his central and customary claim, "Christ is the matter (*materia*) or, if you prefer, the substance (*substantia*) of all the sacra-

47. John Calvin, *Institution of the Christian Religion* (1536), trans. Ford Lewis Battles (Atlanta: John Knox Press, 1975) 140, 145.
48. Ibid., 118, 145, 142.
49. Gerrish, *Grace and Gratitude*, 126.
50. *CO* 15:723.
51. "The Clear Explanation of Sound Doctrine concerning the True Partaking of the Flesh and Blood of Christ in the Holy Supper," in *Calvin: Theological Treatises,* trans. J. K. S. Reid (Philadelphia: Westminster Press, 1954), 266.

ments; "for in him they have all their solidity and they do not promise anything apart from him" (IV.14.16).[52] The efficacy of the sacraments lies neither in the elements nor the celebrants but only in Christ (Com. Eph. 5:26). In these sacramental chapters Calvin's conviction and confession of unity with Christ shine with special refulgence. This point is clearly indicated by the chapter titles in Ronald S. Wallace's *Calvin's Doctrine of the Word and Sacrament*: "The Sacraments of the New Covenant as Signs of Union with the Body of Christ," "The Mystery of Sacramental Union," "Baptism as Ingrafting into Christ," "The Lord's Supper as Communion with Christ."[53] Expounding "This is my body" (Com. 1 Cor. 11:24) Calvin maintains that we share in the benefits of Christ only "when he dwells in us, when he is one with us, when we are members of his flesh, when, in short, we become united in one life and substance (if I may say so) with him. [Christ offers] the self-same body in which he suffered and rose again. My conclusion is that the body of Christ is really (*realiter*) [and] truly (*vere*) given to us . . . a life-giving power from the flesh of Christ is poured into us through the medium of the Spirit." In this statement Calvin affirms the essential elements: union with Christ in one life and substance, meaning the selfsame body, a life-giving power from the flesh of Christ really and truly given to us through the Spirit, but rejects "the idea that the Body of Christ is really and substantially present in the Supper [but insists] this is not at all repugnant to a true and real communion, which consists in our ascent to heaven, and requires no other descent in Christ than of spiritual grace."[54]

During the Reformation time the ferocious supper strife framed the issue of Christ's eucharistic presence in terms of the concept of substance—a situation that obtains today with less legitimacy. When Calvin was charged with "denying that in the Holy Supper we are made partakers of the substance of the flesh and blood of Christ," he answers, "As is declared in my writings more than a hundred times, I am so far from rejecting the term substance, that I simply and readily declare, that spiritual life, by the incomprehensible agency of the Spirit, is infused into us from the substance of the flesh of Christ. I also constantly admit that *we are substantially fed on the flesh and blood of Christ*, though I discard the gross fiction of a local corresponding."[55] Calvin insists that we are one with Christ "not

52. See the "Short Treatise on the Holy Supper," in *Calvin: Theological Treatises*, 146.

53. Ronald S. Wallace, *Calvin's Doctrine of the Word and Sacrament* (Edinburgh: Oliver and Boyd, 1953). According to Boniface Meyer, "Calvin's Eucharistic Doctrine 1536–39," *Journal of Ecumenical Studies* 4 (1967): 55, for Calvin, union with Christ is a special effect of the Lord's Supper.

54. *Westphal*, 2:281.

55. "Clear Explanation of the Holy Supper," 264 (emphasis added). According to Joseph C. McLelland, "Calvin and Philosophy," *Canadian Journal of Theology* 11, no. 1 (1965): 47, Calvin was very wise in trying to take the concept of substance in a more dynamic direction. "This is notably evident in his doctrine of the eucharist. . . . Philosophically he tried to show the logical absurdity of the scholastic teaching, transubstantiation in particular. Theologically he tried to break through into a new dynamism and personalism more suited to the subject. Central was the personal union of Christ: the 'substance' of this living and lordly Person demanded a new framework, only tentatively outlined by the Reformers, especially in their stress on the office of the Holy Spirit."

because he transfuses his substance into us, but because by the power of his Spirit he communicates to us his life and all the blessings he has received from the Father" (Com. Jn. 17:21).

Calvin has already taught that Christ assumed the true substance of human flesh (II.13), meaning, according to Willis, that Calvin is not beginning with substance as a general category "of which Christ and our life in Christ are instances" but with the all-inclusive ontological reality of mystical union.[56] Kilian McDonnell, following Gollwitzer, admits that Calvin's use of the term "substance" is fluid and ambiguous, but it "must be kept in the framework of his larger theological thought on the union with Christ in faith."[57] According to Calvin since we "have our life in Christ our souls should be fed on his body and his blood as their proper food." In the Supper Jesus Christ gives us to feed upon "the real substance of his body and his blood." On earth Christ took our humanity which in his ascension he has exalted into heaven "withdrawing it from its mortal condition, but not changing its nature"! Calvin noted in passing "that to enclose Jesus Christ fantastically under the bread and wine or so to join him to them to amuse our understanding there instead of looking at him in heaven, is a pernicious fancy."[58] Since Christ is ascended to heaven, sharing in the Lord's body "demands neither a local presence, nor the descent of Christ, nor an infinite extension of his body, nor anything of that sort. . . . Christ remains in heaven and is yet received by us." Christ "imparts himself to us by the secret power of the Holy Spirit" who is able to join together things separated by great distances (Com. I Cor. 11:24).

Calvin's great expectations for sacramental peace and unity may be understood in a Pickwickian sense, but his contentions for the truth fell on hard times with the Catholics, Zwinglians, and Lutherans producing (1) a *denial* of the Roman Mass, (2) a *compromise* with the Zwinglians (the Consensus Tigurinus), and (3) a *conflict* with Lutherans (the treatises against Westphal). Since everyone's teaching on the Lord's Supper was a salient point exposed to attack, Calvin was led to construct ever more and more elaborate redoubts, some of which, like the easily misunderstood concept of the flesh and blood of Christ, should be more carefully defended.

1. Calvin and the Catholics

More than a decade before Calvin became Protestant the importance of the Roman Mass had been recognized and attacked by Luther in *The Babylonian Captivity of the Church* (1520). Calvin's opposition to the papal Mass is the subject of IV.18, followed by his objurgation of the other five nonscriptural sacraments: confirma-

---

56. David Willis, "Calvin's Use of Substantia," *Calvinus Ecclesiae Genevensis Custos*, ed. Wilhelm H. Neuser (New York: Verlag Peter Lang, 1984), 300, 291. Surely an ontological mystery is more confessional than philosophical.

57. McDonnell, *John Calvin, the Church, and the Eucharist*, 234. See Helmut Gollwitzer, *Coena Domini* (Munich: Chr. Kaiser, 1937), 117ff.

58. "Short Treatise on the Holy Supper," 147, 148, 159.

tion, penance, extreme unction, holy orders, and marriage (IV.19). The Protestants entirely rejected any power of priest to transform bread and wine into the body and blood of Christ and to offer Christ to God in the sacrifice of the altar. According to Calvin the belief in the Mass as a sacrifice offering up Christ with the expectation of obtaining a meritorious forgiveness of sins is "a most wicked infamy and unbearable blasphemy" (IV.18.14) "perpetrated by the Roman antichrist and his prophets" (IV.18.1). The abomination of the Mass "offered in a golden cup . . . has so inebriated all kings and peoples of the earth . . . that, more stupid than brute beasts, they have steered the whole vessel of their salvation into this one deadly whirlpool" (IV.18.18). In such trenchant terms Calvin contends the word of God proves "that this Mass, however decked in splendor, inflicts signal dishonor upon Christ, buries and oppresses his cross, consigns his death to oblivion, takes away the benefit which came to us from it, and weakens and destroys the sacrament by which the memory of his death was bequeathed to us" (IV.18.1).

To be more specific, the Catholic doctrine, first, denigrates the eternal priesthood of Christ by putting Roman priests in Christ's place as successors and intercessors. Second, by the belief in a repeated or renewed rather than the once-for-all sacrifice, the true cross is torn down and a false altar is raised. "Christ has given us a table at which to feast, not an altar upon which to offer a victim; he has not consecrated priests to offer sacrifice, but ministers to distribute the sacred banquet" (IV.18.12). Third, the Mass is a false new testament. "If Christ is sacrificed in each and every Mass, he must be cruelly slain in a thousand places at every moment" (IV.18.5). Fourth, the purported new redemption offered in the Mass causes people to forget the true redemption and thus to lose its benefits (IV.18.6). Finally, the Lord's Supper is a divine gift, not a human offering. Additionally, the notion of a daily sacrifice leads to private masses, which destroy "the communion by which we all cleave together in Christ Jesus" (IV.18.7).

2. Calvin and the Zwinglians

Whatever his peripheral connections, Calvin had most likely not entered the Protestant corps when Zwingli was killed in 1531. An admirer of Luther, Calvin was aware of Luther's disdain for the sacramental theology of the Zurichers as evidenced by the wound opened and not healed at the Marburg Colloquy of 1529. Nevertheless, Calvin thought agreement could be effected by moderation of temper and care of confession. The unity of church was a fundamental conviction. "For the most important principle of our religion is this, that we be in concord among ourselves" (Com. I Cor. 1:10). Calvin wrote to Bullinger (February 21, 1538), "Oh, if a pure and sincere accommodation could be agreed upon at length among us," and later to Cranmer (April 1552), "The members of the church being severed, the body lies bleeding. . . . Could I be of any service, I would not grudge to cross even ten seas." In the 1536 *First Helvetic Confession* Martin Bucer and Wolfgang Capito of Strasbourg had urged a mediation between the Lutheran and Zwinglian positions on the Lord's Supper, insisting that the sacraments consisting of sign and substance are holy signs, not empty signs. The signs are bodily received and "substantial, invisible, and spiritual things are received in faith" (art. 20). True communion does not require the Lord's body and blood to be naturally united with, nor spacially enclosed within, the bread and wine (art. 22).[59]

In 1543 Luther's "violent outburst" against the Swiss was followed by "his scurrilous parody of the first Psalm: 'Blessed is the man who walks not in the counsel of the sacramentarians, nor stands in the way of the Zwinglians, nor sits in the seat of the Zurichers.'"[60] After some years of correspondence and conferences, Bullinger and Calvin drew up a mutual agreement on the Lord's Supper in twenty-four articles later endorsed by other Swiss churches.[61] The Zurich Consensus is well summarized by Philip Schaff as follows:

> The sacraments are not in and of themselves effective and conferring grace, but that God, through the Holy Spirit, acts through them as means; that the internal effect appears only in the elect; that the good of the sacraments consists in leading us to Christ, and being instruments of the grace of God, which is sincerely offered to all; that in baptism we receive the remission of sins, although this proceeds primarily not from baptism, but from the blood of Christ; that in the Lord's Supper we eat and drink the body and blood of Christ, not, however, by means of a carnal presence of Christ's human nature, which is in heaven, but by the power of the Holy Spirit and the devout elevation of our soul to heaven.[62]

The vaulting question is whether the Zurich Consensus represents a complete victory for Calvin's eucharistic theology or the extent of the territory he was willing to surrender to end the war. Davis devotes nearly forty pages to this topic, concluding that Calvin's more complete explanation in the 1555 *Defense of the Sane and Orthodox Doctrine of the Sacraments* indicates a serious dis-ease, as does his addition of two articles (5 and 23) to the original document of Zurich.[63] Article 5 not only employs Calvin's favorite expression "exhibit" (*exhibere*), but emphasizes that the effectiveness of the sacraments requires "we must be made one with him and grow together into his body." In themselves the sacraments are "nothing," but are used instrumentally by God (art. 13). On reflection Calvin noticed that while the confession used the terms "figure" and "sign," there was

59. *The First Helvetic Confession* was the authoritative confession of faith in the Swiss Reformed Church until superseded in 1566 by *The Second Helvetic Confession*.

60. Ian D. Bunting, "The Consensus Tigurinus," *Journal of Presbyterian History* 44 (1966): 46.

61. Bunting, 48, suggests the *Consensus Tigurinus* "might even have been acceptable to the majority of Lutherans had it not been for the obstruction of men like Westphal and Heshusius. The continuing division on the nature and manner of communion is reviewed by Wilhelm Niesel, "Intercommunion in the German Evangelical Church," *Intercommunion*, ed. Donald Baillie and John Marsh (London: SCM Press, 1952), 281–88. For an account of Farel's role, see Comité Farel, *Guillaume Farel, 1489–1565* (Neuchâtel: Éditions Delachaux et Niestlé, 1930), 578–91. Especially noteworthy is his encouragement for Calvin, profoundly grieved by the death of his wife, Idelette de Bure, on March 29, 1549, to continue negotiations toward concord (585).

62. *The Creeds of Christendom*, vol. 1, ed. Philip Schaff, rev. by David S. Schaff (Grand Rapids: Baker Book House, 1983), 472.

63. Davis, *Clearest Promises of God*, 229–68.

"no mention of the eating of the flesh in the whole work."[64] Therefore article 23 adds, "by the eating of his flesh and the drinking of his blood which are here figured, it is not therefore to be understood as though there was an intermingling or transfusion of substance." Article 24 attacks "the fiction of the papists about transubstantiation" and other "stupid fantasies [that attempt] to place Christ under the bread or to couple him with the bread." The affirmation following these denials states, "But we draw life from the flesh once offered in sacrifice and the blood poured out for expiation" (art. 23). On the important question of the relation of sign and reality, Calvin avoids docetism by insisting the sign participates in the reality it presents.[65]

3. Calvin and the Lutherans

Calvin thought he recognized a "holy union" among the many churches which "preached the same doctrine."[66] Calvin had signed Melanchthon's *Augsburg Confession* of 1530 with the stipulation that he understood the document as its author did. Since Calvin believed he and Melanchthon agreed on the Lord's Supper, he had high hopes of effecting a formula of concord with the Lutherans,[67] expecting that efforts like the Zurich Consensus would provide "an essential first step toward a wider pan-Protestant accord."[68] From the *Short Treatise on the Holy Supper* (1541) Calvin had felt free to criticize aspects of Luther's view. As Heron suggests, "The essential question here is the nature of the humanity of Christ." Calvin insisted that we lose our hope of the resurrection of the body "if we do not firmly and properly hold to the risen corporality of Jesus himself." With Luther's view Calvin detected "an undercutting of the real meaning of union with Christ through a misdirection of the question" of our relation to Christ. Luther is charged with turning Jesus' common humanity with us into a different kind of humanity. Moreover, his particular humanity becomes ubiquity. As Zwingli has fallen into a false subjectivism, so has Luther fallen into a false objectivism.[69]

---

64. Letter of July 6, 1549 (*CO* 13:306).

65. Paul Rorem, "Calvin and Bullinger on the Lord's Supper," *Lutheran Quarterly* (2006): 375, offers an excellent analysis of the complexities of negotiation and the carefulness of nuance, concluding that from beginning to end Calvin understood the sacrament *as an instrument* or means of God's grace while Bullinger believed it to be a *testimony* to God's grace. Therefore, in the Zurich Consensus, "Certain of its articles do represent a finely balanced dialectic between Calvin's concerns for the sacraments as God's means or instruments for conferring grace (on the elect), and Bullinger's concern to counteract any transfer of God's saving activity to the creaturely realm."

66. *Westphal,* 2:251.

67. See Calvin's letter to Melanchthon June 28, 1545. *Letters of John Calvin.*

68. Timothy George, "John Calvin and the Agreement of Zurich (1549)," in *John Calvin and the Church: A Prism of Reform,* ed. Timothy George (Louisville, KY: Westminster/John Knox Press, 1990), 45.

69. See Alasdair I. C. Heron's helpful chapter, "Calvin's Eucharistic Theology," in *Table and Tradition* (Philadelphia: Westminster Press, 1983), 126, 129. Especially interesting is the battle fought physically at the table in Heidelberg by Hechusius and Klebitz and refereed by Melanchthon, who is in the same corner as Calvin and on the way to the Heidelberg Catechism (1563) (135–37).

The specific design of the Zurich Consensus was to set forth sacramental doctrine in terms that were few, simple, clear, and gentle, including a request for discussion, and, if necessary, amendment.[70] "Surely," Calvin asserts, "what we teach perfectly agrees in all respects with Scripture. It contains nothing either absurd or obscure or ambiguous" (IV.17.19). Calvin sincerely believed his view carried the authority of Paul and Luke. Thus, in exasperation he states, those who disagree find "their quarrel is not with me but with the Spirit of God" (IV.17.20). On March 5, 1555, Calvin sent a copy of the Zurich Consensus to Melanchthon, expecting Philip to reveal his true convictions about the false "worship of the bread." Calvin opens his attempt to dissipate the mists of Tileman Heshusius with a passionate, even angry, appeal that Melanchthon stand upright for the sacramental truth.[71]

Earlier Calvin had been surprised and dismayed when Joachim Westphal, a Lutheran pastor at St. Catherine's church in Hamburg, attacked the Zurich Consensus and initiated the second eucharistic war. According to Calvin, this overdone Hamburger "boldly masks all his fictions with the Word of God . . . just as if he were some comic Jupiter carrying a Minerva in his skull."[72] In fact, Westphal appeals to Scripture falsely to support the notion of the body of Christ as immense or ubiquitous, which is a "monstrous phantom" denying the resurrection, ascension, session, and return as taught in Scripture.[73] Calvin understood the relation of the ascended Christ to the earthly Christ, seen especially in the resurrection narratives, to include, not exclude, the risen humanity. Moreover, Calvin thought Westphal's view that the bread of the Eucharist *is* substantially the body of Christ comes perilously close to the "gross gulping" doctrine of the Papists, which is "abhorrent to our sense of piety."[74] Calvin thought to Luther great honor was due and believed that Westphal had misrepresented his views. Still it would be foolish to extol Luther's defects at the price of corrupting Scripture.[75] According to Calvin, Luther would have agreed with the Zurich Consensus.[76] Calvin claims that until Westphal "kindled the torch of discord," he "had never touched him or one of his faction, but had rather humbly begged, that if anything in our doctrine did not please, it might not be deemed too troublesome to correct it by placid admonition."[77] Under the force of Westphal's attack Calvin concludes that the time for discussion has passed, and against Westphal a hard wedge must be used for a bad knot.[78] "All we asked was, that he would not deal

70. *Westphal*, 2:246.
71. "The Clear Explanation of the Holy Supper," 260.
72. *Westphal*, 2:328.
73. Ibid., 2:260.
74. Ibid., 3:374. For a historical introducton see Joseph N. Tylenda, "The Calvin-Westphal Exchange: The Genesis of Calvin's Treatises Against Westphal," *Calvin Theological Journal* 9, no. 2 (November 1974): 182–209.
75. *Westphal*, 3:477.
76. Letter of August 25, 1554.
77. *Westphal*, 3:348.
78. Ibid., 2:248.

roughly with a newly cured sore,"[79] but Westphal opened wounds and Calvin was thoroughly roused to defend "the clear and indubitable truth."[80]

According to Calvin, all bodies are located in a place,[81] which for the risen and ascended Christ is at the right hand of God.[82] Calvin insists that the whole Christ is present everywhere but *in his flesh* Christ is contained in heaven until he appears in judgment.[83] This local, heavenly presence Calvin understands to preserve not only Christ's heavenly glory but most especially the continuing reality and integrity of Christ's human nature, which protects our human nature in union with him and thus our salvation.[84] Calvin affirms the local, heavenly presence by insisting that Christ while present to faith is not present in, with, or under the elements. Christ is absent from us in the body which is in heaven, but Christ dwells in us by his Spirit.[85]

Calvin regards his doctrine of the Lord's Supper as real, true, and also spiritual in contrast with Westphal's carnal view, which understands the substance of Christ's flesh to be on earth.[86] Christ cannot be pulled "down from his throne, that he may lie enclosed in a little bit of bread."[87] Contrary to Westphal's carnal understanding of the Eucharist, "We assert that in the sacred supper we are truly made partakers of Christ, so that by the sacred agency of the Spirit, he instills life into our souls from his flesh."[88] Calvin asserts the analogy of faith supports his view that Christ's flesh itself does not enter into us, but the substance of his flesh breathes life into our souls (IV.17.32). Calvin insists the being is not in the sign (Com. Mt. 3:16), concluding, "Although righteousness flows from God alone,

79. Ibid., 2:314.

80. Ibid., 2:268.

81. *Inst.* IV.17.26. Calvin claims he did not derive this view of body from Aristotle and, in *Westphal*, 2:327, says he did not learn about bodies in the school of Archimedes but of Scripture. Calvin cannot believe that bodies exist if locality is taken away. Therefore, while Christ is ubiquitous in his divinity, with respect to his human nature he is not everywhere present (*Westphal*, 3:382).

82. *Inst.* IV.17.18., where sitting at the right hand of the Father means that Christ's reign is not "bounded by location in space nor circumscribed by any limits."

83. *Inst.* IV.17.30. The fullness of deity dwells in Christ, but he is God manifested in the flesh. "The fact that the body of Christ is finite does not prevent him from filling heaven and earth, because his grace and power are everywhere diffused" (Com. Gen. 28:12). Full ubiquity and true communion are powerfully addressed in two succinct paragraphs in scornful objection to Cardinal Sadolet (*Calvin's Tracts*, 1:45).

84. *Westphal*, 3:391: "The hope of future resurrection is overthrown, if a model of it is not exhibited in the flesh of Christ."

85. Ibid., 2:272.

86. Ibid., 2:240. Joseph N. Tylenda, "Calvin and Christ's Presence in the Supper—True or Real," *Scottish Journal of Theology* 27 (February 1974): 67, points out that both Calvin and Westphal asserted a presence of Christ's flesh in the Supper but they understood it differently. Calvin thought Westphal's view was too carnal; Westphal thought Calvin's too spiritual. "But Calvin's spiritual is not something imaginary or fanciful, it is an actual, real communication" (70). Lutheran theologian Ernst Bizer, "The Problem of Intercommunion in the Reformation," *Intercommunion*, 67, 68, points out that Luther's view of the presence of the body and blood of Christ is finally "completely incomprehensible and irrational." The correct view of presence is appealed to Scripture "for the understanding of which, to be sure, the *analogia fidei*, the *analogia* of *his* faith is normative."

87. *Westphal*, 1:241.

88. Ibid., 2:276.

we shall not have the full manifestation of it anywhere else than in Christ's flesh," which remains in heaven (Com. Jn. 6:51). Likewise in controversy with Heshusius, Calvin declares communion with Christ to be of the flesh but not carnal. Sarcastically Calvin asks, "When I teach that the body of Christ is given us for food by the secret energy of the Spirit, do I thereby deny that the Supper is a communion of the body?"[89]

The fundamental disagreement between Calvin and Westphal and Heshusius concerns differing views on the doctrine of Christ's two natures. Calvin understands the gnesio- (or super) Lutherans to teach that Christ's human nature has disappeared rather than been elevated. In opposition Calvin declares, "We affirm his divinity so joined and united with his humanity that each retains its distinctive nature unimpaired, and yet these two natures constitute one Christ" (II.12.1). Calvin's defense of Christ's human nature insists on an irreducible duality between Christ's divinity and humanity. The Lordship of Christ involves the incarnation (or hypostatic union), and our salvation depends on union with his humanity (or flesh), which is united to his divinity. "We hold that Christ, as he is God and man, consists of two natures united but not mingled" (II.14.1). Our salvation is effected because Christ being God saves us by what he did in *his human nature* (III.11.9). In his Commentary on I Timothy 3:16 Calvin treats the relation of divinity and flesh. "There is great emphasis laid on the contrast between the two terms, God and the flesh. . . . Yet in Christ we see God's infinite glory joined to our polluted flesh so that the two become one." "God's natural son fashioned for himself a body from our body, flesh from our flesh, bones from our bones, that he might be one with us (II.12.2). In the Lord's Supper the real body of Christ is received as bread and the real blood of Christ as drink." "The flesh of Christ is like a rich and inexhaustible fountain that pours into us the life springing forth from the Godhead into itself" (IV.17.9). It is exactly clear that for Calvin communion means a real nourishment by the real flesh (and blood) of Christ, but not exactly clear what real nourishment by real flesh (and blood) means, and made especially confusing with the employment of the term "substance."

Inexplicably, Calvin was not much troubled by the charge of Nestorianism but was greatly agitated by the Eutychian denial of Christ's real and continuing humanity, which in their different ways he perceived in both Luther and Zwingli. Understanding union with Christ required clarity concerning the humanity of Christ and, therefore, an accurate exposition of the flesh of Christ. "There is no doubt that God's purpose was to make entirely explicit that Christ, in truth and in reality, when he put on our flesh, embraced the full role of broth-

---

89. "Clear Explanation of the Holy Supper," 263. Calvin rejects transfusion of substance but insists upon infusion of life. *Westphal*, 1:238, 1:240, 2:248, 2:277, 2:283, 3:447. John R. Meyer, "Mysterium Fidei and the Later Calvin," *Scottish Journal of Theology* 25 (1972): 392–411, takes his survey of this material through the 1561 Colloquy of Poissy.

erly union with men" (Com. Lk. 2:40). "The flesh of Christ gives life, not only because we once obtained salvation by it, but because now, while we are made one with Christ by a sacred union, the same flesh breathes life into us, or to express it more briefly, because ingrafted into the body of Christ by the secret agency of the Spirit we have life in common with him. For from the hidden fountain of the Godhead life was miraculously infused into the body of Christ, that it might flow from thence to us."[90] According to Calvin, "It is as clear as day to me that here the reality is joined to the sign; in other words, we really do become sharers in the body of Christ." The body is not just given to us but given as food for nourishment and growth (Com. I Cor. 11:24). "We eat Christ by faith alone, so long as we grasp how faith unites us to him" (Com. Jn. 6:35). That is, the bread and wine become the elements of sacrament not when the words are pronounced but when they are believed. All that nourishes and advances faith is properly compared to food (Com. Jn. 6:27). Using substance the point is emphasized against Heshusius. "The flesh and blood of Christ are substantially offered and exhibited to us in the Supper [meaning] that the flesh of Christ becomes vivifying to us . . . by the incomprehensible virtue of his Spirit [transfusing] his own proper life into us from the substance of his flesh, so that he himself lives in us, and his life is common to us. . . . This is not a corporeal eating. . . . We become substantially partakers of the flesh of Christ not by an external sign but by the simple faith of the Gospel." The operation of the flesh is mystical and incomprehensible.[91]

According to Max Thurian, "If Calvin had stopped with a simple statement of the real presence, agreement with the Lutherans might have been a possibility, but he was troubled by Zwingli's rationalistic questions. And he was not satisfied with Luther's mystical vagueness."[92] Real presence is not a simple statement, but it is true that in neither his heart nor his mind could Calvin accept the Zwinglian view that nothing grace-full happened in the Lord's Supper. Likewise, he could not accept the Lutheran view that something substantial happened in the bread itself. In his explication of the mystery of Christ's flesh, Calvin defends what he sees as a fundamental and nonnegotiable aspect of the Lordship of Christ related to incarnation and redemption—specifically the human nature of Christ and our union with him. In debate with Osiander Calvin admits the flesh of Christ alone could not effect the work of salvation but insists "that he carried out all these acts according to his human nature. . . . We conclude that in his flesh, righteousness

90. "Exposition of the Heads of Agreement," in *Calvin's Tracts*, 2:238. The difficulty of this concept of flesh is aptly indicated with its denial by so great a scholar as Bohatec. "Die Verbindung mit Christus ist nicht naturhaft, *nicht fleischlich*, physisch, nicht substantiell, sondern qualitativ, spiritual, virtuell, dynamisch" (Josef Bohatec, *Calvins Lehre von Staat und Kirche* [Aalen: Scientia (1937) 1961], 350 [emphasis added]).

91. "Clear Explanation of the Holy Supper," 267, 290, 314.

92. Max Thurian, "The Real Presence," in *Christianity Divided: Protestant and Roman Catholic Issues*, ed. Daniel J. Callahan, Heiko A. Oberman, Daniel J. O'Hanlon (New York: Sheed and Ward, 1961), 208.

has been manifested to us." The sacraments direct our faith to the whole Christ but "salvation resides in his flesh" (III.11.9) because the flesh of Christ, now endowed with immortality, "is pervaded with fullness of life to be transmitted to us, [and therefore] rightly called 'life-giving'" (IV.17.9).[93]

Calvin has used the term "flesh" to distinguish between the outward man and the divine power of the spirit (Com. I Pet. 3:18). Flesh also means bondage to the law—nature without grace (Com. Rom. 7:5). However, in the Lord's Supper flesh refers to Christ's gift of life. The life which Christ bestows "resides in his flesh so that it may be drawn from it," thereby testing "the humility and obedience of our faith by commanding those who would seek life to rely on his flesh, which in its appearance is contemptible. . . . As the eternal Word of God is the fountain of life, so his flesh is a channel to pour out to us the life which resides intrinsically, as they say, in his divinity" (Com. Jn. 6:51). Calvin explains that "the body of Christ is eaten, inasmuch as it is spiritual nourishment of the soul," which means "Christ, by the incomprehensible agency of his Spirit, infuses his life into us." This eucharistic eating of Christ's flesh is a matter of faith, not teeth. Calvin admits the mystery but insists on the reality. He thinks in his definition "there is no quibble, no obscurity, nothing ambiguous or equivocating."[94] He is confident his views are true, his criticisms accurate, and his conclusions to be approved by all godly hearts. The extravagant doctors, on the other hand, strip Christ of his flesh and blood, thereby denying life to us. Still Calvin asserts the mind is not able to conceive and the tongue not able to express the greatness of this mystery.

In summary, union with Christ involves the believers' participation in the humanity of Christ, which is a gift of the Holy Spirit ordinarily made efficacious by the word proclaimed and exhibited in baptism, the sacrament of justification, and in Eucharist, the sacrament of sanctification. Calvin's sense of piety, in confessing the hypostatic union, and affirming the ubiquity of Christ's divine nature, also affirms his humanity in life, death, resurrection, ascension, session, and return, requiring the conception of Christ's local (or fleshly) presence in heaven. Since the divine property of ubiquity is not communicable to the human nature, the presence of Christ in the Lord's Supper must respect Christ's heavenly glory by not binding his body to earthly elements. Likewise, his human nature must be respected by not ascribing infinity to his human body (IV.17.19). The emphasis on Christ's risen humanity is noted by McLelland, who observes that "Calvin relates all his theology [to] the believer's participation in the new humanity of the

---

93. Attempting to be more precise on the "life-giving virtue of Christ's flesh," Nevin writes, "Calvin, it is allowed, teaches the communication of both the natures of Christ in the supper, but only *as regards his theandric spirit, not as regards his theandric body.* That his glorified body should be present as material substance in the bread and wine, Calvin indeed never admitted; for he was too well assured, that a glorified body is no such material substance" (John W. Nevin, "Calvin and Westphal," *Mercersburg Review* [September 1850]: 501). See also B. A. Gerrish, "The Flesh of the Son of Man: John W. Nevin on the Church and the Eucharist," in *Tradition and the Modern World: Reformed Theology in the Nineteenth Century* (Chicago: University of Chicago Press, 1978), 49–70.

94. "The Best Method of Obtaining Concord," in *Calvin: Theological Treatises,* 574–75.

living Christ."[95] Calvin's conception of the life-giving flesh of Christ is an expression of union with Christ, but not an explanation of it.

Of course, flesh locally present in heaven at the right hand of God the Father is no less recondite than flesh locally present on the altar in the Lord's Supper. However, Calvin thought the latter led to "the most fearful and monstrous fascination . . . of stupidly adoring the bread in place of God."[96] Avoiding this "miserable infatuation" and defending the real and continuing humanity of Christ meant confessing the true eucharistic mystery to be the power of the Holy Spirit in really and truly connecting the faithful with the heavenly located, life-giving flesh of Christ. That is, our Lord Jesus Christ in the reality of his divine humanity is in communion with the faithful by the power of the Holy Spirit. Calvin describes this process with the language of both ascent and descent. In faith by the power of the Holy Spirit we ascend to heaven to communicate with the flesh of Christ and, while his body remains in heaven, Christ descends to us on earth by the power of the Holy Spirit (IV.17.24). At heart this is confession of faith, not explanation of it. At best, a declaration of meaning, not an analysis of elements.

C. THE STATE AND THE CHURCH

Calvin's influence on social, economic, and political matters arouses considerable interest.[97] The most notorious economic analysis is Max Weber's *The Protestant Ethic and the Spirit of Capitalism*, which cites Calvin himself only once in over a hundred pages of footnotes. Weber admits, "We are not studying the personal views of Calvin, but Calvinism, and that in the form to which it had evolved by the end of the sixteenth and in the seventeenth centuries." Rather more is made of Benjamin Franklin, who is correctly described as a "colorless deist" but is nevertheless used to illustrate the relation of Calvinism to the spirit of capitalism

95. Joseph McLelland, "Lutheran-Reformed Debate on the Eucharist and Christology," *Marburg Revisited*, ed. Paul C. Empie and James I. McCord (Minneapolis: Augsburg, 1966), 46–47. Keith A. Mathison, *Given for You: Reclaiming Calvin's Doctrine of the Lord's Supper* (Phillipsburg, NJ: Presbyterian and Reformed Publishing Company, 2002), 16–21, 273–76 emphasizes the importance of union with Christ. Also advocating the use of wine (297–313).

96. *Westphal*, 1:219.

97. Lawrence P. Buck and Jonathan W. Zophy, *The Social History of the Reformation* (Columbus: Ohio State University Press, 1972), collect disparate articles, including in our focus Robert M. Kingdon's "The Control of Morals in Calvin's Geneva" (3–16). Out of our focus but worth a sharp glance is Roland H. Bainton, "John Foxe and the Ladies" (208–22). Bainton writes, "One has the feeling that he derived a special relish from relating the tart, smart, pert, audacious and superbly defiant word and deeds of these women to illustrate the point that the weaker vessel, when filled with the Holy Spirit, is powerful enough to pull down strongholds" (208). In addition to Foxe's ladies, one should check out Bainton's three volumes on *Women of the Reformation* (Minneapolis: Augsburg Publishing House, 1971, 1973, 1977). Another strong study of Calvin's social influence is Philip Benedict's *Christ's Churches Purely Reformed: A Social History of Calvinism* (New Haven, CT: Yale University Press, 2002). Benedict surveys the Reformed tradition from its origins to the close of the age of orthodoxy from a sociological perspective under the themes of formation, expansion, and transformation. Zwingli, Bullinger, and Calvin are the main formulators.

because he had a "strict Calvinistic father."[98] Benjamin admits, "I had been religiously educated as a Presbyterian; and though some of the dogmas of that persuasion, such as *the eternal decrees of God, election, reprobation, etc.* appeared to me unintelligible, others doubtful, and I early absented myself from the public assemblies of the sect . . . I was never without some religious principles."[99]

Calvin's views of the state in relation to the church expounded in the final chapter of the *Institutes* (IV.20), while long in historical and political influence, can be short in theological presentation.[100] Some scholars find Calvin's impact on political life and theory the most important single aspect of his work. For example, in an astoundingly vituperative reading of Calvin, Eric Voegelin asserts that while he himself cannot carry out the "smashing operation with [the] thoroughness and gusto" it deserves, "the usual evaluation of the *Institutes of the Christian Religion* as the great systematic presentation of reformed theology" must be corrected. According to Voegelin, we should recognize "Calvin's dictatorial use of unspeakable means for the realization of theocratic ends." "The *Institutes* is a work of pragmatic politics." "In the face of Calvin's argumentative versatility it would be futile to search for an intrinsic meaning of his body of doctrine." "Calvin was a thoroughly unsavory, murderous character" whose purpose was to found a new universal church with himself as the new Saint Peter. Voegelin thinks Calvin's doctrine of predestination served this political purpose.[101]

98. *The Protestant Ethic and the Spirit of Capitalism*, trans. Talcott Parsons (1930; repr. London: Routledge, 1996), 220n7, 53. Weber regards predestination as Calvinism's motivating conviction. W. Fred Graham, *The Constructive Revolutionary: John Calvin and His Socio-Economic Impact* (Richmond, VA: John Knox Press, 1971), surveys both society and economics, including a chapter on the Weber thesis. While I might gnaw a bone of contention over Graham's critique of Calvin's Christology (178–85), the book's marrow is sound. See also Christoph Stückelberger, "Calvin, Calvinism, and Capitalism: The Challenges of New Interest in Asia," in *John Calvin Rediscovered: The Impact of His Social and Economic Thought*, ed. Edward Dommen and James D. Bratt (Louisville, KY: Westminster John Knox Press, 2007), 121–31.

99. *The Autobiography of Benjamin Franklin*, vol. 1, in *The Harvard Classics*, ed. Charles W. Eliot (New York: P. F. Collier and Son, 1909), 80.

100. Doumergue devotes his fifth volume to Calvin's political and social thoughts. Niesel treats secular government in a separate chapter but calls the subject an appendix in Calvin's theology. Wendel subsumes the state into his discussion of the church. John T. McNeill, *The History and Character of Calvinism* (New York: Oxford University Press, 1954), spends a chapter on Calvinism and public affairs. In an essay, "John Calvin on Civil Government," in *Calvinism and the Political Order*, ed. George L. Hunt (Philadelphia: Westminster Press, 1965), 23–45, McNeill suggests some enduring values of Calvin's political insights, which include a positive attitude toward the role of government. In English translation Calvin's political chapter runs to 36 pages. The French study of Marc-Edouard Chenevière, *La Pensée Politique de Calvin* (Geneva: Slatkine Reprints, 1937 [1970]), is 400 pages, and Josef Bohatec, *Calvins Lehre von Staat und Kirche* (Aalen: Scientia, 1961), is 750 pages. Chenevière sees Calvin as a faithful interpreter of the Word (175) and is especially helpful to the magistrates. Disagreeing with both Bohatec and Chenevière, Hans Baron, "Calvinist Republicanism and Its Historical Roots," *Church History* 8 (1939): 30–42, traces Calvinist political thought to Martin Bucer and Strassburg.

101. *The Collected Works of Eric Voegelin*, vol. 22, in *History of Political Ideas*, vol. 4, *Renaissance and Reformation*, ed. David L. Morse and William M. Thompson (Columbia: University of Missouri Press, 1998), 269, 277, 272, 276, 277. To pursue Voegelin's controversial and non-Christian theology, see Michael P. Morrissey, *Consciousness and Transcendence: The Theology of Eric Voegelin* (Notre Dame, IN: University of Notre Dame Press, 1994). Harro Höpfl, *The Christian Polity of John Calvin*

Setting aside Voegelin's monumental fatuity, McNeill emphasizes the democratic elements in Calvin's thought. "Although Calvin's discussions of politics are incidental, his interest in this theme is by no means casual." While Calvin's interest may not be casual, it is also not consuming. McNeill recognizes that Calvin was not the direct author of representative polities but claims "they were inspired in large degrees by his ideas."[102] Ralph Hancock's moderate *Calvin and the Foundation of Modern Politics* expounds Calvin in reverse order. His theology is explained beginning with the last chapter of the *Institutes* and reading back to front. Topics like providence, government, law, reason, justification and sanctification, Holy Son and Holy Spirit are analyzed for their contributions to political science. Hancock's main point argues that the American political appeal to both Locke and Calvin is a fusion, not a confusion. Hancock thinks, "Calvin's view of Christianity essentially mirrors the deep structure of modern 'rationalism.'" This conclusion rejects the theological claim, cited in reference to Niesel, but accepted in this and many other studies that the person of Jesus is at the center of Calvin's theology. As a substitution Hancock suggests the "principle of order is the central teaching or basic doctrine underlying the *Institutes*."[103] Ten years later the same pattern reappears in Stevenson's *Sovereign Grace*, which approaches Calvin's political thought by way of his teaching on Christian freedom (III.19). According to Stevenson the dimensional strands of Christian freedom are woven together in the concept of sovereign grace. Stevenson summarizes Calvin's theology as based on the (1) reality of a sovereign and loving God who reveals himself (2) in the natural order, (3) the Spirit-inspired Scripture, (4) the person and ministry of Christ, and (5) the promptings of conscience. That this summary is for the expository purpose of political philosophy rather than for Calvin's theology is evidenced in the late placing of the person and work of Jesus Christ.[104]

Calvin's obvious and basic teaching is a twofold government for humankind. The first is the church and spiritual. The second is the state and political. The latter regulates outward behavior and instructs people in the necessary duties of humanity and citizenship (III.19.15). Not forgetting humanity's sinful condition, Calvin claims, "Yet the fact remains that some seed of political order has been implanted in all men" (II.2.13). In the context of the *Institutes* this declaration

(Cambridge: Cambridge University Press, 1982), traces the developmental relation between Calvin's practice and his principles of politics. The second appendix is devoted to predestination, and a discussion is promised of "its relationship, or lack of it, to Calvin's political thought" (227). Instead, Höpfl, while noting in Calvin no certitude of salvation except for incorporation in Christ (234), concludes that "it is impossible to derive from Calvin any criteria immune to distortion by wishful thinking or moroseness of spirit . . . whereby an individual might be assured that he is or is not elect" (235). I understand this sentence to mean Calvin's doctrine of predestination can be criticized. The same applies to Höpfl's focus on the affirmation of predestination and denial of works-righteousness to the neglect of the other twin: Calvin's doctrine of sanctification.

102. John T. McNeill, "The Democratic Elements in Calvin's Thought," *Church History*, vol. 18, no. 3 (September 1949), 155, 168.
103. Ralph C. Hancock, *Calvin and the Foundations of Modern Politics* (Ithaca, NY: Cornell University Press, 1989), xiii, 157, 161.
104. William R. Stevenson Jr., *Sovereign Grace* (New York: Oxford University Press, 1999), 8.

seems another example of God's loving providence, but I suppose "the principle of order" could be located with Hancock in the "deep structures" of Calvin's theology. Still the primary focus of this and many other political studies is not on Calvin himself but on his influence on later developments. One of the most hotly debated topics is the relation of Calvin and Calvinism to democracy, which is organized pro and con by the Roberts—Kingdon and Linder—like a tennis match with alternating passing shots from the top-ranked players.[105] Émile Doumergue says Calvin plays in democracy's court. Georges de Lagarde insists Calvin's score with democracy is not "love." John T. McNeill thinks Calvin preferred democracy; Josef Bohatec reads Calvin's preference for aristocracy and so on back and forth across the net. Since the wise men disagree so completely, prudence dictates confining any short exposition to what Calvin actually writes in the *Institutes* rather than what he might mean for the future.[106]

Like Plato, Calvin was suspicious of pure democracy and sympathetic toward real aristocracy, if not monarchy. The hope for Plato's guardians and Calvin's magistrates was that the *best* people would govern, but Calvin, greatly preferring order and greatly fearing anarchy,[107] inculcated the duty of passive obedience to the earthly ruler as a minister of God. Calvin never deviated from his 1537 *Instruction in Faith*: "We must not only render ourselves obedient to superiors who rightly and dutifully administer their higher office, but also it is fit to endure those who tyrannically abuse their power, until, through legitimate order, we be freed from their yoke."[108] The introduction to his commentary on Daniel and the exposition of Romans 13 are paeans to God's providence for those who are obedient in life and in death, where Calvin advises, "If a wicked ruler is the Lord's scourge to punish the sins of the people, let us reflect [on] our own fault" (Com. Rom. 13:3).

A good deal of Calvin's later political influence stems from the fact that his followers, after his death, responding to events like the Massacre of St. Bartholomew's Day (1572), interpreted his theology to sanction "resistance to tyrants" and the rejection of the "divine right of kings." The same position received a gender bend by John Knox against the divine rights of queens in his fierce opposition to Mary Stuart, queen of Scots.[109]

105. *Calvin and Calvinism: Sources of Democracy*, ed. Robert M. Kingdon and Robert D. Linder (Lexington, MA: D. C. Heath, 1970).

106. With a wide interest, Douglas Kelly traces Calvin's influence on liberty in five countries. Douglas F. Kelly, *The Emergence of Liberty in the Modern World: The Influence of Calvin on Five Governments from the 16th through 18th Centuries* (Phillipsburg, NJ: Presbyterian and Reformed Publishing Company, 1992).

107. Ronald S. Wallace devotes part 3 of *Calvin's Doctrine of the Christian Life* (Grand Rapids: Wm. B. Eerdmans, 1961) to "order."

108. Calvin, *Instruction in Faith* (1537) (Philadelphia: Westminster Press, 1959), 77.

109. According to George H. Sabine, *A History of Political Theory*, 3rd ed. (New York: Holt, Rinehart and Winston, 1961), the chief political beneficiary of the Reformation was absolute monarchy. "Thus the Reformation joined with economic forces already in existence to make royal government, invested with absolute power at home and with a free hand abroad, the typical form of European state" (357). Calvin's doctrine of predestination led to an ethics of action (364) although "Calvinism, especially in France and Scotland, was in opposition to governments which it had practically no

In Calvin there is no theory of popular rights, but thinking of the plebian tribunes of ancient Rome he suggested that certain "inferior magistrates" have the duty to resist tyranny (IV.20.31). This minor comment was expanded in the direction of representative government with its necessary checks and balances after his doctrine of passive resistance was abandoned. In a grandiloquent claim George Bancroft characterized the American Revolution as a Presbyterian Rebellion. Calvin, he asserts, bequeathed to the world the principle of republican liberty and concludes, "He that will not honor the memory and respect the influence of Calvin, knows but little of the origin of American liberty."[110] Doubtless the political influence of Calvin would require a lengthy explanation, but his basic political convictions can be briefly stated.

In sweeping overview, (1) Erastian political theory places the state over the church. According to (2) Roman theology (grace perfecting nature), the church is placed over the state. (3) The Radical Reformers taught separation of church and state; saints pure of heart should separate themselves from secularists dirty of hand. (4) Calvin thought the divinely established order produced a twofold government. The spiritual pertains to the inner man and eternal life; the political pertains to civil justice and outward morality (IV.20.1). While the church is chiefly responsible for holiness, and the state for peace, justice, and freedom, there can be no final separation because Jesus Christ is Lord of both church and state. Since we are pilgrims on the earth and not perfect we need the help of civil government, which "has its appointed end, so long as we live among men, to cherish and protect the outward worship of God, to defend sound doctrine of piety and the position of the church, to adjust our life to the society of men, to form our social behavior to civil righteousness, to reconcile us with one another, and to promote general peace and tranquillity" (IV.20.2). This means those who rule are raised to that honor not by chance but by providence (Com. I Pet. 2:13).

For me, these pages with their assertion that politicians are "ministers of God" constitute the most distressing chapter in the *Institutes* because I think Calvin is theologically and theoretically correct but politically and practically wrong. Calvin's confessional and doxological teaching about God's governance of all creation receives here its severest reality test. In discussing the state, Calvin addresses three topics: (1) the rulers (magistrates) who protect and guard the laws, (2) the laws by which the state is governed, and (3) the people governed by the laws and the obedience owed to the magistrates. In the background, "The belief

---

chance to convert or capture" (362). According to J. W. Allen, *A History of Political Thought in the Sixteenth Century* (London: Methuen and Co., 1928), 107, France and Scotland both repudiated Calvin's doctrine of submission to established rulers. "So important was the part played by John Knox in this repudiation by Calvinists of one of the essential points of Calvin's teaching, that he cannot but be regarded as one of the chief personal factors in the history of political thought in the sixteenth century." Allen has a chapter on Calvin, a chapter on the break from Calvin, one on Huguenot thought, and a section on the Calvinist Puritans.

110. George Bancroft, "A Word on Calvin the Reformer," in *Literary and Historical Miscellanies* (New York: Harper and Brothers, 1855), 406.

was general on the side of churchmen that pure doctrine ought to be maintained by public authority, and on the side of statesmen that unity of religion was an indispensable condition of public order."[111]

Calvin assumed the state was neither hostile nor indifferent to the Christian religion (IV.20.9). Therefore, under God's twofold government the civil authorities "have a mandate from God, have been invested with divine authority, and are wholly God's representatives, in a manner, acting as his vicegerents. [This means] that princes are ministers of God, for those doing good unto praise; for those doing evil, avengers unto wrath" (IV.20.4). These "ordained ministers of divine justice" are appointed by divine providence to be instruments of divine truth (IV.20.6). Calvin is aware that the debate concerning the best form of government (mentioning specifically monarchy, aristocracy, and democracy in the French edition of 1560) admits of no simple solution, but hoping for government composed of the best people for the benefit of the most people he preferred "a system compounded of aristocracy and democracy" (IV.20.8). He thought magistrates "are ordained protectors and vindicators of public innocence, modesty, decency, and tranquillity [providing] for the common safety and peace of all" (IV.20.9). This protection requires the right to levy taxes and justifies capital punishment as well as just wars although "surely everything else ought to be tried before recourse is had to arms" (IV.20.12).

Addressing his second topic, Calvin asserts that a discourse concerning the best kind of laws would be endless. Moreover, since he has already dealt with law and gospel in Book II, he thinks a few remarks at this point should suffice. The law is commonly divided into moral, ceremonial, and judicial (IV.20.14). The first commands us to love God with pure faith and to embrace other people with sincere affection (IV.20.15). The ceremonial law guided the Jewish people until the fullness of time revealed the truth that had been foreshadowed. The judicial law "imparted certain formulas of equity and justice, by which [people] might live together blamelessly and peaceably" (IV.20.13).

Turning in the third place to consider the people governed by the laws and their obedience to the magistrates, Calvin thinks Christian plaintiffs and defendants are allowed to appeal to courts of law but only with love in their hearts—a condition quite beyond the capacity of any litigant I have ever known! Calvin recognizes this difficulty but insists litigation must seek equity, not advantage. "For this must be a set principle for all Christians: that a lawsuit, however just, can never be rightly prosecuted by any man, unless he treat his adversary with the same love and good will as if the business under controversy were already amicably settled and composed" (IV.20.18). In summary, "Love will give every man the best counsel. Everything undertaken apart from love and all disputes that go beyond it, we regard as incontrovertibly unjust and impious" (IV.20.21). Since life is "nothing but the bearing of a perpetual cross," Calvin thinks "Christians ought to be a kind of men born to bear slanders and injuries, open to the malice, deceits, and mockeries of wicked men" (IV.20.20).

111. Sabine, *History of Political Theory*, 355.

Civil order is God's will. Therefore, the first duty of citizens is to respect the magistrates' office as a jurisdiction bestowed by God. The second duty is to pay obedience to good and bad rulers. The former is a blessing from God and the latter a punishment from God. The task of ordinary people in the political arena is "to obey and suffer" (IV.20.31), but if there are "magistrates of the people, appointed to restrain the wilfulness of kings," Calvin insists they should protect the people (IV.20.31). Generally Calvin opposes revolution by the people against an unjust ruler following his understanding of Romans 13, but in his commentary on Daniel he also says, "Earthly princes lay aside all their power when they rise up against God, and are unworthy of being reckoned in the number of mankind. We ought rather utterly to defy than to obey them whenever they . . . wish to spoil God of his rights, and, as it were, to seize his throne and draw him down from heaven" (Com. Dan. 6:22). Calvin concludes his reflection on political issues by noting one exception to the advice about obedience to the authority of rulers. Since we are redeemed by Christ whenever obedience to an earthly ruler leads away from obedience to the heavenly King of Kings, "we should not enslave ourselves to the wicked desires of men—much less be subject to their impiety" (IV.20.32).

To his conception of church and state Calvin applied his conviction of God's great government. Intellectually this is commendable and theoretically and theologically satisfying. However, the horrendous choices between two evils and apparently two sins required of modern states seem practically to preclude such a view. I conclude that this subject and this chapter represent an integral and essential part of Calvin's doctrine of God's providence for the beloved community of the faithful. Therefore, the relation of church and state is not an appendage in his theology. Nevertheless, it remains an inchoate inquiry in mine.

CONCLUSIONS TO BOOK IV

According to John T. McNeill the government, orders, and powers of the church occupy nineteen of the twenty chapters of the concluding book of the *Institutes*, which presumably sets apart Calvin's final chapter on the state (IV.20).[112] Book IV is thus divided into the doctrines of the church and the state. More accurately chapter 20 should also be included as a discussion of the power of the church in relation to the state. Calvin outlined his subjects as the church, the sacraments, and the state (IV.1.1), but it is important to recognize that the exposition of the faithful community is an expansion of the treatment of faithful persons. The communal aspects of doctrines already explored in Books I, II, and III being noted were not reengaged. Instead, these important themes central to understanding the church were identified as the head and the body, the true and the false, and the chosen and the responsible.

112. John T. McNeill, "The Church in Sixteenth-Century Reformed Theology," *The Journal of Religion* 22 (July 1941): 259.

The second section of Book IV deals with the sacraments. As a reformer Calvin volunteered to fight in the eucharistic wars with the hope of concluding a lasting peace. Beginning with the conviction of union in Christ, Calvin thought he could explain the "mutual exchange" and avoid superstition, foster faith, and defend the risen humanity of Christ. The result was to open another front until the troops of Geneva and Zurich signed the Zurich Consensus. To whatever extent transubstantiation describes Catholic doctrine and consubstantiation describes Lutheran doctrine, real presence applied to Calvin obscures as much as it clarifies. Since Calvin left unresolved the exact relation between Word and sacrament, a more radical rethinking of the entire issue, while unlikely to occur, would be useful if it did.

The third topic, understanding Calvin's political legacy, will continue to be a concern to the extent his legatees endeavor to resist tyranny and establish representative democracy. Nevertheless, while Calvin's convictions on church and state are theoretically and theologically satisfying, his conclusions are unworkable in modern pluralistic societies.

Breaking Off the Engagement

A Conclusion

This engagement with Calvin's theology is nearly ended. The point of viewing, the introductory conclusions, the expositions, and the evaluations are before the reader. What remains is a summary reflection on the whole.

Calvin's thought can be understood in many ways and for many purposes. One of the most widespread maintains that Calvin provides logical principles, such as the sovereignty or glory of God, from which Calvinistic theologians (or philosophers) can deduce propositions such as predestination and total depravity on the way to constructing a coherent and faithful world view. On the contrary, it is here enounced that Calvin produces not a rational system of belief but a Christian confession of faith, which is not the same thing. *The Institutes of the Christian Religion* is not an appeal to human reason, even to Christian reason (if that nebulous concept could be precisely established). Instead Calvin "calls his book not a *summa theologiae* but a *summa pietatis*," meaning a comprehensive and systematic confession of the love of God the Father revealed in Jesus Christ the Eternal Son, and effected by the work of the Holy Spirit. Calvin, of course, strives to be reasonable and appeals to sound principles, but pride of place belongs to the correct interpretation of Scripture supported by a proper appreciation of the central theological tradition and recognition of the common experience of the faithful.

The enduring value of Calvin's theology is the example he offers in the complexities of confession of the Lordship of Christ and our union with him, which begins "objectively" with what God has done for us as Creator and Redeemer and done "subjectively" in us as faithful persons and the faithful community. Moreover, Calvin's thinking, like ours, involves continually shifting applications of Scripture, tradition, reason, and experience and other human ways of knowing made efficacious by the illumination of the Divine Spirit. Calvin's confession demonstrates both an admirable confidence and a genuine humility, but perhaps not in exactly the places we would prefer. Still, we can learn a great deal from engagement with him while recognizing he does not have all the important answers nor even all the important questions for our time. Obviously, and most especially, no thinker today can rest content with what Calvin knew five hundred years ago about philosophy and history and Scripture and science. Nevertheless, a crucial part of the theological task in any time is the utilization of the best resources available from the past. Among Christian theologians John Calvin is one of the best professors of God.

More than that, if one reads even somewhat carefully, a passionately committed and admirably sympathetic person can be glimpsed behind the lines of text. Calvin cannot be charged with excessive optimism concerning the human condition because he knew a great deal about misery. Yet in the middle of an exposition of sin Calvin writes what I regard as his most touching, winsome, and poignant sentence. "Take courage, my friends; even if we are nothing in our own hearts, perchance something of us is safely hidden in the heart of God" (III.2.25). Calvin is an excellent guide into the central affirmation of the union with Christ declared in Colossians 3:3: "Your life is hidden with Christ in God," calling especial attention to the particles "in God" and "with Christ." He concludes, and so may we, "A beautiful consolation, that the coming of Christ will be the manifestation of our life" (Com. Col. 3:3).

Calvin's Method in Theology

An Excursus

INTRODUCTION

As previously noted, Calvin begins the *Institutes* with an assertion of the knowledge of God and the self. Since the study of the method and grounds of knowing is called epistemology (after the Greek word for knowledge ἐπίστημη), everyone who claims to know anything makes an epistemological statement in some sense. The question, of course, is in what sense? The knowledge of God is a crucial component of theology, but a technical theory of knowledge in itself is not required for confession and by Calvin not provided. Calvin had no intention of making a philosophical contribution as he told Westphal, "I would rather perish a hundred times than put one little word of Christ into the balance, and counter-weigh it by the whole body of philosophy."[1] Put another way, Calvin's purported epistemology is eclectic, not analytical. He appeals to Scripture, reason, history, experience, common sense, and so on, but some scholars isolate these legitimate elements in ways that distort Calvin's actual use of them. Even worse, discussions of these appeals too often ignore their essential connection

1. *Westphal,* 2:289.

with the mystery of union in Christ and their dependent relation on the inner testimony of the Holy Spirit, which are, to say the least, not ordinary epistemological categories. When Calvin's basic theological foundation is set aside, the exposition of his so-called methodology becomes a serious reductionism. Since knowledge of God and the Self is basic to Calvin's theology, his view of knowledge—especially of reason and experience—is crucial to discuss at some length. The main point is that later interest and developments in understanding epistemological categories have been detrimentally imposed on Calvin. Torrance puts the point bluntly, "One of the calamities of traditional exposition and interpretation of Calvin's theology has been, by means of arid logical forms, to make Calvin's own distinctions too clean and too rigid. This has resulted in an oversimplification which has obscured the flexibility as well as the range and profundity of his thought."[2]

Calvin's use of epistemological tools—what, when, where, why, and how they are employed—is impossible to synthesize precisely because Calvin's method is to grab the tool at hand for the purpose in mind without stopping to analyze its general function. Simply stated, fired by any canon, Calvin produces a sophisticated theology that is based on a confessional rather than a philosophical epistemology. This conclusion is exactly opposite that of William J. Bouwsma in his chapter on Calvin's "Rational Religion." Bouwsma thinks his view of doctrine points "to a tendency in Calvin to understand faith less as trust in God's promises than as intellectual assent to a body of propositions."[3] In fact Calvin's tendency is to understand faith as life in Christ. He says, "I am overwhelmed by the depth of this mystery, and with Paul am not ashamed to acknowledge in wonder my ignorance. . . . Reason itself teaches us whatever is supernatural is clearly beyond the grasp of our minds. Let us therefore labor more to feel Christ living in us, than to discover the nature of that communion" (Com. Eph. 5:32).[4]

Calvin's purpose is to articulate the Christian faith aright, which he conceives to require proper interpretation of Scripture. The appeal in faith to Scripture is the primary method of establishing the Lordship of Jesus Christ, but Calvin also cites reason, experience, and tradition, the latter meaning the history of doctrine properly understood. In Calvin these ways of knowing do not constitute a "scientific" method from which a "unified field theory" of knowing is possible. This conclusion could hardly be more trenchantly presented than by Richard Prins in discussing "beclouding problems." "Generally," he thinks, "Calvin's inconsisten-

---

2. T. F. Torrance, *Calvin's Doctrine of Man* (Grand Rapids: Wm. B. Eerdmans, 1957), 7.

3. William J. Bouwsma, *John Calvin: A Sixteenth-Century Portrait* (New York: Oxford University Press, 1988), ultimately argues for "two Calvins." One accepts (99) and one rejects (150) the traditional sovereignty of reason. Reading chap. 6 on rational religion and chap. 9 on knowing (actually unknowing) is an exercise in ambiguity and paradox.

4. As is well known, Plato (*Theaetetus*, 155d) and Aristotle (*Metaphysics*, I, 2) declare that philosophy begins in wonder. Michael B. Foster, *Mystery and Philosophy* (London: SCM Press, 1957), 34, concludes, "It would be correct and I think enlightening to describe Greek contemplation as a form of intellectual worship."

cies, ambiguities, and contradictions are traceable to four sources: (1) the difficulty of maintaining consistency and focus throughout a corpus of some fifty collected volumes; (2) imprecision or incompleteness within his thought; (3) unawareness of conflicts within his thought or reluctance to face those conflicts; (4) the possibility that Calvin's inconsistencies reflect those of the Bible." Certainly Calvin thought he was following the teaching of Scripture. "The prophets of God do not always very anxiously hold to what seems consistent in their discourses" (Com Jl.2:14). Prins accurately evaluates Calvin's work as awesome, comprehensive, embracing, but also diffuse, contradictory, incohesive, and incoherent.[5]

In his masterful consideration of this issue William J. Abraham claims the ecclesial canon appeals to Scripture, creed, liturgy, iconography, the fathers, and the sacraments. In contrast, epistemological criteria include reason, experience, memory, intuition, and inference. The historical conflation of theology and philosophy caused the protocols of Christian faith to be transformed from soteriological to epistemological. "In the course of time the canonical heritage of the West was systematically epistemized: that is, canonical materials, persons, and practices were treated as items in a theory of knowledge."

Agreeing with the main conclusions of Abraham's analysis, his evaluation of Calvin as an important contributor to the transformation of the soteriological to the epistemological is a dreadful mistake. Based on Calvin's view of Word and Spirit, interpreted through a theory of dictation, Abraham associates both Calvin and Luther as theological foundationalists,[6] but the foundation of Christian faith for Calvin is not a dictated Scripture but Jesus Christ.[7] That so learned and perspicacious a scholar could perpetuate this canard concerning "Calvin's Method" is a salutary reminder of the frailty to which all flesh is heir. Moreover, the conflation of faith and logic, theology and philosophy, ecclesial canon and epistemic criteria, personal and communal bias, while important to recognize, is difficult, if not impossible, to avoid. Calvin appeals canonically to Scripture but also to reason and to experience. Nevertheless, many scholars, including Abraham, think he appeals to one or another of these ways of knowing as epistemological norms. Using Abraham's own categories, Calvin's method is more confessional than logical—therefore, more to be located within ecclesial canons than epistemic criteria.

In an earlier and quite unsympathetic reflection, Abraham claims questioning Calvin's view of God is a duty of both faith and logic. According to Abraham, Calvin's doctrines of divine sovereignty and human freedom offer "a bold but hopeless way out." Declaring grace and freedom to be compatible, Abraham

---

5. Richard Prins, "The Image of God in Adam and the Restoration of Man in Jesus Christ: A Study in Calvin," *Scottish Journal of Theology* 25 (1972): 33, 44.

6. William J. Abraham, *Canon and Criterion in Christian Theology: From the Fathers to Feminism* (Oxford: Clarendon Press, 1998), 471, 130–35. Especially helpful are the chapters, "The Rule of Reason" and "Theology within the Limits of Experience."

7. The complicated meaning of dictation in Calvin is helpfully discussed by Edward A. Dowey Jr., *The Knowledge of God in Calvin's Theology*, 3rd ed. (Grand Rapids: Eerdmans, 1994 [1951]), 91ff.

insists, "We can hold to both without committing ourselves to the dubious analysis of freedom presented by the Calvinist tradition." He concludes, "Rather than safeguard divine glory, the Calvinist tradition, therefore, destroys it at its foundation." Sliding seamlessly along his bias between Calvin and Calvinism, Abraham illustrates this distinction by a critique of Paul Helm on credit and merit. However one might define Calvinism, Helm represents one, but not the only, and not the best, interpretation of Calvin. Granted Abraham's Methodist commitments it still appears unseemly for a Wesleyan philosopher of theology to charge a Calvinist philosopher of theology with the opprobrium of displaying "extraordinary theological insensitivity." More substantially, unable to accept Calvin's view of God's irresistible grace,[8] Abraham assures his reader, "We will need to reject Calvin's account of predestination, divine foreknowledge, divine providence, personal assurance, and future hope." Having now demonstrated to his own satisfaction Calvin's inadequacies as a theologian, Abraham suggests all these concepts may legitimately reappear "in a rival theological vision of God and salvation."[9] However, rather than letting us see this rival and better vision, Abraham graciously declares its production to be a task for theologians, not philosophers like himself. The conclusion here is that at least Abraham is a better critic of Calvin than interpreter. Calvin's so-called method does not and cannot bear the weight that some interpreters place on one or another of these elements, meaning Calvin's serious but nontechnical use of epistemological terms should not force his theology to become more rational, more experiential, more scriptural, or more traditional than it actually is.[10]

Since Descartes became too warm in his famous stove-heated room, the general vogue among scholars has decreed beginning with the issue of knowledge. The question, "*How* do you know?" is now placed before "*What* (or *Who*) do you know?" Philosophically (and, to some extent, theologically), epistemology precedes ontology.[11] Even people like Calvin who lived before Descartes are asked to walk their foundational garments down this runway. By some of his dressers Calvin is variously attired in Scripture, faith, reason, experience, or tradition, and in fact Calvin wears all these garments; but Calvin's clothing is more casual and modest than many theological fashion editors are willing to admit. To continue this conceit for one sentence more, Calvin covers himself in Scripture with rea-

8. There exists a presumably non-bodice-ripping Calvinistic romance novel with a cover claim, "Baby, Your Name Must Be Grace Because You Are Irresistible." See http://www.partee.net/grace.htm.

9. William J. Abraham, *An Introduction to the Philosophy of Religion* (Englewood Cliffs, NJ: Prentice-Hall, 1985), 144, 151, 147, 150, 151.

10. See my "Calvin, Calvinism, and Rationality" and the various essays in *Rationality in the Calvinian Tradition*, ed. Hendrik Hart, Johan van der Hoeven, and Nicholas Wolsterstorff (Lanham, MD: University Press, 1983). Also chap. 3, "Reason and Experience in Epistemology" in my *Calvin and Classical Philosophy* (Louisville, KY: Westminster John Knox Press, 2005), and "Calvin and Experience," *Scottish Journal of Theology* 26, no. 2 (May 1973): 169–81.

11. When we lived in the great farm state of Iowa, the philosophers at a major university often complained that veterinary medicine was taken more seriously than philosophical insight. They thought Descartes should come before the horse.

son and experience as important accessories and tradition as an accent, but these items are not presented as uniform.[12]

When Calvin wrote, "Nearly all the wisdom we possess, that is to say, true and sound wisdom, consists of two parts: the knowledge of God and of ourselves," he was neither positing an epistemological antithesis nor accepting a metaphysical dualism.[13] Calvin's central "ontological" confession maintains "our very being is nothing but subsistence in the one God" (I.1.1). Since Calvin's purpose is to confess the truth of the gospel, he does not attempt to develop a methodology in the modern sense, and it may well be doubted whether any technical epistemology could serve his confessional intention. Contrary to many of his proponents, Calvin's working components are neither analytically, synthetically, nor sequentially developed. This point is defended by G. K. Chesterton, who did not like Calvinists, in his chapter on the paradoxes of Christianity. The real trouble with our world, he says, "is that it is nearly reasonable, but not quite. Life is not an illogicality; yet it is a trap for logicians." He concludes, "Christianity got over the difficulty of combining furious opposites, by keeping them both, and keeping them both furious."[14] This situation may be a problem for a putative logical system but not for an actual confession of faith. That is, a confession of faith appeals to a quality of reasonableness but does not claim to forge strong links into chains of reasons. Inevitably and unfortunately, later epistemological developments are often read back into Calvin with the effect of overformulating and therefore oversimplifying his more unsophisticated appeals to knowledge.

Among the fundamental components of knowing, Scripture (in Books I and II) and faith (the chief subject of Book III) were discussed where they appeared in the text of the *Institutes*. Calvin's scattered references to reason, intellect, and understanding created and fallen were briefly noted in Book I. When Calvin defines reason in a positive sense, he means little more than thinking properly. Experience, the other major epistemological category, can be roughly defined as what happens to us, around us, and in us. The precise definitions and their legitimate extensions

---

12. See *Westphal,* 1:241. More systematically presented is the so-called Wesleyan Quadrilateral. According to the Book of Discipline of the United Methodist Church, "Wesley believed the living core of the Christian faith was revealed in Scripture, illumined by tradition, vivified in personal experience, and confirmed by reason" (104). This declaration is followed by several pages of explanation. For a more extended analysis, see William J. Abraham, "The Wesleyan Quadrilateral," in *Wesleyan Theology Today: A Bicentennial Theological Consultation,* ed. Theodore Runyon (Nashville: Kingwood Books, 1985), 119–26. Abraham declares, "None of the other elements in the quadrilateral can be viewed as a coordinate canon of equal standing with the Bible." Additionally, he thinks Wesley more favorable to reason than Calvin, but it is "clear by now that experience had a crucial role in Wesley's theology" (120, 122). See also W. Stephen Gunter, Scott J. Jones, Ted A. Campbell, Rebekah L. Miles, and Randy L. Maddox, *Wesley and the Quadrilateral: Renewing the Conversation* (Nashville: Abingdon Press, 1997).

13. Gerald J. Postema, "Calvin's Alleged Rejection of Natural Theology," *Scottish Journal of Theology* 24 (1971): 423–34, disagrees. He thinks, "The organizing, dominant theme of the *Institutes* is a unique epistemology" (423).

14. Gilbert K. Chesterton, *Orthodoxy* (New York: John Lane Company, 1909), 148, 174. Chesterton's Father Brown stories are, of course, wonderful, but how anyone could enjoy his *The Man Who Was Thursday* baffles me.

as well as the relations of reason and experience to each other is a debate of long duration with no consensus likely to be forthcoming.

Calvin's use of reason is an important aspect of his theology, but it is difficult to describe, easy to exaggerate, and debatable to extend. Among his interpreters focusing on specific aspects of Calvin's method, his view of reason and experience is generally separated and then analyzed because the coherence of all the components is impossible to establish. Calvin employs reason and experience in every part of his exposition, but he does not discuss their uses and limitations as a central topic. This situation allows commentators to divide into sharply opposing camps on these extremely complex issues. Every theologian tries to think reasonably and, seeking to persuade others, appeals to a reasonableness assumed possessed in common. In this way the use of reason in theology is unavoidable. Nevertheless, the precise definition of this "faculty," the proper extent of its employment, and the correct confidence in its adequacy remain hotly debated issues, especially in relation to the effect of sin. In some Calvinistic circles the question is entirely ignored. In "Orthodox Calvinism" a large and definite role is assigned to reason. In "New School Calvinism" a large and definite role is assigned to experience.

A. CALVIN AND REASON

Reason has long been considered the basic and most accurate method of human knowing.[15] Indeed, the entire history of Western thought can be described as the dream of reason, and one of the central aspects of the continuing conversation between Christianity and classical and contemporary culture is its proper role.[16]

---

15. Accepting William James's definition of philosophy as "a particularly stubborn effort to think clearly," Anthony Gottlieb entitles his history of Western philosophy *The Dream of Reason* (New York: W. W. Norton & Company, 2000). This dream continues to haunt Western intellectual culture as evidenced by the socially powerful assumption of American law courts that judgments rendered will be based on the understanding of the "reasonable man." The "reasonable man (or reasonable person) or ordinary prudence" standard plays a critical role in judicial decisions. This legal fiction, tracing its lineage from the guardians (or philosopher-kings) of Plato's *Republic*, assumes society is properly guided by its best (i.e., most reasonable) people. What the average person might think or do is irrelevant. This is an aristocratic rather than a democratic criterion. Presumably, the reasonable person is fair-minded, capable of receiving appropriate information and processing to good judgment. See *Prosser and Keeton on The Law of Torts*, 5th ed., ed. W. Page Keeton (St. Paul, MN: West Publishing Co., 1984), sec. 32.

16. Among the classic studies of reason is the philosopher George Santayana's *The Life of Reason or the Phases of the Human Process*, 5 vols. (New York: Charles Scribner's Sons, 1905 [1933]). The third volume deals with reason in religion. Santayana argues that since reason is the seat of all ultimate values, religion functions in the life of reason by sanctioning, unifying, and transforming ethics. Religion is imaginative and poetic, operating by grace and flourishing by prayer. For a Roman Catholic perspective, see Étienne Gilson, *Reason and Revelation in the Middle Ages* (New York: Charles Scribner's Sons, 1938 [1954]). Especially interesting is the second chapter dealing with Averroës, who tried to reconcile Aristotle's philosophy and Islamic faith. See also *The Unity of Philosophical Experience* (New York: Charles Scribner's Sons, 1937 [1948]). For a Protestant view, see Emil Brunner's *Revelation and Reason: The Christian Doctrine of Faith and Knowledge*, trans. Olive Wyon (Philadelphia: Westminster Press, 1946).

Calvin is, of course, one of the major beneficiaries of the Western intellectual tradition, but his will contains no significant legacy for reason, which is itself significant.[17] The most thorough study of this topic, known to me, is David Jon Van Houten's 1993 University of Chicago dissertation entitled "Earthly Wisdom and Heavenly Wisdom: The Concept of Reason in the Theology of John Calvin." Curiously, the twofold distinction of the title expands into a threefold format for exposition based on the outline Calvin mentions in debate with Tileman Heshusius. In his polemic Calvin suggests three kinds of reason. First, a naturally implanted reason (treated by Van Houten in chap. 3). Second, a vitiated reason corrupted into foolishness by sinful arrogance (chap. 4). The third kind of reason is sanctioned by both the Spirit of God and Scripture (chap. 5).[18] Van Houten takes this outline with programmatic earnestness and develops his thesis on its structure. However, having announced three kinds of reason in this treatise on the Eucharist, Calvin does not analyze them further than to insist he does not "profanely philosophize about the mysteries of God."

Van Houten's thesis is interesting. So are his antithesis and his synthesis, but the issue remains, to put the question anachronistically, whether these three elements form a kind of "Hegelian dialectic," as he thinks, or produce a "Kantian antinomy," as I think. The separating issue is the so-called third stage of reason, which is variously titled illumined, redeemed, sanctified, even right reason. Certainly Calvin praised reason as a good gift of God's creation. He certainly criticized reason as

17. In vigorous advocacy of the contemporary relevance of Calvin's employment of reason, Robert H. Ayers proposes to analyze Calvin's use of language, logic, and reason. That is, "to study critically John Calvin's *Institutes of the Christian Religion* in the light of epistemological and semiotical considerations and issues." Ayers admits that concerning foreordination and theodicy, "Calvin falls into the pit of inconsistency and obscurity" but *insists Calvin has a high regard for reason, which is instructive for modern thought.* "Indeed, it is an indispensable servant and has an essential role to play in the task of faith seeking understanding." Ayers concedes, "To be sure, Scripture, the Word of God, and the experience of faith transcend reason and yet reason is an indispensable servant of faith. For this servant to function properly, attention must be given to the issues in semiotics." Ayers thinks, "It is evident in the *Institutes* that he does in fact proceed by many and various types of arguments and that among them are the categorical syllogisms and the propositional inference schemas." This means "that on almost every page of the *Institutes*, Calvin engages in some sort of semantical analysis in which such problems as the definitional meanings or intentions of important terms, etymologies, common usage, ambiguity, metaphors or symbolic terms and verbal disputes are considered." Likewise, it means, although Ayers has set them aside, that Calvin's epistemological method includes appeals to the Word of God and the experience of faith as well as to reason. Ayers does not explain why Calvin's high regard for reason does not prevent him from falling into the pit of inconsistency and obscurity. Perhaps one can assume the Word of God and the experience of faith lead Calvin to some conclusions at variance with human logic. Still, Ayers demonstrates to his own satisfaction that various contemporary philosophical problems can be found in Calvin's writings. "It seems rather clear" to Ayers but not to me "that Calvin would have agreed with a basic and rather obviously true, claim of the so-called Analytical School in modern philosophy, namely, that the question of the meaning of a claim is logically prior to the question of the truth or falsity of that claim." On the contrary, Calvin assumed he was proclaiming the truth of God not making the "truth claims" of the philosophers. Calvin's theology is a confession of faith, not a clarification of meaning (Robert H. Ayers, "Language, Logic and Reason in Calvin's *Institutes*," *Religious Studies* 16 [1980]: 283, 285, 296, 292, 286, 287).

18. "The Clear Explanation of Sound Doctrine concerning the True Partaking of the Flesh and Blood of Christ in the Holy Supper," in *Calvin: Theological Treatises*, trans. J. K. S. Reid (Philadelphia: Westminster Press, 1954), 272–73.

corrupted by human sin, and he certainly appealed to reason to support his theological confession. Nevertheless, Calvin's theological *use* of reason (also Scripture, and experience, and tradition, etc.), while a constant practice, does not become an epistemological *theory*. Van Houten, of course, disagrees, and in expounding "reason sanctioned by the Spirit of God and Scripture" identifies a third category beyond reason created and reason fallen. He admits, "While Calvin, at times, is vague as to the exact nature of the regeneration, redemption, enlightenment or illumination of reason, he clearly states that both Scripture and the Holy Spirit are involved in the process" (260). Calvin is indeed quite clear about the importance of Word and Spirit in the knowledge of God but not that the enlightenment of reason is a separate epistemological stage. Van Houten declares, "'Illumination' is Calvin's favorite term for this process of spiritual renewal of human reason" (262). On the contrary, having admitted that Calvin is vague about the redemption of reason, Van Houten cannot now claim that the illumination of the Spirit or the inner testimony to the Word becomes a permanent epistemological faculty rather than an occasional gift of divine grace.

The following sketch briefly reviews Calvin and reason under the topics of natural reason, sinful reason, and sanctified reason.

1. Natural Reason

Without doubt Calvin regarded created or natural reason as one of the great gifts of God. Following the philosophers in its praise Calvin taught that the purpose of understanding is to distinguish good from evil and the purpose of the will is to choose and follow the good and to reject evil (I.15.7). Calvin claims the conception of equity "is ample proof that in the arrangement of this life no man is without the light of reason" (II.2.13). Again, "Reason is proper to our nature; it distinguishes us from brute beasts" (II.2.17). This conclusion is reflected in Hamlet's familiar declaration, "What a piece of work is man! How noble in reason / How infinite in faculty" (II.2.315ff.). Our "godlike reason" (IV.4.38) contrasts with the beasts "that want discourse of reason" (I.2.141).

Reason moving about in its natural habitat has many definitions. They include connecting ideas consciously, coherently, and purposively. Reason is the mind's rational, discursive activity of passing from propositions known or assumed to be true to other truths distinct from them but following logically from them. Over the centuries a substantial consensus developed that placed great confidence in reason. In the classical period Plato wrote of the "sacred and golden cord of reason" (*Laws* 1:645a). In the *Phaedo* he recommends that we "follow reason" (84a). According to Aristotle in *De Anima*, there are three souls. We share with plants and animals a *nutritive* soul (the ability to take nourishment). We share with animals a *sensitive* soul (the ability to feel). The *rational* soul is the faculty that sets the human apart from the animal and plant kingdoms. This basic conviction expands into a logic of subject and predicate, of particular and universal propositions, and of syllogisms that still overshadows reflection in the Western world.

The term *logos*—meaning reason, logic, science, and so on—was a dynamite word among Greek thinkers, like Heraclitus, the Stoics, and Philo of Alexandria, for centuries before it was employed to describe Jesus (John 1:1). One group of scholars claims that the employment of the concept of *logos* in Christian theology was a brilliant synthesis of Hellenic and Hebraic thought; others regard the use of *logos* as the introduction of a foreign idea into the biblical witness and therefore an unmitigated disaster. Addressing this issue in his splendid *The Spirit of Early Christian Thought*, Robert Wilken correctly places reason in the service of faith and love, asserting that "the energy, the vitality, the imaginative power of Christian thought stems from within, from the person of Christ, the Bible, Christian worship, the life of the church. . . . Christians reasoned from the history of Israel and of Jesus Christ, from the experience of Christian worship, and from the Holy Scriptures." Of especial importance is the discussion of "The Reasonableness of Faith" (chap. 7). One scholar (unidentified) charged that Christianity "flung itself passionately under the spell of a system of authoritative Revelation, which acknowledged no truth outside itself." The result was "undermining confidence in the power of reason, [and smothering] the spirit of questioning and investigation." Wilken suspects this author "has let his imagination and his rhetoric, not to say his prejudices, roam at will, untethered from sources or facts." The fact is Christian thinkers "used reason to weigh, judge, interpret, and explain what was held to be true."[19]

Calvin is not very interested in the philosophical aspect of the discussion. He declares the term *logos* indicates that God "expresses himself to us by his Speech or Word. The other meanings of ὁ λόγος are not so apt. The Greek certainly means *definition* or *reason* or *calculation*; but I refuse to philosophize beyond the grasp of my faith." This theological refusal applies to the "drivelling nonsense" of Servetus and the Arians, who ascribe a temporal beginning to the Word and of Sabellius who denies the Son a certain subsistence of his own in God. "The Evangelist sends us to the eternal sanctuary of God and teaches us that the Word was, as it were, hidden there before he revealed himself in the outward workmanship of the world" (Com. Jn. 1:1).

Some early Christians believed the conclusions of natural reason should be entirely rejected in favor of God's supernatural revelation to the Hebrew people, a view famously indicated by Tertullian's rhetorical question, "What has Athens to do with Jerusalem?" In his fine essay on faith and reason Robert E. Cushman points out that Augustine opposed Tertullian believing the priority of faith was eminently reasonable. "In showing how this was so, Augustine laid a new and definitive foundation for Christian philosophy."[20] Augustine and other theologians thought the finer elements of pagan antiquity could be accepted, corrected, and understood as part of God's general providence for humankind. According

19. Robert Louis Wilken, *The Spirit of Early Christian Thought: Seeking the Face of God* (New Haven, CT: Yale University Press, 2003), xvi, xvii, 163, 164.
20. Robert E. Cushman, "Faith and Reason," in *A Companion to the Study of St. Augustine*, ed. Roy W. Battenhouse (New York: Oxford University Press, 1955), 288.

to Peter Gay, "The main stream of Christian policy toward antiquity ran some-what unsteadily between these extremes." Christian admirers of antiquity like Origen, Jerome, and Augustine sought anxiously for scriptural permission to uti-lize classical intellectual culture. They believed permission was granted in Deuteronomy 21:10–13.[21] After suitable ablutions the beautiful captive slave woman (probably named Sophia, meaning earthly wisdom) could become the wife of the warrior of God (heavenly wisdom). Once permission to use philoso-phy was assumed, the notion of reason as the defining human characteristic was repeated by countless theologians. Contemplation was thought to be the truest approach to God. In the *Summa Contra Gentiles* Thomas Aquinas writes, "Man's ultimate happiness consists in the contemplation of truth" (3.37).

Calvin's confidence in reason is markedly different from Aquinas's, but it is salutary to remember that Thomas also wrote, "If the only way open to us for the knowledge of God were solely that of the reason, the human race would remain in the blackest shadows of ignorance" (*SCG* 1.4.4). According to Calvin, the fac-ulty that may be called created or natural reason was one of the good gifts God bestowed on the human race in the beginning, but the result of sin is that human reason can understand neither who God is nor his relation to mankind (II.1.18). Human philosophy is based on reason alone, but "Christian philosophy bids rea-son give way to, submit, and subject itself to, the Holy Spirit" (III.7.1; II.2.26). Calvin occasionally appeals to a distinction between "earthly things," for which reason is more or less adequate, and "heavenly things," for which it is not (II.11.13), but the sharp point of Calvin's cut direct is that philosophers are igno-rant of the corruption of nature that originated from the penalty for human defection (I.15.7). Concerning intellect and will, the philosophers (and theolo-gians like Thomas) face great obscurity since they seek a building in a ruin, and in scattered fragments, a well-knit structure (I.15.8).[22]

---

21. Peter Gay, *The Enlightenment: An Interpretation, The Rise of Modern Paganism* (New York: W. W. Norton & Company, 1966), 218–20. In 1939 Peter Gay (born Peter Joachim Fröhlich), *My German Question: Growing Up in Nazi Berlin* (New Haven, CT: Yale University Press, 1998), was sched-uled to escape from Hamburg, Germany, to Havana, Cuba, on a ship called the *St. Louis* but switched to the *Iberia*, which departed two weeks earlier. When the *St. Louis* arrived in Havana, the Cuban gov-ernment revoked the landing permits of the 907 Jewish refugees and barred them from leaving the ship. With Peter Gay watching from the Havana harbor the *St. Louis* left to circle the Caribbean, seeking asylum for its passengers, but no country, including the United States, would accept them. The ship finally returned to Europe where Belgium, France, Holland, and England each accepted a fourth of the refugees. Except for about forty, all those who did not go to England died in the Nazi occupation. Also traveling on the *Iberia* was a nineteen-year-old Hungarian Jew named George Jellinek who later hosted classical music for thirty-six years on *The Vocal Scene* at New York's WQXR radio station.

22. In his study of Calvin's humanism using the dialectic between wisdom and holiness and see-ing the fall as the pivot, Jean Boisset treats parallels between Plato and Calvin on the theme of con-templation. *Sagesse et Sainteté dans la Pensée de Jean Calvin: Essai sur l'Humanisme du Réformateur Français* (Paris: University of Paris, 1959), 273–75. See also Nicholas Wolterstorff, *Reason within the Bounds of Religion* 2nd ed. (Grand Rapids: Wm. B. Eerdmans, 1984), 27, who suggests that "Aquinas offers one classic version of foundationalism. There is, he said, a body of propositions which can be known by the natural light of reason—that is, propositions which can become self-evident to us in our present earthly state" (26). According to Wolterstorff, Calvin can be identified with "a second

2. Sinful Reason

Sin is not so much a part of Calvin's doctrine of reason as reason is part of his doctrine of sin. Calvin thus devotes five chapters of the *Institutes* to sin and none to reason. For Plato and the philosophers the human problem is ignorance and the answer is education (παιδεία). For Calvin and the theologians the human problem is sin and the answer is redemption. The concept of a totally natural reason has some function in theology, but a totally sinful reason has none in philosophy. Although Calvin believes that traces of created reason survived the devastation of the fall, he does not attempt to analyze the sinful reason by the use of the natural reason. Instead he confesses that the disobedience of Adam "perverted the whole order of nature in heaven and earth" (I.1.5). Total sinful perversion and some natural continuance seem logically contradictory, but Van Houten thinks natural reason functions adequately in the earthly kingdom and is vitiated by sin in relation to the heavenly kingdom. "The complete shift in Calvin's attitude is striking. A faculty that in the earthly kingdom appears as wise, insightful, and productive is portrayed as foolish, arrogant, and fatuous in the celestial realm. Natural reason falls short in its consideration of heavenly mysteries because of the lasting effects of the fall of Adam."[23]

In Calvin's opinion the diversity of the conclusions of the philosophers "who have tried with reason and learning to penetrate in heaven" is shameful (I.5.12). Therefore, given Calvin's remarks on the fallen reason, the question of accurate thinking immediately arises. Van Houten believes in the existence of a third stage a synthetic and sanctioned reason beyond natural and sinful reason. Calvin's view of the nature of created reason is treated in terms of his doctrines of creation and providence (Book I); his doctrine of the nature of fallen reason is treated in terms of his view of sin (Book II). And while Calvin does teach a use of reason beyond its corruption, this use is a first matter of God's grace, not a third stage of human nature. That is, Calvin's exposition moves from nature created and fallen to the confession of God's grace revealed in Word and Spirit. According to Calvin, the human mind is in the hands of God (Com. Gen. 26:26). Those whom God governs by his Spirit are spiritual, "not those who obey reason on their own impulse." It is true that the Spirit "cannot dwell in them without taking hold of the higher faculties," but this passage is not developing a concept of redeemed reason but offering a testimony to the work of the Holy Spirit, concluding, "We must either deny Christ, or confess that we become Christians by his Spirit" (Com. Rom. 8:9). According to Calvin, those who have not been born anew of the Spirit of Christ have minds condemned for vanity. The "theologasters of the Sorbonne" think of reason as "the Queen," but in relation to the kingdom of God and the

---

classic view of the relation of faith and reason [that] can be called the *pre-conditionalist* view. Faith is seen as a condition for arriving at a fully comprehensive, coherent, consistent, and true body of theories in the sciences."

23. David Jon Van Houten, "Concept of Reason in Calvin," 167–68.

spiritual life, "The light of human reason differs little from darkness; for, before it has shown the way it is extinguished and its perspicacity is worth no more than blindness." Paul asserts that men "are blind in reasoning, even on the highest matters" (Com. Eph. 4:17). This bleak assessment of reason's power seems clear, but it is ignored by Abraham Kuyper, who praises Calvin's theology as superior to Augustine's because of its "thoroughgoing logical consistency."[24] More recently, R. H. Murray connects "Calvin with the pitiless logic so characteristic of the French temper, so unassailable in his conclusions when his premises are granted."[25] However, with his view of fallen reason Calvin cannot appeal his theological views to reason alone or even preeminently. Calvin's goal is not rational speculation on reality nor logical consistency in knowing, but faithful obedience to God's revelation in Scripture in the light of the testimony of the Spirit. Calvin's theology is inaccurately viewed as a logical system and should neither be read, nor expounded, nor defended as if it were.

3. Sanctified Reason

Some of Calvin's followers, feeling the need for a stronger view of reason than Calvin provides, passed over his severe strictures on reason and returned for guidance to the concepts of Aristotle and Aquinas.[26] R. C. Sproul testifies that the Thomistic synthesis of reason and revelation was a great loss to Reformed theology when he identifies himself as a "Reformed, Calvinistic, evangelical Protestant" and laments "the loss of the medieval synthesis of Christian theology and philosophy achieved by St. Thomas Aquinas."[27]

The Christian narrative begins with creation and the good gifts of reason; it continues into sin and the devastation of reason with the fall. The next stage is

24. Abraham Kuyper, "Calvinism and Confessional Revision," trans. Geerhardus Vos, *The Presbyterian and Reformed Review* 7 (July 1891): 377. The interpretation of Augustine as theologian and philosopher is an interesting chapter in the history of ideas, especially his conception of the priority of will in relation to reason, which powerfully influenced Calvin. Augustine's doctrine of God, often accused of being Neoplatonic, is intriguingly corrected by Cushman. "Even of the *Confessions*, it is incautious and ill-considered to accentuate the 'theo-centrism' of Augustine's form of piety. The Mediator is the indispensable instrument through whom confession is educed and without whom there could be none." He continues, "In spite of all he has said to exalt the role of reason, Augustine's pervasive insistence is that Jesus Christ, the eternal Word *incognito*, disguised in the flesh, is the principium or the beginning point of knowledge." True knowledge requires commitment, and therefore believing leads to knowing since will is superior to reason. Christ is the mover of the will (Cushman, "Faith and Reason," 308, 295, 306).

25. R. H. Murray, *The Political Consequences of the Reformation* (New York: Russell and Russell, 1960), 81.

26. See, for example, my favorite Jesuit, John Patrick Donnelly, "Italian Influences on the Development of Calvinist Scholasticism," *The Sixteenth-Century Journal* 7 (April 1976): 81–101, and his "Calvinist Thomism," *Viator* 7 (1976): 441–55. The Aristotelianism at the core of Reformed scholasticism is explored in *Calvinism and Scholasticism in Vermigli's Doctrine of Man and Grace* (Leiden: E. J. Brill, 1976).

27. Quoted in Jack B. Rogers and Donald K. McKim, *The Authority and Interpretation of the Bible: An Historical Approach* (New York: Harper and Row, 1979), 197–98.

redemption of the individual and the community of the faithful, but whether, and to what extent, the reason in itself is redeemed remains a problematic topic. The great preponderance of Calvin's discussions of the issue are bifold and antinomic. The evangelist warns us that the light shining in the darkness is not to be understood as the light given in the beginning. In the present state this "light has been turned to darkness. And yet he denies that the light of reason is completely put out: for in the darkling gloom of the human mind there still shine some sparks of that brightness" (Com. Jn. 1:5). These few remaining sparks are not a full-scale third stage of reason. Calvin does mention a "reason sanctioned by the Spirit of God and Scripture," but this concept belongs to his doctrine of Word and Spirit, not to his so-called doctrine of reason.[28] If Calvin possessed a clear concept of sanctified reason he could appeal to it simply and directly to resolve all intellectual controversies. He would not need to appeal to the experience of faith if redeemed reason had the answer wholly and holy. The prophet Daniel being truly and clearly taught by the angel retained no strength in himself, which Calvin takes to demonstrate that "we must always remember how hostile all our natural thoughts are to the will of God" (Com. Dan. 10:8).

After Calvin the dream of reason was a distinctive characteristic of the Puritans who believed that right reason was the candle of God shining in human beings. Their sanction was Seneca's dictum that "Right reason is nothing else than a portion of the divine spirit set in a human body" (*Epistulae* 66).[29] The theological confidence in reason during the Puritan period was subtly but powerfully expressed within the Reformed tradition in the either/or of the Westminster Confession, notably the phrase which reads, "The whole counsel of God, is *either* expressly set down in Scripture, *or* by good and necessary consequence may be deduced from Scripture" (1:6, emphasis added). On first reading, one might assume the authors of the Confession naively believed that their own deductions and conclusions were, or ought to be, valid and true for everyone in the world. However, the learned divines at Westminster[30] made an interesting and sophisticated logical move consciously accepted from Thomas Aquinas[31] who learned it from Aristotle.[32] The claim is that necessary consequences are not located in

28. In his study of Calvin's doctrine of the Holy Spirit, Werner Krusche devotes a long section to the blindness of reason (*Das Wirken des Heiligen Geistes Nach Calvin* [Göttingen: Vandenhoeck & Ruprecht, 1957], 67–89).

29. If poets are, as Shelley thought, "the unacknowledged legislators of the world," then on right reason our most learned poet should be acknowledged. In his *Areopagitica* John Milton makes a passionate appeal for obedience to "the voice of reason from what quarter soever it be heard speaking." The angel Michael tells Adam, "Reason in man obscured, or not obey'd, / Immediately inordinate desires / And upstart Passions catch the Government / From Reason" (*Paradise Lost* 12.86–89). See William J. Grace's section on "Milton's Concept of Right Reason" in *Ideas in Milton* (Notre Dame, IN: University of Notre Dame Press, 1968). Against Milton's dream of right reason should be posed Jonathan Swift's nightmare of wrong reason in chap. 5 of *Gulliver's Travels*. The Yahoos were vile creatures in human form.

30. Minutes of the Sessions of the Assembly of Divines, Session 640, May 15, 1646.

31. Thomas Aquinas, *Commentary on the Metaphysics of Aristotle*, 1015a20–b15.

32. Aristotle, *Metaphysics*, 1015a20–b15.

the mind of the deducer but in the text itself! Thus, theological affirmations can be drawn from Scripture exactly without adding to or diminishing from its meaning. To put the matter another way, conclusions drawn from biblical premises are as essentially true as the source. A conclusion necessarily (as opposed to possibly) deduced from Scripture is itself divine truth.

Of course, both true premises and good and necessary consequences may be denied by ignorant and sinful thinkers. Therefore the ontological relation between source and deduction requires expansion into an epistemological context containing individuals and communities who possess rectified, regenerate, or sanctified reason as the Westminster divines recognized and as a third-stage development would require. Interestingly, the Westminster Confession precisely defined the first two parts of this sequence (Scripture and deduction) but left the latter two (sanctified reason in individual and community) without careful analysis.

Of these four components—Scripture, reason, individually sanctified reason, and communally sanctified reason—the last three have been quietly abandoned with the result that an essentially unmodified Westminster view of Scripture stands alone as the single and logically privileged basis for the knowledge of God's will. The difficulty, of course, is that the appeal to the Scripture also appeals to the judgment of human thinking. Even if the Bible itself is pure divine revelation, entirely unmodified by human elements, its understanding by human beings requires some kind of human reasoning—natural or sanctified. Pure revelation is not purely self-interpreting. It would be interesting to know if sanctified reason applies only to thoughts about God or affects thoughts about other subjects like physics, mathematics, history, and so on. Moreover, it would seem difficult, if not impossible, to establish which individuals and groups possess sanctified reason and whether their possession is permanent or only occasional. The criteria, whether spiritual or rational, employed to determine who is sufficiently sanctified to be reasonable presents an apparently insurmountable problem. Progressive distinctions among (1) natural reason, which every normal person possesses; (2) vitiated reason, which every sinful person possesses; and (3) sanctified reason, which only some special persons possess, is an intriguing concept, but one that Calvin does not develop. His nearest approach to the subject is a comment like when we come to Christ, drawn by the Holy Spirit, we are lifted up in mind and heart above our understanding so that the soul illumined by the Holy Spirit takes on a new keenness, as it were, to contemplate the heavenly mysteries (III.2.34). This statement, and others like it, does not assert a general power given to redeemed and restored rationality but a specific affirmation of the work of the Holy Spirit in interpreting the Word.

Recently some philosophers have argued for nonrational, nonlogical mental processes that lead to truth. These "unreasoned beliefs" include facts, like the existence of the world and the existence of other minds, and values.[33] More precisely

---

33. W. T. Stace, "The Problem of Unreasoned Beliefs," *Mind* (January–April 1945): 27–49, 122–47.

than Calvin, Emil Brunner forthrightly points out that in dogmatic reflection an immense role is played "by the purely rational element, the logical power of thought." While the devastating effect of sin on reason cannot be ignored, a theological panegyric concerning the sinful corruption of human reason must be tempered. "Even if it is divine revelation about which he is thinking, still this process of reflection takes place by means of the *natural human reason*, with its concepts and thought-forms and its logical processes of proof." To which must be added individual habits (or dispositions) of heart and mind as well as the pervasive influence of cultural context. Crucial to recognize, Brunner also asserts theology is not a purely rational reflection of the truths of faith because faith pulls logic away from the straight line to the center. "Theological thinking is a rational movement of thought, whose rational tendency at every point is continually being deflected, checked or disturbed by faith." The center of this "believing thinking" is Jesus Christ,[34] and the basis of dogmatic reflection is in personal encounter. In this concluding conviction Brunner echoes Calvin. Theological reflection can proceed with confidence only in connection to God revealed in Jesus Christ through the work of the Holy Spirit. *Apart from him*, confidence in reason, experience, tradition—even in Scripture and faith—is misplaced.

The analysis of religious faith is a rational activity, but religious faith is not based on reason. George S. Hendry asserts the deep root of the Protestant Reformation of the God of free grace revealed to faith in Jesus Christ is a protest against the doctrine of a God cognizable by reason. In other words, a belief in a personal God based in philosophy is a contradiction in terms.

> Modern thought is characterized by a profound conviction in the validity of reason [including] the ability of reason to attain a true knowledge of God. . . . The knowledge of God is sought as the ultimate principle or explanation of the world; the interest in God is primarily as an object of thought, a metaphysical entity, a means of satisfying man's intellectual curiosity. And the underlying assumption is that God can be thought either by way of extension or analogy of what reason finds in the world. . . . But this conception of God, *Deus philosophorum*, has only the properties of a conception; it is static and impersonal; it has no self-evidencing objective existence.

Hendry concludes, "No process of thought can reach a living and personal God."[35]

A better conclusion is offered by John H. Leith in his fine article "Calvin's Theological Method and the Ambiguity in His Theology": "Calvin was ready to sacrifice logical consistency in order to do justice to the complexity of Christian revelation and experience."[36] This continues the interpretation made famous by

34. Emil Brunner, *The Christian Doctrine of God (Dogmatics I)*, trans. Olive Wyon (Philadelphia: Westminster Press, 1950), 75, 76. On encounter, see Brunner's *Truth as Encounter* (Philadelphia: Westminster Press, 1943) and Andrew Purves and Charles Partee, *Encountering God: Christian Faith in Turbulent Times* (Louisville, KY: Westminster John Knox Press, 2000).
35. George S. Hendry, *God the Creator* (London: Hodder & Stoughton, 1937), 24, 25, 26, 27, 28.
36. *Reformation Studies: Essays in Honor of Roland H. Bainton*, ed. Franklin H. Littell (Richmond, VA: John Knox Press, 1962), 108.

Hermann Bauke, who thought Calvin addressed the problems of theology with a *complexio oppositorum*, that is, by expounding in combination doctrines that are logically opposed.[37] The same point is made by Edward Dowey, who thinks that Calvin is too much aware of the mysteries of God's will and "too little a lover of logical symmetry" to be "condemned for excessive curiosity on the one hand or for ingratitude on the other" (III.21.4). Calvin was "so utterly submissive before divine mystery as to create a theology containing many logical inconsistencies rather than a rationally coherent whole." "Clarity of individual themes, incomprehensibility of their interrelations—this is a hallmark of Calvin's theology."[38] Perhaps the point is best made by Quirinius Breen. "There is a logic in the *Institutes*. In fact, it is full of logic. But the logic is not syllogistic. It is rhetorical logic. Syllogistic logic uses induction and the syllogism; rhetorical logic uses example and the enthymeme."[39] The narrative of confidence in reason to reach sure and certain knowledge skips over Calvin and is caught by Descartes, Leibniz, and Spinoza, who believed the mind properly employed in clear and distinct thinking was able to discover self-evident concepts and principles, meaning all our ideas, and therefore all truth is the product of reason.[40] This conclusion of the Continental rationalists was mightily challenged by the British empiricists, as will be noted in the following discussion of experience.[41] Calvin does appeal to reason on occasion but Étienne Gilson is correct in judging Calvin a theologian of faith not reason.[42] Calvin's relation to the dream of reason is marginal at

37. Hermann Bauke, *Die Probleme der Theologie Calvins* (Leipzig: J. C. Hinrich'schen, 1922), 16–19. In 1909 Willy Lüttge, *Die Rechtfertigungslehre Calvins* (Berlin: Reuther und Reichard, 1909), 78–79, pointed to tensions (*Spannungen*) or contradictions (*Widerspruchen*) in Calvin's theology.

38. Dowey, *Knowledge of God*, 39, 40.

39. Quirinius Breen, "John Calvin and the Rhetorical Tradition," *Church History* (March 1957): 13. (Yet see Calvin's syllogism at Com. Phil. 1:6.) George A. Kennedy, *Classical Rhetoric and Its Christian and Secular Tradition from Ancient to Modern Times* (Chapel Hill: University of North Carolina Press, 1980), is a helpful introduction but does not consider Calvin (or Luther), although Melanchthon is briefly mentioned.

40. The denial of the adequacy of reason to support Christian life finds a powerful, sarcastic, and dangerous modern ally in William James. Of God's metaphysical attributes like aseity, James asserts, "I must frankly confess that even though these attributes were faultlessly deduced, I cannot conceive of it being of the smallest consequence to us religiously that any one of them should be true. . . . So much for the metaphysical attributes of God! From the point of practical religion, the metaphysical monster which they offer to our worship is an absolutely worthless invention of the scholarly mind" (*The Varieties of Religious Experience* [Gifford Lectures of 1901–2] [Cambridge: Harvard University Press, 1985], 352–53). According to Ernst Troeltsch, "Empiricism and Platonism in the Philosophy of Religion: To the Memory of William James," *Harvard Theological Review* 5, no. 4 (October 1912): 401–22, James's "radical empiricism" is not only an attack on Platonic rationalism but a substitution of a psychology for a philosophy of religion rejecting "dogmatic theology, church, ecclesiastical worship, ritual, sacrament, and canonical law" (417).

41. To the preeminent human faculty of reason as developed in this long conversation are added other faculties such as will. That the will is informed and guided by the reason is poetically expressed by Lysander in Shakespeare's *Midsummer Night's Dream*, "The will of man is by his reason swayed" (II.2.115).

42. Étienne Gilson, *Christianity and Philosophy*, trans. Ralph MacDonald (New York: Sheed and Ward, 1939), 13–21, a brilliant essay from a Roman Catholic perspective.

best. Appealing to mystery, Calvin says, "Let us, however, learn from this that the Gospel can be understood by faith alone, not by reason" (Com. Col. 2:2).

B. CALVIN AND EXPERIENCE

For centuries experience was evaluated and judged by reason, but more recently the reverse is being argued by philosophers and theologians. Calvin certainly appeals to experience, especially the experience of faith,[43] but the modern discussion begins with the British empiricists and was synthesized by Immanuel Kant. Since the issue becomes focused after Calvin's death, he obviously did not contribute to this conversation directly. However, some modern interpreters—living after the Continental rationalists Descartes, Spinoza, and Leibniz; after the British empiricists Locke, Berkeley, and Hume; after Kant's critical resolution and Schleiermacher's theological response—double back from Schleiermacher to Calvin. For contemporary Calvin interpretation this movement is important enough to warrant a few paragraphs of background.

David Hume denied the creative power of reason in favor of its receptive function, writing, "All the philosophy in the world and all the religion . . . will never be able to carry us beyond the usual course of experience."[44] In denying reason's suzerainty, empiricism concluded that exact knowledge of God, the world, and the soul are beyond human reach. Even the knowledge of matters of fact is only probable, not certain. We have no perception of rational or necessary connections. According to Hume, life is neither actually nor properly guided by reason and logic but rather by social customs and personal habits. In a real sense the great skeptic David Hume remains unburied. Theological conservatives pretend he never lived, and theological liberals dance in his shadow.[45]

Hume's conclusions about God and reason and causality were powerfully attacked by Immanuel Kant, who asserted that the remembrance of Hume's arguments caused him to awaken from his dogmatic slumbers. Kant's "critical philosophy" agreed with the empiricists in holding that the *matter* of ideas is given

43. See H. Obendiek, "Die Erfahrung in ihrem Verhältnis zum Worte Gottes bei Calvin," *Aus Theologie und Geschichte der Reformierten Kirche: Festgabe für E. F. Karl Müller* (Neukirchen: Buchlhandlung des Erziehungsvereins Neukirchen, 1933), 180–211; W. Balke, "The Word of God and Experientia according to Calvin," *Calvinus Ecclesiae Doctor*, ed. W. H. Neuser (Kampen: J. H. Kok, 1978), 19–38; and my "Calvin and Experience," *Scottish Journal of Theology* 26, no. 2 (May 1973): 169–81.

44. David Hume, *An Inquiry Concerning Human Understanding* (Chicago: William Benton, 1952), sec. 11:113. See F. W. Dillistone, *Religious Experience and Christian Faith* (London: SCM Press, 1981).

45. The use of reason among the empiricists is not a simple subject. For example, while Locke uses the word "reasonableness" only once in his text (112), he concludes, there cannot "be any thing plainer, than that the assenting to this Proposition, that Jesus was the *Messiah*, was that which distinguished the Believers from the Unbelievers" (John Locke, *The Reasonableness of Christianity as Delivered in the Scriptures*, ed. John C. Higgins-Biddle [Oxford: Clarendon Press, 1999], 30).

316 Calvin's Method in Theology: An Excursus

in sensation, but he agreed with the rationalists that their *form* is the product of reason. Among the other purposes of his work, Kant set out to defend the truth of religion by diminishing reason in order to enhance faith. In the preface to *The Critique of Pure Reason* he wrote, "I must, therefore, abolish *knowledge*, to make room for *belief*."[46] Of Kant's two realms of reality: the *noumenal* refers to things as they are in themselves and the *phenomenal* refers to things as they appear to us. Since God does not appear in the phenomenal world, God cannot be known directly by reason. However, while the existence of God is not a *logical* necessity for Kant, God is a *moral* necessity. The existence of God, the Self, and Immortality cannot be perceived in the phenomenal world, but they *ought* to exist in order to provide for the ultimate harmony of goodness and happiness. As a result, theology becomes a branch of ethics. The noumenal existence of the divine God is a concept understood by a phenomenal extension of the human good. Kant's attempt to synthesize the best insights of rationalism and empiricism succeeded well enough to become the subject of this aphorism: One can think with Kant or against him, but not without him.[47]

More directly concerned with theology, Kant intended his *Religion within the Limits of Reason Alone* as a stout defense of Christian faith, but his view of both reason and experience rejects many central convictions of Christianity's faith alone. More importantly, Kant's critiques have set a central agenda for modern thinking about reason and experience. Of special note is embarrassment over the historical Jesus. Kant thinks it would be unethical and unreasonable for God to offer salvation to the world in a single historical person.

According to Kant, God, who cannot be experienced, is defined as the supreme good based on the idea of moral perfection, which is framed by reason. The only God worthy of worship and service is associated with morality. No real God could demand obedience to an immoral command. (Kant thought the command to Abraham to slay Isaac was probably an error.) It is an illusion to wish to be well-pleasing to God through actions that could be performed without being a moral person. "Whatever, over and above good life-conduct, man fancies that

46. Immanuel Kant, *The Critique of Pure Reason*, trans. J. M. D. Meiklejohn (Chicago: William Benton, 1952), 10 (emphasis in original).

47. This point is developed in considerable detail by Cornelius van der Kooi, *As in a Mirror: John Calvin and Karl Barth on Knowing God*, trans. Donald Mader (Leiden: Brill, 2005). Obviously Calvin and Barth thought God as subject could be known. It is true for Calvin "that God existed, that He revealed certain things about himself, was a deep conviction" (226), although the proof of the existence of God is not nearly so important as what God requires of us. Moreover, Calvin is more interested in God's incarnate presence with us than in the revelation of "certain things" about himself. Nevertheless, the depth of Calvin's conviction is clear. Van der Kooi correctly sees Kant's epistemology as the hinge on which a great deal of modern theology, including Barth's, swings. The central issue is the validity of Kant's noumenal-phenomenal distinction, which Calvin, of course, never addressed and which his conviction of union with Christ simply denies. The turn to the subject in Kant's philosophy is to the Self and away from God. In other words, for Kant true wisdom does not consist of two interlocking parts: "the knowledge of God and of ourselves" (I.1.1). Granting the observation that the knowledge of God "is no longer rooted in the generally accepted metaphysics of being" (10), the larger question is the value of modern epistemology and ontology in theology.

he can do to become well-pleasing to God is mere religious illusion and pseudo-service of God."[48] Ethical behavior is a universal obligation, but commitment to a historic religion is not. It follows, says Kant, that "even the Holy One of the gospels must first be compared with our ideal of moral perfection before we can recognize Him as such."[49] For Kant Jesus Christ is an ideal or an example, an abstraction of moral perfection. As such, his historical reality is not required since the archetype exists in the human reason. Each person must live as if everything depended on one's self, not on a heteronomous providence.[50] Allen Wood is para-doxically correct. "No thinker ever placed greater emphasis on reason's bound-aries than Kant; at the same time, none has ever been bolder in asserting its unqualified title to govern our lives."[51] The importance of Immanuel Kant for modern academic and theological thought is difficult to overestimate.[52]

Kant's declaration in the opening sentence of the *Critique of Pure Reason*—that all our knowledge begins with experience—connects directly with the the-ology of Friedrich Schleiermacher and, thus, with Calvin interpretation. Schleiermacher, often called the father of modern liberal theology, seeks to obvi-ate Kant's understanding of religion as a subcategory of ethics, by locating reli-gion in the experience of feeling. On this view religion is not ultimately a rational but a psychological activity. As such it is impervious to rational or moral critique. In much the same way that Kant towers over the modern Western philosophical world, so does Schleiermacher over the theological. As Kant's view of reason plays a dominant role in the contemporary intellectual scene, so does Schleiermacher's view of experience. Wayne Proudfoot claims the roots of the category of "reli-gious experience" can be traced to Schleiermacher. Proudfoot observes, "Schleier-macher's conception of religion was inspired by the pietistic tradition in which

48. Immanuel Kant, *Religion within the Limits of Reason Alone*, trans. Theodore M. Greene and Hoyt H. Hudson (New York: Harper and Brothers, 1960), 175, 158.

49. Immanuel Kant, *Fundamental Principles of the Metaphysic of Minds*, trans. Thomas Kingsmill Abbott (Chicago: William Benton, 1952), 263.

50. *Religion within the Limits of Reason*, 92. Surveying the rise and fall of faith, the names of Hume, Gibbon, Kant, and George Eliot (Mary Ann Evans) figure prominently in A. N. Wilson's arresting *God's Funeral: A Biography of Faith and Doubt in Western Civilization* (New York: Ballantine Books, 1999). According to Nancy Etcoff in *Survival of the Prettiest: The Science of Beauty* (New York: Anchor Books, 1999), 245, when the novelist Henry James met the fifty-year-old George Eliot he wrote to his father, "She is magnificently ugly—deliciously hideous. She has a low forehead, a dull grey eye, a vast pendulous nose, a huge mouth, full of uneven teeth and a chin and jaw-bone *qui n'en finissent pas*. . . . Now in this vast ugliness resides a most powerful beauty which, in a very few min-utes, steals forth and charms the mind, so that you end as I ended, in falling in love with her."

51. Allen W. Wood, "Rational Theology, Moral Faith, and Religion," in *The Cambridge Com-panion to Kant*, ed. Paul Guyer (Cambridge: Cambridge University Press, 1992), 414.

52. The serious challenge of Kant is addressed by Nicholas Wolterstorff in "Is It Possible and Desir-able for Theologians to Recover from Kant?" (*Modern Theology* 14, no. 1 [January 1998]: 1–18). Exploring the concept of boundaries, he asks, "Must one experience the Kantian agony to be a mod-ern theologian?" (16). In answer Wolterstorff points to the thought of Thomas Reid, whom he regards as an antidote to Kant. For both Reid and Kant the problem is Hume. Kant tries to think past Hume; Reid tries to think around Hume. For an account of his detachment from his early Calvinism, see the short essay on "Hume's Relations to His Calvinist Environment," in *Dialogues Concerning Natural Religion*, ed. Norman Kemp Smith (New York: Bobbs-Merrill, 1947), 1–8.

he was nurtured, and it was intended as a response to Kant's critique." In responding to Kant, Schleiermacher became "the earliest and most systematic proponent of the autonomy of religious experience and of religious judgments and doctrine." Proudfoot's chapter 1 is devoted to an examination of Schleiermacher's theory of religious experience. According to Proudfoot, Schleiermacher intends to convince his sophisticated friends that religion should not be depicted "as a system of beliefs or doctrines or as a moral code prescribing behavior." Rather, "Real piety is identical with the spiritual integrity and sense of harmony with the universe which they sought in the aesthetic and cultural life."[53] Schleiermacher posits a direct contact with a reality that transcends the mind and its categories. He finds this reality in the immediacy of religious experience or feeling, which he believes to be independent of beliefs and practices. According to Schleiermacher, religion is expressed in thoughts and actions but is not primarily about knowing or doing but about feeling. Christian doctrines are accounts of religious affections set forth in speech,[54] meaning theology is not about God but about what a particular community believes about God. Schleiermacher restricts religious experience to itself with no real and personal encounter with something (or Someone) outside the consciousness of the self.

Proudfoot's main criticism is that Schleiermacher thinks "he has identified a moment of consciousness independent of thought and yet having cognitive significance." "This combination, required for Schleiermacher's program, is an impossible one." In other words, Schleiermacher does not sufficiently recognize that experience is not a simple inner awareness. Experience involves sets of complex concepts, beliefs, expectations, dispositions, and practices. Religion is not a matter that escapes "Kant's contention that our experience is structured by the categories and thoughts we bring to it." That is, "Religious language is not only the expressive, receptive medium Schleiermacher takes it to be. It also plays a very active and formative role in religious experience."[55] Interestingly, Protestant scholastics ignore Hume's critique of reason and Kant's resolution while their liberal opponents accept Kant's critique and embrace Schleiermacher's resolution.

However one evaluates Schleiermacher's theology in itself, it is even more problematic in relation to Calvin. While Karl Barth and Emil Brunner vigorously opposed each other on points of Calvin interpretation, they agreed that Calvin

53. Wayne Proudfoot, *Religious Experience* (Berkeley: University of California Press, 1985), xiii, 31, 6, 2.

54. Friedrich Schleiermacher, *The Christian Faith*, ed. H. R. Mackintosh and J. S. Stewart (New York: Harper and Row, 1963), sec. 15.

55. Proudfoot, 11, 2, 40.

56. Heinrich Emil Brunner, *Dië Mystik und das Wort: Der Gegensatz Zwischen moderner Religionsauffassung und christlichem Glauben dargestellt an der Theologie Schleiermachers* (Tübingen: J. C. B. Mohr, 1924). For criticism of Brunner, see B. A. Gerrish, "Continuity and Change: Friedrich Schleiermacher on the Task of Theology," in *Tradition and the Modern World: Reformed Theology in the Nineteenth Century* (Chicago: University of Chicago Press, 1978), 13–48. Especially interesting is Gerrish's critique of Brunner's *Dië Mystik*.

should not be understood in Schleiermacher's frame of reference.[56] This interpretation is challenged by the recent and interesting development of a small Schleiermacher sodality in Calvin studies. As the proponents of Reformed Scholasticism insist their doctrine *conserves* Calvin's true theology, so do the friends of Schleiermacher insist their Reformed doctrine *liberates* Calvin's true theology. In other words, modern conservatives and liberals both produce documentation that understanding Calvin correctly requires developing his thought in continuity with their direction.[57] Each claims to be the legitimate heir of Calvin's legacy. In his "Schleiermacher as a Calvinist," Walter L. Moore points out similarities in such areas as the exposition of providence in relation to creation, the universality of divine control, the centrality of special providence, and predestination treated within an ecclesiological context rather than as part of the doctrine of God. Accordingly, "Schleiermacher is faithful to the Reformer when he treats the subject of election as the church's reflection upon its origin," but Moore also calls attention to differences in their views of Scripture, sin, and especially the activity of God in individual lives.[58]

In his essay on Schleiermacher's and Calvin's doctrine of God, Gerrish focuses on the common opposition of Calvin and Schleiermacher to intellectual speculation and their common affirmation of the role of piety in theology. Of special interest is Gerrish's comparison of their doctrines of Trinity as like and unlike. Schleiermacher thought the doctrine was muddled and obsolete while Calvin thought the traditional terms were valuable because they defended piety. "The doctrine of the Trinity, in Calvin's view, did not transgress the limits of piety."[59] If the purpose of the doctrine of Trinity were simply the service of piety, then Calvin and Schleiermacher might be close, but Schleiermacher finds the doctrine of Trinity a theological embarrassment while Calvin thinks the doctrine of Trinity serves piety because it is the truth of God. To my mind the most telling difference in "style of theology" between Schleiermacher and Calvin is reflected in Gerrish's rhetorical question, "Is it not just to conclude, then, that the subject of

57. In a collection of essays dedicated to Gerrish, Randall C. Zachman, "The Awareness of Divinity and the Knowledge of God in the Theology of Calvin and Schleiermacher," in *Revisioning the Past: Prospects in Historical Theology* (Minneapolis: Fortress Press, 1992), 143, claims both Calvin and Schleiermacher anchor all religion in human awareness of divinity. Bruce McCormack, "The Sum of the Gospel: The Doctrine of Election in the Theologies of Alexander Schweizer and Karl Barth," *Toward the Future of Reformed Theology: Tasks, Topics, Traditions*, ed. David Willis and Michael Welker (Grand Rapids: William B. Eerdmans Publishing Company, 1999), 493, thinks Barth and Schweizer (and also Schleiermacher) cannot be reconciled on the level of method but they share many of the same dogmatic concerns. "At the very least, they were chewing on two ends of the same bone." Presumably all three are legitimate heirs of Calvin. See also the essays in *Barth and Schleiermacher: Beyond the Impasse?* ed. James O. Duke and Robert F. Streetman (Philadelphia: Fortress Press, 1988).

58. Walter L. Moore, "Schleiermacher as a Calvinist: A Comparison of Calvin and Schleiermacher on Providence and Predestination," *Scottish Journal of Theology* 24 (1971): 173.

59. Gerrish, "Theology within the Limits of Piety Alone: Schleiermacher and Calvin's Doctrine of God," in *The Old Protestantism and the New: Essays on the Reformation Heritage* (Chicago: University of Chicago Press, 1982), 206.

Schleiermacher's theology is not *homo religiosus* (as the neoorthodox critics tire-lessly maintained), but *homo evangelicus*—the man of faith under the Word of the gospel?"[60] In either case the subject of Schleiermacher's theology is man, while the subject of Calvin's theology—unmodern, meaning un-Kantian, as it may be—is God revealed in Jesus Christ. Gerrish counters, "It will no longer do to measure Schleiermacher with the external norm of 'Christocentricity,' it being presupposed in advance that to be Christocentric is a very good thing." Roused from my own dogmatic slumbers, I maintain that Christocentricity is not an *external* but an *essential* norm of the Christian faith. According to Gerrish, "Schleiermacher found two elements *inseparably* present together in Christian experience, a general consciousness of God and a specific relation to Christ."[61] This "two-sidedness" that Schleiermacher and Gerrish find congenial, I find unacceptable. Calvin's doctrine of Trinity cannot be reduced to "two elements."

Happily for the cause of connubial felicity, Dawn DeVries agrees with Brian Gerrish, her husband, on the relation between Calvin and Schleiermacher. Schleiermacher called himself a Moravian of a higher order, and DeVries declares Gerrish to be a Calvinist of a higher order. Among the tasks taken up by higher-order Calvinists is the correction of the neo-orthodox misunderstanding of Schleiermacher and then the demonstration that Schleiermacher's theology is a faithful development from Calvin's. For the present purpose, the most important of DeVries' claims is this:

> Schleiermacher is more able than Calvin to formulate coherently the rela-tionship between Christology and soteriology. Calvin's entire soteriology is based on the notion of a union with Christ that is effected by the work of the Holy Spirit through the Word and faith. Although he is clear in insist-ing that this union is necessary for salvation, Calvin is, however, unclear about how it relates to the objective, and presumably self-sufficient, "work" of Christ that he set out in Book 2 of his *Institutes*. Schleiermacher, on the contrary, defines the work of the Redeemer from beginning to end in terms of a necessary union of Christ and the believer. And while, like Calvin, he argues that this union with Christ requires a conjunction of Word, faith, and Spirit, Schleiermacher is better able than Calvin to explain this con-junction as a hermeneutic event that entails a human act of interpretation. The preacher's words "embody" the Word; that is, preaching becomes the continuing locus for the ongoing redemptive work of Christ.[62]

It is not clear to me how Schleiermacher's "hermeneutic event" is better able to explicate union with Christ and thus "more able than Calvin to formulate coher-ently the relationship between Christology and soteriology." What is clear is that some scholars believe Schleiermacher's theology is an improvement on Calvin's.

60. Gerrish, "Schleiermacher on the Task of Theology," 39.

61. Gerrish, "Schleiermacher and the Reformation: A Question of Doctrinal Development," in *The Old Protestantism and the New*, 194, 374.

62. Dawn DeVries, *Jesus Christ in the Preaching of Calvin and Schleiermacher* (Louisville, KY: Westminster John Knox Press, 1996), 9. DeVries does not consider Proudfoot's critique.

A plausible case can be made for some genuine commonalities between Calvin and Schleiermacher. Certainly full credit can be extended to both theologians for their desire to interpret the traditional biblical faith with integrity. Moreover, each may be accurately called a "theologian of Christian experience," but even such points when carefully argued in particular are not finally convincing in general because the real differences outweigh the real similarities. The question asked of Calvinistic Scholasticism, "Have Calvin and the Reformation been abandoned?" is the same for Calvinistic liberalism. Both persuasions give the same answer, insisting their views are not a distortion but a helpful development of Calvin's thought. While one can appreciate the testimony of each group to the importance of a proper understanding of Calvin's theology, the sharpest difference between Calvin and Schleiermacher is that Calvin thought theology was the true explication of the truth of faith while Schleiermacher thought theology was the true explication of the believers' consciousness. For Calvin the referent for Truth is God revealed in Jesus Christ; for Schleiermacher it is Self come to correct awareness. Moreover, Schleiermacher, an expert in Plato, seems to me more exercised by the Kantian dualism between phenomenal and noumenal than the Platonic dualism between ideas and things. In any case, the resulting epistemological reserve precludes for Schleiermacher a direct encounter *with* God in favor of the feeling of absolute dependence *on* God. Since Calvin had not studied Spinoza or Hume or Kant, his theology, unlike Schleiermacher's and contemporary theologians', is not an attempt to reason with them.

Experience in general and religious experience in particular is a vast and complicated topic.[63] Arthur E. Murphy considered experience to have informational primacy for all reasonable beliefs. "Rationality," he insisted, "is not a property of selected ideas in their own nature, but of the manner of their use in the *organization of experience* in the light of the best knowledge and widest understanding relevant to the specific purposes with respect to which enlightenment is sought." "The ability to *learn* by experience, that is, to derive ideas from what we observe and to correct beliefs in terms of what is found to be the case, is the most basic

---

63. W. R. Matthew, in *God and Christian Thought and Experience* (London: Nisbet & Co., 1930), illustrates two difficulties. First, he repeats the taradiddle about Calvin's logical abstractions. He admits Calvin's "conception of God is not a rationalist one in the same degree as that of Thomas; but he, too, has in effect taken an abstraction and treated it as constituting the essence of Deity. Calvinism is built up round the idea of sovereignty considered as a logical notion. The God of Calvinism may perhaps be less remote than the God of the Aristotelians, but He is the presiding genius of a terrific tyranny. By abstracting the concept of sovereignty or power and making God practically equivalent to this idea, Calvin really destroyed the validity of moral distinctions. He is logically bound to deduce them from the arbitrary will of God and to hold that they depend solely on that will. . . . It follows that *God in Calvinist theology is even more remote from human experience than in the rival systems of medieval philosophy*" (106–7, emphasis added). Second, the Library of Constructive Theology series, in which Matthew's book appears, and of which he is an editor, demonstrates the extreme difficulty of defining "experience." One only needs to compare Matthew's use of the term, instanced above, with H. R. Macintosh's (*The Christian Experience of Forgiveness*) with H. Wheeler Robinson's (*The Christian Experience of the Holy Spirit*) with H. H. Farmer's (*The World and God: A Study of Prayer, Providence, and Miracle in Christian Experience*).

factor in our intellectual progress, when such progress actually occurs." Experience is "an intellectual, and not merely a physiological, achievement." Murphy insisted that perceptual observation is fallible, corrigible, and quite ultimate, leading to self-correcting inquiry.[64]

Testifying to the centrality of experience, A. Seth Pringle-Pattison suggests in his Gifford Lectures of 1912–13, "Philosophy is just the attempt of the reason to realise the coordination of the different aspects of experience, and thereby to express, as far as may be, the nature of the total fact." He continues, "It is to the moral and religious man himself that we must go, not to the philosopher weaving theories about him, if we are to understand his experience aright. . . . The fundamental presuppositions of any experience must be accepted from the experience itself: they may be explained, but not explained away. Even the ideals operative in experience are themselves part of experience."[65] The importance of the role of experience in defining religion is recognized by recent introductory texts in the philosophy of religion like Abraham's, Miller's, and Davies's, which devote a chapter to the topic. Dane R. Gordon entitled his book on philosophy of religion, *A Feeling Intellect and a Thinking Heart*.[66] In the lecture on philosophy in his classic *The Varieties of Religious Experience*, William James declares, "Ratiocination is a relatively superficial and unreal path to the deity." Like Schleiermacher, he insists "that feeling is the deeper source of religion, and that philosophic and theological formulas are sec-

---

64. Arthur E. Murphy, *The Uses of Reason* (New York: Macmillan Company, 1943), 183 (emphasis added), 34, 35. Given the importance of interpreted experience (184–96), one can hold for its confessional nature and impenetrable mystery. Further theology need not be described as a reflection on religious experience if experience is entrained along Kantian tracks. As I interpret my own experience of jumping to conclusions with knee-jerk reactions, the nonrational aspect of life seems huge. Therefore I do not understand this claim of J. Wentzel van Huyssteen, *The Shaping of Rationality: Toward Interdisciplinarity in Theology and Science* (Grand Rapids: William B. Eerdmans, 1999), "A postfoundationalist notion of rationality will highlight the fact that one's own experience is always going to be rationally compelling" (219). The three physicists in my family see a much sharper difference between the "empirical adequacy" needed for the science they practice and the "experiential adequacy" needed for the theology we espouse (183).

65. A. Seth Pringle-Pattison, *The Idea of God in the Light of Recent Philosophy* (New York: Oxford University Press, 1920), 57, 252, 243. Among other important contributions is William Ernest Hocking's massive *The Meaning of God in Human Experience* (New Haven, CT: Yale University Press, 1923), which attacks the Hegelian rationalism that "thinking is also worship of God" (*Denken ist auch Gottesdienst*) by vigorously insisting *Denken ist nicht Gottesdienst*. Hocking believes what we want is "mysticism as a practice of union with God, together with the theory of that practice" (xviii). Hocking caused a furor among more conservative Christians with his perceived attack on the Christian missionary enterprise in his *Re-Thinking Missions: A Layman's Inquiry after One Hundred Years* (New York: Harper and Brothers, 1932). Also H. D. Lewis, *Our Experience of God* (London: George Allen and Unwin, 1959), 138, suggests "The imagination is not a thing apart, but a feature of total experience." Lewis is especially sound in his analysis of religious imagery. The role of colorful metaphors and parables is to give particularity and concretion to the process of revelation. They sum up, reflect, guide, and sustain the life of the individual and community.

66. Ed. L. Miller, *God and Reason: An Invitation to Philosophical Theology* (Upper Saddle River, NJ: Prentice-Hall, 1995); William J. Abraham, *An Introduction to the Philosophy of Religion* (Englewood Cliffs, NJ: Prentice-Hall, 1985); Brian Davies, *An Introduction to the Philosophy of Religion*, 3rd ed. (Oxford: Oxford University Press, 2004), has an interesting discussion of personal encounter and rational inference. Dane R. Gordon, *A Feeling Intellect and a Thinking Heart* (Lanham, MD: University Press of America, 2003).

ondary products." James wants to discredit the intellectualism that "assumes to construct religious objects out of the resources of logical reason alone, or of logical reason drawing rigorous inference from non-subjective facts." If reason is not exactly the slave of the passions, reason is certainly not passion's master. Human beings often find reasons (or excuses) for behaviors that are not initiated by logic, such as falling in love. "The logical reason of man operates, in short, in this field of divinity exactly as it has always operated in love, or in patriotism, or in politics, or in any other of the wider affairs of life, in which our passions or our mystical intuitions fix our beliefs beforehand. It finds arguments for our conviction, for indeed it *has* to find them. It amplifies and defines our faith, and dignifies it and lends it words and plausibility. It hardly ever engenders it; it cannot now secure it." James summarizes, "In all sad sincerity I think we must conclude that the attempt to demonstrate by purely intellectual processes the truth of the deliverances of direct religious experiences is absolutely hopeless."[67] James takes experience as equivalent to the whole of reality, including the actual, possible, and imaginary. Among these the widespread reports of the experience of alien abductions are difficult to understand. A skeptic can argue that mystical experience "is wholly shaped by a mystic's cultural environment, personal history, doctrinal commitments, religious training, expectations, aspirations, and so on."[68] According to William James, life exceeds logic. However, philosophy, thinking there is an intellectual answer to intellectualism's difficulties, has been strolling along a false path since the days of Socrates and Plato. The true answer "consists in simply closing one's ears to the question" posed with the logicians' bias. Idealists cannot believe with the radical empiricists that true philosophy lies "flat on its belly in the middle of experience . . . never getting a peep at anything from above," but intellectualism "can only approximate to reality and its logic is inapplicable to our inner life, which spurns its vetoes and mocks at its impossibilities." James concludes that religious experience, properly understood, leads to consciousness of the deeper reaches of reality.[69]

The sole suzerainty of reason has also been challenged from other directions, such as emotional or social intelligence, that are more intuitive than discursive. According to Daniel Goleman sociobiologists point out that evolution has given the heart preeminence over the head in facing predicaments and tasks too important to leave to intellect alone.[70] Among the most intriguing

67. James, *Varieties*, 353, 341, 342, 344–45, 359.

68. See Robert H. Sharf, "Experience," in *Critical Terms for Religious Studies*, ed. Mark Taylor (Chicago: University of Chicago Press, 1998), 108ff., 98.

69. William James on "The Continuity of Experience," in *A Pluralistic Universe* (New York: Longmans, Green, 1909), 291, 277, 289, 329.

70. Daniel Goleman, *Emotional Intelligence* (New York: Bantam Books, 1995), 4. In a considerable overstatement Paul T. Fuhrmann, "Philosophical Elements in the Early Reformed Tradition," *Columbia Theological Seminary Bulletin* 57, no. 3 (July 1964): 61, opines, "Emotion paralyzes and constricts while Reason considers and includes." See Goleman's companion book, *Social Intelligence: The New Science of Human Relationships* (New York: Bantam, 2006). Also Martha C. Nussbaum, *Upheavals of Thought: The Intelligence of Emotions* (Cambridge: Cambridge University Press, 2001).

contemporary studies of reason and experience are those of John E. Smith. According to Smith, "Christianity alone has developed *theology* with systematic rigor and with a logical conscience surpassing that of religions content to rely upon *mythos* alone."[71] At the same time, "All that man knows and does takes place within the medium of experience."[72] "An impasse in thought calls for further thought, and ultimately for a return to the experience that is at the base of all thought."[73] Experience is not a matter of pure subjectivity but rather "the medium of an objective encounter with the real world." Smith thinks human *experience* reveals a directly present, though mediated, reality that makes belief in God *reasonable*. Experience "is an objective and critical product of the intersection between reality in all its aspects on the one hand and a self-conscious being capable of receiving that reality through significant form on the other."[74] Experience encounters, reflects, and refracts reality.[75] In evaluation of Smith, Vincent Colapietro writes, "His goal was to articulate a concept of experience richer and more inclusive than the narrowly empiricistic . . . concept symbolized by the notion of sense data and to articulate a concept of reason richer and more inclusive than the narrowly formal and calculative concept symbolized by the notion of symbolic logic as an ideal language." In other words, Smith wanted to show that reason permeated by experience could be in touch with both scientific and religious reality.[76]

Of more direct interest is Smith's claim that Calvin and the other Protestant reformers of the sixteenth century recognized the limitations of reason, giving preference to experience. "It was, as we now understand so well, the momentous task of the Reformers to recover the conative side of faith in a *return to personal experience* and to put emphasis on the relation of the creature to God."[77] Such judgments about experience and reason may be quite insightful, but they represent a modern perspective on the Reformation. Calvin cites reason and experience in certain instances, but he does not offer a general theory of their role. Experience alone is not superior to reason alone. "For seeing that we are slow and dull, bare experience by no means suffices to attest the favor of God towards us, unless

71. John E. Smith, *Reason and God: Encounters of Philosophy with Religion* (New Haven, CT: Yale University Press, 1961), 140.

72. John E. Smith, *Experience and God* (New York: Oxford University Press, 1968), 69.

73. Ibid., 4.

74. Ibid., 12.

75. See also John E. Smith, *The Analogy of Experience: An Approach to Understanding Religious Truth* (New York: Harper and Row, 1973).

76. *Reason, Experience and God: John E. Smith in Dialogue*, ed. Vincent M. Colapietro (New York: Fordham University Press, 1997), 3. Thomas Molnar, *The Pagan Temptation* (Grand Rapids: Wm. B. Eerdmans, 1987), suggests Christianity became so fascinated by the quest for rationality that the vitality of myth and symbol were surrendered to neopaganism. In opposition the professional group known as the Society of Christian Philosophers examines theological "presuppositions, implications, and central components with philosophical tools." See *Philosophy and the Christian Faith*, ed. Thomas V. Morris (Notre Dame, IN: University of Notre Dame Press, 1988).

77. Smith, *Analogy of Experience*, 6 (emphasis added).

faith arising from the word be added" (Com. Gen. 35:1). Since Calvin lived before both Kant and the German idealists, he assumed that human experience encounters and is taught by a genuine reality. Experience is not merely self-referential. According to the famous statement of Anselm, faith seeks understanding, but it is also true that understanding seeks faith—something or Someone to trust.

The interlocking relation among Scripture and faith, reason, experience, and tradition concerns every theologian. Karl Barth treats reason and experience in a section entitled "Freedom under the Word" (1.2). Barth's so-called positivism seems to appear and to be most questionable in the claim, "Scriptural exegesis rests on the assumption that the message which Scripture has to give us, even in its apparently most debatable and least assimilable parts, is in all circumstances truer and more important than the best and most necessary things that we ourselves have said or can say."[78] The greatest confidence in the canonical Scriptures and the traditional historical context from which they proceed, allied with the most profound humility concerning the accuracy of our judgment concerning "the best and most necessary," does not warrant the conclusion that the "apparently most debatable and least assimilable parts" of Scripture are "truer and more important." Barth recognizes we cannot abandon our ideas, thoughts, and convictions any more than we can walk away from our shadow. However, he insists, we must subordinate "our ideas, thoughts, and convictions to the witness which confronts us in Scripture." "With the whole weight of our reason and experience we have to follow in the path of [the testimony of the prophets and apostles] and become compliant to it."[79]

On the subject of reason and experience a massive reorientation will soon be required as a result of the work of a new group of scholars, the anthropologists, who have joined the centuries-old discussion. Their major and obvious point is that not every human society has been influenced by the *Prior Analytics*, Aristotle's logical works. In an essay on rationality from an anthropological perspective, Paul Stoller describes his December 1979 experience in a West African city widely known for its sorcerers. After hearing steps on the roof, a dangerous presence entered Stoller's room and paralyzed his lower body until he remembered the antidote, a Songhay incantation. Stoller concludes, "I may never discover reasonable explanations for my experiences there. And yet those experiences have kept me suspended in uncertainty and ambiguity that have fired my imagination and fed my hunger for knowledge."[80] Stoller asserts that the problem of rationality "has long been at the forefront of scholarly debate in anthropological, philosophical, and religious studies."[81] At the center of Stoller's reflection is E. E. Evans-Pritchard, "whose monumental *Witchcraft, Oracles, and Magic among*

---

78. *CD*, 1.2, 719.
79. Ibid., 718–19. *Diesem Zeugnis haben wir mit dem ganzen Bestand unserer Vernunft und Erfahrung Folge zu leisten, fügsam zu werden.*
80. Paul Stoller, "Rationality," in *Critical Terms for Religious Studies*, 239–55, 254.
81. Ibid., 239.

the Azande was to become the first—and perhaps the best—empirically grounded disputation on rationality."[82]

The experience of rationality is not only different but appropriately different in different cultures. And within the same culture at different times. Farnell quotes, "It has always been found possible to hold together at one period thoughts that later reflection discovers to be contradictory."[83] In other words, among human beings there is no normative description of reason. Habits of mind and heart are culturally conditioned, perhaps even culturally determined. At the very least rationality remains an open question. To my great surprise, I once heard an educated Scot assert in a matter-of-fact aside that in Africa where she was buried he often talked to his dead daughter, but *never* in Europe. Occurrences like this raise the question in what sense rationality can be comfortably reconciled with experience. As always Shakespeare has the apt expression, "There are more things in Heaven and earth, Horatio, / Than are dreamt of in your philosophy" (*Hamlet,* 1.5.166–67). Over time the anthropologists will make a significant impact on the discussion of reason and experience.

CONCLUSION

This brief review of the immense amounts of intellectual energy expended over the centuries by philosophers and theologians on reason and experience illustrates that no easy resolution of their proper definitions or their relation is likely to be forthcoming any time soon. Moreover, it demonstrates that Calvin's appeal to these categories does not include any deep analysis of them.

Calvin's theology constantly employs his understanding of Scripture, his appropriation of Christian tradition, his sense of reasonableness, and his experience of faith. These four elements exist in a complex, interlocking, and generally descending relationship. Each of the latter three is essential and sometimes primary (behind Scripture). The church's tradition is to be accepted only when it properly

82. Ibid., 241. I always notice the name of Evans-Pritchard because Mussolini's African war forced the McClures, my wife's family, to abandon their home among the then-primitive Anuak tribe on the Sudanese border with Ethiopia. Edward Evan Evans-Pritchard, professor of social anthropology at Oxford from 1946 to 1970 came to Sudan to lead a band of Anuak volunteers in resisting Italian incursions into southeast Ethiopia. Evans-Pritchard later paid generous tribute to the loyalty and courage of the Anuak soldier. During his time in Sudan the warrior-scholar lived in the McClures' house (actually three connected mud huts). When he was not fighting, Evans-Pritchard spent his time compiling a dictionary of the then-unwritten Anuak language that he left behind for Don McClure to use on his return. See my *Adventure in Africa: The Story of Don McClure,* 3rd ed. (Lanham, MD: University Press of America, 2000), 436–37.

83. Lewis Richard Farnell, *The Attributes of God* (Gifford Lectures 1924–25) (Oxford: Oxford University Press, 1925), 3, quoting Nicol MacNicol, *Indian Theism, from the Vedic to the Muhammadan Period* (Delhi: Murshiram Monoharlal, 1968), 26. Among recent studies of religious experience, Ann Taves reminds, "We can talk about the making of evangelical religious experience on two levels, the level of theories about religious experience and the level of personal narratives of religious experience; at the level, that is, of theology or of testimony" (*Fits, Trances, and Visions: Experiencing Religion and Explaining Experience from Wesley to James* [Princeton, NJ: Princeton University Press, 1999], 47).

explains the Scripture—a conviction demonstrated in Calvin's discussion of the doctrine of the Trinity, as we have seen. Likewise, within the general context of expounding the truth of Scripture, Calvin cites the specific values of both reason and experience. He insists there "is a conviction that requires no reasons; such a knowledge with which the best reason agrees—in which the mind truly reposes more securely and constantly than in any reasons; such, finally a feeling that can be born only of heavenly revelation. *I speak of nothing other than what each believer experiences within himself*—though my words fall far beneath a just explanation of the matter" (I.7.5, emphasis added). Statements like this suggest that experience is superior to reason in that the proper relation among conviction, no reason, and best reason is appealed to experience. Calvin opposes speculative reason because "it is becoming in us not to be too inquisitive: only let us not dare to deny the truth of what Scripture teaches and experience confirms, or to keep nagging that it does not reach agreement in God."[84] In this quotation Calvin appeals to Scripture, experience, and an ultimately rational coherence found in God.

As reason has been overemphasized in Calvin studies, so has experience been undervalued. Most modern interpreters cannot see Calvin through the lens of Schleiermacher's glasses, but Calvin is certainly an experiential theologian—a theologian of the heart. As a theologian of the Holy Spirit, Calvin's theology begins with a divine encounter that progresses by God's grace to the recognition of union with Christ.[85] In most cases Calvin thought a simple appeal to Scripture answered the question. More promising for modern reflection is the complicated appeal to the experience of Scripture—what Calvin calls the inner testimony of the Holy Spirit.

In addition to its connection with Scripture, experience is often associated with faith. Since Calvin understands faith as a gift of God, the experience of faith is sure and certain (III.2.7). At the same time faith is never perfect, and the conflict between belief and unbelief "is what every one of the faithful experiences in himself daily" (Com. Ps. 22:2; cf. III.2.18). In a negative vein Calvin writes, "Faith cannot arise from a naked experience of things but must have its origin in the Word of God" (Com. Jn. 20:29). More positively Calvin asserts that "with experience as our teacher we find God just as he declares himself in his Word" (I.10.2).

Experience is also closely related to the work of the Holy Spirit. In the *Catechism of the Church of Geneva* the child says, "Scripture teaches that [faith] is the special gift of God, and experience confirms this." The minister responds, "Tell me

84. *Concerning the Eternal Predestination of God*, trans. J. K. S. Reid (Louisville, KY: Westminster John Knox Press, [1961] 1997), 185.

85. Gerhard Ebeling ("The 'Non-religious Interpretation of Biblical Concepts,'" in *Word and Faith*, trans. James W. Leitch [Philadelphia: Fortress Press, 1963], 108–9) asks rhetorically why Dietrich Bonhoeffer was so exercised "by the question what Christ really *is* for us today." He asserts, "The answer to the first part of the question cannot escape concepts so taboo in theology today as 'experience' in both senses of the word (Erfahrung oder gar Erlebnis). The simple fact is: Jesus Christ has met him, he knows himself called and claimed by Jesus Christ, he too has allowed himself to be caught up into the way of Jesus Christ, he has become sure of Jesus Christ as the Lord. He has experienced him as the hope and driving-force of his life."

what experience you mean." The child answers, "Our mind is too rude to be able to grasp the spiritual wisdom of God which is revealed to us through faith; and our hearts are too prone to distrust or to perverse confidence in ourselves or other creatures to rest of their own accord in God. But the Holy Spirit by his illumination makes us capable of understanding those things which would otherwise far exceed our grasp, and brings us to a sure persuasion by sealing the promises in our hearts."[86]

The point Calvin makes is that faith is not only a matter of the head but the heart. The centrality of piety is indicated by the title of the first edition, which declared that *The Institutes of the Christian Religion* contained almost the whole sum of piety. Early in the *Institutes* Calvin writes that God cannot be properly known where there is no piety (I.2.1). Again, the pious mind observes God's authority, reverences his majesty, advances his glory, and obeys his commandments (I.2.2). The faithful should "not indulge in curiosity or in the investigation of unprofitable things because the Lord willed to instruct us, not in frivolous questions, but in solid piety, in the fear of his name, in true trust, and in the duties of holiness" (I.14.3).

To repeat, Christian truth "is a doctrine not of the tongue but of life. It is not apprehended by the understanding and memory alone . . . but it is received only when it possesses the whole soul and finds a seat and resting place in the inmost affection of the heart" (III.6.4). Calvin is aware that in Scripture "heart" can mean "mind." In commenting on "He hath blinded their heart" Calvin identifies the two faculties. "In Scripture *the heart* is sometimes taken as the seat of the affections. But here, as in many other places, it means the so-called intellectual part of the soul" (Com. Jn. 12:40). Later in this same comment Calvin speaks of God's enlightening the heart. Calvin also contrasts the two faculties when he insists, "The seat of faith is not in the head but in the heart. I am not going to argue about the part of the body in which faith is located, but since the word *heart* generally means a serious and sincere affection, I maintain that faith is a firm and effectual confidence, and not just a bare idea" (Com. Rom. 10:10). Both faith and its theological expression arise not from the head alone but from the serious and sincere affection of the heart. However they may be distinguished, heart and head are obviously interlocking in everyone's life. Calvin always uses his head, but he also puts his hand over his heart. The heart does not exclude the head and its bare ideas, but full persuasion includes sincere affection. Experience and the heart, reason and the head are important categories in Calvin's thought, but while he uses the terms frequently he does not analyze them at any length or in any depth.

Calvin both praises and blames reason. For example, Calvin says that no one is without the light of reason (II.2.13) and that reason is proper to human nature, separating humans from animals (II.2.17; II.2.12). On the other hand he argues that reason is blind (Com. Jn. 3:31) and should be renounced.[87] Calvin recognizes that our reason dissents from the judgment of God concerning the death of Achan and all he possessed (Com. Josh. 7:24) as well as the murder of kings

---

86. *Calvin Theological Treatises*, trans. J. K. S. Reid (Philadelphia: Westminster Press, 1954) 105.
87. "On the Necessity of Reforming the Church," *Selected Works of John Calvin, Tracts*, ed. and trans. Henry Beveridge (Grand Rapids: Baker Book House, 1983 [1844]), 1:147.

(10.18) and the massacre of women and children (10.40). Human reason can understand neither who God is nor his relation to mankind (II.1.18). Calvin three times repeats, "We are not our own." Since "we are God's," let us live and die for him and not be swayed by our reason or will. The philosophers are ignorant of self-denial. "For they set up reason alone as the ruling principle in man, and think that it alone should be listened to . . . but Christian philosophy bids reason give way to, submit and subject itself to, the Holy Spirit" (III.7.1; II.2.26). Calvin denounces the theologasters of the Sorbonne because they think "the primacy in the life of man, is the seat of reason, presides over the will, and restrains vicious desires," but as it relates to the spiritual life, "the light of human reason differs little from darkness" (Com. Eph. 4.17). He also says that reason is a natural gift which could not be completely wiped out by sin, meaning human understanding by its nature searches for truth (II.2.12). These conflicting statements demonstrate that Calvin does not focus on either reason or experience as a technical, epistemological warrant for theological conclusions.

Contemporary thinkers interested in Calvin cannot ignore complicated methodological issues raised by modern thought, but Calvin himself does not deal with them directly, and whether his work provides indirect answers is debatable.[88] Recently the conviction that the human creature is preeminently rational has been challenged by the notion that experience evaluates reason rather than the reverse. Of course, Calvin is not part of this development of reason and experience, and his employment of the concepts does not comport with the more sophisticated usages of today. To isolate and then enhance Calvin's actual usage is to overemphasize and thus to misrepresent. Calvin's appeals to reason and experience will not bear the weight of the epistemological interpretations sometimes offered since Calvin's purpose is more confessional than logical. Reason and experience are tools in constant use by Calvin (and by his readers). The ordinary use of reason in Calvin means trying to think properly or sensibly about the topic being discussed, but Calvin's use of reason differs in confidence and therefore in tone from Reformed Scholasticism's "argumentative techniques, distinctions, and proposition analyses, all within a framework determined by revelation."[89] Calvin takes his intellectual work seriously and tries to do it thoroughly, but he is not constructing a unitive argumentative logical structure. Sophisticated concepts of rationality and experience are available in modern philosophy and theology, but none can be regarded as fixed and unproblematic, and none of them is employed by Calvin.

Giving a helpful list of rational difficulties in Calvin's (and all theologians') thought, François Wendel includes the relation of God's love and wrath, human justification as complete and sanctification as incomplete, both gratitude and contempt for earthly goods, divine omnipotence and human responsibility, the

---

88. The confident answers provided by Francis A. Schaeffer, *A Christian View of Philosophy and Culture*, 2nd ed., vol. 1 (Westchester, IL: Crossway Books, 1982), are truly remarkable. According to G. P. Gooch, *History and Historians in the Nineteenth Century* (Boston: Beacon Press, 1965), 281, "Melbourne wished that he was as cocksure about anything as Macaulay was about everything."

89. "Introduction" to *Reformation and Scholasticism: An Ecumenical Enterprise*, ed. Willem J. van Asselt and Eef Dekker (Grand Rapids: Baker Academic, 2001), 32.

goodness of God and the existence of evil. Wendel concludes, "It would be better, we think, to confess that Calvin's is not a closed system elaborated around a central idea, but that it draws together, one after another, a whole series of Biblical ideas, some of which can only with difficulty be logically reconciled."[90] This comment demonstrates not only Wendel's perspicacious unwillingness to force a *logical* unity on Calvin's theology but also his suspicion that no thread exists which binds the "whole series of biblical ideas." A better summary asserts that while Calvin's thought is not a rational synthesis, it is a theological confession of the truth which is revealed in Jesus Christ, informed by Scripture, guided by tradition, certified by experience, and elaborated by reason.

The relations among Scripture, tradition, reason, and experience and other ways of knowing do not admit to exact formulaic resolution as once and often dreamed. Since each term refers to a range of meanings, examination leads to sensitivity but not resolution. Philosophers from Plato to Wittgenstein have been arguing with each other for centuries[91] because reason and experience, like love and fidelity, are mysteries impossible to define precisely in theory or practice. Likewise, theologians cannot agree concerning their uses and limitations. The main reason (to use the word again) is that theological convictions about sin render a precise definition of rationality problematic. This fact need not be too troublesome if perfect rationality is understood to be an impossible, and perhaps even undesirable, dream. By any standard, human beings are only occasionally rational. We are ultimately historical creatures, not essentially rational ones. According to the poet:

> The troubles of our proud and angry dust
>   Are from eternity, and shall not fail. . . .
> But men at whiles are sober
>   And think by fits and starts,
> And if they think, they fasten
>   Their hands upon their hearts.[92]

Experience teaches that within the work of single theologians there are various and strongly defended doctrines that do not appear rationally compatible— a fact that demonstrates that neither reason nor experience nor for that matter Scripture or tradition is absolute sovereign in theological reflection. They are, as in Calvin, bound together with Scripture the primary focus and the other witnesses in shifting ascendancy.

90. François Wendel, *Calvin: The Origins and Development of His Religious Thought*, trans. Philip Mairet (New York: Harper and Row, 1963), 358–59.

91. In the *Cratylus* Plato considers the instructive power of words connected to the nature of things by the rarest of artists, those who are able to apply right names. Cratylus suggests that only a god can be the first giver of names (438b), but Socrates' main interest is the insistence that knowledge is only possible if words have a fixed meaning or essence—a view successfully challenged by Ludwig Wittgenstein.

92. *The Collected Poems of A. E. Housman* (New York: Henry Holt & Company, 1965 [1922]), 108–9.

Index of Names

Abelard, Peter, 158–59
Abraham, William J., 301–3, 321, 322n66
Achtemeier, Mark, 41n142
Adams, Marilyn McCord, 130n17
Ahmed III, 127n12
Alexander, Archibald, 24n91
Alighieri, Dante, 43, 77, 78n74, 151n61, 203, 256n124
Allen, J. W., 293n109
Althaus, Paul, 99n128
Amyraut, Moïse, 15n49, 39n137
Anderson, Owen, 24n91
Anselm, 158–62, 168, 325
Aquinas, Thomas. *See* Thomas Aquinas
Aristotle, 3, 13–14, 25, 44, 84–85, 90, 109–10, 129, 171n105, 203, 241, 278, 285n81, 300n4, 304n16, 306, 310–11, 325
Arius, 120, 149
Armstrong, Brian, 38–39, 91n99, 100n131, 156n73, 204n20
Atwater, Lyman H., 240
Augustine, 22, 62, 70, 74, 84–85, 90, 92, 107, 132–35, 143, 154, 156, 171–72, 180, 198, 203, 211, 221, 272, 307–8, 310
Aulén, Gustav, 158
Austen, Jane, 97
Ayers, Robert H., 25n93, 113n168, 305n17

Baelz, P. R., 234
Baepler, Richard, 106n152
Bagchi, David, 25n95
Bainton, Roland H., 41n141, 289n97, 313n36

Bakhtin, Mikhail, 9–10
Balke, William, 255n122, 315n43
Bancroft, George, 293
Baron, Hans, 290n100
Barr, James, 57–58
Barth, Karl, xiiin7, xv, 12n39, 14n47, 30–31, 34n119, 42, 46n159, 47, 48, 65, 92, 95–96, 98–105, 121n1, 125n8, 137n26, 141, 144n49, 148n59, 153, 155n70, 156, 160n82, 172n110, 174n120, 188n152, 195, 197n6, 200n11, 203n16, 211, 213–14, 224n62, 245n109, 254n120, 316n47, 318, 319n57, 325
Basinger, David, 234
Battenhouse, Roy W., 70, 84, 87–88, 150n60, 307n20
Battles, Ford Lewis, xivn9, 107n158, 111n161, 154–55, 156n71, 278n47
Bauke, Hermann, 314
Bavinck, Hermann, 2n1, 117, 118n177
Beard, Charles, 28
Beardslee, John W., III, 216
Beaty, Michael D., 93n113
Benedetto, Robert, 155n70
Benedict, Philip, 289n97
Bennett, Jonathan, 97n122
Benoit, Jean-Daniel, 4n4, 227n68, 260, 270
Bent, Charles N., 125n8
Berkhof, Louis, 21n81, 26, 32, 60, 196, 234n86
Berkouwer, G. C., 101n137, 130n17, 214
Beyerchen, Alan D., 100n128

331

Beza, Theodore, xv, 8–9, 15–16, 152n65, 214, 266
Billings, J. Todd, 175–76, 227n67, 229
Bizer, Ernst, 285n86
Boethius, 198n9
Bohatec, Josef, 105, 108, 141, 221n57, 245, 287n90, 290n100, 292
Bois, H., 246n111
Boisset, Jean, 209n37, 308n22
Bolsec, Jérôme, 245
Bonnet, Jules, xivn8, 268n24
Bosco, David, 95
Boswell, James, 253n119
Bouwsma, William J., 29, 300
Bouyer, Louis, 236
Bowden, John, 30n113, 99n128
Bowman, John C., 46n161
Braaten, Carl E., 178n133
Bratt, James D., 291n98
Bray, Gerald L., 64
Breasted, James Henry, 96n120
Breen, Quirinus, 25n94, 45, 314
Bressler, Ann Lee, 218n55
Brown, James, 2
Brown, William Adams, 235
Brunner, Emil, 71, 92, 98–105, 123, 141, 144, 155n70, 160, 177, 188, 304n16, 313, 318, 319n57
Buber, Martin, 170n102, 177
Buck, Lawrence P., 289
Bullinger, Heinrich, 3, 145, 184n140, 272n33, 281–82, 283n65, 289n97
Bultmann, Rudolf, 61, 102
Bunge, Marcia J., 274n37
Bunting, Ian D., 282nn60, 61
Bure, Idelette de, 282n61
Busch, Eberhard, 30n113
Butin, Philip Walker, 39, 197, 212–13
Bynum, Caroline Walker, 277n46
Byron, Lord, 127

Cahill, Thomas, 8n16
Campbell, McLeod, 159, 163n87
Canlis, Julie, 167–68, 169n99, 170n103, 227–29, 230n77
Carlyle, Thomas, 9
Caroli, Peter, 65
Carpenter, Craig B., 230n78
Carus, Paul, 74n63
Cary, Phillip, 171n107
Case-Winters, Anna, 209n37
Casteel, Thomas W., 230n78
Chaucer, Geoffrey, 92n102, 131n18

Chaulker, W. H., 251n116
Chenevière, Marc-Edouard, 290n100
Chesterton, Gilbert K, 303
Cicero, 111–12
Clark, R. S., 24
Clive, H. P., 79n76
Coakley, John W., 209n37
Coates, Thomas, 223
Cochrane, Arthur C., 99n128, 141
Colapietro, Vincent M., 324
Coligny, Admiral de, 12n39, 260
Cooke, Charles L., 12n39
Copernicus, 69
Cowper, William, 187
Craig, Samuel G., 132n22
Crawford, John R., 266n17
Cullmann, Oscar, 83n84
Cushman, Robert E., 307, 310n24

Dakin, A., 36n126
Dalferth, Ingolf Ulrich, 172n110
Daniel, Francis, 10n24
Davies, Brian, 322
Davies, G. I., 86n89
Davies, Rupert E., 57
Davis, Thomas J., 242, 276–77, 282n63
Deason, Gary B., 69n57
de Greef, Wulfert, 3n4
Dekker, Eef, 16n54, 21n80, 22n84, 329n89
Descartes, René, 2–3, 34–35, 66n51, 71n62, 302, 314–15
DeVries, Dawn, 320
DeVries, Peter, 127n11
Dickens, Charles, 56n12
Dillistone, F. W., 161–62, 315n44
Dionysius the Areopagite, 72, 167, 172–73
Dominicé, Max, 171n101
Donne, John, 69n55
Donnelly, John Patrick, 310n26
Dostoevsky, Fyodor, 107, 131, 220n56
Doumergue, Émile, 8, 10, 12, 45, 202n14, 206, 245n108, 260n6, 290n100, 292
Dowey, Edward A., Jr., 36–38, 47n162, 91n99, 93, 95, 99n129, 154–155, 310n7, 314
Duffus, R. L., 6, 8

Ebeling, Gerhard, 60n32, 96, 139n30, 327n85
Edmondson, Stephen, 21n81, 142–44, 146, 152, 158–59, 162
Edwards, Jonathan, 97n122, 162, 218n55
Eire, Carlos M. N., 62–63, 129
Elwood, Christopher, 272n32

Emerson, Everett, 20
Emerson, Ralph Waldo, 124n6
Engel, Mary Potter, 81, 88–89, 101n135, 206n29
Engelbrecht, B. J., 198n7
Epicurus, 110
Erasmus, Desiderius, 62n36, 85, 129n14, 132, 221n59, 245n110
Ericksen, Robert P., 99n128
Etcoff, Nancy, 317n50
Evans, Mary Ann (George Eliot), 317n50
Evans-Pritchard, Edward Evan, 325–26

Farel, William, xivn11, 3, 8n15, 65n45, 282n61
Farley, Benjamin Wirt, 106, 107n155, 224n19
Farmer, H. H., 235n93, 321n63
Farnell, Lewis Richard, 326
Farrer, A. J. D., 101n138
Farris, Allan L., 263, 266n18
Faulkner, William, 5
Febvre, Lucien, 9n21
Fiddes, Paul, 161–62
Forstman, H. J. (Jack), 61, 99n128, 106, 206–7
Foster, Herbert Darling, 132n21
Foster, Michael B., 300n4
Foxgrover, David, 29n105, 242n102, 272n33
Fraenkel, Peter, 98n126
Franklin, Benjamin, 289, 290n99
Fremantle, Anne, 170n101
Freud, Sigmund, 9n20, 35, 96–97, 101n135
Friedman, Jerome, 67n52
Fuhrmann, Paul T., 323n70

Gaffin, Richard B., Jr., 41, 160n81
Ganoczy, Alexandre, 29
Garrigou-Lagrange, Reginald, 94n115
Garside, Charles, Jr., 79n76
Gathercole, Simon J., 148n58
Gay, Peter, 308
George, Timothy, 12n39, 46n161, 64n41, 283n68
Gerrish, Brian A., xvn13, 23n88, 47–48, 69n57, 161n84, 272n33. 275, 287n43, 278, 288n93, 318n56, 319–20
Gerstner, John H., 7, 46n159
Gibbon, Edward, 35, 124n5, 317n50
Gilhus, Ingvild Sælid, 10n28
Gilkey, Langdon, 55n7, 107, 194n2
Gilmont, Jean-François, 3n4
Gilson, Etienne, 304n16, 314
Gloede, Günter, 99n129

Gogarten, Friedrich, 102
Göhler, Alfred, 209n37, 217n54
Goldstone, Lawrence and Nancy, 67n52
Goleman, Daniel, 323
Gollwitzer, Helmut, 107n156, 280
Gomarus, Franciscus, 214
González, Justo, 13
Gooch, G. P., 329n88
Goody, Jack, 128n12
Gordon, Dane R., 322
Gordon, Ernest, 107n156
Gottlieb, Anthony, 305n15
Grace, William J., 311n29
Graham, W. Fred, 12n41, 47n162, 290n98
Grant, Robert, 53n3
Gray, Hanna H., 46n154
Greene, Robert A., 92n102
Greene, Theodore M., 234n90, 317n48
Grislis, Egil, 274
Gross, Jules, 173n117
Grosshans, Hans-Peter, 173n110
Gründler, Otto, 42n147, 91
Gunton, Colin E., 46n159
Guyer, Paul, 317n51

Habets, Myk, 176
Hall, Basil, 6n8, 12n42, 15
Hall, Thomas, 271
Hamilton, Edith, 79n76
Hamilton, William, 23n89
Hancock, Ralph C., 291–92
Hardy, Daniel W., 43n151
Harkness, Georgia, 55n8
Harnack, Adolf, 14n45, 173–74
Hart, Trevor, 98–100, 102n142, 103, 104n146
Haught, John F., 69n56
Hauke, Rainer, 178n133
Hebert, A. G., 158n78
Heiler, Friedrich, 234, 235n92
Helm, Paul, 15–16, 94, 127n11, 302
Henderson, G. D., 266n15
Henderson, Robert W., 265n12
Hendry, George S., 46, 198n7, 313
Henry, Paul, xiin3
Heppe, Heinrich, 18, 32n118, 106n154, 206, 216, 217n52
Herodotus, 221
Heron, Alasdair I. C., 15n51, 283
Herrick, Robert, 250n114
Heshusius, Tileman, 282n61, 284, 286–87, 305
Hesselink, I. John, 4, 89n95, 137n27, 139, 140n33, 195n4, 233n84

Heynen, Willem, 255n122
Hick, John, 26n96, 47n162, 144, 187–88, 200n56, 220n56
Higman, Francis, 9n21, 45
Hill, Thomas E., 203n18
Hiller, Marian, 67n52
Himmler, Heinrich, 97n122
Hirsch, Emanuel, 99n128, 225n64
Hitchens, Christopher, 7–8
Hitler, Adolf, 99–100, 141
Hocking, William, 322n65
Hodge, Archibald Alexander, 32
Hodge, Charles, 18, 21n81, 22–24, 26, 32n118, 41n143
Hoekema, Anthony A., 140n33
Hoffmeyer, John F., 277n46
Hogge, Allen, 12n39
Holder, Ward, xiii
Höpfl, Harro, 290n101
House, Humphry, 56n12
Housman, A. E., 330
Hughes, Merritt Y., 15n47
Hume, David, 253n119, 315, 317nn50, 52; 321
Hunt, Dave, 7–8
Hunt, George L., 290n100
Hunter, A. M., 55–58, 181n136, 244n105, 246–47
Hyers, M. Conrad, 9n20

Inge, W. R., 171

Jaeger, Werner, 83n84
James, Henry, 317n50
James, William, 169n100, 314n40, 322–23
Jansen, John F., 142, 163n87, 165, 166n90
Jefferson, Thomas, 217n53
Jellema, Roderick, 127n11
Jellinek, George, 308n21
Jenson, Robert W., 178n133
Johnson, George, 47n161
Johnson, Robert Clyde, 60
Johnson, Sam, 77n72
Jones, Serene, 93
Jones, William, 73n65
Jüngel, Eberhard, 172n110

Kaiser, Christopher B., xvn13, 69n57, 209n37, 246n111, 280n57
Kant, Immanuel, 2–3, 14n45, 23n89, 60n29, 66n51, 97, 187, 198n7, 234, 271, 315–18, 321, 325
Karlstadt, Andreas, 64n40

Keeton, W. Page, 304n15
Kehm, George H., 162
Keller, Carl A., 167
Kelley, Maurice, 198n7
Kelly, Douglas F., 4n4, 292n106
Kempis, Thomas à, 221
Kendall, R. T., 15
Kennedy, George A., 314n39
Kingdon, Robert M., 292
Kinross, Lord, 127n12
Kirk, Kenneth E., 91n98
Kittel, Gerhard, 99n128
Klauber, Martin I., 22n81
Klooster, Fred H., 118n177
Knox, John, 292
Kolfhaus, W., 41n143, 42n145
Kraemer, Hendrik, 263n10
Kraus, Hans-Joachim, 54
Krusche, Werner, 199n11, 311n28
Kuiper, Herman, 117
Kuiper, R. B., 128n13
Kuyper, Abraham, 188n177, 310

LaCugna, Catherine M., 33n119, 66n51
La Faye, Antoine de, 24n92
Lagarde, Georges de, 292
Lake, Kirsopp, 235
Lampe, G. W. H., 197n6
Lane, A. N. S., 86n89, 251n116
Lecerf, A., 118n177
LeFranc, Abel, 9n21
LeGuin, Ursula K., 147n57
Lehmann, Paul L., 25n94, 97–98, 103n144
Leith, John H., 46, 64n40, 260, 313
Léonard, Emile G., 65
Letham, Robert, 16n54, 188n152
Lewis, Gillian, 12n41
Lewis, H. D., 235n93, 322n65
Liddle, Eric, 107n156
Lifton, Robert Jay, 99n128
Lillbeck, Peter, 19n65
Lindberg, Carter, 91
Linder, Robert D., 292
Little, David, 141
Locher, G.W., 47n162
Locke, John, 66n51, 291, 315
Lombard, Peter, 216
Louth, Andrew, xivn10
Loux, Michael J., 226n66
Lovejoy, Arthur O., 73n64
Luther, Martin, xi–xii, xiiin5, xivn8, xviin19, 6, 14, 30, 57n17, 64n40, 71n62, 85, 91, 96–97, 132, 137, 139n30, 145, 146n54,

150–51, 161n84, 170n101, 178, 213,
  223–24, 229, 244n105, 245n110, 256,
  266, 271, 277, 280–81, 283–84, 286, 301,
  314n39
Lüttge, Willy, 314n37

MacDonald, Dwight, xviin19
MacGregor, Geddes, 262, 269n26
Mackerel, Andrew, 127n11
Mackinnon, D. M., 234n88
Mackintosh, H. R., xvi, 14, 30, 163n87, 166,
  168, 185n141, 226n66, 277, 278n54
Mackintosh, Robert, 163n87
Macmurray, John, 34n119
Malcolm, Norman, 161n82
Mannermaa, Tuomo, 178
Mansel, Henry, 23n89
Marcel, Gabriel, 130n17
Marcel, Pierre, 31n115, 211n40
Margerie, Bernard de, 198n8
Maritain, Jacques, 71n62
Marlowe, Christopher, 12n39
Martin, Malachi. 76
Masselink, William, 118n177
Mathison, Keith A., 289n95
Matthew, W. R., 321n63
Mauser, Ulrich, 64n40
McClure, Don, 77n70, 326n82
McCormack, Bruce L., 102n140, 172n110,
  223, 224nn62, 63; 319n57
McDonnell, Kilian, 275n41, 280
McGiffert, Arthur Cushman, 13, 14n45
McGinn, Bernard, xivn10
McGrath, Alister E., 13, 16n54, 20n79,
  66n50, 69n57, 224
McIntyre, John, 159n79
McKee, Elsie Anne, 38n131, 91n99
McKim, Donald K., 4n6, 22n83, 23n86, 52,
  54n5, 55, 62, 105n150, 310n27
McLelland, Joseph C., 46n160, 173, 184, 229,
  279n55, 288, 289n95
McNab, James Strathearn, 137n26
McNeill, John T., xivn9, 2n1, 6, 8, 58–59, 61,
  137n26, 141, 266, 290n100, 291–92, 295
Meeter, H. Henry, 118n177
Meeter, John E., 234n86
Melanchthon, Philip, 139n30, 144n49, 245,
  268, 283–84, 314n39
Melville, Herman, 48
Mencken, H. L., 6, 8, 12
Meyer, Boniface, 279n53
Meyer, John R., 286n89
Meylan, E. F., 268n22

Miles, Margaret R., 83n85
Miller, Ed. L., 322n66
Miller, Perry, 18–20, 135n23, 140n33
Milner, Benjamin Charles, Jr., 259
Milton, John, 14n47, 71, 73n64, 76, 77n72,
  82, 94, 104n145, 198n7, 235, 250n114,
  311n29
Molnar, Thomas, 324n76
Moore, W. G., 9n21
Moore, Walter L., 319
Morrissey, Michael P., 290n101
Mosser, Carl, 168, 172, 175
Mouw, Richard J., 127n11
Mozart, Wolfgang Amadeus, 77n70
Mozley, J. K., 235n94
Mülhaupt, Erwin, 46n159
Muller, Richard A., xvn13, 14n46, 16n54,
  21–22, 24–27, 32n118, 41, 101n136, 206
Murphy, Arthur E., 321–22
Murphy, Nancey, 83n84
Murray, John, 177, 212
Murray, R. H., 12n39, 310
Mützenberg, Gabriel, 8n15

Nestorius, 120, 149
Neuser, Wilhelm H., 22n83, 42n144, 53n2,
  143n42, 156n73, 204n20, 208n36,
  209n37, 236n96, 280n56, 315n43
Nevin, John W., 41n143, 288n93
Newman, John Henry, 26n96
Nichols, James Hastings, 43n149
Niebuhr, H. Richard, 266n16
Nielsen, Kai, 140n34
Niesel, Wilhelm, xvn13, 62, 65, 77, 84,
  99n129, 113, 136, 159, 167n95, 179, 202,
  214, 235n85, 244, 266, 273, 282n61,
  290n100, 291
Noll, Stephen F., 76
Norris, F. W., 174–75
Nussbaum, Martha C., 323n70

O'Brien, George Dennis, 130n17
O'Donovan, Joan E., 98n125
O'Hanlon, Daniel J., 287n92
Obendiek, H., 315n43
Oberman Heiko A., 41, 43, 68n53, 231n80,
  287n92
Old, Hughes Oliphant, 43n149
Olivétan, Pierre, 10
Oorthuys, G., 246n111
Osgood, Charles Grosvenor, 77n72
Osiander, Andreas, 145, 167n95, 168–70, 172,
  176, 178, 225–30, 287

Ott, Heinrich, 47–48
Otten, Heinz, 245, 246n111
Otto, Rudolf, 60n29, 169n100
Outka, Gene H., 141n38

Palamas, Gregory, 174n122
Parker, T. H. L., 37, 46n159, 55n8, 234n88
Partee, Charles, 4n6, 25n94, 62n35, 77n70,
    90n96, 113n169, 114n171, 117n173,
    131n18, 168n96, 171n105, 204n20,
    205n25, 209n37, 236n96, 245n108,
    252n117, 302n10, 313n34, 326n82
Pauck, Wilhelm, 266
Peck, M. Scott, 76
Pelkonen, J. Peter, 97n123
Pepper, Stephen C., xvin15
Perrot, Alain, 11n36, 12n40
Peterson, Robert A., 159
Petry, Ray C., 269
Pettegree, Andrew, 3n4, 10n21, 12n41
Peyer, Étienne de, 117
Pierce, C. A., 97n124
Pighius, Albert, 86, 92n101, 129n15,
    244n105, 245
Pitkin, Barbara, 274n37
Pitkin, Horace Tracy, 107n156
Plantinga, Alvin, 93–94
Plato, xivn10, 12, 28–30, 32, 35, 74n65,
    83–85, 100n132, 106n152, 171, 173–74,
    203, 221n59, 254, 292, 300n4, 306,
    308n22, 309, 321, 323, 330
Plotinus, 70, 84, 171
Polanus, 22, 27
Postema, Gerald J., 303n13
Prestwich, Menna, 12n41
Pringle-Pattison, A. Seth, 198n7, 322
Prins, Richard, 87, 300–301
Proudfoot, Wayne, 317–18
Puckett, David L., 55n9, 138
Purves, Andrew, 41n142, 62n35, 90n96,
    131n18, 205n25, 209n37, 313n34

Quistorp, Heinrich, 216n50, 221, 253n118,
    256

Rabelais, François, 9n21, 10
Rahner, Karl, 34n119
Rainbow, Jonathan H, 127n11
Raitt, Jill, 143n42, 152n65
Ramsey, Paul, 141n38
Reardon, P. H., 112, 116, 117n173
Redding, Graham, 234

Reid, J. K. S., 30, 44n152, 57, 65n46, 80n78,
    123, 203n16, 209n39, 264n11, 279nn52,
    55; 305n18, 327n84
Reid, Thomas, 317n52
Reist, Benjamin, xiiin6, xivn9
Renan, Ernest, xiiin7
Richard, Lucien Joseph, 172n109
Ritschl, Albrecht, 133n22, 163n87
Ritschl, Dietrich, 47n162
Roberts, J. M., xi
Robinson, A. T., 234n91, 262n8
Robinson, H. Wheeler, 198n7
Robinson, J. A. T., 234n91, 262n8
Robinson, Marilynne, xiii, 6, 12n39, 42,
    126n9, 132n20
Rogers, Jack B., 23n86, 55, 310n27
Rohde, Edwin, 83n84
Rolston, Holmes, III, 15, 17–18
Rorem, Paul, 283n65
Rosen, Edward, 69n57
Rounder, Leroy S., 242
Russell, Norman, 173n117

Sabine, George H., 140n34, 292n109,
    294n111
Sadolet, Jacopo, 29, 59, 68n53, 204–5, 231,
    267, 270, 295n83
Santayana, George, 56n12, 304n16
Sayers, Dorothy L., 78n74
Schaeffer, Francis A., 329n88
Schaff, Philip, xii, xiiinn4, 7; 9, 11, 12n38,
    65, 282
Schiller, Friedrich, xin1
Schleiermacher, Friedrich, xiiin7, xv, 14n47,
    23, 47n164, 60n29, 99, 101n135,
    106n152, 119, 144, 169n100, 177, 179,
    185–86, 198n7, 274n37, 315, 317–22,
    327
Schlemmer, A., 167
Scholder, Klaus, 99n128
Schrader, Paul, 127n11
Schreiner, Susan E., 71n62, 106, 140n32, 205,
    206n26
Schulze, Martin, 221
Schweizer, Alexander, 244–45, 319n57
Schwöbel, Christoph, 46n159
Scott, Nathan A., Jr., 9n20
Scott, Sir Walter, 74n65
Seban, Jean-Loup, 99n128
Seneca, 111
Servetus, Michael, 12n39, 41n141,
    67, 307

Shakespeare, William, 35, 78, 326
Sharf, Robert H., 323n68
Shelley, P. B., 311n29
Shepherd, Victor A., 46n159, 196n5
Shorey, Paul, 28
Smart, Ninian, 169n100
Smith, Elwyn A., 141n36
Smith, Gary Scott, 126
Smith, Henry B., xiiin7
Smith, John E., 125, 170, 324
Smith, Ronald Gregor, 170n102
Smits, Luchesius, 70n60
Sproul, R. C., 7, 310
Spurgeon, Charles Haddon, 7, 242, 243n103
Stace, W. T., 169–70, 171n104, 312n33
Stadtlund, Tjarko, 224n63
Stancaro, Francesco, 145, 225
Stauffer, Richard, 4n5, 6n8, 8n16
Steinmetz, David C., 2n1, 25nn92, 95; 41, 54n5, 225n64
Stephanopoulos, Robert G., 173, 176, 216
Stevenson, William R., Jr., 291
Stewart, J. S., 318n54
Stickelberger, Emanuel, 8, 12
Stoller, Paul, 325
Street, T. W., 268n22
Stückelberger, Christoph, 290n98
Swift, Jonathan, 311n29

Tamburello, Dennis E., 42, 174n120, 209n37
Tan, Seng-Kong, 194n1
Tavard, George H., 255n122
Taves, Ann, 326n23
Taylor, Mark, 323n68
Thomas Aquinas, xviin19, 6, 30, 32, 33n119, 71, 85, 89, 94n115, 97, 103, 128, 137, 173n115, 199, 203–4, 252, 308, 310–11
Thompson, John L., 54n6, 206n26
Thompson, William M., 2, 229, 290n101
Thurian, Max, 287
Thurneysen, Eduard, xiiin7
Tillich, Paul, 107n156, 166n91
Torrance, Alan J., 200n11
Torrance, James B., 15n51
Torrance, Thomas F., xivn9, xvin17, 31n116, 64n43, 88–89, 123n4, 200, 266n15, 300
Tracy, David, 53n3
Troeltsch, Ernst, 2n1, 259, 265, 314n40

Trueman, Carl R., 22n83, 24n92
Trumper, Tim J. R., 41
Tulloch, John, xiii
Twain, Mark, 97n122, 235n92
Tylenda, Joseph N., 145, 146n54, 284n74, 285n86

Underhill, Evelyn, 169n100, 170

Van Buren, Paul, 41n143, 125n8, 152n63
van der Kooi, Cornelius, 316n47
Van Houten, David, 305–6, 309
van Huyssteen, J. Wentzel, 322n64
Van Til, Cornelius, 24n91, 118n177
Van 't Spijker, Willem, 43n144
van Asselt, Willem J., 16n54
Vance, Lawrence M., 7–8, 12
Vermigli, Peter Martyr, 278
Viret, Pierre, 8n15, 10
Voegelin, Eric, 290
von Balthasar, Hans Urs, 26n96
Vos, Arvin, 204n19
Vos, Geerhardus, 2n1, 310n24

Wainwright, Geoffrey, 47–48
Walder, Dennis, 56n12
Walker, G. S. M., 267n21, 276n43
Walker, Williston, 260n5
Wallace, Roland S., 46n158, 217n54, 234n85, 279n53, 292n107
Walls, R. C., 174n122
Walzer, Michael, 4n6
Warfield, Benjamin B., 11, 24n91, 35, 39, 59, 64n42, 66n50, 132n22, 234n86
Webb, Clement C. J., 198n9
Weber, Max, 309, 310n98
Weir, David A., 19n65
Weis, James, 225n65
Welker, Michael, 277n46, 319n57
Wencelius, Léon, 79n76
Wendel, François, xvn14, 29, 62, 65, 116, 137, 139, 144–45, 150, 151n61, 152n65, 159, 174, 178, 179n134, 196, 200, 226, 227n67, 228, 244n106, 245, 255, 274n36, 275, 290n100, 329–30
Wenger, Thomas L., 41
Wesley, John, 132, 242, 303n12, 326n83
Westphal, Joachim, 13, 145, 268n25, 276, 279n54, 280, 282n61, 283n66, 284–86, 288n93, 289n96, 299, 303n12
Wilcox, Donald J., 35n120
Wilken, Robert Louis, 307

Williams, Daniel D., 101n138, 266n16
Willis, E. David, 25n94, 42, 64n40, 144, 146,
    151, 152n66, 208, 235, 280, 319n57
Willis, R., 67n52
Wilterdink, Walter, 31n117
Wittgenstein, Ludwig, 330
Wolf, Hans Henrich, 136n25
Wolsterstorff, Nicholas, 302n10
Wood, Allen, 317
Wordsworth, William, 77, 171n106
Wren, Brian, 147n57
Wright, David F., 105n150, 154, 156
Wübbenhorst, Karla, 224n63

Young, Davis A., 79n75
Young, William, 118n177

Zachman, Randall C., 87n90, 96, 101n135,
    156, 319n57
Zaehner, R. C., 169n100, 172
Zanchi, Jerome, 22, 27, 91
Zimmerman, Gunter, 228n70
Zizioulas, John, 34n119, 199
Zophy, Jonathan W., 289n97
Zwingli, Huldreich, 3, 11, 47n162, 57n17,
    184n140, 258, 271, 272n33, 274–75,
    277–78, 280–83, 286–87, 289n97

Index of Subjects

accommodation, 99, 100n131, 142, 145, 150n60, 154–57, 162
adiaphora (indifferent things), 233, 267–68
adoption, 151, 160, 173–75, 188n152, 201, 203, 205, 217, 241, 248
analogy
  of being, 32, 34, 101n137
  of faith, 32, 34, 68, 285
angels, 44, 70, 71–72, 73, 75–78, 106, 150, 153, 262
antinomianism, 18, 20, 135n23
Apostles' Creed, 35–36, 37, 39, 121, 180–82, 185, 189, 256
Arianism, 65n45, 125, 187n148, 307
Arminianism, 18, 20, 132, 135n23, 242
ascension, 178, 184–85, 280, 284, 288
assurance (certainty), 2, 18, 94, 96–97, 131, 133, 141, 181, 205, 206–8, 213–15, 218, 220, 229, 230n78, 232, 237, 239, 240–52, 253
atonement, 7, 15, 121, 125n8, 126, 127n11, 138, 155, 158–62, 166, 180, 185, 187–88, 205, 255

baptism
  infant, 44n153, 273, 274n36
  sacrament of, 175, 210, 273–75, 282, 288
beauty (delight), 77, 79–80, 222, 317n50
Bible (Scripture), inerrancy of, 54–60
body
  church as, 152, 178, 226, 261, 271
  glorified, 288n93

head and, 152–53, 262–63, 269
locality of, 184, 278, 280, 282–85, 288–89
members of, 35, 75, 208, 228, 240–41, 247, 250, 259, 270
resurrection, 252–256
soul and, 83–85, 227, 255
blood (of Christ), 162, 179–82, 187–88, 216, 224, 262, 273, 275–83, 286–88

calling, effectual, 241n101
Calvin
  childhood, 10–11
  enemies—caricature, 2, 5–13, 28, 79, 81, 121, 240, 252, 262
  friends—proponents, 5, 8, 12n40, 13–27, 28, 240, 303
  health, 9, 12
  humanness, 6, 8, 12
  humor, 10–11
  letters, 3–4, 8, 260
  pastor/preacher, 4n5, 8, 12n40, 45–46, 48, 78, 248, 260, 266
  treatises, 3, 8, 145, 280
  tributes, xiiin7, 8–9
Calvinism, xii, xv, 2n1, 3, 5–8, 12, 13–16, 25–26, 32, 41n143, 46n159, 84, 121, 126–29, 140n33, 194n2, 229, 234nn86, 87; 240, 242–43, 259, 289–90, 292, 302, 304, 317n52, 321n63
Canons of Dort, 13, 127–28
capacity, 66, 72, 93, 98–100, 102–5, 139, 154–55, 157, 162, 175, 180–81, 252

339

cause, 64, 90, 109–10, 112, 114, 160, 205,
    214–15, 241–42
central dogma (doctrine), xv, xvin18, 1, 12n42,
    16n52, 29, 41n143, 129, 240, 244–48
Chalcedon, Council of, 120, 145
chance (fortune) (luck), 86, 108, 109–13,
    218–20, 293
chosen. *See* elect
Christ
    ascension of, 184–85, 189, 276n43, 178,
        280, 284, 288
    descent to hell, 179, 182–83
    divinity of, 65, 67, 122, 143, 145–47,
        148n59, 149–52, 158, 227, 285n81,
        286, 288
    eucharistic presence, 279–80, 281–89
    humanity of, 121, 145–53, 169, 175, 184,
        199, 253, 283–84, 286, 288–89, 296
    hypostatic union, 42, 121n1, 122, 146, 153,
        157, 286, 288
    Lordship of, 1, 35, 42, 124n5, 145, 153,
        172, 178, 184–85, 200, 242n102, 246,
        286–87, 298, 300
    Mediator, 32n118, 85, 121, 130, 136–38,
        143–45, 147–48, 151n61, 152n65, 162,
        168, 174n120, 175, 179, 185, 220,
        225–28, 234, 276, 310n24
    person of, 2, 16n54, 121–24, 142–58, 162,
        178, 185, 226, 291, 307
    offices of, 142–43, 153, 163, 166, 264
    Redeemer, 36n126, 37, 40, 51–52, 95, 108,
        113n170, 120–89, 225, 228, 245, 247,
        255, 257, 298, 320
    union with, xv–xvi, 3, 16n52, 19n65, 27,
        29, 35, 40–42, 47n162, 81, 84, 87, 89,
        91, 108, 125n8, 130n17, 140n33, 144,
        161–62, 166, 167–78, 181–82, 185,
        188n152, 195, 200–202, 206, 208–9,
        211–12, 214–15, 223–29, 230n78, 234,
        236–37, 242n102, 243, 244n106,
        245–48, 252–54, 259, 261–62, 267, 269,
        271, 273, 275–80, 283, 285–89, 298,
        316n47, 320, 327
    work of, 15n51, 37, 121, 125n8, 142, 144,
        148, 158–67, 176, 180, 185–87, 196,
        209n37, 223, 320
Christian life, 30, 47, 86, 91n98, 95, 133, 139,
    140n33, 173, 217–22, 257, 260, 272,
    314n40
church (company of the faithful), 12, 27, 48,
    65, 78, 258–96, 311
clergy, 263–64, 266, 270

communication of idioms, 152
communion, 43, 87, 103, 146, 169, 173–74,
    177–78, 188, 194–95, 198n7, 199n11,
    205, 208–9, 217, 224, 226, 239, 240,
    248, 262, 268, 271–89, 300
community, 40, 46, 185, 193–94, 258–296,
    298, 311–12, 322n65
confession
    of faith, xivn8, 31, 80, 119, 145, 157, 211,
        249, 289, 297, 303, 305n17
    of sin, 215
confidence, 2, 23, 60, 69, 86, 131, 156–57,
    160–61n82, 185, 207–8, 214, 220,
    237–40, 247, 269, 274, 298, 306, 308,
    311, 313–14, 325, 328–29
conscience, 89, 92–98, 101n135, 140, 208,
    215, 233, 271–72, 291
contrition, 215
conviction, 1–2, 24, 26, 42, 122, 147–48,
    158, 173n119, 189, 197, 247, 279,
    281, 290
covenant
    new, 138, 188, 272–73, 279
    old, 123, 138,
    of grace, 17–20, 32n118, 137, 140, 196,
        206
    of works, 17–20, 32n118, 137, 139–40,
        196, 206
creation, 17, 32n118, 40, 51–53, 64, 69–105,
    106, 108, 115, 119, 121, 123, 129–30,
    133, 148–49, 151, 160, 161n82, 174,
    225, 227, 243, 245n110, 250, 257, 259,
    269, 309–10, 319
cross, 11, 67, 150, 152, 159, 165, 177, 179,
    182, 188, 195, 216, 219, 270, 281, 294
crucifixion, 64, 166, 181–82, 188

deacons, 264–65
death (mortification), 179, 182, 210
deification (divinization), 121, 167–69,
    172–78, 216, 226, 228–29, 266, 272
devil(s), 70–78
discipline, 260, 262, 264, 270–71
doctors, 134, 264
dogma, dogmatic(s), xiv, xvin15, 14, 26, 28,
    30, 32, 42, 47, 58, 60n29, 101, 105, 144,
    148n59, 154, 157, 160n81, 167, 170,
    172, 173n117, 200n11, 245, 290, 313,
    315, 319n57
doubt, 34, 59, 89, 106–7, 202, 207–8, 220,
    249
doxology, 34n119, 159, 230, 247

elders, 264–65
elect (chosen), 15, 19–20, 66, 90–91, 107–8,
    116–17, 149, 160, 162, 167, 169,
    187n149, 202, 205–6, 210, 219, 240–44,
    247–49, 251–56, 260–62, 269–70, 282,
    283n65, 291n101, 295
election (eternal), 7, 105, 116, 195, 240–49,
    252, 259–60, 269. See also predestination
eloquence (rhetoric), 18, 45n154, 22, 25n94,
    38, 45, 155, 307
encounter, 16, 43, 54, 76, 101, 124, 153, 313,
    318, 321, 322n66, 324, 327
Epicureans, 106, 108, 109–13
eschatology (future life; last judgment), 133,
    164, 174, 195, 217, 220–21, 253–54,
    256
essence, xvin18, 21, 33, 63, 66–68, 84, 120,
    121n1, 123, 125, 145, 149, 155, 163,
    168, 170–71, 173–74, 181, 195, 197–99,
    226, 228
Eucharist (Lord's Supper), 145, 150, 152–53,
    168n98, 175, 188, 226, 254, 260,
    271–89, 305
Eutychian, 151, 286
experience, xvi, 16, 24n89, 33, 62, 66n50, 73,
    76, 114, 119, 124–25, 169–72, 178, 185,
    198n7, 202, 207, 244–47, 278, 298,
    301–4, 305n17, 311, 313, 315–30
extra Calvinisticum, 151–53

faith
    analogy of, 32, 34, 68, 285
    certainty of, 94, 96, 208, 240–52
    Christian life of, 217–22
    exercise of, 201, 233–40
    experience of, 16, 117, 202, 305n17, 311,
        315, 326–28
    gift of, 18, 40, 137, 176–77, 181, 196n5,
        200–205, 208, 210, 214, 227, 230, 232,
        237, 240, 243, 247–48, 252, 269, 327
    justification by, 38, 95, 196, 208, 210, 214,
        222–33
    narrative of, 179–88
    sanctification through, 208–17
    victory of, 252–56
    work of Holy Spirit in, 199n11, 200–208
fall, 64n73, 75, 82, 85, 87–91, 98, 103–4,
    121, 126, 128–29, 131–32, 135, 137–38,
    140n32, 148, 159, 193, 203n17, 204n19,
    225, 241, 254, 259, 308n22, 309–10
fate (necessity, determinism), 86, 108–9,
    111–12, 115

First Helvetic Confession, 19n65, 281–82
flesh. See Eucharist
foreknowledge, 77n71, 250, 252, 302
foreordination, 77n71, 113n168, 240, 242,
    250, 252, 305
forgiveness, 38, 132n20, 159, 162, 180–81,
    210, 215–16, 224–25, 260, 271, 274,
    281
foundation, 37, 47, 59, 85, 91, 106, 123–24,
    132, 146, 170, 188n52, 208–9, 217, 261,
    263, 269, 300–302, 307
free will (liberty), 44, 75, 82, 86, 89, 91, 109,
    126, 129, 131–34, 231, 239, 242
future life. See eschatology

gifts, 70, 80, 85–86, 118, 129, 133, 176, 179,
    202–4, 208–9, 222, 230, 262–66, 269,
    273, 306, 308, 310
God
    being, attributes of, 27, 32–34, 51, 81, 199,
        314n40
    glory of, 29, 79, 83n85, 172n109, 213, 216,
        297
    kingdom of, 45, 131, 151n61, 186, 255,
        309–10
    sovereignty of, 1, 2n1, 12, 123, 140n33,
        223, 245–47
    will of, 34, 56, 74, 95, 117, 135, 139, 222,
        237, 311, 321n63
gospel
    and law, 121, 136–42, 189, 257, 294
    preaching of, 43–48, 264, 274–75
governance, 108–9, 111, 116, 240, 250, 293
government
    civil, 40, 257, 289–95
    ecclesiastical, 258, 261–71
grace
    common, 16n52, 114, 116–19
    cooperating, 90–91, 94, 98, 103, 105, 129,
        215–16, 252
    covenant of, 17–20, 32n118, 137, 140, 196,
        206
    means of, 40, 234, 257, 273–74
    operating, 90, 98, 103, 129, 216, 252
    special, 79n76, 90, 105–6, 113, 116–19,
        129, 241n101
guilt, 129, 134, 165, 182, 210

habit, 90, 92n101, 94n115, 104, 204n19, 313,
    326
happiness, 109, 174, 236, 256, 308, 316
head. See intellect

heart, xiv, 2–3, 27, 53, 60, 69n55, 88, 96n120, 97, 133, 159, 161n82, 208, 216, 221, 234–35, 239, 246, 287, 312, 313, 323, 326–28

heaven, 43, 45–46, 57, 71, 80, 110–12, 124, 150, 152–53, 167, 173, 179, 184–85, 203, 215, 220–22, 227, 238, 252–53, 256, 274, 276n43, 277n46, 278–80, 282, 285–86, 288–89, 309

hell, 43, 71, 77, 162, 179, 182–83, 215, 218, 250n114, 252

holiness. *See* sanctification

Holy Spirit
    person of, 36, 39, 67–69
    testimony of, 59, 171, 300, 327
    work of, xvi, 36–37, 39–40, 43, 52n1, 60, 64, 86, 140n33, 167–69, 180, 194, 196–97, 199n11, 200–209, 211–13, 217, 222, 227, 230, 236–37, 243, 247, 252, 254, 257, 271, 273–74, 276, 297, 309, 312–13, 320, 327

hope, 72, 91, 111, 113n168, 124n6, 128, 138, 142, 164, 167, 185, 203, 219–21, 232, 236–37, 249, 252–54, 256, 261–62, 283, 285n84, 302, 327n85

humanity of Christ. *See* Christ: humanity of

humility, 31, 54, 85, 108, 132–33, 139, 141, 148, 154, 156, 237, 243, 247, 263, 288, 325

hypocrisy, 10n24, 248

idolatry, 62–64, 93

image of God, 63, 72, 87–89, 98, 100, 102, 106, 123, 125, 140, 150, 174–75, 193, 203n17, 218, 225, 227, 253

impartation, 181, 223, 226, 228–29

incarnation, xiv, 3, 40, 41n143, 42, 73n64, 125, 129, 143, 145–46, 148–51, 153, 157–60, 166, 170, 172, 174, 178, 181, 187–88, 225–27, 262, 286–87

infusion, 174, 226, 228, 230, 286n89

ingrafting, 174–75, 197, 223, 226–28, 273, 275

inspiration, of Bible, 15, 55n9, 56–58

intellect (head, mind), 2–3, 24, 34, 43, 53, 66n50, 77, 82, 86, 88, 92, 114, 120, 122n2, 154, 157–60, 161n82, 182, 208, 212, 221, 226n66, 234, 239, 243–44, 278, 287–88, 303, 308–9, 311–12, 314, 318, 323, 327–28

Jehovah, 122, 143, 149

Jesus Christ. *See* Christ

judgment, 33, 73, 94, 96, 153, 164, 174, 179–81, 183, 185, 224, 231, 249, 255–56, 285, 328

justification, 2n2, 38, 41, 61n32, 95, 103, 108, 133, 135, 161, 166–67, 169n100, 176, 178, 188n152, 195–96, 205, 208–17, 222–33, 243, 244n106, 247, 249, 257, 270, 272–73, 275, 288, 291, 329

king, kingdom, 45, 73–74, 121, 131, 151n61, 163–65, 174, 179, 184, 186, 215, 222, 238, 251, 255, 264, 274, 295, 309

knowledge
    of God, 2, 16n52, 23n89, 27, 32–40, 51–52, 54, 64–65, 70, 81, 85, 87n90, 92–93, 97–98, 104, 121–22, 125, 130, 136–38, 142, 149, 155–56, 159–60, 172n109, 180, 206–7, 234n88, 263, 299–300, 303, 306, 308, 313, 315, 316n47
    of self, 27, 33–35,
    in theory, 32, 60, 299, 301–3

laity, 262–63, 266, 270

laughter (humor), 9–11, 56n12

law (legal), 18, 20, 54, 95, 106, 121, 136–142, 148, 156, 160–63, 165, 172, 180, 183, 205, 223–24, 228–29, 232, 288, 294

logic (paradox, contradiction, antinomies, ambiguities), 9, 12, 14, 15n47, 22, 23n89, 25n94, 26, 28, 31n117, 32, 45, 93, 127n11, 135, 160–61n82, 180, 208, 231, 234, 239, 242, 251, 300n3, 301, 305n17, 310, 313–15, 323–24

logos, 92, 112, 307

love
    divine, 106, 109, 130n17, 137, 154, 159–60, 166, 180–81, 187–89, 201, 216, 235, 241, 243–44, 247, 250–51, 277, 297, 329
    human, 78, 205, 215, 218, 231n80, 232–33, 248, 256n124, 273n35, 294, 317n50, 323
    as supernatural virtue, 91, 128, 203–4

man (humanity, humankind, human beings), 2, 19, 32, 40, 43, 47, 60, 63, 70–71, 74–75, 78, 81, 87, 89–90, 92, 100, 102–4, 112, 117, 121, 126, 128–31, 133, 135, 137–38, 140n33, 147, 156, 158, 173n115, 175–76, 178, 180, 194, 196, 198, 206–7, 212–13, 225, 230, 237, 251,

283, 291, 306–7, 311–12, 316, 320,
323–24, 326, 329–30
Mass, 165, 277, 280–81
Mediator. *See* Christ
mercy, 33, 94, 129, 136, 142, 180–81, 203,
205, 208, 216, 231–32, 239–41, 247–49,
251, 269, 274
merit, 90, 104, 131, 161, 211, 214–16,
231–32, 243, 302
Messiah, 163, 165, 315n45
metaphor, root, xvin15, 105, 245
ministry, 40, 43–48, 52n1, 58, 72, 142,
262–71, 291
music, 79, 233
mystery, xiv–xvi, 3, 13, 30–31, 40–41, 60,
64–67, 69, 77, 89, 101n138, 107–8,
119–20, 122, 130n17, 142, 145–46,
148–49, 153–54, 162, 171, 181–83,
188, 194, 198–99, 220n56, 235, 240,
242–43, 247, 252, 255, 262, 271,
273–74, 277–80, 287–89, 300,
314–15, 322n64
mystical, xiv–xv, 39, 41–42, 86, 167–73,
177–79, 185, 199n11, 202, 223, 229–30,
261, 280, 287, 323
mysticism, 24, 42, 121, 167–72, 177–79,
202n14, 322n65
myth, 29, 71, 187, 324n76

nature, 17, 32, 78–79, 84, 89–92, 95, 98–100,
102–4, 106, 112, 114, 116–19, 129–30,
134, 140, 148, 171, 203, 221, 259, 288,
293, 308–9
natures of Christ. *See* incarnation; Christ:
humanity of; Christ: divinity of
neoorthodoxy, 22, 320
Nestorian, 151–52

obedience, 17–18, 20, 71, 107n156, 121, 155,
159, 161n82, 163, 172n109, 176, 178,
182, 217, 219, 248, 261, 265, 270, 288,
292–95, 310, 311n29, 316
offices. *See* Christ
order (structure), 30–31, 35–43, 106–8, 137,
196, 260–71, 291–95
Orthodox Church, xii, 173–74, 178, 216

pardon, 215, 229, 231–32, 239, 251
participation, 41n143, 87, 143, 167–68,
173–76, 178, 201, 213, 223, 226–30,
272, 276–77, 288
pastor, xiii, 4, 8, 12n40, 260, 264–66
Pelagius, Pelagians, 132, 231, 239

perfection, 32–33, 58, 60, 72, 113n168,
132–33, 142, 154, 186, 211, 217, 232,
239, 261, 316–17
permission, 74–75, 77n71, 86, 114, 135, 156,
250, 308
persuasion (rhetoric), 22–23, 38, 45, 155, 208,
239, 307, 328
petition, prayer of, 234–37
philosophy, 1–2, 10n21, 13, 16, 20, 22,
23n89, 28, 32, 55n7, 61, 84–85,
100–102, 129–31, 118n177, 124, 132,
170, 199, 203, 219, 221, 234n88, 291,
298–301, 304nn15, 16; 305n17, 307–10,
313–16, 323–24, 329
piety, xv, 18, 47, 85, 90, 111–12, 121,
172n109, 220, 270, 272, 273n35, 275,
284, 288, 293, 310n24, 318–19, 328
point of contact, 89, 98, 100–105
politics, 4n6, 15n47, 290–91, 323
prayer, 45, 47, 123, 171, 195–96, 201,
233–40, 243, 260–61, 304n16
preaching, preacher, proclamation, sermon, xvi,
4, 43–47, 53, 63, 75, 107n156, 131, 183,
241, 243, 246n111, 248, 256, 264–65,
272, 274–75, 320
predestination, 7, 55, 105, 107–9, 112, 116,
135, 224n63, 231n80, 233, 236, 240–52,
259, 290, 291n101, 292n109
pride, 7, 86, 132, 134, 141, 218–19
priest, 121, 143, 163–66, 181, 215, 263, 266,
273, 281
principles, 1–2, 15–16, 22, 24, 26–27, 29, 26,
54–55, 194n1, 201, 269, 290, 291n101,
297, 314
propositions, 18, 24–26, 55, 173n119, 297,
300, 306, 308n22
providence, 12n39, 69–72, 86, 92, 105–19,
130, 131n18, 135, 140n32, 220n56,
237–38, 241–43, 245–46, 251, 292–95,
307, 309, 319
purgatory, 151n61, 215–16
Puritans, 6, 15–16, 18, 20, 293n109, 311

reason, xv, 13, 15, 18–19, 21–22, 23n89,
24–27, 30–34, 59–60, 62, 66n50, 82–86,
92, 94–95, 99, 102, 104, 111–13,
127n11, 129–30, 134, 140nn33, 34; 157,
161n82, 194, 202, 203n17, 204n19,
207–8, 217–18, 278, 297, 299–315,
323–30
reconciliation, 104, 160, 165–66, 179–81,
265, 277n46
Redeemer. *See* Christ

redemption, 20, 36, 51, 73n64, 75, 81–82, 85, 87–89, 92, 95, 101–2, 106, 108, 121, 129–31, 148, 154, 159, 162–63, 166, 179, 182–83, 185–87, 193, 212–13, 225, 227, 243, 247, 254, 281, 287, 306, 309, 311

relics, 30–31

repentance, 113n168, 154, 159, 176, 209n38, 210, 237, 248

reprobation (damnation), 108, 208, 241–42, 244–45, 248–50, 290

responsibility, 18–19, 24, 98, 109, 115, 130–32, 134, 136, 140n33, 200, 210–11, 216–17, 236, 240, 252, 270, 329

resurrection, xvin17, 81, 83–84, 150, 160n81, 174, 178–79, 181, 183–84, 195–96, 200, 210, 212n42, 220–21, 227, 252–56, 277n46, 283–84, 285n84, 288

righteousness, 19, 20n76, 33, 41, 44, 47, 74, 91, 96, 122, 125, 128, 132, 136, 140–41, 153, 162, 178n133, 180–81, 185, 200–201, 209–10, 217, 219, 223–33, 250, 255, 285, 287–88, 291n101, 293

Roman Catholic
    Papists, Romanists, 45, 54, 165, 205, 208, 220, 230–31, 239, 270, 283–84
    theology, xii, 21–22, 32, 33n119, 101n137, 209–10, 214–17, 229–30, 232, 280–81, 293, 304n16
    tradition, 43, 33n119, 53, 62, 66n51, 263–64, 266–68
    worship, 63 (see also Mass)

sacraments, 43–44, 90, 176, 201, 249, 258, 264, 267–68, 270–89, 296 (see also baptism; Eucharist)

sacrifice, xivn11, 159, 165–66, 179, 182, 187–88, 229, 272, 281, 283

salvation, xvin17, 7, 17–20, 40, 44, 59, 61n32, 65, 66n50, 81, 85–86, 90–91, 107, 109, 112, 121–22, 125n8, 130–31, 136–39, 142, 144, 150, 152, 159, 160n81, 172, 174n122, 179–83, 187–88, 195, 200–201, 203n16, 204–11, 214–15, 219–20, 228–29, 231–32, 238–42, 244, 248–53, 259, 261, 265, 269, 276, 277n46, 281, 285–88, 291n101, 302, 316, 320

sanctification, 2n2, 20–21, 38, 41, 95, 103, 107–8, 133, 135, 139, 161, 163, 166–67, 174, 176, 178, 188n152, 195, 208–17, 222–24, 229–30, 232, 243–44, 247, 249, 260, 270, 273, 288, 291, 329

Satan, 71, 73–77, 216, 241, 249, 261

satisfaction, 159–62, 165, 179–80, 182, 215

scholasticism, xv, 13–16, 21–26, 33, 55, 173n119, 310n26, 319, 321

Scripture. See Bible; word

Second Helvetic Confession, 25, 47, 183n138, 282n59

seed, of religion, 92–94, 97

self, xvi, 27, 34–35, 37, 39, 66n51, 81, 101, 143, 170–72, 177, 185–86, 194, 206–8, 241, 300, 316, 318, 321

self-denial, 217–18, 329

signs, 91n98, 214, 272–73, 275, 282

sin
    actual, 126, 133–36
    evil, 71, 73–74, 75–78, 82, 85–86, 90, 92, 94n115, 130–32, 134, 167, 171, 173, 187, 210, 218–19, 220n56, 250, 261, 306, 330
    original, 97, 126, 133–36
    total depravity, 12, 28, 78, 80–81, 126–36, 230n78, 297

soul, immortality of, 83–84, 111, 254, 256

speculation (curiosity), 4n6, 33–34, 54, 63, 66, 72, 81, 146, 148, 169n99, 202, 220, 225, 227, 243–44, 246–47, 251, 255, 310, 313–14, 319, 328

Stoics, 108–9, 111–13, 219, 307

subject and object, xvi, 2, 23n89, 226, 211–12

substance (essence), 33n119, 34, 41n143, 64, 66n51, 69, 100, 120, 168, 174, 176, 199, 202, 226–27, 258, 261, 271–72, 274, 276, 278–80, 283, 285–88

substitution, 161–62, 224

syllogism, practical, 214

symbol(s), 63, 107n156, 124n6, 271–75, 324n76

T. U. L. I. P., 126

theology
    natural, 24n91, 95, 98, 101n137, 103n144, 141
    revealed, 31–34, 38–39, 51–52, 54, 56, 61, 63, 65, 66, 68, 79, 98, 103n144, 104–5, 123–25, 133, 135, 138, 141–42, 148, 150, 166, 180–81, 183, 188–89, 195, 200, 202, 208, 216, 237, 242, 247, 254, 294, 297, 307, 309, 313, 316n47, 320–21, 328, 330
    tradition, xii–xiv, 3, 6, 21n81, 22, 25, 33n119, 42, 45, 53–55, 62, 66n51, 68, 92n102, 144, 167, 170, 198n7, 228, 250n114, 252, 264, 273, 289n97, 298,

300, 302, 303, 306, 311, 313, 317,
325–26, 330
Trinity, xiv, 33, 39–40, 51–52, 64–69, 80, 120,
145, 147, 149, 157–58, 168, 174–75,
194, 196, 197n6, 198–99, 212, 226, 273,
319–20
truth, xiii–xiv, 15, 24, 30–31, 38, 45–46, 54,
66, 68–69, 73, 77, 85, 107n156, 112,
124, 153–54, 157, 177, 202, 208,
242–43, 260, 271, 274, 294, 305n17,
307–8, 312, 314, 316, 319, 321, 328–30

ubiquity, 153, 283, 285n83, 288
understanding. *See* intellect
union
    with Christ (*see* Christ: union with)
    with God, 41, 152–53, 167, 169–70,
        171n104, 172–74, 176–78, 195, 209,
        217, 252, 254, 273, 322n65
    with others, 261–62 (*see also* body:
        members of)

vice, 90, 128, 134, 183
virtue, 78n74, 90–91, 94n115, 134, 141, 166,
203–4, 286–87

Wesleyan Quadrilateral, 303n12

Westminster Confession, 15–17, 33, 55,
128, 160n81, 234n87, 241n101, 243,
311–12
will
    bound, 86, 126, 131–33, 135
    divine, 13, 18, 44, 70, 74, 81, 86, 94, 111,
        113–15, 118, 155, 163, 176, 186, 220,
        236, 241, 250, 259, 295, 312, 314
    free, 75, 82, 86, 91, 109, 126, 129, 131–32,
        134, 231, 239, 242, 268
    human, 74, 86, 90, 133, 194, 211–12,
        217–18
word
    of God, 2, 10, 43–44, 46n158, 47, 53, 57,
        59, 61, 66, 101–2, 104, 214, 220, 251,
        264, 267–68, 270, 275, 284, 288,
        305n17, 327
    Scripture as, 22, 46n159, 52–63, 67–68,
        251, 272, 305n17, 311
works, good, 90, 133, 205, 209n37, 214–16,
231–32
worship, 3, 43, 47, 63, 124, 133, 172n109,
200n11, 203–5, 260–61, 293, 307,
314n40, 322n65

Zurich Consensus (Consensus Tigurinus), 145,
280, 282–84, 296